THE FAMILY in SOCIAL CONTEXT

The Family in Social Context

SECOND EDITION

GERALD R. LESLIE

NEW YORK

OXFORD UNIVERSITY PRESS

LONDON   TORONTO   1973

Copyright © 1967, 1973 by Oxford University Press, Inc.
Library of Congress Catalogue Card Number: 72-86130

Printed in the United States of America

Preface | *to the Second Edition*

DURING the past four and one-half years, many teachers have written to the author praising *The Family in Social Context* and occasionally offering suggestions for incorporation into the revision. Others have made their contributions at professional conferences. While the author has attempted to thank each of these people personally, he would like to extend his collective thanks to them publicly now. These contacts with professional colleagues have been as satisfying as the widespread and enthusiastic reception that the book has received in the United States, Canada, and abroad.

The revision files for *The Family in Social Context* were begun even before the first edition was published. Because of the tremendous outpouring of research, they grew large and pressed for enlargement of an already large book. By wielding a sharp editorial pencil, however, some 200 new works have been included without any increase in over-all length. The result is a more tightly written book.

Generous colleagues have specified its comparative perspective, its linkage of theory and research, and the flexibility it offered to teachers as prime reasons for the success of the first edition. All of these have been preserved in the revision.

Although it has been less than five years, there have been striking developments on the American family scene since the first edition was published: the new emphasis upon the strengths of black families; Women's Liberation; and the search for alternative life styles. Each of these has been treated in the revision, hopefully not stridently or defensively, but in the larger contexts in which they appear. The true importance of each is thus affirmed.

Finally, the revised materials have been tested on several classes of students for readability and significance. Their responses have shaped the final product. The author acknowledges his gratitude to them.

Gainesville, Florida   Gerald R. Leslie
January 1972

Preface | *to the First Edition*

THIS BOOK is the product of 17 years' experience in teaching courses on the family at half a dozen major universities. It contains materials and emphases that the author has found especially useful in bringing understanding to students. The purpose of a textbook, after all, is to make learning more efficient and pleasurable for both professors and students.

It is a big book, designed to include most of the material usually covered in courses offered under titles such as, the Modern Family, the Sociology of the Family, and Marriage and the Family. Not all instructors will be able to cover all of it in one semester. Most instructors, however, should find ample material to get into their courses the specific emphases that they want. In addition, by assigning the whole book to be read, they will be able to give to their students what often requires a textbook and a book of readings combined.

One of the features of the book is unusually extensive coverage of cross-cultural material. With the marked trend toward the inclusion of more cross-cultural material in family courses, many instructors will want to spend considerable time on Part I. Those instructors who do not emphasize cross-cultural material will want to move more quickly to the materials on the American family system.

Part II, consisting of two chapters, provides more adequate historical perspective on American family patterns than ordinarily is found in textbooks that are not devoted principally to historical analysis. Historical influences on the contemporary American family system are traced in detail sufficient to give students genuine understanding and not merely academic indigestion.

The chapter on theories of family structure and family change is unique to this book. It could not include, of course, all the major theoretical contributions to our understanding of the family that have been made. It is designed to correct for the fact that family textbooks seldom reveal much connection between study of the family and sociological theory. Essentially, the ideas of three men—William Ogburn, Carle Zimmerman, and Talcott Parsons—who have had significant and lasting influence on our thinking about the family are treated in detail. With this material as background, some instructors undoubtedly will choose to introduce their students to other historical and contemporary theorists. The systematic inclusion of such material should help to raise family courses above the simple descriptive level.

Part IV presents the core of sociological material on the contemporary American family system. The chapter on the middle-class family model orients the rest of the book to the family system of the 1960's and 1970's rather than to that of the 1930's and 1940's. The chapter on the kin network also reflects the most recent research on the relation between the nuclear family and the larger circle of kin.

From there, the last nine chapters are organized in terms of a family life-cycle framework. They contain a wealth of detail concerning the functioning of contemporary families in the experience of people from adolescence through old age. Some instructors will want to interpret this material in strictly institutional terms; some will want to use a more functional approach. The material is organized and presented to lend itself to either approach. There are no hints on "how to do it," for the author assumes that the most truly functional textbook is one that is not self-consciously so.

Certain other distinguishing features of the book deserve mention. It draws heavily and systematically upon the body of family research that has been accumulating over the past two decades. It assesses the research and then lets the chips fall where they may, rather than using research findings to support a point of view. Systematically, it identifies research with the people who have done it and presents enough information about the research process to excite students to learn not only about the family but also about how knowledge is acquired and systematized.

Finally, the book strives to avoid the confusion of profundity with obscurantism. It assumes that the conceptual apparatus essential to an understanding of the field can be employed in a clear and simple writing style that makes learning a pleasure rather than a chore.

Stillwater, Oklahoma   Gerald R. Leslie
August 1966

Contents

Part V. THE FAMILY LIFE CYCLE

Part | I

CROSS-CULTURAL PERSPECTIVE

1 | *The Nature of Family Organization*

The family is, as far as we know, the toughest institution we have. It is, in fact, the institution to which we owe our humanity. We know no other way of making human beings except by bringing them up in a family. Of course this does not mean that widows cannot bring up children; but the widowed mother brings up her children to know that their father is dead, that they had a father, and that the children next door have a father. The model is still there. And of course this holds for the widower as well. But we know no other way to bring children up to be human beings, able to act like men and women, and able to marry other men and women and bring up children, except through the family.[1]

T HE quotation above indicates how fundamental the family is in human life. Families exist everywhere and have existed throughout human existence on this planet. Everyone belongs to at least one family, and virtually everyone lives in one or more family groups. Although there are occasional individuals in most societies who live apart from their families for a time, both they and their kinsmen are conscious of the living apart and still think it best to live in families. The family is the very cradle of human nature. Family experience is necessary to turn a newborn infant—a less-than-human puking, bawling brat with visceral urges—into a fully human being with values and standards and the ability to live harmoniously with other people.[2]

The term, family, embraces a tremendous range of characteristics, behavior, and experience. To understand it fully would require lengthy excursions into genetics, embryology, anatomy, and physiology, to say nothing of law, economics, and politics. Obviously we cannot do all of this: some restrictions

[1] Margaret Mead, "The Impact of Cultural Changes on the Family," in *The Family in the Urban Community*, Detroit: The Merrill-Palmer School, 1953, p. 4.

[2] Kingsley Davis, "Final Note on a Case of Extreme Isolation," *American Journal of Sociology* 52 (March 1947), pp. 432-7.

must be placed upon the scope of our inquiry. This is a textbook in social science, and, though the boundaries of the area are fuzzy, it concentrates upon the study of the family as a social institution.

THE SOCIETAL CONTEXT

No one knows exactly how many societies there are, and have been, in the world. The boundaries separating one society from another are often exceedingly difficult to define, and human societies existed long before adequate means of recording their existence came into being. One scholar estimates that there have been at least 4000 separable human societies [3] ranging from small, preliterate societies of fewer than 400 people to modern societies of up to 750 million people.

Not even a majority of these societies has been systematically studied by social scientists. The most adequate analysis, to date, has been done by Murdock who has compiled an *Ethnographic Atlas* of 862 carefully selected societies.[4] Among those 862 societies, some are known through history and some exist now, some are preliterate and some are so-called civilized societies.

Few people, except for social scientists, have any idea that there have been so many societies. Moreover, when they first become aware of this tremendous range of human groups many people are prone to wonder how relevant the experience of small preliterate societies in the mid-Pacific, the Andes, or Africa is to the problems of large, complex societies such as that in the United States. They wonder whether the experience of 178 people isolated in a jungle and virtually without material possessions should be compared with the customs of a society of 205 million people who have created an automated, computerized economy and one in which the arts and humanities flourish.

The problems of comparing societies are complex and we need not get into them here. Suffice it to say that anthropologists believe that it is legitimate and useful to compare large and small societies in this fashion when the purpose is to try to understand the full range of solutions to universal human problems. Regardless of the size or technological advancement of the societies involved, each society's customs and institutions constitute an independent solution to the problem of ensuring survival. The family system of a society of 178 people in Peru might not be at all practical in the United States, but it does represent another means of coping with the same general human

---

[3] George P. Murdock, "World Ethnographic Sample," *American Anthropologist* 59 (Aug. 1957), pp. 664–87.

[4] George P. Murdock, *Ethnographic Atlas*, Pittsburgh: University of Pittsburgh Press, 1967.

problems that we face. Moreover, if we see that the majority, or even a significant minority, of societies have family systems that differ significantly from our own, it becomes more difficult for us to believe that our own system is divinely ordained or even inherently superior.[5]

SOCIAL INSTITUTIONS

The concept of *social institution*, or just institution, will appear throughout this book, for social scientists are much concerned with the institutional aspects of the family. At this point our task is to discuss briefly the major social institutions and to place the family institution within the context of the society's larger institutional structure.

Sociologists generally use the term institution in a slightly different and more technical way than does the man on the street. Sociologists view institutions as systems of social *norms*. Norms, of course, are a society's rules of conduct for its members. Norms range from the very formal—each person may have only one spouse—to the quite informal—letting father have the largest piece of pie for dessert. The number of such rules, or customary behaviors, is exceedingly large and covers almost every aspect of life. Growing up in a society means learning its system of norms so that as an adult one will be able to function successfully with other similarly socialized people.

Although most people may not be aware of it, norms are organized into patterns. In the family area, for example, there are norms that specify which persons in the society are eligible to marry, how many spouses they may have, who is eligible to marry whom, when they should marry, who should be the boss in the family, where they should live, what the division of labor between the family members should be, the proper attitudes toward children and oldsters, and so on. Detailed examination of the normative system controlling family behavior is a major task in subsequent chapters. And similar examples could be given for many other areas of social life.

In all societies, complex normative patterns appear in certain basic areas. There is always a normative system governing the legitimate use of power in the society. We call this system of norms government or, in sociological terms, the political institution. Similarly, another normative system defines the

[5] The tendency of peoples everywhere to regard their own ways of doing things as the best ways is, of course, the basic social science concept of *ethnocentrism*. Ethnocentrism serves the valuable function of promoting loyalty to one's own society and its institutions but it makes it difficult for us to see the essential relativity of cultural practices. The principle of *cultural relativity* holds that the functions and meaning of institutions and practices can be understood only in the context of the larger culture in which they are found—not in the context of our values and our practices.

production, distribution, and consumption of goods and services: the economic institution. A third normative system regulates man's relation to the supernatural: the religious institution. The educational institution is concerned with the transmission of values, attitudes, knowledge, and skills from one generation to the next. And there are always rules regulating adult sex relationships and procreation: the family institution.

All societies have these major institutions: family, government, economic system, education, and religion. The content of its institutions determines in large measure the character of the society. Understanding these basic institutions leads to understanding of the society.[6]

The various institutions of a society are related to one another. Government, for example, impinges upon the family in many ways. The authority wielded within the family may well stand in some inverse relation to the power vested in the government: when the government is weak the family may need to exercise considerable control of individual behavior and vice versa. Government may provide a host of services to families and their members or it may require that families be largely self-sufficient.

Moreover, the interrelations among a society's institutions may vary over time. As we shall learn, there was a time in our own history when there was relatively little differentiation among the major institutions: when the family performed many of what today are the functions of government, religion, and the schools. Somewhat later on, Western religious institutions became quite powerful and restricted and controlled family life. Still other changes saw government come to exercise great regulatory power, and current interrelations between the family and the economic system have much to do with the nature of present-day family problems. One social institution can be understood adequately only in the context of its relations with other institutions.

FUNCTIONAL REQUISITES FOR SOCIETAL SURVIVAL

The fact that certain institutions are found in all known societies suggests that societies may not be able to exist without them. Or, to put it differently,

[6] Unfortunately for precise analysis, sociologists occasionally use the term institution not only in its technical sense but also in its lay usage. Thus the man on the street is likely to refer to prisons and hospitals as institutions. Actually institutionalization is a sociological process, going on in many areas of life simultaneously. Students who are interested in fuller understanding of institutions and the process of institutionalization are referred to J. O. Hertzler, *American Social Institutions: A Sociological Analysis*, Boston: Allyn and Bacon 1961, and to Robert K. Merton, *Social Theory and Social Structure*, Glencoe, Illinois: The Free Press, 1957.

the major social institutions play a very large role in accomplishing those basic functions which are essential to a society's survival.

Apparently there are certain minimum tasks that must be performed in all societies. Unless they are performed adequately, the society would cease to exist. An analogy may help to make the point clear. We might hypothesize that a quality-control department is essential to the survival of a manufacturing company. A company might survive if it put out an occasional defective piece of merchandise, but if much of its product were defective, customers would take their business elsewhere and the company would go bankrupt. Perhaps the only way to prevent this from happening is to have a quality-control department to oversee the production process and to make sure that the company's product uniformly meets predetermined standards.

Notice that we are not saying that the conscious purpose of a quality-control department is to keep a company in business. Nor are we saying that a company could not be established and operate without a quality-control department. We are saying that, in the long run, a company that does not develop effective means of quality control is likely not to be able to meet the competition and, hence, is likely not to survive.

So it is with societies. To speak of there being functional requisites to a society's survival does not mean that each society is aware that certain tasks must be performed and that it consciously creates arrangements to provide for them. Nor is it to say that there have never been societies in which these tasks were not properly provided for. It is to say that if such societies existed, they have long since ceased to exist.

Social scientists, through study of what societies actually do, have concluded that there are certain minimum conditions that must be met. These generally agreed upon functional requisites that are met principally through a society's major institutions include the following. (1) There must be provision for the continued adequate biologic functioning of the members of the society. (2) There must be provision for the reproduction of new members of the society. (3) There must be provision for the adequate socialization of new members of the society. (4) There must be arrangements for the production and distribution of goods and services. (5) There must be provision for the maintenance of order within the group and with outsiders. (6) The meaning of life must be defined and the motivation for group and individual survival must be maintained.[7]

Continued Biologic Functioning. In our analysis of human social life, we

---

[7] For an extended treatment of the nature and role of functional requisites, see John W. Bennett, and Melvin M. Tumin, *Social Life: Structure and Function*, New York: Alfred A. Knopf, 1948, Ch. 4.

should never forget that man is fundamentally a biological organism who shares problems of survival with all other animal species. His survival depends at least upon provision of the basic necessities of food, clothing, and shelter. Without these he could not remain healthy—and the maintenance of health is a part of this requisite to societal survival. Man must be relatively healthy also in order to successfully reproduce his kind, and reproduction is a part of the maintenance of continued biologic functioning. The provision of food, clothing, and shelter of course implies that there must be an organized pattern of work. Food, clothing, and shelter must be produced and they must be distributed, according to some notion of equity, among the society's members. Except in the technologically simplest of societies, the provision for continued biologic functioning does not stop at this rudimentary level. In societies that operate above the subsistence level, the basic necessities are elaborated into standards of nutrition, comfort, style, medical care, family planning, and so on. But whatever the level at which the society operates, certain minimum provisions in this area are essential to its survival.

It should be apparent that two major social institutions are deeply involved in meeting this functional requisite for societal survival. The production and distribution of goods and services occurs through the operation of the economic system. The usual consumption unit for these goods and services is the family. Moreover, the family is the unit of reproduction and the primary source of care for ailing persons. It is no accident that the meeting of functional requisites is accomplished significantly through social institutions. Institutions develop originally in response to societies' needs to survive.

Adequate Reproduction. That the various functional requisites are interrelated has been shown by our reference to reproduction when talking primarily about continued biologic functioning. The problem of replacement of members of the society is so fundamental, however, that it deserves separate discussion.

It should be obvious that unless a society makes provision for an adequate number of children to be born and for those children to be protected and cared for, the population will dwindle and eventually disappear. All societies have normative systems which regulate the processes of child-bearing and child-rearing. These societal rules define who is qualified to bear children, when reproduction may begin, how many children should be born, how the children should be cared for, and so on. These norms make up part of the institution that we call the family.

Even in this area, which seems to fall squarely within the institutional sphere of the family, other social institutions are involved. The educational system, for example, shares with the family the care and training of the young. The replacement of societal members may occur also through the recruitment of members from other societies. In the modern world this process sometimes assumes large proportions through the process of immigration. Immigrants require resocialization into the normative system of the new society, again involving the educational institution. No society for long, however, depends too much upon immigration to provide new members. New adults are not a dependable source of replacements as are infants born into the society, and infants born into the group are not faced with conflicts between two normative systems. In all societies, the replacement of members occurs primarily through reproduction.

Socialization of New Members. The term, socialization, encompasses the whole process of learning the values, attitudes, knowledge, skills, and techniques which a society possesses—in short, it involves learning the culture. A very important part of the culture is the normative system, including the major social institutions. Socialization molds the child's biological potential into the pattern of functioning that we call human personality.

Socialization is equivalent to education in the very broadest sense. It includes the indirect and unanticipated learning that occurs whenever the child observes parents or others in interaction. Thus the child learns socially disapproved as well as approved behaviors and masters the nuances which are not taught in school, college, or in apprenticeship.

No society allows socialization to proceed purely according to chance. The family institution includes norms defining proper parental behavior in front of and in relation to children. It defines what things parents properly may teach children and what they may not. Beyond the familial contribution, and intertwined with it, there always lies a body of knowledge and practice shared by the society at large which the society transmits to all new members. For unless the members of a society share a common core of values, beliefs, and practices, the organization of the society cannot be maintained.

The organization of the socialization process outside the family is, of course, what we call the educational institution. It may be rudimentary and nonspecialized, involving only a few wise men passing on the ancient lore and youngsters working in informal apprenticeship with adults, or it may be highly organized and complex, including nursery schools, schools, colleges, and graduate schools.

The socialization function does not cease when adulthood is reached. The socialization of the young is so dramatic that historically most of our attention has focused upon it. And the essentially Freudian emphasis in psychology has concentrated attention upon the development of personality occurring during the first few years of life. We are learning more and more, however, that significant learning occurs throughout life. The college senior has only begun to prepare for his occupational role, and it takes a very fundamental and pervasive pattern of learning to transform him from callow youth into the mature, poised, knowledgeable, self-confident leader he may be as a middle-aged adult. Similarly, becoming a husband or wife and a parent involves learning attitudes, sentiments, and skills that are not learned in school. Even the process of becoming old involves complicated learning that the young and middle-aged cannot appreciate. The need for society to socialize its members may be most dramatic in the early years of life, but the successful continued functioning of a society is equally dependent upon the continued socialization of its adult members.[8]

Production and Distribution of Goods and Services. All known societies have norms defining what goods shall be produced, how, and by whom. At bottom is the problem of ensuring the survival of individual biological organisms. But the regulation of economic activity does not stop here. All societies elaborate their regulations in this area to provide for a division of labor among the members of the society. The economic and family institutions become intertwined, for there is always a division of labor between the sexes and between adults and children. The definition of what is man's work and what is woman's work both derives from the family and is further influenced by it. The division of labor among age groups similarly is partly a family and partly an economic matter. Further, the production of goods results in the accumulation of property and necessitates the development of rules for transmitting property from one generation to the next. Such rules again are involved in both the family and the economic system.

The adequate functioning of these various sets of norms ensures that the necessary goods will be produced, that they will be distributed in predictable fashion, and that competition among the members of the society will be limited and controlled.

Maintenance of Order. The rules which serve to maintain order within societies range from informal customs to carefully formulated and legally enforced codes. All societies have such customs and codes to govern relationships among members of the society and between members of the society and outsiders.

This is the general area involving the legitimate use of power and force through what we call the political institution. Through organizations ranging from a few tribal elders to large nation states, societies regulate behavior in

[8] The recently emerged major emphasis, among sociologists, upon socialization throughout the life cycle is reflected in, Orville G. Brim, Jr., and Stanton Wheeler, *Socialization After Childhood: Two Essays*, New York: John Wiley and Sons, 1966. See also, John A. Clausen, ed., *Socialization and Society*, Boston: Little, Brown and Company, 1968.

the interests of the group. Police forces, regulatory commissions, courts, prisons and the like are representative of the enforcement apparatus. Such apparatus usually is quite conspicuous in the society, and people tend to remain quite aware of the potential threats thus presented.

Yet it is inherent in the nature of human social organization that the threat of force is a far more effective deterrent to deviation from approved behavior than is the actual use of force. In fact, the need to use force on any great scale is likely to be symptomatic of ineffective social organization. Even in the most complex society with the most elaborate regulatory and enforcement agencies, there simply cannot be enough policemen and other officers to force people to conform. Imagine, for example, what would happen if most citizens did not habitually obey traffic laws or voluntarily abstain from stealing. The vast majority of violators would go unapprehended, and those who were caught would overflow the jails and swamp the courts.[9] The threat of force is effective only when it does not often have to be used, and all societies depend primarily upon other means for securing conformity to expected behavior.

The primary technique for gaining conformity to social norms in all societies is the thorough socialization of society's members. The socialization process normally produces persons who have so thoroughly learned the official and unofficial norms that not only do they not want to violate the norms but it does not often occur to them that they might do so. It is common knowledge, for example, that small children are notoriously light-fingered. A five-year-old is likely to pick up attractive items in a store with little sense of guilt because he has not yet learned how much other people disapprove of such behavior. A few years later, he may still steal small items he wants, but now with furtiveness and guilt. By the time he reaches adulthood, he ordinarily does not have to be watched and he now helps teach other younger persons that stealing is reprehensible. The word, conscience, is used to refer to this internalization of norms within the personality.

Here, again, the family institution and the political institution interpenetrate. Parents and siblings, aided by the formal educational system, assume the basic task of teaching conformity to the norms which the political system has the official responsibility for enforcing. Without effective cooperation among the various institutions, order would soon break down and the society would disintegrate.

---

[9] A good illustration is provided by sit-ins and other demonstrations used by the civil rights movement in the middle 1960's. The police ordinarily were not able to cope with hundreds of Negroes and whites who marched and sat in violation of law and police orders. Mass arrests simply filled the jails but did little to restore the *status quo ante.* Eventually the police were forced to compromise and to depend upon voluntary compliance with the law.

Maintaining Motivation for Survival. To some degree the adequate performance of all of the preceding functional requisites depends upon this last one. There is a universal human problem of ascribing meaning to life itself and providing the society's members with motivation for their own survival.

The societal rationale for valuing existence varies from society to society, but some rationale always is provided. In one society the primary purpose of life may be to provide for the worship of the Almighty. In a second, the overriding goal may be the production of sons and continuation of the family line. Alternative and overlapping goals in life might include the appreciation of nature, the destruction of enemies, and purely hedonistic enjoyment. Some combination of goals is often found.

The religious institution is usually deeply involved in this area. One of the functions of religion is to define and strengthen ultimate values and to define man's relation to the supernatural. The interpenetration of the religious and the family institution in this connection probably is obvious. In relatively undifferentiated societies it may be the father, himself, who serves as priest and as intermediary with the Almighty. In more complex societies, it is still likely to be the family that guides the young into participation in the formal religious organizations and which complements the instruction of the church with family devotions and home worship. This complementariness is well illustrated by holidays such as Christmas and Easter, Chanukah and Yom Kippur, in which family, church, and synagogue are deeply involved.

In this discussion of the functional requisites for societal survival we have tried to show the minimum conditions for a society's continued existence and something of the various roles played by the major social institutions. We have stressed the family's involvement in these tasks and the overlapping of the roles of the family and those of other institutions.

The Nature of Family Organization

The family is sometimes called the basic social institution. For, although the several major institutions are to be found in all known societies, their relative importance and even the clarity with which they are defined and differentiated varies from one society to another. The family is always a conspicuous feature of the social organization. The family is always easy to locate, is in the constant awareness of the society's members, and is deeply involved in the performance of the functional requisites. These are sweeping generalizations. They are true enough—but not without qualification. There follow several hundred pages of qualifications!

THE NUCLEAR FAMILY

Not only is the family a universal institution, but a specific form of the family—the nuclear family—is found in all known societies.[10] Americans have little difficulty understanding the concept of the nuclear family because in our society we tend to equate the nuclear family with family organization in general. The United States has the nuclear family as the basic residential family unit.

The term, nuclear family, refers simply to a group of at least two adults of opposite sex, living in a socially approved sex relationship, with their own or adopted children. It is the familiar unit of mother, father, and children. Most anthropologists believe the nuclear unit to be a distinct functional unit in all societies.[11] Often it is to be found existing as part of a larger kinship unit, embedded in a network of grandparents, grandchildren, uncles, cousins, and so on, but even in these cases the nuclear family is recognized by all concerned as a distinct unit and it usually has its own private living quarters. Moreover, the nuclear family ordinarily is the smallest kinship unit which is treated as a separate unit by the rest of the society.

In specific instances the nuclear family may contain only one adult or more than two adults. Similarly there may or may not be children present. If the husband has died or been divorced, the wife may continue the family alone and vice versa. Or there may be a grandparent or unmarried brother or sister living with the family. Either the married couple may have had no children or the children may be grown and gone. The important thing about these exceptions is that they are exceptions. The "normal" way to live is with one's own spouse and one's own children, and it is toward this model that societies strive.

Before proceeding further, it may be helpful to distinguish the *family*, as we

[10] George P. Murdock, *Social Structure*, New York: The Macmillan Company, 1949, Ch. 1.

[11] Ibid. Murdock's view apparently is shared by most anthropologists. See, for example, Robert H. Lowie, *Primitive Society*, New York: Boni & Liveright, 1920, pp. 66-7; and Franz Boas, *et al.*, *General Anthropology*, Boston: D. C. Heath, 1938, p. 411. For a contrary view, see Ralph Linton, *The Study of Man*, New York: D. Appleton-Century, 1936, p. 153. A widely discussed apparent exception is alleged to be the Nayar of Malabar. The Nayar until fairly recently had an arrangement in which the husband lived with his sister's family and visited his wife only at night for sexual purposes. The Nayar are not a separate society, however, but are a caste group in the south of India. Even among the Nayar, the nuclear family is becoming a more prominent residential unit. See Joan P. Mencher, "The Nayars of South Malabar," pp. 163-91, in Meyer F. Nimkoff, ed., *Comparative Family Systems*, Boston: Houghton Mifflin, 1965. The general problem of the universality of the nuclear family is discussed further in Chapter 5, Utopian Family Experiments.

define it, from *marriage*. We reserve the term, marriage, not for the married couple themselves but for the complex of customs which regulates the relationship between them and which provides for the creation of a family. Marriage specifies the appropriate way of establishing a relationship, the normative structure for ordering the relationship, and often includes provision for terminating it.[12]

The Family of Orientation and the Family of Procreation. To view the nuclear family as a set of parents and their children is to view it in static, cross-sectional fashion. It describes the nuclear family at any given point in time but it fails to describe the experience in the nuclear family of any given person.

Normally, during his lifetime, each person in the society is a member of two different, overlapping nuclear families. He is born into a nuclear family composed of himself, his siblings (brothers and sisters), and his parents. This nuclear family is called the family of orientation. At marriage the individual leaves his family of orientation to create a new nuclear family composed of himself, his spouse, and his children. This new nuclear family in which the individual lives as an adult is called the family of procreation.[13] The families of orientation and procreation are diagrammed in Figure 1. The word, ego, the Latin word for self, is used to stand for any particular individual.

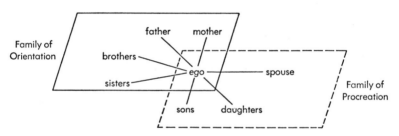

FIGURE 1. *Diagram of the families of orientation and procreation.*

The term, nuclear family, refers either to the family of orientation or to the family of procreation. Note that ego is the only person who is a member of both of these particular nuclear families. If we were to diagram the nuclear families of each other member of ego's nuclear families (his mother, or his wife, or his sister), the same thing would be true. Each pair of nuclear families would have only one member in common. As will be shown in the next chapter, this has much to do with the complexity of kinship structure.

Nuclear Family Functions. If we look at the common characteristics and

---

[12] Murdock, *Social Structure*, p. 1.

[13] W. Lloyd Warner, "A Methodology for the Study of the Development of Family Attitudes," *Social Science Research Council Bulletin*, No. 18, 1933.

functioning of nuclear families in various societies, we see that they parallel very closely the functional requisites for societal survival discussed in the preceding section. We find that: (1) the marriage relationship always provides for meeting the sex needs of adult members of the society; (2) the nuclear family is the unit of reproduction; (3) the nuclear family is a unit of common residence; (4) the nuclear family is the primary unit of economic cooperation; and (5) the nuclear family has important responsibility for the socialization of children.

1. The nuclear family, through the marital relationship, always provides for meeting the sex needs of its adult members. Sex is an exceedingly powerful impulse that is nowhere permitted expression without regulation; unregulated sexual expression would threaten the cooperative relationships necessary within the family and within the society. Neither do societies deny the opportunity for regular sexual gratification to any sizable proportion of their adult members. Occasional adults, or even defined groups of adults, may remain celibate, but what evidence is available suggests that whenever sexual gratification is denied to a sizable segment of men or women the society is likely to become unstable and major social change will occur.

> Marriage has many pains, but celibacy has no pleasures.
>
> —Dr. Johnson

It would be a mistake, however, to assume that the availability of sex relationships within marriage accounts for its existence. In our own society, whose formal norms prohibit sexual intercourse before marriage, this might seem to be true. Many other societies, however, grant considerable sex freedom to unmarried adolescents and young adults, imposing more restrictions upon the availability of sex partners after a person is married than before. If sex were the only, or even the chief, reason for marriage, we would expect persons in these societies to resist the idea of marriage. Such is not the case. People marry just as predictably in these societies as in our own. Most societies appear to assign full adult status only to married people, and adult functioning with its sexual division of labor is more difficult for the single person. We need to look to the full pattern of relationships between men and women to account for the universality of marriage.

2. The sex relationship between husband and wife is expected to result in

the production of children. The fact that all societies place high value upon children testifies to the necessity of children to the society's survival. Generally, all children are loved and cared for, but important distinctions may be made among them. Male children, for example, often are preferred to female children, with the occasional practice of female infanticide being found. In all societies the reproductive function of the nuclear family is emphasized.

It even appears that some societies make the sex relationship between husband and wife contingent upon the fact of reproduction rather than the other way around as in our own society. The Banaro of New Guinea, for example, forbid the new husband to have sexual intercourse with his wife until after she has borne a child by another man who is carefully chosen for this purpose.[14] The husband is granted sexual access to the wife only after her ability to produce children has been established.

3. In most societies, residential kin groups are not limited to the nuclear family. There may be grandparents and grandchildren present. The group may include brothers and their wives, or sisters and their husbands. There may also be unmarried siblings, aunts, nephews, and so on. The residential kin group may be larger than the nuclear family. Always included within the residential kin group, however, and identifiable within it, is the nuclear family.

Where larger residential kin units are found, there may be common facilities, such as cooking space, dining space, and space for relaxation, but there are usually separate dwellings or apartments also. Each nuclear family ordinarily has some private quarters.

4. Economic cooperation within the nuclear family, along with the sex relationship between the father and mother, serves to bind it tightly together. This cooperation is rooted in biological differences between the sexes and is reinforced by the culturally defined division of labor. Males everywhere are the physically more powerful sex, while females everywhere have their freedom of movement hampered by the facts of pregnancy and nursing. All societies have developed a sex division of labor which assigns much of the heavier work and most of the roaming to men. Women, of course, are assigned more household tasks and the routine caring for children.[15] Neither the man nor the woman can function at full efficiency without the services of the other.

All societies also have a division of labor by age, assigning certain lighter tasks to children. Our own urban industrial society has restricted the number of such childhood tasks severely, but even among us there exist tasks ranging from mowing the lawn to walking the dog, and from going to the grocery to

[14] Murdock, *Social Structure*, p. 5.

[15] There also is great variation from one society to another in the tasks deemed appropriate for men and women. The sex division of labor is a product both of biological differences and learned behavior patterns. See Margaret Mead, *Sex and Temperament in Three Primitive Societies*, New York: Mentor Books, 1950.

baby-sitting with younger siblings. In most of the world's more agriculture-oriented societies, the economic contribution of children is more obvious and greater. This division of labor continues into subsequent stages of the family life-cycle when the dependency patterns may become reversed. One day the parents will need more support, and the children, now adult, will be in a position to provide it. Both across sex lines and generational levels, the fact of economic cooperation helps to account for the universality of the nuclear family.

Nowhere else except in marriage can we find one other person concerned with so many of our needs. No doubt many people are capable of doing the same thing for us, but there are many advantages in having one person perform these various functions.

—Allan Fromme

---

5. Even in the most highly specialized societies, the nuclear family has the basic responsibility for the care and socialization of children during their early years. The facts of parturition and nursing determine that there will be an earlier and more intense contact with the mother. Ordinarily she assumes most of the responsibility for physical care of the infant and only gradually does the father become involved in training the child. The training process ultimately is much more complex than the mere physical care, and it requires the combined efforts of both parents, and frequently siblings, to prepare the child for each subsequent stage in life. Only the father can transmit to his sons the skills required of adult males in the society, and only the mother can provide comparable training for her daughters. Boys learn partly from their fathers and partly from their mothers how to interact with members of the opposite sex, and it takes a father as well as a mother to teach a girl how to become a woman. The more elaborate the society the more agencies are likely to share in this socialization process, but the nuclear family everywhere plays an important role in it.

The nuclear family everywhere is characterized by sexual, reproductive, residential, economic, and socialization functions.[16] Groups and agencies out-

[16] An analysis by Ira Reiss re-argues the position that most of these functions may be exercised by groups other than the nuclear family and that only the key function of nurturant socialization is the exclusive prerogative of a small family group. See Ira L. Reiss, "The Universality of the Family: A Conceptual Analysis," *Journal of Marriage and the Family* 27 (Nov. 1965), pp. 443–53. For another challenge to this position, see S. C. Lee and Audrey Battrud, "Marriage Under a Monastic Mode of Life: A Preliminary Report on the Hutterite Family in South Dakota," *Journal of Marriage and the Family*, 29 (Aug. 1967), pp. 512–20.

side the family often share in the fulfillment of these tasks but never to the exclusion of the nuclear family. No society has yet found a satisfactory substitute for the nuclear family.

As far as we know there is no biological instinct that makes a man into a good father. It is necessary to persuade him to want to be a father, and each society uses different means of doing so. Sometimes he is persuaded to be a father because he needs an heir to inherit his land. The French-Canadians used to persuade him to be a father by not giving bachelors hunting or fishing licenses. Sometimes he was persuaded to be a father through a system of ancestor worship, in which a man lacking children to worship him after death had no proper existence in the next world.

There have been all varieties of inducements, and they all tend to break down. The real variation through history has been in what has been done with the role of fathers. What has been done with mothers has been extremely monotonous on the whole, and heavily determined biologically, although it has varied, of course, with the invention of baby carriages and feeding bottles and things of that sort.

Margaret Mead, "The Impact of Cultural Changes on the Family," in *The Family in the Urban Community*, Detroit: The Merrill-Palmer School, 1953, pp. 3–4.

KINSHIP ORGANIZATION

The nature of Western family organization makes it easy for American students to grasp the concept of the nuclear family. To a very large extent the nuclear family is the family in the United States. This same family structure is a handicap, however, when it comes to understanding the larger phenomenon of kinship organization as it exists over most of the world. For in most societies, nuclear families do not exist in the relative isolation from other kin units which is true of the United States. Most societies have additional forms of family or kinship organization. Nuclear familes may be combined through the practice of plural marriage or through extension of the parent-child relationship into composite families. In addition, the means of tracing descent or relationship often produce larger kinship units known variously as lineages, moieties, clans, and so on. None of these other forms of kinship organization is universal, so discussion of them is contained in the next chapter rather than here. It is important, however, to emphasize, along with the universality of the nuclear family, that most societies have a kinship organization more elaborate and more complex than our own.

THE FAMILY AS A SOCIAL GROUP

So far we have emphasized the family as a social institution. As an institution, the family is a normative system. It consists of more or less formal rules and regulations concerning the conduct of a major aspect of life. As such, the family institution is not limited to the particular form of expression given to it by a particular group of people, by the Jones family, say, or the Kowalskis. The family institution does not come into existence with the Joneses or the Kowalskis, and it does not die with them. The family as an institution is an abstraction or, rather, a series of abstractions from behavior. By observing the behavior of a sufficiently large and representative group of people in a society and by studying its official codes, we can state that the family institution of that society has certain features. This form of analysis provides a powerful tool for understanding human behavior.

There is yet another way of viewing families and their behavior, however. This way involves focusing upon the specific groups of people through whom the family institution is enacted and transmitted to subsequent generations. The distinction is not completely clear-cut: it is a matter of emphasis. The nuclear family, for example, is an institutional form—a series of prescriptions and proscriptions—about the relationships among its members and also refers to a specific group of people—mother, father, sons, and daughters.

There are a number of fairly common family groups in the United States in addition to the nuclear family. They are not fully institutionalized in the sense that they present models for people to strive toward. Instead, they constitute variations on the nuclear family theme. People who think that it is normal and desirable to live in independent nuclear families sometimes live in different circumstances. And to fully understand the operation of our nuclear family system requires some awareness of some of these variations.

The Household. A household is simply a group of people who share a common dwelling. Normally a group united by ties of marriage, blood, or adoption at least forms the core of a household. There usually is a nuclear family with perhaps some unmarried relatives or aged parents in addition. A household may comprise, on the other hand, an unmarried brother and sister who live together. Even several bachelors living together constitute a household. A household often is a family group but it need not be: it may be an unrelated group of people who share the customary living arrangements of a family group.[17]

Primary Family. A primary family consists of the head of a household and all other persons in the household who are related to him. In the normal course of events, the head of the household is the husband and father and the related persons are his wife and children.

Secondary Family. A secondary family comprises two or more persons who are related to one another and who live with a primary family to whom they are not related. A servant couple provides one illustration, and a pair of married college students living in a professor's home provides another.

Subfamily. A subfamily is a married couple with or without children, or one parent with one or more children under 18 years of age, related to and living with a primary family. Young married couples living with one set of parents, or a widowed wife and her children who have returned to the parental home, provide illustrations.

These definitions are essentially those of the United States Census and they are given here because the Census is the primary source of statistical information about the structure of families and the living arrangements of families

TABLE 1. *Households, Families, Subfamilies, Married Couples, and Unrelated Individuals in the United States, 1969.*

TYPE OF UNIT	1969	PER CENT CHANGE 1960-1969
Households	61,805,000	+17.1
Families	50,510,000	+12.0
Primary Families	50,416,000	+12.3
Secondary Families	94,000	−54.6
Subfamilies	1,163,000	−23.2
Married Couples	44,440,000	+10.5
Unrelated Individuals*	14,063,000	+26.8

* Persons who are not living with any relatives.
Source: U. S. Bureau of the Census, *Statistical Abstract of the United States: 1970* (Washington, D. C.), p. 35.

[17] For analyses of recent changes in the composition of American family groups, see Hugh Carter and Paul C. Glick, *Marriage and Divorce: A Social and Economic Study,* Cambridge, Mass.: Harvard University Press, 1970, Ch. 6; and Abbott L. Ferriss, *Indicators of Change in the American Family,* New York: Russell Sage Foundation, 1970, pp. 30–49.

and unrelated individuals in the United States. Summary figures from the Census for the year 1969 are shown in Table 1.

When one focuses on the family as a social group his attention is directed inward toward the relationships within the family unit. It may be some exaggeration to say that institutional analyses emphasize relationships between the family and other aspects of the society while group analyses are more social psychological, focusing upon the emotional dynamics within the family. But a difference in emphasis, at least, is there. Both institutional and social psychological analyses will be used throughout this book.

Summary

No one knows just how many human societies there are and have been, for societal boundaries often are difficult to define. There are, however, at least 4000 identifiable societies, ranging from preliterate to modern. The culture of each of these societies constitutes an independent solution to the common human problem of group living. Study of these societies will aid us to understand our own society and our own family system.

The term, institution, is used by social scientists to refer to complex systems of social norms organized about the preservation of basic societal values. All societies have certain basic institutions—government, an economic system, an educational system, a religious institution, and the family. The various institutions in a society are interrelated. Each impinges upon all of the others and the various relationships among them change over time.

A society's institutions play major roles in performing the tasks essential for the society's survival. Such fundamental tasks are called functional requisites. Functional requisites include: (1) provision for the continued adequate biological functioning of the society's members; (2) provision for reproduction; (3) provision for the socialization of new members of the society; (4) provision for the production and distribution of goods and services; (5) provision for the maintenance of order within the group; and (6) maintenance of the motivation for individual and group survival. The family plays an important role in the performance of each of these essential tasks, sharing the responsibility differentially with the other major institutions.

The nuclear family, composed of a married pair and their offspring, is a somewhat distinct human unit in all known societies. During his lifetime each individual normally is a member of two such units, the family of orientation and the family of procreation. The nuclear family: (1) provides regular sexual outlet for most of its adult members; (2) is the basic unit of procreation; (3) is the basic unit of economic cooperation; (4) maintains a common residence; (5) and has basic responsibility for the indoctrination of the young.

In most societies, nuclear families are organized into larger kinship units. Adequate understanding of social structure requires analysis of the whole of kinship organization, not just of the nuclear family.

The family may be conceived of not only as an institution but also as a social group. When one focuses upon the family as a social group, his attention is directed toward its internal functioning more than toward its relationships with other aspects of the society. Some common forms taken by family groups in the United States include primary families, secondary families, and subfamilies. These units are organized into households, which are residential units.

SUGGESTED READINGS

Bell, Norman W., and Vogel, Ezra F., eds., A Modern Introduction to the Family, New York: The Free Press, 1968. An excellent book of readings on the family from the structure-function theoretical framework.

Bennett, John W., and Tumin, Melvin, Social Life: Structure and Function, New York: Alfred A. Knopf, 1948. Includes a whole chapter on the nature of functional requisites for societal survival. Sophisticated but good introductory treatment.

Farber, Seymour M., Mustacchi, Piero, and Wilson, Roger H. L., Man and Civilization: The Family's Search for Survival, New York: McGraw-Hill, 1965. This volume constitutes the proceedings of a multidisciplinary conference concerned with the apparent drift of modern society away from the family as the fundamental social structure. Re-affirms the indispensability of the family and provides a broad body of facts and interpretations to permit the making of wise choices concerning the society's and the family's future.

Hertzler, Joyce O., American Social Institutions: A Sociological Analysis, Boston: Allyn and Bacon, 1961. A thorough and excellent treatment of American institutions.

Merton, Robert K., Social Theory and Social Structure, Glencoe, Illinois: The Free Press, 1957. One of the most sophisticated analyses of the whole concept of social institution. Assumes considerable background in sociology.

Murdock, George P., Social Structure, New York: The Macmillan Company, 1949. The best single source available on the nature of the nuclear family and the combination forms into which the nuclear family frequently is integrated.

Nye, F. Ivan, and Berardo, Felix M., eds., Emerging Conceptual Frameworks in Family Analysis, New York: The Macmillan Company, 1966. Systematic analysis of eleven different theoretical approaches to the analysis of family data. Includes anthropological, psychoanalytic, economic, legal, and religious approaches in addition to sociological approaches.

Skolnick, Arlene S., and Skolnick, Jerome H., eds., *Family in Transition: Rethinking Marriage, Sexuality, Child Rearing, and Family Organization*, Boston: Little, Brown and Company, 1971. A provocative series of essays, the thrust of which is to challenge conventional views of marriage and family life.

FILMS

A House, a Wife, and a Singing Bird (available through Oklahoma State University Audio-Visual Center, Stillwater, Oklahoma), 30 minutes, color. A wise man tells a youth that old men dream dreams but it is the young men who make them come true, and to be happy, he must have a wife, a house, and a singing bird. Shows the young Indonesian searching for a place to live, ways that people make a living, customs, and finally the marriage ceremony.

Beginnings of Conscience (McGraw-Hill Book Company, Text-Film Division, 330 West 42nd St., New York, N. Y., 10036), 16 minutes. The social conscience which James Bryce, the adult, manifests is traced back to his socialization as a child. The conscience which he gradually develops in childhood through the experiencing of such social sanctions as force, exclusion, and ridicule, later functions almost automatically in adulthood to make him a social being.

Excited Turkeys (Grove Press Film Division, 80 University Place, New York, 10003), 10 minutes. Focuses on the traditional Thanksgiving dinner to examine the "apple pie" family. Studies the myths that Americans have created about their cultural and national identity.

Families First (R.K.O. Pathé, 1270 Avenue of the Americas, New York, N. Y., 10020), 17 minutes. Portrays the relationship of the home to the future happiness of children, emphasizing their need for affection, security, success, and new experiences. Dramatizes everyday happenings in the lives of two contrasting families to illustrate the causes of tension, frustration, and antisocial attitudes.

Family Life (United World Films, 211 Park Avenue South, New York, N. Y., 10003), 20 minutes. Each member of the family, in his own way, participates in the tasks of providing food, clothing, and shelter amid an atmosphere of cooperation and mutual concern.

Roots of Happiness (Sun Dial Films, 341 E. 43rd, New York, N. Y., 10017), 24 minutes. The story of a family living in a poor, rural area of Puerto Rico shows the needs and desires of small children as they grow to maturity. Demonstrates how boys imitate older men and the importance of both parents in providing adult role models.

Windy Day (Grove Press Film Division, 80 University Place, New York, 10003), 12 minutes. An animated film, featuring the voices of two young girls, deals with the responses of children to romance, marriage, and adulthood. The children muse about their parents getting married, growing old, and dying.

QUESTIONS AND PROJECTS

1. Explain how we have something to learn about the American family system from knowledge of the family systems of preliterate societies.
2. Define the concept of social institution. How are institutional patterns inferred from behavior?
3. Name the basic social institutions and give a brief definition of each. In what ways are the various institutions of a society interrelated? Illustrate.
4. Define the term, functional requisites. Have there ever been societies that did not provide for meeting the functional requisites? If so, what happened to them?
5. Show, through illustration, how the family is involved in meeting each of the functional requisites.
6. Why is the family sometimes called the basic social institution?
7. Define the term, nuclear family. Does the fact that some members of a society do not live in nuclear units detract from the universality of the nuclear family? Why or why not?
8. Distinguish between *the family* and *marriage*. What is the relationship between the two?
9. What is the family of orientation? The family of procreation? Draw a diagram indicating the relationship between them.
10. What are the universal functions of the nuclear family? Illustrate each.
11. What is meant by the family "as a social group"? How is the family as a social group different from the family as an institution?
12. Define each of the following terms: household; primary family; secondary family; subfamily.

2 | *Family Structure in World Perspective: I*

President Sékou Touré is trying to persuade Guinean males to marry only one wife.

It's an idea unlikely to spread to West Africa's largest Moslem country, Nigeria, where there is even a whisper of support for the female version of multiple marriage, polyandry.

"Wake up fellow women and let us march to freedom," a determined feminist has written to the Ibadan newspaper, *Daily Sketch*. "Let us show our male counterparts that we are also capable of managing and directing them . . . polyandry is the only answer."

Polygamy is common in Nigeria where about 13 million Moslem males are allowed four spouses by the Koran and where non-Moslem tribes nurture traditions of many wives.

The practice is common enough to inspire one French automobile manufacturer to advertise a new compact model as exactly what " a man with four wives needs." The maker claims the compact "is big enough to seat yourself and four buxom ladies in complete comfort." . . .

Women with several husbands are hard to find.

The Ibadan letter writer, lamenting the sad state of women in Nigeria said, "Perhaps it would be a happier life if the women were to have more than one husband instead of the men having many wives.

"I am not advocating that all these husbands should stay under the same roof because I know this will not be practicable—the woman may live alone. All she has to do is to rotate her husbands as to whom should spend the night with her and on what day."

. . . a newspaper columnist recently wrote, ". . . The truth is that men are polygamous by nature." . . .

The custom of marrying several women goes back to farm society when a man needing all the help he could get for his crops, married it. . . . Two of Nigeria's most widely known actors keep their troupes outfitted with leading ladies by marrying them all.

Polygamy also filled a need dictated by custom. A woman is likely to have nothing to do with her husband during her pregnancy and until she weans her child—a period of two years or more. The man solves his problem by finding another wife.

Despite [the columnist's] belief that the idea of "one man, one wife" is fast losing ground, some younger Africans see disadvantages in plural marriage.

According to one male student: "A man having two wives can hardly get peace of mind and can take but minor part in world affairs. If these wives are so jealous of each other, one may kill the other or the husband will die instead. And if Africans keep dying in this way, how can they concentrate on their unity?"[1]

T HIS quotation reveals both the timelessness and the contemporary urgency of some of the basic facts of family structure which are the subject matter for this chapter. The entire Mohammedan world has had a tradition of polygamy (more precisely, polygyny) for many hundreds of years. As we shall soon see, polygyny has been more highly valued over most of the world than has monogamy. Another common feature of family structure over much of the world has been a fairly drastic subordination of women to men. Some women, at least, have been regarded almost as the property of men—to be bought, sold, and disposed of by will. The divorce of a wife by her husband often has been very easy, while the reverse process, the divorce of a husband by his wife, often was difficult or even impossible.

It is easy both to underestimate and to overestimate the degree to which these things are still true. The average American's ignorance of other cultures and his naïve ethnocentric faith in the inherent superiority of his own patterns often results in his being unaware of how different we are from much of the rest of the world. At the same time, however, the past few decades have seen an unparalleled increase in communication among societies and a startling change in concepts of appropriate man-woman relationships. There are many parallels to the African situation described above. We may be experiencing a true world revolution in family patterns.[2]

The problem of large-scale change in family patterns will be treated later in this chapter. First, however, we need to establish the base from which change might be measured. Something of the basic nature of family organization was pointed out in Chapter 1. There the universality of the family, and of the nuclear family unit, was stressed. We pointed out, also, that nuclear families generally are combined into larger family units. The major part of this chapter deals with some of the resulting uniformities and variabilities in family patterns over the world.

1 Associated Press, March 15, 1968.

2 William J. Goode, *World Revolution and Family Patterns*, New York: The Free Press of Glencoe, 1963.

Composite Family Forms

Nuclear families, in various societies, are combined into larger family units in two basic ways. Either they are combined through the practice of plural marriage, or they are combined through extension of the parent-child relationship. Nuclear families combined through plural marriage are called *polygamous families* and those combined through the parent-child relation are called *extended families*.

POLYGAMOUS FAMILIES

Americans are prone, when they hear the word polygamy, to think immediately of the sexual aspects of marriage. Because of our traditional restriction of sexual activity outside of marriage and our frequent preoccupation with the erotic, we are likely to imagine polygamy as one long sexual orgy. Nothing could be further from the truth.

In the first place, polygamous marriage is based upon more than extension of the sexual privilege to additional partners. Most societies grant sexual privileges with persons to whom the individual is not and probably never will be married. Moreover, marriage involves more than just a socially approved sex relationship. For a marriage to exist, there must also be the expectation of reproduction by the couple, common residence, and economic cooperation. To understand polygamy it is necessary to emphasize these latter aspects of marriage.

One of the common errors made by Americans is to assume that polygamy is to some degree forced upon unenthusiastic women by lecherous men. In our own society, men do most of the more vigorous sexual pursuing and such a situation seems to make sense. Such attitudes, however, are not necessarily characteristic of polygamous societies. Where polygamy is fully institutionalized, women may be just as involved in its perpetuation as men are, and it is even conceivable that some men are pressured, by their wives, into taking additional marriage partners.

Perhaps an analogy will help to make the point. In the United States, women have been known to pressure their husbands to acquire possessions and other status symbols which the wives can use to raise their status with other wives. A woman may urge her husband, for example, to acquire a larger house, newer or more automobiles, domestic help, a new fur coat, or perhaps to take her on a lavish, expensive vacation. In a polygamous society, a woman might similarly urge her husband to take a second wife. After all, what kind of man is it who cannot afford a second wife? If he truly loved her, he would get another

wife to help her with all of her domestic duties. The first wife in polygamous societies often occupies a preferential or supervisory position and the second wife
may gain her something of a servant as well as a co-wife. Moreover, if women
over most of the world believe that their husbands are sexually too demanding,
a second wife might serve the useful function of periodically relieving the first
wife of sexual duty.

---

*Certainly the Chinese women's attitude toward polygyny was dif-
ferent from that of the women in the West who were brought up in
the idea of monogamy. In old Chinese fiction a great number of
women take their husbands' concubines for granted. The wife of an
official who does not accompany her husband on his travels but stays
home to care for his children and his parents readily understands his
taking a concubine. Others willingly accept concubines in their home.*

*The most striking example is perhaps the wife of Chia She in The
Dream of the Red Chamber, who tries to help her husband win a girl
who had caught his fancy. "What," says she indignantly, "other distinguished people can have several concubines, why not we?"*

*The wife of Hsi Men, in Chin Ping Mei, amiably receives the new
concubines of her insatiable husband; she cooperates with them in
arranging house parties, mediates their conflicts, and reprimands her
husband when he favors one concubine to the neglect of another: "You
are completely captivated by Chin-lien," she says, ". . . one of us,
Meng Yu-lo, suffers because you neglect her. You should go to her."*

—Olga Lang, *Chinese Family and Society*, New Haven:
Yale University Press, 1946, p. 50.

For his part, we might imagine the husband saying to his first wife, "But I
can't afford another wife. Sure Jones got his wife another wife, but he makes
more money than I do." As for the sexual privilege, even if we accept the
stereotype of males being highly sexed and desirous of sexual variety, it is
sexual privilege that men seek—not sexual duty. The most ardent Don Juan
might give up seduction if he knew he was going to have to sleep twice a week
with each of his conquests. Under polygamy the husband normally is required
to treat his wives equally, to live with them in regular rotation, and to have
sexual intercourse with them. Nothing dulls the sexual appetite more than
obligation! A twenty-year-old man might not think that he would be too
oppressed by such a burden. But twenty-year-old men can afford extra wives
just about as regularly as twenty-year-old men can afford large houses and fur

coats. The forty- or fifty-year-old man who can afford the extra wife may not be quite so confident of his sexual prowess.

This was an analogy, of course, and it should not be pressed too far. The basic points involved are these. First, polygamy involves far more than sex. It is intimately tied up with economic functioning and status considerations. Second, where polygamy exists it is likely to be supported by the values and attitudes of women as well as by those of men. And, third, polygamy is a normative system involving a whole series of obligations upon men and women. People in polygamous societies may react to those obligations much as we react to the obligations inherent in our monogamous system.

So far, in this discussion, we have been using the term, polygamy, in its lay sense. Technically, polygamy is the general term used to refer to all marriage forms that involve the taking of plural spouses. Under polygamy, the plural spouses may be either husbands or wives. Polygamy is subdivided into two types, *polygyny* and *polyandry*. Polygyny is the more common form, involving the taking of plural wives. Polyandry, the taking of plural husbands, is rare.

Polygyny. Again, because of our own cultural biases, it is not too difficult for most Americans to imagine polygynous societies. We may misunderstand polygyny, but at least we can imagine it. Polygyny further subdivides into two basic types, *sororal* and *nonsororal*. The Latin word *soror* means sister. Under sororal polygyny the wives are sisters. Under nonsororal polygyny, the wives may be unrelated.

The society best known to most Americans and practising sororal polygyny may be that of the Hebrews of scriptural times. Many students will remember the story of Jacob, Rachel, and Leah. Jacob wished to marry Rachel who was the younger daughter of Laban. Jacob worked for Laban for seven years in order to earn the "bride price" for Rachel only to be told that the younger daughter could not be married until the elder daughter was married. So Jacob took Leah and worked another seven years for Rachel.

Sororal polygyny is exceedingly widespread among the societies of the world.[3] Polygyny does produce problems of adjustment for the people who practice it (as does any form of marriage), and sororal polygyny seems to minimize some of these problems. Co-wives who are sisters are more likely to get along with one another than are co-wives who are not sisters. Having grown up together, they are likely to have similar values, attitudes, and ways of doing things. Jealousy between them is also less likely than is the case between unrelated women. This situation is often reflected in housing arrangements. The separa-

[3] George P. Murdock, *Social Structure*, New York: The Macmillan Company, 1949, p. 31.

tion of the dwellings of the co-wives is likely to be more marked if they are not sisters.

A special form of sororal polygyny is the *sororate*, which is a cultural rule specifying that the preferred mate for a widower is the sister of his deceased wife. Under the sororate, the marriages are successive rather than concurrent.

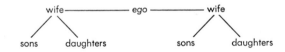

FIGURE 1. *Diagram of independent, polygynous family.*

In many societies, both sororal and nonsororal polygyny are found. The Mormons and the Crow Indians in the early United States are examples.[4] The breakdown of Mormon polygyny often is attributed to the fact that the Mormons permitted unrelated wives to live in close contact with one another and to the fact that Mormon husbands often showed definite preference for the most recently acquired wife.

Murdock has prepared estimates of the incidence of polygyny for one sample of 250 societies and for an expanded sample of 565 societies. Polygyny was found in 75 per cent of the first sample of societies and in 81 per cent of the second.[5]

Where it exists, polygyny usually is accorded higher status than is monogamy. Yet, even where polygyny is preferred, it tends to be practised only by a small segment of the population. In some instances the right to take multiple wives is limited to ruling families or to high-status persons. But even where such restrictions do not exist, most persons in polygynous societies remain monogamous. There are at least two reasons for this: (1) the economic factor and (2) the sex ratio.

1. The very existence of polygyny implies relatively high living standards. It means that one man must be capable of supporting at least two women and the children of each. Even where the highest living standards prevail, not very many men can afford to do this. Most men in the United States, with probably the world's highest standard of living, could not afford two wives even if it were permitted. Thus, as a matter of sheer economic necessity most men in polygynous societies have only one wife. Only the wealthy are likely to be able to afford more than one.

2. The second factor which exerts a push in the direction of monogamy is

4 Ibid.; and Kimball Young, *Isn't One Wife Enough?*, New York: Holt, 1954.

5 George P. Murdock, *Social Structure*, p. 28, and "World Ethnographic Sample," *American Anthropologist* 59 (Aug. 1957), p. 686.

biological. In all known societies the sex ratio hovers about one hundred. The sex ratio is, technically, the number of men per one hundred women in the society. The denominator of the fraction usually is not stated. Thus if there are 110 men for every 100 women in the society, the sex ratio is 110. If there are 97 men for every 100 women the sex ratio is 97, and so on.

There are *primary*, *secondary*, and *tertiary* sex ratios. The primary sex ratio is the ratio at the time of conception and is variously estimated to range from 120 to 150. Mortality rates are higher among male fetuses than among female fetuses and, by the time of birth, the ratio is down to 105 or 106. This is the secondary sex ratio. Males continue to have higher mortality rates during childhood and by the time adulthood is reached, the sex ratio in most societies (the tertiary sex ratio) is down to around 100.

As indicated in Chapter 1, all societies afford marriage and the opportunity for regular sexual intercourse to most of their adult members. Since there are approximately equal numbers of men and women, monogamy for most people is the only circumstance which will permit this. For every man who has three wives, there may be two men who will have none at all. The number of males might be held in check through male infanticide, but children, and particularly male infants, tend to be highly valued. The result of all of this is that polygyny is found in many places over the world but it is not common even where preferred. Polygyny is more widely valued but monogamy is more widely practised.

TABLE 1. *The Incidence of Plural Marriages in Two World-Wide Samples of Societies.*

FORM OF MARRIAGE	FROM *Social Structure*		FROM *World Ethnographic Sample*	
	NUMBER	PER CENT	NUMBER	PER CENT
Monogamy	43	18	135	24
Polygyny	193	81	415	75
Polyandry	2	1	4	1
Totals	238	100	554	100

Source: George P. Murdock, *Social Structure*, New York: The Macmillan Company, 1949, p. 28; and "World Ethnographic Sample," *American Anthropologist* 59 (Aug. 1957), p. 686. Reprinted by permission.

Polyandry. In a society where the phenomenon of masculine jealousy is conspicuous and where no "nice" woman would think of having intercourse with several men, polyandry is difficult to imagine. As a matter of fact, polyandry is difficult to imagine outside of our society too, and is very rare. Murdock found only four societies out of 565 to practise it—less than 1 per cent of all societies.[6]

Polyandry also is divided into two main types: *fraternal* polyandry where the husbands are brothers; and *nonfraternal* polyandry where the husbands may be unrelated. When nonfraternal polyandry is practised, the husbands are likely to have separate dwellings. The Todas, in Southern India, practise fraternal polyandry,[7] and the Marquesan Islanders provide an example of nonfraternal polyandry.[8]

A special variant of the practice of taking brothers as husbands is the custom of *levirate*. The levirate is a cultural norm specifying that the preferred mate for a widow is the brother of her deceased husband. The brother may be required to marry his deceased brothers' wife, as was the case among the ancient Hebrews. In a polygynous society where the brother already is married, the widow often becomes a secondary spouse to him. The caution should be added that the terms levirate and sororate are appropriate only when there is a definite societal preference and some resulting social pressure for the arrangement to be followed. The terms do not apply to societies like our own, where such marriages occur occasionally but are not the general practice.

Polyandry creates one special problem that polygyny does not: that of determining paternity. Obviously the biological father of a particular child generally remains unknown. The customs of the Todas are instructive in this respect. First of all, there is no great emotional investment on the part of the the husbands in establishing paternity. For legal and ceremonial purposes, paternity is established through a ceremony in which one of the husbands presents a toy bow and arrow to the pregnant wife. That husband becomes the father of the child. During subsequent pregnancies, the rite may be repeated by other husbands if they wish to become fathers. Thus, the social status of father has no necessary connection with the biological fact of having sired a child.

There are so few cases of polyandry in the world that only tentative explanations for its existence have been developed. It does appear that polyandry is associated with extreme societal poverty; that it is found in societies existing very close to the minimum subsistence level. It would not be correct to say that poverty causes polyandry, because there are many poverty-ridden societies

    [6] Murdock, "World Ethnographic Sample," loc. cit.

    [7] His Royal Highness, Prince Peter of Greece and Denmark, "The Tibetan Family System," in Meyer F. Nimkoff, ed., *Comparative Family Systems*, Boston: Houghton Mifflin, 1965, pp. 192–208.

    [8] Murdock, "Sample," pp. 675–86.

which are not polyandrous. A true cause-and-effect relationship exists only where the alleged cause invariably is followed by the supposed effect.

As an adjustment to poverty, polyandry has certain advantages. If the level of living were so low that a man could not produce sufficient food for a wife and children by himself, he might be able to have a wife and children by sharing the burden of their support with one or more other men. Polyandry also serves to keep the birth rate low and, thus, to keep the population in check. The reproductive potential for any society is set basically by the number of nubile females who have the opportunity for regular, socially approved sexual outlet. Since each married woman can produce only one child every nine months, it does not matter, reproductively, how many husbands are involved. The polyandrous society thus can provide sexual outlet for a large number of males and still keep the birth rate low. There is some evidence of a tendency in polyandrous societies to keep the sex ratio in proper balance through ritual female infanticide. His Royal Highness Prince Peter of Greece and Denmark, a foremost student of the Tibetan family system, believes that fraternal polyandry among the Tibetans is a device for keeping the family property intact. Polyandry permits all the brothers to continue living on the land and permits them to transfer it intact to the next generation.[9] Such an explanation, of course, is quite consistent with the idea of an association between poverty and polyandry.

Group Marriage. Continuing anthropological debate over whether or not group marriage exists in the world illustrates a startling fact about the nature of our own society and particularly its kinship system. We are accustomed to thinking of our society as being quite complex and of other societies as being much less so. In fact, we often use value-laden adjectives such as "simple" and "primitive" to describe, particularly, preliterate societies. In some respects, our society *is* complex. Its technology, certainly, and probably its economic and political institutions are intricate and involved. But when we come to family and kinship, we find that the institutions of many so-called simple societies are almost unbelievably more complex than our own. It appears, literally, that persons reared in the context of our relatively simple system, and handicapped by a language associated with such simplicity of kinship, are unable to conceptualize adequately the marital, family, and kinship customs of many other societies.

Western anthropologists use the term, group marriage, to refer to a situation in which a group of men and a group of women are married in common to one another. And they cannot agree on whether or not such practices exist. Murdock says that group marriage "appears never to exist as a cultural

[9] Op. cit., pp. 197–8.

norm." [10] He acknowledges, however, that among the Kaingang of Brazil,[11] 8 per cent of all recorded marriages over a period of 100 years were group marriages. Linton describes the Marquesan Islanders as practising group marriage.[12] The Dieri of Australia and the Chukchee of Siberia also have been reported to practise group marriage.

In fact, it appears that the categories of polygyny, polyandry, and group marriage are inadequate to describe satisfactorily the marriage forms in some preliterate societies. Both polygyny and polyandry and combinations of polygyny and polyandry exist in some of these societies. In addition, there may be the sharing of sexual privileges without the common residence and economic cooperation which we regard as essential to true marriage. Whether or not group marriage exists seems to reduce almost to a problem of semantics. It may be concluded that the answer to the question of whether or not group marriage exists is less significant than the fact that we are ill equipped to understand fully the complex kinship institutions of many societies which we are prone to dismiss as not being very creative.

Polygamy and the Economy. Monogamy, polygyny, and polyandry are widely scattered over the world. Moreover, what associations have been discovered between them and other aspects of the social structure are far from perfect. There is some evidence of certain very rough relationships between the type of marriage system and the economic situation in the society. The following very tentative generalizations may be hazarded. First, when small family units are as efficient as large ones, monogamy may be favored. Second, where women have relatively little economic contribution to make, polyandry may be preferred. Finally, in those societies where large family units are advantageous and one man can support several women, polygyny may be favored.[13] In so-called pastoral societies dependent upon the keeping of herds and flocks, one man and his sons may be able to shepherd enough animals to keep several women busy processing meat, hides, and milk, and operating the household.

EXTENDED FAMILIES

The second mode of combining nuclear families into larger family units is through extension of the parent-child relationship. Such combination pro-

[10] *Social Structure*, p. 24.

[11] Jules Henry, *Jungle People*, New York: Vintage Books, 1964, p. 45. Henry uses the term, "joint marriage," instead of the term, "group marriage."

[12] Ralph Linton, *The Study of Man*, New York: D. Appleton-Century, 1936, pp. 181–2.

[13] Murdock, *Ethnographic Atlas*. For an analysis of how demographic conditions limit opportunities to maintain extended family households, see Karen K. Peterson, "Demographic Conditions and Extended Family Households: Egyptian Data," *Social Forces* 46 (June 1968), pp. 531–7.

duces residential units of three or more generations—at least grandparents, parents, and children. Actually, extended families may be compounded of either monogamous or polygamous families. Families need not be either polygamous or extended; they can be both. A simple diagram of a three-genera- tion extended family is given in Figure 2. For purposes of simplicity, a monoga- mous family is shown. Note that in Figure 2 there are three separate nuclear families—the families of procreation of ego's father, of ego, and of ego's brother. These are dependent nuclear families in contrast with the inde- pendent polygynous family diagrammed in Figure 1. Nuclear families or polyg- amous two-generation families are called independent. The nuclear families included in an extended family unit are referred to as dependent families.

Consanguine and Conjugal Family Types. In the structuring of kinship, priority tends to be assigned either to marital ties or to blood ties. When priority is given to marital ties, the kinship system is called a *conjugal* system. Our own family system is a conjugal one. Independent nuclear or polygamous family systems are ordinarily conjugal systems.

In contrast, extended family systems tend to emphasize blood ties—those between parents and children or between brothers and sisters—over marital ties. These are *consanguine* systems. In a conjugal system, a man may leave his parents and "cleave unto his wife." In a consanguine system, the wife (or husband) is an outsider whose wishes and needs must be subordinated to the continuity and welfare of the extended kin group.

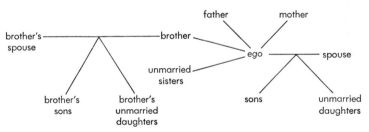

FIGURE 2. *Diagram of three-generation extended, patrilocal, monogamous family.*

Conjugal family systems, including only two generations, are transitory in character. They disintegrate with the death of the parents and with the mar- riage of offspring. The family of orientation of the offspring ceases to exist and the family of procreation comes into being. The family of procreation creates a new family of orientation for its offspring and in turn will disappear with the death of the new parents. Thus, conjugal families are short lived. With their short duration and the drastic break from one generation to the next, they are not especially good vehicles for the maintenance of family traditions or for keeping family property intact over the generations. On the other hand, since conjugal families involve relatively few people, there may be little need for each family member to carefully follow a series of roles prescribed in great detail. There may be far more improvisation permitted on the role of husband, daughter, and so on. We pride ourselves, in the United States, on the opportunities for personal development and personal freedom that our system provides. At the same time, many of us know little about our great grandparents, and few of us hold substantial property that might properly be called "family property."

In contrast, consanguine families tend to be immortal. The continued existence of the family does not depend upon any one person or any couple. At marriage, one of the spouses remains with the family of orientation and is joined there by husband or wife. The couple raise their children in a large family setting, and, even if the mother or father should die prematurely, there are other kin present to absorb the several facets of the parental role. Eventually when the grandparents retire or die, control and property tend to pass without great fanfare to the next generation.

The advantages and limitations of the consanguine family tend to be the reverse of those of the conjugal family. Whereas the conjugal family tends to produce the splitting of family property at each generation, the consanguine family permits it to be transmitted intact. Since consanguine families ideally involve a sizable number of persons spread over at least three generations, the appropriate role behaviors for each family member at each stage in life tend to be laid down in considerable detail. One is under considerable pressure to enact the roles of son, elder brother, husband, father and eventually grandfather, as they have been traditionally enacted. Whether one is well suited temperamentally to playing these roles in this fashion has little to do with it. Instead of the personal freedom likely to be emphasized in a conjugal family system, emphasis is placed upon the faithful performance of prescribed roles.

A widely discussed variant of the extended family deserves brief mention here. This is the so-called *joint family* of India.[14] The joint family is the traditional Indian family in which adult brothers live together with their respective families of procreation. In addition to maintaining a common residence, they hold property in common and assume joint responsibility for the education of younger siblings.

[14] M. S. Gore, "The Traditional Indian Family," in Meyer F. Nimkoff, ed., *Comparative Family Systems*, Boston: Houghton Mifflin, 1965, pp. 209–31. See also Joseph S. Himes and Vernaline Watson, "The Changing Indian Joint Family: Essence and Accident," unpublished manuscript available from the authors.

This Indian joint family actually is characteristic of just one stage in the life-cycle, with persons typically passing through several stages during their lifetime. The process may be said to begin when the sons remain in the parental home following their marriage. While the father is alive, the Indian family does not differ significantly from other extended families. Following the father's death, the true joint family comes into existence when the brothers keep the extended household intact. This joint family is preserved until all of the younger siblings are educated and married, at which time the brothers split off their families of procreation and divide the family property between them. Thus, for a time, nuclear units exist separately. Soon, however, the sons of the brothers are ready for marriage and the process begins over again.

COMPOSITE FAMILIES AND THE ECONOMY

In Murdock's analysis of 250 societies, he found adequate data on composite family forms for only 192 societies. Of these 192 societies, 47 had the nuclear family only, 53 had polygamous but not extended families, and 92 had some form of extended family.[15] Roughly, this indicates that about one-fourth of all societies may have the nuclear family only, another one-fourth may have polygamous but not extended families, and about one-half may have extended family systems. The extended families may be composed, of course, of either monogamous or polygamous families.

Nimkoff and Middleton carried this kind of analysis further when they analyzed data from 549 of the cultures included in Murdock's world ethnographic sample.[16] They correlated the type of family system with certain economic factors, particularly the subsistence pattern and the amount of family property. Their study produced the following tentative generalizations. First, the independent nuclear family tends to be found at both ends of the economic scale. It predominates in societies with the most primitive hunting and gathering societies where the food supply is very uncertain, and also is found in modern, industrial societies such as the United States, England, and the Soviet Union. Second, the extended family predominates in agricultural economies and reaches its fullest development in farming economies that combine agriculture with animal husbandry. Finally, independent nuclear families and

---

[15] *Social Structure*, p. 2.

[16] Meyer F. Nimkoff and Russell Middleton, "Types of Family and Types of Economy," *American Journal of Sociology* 66 (Nov. 1960), pp. 215–25. See also Hsien-Jen Chu and J. Selwyn Hollingsworth, "A Cross-Cultural Study of the Relationship Between Family Types and Social Stratification," *Journal of Marriage and the Family* 31 (May 1969), pp. 322–7; and Marie W. Osmond, "A Cross-Cultural Analysis of Family Organization," *Journal of Marriage and the Family* 31 (May 1969), pp. 302–10.

extended families occur with about equal frequency in societies which depend on hunting and fishing, in societies that depend primarily upon animal husbandry, or where animal husbandry exists along with fishing. Thus, the independent nuclear family is found both at the top and the bottom of the scale, with extended family systems being more prevalent in the middle.

FAMILY STRUCTURE AND THE REGULATION OF SEX

The regulation of sexual behavior is one aspect of each society's normative system. All societies provide for regular sexual outlet for most adults, but nowhere is the selection of partners simply a matter of personal choice. Instead there is to be found a series of obligations, alternatives, possibilities, discouragements, and prohibitions. Moreover, these prescriptions and proscriptions are intricately bound up with the family and kinship system.

As with the more complicated combinations of plural marriage, intercultural variation in the regulation of sexual behavior is difficult for many Americans to put in proper perspective. Our own society is one of a very few societies that traditionally have completely prohibited sexual intercourse outside of marriage. Murdock estimates the proportion of such societies in the world to be less than 5 per cent.[17] People who have grown up in such a society are prone, perhaps, to make moralistic judgments about patterns that provide for a range of sex partners both before and after marriage. It is well to keep in mind that patterns different from our own can be understood only in the larger social context in which they are found.

In the United States, and in much of the Western world, sex itself has been the focus of regulation. Sex still is seen frequently as a necessary evil. It is not so in most other societies. Most commonly, sexual regulation is one part of the broader regulation of marriage, reproduction, kinship, and social status. What we encounter is a series of permissions and restrictions in relation to these other phenomena.

PREMARITAL SEX RELATIONSHIPS

The marriage relationship is one of the major foci of sexual regulation. Most societies see nothing inconsistent between the careful regulation of sex in marriage and considerable sex freedom before marriage; consequently complete premarital chastity is a minority pattern over the world. In some societies there is almost complete freedom of premarital sexual relationships, with boys and girls being allowed to take and to change partners at will. Surpris-

[17] *Social Structure*, p. 264.

ingly, the incidence of pregnancies resulting from such unions appears to be quite low. Some writers attribute this to the relative youthfulness and undeveloped fecundity of the persons involved. In some cases birth control techniques may be employed, although this is difficult to establish. Generally, when a pregnancy does occur it is not the tragedy that a premarital pregnancy in our society is likely to be. It may even be that the girl's marriageability will be enhanced by virtue of her proven ability to have children.

Murdock found premarital sex relationships to be fully approved in 65 societies, to be conditionally approved in 43, to be mildly disapproved in 6 and to be forbidden in 44.[18] In some societies where complete premarital freedom is not sanctioned, intercourse with selected persons, such as cross cousins,[19] who are potential marriage partners is permitted. In sum, about 70 per cent of the societies for whom such data are available permit premarital intercourse. In most of the others the taboo falls particularly upon females

TABLE 2. *The Incidence of Sex Taboos Outside Marriage, 250 Societies.*

INFORMATION ON SEX TABOOS	NUMBER OF SOCIETIES	
Indications of probable presence of a generalized sex taboo		3
Definite evidence of absence of a generalized sex taboo		
Permissive premarital unchastity	49	
Fully or conditionally permitted adultery	3	
Privileged relationships	23	
Two or all three of the above	40	
Total		115
Inadequate information		
No data on premarital unchastity	7	
No data on premarital or postmarital relationships	35	
Total		42
No relevant data whatsoever		90
Total		250

Source: Reprinted with permission of The Macmillan Company from *Social Structure* by George P. Murdock. Copyright 1949, The Macmillan Company.

and seems to be based upon the necessity to prevent premarital pregnancies. In most societies it is far less of a moral issue than with us.

[18] Ibid. p. 265.

[19] Cross cousins are the children of a father's sister or of a mother's brother. In many societies, cross cousins are preferred marriage partners. Parallel cousins are the children of a father's brother or of a mother's sister.

SOCIAL STATUS AND SEX RELATIONSHIPS

The rules of *endogamy* and *exogamy* are two conspicuous examples of the relation between sexual regulation and social status. Technically, endogamy and exogamy define the range of potential marriage partners and, indirectly, of sexual partners. Endogamy is a rule of marriage which requires a person to select a marriage partner from within his own tribe, community, social class, nationality, race, or other social grouping. Such requirements exist in virtually all societies and often have strong sanctions attached to them. Conversely, exogamy requires a person to select a marriage partner from outside certain defined groups to which he himself belongs. Exogamous requirements appear basically to result from extensions of the incest taboos which prohibit sex relationships with close kin.

Exceptions to existing sexual regulations sometimes are made for high-status persons in a society. The custom of *jus primae noctis* in medieval times and as it exists in some preliterate societies has received considerable public attention. Under *jus primae noctis*, the feudal lord, a priest, chief, or other high-status male selected for the purpose is privileged to have the first sexual intercourse with a bride. This custom has been variously interpreted to reinforce the head-man's proprietary interest in the persons and property of his subjects and as a means of offering proof to the society that the bride is virginal.[20] Exceptions to prevailing incest taboos are also known to have existed for members of royal families in a number of societies.

KINSHIP AND SEXUAL REGULATION

Sexual freedom before marriage does not necessarily mean sexual freedom in marriage, for virtually all societies regulate closely the sexual behavior of married people.[21] The majority of societies forbid intercourse between a married man and an unrelated woman. At the same time, however, few so-

[20] This is another instance of a practice regularly misinterpreted by many Westerners. Many of us are prone to think of *jus primae noctis* as a highly erotic situation and as an uncomplicated privilege of rank. It is somewhat sobering to realize that privilege tends to shade off into duty and that the lord or chief may not really be free to take only the attractive brides. The duty might become more than onerous in the case of a bride who was fat, dirty, and ugly.

[21] The two most obvious exceptions to this rule are the Kaingang of Brazil and the Todas of southern India. Regulations for the control of sexual behavior exist in both these societies but their control of sexual behavior appears to be weak, just as many other aspects of their social structures appear to be quite inadequate. See Jules Henry, op. cit., and His Royal Highness Prince Peter of Greece and Denmark, op. cit.

cieties are as restrictive as ourselves in allowing intercourse only between spouses.

Most societies recognize some "privileged relationships" both before marriage and for married persons that give the person legitimate sexual outlet with certain classes of kin. Before marriage the most common of privileged relationships is with cross cousins where cross cousins are preferred marriage partners. In Murdock's sample of 250 societies, 11 allow premarital intercourse with a father's sister's daughter and 14 allow it with a mother's brother's daughter.[22]

Within marriage a comparable situation exists, particularly where the levirate and sororate are found. In this case the privileged relationships are with the siblings-in-law who are potential spouses. Nearly two-thirds of the sample societies for whom data are available permit sexual intercourse with brothers-in-law or sisters-in-law.[23]

In many societies there appears to be an assumption that men, particularly, suffer if they are denied sexual outlet for very long. The assumption for women is less explicit, the argument sometimes being made that women do not experience sexual frustrations comparable to those of men. In some societies, also, there are taboos upon sexual intercourse during menstruation, pregnancy, and during a lactation period that may last for three or four years. The granting of sexual access to other female relatives often is rationalized as a means of relieving the sexual frustration and tension that otherwise would be experienced during these periods.

This logic has been institutionalized in a few societies scattered widely over the world in the custom known as *sexual hospitality*. The custom is found in a few societies in which men travel a good deal and are away from their wives during their travel. When they stop with a family for the night, it is obligatory upon the host to provide a female sleeping partner, just as he provides food and shelter. It is generally equally obligatory upon the guest to accept the sexual partner, just as he accepts food. The American university student's interpretation of sexual hospitality should be made in full awareness of the fact that the partner proffered may not be a luscious young girl but may be one's obese aunt or even a toothless grandmother.[24]

The regulation of sexual behavior in and out of marriage is related to and part of the regulation of family behavior. Sexual regulation, in our society or

[22] Murdock, *Social Structure*, p. 268.

[23] Ibid.

[24] Genuine appreciation of the marital and sexual customs of one composite people practising sexual hospitality may be gained from the novel by Hans Reusch entitled *Top of the World* (Pocket Books, 1959). This fascinating novel is anthropologically sound and illuminating.

in any other, cannot be understood apart from the larger normative system of which it is a part. Moreover, understanding of the larger normative system requires understanding of its constituent parts. One general set of sexual regulations having great significance for family structure has yet to be discussed. These regulations are included under the heading of incest taboos.

THE STRUCTURAL IMPLICATIONS OF INCEST TABOOS

An important factor in the analysis of family structure is the understanding of the nature and effects of incest taboos. The term, incest, refers to the prohibition of sexual intercourse with close blood relatives. Such taboos exist in all known societies.

Sexual intercourse between members of the nuclear family always is taboo except, of course, between husband and wife. No society regularly permits intercourse between father and daughter, mother and son, or brother and sister. Virtually all societies also proscribe sex relationships with adoptive parents, adopted children, step children, godparents and godchildren—persons who occasionally stand in lieu of regular members of the nuclear family. Not only are such relationships prohibited, but most people in all societies react even to the idea of incestuous relationships with aversion and disgust.

As with most rules of social behavior, there are a few partial exceptions and one or two general exceptions have been proposed. It is known, for example, that intermarriage of brothers and sisters has been permitted or required in certain royal families. Among the ancient Egyptians of the Ptolemaic period, among the Inca Indians, and within the old Hawaiian aristocracy, brother-sister marriage occurred within royal families. The practice generally is interpreted as a device for keeping property and power within the family. Murdock also reports that the Dobus, a Melanesian people, regard intercourse with one's mother after the father's death, as a private sin but not as a public offense.[25] The Balinese permit twins to marry on the assumption that they have already been too intimate in the womb. And an African people, the Thonga, are reputed to permit father-daughter incest in extraordinary preparation for a great hunt. These exceptions, of course, do not apply to whole societies and their very nature serves to emphasize the universality of incest taboos.

There are two instances reported of societies where incestuous relationships within the nuclear family may have been more widespread. Slotkin claims that father-daughter, mother-son, and brother-sister incest all were generally per-

[25] *Social Structure*, p. 13.

mitted in ancient Persia.[26] Middleton, in a recent article, presents evidence that brother-sister marriage, at least in Roman Egypt, occurred among commoners as well as within the royal family.[27] He interprets these marriages as a device for keeping property within the family. Unfortunately, it is not possible to gather additional data concerning these possible major exceptions. Comparable situations apparently do not exist in any contemporary society. Suffice it to say that even should these two interpretations prove valid, the prohibition of sexual intercourse within the nuclear family is the most nearly universal social custom.

DISCONTINUITY IN THE NUCLEAR FAMILY

A primary effect of universal incest taboos is to make the nuclear family discontinuous over time. Sons and daughters are forced to go outside the nuclear family to find mates, resulting in a major break between the family of orientation and the family of procreation. Were this not true, the nuclear family would be immortal. Brothers would marry their own sisters and family property, traditions, and other folkways would be transmitted undisturbed from generation to generation. Kinship structure would be very simple. Except for distinctions by age and sex, no other differentiation would be necessary.

The selection of mates from outside the nuclear family produces a universal, continuous overlapping of nuclear families. The nuclear family experience of any two persons, over their lifetimes, is different. Each person becomes related biologically to an ever-expanding number of people. This process is illustrated in Figure 3.

Anthropologist A. R. Radcliffe-Brown coined the terms "primary," "secondary," and "tertiary" relatives to describe the degree of relationship between a person and his ever-expanding circle of relatives.[28] Primary relatives are the categories of members of ego's nuclear families—mother, father, brothers, sisters, spouse, sons, and daughters—seven categories in all. Secondary relatives are composed of the primary relatives of ego's primary relatives—33 categories in all. Tertiary relatives are the primary relatives of ego's secondary relatives—151 different categories. Note that these are categories of relatives and that most categories may include several different people. Some per-

---

[26] J. S. Slotkin, "On a Possible Lack of Incest Regulations in Old Iran," *American Anthropologist* 49 (Oct.–Dec. 1947), pp. 612–15.

[27] Russell Middleton, "Brother-Sister and Father-Daughter Marriage in Ancient Egypt," *American Sociological Review* 27 (Oct. 1962), pp. 603–11.

[28] A. R. Radcliffe-Brown, "The Study of Kinship Systems," *Journal of the Royal Anthropological Institute* 71 (1941), p. 2.

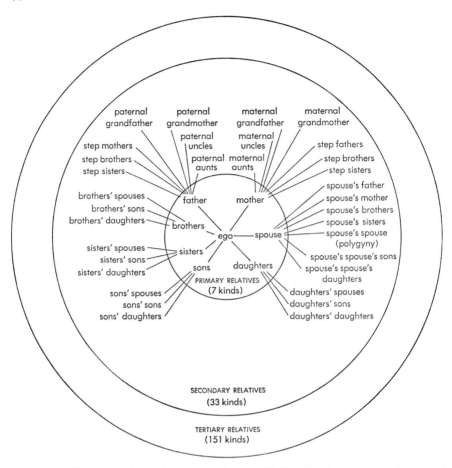

paternal grandfather
paternal grandmother
maternal grandfather
maternal grandmother

paternal uncles
maternal uncles

step mothers
step brothers
step sisters

paternal aunts
maternal aunts

step fathers
step brothers
step sisters

brothers' spouses
brothers' sons
brothers' daughters

father   mother

spouse's father
spouse's mother
spouse's brothers
spouse's sisters
spouse's spouse (polygyny)

brothers

ego ——— spouse

sisters' spouses
sisters' sons
sisters' daughters

sisters

spouse's spouse's sons
spouse's spouse's daughters

sons   daughters

PRIMARY RELATIVES
(7 kinds)

daughters' spouses
daughters' sons
daughters' daughters

sons' spouses
sons' sons
sons' daughters

SECONDARY RELATIVES
(33 kinds)

TERTIARY RELATIVES
(151 kinds)

FIGURE 3. *Diagram of maximum number of kinds of primary, secondary, and tertiary relatives, polygamous marriage.*

spective on these degrees of relationship may be gained by realizing that first cousins, generally recognized relatives in our own society, are tertiary relatives.

Where we stop tracing relationship, biologically, is purely arbitrary. What should be obvious is that even by the time we trace relationships out three degrees we have included so many categories, to say nothing of the larger number of people, that we cannot possibly have close social relationships with all of them. How many of us can name even one person who belongs to each of the 151 different categories of tertiary relatives?

Because of the large and ever-expanding number of biological kinsmen, all societies have found it necessary to select certain categories of kinsmen for recognition and to ignore others. To put it differently, all societies have developed *social* definitions according to which priorities are established with certain biological kin. Family relationships are social relationships that include norms governing the sharing of affection, economic cooperation, and the provision of mutual aid in time of need. There isn't enough affection to be scattered indiscriminately over several hundred people, and to be entitled to aid from several hundred people would be tantamount to receiving aid from no one at all. The satisfactory performance of family duties requires that there be a group of kin of manageable size with whom orderly relationships may be maintained. In order to reduce the number of biologically related kin to a manageable social group, all societies have developed *rules of descent*.

RULES OF DESCENT

Rules of descent are social definitions that determine for the individual who, among the myriad of biological kin, he considers himself related to. Rules of descent define the family as a social group in contrast to the family as a biological group.

There are four general rules of descent that warrant definition and description here. We shall take them in order of the frequency of their appearance among Murdock's 250 societies.

Patrilineal descent is the most common form and is found in 105 of the 250 societies—just over 40 per cent. Under patrilineal descent, the person is assigned at birth to a group of kin who are related to him through males only.[29] To put it technically, descent is traced through the male lineage. The most important ties are those which extend from father to son to grandson. Wives typically marry into their husbands' families and their children become members of the husband's family but not of the family into which the wife was born.

Such unilineal systems of descent obviously are not in accord with the facts of biological relationship. Relationship to biological kin on the father's side is affirmed while relationship to the mother's biological kin is ignored. Some early anthropologists believed that patrilineal descent generally meant that the people were ignorant of the ties to the maternal kin. This is not true, however. Neither is patrilineal descent confined to preliterate peoples. As we shall see in two succeeding chapters, patrilineal descent has a long history in both Eastern and Western civilizations. Unilineal systems of descent do not mean that people in those societies deny their biological relationship to the opposite lineage. They do mean that systems of descent are means of defining

---

[29] Murdock, *Social Structure*, p. 15.

social relationships and that family structure, while it is rooted in the facts of biological relationship, is by no means limited by them. Family structure is social structure.

The second most common system of tracing descent is called *bilateral*. As the term implies, it involves tracing relationships through two sides of the family—through the mother's biological kin and the father's biological kin equally. The size of the kin group is regulated by limiting it to very close relatives on each side. Such a system of tracing social relationships is in accord exactly with the facts of biological relationship. Because it is the system of descent used in our own society, it makes sense to most Americans. Some sociologists have suggested that a more accurate designation of this descent system would be *multilineal*.[30] Since the incest taboos require that each person seek his mate outside his own family group, there is a continuous interpenetration of family lines. Murdock found just 30 per cent of his 250 societies to follow this system.

Matrilineal descent is the obverse of patrilineal descent. It traces relationship through females and the female line, discarding all of the father's relatives. Matrilineal descent is less common, occurring in about 20 per cent of the 250 societies. As we shall see, descent, residence, inheritance—indeed virtually all family phenomena—are more frequently determined through males than through females.

The fourth descent system, *double descent*, is most useful for our purposes, simply to provide a bit of insight into how complicated kinship systems can and do get. It is not common over the world, occurring in only about 7 per cent of societies. Where double descent exists, each person at birth is assigned to two kin groups, one traced through the paternal relatives and one through the maternal relatives. He becomes a member of his father's patrilineal group and a member of his mother's matrilineal group. This arrangement involves, of course, discarding the father's matrilineal kin group and the mother's patrilineal kin group. There are, in the world, even more complex systems of descent in which relationships are traced differently for sons and daughters and which zigzag between the sexes, from generation to generation.[31]

The rules of descent select from the ever-expanding group of biological kin those with whom close social relationships are to be maintained. Associated with rules of descent are rules of inheritance.

[30] Talcott Parsons, "The Kinship System of the Contemporary United States," *American Anthropologist* 45 (Jan.–March 1943), p. 26.

[31] Students who wish to read more on this system of descent are referred to Margaret Mead, *Sex and Temperament in Three Primitive Societies*, New York: Mentor Books, 1950, pp. 119–63.

RULES OF INHERITANCE

Inheritance patterns are in some ways more complex than systems of descent and they have been studied less thoroughly. They are complicated by the facts that some possessions such as clothing, ornaments, and tools are used only by members of one sex while other possessions, such as money, are easily transmitted to either sex. Throughout most of human history and over much of the world, inheritance rights have centered on land, dwellings, animals, and, generally, the means of production. If such property passes to the heir or heirs through males, the rule is said to be that of *patrilineal* inheritance; if the route is through females (from a man to his sister's son) then it is *matrilineal* inheritance.

Inheritance patterns are further complicated because men and women may or may not inherit equally, and even within the same sex the siblings may or may not inherit equally. More often than not, the inheritance of major property items is through males to other males. The inheritance rights of women often are circumscribed and sometimes are nonexistent.

The inheritance rights of males may vary with birth order. If all sons do not inherit equally, the most likely situation is for the eldest son to inherit all or a disproportionate part of the property. This arrangement is known as *primogeniture*. Less commonly found is *ultimogeniture*, where the youngest son is favored.

RULES OF RESIDENCE

The nuclear family, it will be remembered, is virtually everywhere a common residential unit. At marriage the husband and wife take up residence together. Since they come from different families of orientation, this means that one or the other or both of them must move at the time of marriage. The alternatives available to them, in relation to their respective families, are relatively few: they can locate with the husband's family of orientation, with the wife's family, away from both families of orientation, or in some combination of these. All societies have developed certain normative prescriptions to determine which alternative shall be followed. These norms are generally called rules of residence.

The most common rule of residence is that which is called *patrilocal*. Under patrilocal residence the bride leaves the locale of her family of orientation and sets up housekeeping with her husband in the same dwelling with, or adjacent to, his family of orientation. Note that patrilocal residence does not refer to the wife's going to live with the husband but to her going to live with the husband's family. Patrilocal residence is most common over the world, being found in 146 of Murdock's 250 societies. A special variant of patrilocal residence is the rule known as *matri-patrilocal*, where residence is with the bride's family of orientation for a prescribed period after which the couple take up permanent residence with the groom's family. The couple may live with the bride's family for one year or until the first child is born. Murdock found 22 of 250 societies to have matri-patrilocal residence.

Matrilocal residence involves the husband leaving the home of his family of orientation to take up residence with his bride in the locale of her family of orientation. Thirty-eight of 250 societies have matrilocal residence. Closely related to matrilineal descent and inheritance is another rule of residence known as *avunculocal*. Under avunculocal residence, the newly married couple take up residence with the maternal uncle of the groom. Thus, the residence rule is built around males of the female line. Only 8 of the 250 societies have avunculocal residence.

Nineteen of the 250 societies were found to have *bilocal* residence. Under this rule, the couple is permitted to choose whether they will locate with the husband's kin or the wife's kin. The strength of the personal ties between the couple and their parents, the relative wealth of the two sets of parents and their power in the community, and the need for assistance from the young couple may be determining factors.

Students should note that of the rules of residence discussed so far, all favor the development of extended families. All create units of at least three generations and including several nuclear families. They also tend to put one of the spouses into a favored position. The spouse who stays with his or her family of orientation is surrounded by a large kin group likely to be sympathetic to his or her cause in any disputes with the other spouse. The spouse who has to move, in contrast, is relocated among relative strangers and somewhat isolated from the support of his own kin group. Thus the prevailing rule of residence may have much to do with the distribution of power between the spouses in marriage.

The final rule of residence to be discussed here is *neolocal*. As the term implies, this rule involves the establishment of a new residence for the couple, apart from both families of orientation. This is the only rule of residence which militates against the development of extended family units and encourages the isolation of the nuclear family. This is the rule of residence followed in our society, but is found in only 17 of 250 societies.

It is probably apparent by now that there are certain logical associations among patrilineal descent, patrilineal inheritance, and patrilocal residence, and among matrilineal descent, matrilineal inheritance, and matrilocal residence. Table 3 verifies these connections. Of 105 societies having patrilineal descent, 97 have either patrilocal or matri-patrilocal residence. Within the maternal line, the connections are still there but are not as strong. Of 52 societies having matrilineal descent, 33 are either matrilocal or avunculocal. Bilateral descent does not show the same association with neolocal residence,

TABLE 3. *Rule of Descent, by Rule of Residence, 250 Societies.*

RULE OF RESIDENCE	PATRI-LINEAL DESCENT	MATRI-LINEAL DESCENT	DOUBLE DESCENT	BILATERAL DESCENT	TOTALS
Patrilocal and matri-patrilocal	97	15	17	39	168
Matrilocal and avunculocal	0	33	0	13	46
Neolocal and bilocal	8	4	1	23	36
Totals	105	52	18	75	250

Source: Adapted from George P. Murdock, *Social Structure*, New York: copyright The Macmillan Company, 1949, p. 59. Reprinted by permission.

for, of 75 societies following bilateral descent, more than half follow essentially patrilocal residence and fewer than one-third are neolocal or bilocal.

Murdock has concluded that patrilocal residence is associated with polygyny, warfare, slavery, and an economy which depends upon the chase rather than upon collecting. Matrilocal residence, he says, is favored by the development of agriculture in a previously hunting and gathering economy and by the ownership of land by women. Bilocal residence is accompanied by a migratory life in unstable bands and, at a higher economic level, by an approximate equality of the sexes in the ownership of property. Finally, neolocal residence is associated with approximately equal economic contributions by men and women, monogamy, extensive poverty, and individualism.

Murdock also assigns a certain priority to rules of residence in determining systems of descent and inheritance. His data lead him to conclude that rules of residence are likely to be affected first by changes in the economic base and by technological development. As the residential kin group alters, changes gradually come about in the means of tracing relationships.

One final set of associations with rules of residence deserves mention. The general phenomenon known as *bride price* is found to exist in approximately two-thirds of the societies for whom adequate data are available (see Table 4). The bride price refers variously to a payment of money or goods made to the bride's family at the time of marriage, to the exchange of one of the husband's female relatives for the bride, or to a period of work-service for the bride. Students will recall here, again, Jacob's seven years of service to Laban for each of his daughters.

TABLE 4. *Form of Bride Price, by Rule of Residence, 241 Societies.*

RULE OF RESIDENCE	MARRIAGE WITH BRIDE PRICE			MARRIAGE WITHOUT BRIDE PRICE	TOTALS
	GOODS OR MONEY	EXCHANGE OF WOMEN	BRIDE SERVICE		
Patrilocal	103	10	2	25	140
Matrilocal	4	0	8	24	36
Matri-Patrilocal	6	0	13	2	21
Bilocal	6	2	1	10	19
Neolocal	0	0	2	15	17
Avunculocal	2	0	4	2	8
Totals	121	12	30	78	241

Source: Adapted from George P. Murdock, *Social Structure*, New York: copyright The Macmillan Company, 1949, p. 20. Reprinted by permission.

The payment of some form of bride price is found to be associated with rules of residence that remove the bride most drastically from her family of orientation. In Table 4, it may be seen that bride price exists in only one-third of the societies which have matrilocal residence but is to be found in more than four-fifths of societies having patrilocal residence and in 90 per cent of those having matri-patrilocal residence.

. . . That hallowed tribal custom, the bride price, is coming under fire. Africa's young bachelors, caught between higher education and even higher inflation, are growing increasingly unhappy at the ancient laws that force the prospective groom to buy his bride from her parents. In Kenya the [bride price] is often the equivalent of five years of the groom's expectable income, usually payable in postmarital installments of livestock, bicycles, and money. By the time the bartering is over and the wedding rolls around, only his in-laws have much cause for celebration: rather than losing a daughter, they are gaining a herd of cattle.

Leading the attack is a generation of young Kenya urbanites who look upon the [bride price] as institutionalized blackmail. . . . The *campaign is gaining support.* The East African Standard, *largest paper in Nairobi, told its readers that bride prices, if not actually subversive to an emerging nation, are far too high. "No young girl can feel other than ashamed, in these times of personal freedom, to think she is sold by her parents to the highest bidder," the paper wrote. . . .*

Few educated Africans are willing to destroy the custom entirely, for despite its iniquities, it is the only form of marriage insurance in many African societies. Tribal laws dictate that if a marriage breaks up because of the wife's misdeeds, her husband gets his money back; if the fault is his, however, he can lose both bride and bride price. . . .

—Reprinted by permission from *Time*, The
Weekly Newsmagazine; copyright Time Inc., 1965.

Some early students of kinship structure were inclined to interpret bride price as outright purchase of the wife, as one would purchase cattle or other property. Such an interpretation appears to be erroneous and to miss the true functions of bride price. These functions appear essentially to be two. First, the bride price offers some recompense to the bride's family for loss of her services. Particularly when the bride's and groom's families live in different communities and patrilocal residence is followed, the bride's family's economic loss may be very real. Second, the bride price is a form of insurance against maltreatment of the bride by the husband or his family. The sum involved usually is substantial and if the bride is unjustly divorced or forced to return to her parental home because of mistreatment, her family generally retains possession of the bride price. True wife-purchase appears to be rare.

AUTHORITY PATTERNS IN THE FAMILY

Strictly speaking, the distribution of authority between the husband and wife does not derive directly from the existence of incest taboos. The relationships between family authority patterns and rules of descent and residence, however, are such as to make brief discussion of them relevant here. We may describe three principal types as patriarchal, matriarchal, and equalitarian.

A *patriarchal* family system is one in which power and authority are vested in the hands of males, with the eldest male usually wielding great arbitrary power. Patriarchal family systems have been very common through history and over the world. The ancient Hebrews, Greeks, and Romans; the Hindus and Mohammedans; and the Chinese and Japanese provide just a few examples.

Woman is given to man to bear children; she is therefore his property, as the tree is the gardener's.

—Napoleon Bonaparte

Since 1840, when the Code Napoléon was enacted as France's basic
civil law, married French women have enjoyed all of the legal privileges one might expect from the Emperor's opinion of them. Novelist
George Sand watched in despair in the 19th century while her husband squandered her immense dowry and made her ask permission
to spend the money she earned from her books and plays. A present-
day Frenchwoman told her lawyer that her husband had just sold her
store, and now wanted a divorce. What could she do? "Cry, madame,
cry," she was advised.

Some of madame's tears would be wiped away by sweeping changes
in marriage laws proposed last week. . . . What the government had
in mind . . . was "a veritable emancipation of women." Under the
new bill, a married woman for the first time will be able to take a
job or open a bank account without her husband's permission. She
will have the legal right to help decide where her children can go to
school, to veto his plans to sell her property, and retain her own
possessions if there is a divorce.

Actually through a delicate balance of finesse and commanding
personality, many Frenchwomen are already freer than the laws would
indicate. Madame de Pompadour, after all, ruled France from the
boudoir of Louis XV, and fully three-quarters of all French blue-
collar workers voluntarily (so to speak) turn over their weekly pay
envelopes to maman who passes back a few francs for Gauloises and
wine. Economically, French housewives are growing increasingly independent. With the growth in popularity of household time-savers
like the automatic washer and le sandwich, some 30% of all married
women find the time and energy to hold jobs outside the home,
roughly the same proportion as in the U.S.

—Reprinted by permission from *Time*, The
Weekly Newsmagazine; copyright Time Inc., 1965.

Kirkpatrick has listed and discussed the characteristics of the patriarchal
family in some detail.[32] He concludes that patrilineal descent, patrilineal inheritance, patrilocal residence, and primogeniture all are associated with male
dominance. In addition, polygyny, a double standard of sexual morality,

[32] Clifford Kirkpatrick, *The Family: As Process and Institution* (New York: Ronald
Press, 1963), pp. 79–84.

masculine privilege with regard to divorce, the arrangement of children's marriages by adults, and a low status for women are frequent accompaniments of patriarchy. Unfortunately, we do not have quantitative data to indicate what proportion of the world's societies are and have been strong patriachies, but abundant descriptive data exist. Few would question the fact that male dominance is the rule rather than the exception.

Logically, the construction of a *matriarchal* family type is very simple. Logically, a matriarchy should involve the almost complete vesting of power in the hands of females. Except in the comic strips of tabloid newspapers, however, and in D-grade Hollywood movies, true matriarchies are never found. The fabled Amazon women are just that—a fable. Even in societies which are organized about women, in societies which follow matrilineal descent and inheritance and matrilocal residence, power tends to be held by males in the female lineage. Power usually is held by the women's brothers—from the viewpoint of ego, by the maternal uncle. Male dominance, or at least a tendency toward it, appears to be one of those basic features of human existence that culture cannot completely contradict. A minority of societies are organized around the female lineage, but even among them, power, status, and property tend to be held by males.

One common feature of human existence which has worked to put women into positions of power whether or not the official norms provide for it is the tendency for women to outlive men. Men are physically stronger but women live longer. Patriarchal societies often accord high status to older people, and sons usually are trained to respect their mothers. When the father dies first, the son who nominally assumes power may continue to defer to his mother, thus creating by default a degree of female dominance in the society which could not be created by design.

The third logical type, the *equalitarian* family, implies a somewhat equal distribution of power and authority between husband and wife. This arrangement, too, appears to be in accord with some of the basic facts of human existence. Few fair-minded people would question the fact that, except perhaps for brute strength, there are many women in any society who are as strong, intelligent, clever, and ambitious as their husbands. Even in the most patriarchal of societies strong wives probably have dominated weak husbands. One of the traditional ways of writing "wife" in Chinese characters was to show a woman's hand holding onto a man's ear. The equalitarian family simply represents some degree of institutionalization of this situation. It is often said that the Western family, and particularly the family in the United States, has been tending for many decades toward an equalitarian form.

EXTENSION OF INCEST TABOOS OUTSIDE THE NUCLEAR FAMILY

All societies taboo all cross-sex relationships within the nuclear family, but no society stops there. Some additional kinsmen are always included within the tabooed circle. Interestingly, however, there is no one kinsman, or class of kin, outside the nuclear family who is not an acceptable sex partner in some society. First cousins, aunts, nephews, and so on, are taboo in some societies but not in others. At first glance there does not appear to be much rhyme or reason to the way in which these extensions are accomplished.

Obviously the taboos are not extended strictly in accord with the degree of biological relationship. In most societies, intercourse is permitted with some fairly close blood relatives and prohibited with some more distantly related ones. The key to these extensions is the family as a socially defined group rather than the family as a biologically constituted group. Those persons and groups who are prohibited to the individual tend to be those whom the system of descent defines as being closely related to him. Thus the *extension* of incest taboos, at least, tends to be rooted more in sociology than in biology.

A peculiar feature of incest taboos is their strength and the emotional attitudes which surround them. A peculiar horror attaches to the prospect of their violation; scarcely can a more heinous offense be imagined. The repugnance is greatest at the prospect of incest within the nuclear family and becomes less strong as one moves outward from the nuclear family along the socially defined lines of kinship.

THE ENFORCEMENT OF INCEST TABOOS

The basic technique upon which most societies depend for the enforcement of incest taboos is to so thoroughly instill them in the society's members that violations become virtually inconceivable. The learning of the incest taboos is a basic part of the socialization process. It is commonplace in American society today that many small children are relatively free in acting upon their sexual impulses and relatively indiscriminate in their choice of partners. It is not unusual, for example, for young brothers and sisters to join in sex play. By the time adulthood is reached, however, the taboos have been so thoroughly learned that aversion, bordering upon physical illness, may be the response to any prospect of sexual intercourse within the nuclear family. Adult brothers and sisters may sleep in adjoining bedrooms and appear before one another in partial states of undress without arousing any sexual response in either person. This internalization of the taboos within the personality is far more effective than any external restraints might be and is the primary mechanism upon which most societies depend.

Not all societies, however, depend upon internalization alone. In some societies there are, in addition, certain patterns of avoidance behavior between persons who are tabooed but between whom intercourse might occur. At puberty, for example, the norms may prescribe that the brother and sister shall no longer be alone in the same room together. If the sister enters a room and only her brother is present, he may be required to leave. Similarly, the norms may provide that a man may not look directly upon his mother-in-law. Whenever they are together, he may be required to keep his face turned away. Murdock found 17 societies in which behavior toward both sister and daughter was characterized by prescribed avoidance or marked respect.[33] He also found the relationship between a man and his mother-in-law and between a father and his son's wife to be classic avoidance relationships.

Avoidance relationships appear not to be depended upon by any society to the exclusion of internalization of incest taboos, but rather as supplements thereto in the case of specific relationships where the internalization process is not wholly effective. Relationships with a mother-in-law or a son's wife, for example, are not likely to be so strongly tabooed as those with a sister or daughter. The avoidance relationships also are quite effective, up to a point. People who cannot be alone together or who cannot look at one another ordinarily are not in great danger of sexual involvement. The superiority of internalization of the taboos as a means of control is to be found in the fact that they continue to be effective even when the situational restraints are removed.

The indoctrination of people with social norms is never perfect, and violations of the incest taboos apparently do occur in all societies. The very few violations which do occur appear to be the exceptions which validate the rule. Kinsey reports that violations in our own society are so rare that it would be misleading even to mention specific figures.[34] Weinberg studied 203 cases of incest known to the authorities in Illinois, in detail,[35] and reports that the detected incidence of incest in the United States in 1920 was 1.9 offenders per one million population, and in 1930 was 1.1.

These are detected incidence figures, of course, and probably underestimate the actual incest rates. One might speculate that true incest rates are considerably higher; certainly the experience of social workers and clinicians

---

[33] *Social Structure*, p. 274.

[34] Alfred C. Kinsey, Wardell B. Pomeroy, and Clyde E. Martin, *Sexual Behavior in the Human Male*, Philadelphia: W. B. Saunders, 1948, p. 558.

[35] S. Kirson Weinberg, *Incest Behavior*, New York: Citadel Press, 1955, p. 39.

would indicate so. It is most significant, however, that great effort is made to suppress knowledge of specific cases of incest. The maintenance of the taboo is too crucial to the welfare of the larger society to permit open discussion of the violations which do occur.

EXPLANATION OF INCEST TABOOS

Men have long sought for an adequate explanation of the universality of incest taboos. Literally dozens of explanations have been proposed, most of them so bizarre that no discussion of them need be given here. Of the many proposed explanations, only a few have more than superficial plausibility. Upon detailed examination most of those also prove inadequate to account for universal incest taboos. We will examine four of the more commonly accepted explanations before arriving at the one which, on the basis of present knowledge, appears most plausible.[36]

Alleged Harmful Effects of Inbreeding. An explanation advanced by a variety of writers from different academic backgrounds attributes the prohibition of intercourse between close blood relatives to the adverse effects of inbreeding upon the quality of the population. It is claimed that inbreeding leads to deterioration of the stock (the perpetuation of hemophilia within certain closely inbred European royal families often is used as an illustration) and recognition of this fact has led men everywhere to prohibit such relationships.

This explanation has some appeal, for inbreeding does tend to bring genetic deficiencies into expression. It is believed that most human genetic deficiencies are carried as recessive genes and do not produce harmful effects when the carrier is mated with a person of different genetic stock who does not carry the same recessive gene. The odds are much greater that a closely related person also carries the harmful recessive gene and that if these closely related persons are mated, the defect will appear in their offspring. Thus, intermarriage may to some degree promote the biological welfare of the species.

There are several problems with this logic as a full explanation of incest taboos, however. For one thing, this same logic might be reversed to promote the biological improvement of the species. Inbreeding is precisely what is used in the field of animal husbandry to produce steers which yield more and higher quality beef, chickens which contain more white meat, faster race horses, and so on. If man were to be completely rational about reproduction, he might promote inbreeding within certain lines along with prohibiting it in others. It can be argued that until recently, if even now, man did not have

---

[36] The following section follows closely Murdock, *Social Structure*, pp. 289–301.

sufficient knowledge of human genetics to make such selective regulation possible. Granting this argument, it appears unlikely that even vastly improved knowledge of genetics would have much influence upon incest taboos.

A more serious difficulty with this explanation is that it assumes a rationality which in some cases is literally impossible. Until recently, at least, some preliterate peoples have lacked adequate knowledge of the reproductive process, occasionally being completely unaware of the role of the father in procreation. The Arunta and the Trobriand Islanders are illustrations. Incest taboos are no less complex and are just as strong in these societies who could not possibly connect genetic problems to inbreeding.

Still another problem with this explanation is that incest taboos in most societies do not coincide with the closeness of biological relationship. Rather distant biological relatives may be prohibited while intercourse and procreation with much closer relatives are permitted. Thus, we must conclude that while the prohibition of inbreeding has some salutary effects in some instances, the total weight of evidence is against this explanation for most of the incest taboos.

Alleged Instinct Against Inbreeding. The internalization of the norms against inbreeding among most people is so effective that the revulsion against incestuous relations seems almost to be a part of the biological structure of the organism. This fact led some early writers to posit the existence of an instinct against incest.[37]

Early in the twentieth century, before there was sufficient knowledge of the socialization process, the concept of instinct was seized upon to explain a tremendous variety of human behaviors ranging from simple autonomic reflexes to complex and variable patterns of behavior such as parenthood and war. Gradually, however, the absurdity of postulating the existence of hundreds of human instincts became apparent.[38] It was generally concluded that the term, instinct, has utility only to refer to complex patterns of behavior which are biologically fixed for the species and which cannot be explained as a product of learning.

Such a concept of instinct cannot begin to explain incest taboos. In the first place, we know that violations of the taboos do occur. If there were an instinctive mechanism operating, this could not happen unless one were to make the implausible assumption that some people are born without the instinct. Second, the incest taboos are highly variable. It makes no sense biologically to claim that instincts prohibit sexual intercourse with first cousins in one social group and not in another. Third, if there were an instinct against

[37] Robert H. Lowie, *Primitive Society*, New York: Liveright, 1947.
[38] Luther L. Bernard, *Instinct: A Study in Social Psychology*, New York: Holt, 1924.

incest, there would be no need for the widespread horror of incestuous relationships. A biological mechanism should operate automatically without the need for buttressing by such emotional reactions. The instinctual explanation has been generally discarded by biological scientists as well as by social scientists.

Familiarity Breeds Disinterest. The anthropologist, Edward Westermarck, proposed to explain incest taboos by the fact that continued close association between persons of opposite sex tends to lessen their sexual attraction for one another. [39] That some general lessening of sexual interest does occur with continued close association seems to be an unassailable fact. Virtually all husbands and wives recognize it even in a context where sexual participation is expected. Recently in the Kibbutzim of Israel it has been found that among children reared together in a group situation where there are few taboos upon nudity and where sexual interest might be expected to develop, it does not. [40] It was also usual in ancient Egypt where royal brother and sister were expected to marry, to separate them in childhood and to keep them apart until adulthood so that they would be sexually attracted to one another.

The problem here is not so much with the facts themselves as with the facts as an explanation of incest taboos. The effects of growing up together cannot possibly be used to explain the frequent extension of incest taboos to kin who are not members of the household and with whom one might not have continuing close association. In the reverse situation, preferential mate selection (the levirate, sororate, and cross-cousin marriage) often call for marriage with persons with whom one has been associated long and intimately.

There is also some reason for questioning the facts in this case. We know that there are many exceptions to the rule and that some persons are strongly attracted sexually to other members of their own nuclear families. The logic of lessened sexual attraction would not explain why sex relationships should be prohibited in those cases where sexual attraction does exist.

Frustrations Encountered in the Oedipal Involvement. Another explanation for incest taboos has come out of classical psychoanalytic theory. Freud developed the notion of universal sexual attraction of a boy to his mother from Sophocles' *Oedipus Rex*, in which the son, Oedipus, unknowingly slays his own father and marries his mother. When he learns what he has done, he is overwhelmed with guilt and blinds himself. In psychoanalytic theory, this has been transformed into the universal situation where the child's sexual attrac-

[39] Edward Westermarck, *The History of Human Marriage*, New York: Allerton Book Company, 1922, Vol. 2, p. 192.

[40] Melford E. Spiro, *Children of the Kibbutz*, Cambridge: Harvard University Press, 1958.

tion to the parent of opposite sex must be repressed because of the harm that would be done to the child should the parent of the same sex become aware of the incestuous desires. The repression is only partly successful, and the horror which is attached to violations of the incest taboos is interpreted as reaction formation against the partly repressed impulses.

This psychoanalytic interpretation makes sense in the context of Western family organization but is not as adequate in societies with a radically different family organization. Malinowski attempted to test the notion of a universal oedipal complex through study of the Trobriand Islanders, a matrilineal society in which the role of paternity was not understood and in which the maternal uncle performs most of the functions associated with the father role in Western society. He found that the child's hostility was directed toward the uncle rather than toward the father and concluded that the basis for the hostility was not sexual jealousy but was resentment against authority. Thus Malinowski suggested that the oedipus complex is not a universal phenomenon but is, instead, a product of middle-class family structure in Western society.[41]

The Oedipus hypothesis is inadequate in other respects. It cannot satisfactorily account for the universal extension of incest taboos beyond the nuclear family. Nor can it account for the variability from one society to another in the definitions of which relatives are taboo. Psychoanalysis usefully focused attention upon the dangers of sexual conflict within the nuclear family but by itself it did not provide an adequate explanation of the incest taboos.

An Eclectic Explanation. The term "eclecticism" refers to the combination of elements of existing theories into a new, more comprehensive theory. Murdock has proposed such an eclectic theory of incest taboos which provides the most satisfactory explanation of them to date. In so doing, he draws upon contributions from sociology, cultural anthropology, psychoanalysis, and behavioristic psychology.[42]

The explanation begins by assuming, with the psychoanalysts, that immature sexual responses, or at least responses which adults interpret as potentially sexual, are made by the infant toward its parents as part of its responses to feeding, protection, and general care. These incipient responses meet with

[41] Bronislaw Malinowski, *Sex and Repression in Savage Society*, New York: Harcourt, Brace, 1927.

[42] *Social Structure*, pp. 292–300. For other analyses of the incest taboos, see Christopher Bagley, "Incest Behavior and Incest Taboo," *Social Problems* 16 (Spring 1969), pp. 505–19; and Richard L. Means, "Sociology, Biology, and the Analysis of Social Problems," *Social Problems* 15 (Fall 1967), pp. 200–212.

rebuffs and frustration both because of lack of interest by parents and siblings and because of the threats which are inherent in such behavior.

The parents, as sexually experienced adults, will feel some sexual attraction toward their children. Having themselves been indoctrinated with the culturally sanctioned restraints upon sexual behavior with children and within the nuclear family, the parents react with guilt and anxiety. Their anxiety is heightened because each parent would be threatened by the other's sexual attraction to one of the children. As a consequence, both parents strongly discourage their children from making any sexual overtures within the nuclear family.

The explanation of the cultural sanctioning of these tendencies within individual families comes from sociology. The family is the basic unit of reproduction, economic cooperation, and socialization. Sexual rivalry within the group would jeopardize its efficient functioning and even its existence. Fathers competing with their sons for the mother and the daughters, and mothers competing with their daughters for the father and the brothers would tear the group apart. Thus the self-interest of individuals and the societal interest are completely consistent with one another. The spontaneously developing sexual restraints within the family receive normative support from the society at large.

Kingsley Davis points out, further, that should inbreeding occur, the resulting confusion of statuses would be unbelievable. As he says, "The incestuous child of a father-daughter union . . . would be a brother of his own mother, i.e. the son of his own sister; a stepson of his own grandmother; possibly a brother of his own uncle; and certainly a grandson of his own father." [43] All family systems provide definitions of proper behavior between various family members: these definitions would break down completely in the face of widespread inbreeding.

The extension of incest taboos beyond the nuclear family is explained through the psychological concept of "stimulus generalization." According to the principle of stimulus generalization, any response elicited by a given stimulus will tend to be elicited by other stimuli in direct proportion to their similarity to the original stimulus. Thus, if the mother is tabooed, other women will be tabooed in proportion to their perceived similarity to the mother. Where maternal aunts are called by the same kinship term as the mother (as they sometimes are), where they live in the same household, and

---

[43] Kingsley Davis, "Legitimacy and the Incest Taboo," in Norman W. Bell and Ezra F. Vogel, eds., *A Modern Introduction to the Family*, The Free Press of Glencoe, Illinois, 1960, p. 401.

where the sororate exists, the maternal aunts are likely to be tabooed also. Countless other examples could be given.

There still remains the problem of why the taboos are extended further in some cases than in others, both within and among societies. This is a technical problem in cultural anthropology which goes far beyond the scope of this book. Suffice it to say that anthropologists have determined that kinship systems have both a history and a structure that is somewhat self-limiting. To explain why a particular society has an irregular extension of incest taboos outside the nuclear family, it is necessary to know both its historical connections with other societies and the particular directions of change which are facilitated and restricted by its existing kinship structure.

SUGGESTED READINGS

Since Chapters 2 and 3 form a single unit, the summary, suggested readings, films, and study questions will be found at the end of Chapter 3.

Family Structure in World Perspective: II

WORLD TRENDS IN FAMILY STRUCTURE

THE quotation that opened Chapter 2 described marital patterns that are very different from our own. In addition, it revealed a family system in the throes of drastic change. This quotation was used not because the Nigerian situation is unique but because what is happening there reflects what is happening in much of the rest of the world. There are signs of major change in family patterns and a trend toward the conjugal form of family organization. Let us address ourselves to this situation in some detail.

EVOLUTIONARY THEORY

Before attempting to present and evaluate the data on present world trends in family patterns, it may be helpful to review, briefly, earlier attempts to trace the evolution of family structure from its primeval beginnings to modern times.

Sociological and anthropological interest in the family as a social institution traces back to the mid-nineteenth century. The publication of two books in 1861 might be taken to establish an arbitrary beginning. One of these books, *Das Mutterrecht*, was written by a Swiss jurist, J. J. Bachofen; the other, *Ancient Law*, was written by the anthropologist Sir Henry Sumner Maine. The two books proposed quite different theories of the development of family organization, but both became part of a general academic movement attempting to trace the evolution of family structure from its beginnings in primitive promiscuity to the final penultimate form of permanent monogamy.

Most early writers did not state directly that man lived originally in a promiscuous horde, but believed instead that such a condition could be logically inferred from the widespread "promiscuous" mating being discovered among preliterate peoples. What appeared to be promiscuity to early anthropologists, ship captains, and missionaries was not that at all, of course, but only forms of sexual regulation different from the familiar Western ones. Nevertheless this ethnocentric interpretation of preliterate sexual behavior prevailed, and the assumption of an original human state of promiscuity was widespread.

From this beginning, many writers reasoned that family systems everywhere passed through a regular series of stages eventuating in Western-style monogamy. Sumner's analysis may be taken as representative.[1] From an hypothesized original promiscuity Sumner believed that the next stage might have been a more or less durable informal monopoly of one or more women by a man. This stage he called monandry. From monandry, the next stage probably was group marriage. Group marriage developed into polyandry, and polyandry into polygyny. The stage of monogyny, one wife plus additional consorts, preceded the final development of monogamy. Note the regular progression of stages from forms very different from our own to those more like ours.

There were many other variants of the evolutionary scheme. Bachofen assumed an original promiscuity and along with it postulated an actual supremacy of women which resulted in the development of a matriarchal, matrilineal society.[2] Gradually, he says, women lost their power and the final stage of the patriarchate emerged. A contrary view was proposed by Maine who secured his data from the study of ancient legal codes.[3] Not surprisingly, since the societies he studied were strongly patriarchal, he concluded that the human family has been basically patriarchal.

These theories, and many similar ones, have only historical interest today. More sophisticated anthropological study has long since rendered implausible the proposition that families everywhere have passed through similar stages or that there is any unilinear trend toward the monogamous family. The question of family origins is lost in prehistory, and social scientists have ceased to pursue a problem upon which data can never be brought to bear.

These evolutionary theories are mentioned here to provide background for consideration of the ways in which family systems are changing today. To realize that only 40 to 100 years ago social scientists should have engaged in what is today such an obviously ethnocentric exercise may encourage us to be somewhat cautious in interpreting present trends.

CURRENT WORLD TRENDS

Later chapters in this book will analyze the American conjugal family system in detail. At this point it is necessary only to indicate that most sociol-

---

[1] William Graham Sumner and Albert G. Keller, *The Science of Society*, Vol. 3, New Haven: Yale University Press, 1927.

[2] J. J. Bachofen, *Das Mutterrecht*, Stuttgart, 1861.

[3] Sir Henry Sumner Maine, *Ancient Law*, London: Murray, 1861.

ogists trace major changes in the American family system to the Industrial Revolution and the consequent urbanization of society. They believe that industrialization was instrumental in transforming the authoritarian, large, stable, rural family system into a more equalitarian, relatively isolated unstable nuclear family. They ask whether there may not be a causal connection between industrialization and the nuclear family.

The logic associated with this position is simple. In an agricultural society, members of the family work together as an economic unit. Sons become apprenticed to their fathers and eventually inherit the land. There is a clear division of labor between men and women but the division of labor among men is minimal. A person's status in the community is clearly fixed by the family into which he is born. Large families are advantageous. With industrialization, all of this changes. Work is removed from the home to factories. The division of labor becomes complex, and schools, not fathers, teach many occupational skills. The use of specialized occupational skills requires that sons move away from their families to the cities. Occupational success produces mobility upward in the social class structure and further isolates parents and children from their grandparents. Property becomes more intangible and the ties to the land are lost. Thus, the argument runs, industrialization tends to change extended family systems into nuclear systems.

The argument is persuasive. It accords with the American experience; it appears to be consistent with current happenings in other areas of the world. In order to provide some test of the argument, Goode assembled family data covering roughly the past fifty years in the West, in Arabic Islam, in Sub-Saharan Africa, in India, China, and Japan.[4]

As the Saudi Arabian Airlines jet descends into Jedda, the dark-haired stewardesses dressed in swingy green miniskirts disappear behind a curtain.

They emerge a few minutes later shrouded in full-length, black-veiled robes, now properly garbed to set foot in the homeland of the prophet Mohammed.

"When you put on the abaya," said the English-speaking Saudi stewardess, "you lose your shape, your age and your identity. You become a non-person."

The transformation was repeated in reverse recently in Kuwait. There, two wives of government officials boarded an airliner for Beirut, wearing abayas.

[4] William J. Goode, World Revolution and Family Patterns, New York: The Free Press of Glencoe, 1963.

As soon as the plane was airborne, the women doffed their robes, revealing chic and colorful dresses, settled back and ordered whisky sodas.

Thus does jet travel, crossing the cultural gap of centuries, dramatize the vast contrast in the feminine condition of the Arab world—from the Western freedom of Beirut and Cairo city life to the Oriental seclusion of the Arabian desert.

—Wire Services, September 9, 1970.

Goode concluded from his analysis that "the alteration appears to be in the direction of some type of conjugal family pattern—that is toward fewer kinship ties with distant relatives and a greater emphasis on the nuclear family unit of couple and children." [5] Note that Goode does not say that family systems all over the world are becoming more like our own. He says that the trend is toward *some type* of conjugal system. In fact, Goode's study indicates that the problem is far more complicated than simply whether other family systems are becoming more like ours. He adds the following cautions.

1. Even if the family systems in diverse areas of the world are moving *toward* similar patterns, they *begin* from very different points, so that the trend in one family trait may differ from one society to another—for example, the divorce or illegitimacy rate might be dropping in one society but rising in another.
2. The elements within a family system may each be altering at different rates of speed. . . .
3. Just *how* industrialization or urbanization affects the family system or how the family system facilitates or hinders these processes is not clear.
4. It is doubtful that the amount of change in family patterns is a simple function of industrialization; more likely, ideological and value changes, partially independent of industrialization, also have some effect on family action.
5. Some beliefs about how the traditional family system worked may be wrong. . . .
6. Correlatively, it is important to distinguish *ideal* family patterns from *real* family behavior and values, . . . [6]

Women have long been rejecting home economics in order to assist with home economy—by going to work earning money. Partly because

[5] Ibid. p. 1.
[6] Ibid. pp. 1–2.

of continued inflation, women in ever-increasing numbers are leaving their dishes in the sink and their babies in the nursery to move into offices and factories. As a result, less than half the nation's women are now keeping house full time. . . .

Despite the spread of "liberation" movements and antidiscrimination laws, women's jobs are far from the board room variety. Five of the ten occupations employing the largest number of women—teaching, nursing, making clothes, cooking and cleaning—are simply functions that have been transferred from the home to some institution. Whatever the job, a woman's wage seldom matches a man's. In 1957, fully employed women earned a median wage of $3,008 a year and men, $4,713. By 1968, men's income had risen 65%, to about $7,800, while women's had gone up 51% to $4,550. . . .

—Reprinted by permission from *Time*, The Weekly Newsmagazine; copyright Time Inc., 1970.

Zelditch, in summarizing an independent analysis of the relation between industrialization and family change, reaches somewhat similar conclusions. He states that "apparently, any kind of nonsubsistence expanding economy, or even political changes can destroy the authority structure on which the descent group and extended family depend." [7] He summarizes the conditions for change as:

1. any change by which kinship and occupational structures become differentiated.
2. where income and status come to depend upon factors not controlled by the extended family.
3. where sons begin to contribute more status and income to the family than do their fathers.
4. where the self interests of family members are not identified with continuity of the family.

These conditions, he says, may produce a trend toward the conjugal family whether or not industrialization is involved. In just a few generations, all that is left may be a sense of personal obligation and affection toward kin. Gradually these sentiments are restricted to fewer and fewer kin, with the relatives included being increasingly bilateral.

That there is no simple cause-and-effect relationship between industrialization and the development of the nuclear family is quite clear. Nuclear family

[7] Morris Zelditch, Jr., "Cross-Cultural Analyses of Family Structure," in Harold T. Christensen, ed., *Handbook of Marriage and the Family*, Chicago: Rand McNally, 1964, p. 496.

systems are found in primitive, non-industrialized societies as well as in modern societies.[8] Nor is it at all clear that it is simply industrialization which is producing the changes that are evident in much of the world today. Goode points out that we cannot assume that non-Western family systems were basically similar to Western family systems at some undefined historical period just before industrialization.

Goode also emphasizes the role of ideological changes—changes in values— that are helping to transform non-Western family systems. He sees all family systems as containing some points of stress and strain—features which make them vulnerable to change. Consanguine extended family systems over the world have tended to subjugate women and to subordinate the young to their elders. Among women and the young and among intellectuals, radical ideologies have been emerging concurrent with and even prior to industrialization.

One such new ideology is that of economic progress, the radical notion that technological development and the production of wealth is more important than the preservation of traditional customs. A second radical ideology is that of individualism, the heretical notion that personal welfare is more important than family continuity. A third emerging ideology is that of equalitarianism, the notion that women should have equal rights with men. Taken together, these emerging values may be as instrumental in producing family change as are the effects of industrialization.

It remains now only to summarize the general changes involved in the widespread trend toward some variant of the conjugal, nuclear family. The changes include trends toward: (1) free choice of spouse, (2) more equal status for women, (3) equal rights of divorce, (4) neolocal residence, (5) bilateral kin, and (6) the equality of individuals against class or caste barriers.

Free Choice of Spouse. Extended family systems and the arrangement of the marriages of youth by their parents have long been associated. Love as a basis for marriage is discouraged because affectional ties between the young married couple cannot be permitted to conflict with their obligations to the large family group. The spouse who moves at marriage often is completely subordinated to members of his or her new family until he or she has been so completely socialized into the new family that any opposition to its customs or goals has been completely eliminated. Most often, of course, it is the woman who moves at marriage and who suffers most.

---

[8] Meyer F. Nimkoff, and Russell Middleton, op. cit. See also, Sydney Greenfield, "Industrialization and the Family in Sociological Theory," *American Journal of Sociology* 67 (Nov. 1961), pp. 312–22. A recent analysis suggests that the American family possessed, before industrialization, many of the features that most writers assume to have derived from industrialization. See Frank F. Furstenberg, Jr., "Industrialization and the American Family: A Look Backward," *American Sociological Review* 31 (June 1966), pp. 326–37.

*Friends are informed that the announcement on January 13, 1959,
that I and Ma Mya Kyaing had been divorced was merely a propitiatory
act astrologically executed to prevent the actual event from taking place.*

—advertisement in the newspaper, *Bamakhit*, Rangoon, Burma

The conditions of urban living often include separation from both families of orientation so that the ability of the new spouse to get along with one's parents is no longer so important. Instead, the relationship between the husband and wife assumes great importance. Probably in all times and places certain men and women have experienced attraction to one another, but, whereas extended family systems work to exclude such attractions as bases for marriage, conjugal family systems tend to make romantic love the primary basis for marriage. Until recently, the encouragement of romantic love and the right to choose one's own marital partner were not widespread in non-Western countries. Now they are spreading rapidly.

More Equal Status for Women. Patrilineal descent and inheritance and patrilocal residence have been associated with some degree of patriarchy and the subordination of women. Polygyny has been widespread, with some women assigned the status of secondary wives. The custom of *concubinage* in which women have approved status as additional sex partners but not the full legal and other rights of wives also has been widespread. Then there are the more informal, socially disapproved situations where wealthy and influential men have had mistresses who had no rights at all.

The emerging right of women to choose their husbands is doing much to change all this. When men must compete for the favor of women, inevitably the women gain a certain amount of power. Coupled with this is the fact that education for women, and particularly higher education, is spreading rapidly. Women find the possibility of taking jobs in the expanding economy and often their pay approaches that of men. The cities, moreover, offer independent living opportunities for women who cannot achieve favorable terms in their relationships with men.

Goode points out, interestingly, that while the philosophy of equal rights for women receives more verbal acceptance in upper social-class levels, the equal rights are more effective at lower-class levels.[9] Upper-class men may believe that they should grant equal rights to women but their own positions of wealth and power lead them to expect considerable deference from their wives. Lower-class men, on the other hand, have less real power over their

[9] Op. cit. pp. 21-2, 372.

wives because of the greater direct economic contribution lower-class wives make to the family. Goode also warns that no family system now grants *full* equality to women and none is likely to do so as long as much of the daily work involving house and children is regarded as woman's responsibility.[10]

The big bridal dowry would be an offense punishable by up to six months in jail and/or $1,050 (equivalent) fine under a new bill in India's parliament. It would let a bride be given jewels and clothing to the value of $420.

—Associated Press

Equal Rights of Divorce. The modern term, divorce, is somewhat misleading when applied to many non-Western and ancient societies. What has often been found among them might be more usefully referred to as the husband's right of *repudiation* of his wife. The distinction is important. The modern concept of divorce implies that divorce may be secured only on specified grounds and with some official body such as the courts determining the equity of the matter. In many non-Western and ancient societies, however, the husband or his family has been the sole judge. With no more ceremony than telling the wife before witnesses, or handing her a slip of paper, a so-called bill of divorcement, the husband could end the marriage. The wife often had no recourse and no corresponding rights.

Women in many countries now are demanding that they have protection against their unjust repudiation by the husband or his family—that their husbands be permitted divorce only for cause. Similarly, they are demanding that they be given equal rights; that the same or comparable grounds for the divorce of a wife should also be grounds for the divorce of a husband. Again the caution should be added that divorce rights in many societies still favor the husband. There is a *trend only* toward more equal divorce rights for women.

Neolocal Residence. Patrilocal residence has been far and away the most common pattern over the world. Even matrilocal residence, also reflecting extended family organization, has been more common than neolocal residence. As urbanization and industrialization proceed, more and more families of procreation find their residences being determined for them by the location of the husband's job. By default, if not by design, neolocal residence is be-

[10] For vigorous protest against this state of affairs, see Kate Millett, *Sexual Politics*, New York: Doubleday, 1970; and Robin Morgan, ed., *Sisterhood is Powerful*, New York: Random House, 1970.

coming more common. In some cases nuclear families plan for decades eventually to return to their extended families. Sometimes they do; often they do not. If Murdock is correct, such changed residential patterns will eventually lead to changes in the formal rules of residence.

Bilateral Kindred. Technically, the term *kindred* refers to a bilateral kin group. The evidence indicates that even where formal unilineages exist, social and geographical mobility and neolocal residence lead to weakening of ties with the extended kin group. The tasks formerly performed by the lineage either are assumed by the conjugal family or by public and private agencies— the police, the courts, welfare agencies, and so on. Gradually the ties with kin are reduced to a smaller and smaller group, typically drawn from both the husband's and the wife's lineages. Whether ties are maintained with any kin at all come to depend upon whether affection is felt for those kin rather than upon any great sense of obligation to them.

Equality of Individuals Against Caste or Class Barriers. To some degree, the trends toward free mate choice, equality for women, and equal divorce rights, are part of a larger ideological change. A pervasive philosophy of individualism appears to be spreading over much of the world—a philosophy which militantly asserts the importance of the welfare of the person over any considerations of the continuity of the group. This is a radical philosophy, at least as radical as the movement for redistribution of large land holdings which has attracted so much Western attention. The worth of the individual comes to be more important than inherited wealth or ethnic group. The individual's status comes to be evaluated not so much by the lineage into which he was born as by his own accomplishments. The status of the family, then, must be determined for each generation anew.

In closing this section, a few reminders and cautions are in order. First, the trends described are just that—trends. It would be a serious mistake to conclude that extended family systems the world over have broken down. Most societies in the world today have unilineal descent systems, extended families, and male domination. The trends toward conjugal family systems, widespread as they are, generally are confined to the more urbanized, industrialized regions. The great masses of population in the hinterlands of countries like China and India, to say nothing of preliterate societies, are relatively unaffected. Moreover, these changes, where they appear, often are viewed as social problems, as symptoms of the breakdown of time-honored ways. Men and women, young and old are pitted against one another. One should not construct a stereotype of societies emerging from the darkness of autocratic extended family systems into the light of conjugal systems held together by ties of affection. It has yet to be shown that the sum total of human happiness is greater under one system than under another.

. . . For the evaluation of (current) changes the individual reader must rely on his own philosophy. Some will see them as the advent of a new and fruitful era, a period in which men and women will find a richer personal life, in which they will have a greater range of choices in their own emotional fulfillment. They will rejoice to learn that young Chinese brides do not have to bring tea to their mothers-in-law in the morning or wash their feet, that young Chinese grooms and brides may openly express their love for one another. They will be pleased that the Indian husband who has tired of his wife may not take an additional secondary mate into his household, or that the Arab husband finds divorce a much more tedious, awkward, and expensive affair than it once was. They will be glad that it is only the rare young European woman who now has to acquire a dowry in order to make a desirable marriage, and they will be pleased that increasingly in the major family systems, when either a husband or wife finds no happiness in marriage, either can break it and perhaps find happiness with someone else.

But still others will view all of these processes with suspicion, skepticism, or dismay. They may see them as the breakdown of major civilizations. They will see the Western pattern of the conjugal family spreading like a fungus over other societies, leading inevitably to a decline in their quality and the ultimate destruction of the achievements of our time. They will know that although under a system of arranged marriages some people did not find love, but almost everyone had a chance at marriage; and more pain and trauma can come from the disruption and dissolution of love under the conjugal system. They will insist, moreover, that although the older systems weighed heavily upon the young and upon women, the elders did, in fact, have more wisdom, and the young in time grew older and took their place in the community, while both men and women in their turn, and according to their positions, received the honor, respect, and power to which they once had to submit.

Finally, we should remember how little we know of the cause-and-effect relations underlying these trends. That urbanization and industrialization are involved is obvious; that urbanization and industrialization alone cannot account for the trends is equally obvious. Ideological factors—individualism, democracy, economic progress—are involved and appear to be both cause and effect. To some degree, the ideals, the technology, and the family system are being exported to the rest of the world from the West. But, just as surely, other societies cannot be seen properly as following the model of the West. Other societies, exposed to the influences of technological and ideological change, will incorporate the effects of those changes in ways unique to themselves. Each society has a history and a present structure into which change must be incorporated. Other societies, even if they are profoundly altered by it, will adapt the conjugal family system to their own needs.[11]

THEORETICAL TYPES AND EMPIRICAL REALITY

Before proceeding to the further description and analysis of family behavior, it may be desirable to make explicit some of the mental operations that we are using. For what we see when we look at families and family behavior depends very much upon the nature of our conceptual tools.

It would be impossible for us to describe the full behavior of even a single family for a period of one year in a book of this size. Indeed, many books larger than this one have been written about individual families. Nor would the detailed description of the behavior of just one family tell us as much about family behavior in general as can be learned from the study of limited aspects of the behavior of a large number of families.

To study the behavior of a large number of families it is not only necessary to focus upon what we think is important in their behavior to aid us in the understanding of other families, but it also is necessary to conceptualize those few aspects of behavior. To conceptualize, of course, means to select out common properties of that which is being observed and to focus upon those common properties rather than upon the range of differences to be found.

To take a very homely illustration, consider for a moment the concept of "a man." Actually there is no such thing as a man. There are only specific men—Joe Gronowski who is tall, dark, and intelligent, and Bill Smith, who is short, heavy, and aggressive. When we use the concept of "a man" we ignore, for the moment, the fact that men differ in height, weight, coloring, intelligence, and aggressiveness, and focus upon those characteristics men have in common and in relation, perhaps, to women. In relation to women, men are tall, heavy, bearded, angular in construction, aggressive, and so on. By thus conceptualizing man (and woman) we can explore differences between men and women that otherwise would be obscured in a bewildering mass of details.

All analysis involves the use of concepts, and the analysis of the family is

[11] William Graham Sumner, *Folkways*, Boston: Ginn, 1906, pp. 5–6.

no exception. To make sense out of family behavior we must select certain abstract properties for study and, meanwhile, ignore a mass of detail. This process is necessary but it also is fraught with some hazard. One danger is that the concepts we use may become confused with empirical reality. We may develop such a firm notion of what a man is like that we can no longer see that Ray Jones or Tom Andre do not conform in all respects to our idea of what a man is like. If we are not careful, we may actually substitute *our idea* of a man for the specific characteristics of individual men that we are supposed to be observing. Academicians call this process, of confusing the concept with reality, the error of *reification*. The analyst reifies, that is, gives reality to, his idea. The error of reification must be carefully avoided.

IDEAL TYPES

Much sociological analysis makes use of a particular form of concept which is known as an "ideal type." This form of conceptualization and the techniques for its proper use were developed originally by the German sociologist Max Weber.[12] As currently used by sociologists, the ideal type has three features which merit discussion.

Not a Normative Concept. The very term, ideal type, is unfortunate. It is unfortunate because the word, ideal, in English has normative connotations; that is, the word, ideal, implies the making of an evaluation to the effect that what is described as ideal is also good. When we say that a man and woman make an ideal couple, we mean that we approve of their relationship, that they make a perfect couple. These normative connotations in the everyday use of the word, ideal, are an endless source of confusion to students when they try to grasp the sociological concept of the ideal type. *The ideal type in sociology has no normative connotations whatever!*

When we refer to the patriarchal family as an ideal type we make no value judgments concerning it whatever. We do not assume that it is good or that it is bad. We refer instead to a family system where authority is concentrated in the hands of the eldest male and which often includes patrilineal descent, patrilocal residence, a low status for women, arranged marriages, and so on. Ideal types are descriptive and analytic types. They are not normative types.

A Logical Construct. An ideal type is constructed by taking one or more characteristics which are believed to be typical of a phenomenon and accentuating those characteristics to their logical maximum or reducing them to their logical minimum. Take, again, the matter of the distribution of authority in

---

[12] Max Weber, *The Methodology of the Social Sciences* (translated and edited by Edward A. Shils and Henry A. Finch), Chicago: The Free Press of Glencoe, 1949.

the family between the husband and wife. Women are never completely without power in the family. Nor, for that matter, are the younger brothers of the patriarch without some power. In some family systems, the eldest male (and males generally) holds more power than in others. In some family systems that power is great. The ideal type of the patriarchal family involves taking this factor of disproportionate concentration of power in male hands and constructing a theoretical type in which *all* power would be held by males. An ideal type, by definition, does not accurately describe the situation which exists in any given society. It represents, instead, a logical exaggeration of one or more features of the society.

Most students should be familiar with the idea of a continuum. A continuum is simply a scale, infinitely divisible, and with the ends of the continuum represented by logically extreme cases. Thus a continuum of adult height might range from short to tall. How short is short, and how tall is

short   tall
CONTINUUM OF HEIGHT

tall? There is no such thing as "tall." There are men who range in height up to seven feet and slightly above. If one wants to describe the range and distribution of adult heights the idea of a continuum is useful and the ends of the continuum may be usefully represented by the words short and tall, even though no person will be found at either end of the continuum. A hypothetical distribution of adult male heights is shown below. Note that the greatest concentration of men is to be found in the center of the con-

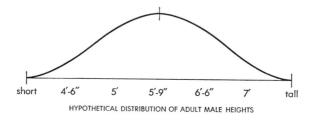

short   4'-6"   5'   5'-9"   6'-6"   7'   tall
HYPOTHETICAL DISTRIBUTION OF ADULT MALE HEIGHTS

tinuum. Five feet nine inches may be the average, or most representative, male height. For certain descriptive purposes one might want to emphasize the average height. For other purposes one might want to focus on the ends of the continuum—the ideal types of short and tall.

Ideal types always represent the ends of the continuum. They are extreme types rather than most representative types. They do not represent reality. They are analytic tools to be used in the study of reality.

The Ideal-Typical Methodology. The proper use of ideal types is as reference points. One constructs a series of theoretically relevant ideal types and then uses these constructions as standards with which to compare the reality situation. Thus we are not interested in trying to find a society which completely fits the ideal type of the patriarchal family. Instead we study the distribution of power in different family systems and compare them one with another and all of them against the ideal type. In so doing, we can gain perspective on the distribution of power in existing societies and on the significance of power distribution for other aspects of family structure. This use of ideal types has been found uncommonly useful in sociological analysis.

THEORETICAL FAMILY TYPES

Without being explicit about it, the major part of this chapter has been devoted to the development of a series of types of family structure. Thus patriarchal and matriarchal; patrilineal, matrilineal, and bilateral; patrilocal, matrilocal, and neolocal; polygynous, polyandrous, and monogamous; extended and nuclear; and consanguine and conjugal all represent classifications of family types.

Most of these types may be conceived of as ideal types, involving the abstraction and logical extension of the characteristics used as the basis for classification. Throughout this book we will find these types useful as standards against which to analyze family structure and family behavior in this and other societies.

It should be recognized that the use of such theoretical types makes it easy to exaggerate the differences in day-to-day family behavior from one society to another. We should not become so enamored of our typologies that we forget the common human character of family relationships. There is a biological and a social psychological foundation upon which the cultural regulation of family behavior is built. In almost any society in the world an observer could witness the play of children, the flirting of adolescents, and the lovemaking, quarreling, and economic cooperation of marriage partners and perceive the similarity of those experiences to similar events in his own life.

SUMMARY

Nuclear families are combined into composite families either through plural marriage or through extension of the parent-child relationship. Polygamous marriage, which involves common residence and economic cooperation as well as extension of the sexual relationship, is divided into polygyny, the taking of plural wives, and polyandry, the taking of plural husbands. Polygyny is widespread over the world, polyandry is rare, and group marriage, several men married in common to several women, is nowhere the societal norm. Polygamous marriages may involve the taking of siblings as spouses, or the multiple spouses may be unrelated. The terms, levirate and sororate, refer to preferential marriage with the sibling of a deceased spouse. Though polygyny usually is accorded higher status than monogamy, most persons in any society are monogamous. The sex ratio and the cost of polygynous marriages are influential here.

Extended families may be compounded either of monogamous or polygamous families. Nuclear families become dependent units in extended family systems. Extended families tend to emphasize blood ties over marital ties and are labeled consanguine. Nuclear families emphasizing marital ties are called conjugal. Consanguine families provide for continuity over the generations, serve to hold property intact, and prescribe the roles of family members in detail. Conjugal families are short-lived, tend to split up the family property, and emphasize flexibility in role performance.

About one-fourth of all societies have the nuclear family only, another fourth have polygamous but not extended families, and about half have some form of extended family. The independent nuclear family is found at both the bottom and top of the economic scale. The extended family predominates in agricultural and pastoral economies.

Since one spouse must move at marriage, rules of residence also are necessary. Patrilocal residence is most common, followed by matrilocal residence. Neolocal residence, in which the young couple establish residence apart from both parental groups, is found in only 17 of 250 societies. Some form of bride price is associated with removal of the bride from the community of her parents and is a guarantee of her good treatment. Women seldom are purchased outright.

Authority patterns in the family may be patriarchal, matriarchal, or equalitarian. Even in alleged matriarchies, power is wielded by males of the female lineage.

All societies regulate sex behavior. Only about 5 per cent of the world's societies prohibit all sex behavior outside of marriage, however. About 70 per cent of societies permit premarital intercourse, sometimes with persons who are preferred marriage partners. Intercourse between a married man and an unrelated woman generally is forbidden, but men, in most societies, are granted sexual access to one or more female relatives. The cultural rules of endogamy and exogamy require marriage either within or outside the group.

Universal incest taboos within the nuclear family have striking effects upon family structure. The constant overlapping of nuclear families requires that social definitions of kinship be established. This is accomplished through rules of descent. The structurally significant rules are patrilineal, descent traced through the father's lineage; matrilineal, descent traced through the mother's lineage; and bilateral, the tracing of descent through a group selected from both father's and mother's biological kin. Rules of inheritance may also be patrilineal or matrilineal, with primogeniture—preference given to the eldest son—often being found.

Incest taboos are always extended beyond the nuclear family but not universally to any specified relative outside the nuclear family. The key to these extensions is the family as a defined social group rather than the family as a biological group. Societies enforce incest taboos primarily through internalization of the taboos during socialization and secondarily through avoidance relationships.

Among explanations proposed for the universal incest taboos are the alleged ill effects of inbreeding, alleged instincts against inbreeding, the sexual disinterest which allegedly accompanies intimate familiarity, and the frustrations encountered in the oedipal situation. All of these explanations are found wanting. An eclectic explanation finds the roots of the taboos in the suppression of sexual rivalries within the nuclear family and the necessity to preserve the family as a cooperative unit.

Research indicates that family systems over a wide area of the world are tending toward some variant of the conjugal family. Urbanization and industrialization are involved in this trend, but it is too simple to say that they are the cause of the trend. For one thing, conjugal families are found in pre-industrial societies. Moreover, ideological changes appear to play a partly independent causal role.

The analysis of family systems requires the use of theoretical types. One form of construct, the ideal type, has been widely used in this chapter and will be used throughout the book. Care should be taken not to confuse the theoretical types with empirical reality.

SUGGESTED READINGS

Bohannon, Paul, and Middleton, John, eds., *Marriage, Family and Residence*, Garden City, New York: The Natural History Press, 1968. A collection of classic articles on incest, marriage forms, the universality of the family, and patterns of residence.

Edwards, John N., *The Family and Change*, New York: Alfred A. Knopf, 1969. Includes an excellent collection of essays and research articles on the impact of industrialization and urbanization on the family.

Eshleman, J. Ross, *Perspectives in Marriage and the Family: Text and Readings*, Boston: Allyn and Bacon, Inc., 1969. Contains a valuable collection of articles on the American family in the process of change.

Farber, Bernard, *Comparative Kinship Systems: A Method of Analysis*, New York: John Wiley and Sons, Inc., 1968. Relates incest taboos to the organization of kinship groups, and patterns of inheritance, mate selection, and divorce.

Houston, James, *The White Dawn: An Eskimo Saga*, New York: Harcourt Brace Jovanovich, 1971. Fascinating novel set in an imagined Eskimo community at the moment of its intersection with Western life. Sympathetically presents sexual, marriage, and family patterns diverging widely from our own.

Stephens, William N., *The Family in Cross-Cultural Perspective*, New York: Holt, Rinehart, and Winston, 1963. A general cross-cultural survey of family customs in preliterate and literate societies. Contains three very useful bibliographies for the student who wishes to delve deeper into cross-cultural analysis.

Young, Frank W., "Incest Taboos and Social Solidarity," *American Journal of Sociology* 72 (May 1967), pp. 589–600. Presents a provocative analysis of incest taboos as a mechanism for the promotion of group solidarity.

FILMS

Courtship and Marriage: A Comparison of Courting Customs Around the World (National Film Board of Canada, Mackenzie Building, Toronto), 60 minutes. Examines courtship customs in Sicily, Iran, Canada, and India. Contrasts arranged marriage with marriage based upon romantic love.

Fifty Miles From Poona (National Film Board of Canada, Mackenzie Building, Toronto), 20 minutes. From the heart of India, the story of a Hindu family. An engrossing view of people whose ways are strange to us promotes understanding of things people everywhere have in common—the love of a farmer for his land, the devotion of a mother to her children.

Four Families (National Film Board of Canada, Mackenzie Building, Toronto), 61 minutes. Comparison of family life in India, France, Japan, and Canada. Margaret Mead discusses how the upbringing of a child contributes to a distinctive national character.

Japan's New Family Pattern (available through Oklahoma State University Audio-Visual Center, Stillwater, Okla.), 15 minutes, color. Points out the change since World War II in the home life of the Japanese people.

Married Life (Time-Life Films, 43 West 16th Street, New York 10011), 45 minutes. Married life in five different settings: a wife with three husbands in the Himalayas; a couple in a prosperous English community; a man with three wives in New Guinea; another with two wives in Botswana; and a young couple in Lancashire.

Meaning of Adolescence (McGraw-Hill Book Company, Text-Film Division, 330 West 42nd St., New York 10036), 16 minutes. Film begins with a definition of "adolescence" and then contrasts the adolescent in a preliterate culture with one in our Western 20th century culture. Points to the unsure status of the adolescent. Revolves around a boy and girl in the 14–16 years age group and shows how they must adjust to five major aspects of modern life.

Wedding Day (National Film Board of Canada, Mackenzie Building, Toronto),
   29 minutes. In Nigeria, Brazil, Ontario, three weddings showing how the
   ceremony and its preliminaries compare in these widely separated areas.

QUESTIONS AND PROJECTS

1. Describe the two ways in which nuclear families may be combined into composite forms. What general terms are used to refer to the two types of
   composite families?
2. Differentiate among polygamy, polygyny, and polyandry. Why are most
   people monogamous even in societies which value polygyny highly?
3. What economic conditions in a society favor monogamy? Polygyny? Polyandry? How widespread is each over the world?
4. What are the levirate and the sororate? Does either custom exist in our own
   society? Why or why not?
5. Distinguish between dependent and independent nuclear families.
6. What is meant by a consanguine family system? A conjugal family system?
   Detail the advantages and problems associated with consanguine and conjugal
   systems.
7. What economic subsistence patterns are associated with independent nuclear
   family systems? With extended family systems?
8. Evaluate the proposition: that most societies do not regulate sex per se. What
   are the societal bases for the regulation of sexual behavior? Does any society
   grant complete freedom in sexual behavior? Explain.
9. What are incest taboos? Differentiate between incest taboos and endogamy
   and exogamy. Illustrate rules of endogamy and exogamy in the United States.
10. How does the existence of universal incest taboos necessitate the development
    of complex kinship systems? Evaluate the proposition: that kinship systems
    are social systems.
11. Define and describe the major rules of descent; the rules of inheritance; the
    rules of residence. Which are more common over the world? What associ-
    ations exist among rules of descent, inheritance, and residence?
12. What is a patriarchal family system? Are there any true matriarchies? In what
    persons is power usually vested in so-called matriarchal societies?
13. What explanations have been proposed for the universality of incest taboos?
    Evaluate the strengths and weaknesses of these explanations. What is the
    most adequate explanation of incest taboos?
14. Toward what general form are family systems over the world changing? Eval-
    uate, critically, the proposition: that family systems in other parts of the
    world are coming to be modeled after the American system.
15. Discuss, as thoroughly as you can, the basic causes for the world revolution
    in family patterns.
16. What is an ideal type? What is the ideal-typical methodology? What is meant
    by the statement that the ideal type is not a normative concept?

4 | *The Family System of China*

The Chinese family was patriarchal. The grandfather or father was the ruling head and had authority over all the members of the family, including his wife and concubines, his sons and grandsons, their wives and children, his unmarried daughters, his collateral relatives who were junior to him and who shared his domicile, his slaves and servants. His control of the family economy and his power to make financial decisions strengthened his authority. In addition, since the concept of ancestor worship was central to the perpetuation and solidarity of the family, the authority of the family head, who was also the family priest, was further enhanced. Finally, his authority was recognized and supported by the law.[1]

. . . He is foreman of a crew of ten men who install and repair machines. By going to night school he has completed six years of secondary education which helped him qualify for his job.

Mr. Chou earns 71 yuan ($28.40) a month, and works a six-day, 48-hour week. He and his family live well, and save money, because three others also work.

With two of his four children holding jobs and two in school, his wife recently became an apprentice in the factory. . . .

The family lives half a mile from the factory in a sparsely furnished apartment that has two small bedrooms with tiny outside balconies, a kitchen and lavatory. For this they pay 7 yuan a month. . . .

Mr. Chou remembers the old days and says he is well off now. More than anything else, he is grateful to Chairman Mao for the opportunity to become a skilled worker.

His children also are reminded constantly how fortunate they are to be living now rather than in the capitalist days. With other Peking children, they go to . . . hear lectures and look at life-size clay figures depicting cruelty of landlords and Nationalist soldiers.

[1] T'ung-tsu Ch'u, *Law and Society in Traditional China*, Paris: Mouton and Co., 1961, p. 20.

Landlords are shown cheating peasants of their grain, beating them, and dragging their daughters off to serfdom.

After the lecture, the children shout in unison: "Long live Chairman Mao."[2]

THE first of these two quotations refers to the traditional Chinese family system—a strong, stable family system which persisted for some 2000 years. The second quotation refers to the new family system that is being promoted by the government of the People's Republic of China.

Literally hundreds of family systems from all over the world might have been selected for analysis in this chapter. Selection of the Chinese family system was not completely arbitrary. Indeed, study of the Chinese family has many special advantages. We will make those advantages explicit before proceeding to analysis of the family system itself.

ADVANTAGES IN STUDY OF THE CHINESE FAMILY SYSTEM

MAJOR FAMILY TRADITION DIFFERENT FROM OUR OWN

The principal part of this book will be devoted to the analysis of Western family organization, and more specifically to the family system in the United States. Chapters 2 and 3 already have provided some world perspective but, necessarily, that cross-cultural analysis could not provide a comprehensive, integrated portrayal of any one family system that is very different from our own. Given family practices take on meaning only in the total context in which they appear. Lest strange family customs remain merely as curiosities, we need to present some of them in a context in which they will be wholly intelligible and, at the same time, to present another major type of family system with which our own can be systematically compared.

The traditional Chinese family system is very different from our own. Just as ours may be used to represent Western family systems, the Chinese can be used to represent Eastern systems. Instead of choosing a preliterate society of a few hundred people and with tenuous ties to any of the major civilizations in the world, we have selected a society of approximately 780 million people,[3] the largest nation in the world, and a society whose general practices are at least somewhat applicable to additional hundreds of millions of people. The cultural stream from which Chinese family practices derive has as long and distinguished a history as does our own.

[2] From *The New York Times*, June 21, 1971. © 1971 by The New York Times Company. Reprinted by permission.

[3] United Nations estimate, 1970.

A MODEL OF STABILITY AND CHANGE

The Western family, and the American family in particular, has been characterized by great and rapid change. In contrast, the Chinese family system remained *relatively* unchanged for approximately 2000 years. No society is ever completely static, of course, and some of the apparent lack of change in Chinese society is a function of the inability of Western scholars to see and interpret the change which has occurred. Nevertheless, by Western standards, Chinese social change has been very slow and China has shown great capacity for simply absorbing potential agents of change from the outside. Neither Christianity nor Judaism, for example, has had the impact upon China which might have been expected. The Jews who settled there centuries ago were absorbed so that few traces of them remain today.[4] Christianity has had somewhat more impact, but there is no evidence of basic change in Chinese institutions which can be traced directly to the religious character of this influence.[5] Similarly, both Mongol and Manchu invasions of China resulted ultimately in the conquerors' adoption of Chinese ways rather than in major social change.[6] Though change was present, the appearance presented by the Chinese family and Chinese society, to the West, was one of great strength and stability.

Even as it serves as a model of stability, however, the Chinese family also presents a model of change. About 100 years ago, urbanization and industrialization began to make their influence felt and China embarked upon a period of rapid change which today is still in process. The family system, which had seemed impervious to change, underwent drastic alteration. The nature of China's sharing in the world revolution in family patterns will be treated in the latter part of this chapter.

UNUSUALLY COMPREHENSIVE DATA AVAILABLE

There may well be more reliable literature on the Chinese family than on any other non-Western family system. Both Oriental and Western scholars have been studying China's history and social patterns for decades and, in some cases, centuries. This concerted attention to China has resulted not only in a great mass of literature but also in literature of unusual trustworthiness.

---

[4] S. M. Perlmann, *The History of the Jews in China*, London, 1913, as discussed in Marion J. Levy, Jr., *The Family Revolution in Modern China*, Cambridge: Harvard University Press, 1949, p. 286.

[5] Levy, ibid.

[6] Ibid. pp. 329–30.

The interaction, particularly between Chinese and non-Chinese scholars, has produced modification of many early ideas concerning Chinese family patterns and has produced understanding in great depth. The descriptions which follow are not based upon the work of one or two people with two or three years of field work experience; they represent the combined efforts of a veritable army of scholars. What limitations inhere in this chapter are more a product of the present author's incomplete mastery of the literature rather than being due to faults in the literature itself.

SIGNIFICANCE IN THE MODERN WORLD

At the close of World War II when the United Nations was organized, China was selected as one of the five great world powers along with the United States, England, France, and the Soviet Union. At that time China's greatness lay in her tremendous land area, her huge population, and, largely, in her history of greatness. The government of the Republic of China was beset by revolution and in dire trouble. The troubles worsened and soon there were "two Chinas," the new People's Republic on the mainland and Nationalist China on Taiwan.

The past twenty-five years have made it quite clear that the People's Republic of China is in firm control of the country. China has become a modern nation, presenting formidable ideological, military, and economic challenge to the rest of the world.

The early policies of the Chinese communist government were aggressively hostile to the family system that had been the mainstay of traditional society. The government perceived that family system as a threat and sought gross alteration in it. The struggle between the two institutions is not ended yet, but the government now seems secure and has turned most of its attention elsewhere. A new Chinese family system is emerging.

The Traditional Chinese Family

At the outset, the phrase "traditional Chinese family" requires qualification. In the broadest sense it refers to Chinese family patterns up to about 75 to 100 years ago. The extensive social change which has produced the "transitional family" first became evident at about that time. More narrowly, the traditional family, as we will discuss it here, was most characteristic of the Ch'ing dynasty which lasted from A.D. 1644 to 1911.[7] Earlier variations of

[7] The discussion of the traditional Chinese family will depend heavily upon that of Marion J. Levy, Jr., ibid. pp. 41–269.

the traditional family did not differ greatly from that which prevailed during the Ch'ing dynasty. Moreover, it was the Ch'ing dynasty which gave way to the modern Republic of China.[8]

It should be remembered that during most of this traditional period China was a land of over three and a half million square miles (larger than the United States),[9] a land where dozens of dialects were spoken, and one in which there was great variation from one section of the country to another and from rural to urban areas. Far from there being one family pattern in such a vast land, there were innumerable variations. Some of these variations we will touch upon in the ensuing discussion. For the most part, however, we will concentrate upon the dominant patterns which were reflected in Confucian teachings, in literature, and in the law.

THE GENTRY AND THE PEASANTRY

A basic distinction required for understanding of the traditional Chinese family separates the so-called gentry from the vast majority of Chinese peasants. The gentry were defined by several criteria. First, they were distinguished by income from land which they, themselves, did not cultivate. Abstinence from manual labor of all sorts was a source of pride among them and essential for acceptance into the class. By and large the gentry were intellectuals for whom mastery of knowledge was the route to social advancement. China developed very early a massive examination system, somewhat analogous to our civil service system, which theoretically was open to virtually all Chinese and through which positions in government were awarded. Actually the examination system was controlled by the gentry whose opportunities for leisure also gave them great advantage in acquiring the knowledge necessary for success in the system. In addition to their income as landlords, the gentry received income from the governmental offices and academic positions which they held. As China began to move into the modern era, the gentry also became involved in industry and commerce as owners and managers, and in banking. The gentry probably accounted for less than one-fifth of the population.

China was basically an agricultural nation and the term peasantry accurately described the overwhelming proportion of the population. The peasantry, who actually worked the land, were very poor by modern standards; sheer physical survival was their primary goal. There was little room in their existence for the elaboration of social customs and their family patterns were

---

[8] The Republic of China is represented by the present nationalist government on Taiwan.

[9] Sripati Chandrasekhar, *China's Population: Census and Vital Statistics*, London and New York: Oxford University Press, 1960, p. 37.

similar to those of poverty-ridden people everywhere. Men and women worked together in the fields and children were pressed into work as soon as they were able. There appears, however, to have been widespread aspiration among the peasants for the attainment of gentry status and just enough upward mobility to keep the dream alive. Consequently, even among the peasantry who lived quite differently, the family ideals were frequently those of the gentry.[10]

The influence of the gentry in traditional China cannot be overemphasized. Their ways were so highly regarded as to set the standards for the entire country. It was the gentry patterns that were referred to in literature and song and in law and official records. This preoccupation with gentry patterns was so great that very little is actually known about the wide variety of peasantry patterns that existed. The gentry patterns were the ideal patterns[11] and it is with these ideal patterns that we shall mainly deal.

THE GENTRY FAMILY

The traditional gentry family was patriarchal, patrilineal, patrilocal, and monogamous. It included the patriarch and his wife, all their sons and the sons' wives, all unmarried daughters, all grandsons and their wives, all unmarried granddaughters, all great-grandsons and their wives, all unmarried great-granddaughters, and so on. The ideal was to have six generations of the family living under one roof and for the family to go nine generations without a division of property. The gentry family ideally was a very large family, all living together, and maintaining themselves intact for as many generations as possible.

Family Size. The real gentry patterns, however, deviated somewhat from this ideal. In practice China appears not to have been a nation of exceptionally large families. Comprehensive and accurate data are difficult to come by, but several studies have shown an average household size of around five persons. Ping-ti Ho reports that a respectable census in A.D. 2, yielded an average household of 4.87 persons and that Chinese family size has not changed appreciably

---

[10] In addition to the gentry and peasantry there were small merchants, artisans, soldiers, servants, and the like. These groups were relatively unimportant in the social structure and generally followed the social patterns of the peasantry. If their economic status was high enough, they tended to follow the gentry patterns.

[11] Care should be taken not to confuse ideal culture patterns with ideal types. Ideal culture patterns are the models of exemplary conduct toward which a society strives. Real culture patterns, in contrast, refer to the actual behavior patterns prevailing in the society. See Ralph Linton, *The Cultural Background of Personality*, New York: D. Appleton-Century, 1945, pp. 52–4.

over the past 2000 years.[12] He states further that, "the size of the Chinese peasant family was determined primarily by its basic economic needs and by the fiscal burden it bore." [13]

> . . . having been born and nurtured in a traditional Chinese family of considerable size, and having, naturally, observed many others, the present writer is in a position to state that, in spite of every social training, restraint, and sanction against the cohesion of the individual marriage unit, as the traditional Chinese family ideal dictated, the distinctive "cohesive tendency of the individual marriage unit" was and is ever ready to show up, leading finally toward the breaking-up of the larger family unit.
>
> —Francis L. K. Hsu, "The Myth of Chinese Family Size," American Journal of Sociology 48 (March 1943), p. 556. Reprinted by permission of the University of Chicago Press.

Census figures, of course, would yield averages much closer to the typical size of the peasant family than to that of the gentry family. Yet, there is reason to think that the typical gentry family probably fell far short of the large, six-generation ideal.

If nothing else, longevity patterns generally would prevent there being six generations of the same family living together. Even in modern America where longevity is greater, we do not often find living families extending from great-grandparents through great-grandchildren. It seems obvious that three or four generations must have been the usual maximum in traditional China.

Even this three- or four-generation group probably was not the most common gentry family. Though the gentry were relatively wealthy, it appears that such large family units were not economically feasible for most of them. When a man achieved additional wealth it appears that he was very likely to use that wealth to increase the size of his household in accord with the con-

[12] Ping-ti Ho, "An Historian's View of the Chinese Family System," in Seymour Farber, Piero Mustacchi, and Roger H. L. Wilson, eds., Man and Civilization: The Family's Search for Survival, New York: McGraw-Hill, 1965, p. 18. He reports that in A.D. 755, the average was 5.95; in 1393, it was 5.68; and in 1812, it was 5.33.

[13] Ibid. For convincing arguments that actual variations in family size from one society to another are considerably less than differences of family ideals would indicate, see Ansley J. Coale, Lloyd A. Fallers, Marion J. Levy, Jr., David M. Schneider, and Sylvan S. Tomkins, Aspects of the Analysis of Family Structure, Princeton, New Jersey: Princeton University Press, 1965.

cept of the ideal family. But it also appears that economic necessity forced most of the gentry to live in smaller units.

Levy believes that the typical Chinese family probably was the stem family.[14] Under this arrangement one of the sons brings his bride to live with his parental family while all of the other sons go out of the family unit to earn their living. Even though large families could not generally be maintained, there probably were several factors operating to prevent the Chinese family from breaking down into a simple conjugal unit. One such factor was the practice of ancestor worship. Taoism, Buddhism, and Confucianism were all major religions in China, but, in addition, virtually all Chinese practised ancestor worship. Provision for the worship of ancestors was both a major responsibility and a major goal in life. If one worshipped one's ancestors dutifully and, in addition, raised sons properly, one would eventually be worshipped as an ancestor himself. It was necessary for at least one son to remain with the parental family to maintain the family burial ground and continue the ancestor worship.

Supporting factors in this arrangement were the doctrine of filial piety which stressed the absolute subordination of the child to the wishes of the parents and the practice of holding family property in common. These forces were strong enough to perpetuate the large family ideal in circumstances where economic factors did not at all favor it. Many married sons were forced to live in simple conjugal units for much of their adult lives. Apparently many of those sons lived as meagerly as possible, sending much of their earnings back to the family home and paving the way for the day when they would be able to return to the family and take their places in it as distinguished elders.

Division of Property. Ideally, the Chinese family was to go nine generations without a division of property. The inheritance rules provided that all sons should inherit equally. There was no institutionalized primogeniture, although the eldest son appears often to have received a larger share. This informal inequality reflected what Levy calls a "ceremonial primogeniture," in which the eldest son assumed major responsibility for the family's ancestor worship.[15] The eldest brother also was destined, in the event a division of property did not occur, eventually to succeed his father as the patriarch. The greater prestige of the eldest brother, and the expenses he incurred in maintaining the ancestors' graves, often were enough to militate against a strictly equal inheritance of property. In peasant families it appears that younger sons often turned their inheritances over to the eldest son completely, in which case he

---

[14] This concept was developed by Frederic Le Play who used the term, *famille souche.* See his *Les Ouvriers europeens,* Tours, 1879, Vol. I, p. 457.

[15] Op. cit. p. 137.

assumed full responsibility for the ancestor worship and they were relieved of further obligation.

While the family remained intact, property normally was held in common under the control of the patriarch. Given the norms of filial piety, sons were unlikely to ask for a division of property during the father's lifetime. The same allegiance was not owed to the elder brother, however, and there were forces operating to encourage younger brothers to ask for a division at the time of the father's death or retirement. Particularly if the family wealth was not increasing significantly, expansion of the family would reduce each brother's potential wealth accordingly. Thus the brothers were encouraged to request their inheritances while there still was something to inherit. Any tensions among the brothers, of course, increased the probability that a division of property would be sought, and, especially, dissatisfaction on the part of wives of the brothers led them to urge their husbands to seek a division.

When a division of property occurred, each brother separated his straight-line descendants from the larger group and established a new branch of the family with himself as patriarch. Such a move permitted younger brothers to attain the status of family head which otherwise would be denied to them, but the division of property also was regarded as very undesirable and it appears that this kind of motivation was not prominent. Few families were wealthy enough and sufficiently well integrated to avoid a division of property for the desired nine generations. In fact, it appears that division often occurred at the death of the patriarch. The strength of the family ideals is illustrated by their continuance in the face of widespread deviation from them in fact.

The Tsu. The traditional family was much more important in the institutional structure of China than almost any family system is in the institutional structure of any contemporary nation. This was before the development of modern nation-states even in Europe, and there was no strong central government in China. The family performed most of the enforcement, judicial, and welfare functions that we associate with government.

Moreover, the Chinese concept of obligation to, and fair play with, others was quite different from the Western concept. Whereas Western culture assumes a generalized obligation to other people, resulting in strangers being able to interact according to the universal norms of fair play, no such notion existed in China. Instead the Chinese concept of obligation to others extended more radically to family members than does our own but did not extend at all to people outside the family.[16] This resulted in considerable isolation,

---

[16] Many American students tend to make ethnocentric evaluations of this difference between Western and Eastern norms, deploring the apparent insensitivity of Orientals to distress on the part of persons who are not members of their own families. The American's

particularly of gentry families who could afford and manage it, from contacts with persons outside the family. Virtually all contacts with outsiders were made through the patriarch and even the patriarch avoided such contacts whenever possible.

Beyond the family, the chief group of major significance in traditional China was the clan or *tsu*. The *tsu* included all persons with a common surname who could trace their descent from a common ancestor. With the care given to tracing ancestry, the *tsu* might number thousands of persons, and gentry, peasants, servants, and soldiers might be members of a single *tsu*. The importance of the *tsu* varied from one section of the country to another, but in some areas there were whole villages where everyone had the same surname and belonged to the same *tsu*.

The *tsu* operated generally through a council of elders and intervened in those matters which could not be handled adequately by individual families. Its will was implemented through the patriarch and, in rare instances, might be exerted against the patriarch himself. A major function of the *tsu* was to aid in the maintenance of the ancestral tablets and the ancestral graves. Its resources were thus used to ensure the continuation of the group when that continuance might be placed in jeopardy.

The *tsu* also exercised broad welfare functions, paid for by the income from land and property held for this purpose. It paid for the education of an occasional bright son from a poorer branch of the *tsu* and thus supported some upward mobility in the society. It loaned money to *tsu* members. It also helped families to organize and to pay for lavish weddings and funerals.

Certain enforcement and judicial functions were handled by the *tsu*. It arbitrated disputes between branches of the *tsu* and enforced its rulings. It served as a tax collection agency for the government. It mediated between family members and government authority, protecting *tsu* members from outside aggression and serving as a parole body for *tsu* members who had committed offenses but who had reformed.

The *tsu* was one of a very few sources of power in China outside the indi-

---

learned reaction is that aid should be provided to any human being in trouble and that anyone who does not almost automatically provide such aid is morally deficient and despicable. It may be appropriate here to point out that, conversely, the traditional Chinese is likely to be horrified at American treatment of older family members. No self-respecting Chinese would think of incarcerating his aged parents in an institution but would automatically accord them the place of greatest honor in his home.

American notions of obligation to others also appear to be changing with increased urbanization. Witness the widespread publicity being given to situations where citizens, obviously aware of what was happening, have refused to aid in cases of rape, drowning, accidents, illness, and even murder.

vidual family unit. It played a role in helping to maintain the integrity of
the family which will become clear later in this chapter. The *tsu* also came
under concerted attack as a competing source of power when the present
communist government came into being.

AGE AND SEX ROLES

The traditional Chinese family system is an excellent example of a consanguine system. Consistent with the large family ideal, prescribed roles for
various family members were laid down in great detail. Position in the family
was the all-important thing; little opportunity was provided for the expression
of personal idiosyncrasies. What mattered was whether one was an eldest
son in a well-to-do family or the newest daughter-in-law—not personality
characteristics such as whether one was extraordinarily intelligent, phlegmatic,
or what have you. Little ad-libbing on the prescribed roles was permitted.
Everyone knew pretty much how the eldest son or the newest daughter-in-law
was supposed to think, feel, and act in most situations, and most people con-
formed closely to expectations.

Traditional China was highly structured according to definitions by age and
sex. The roles for various family members can be described in detail according
to the specific age groups to which they belonged. Moreover, not only was
absolute age important—not only were 40-year-olds treated quite differently
from 20-year-olds—but relative age was also very important. By relative age,
we mean the age of one person in relation to the age of another person. The
Chinese placed great emphasis not only upon whether one was 20 years or 40
years old but also upon whether, at those ages, one was younger or older than
the other people with whom he interacted. Prescribed behavior was also
closely defined by sex. There was marked segregation of sex roles with quite
different behavior expected of males and females.

Understanding of the prescribed age and sex roles is essential to understanding of the functioning of the traditional family. We will trace these definitions
from infancy to old age, specifying sex differences, and emphasizing the gentry
patterns.

Infancy. Paradoxically, although the Chinese held old age in great deference,
they were kind and affectionate toward small children. Children were highly
valued in the family, particularly sons. Sons were the means to continuation
of the family line and provided for continued worship of the ancestors. A
marriage which did not soon produce sons was unfortunate indeed.

Girls, too, were valued and were welcomed into the family when their birth
did not present grave financial problems and when daughters were not born to

the exclusion of sons. In poor peasant families the situation was somewhat different. There is evidence that female infanticide occasionally was resorted to by poverty-stricken parents and that girl babies occasionally were sold. If resources were scarce, it was also true that the sons, as the most important children, had first priority on the material goods and upon the care of their parents.

The length of the infancy period was not hard and fast. Upon the average it may have lasted about four years, depending upon the wealth of the parents and whether children were born subsequently. Wealthy parents could afford to indulge their children more and if no other siblings were born, the infancy period could be prolonged.

The child's first years were easy, pleasant ones. Both boys and girls received affection and attention from both parents, while discipline was held to a very minimum. Weaning and toilet training were accomplished during this period but both were accomplished gradually and without undue strain. During the latter part of the period, training in filial piety was begun. This training often took the form of stories that were read or told to the children in which the implicit message was that the child was the property of his parents and ancestors. Children learned to be obedient to their parents and even to older brothers and sisters.

Childhood. The term, childhood, is American, not Chinese. The Chinese term for this second age period, *yu-nien*, stressed the immaturity and inexperience of the persons involved.

Early in this period, sex differentiation became marked. Among the gentry, boys normally moved to the father's section of the house where they came under his direct supervision. Schooling began for the boys also, and the schoolmaster or tutor wielded an authority over boys that closely paralleled that of the father. The mother remained as a source of refuge for the boy against unduly harsh treatment by the father but her position was essentially without power, enabling her only to comfort him emotionally. Girls remained under their mother's care and began preparation for their future roles as wives and mothers.

The severe discipline of Chinese life began during this period. Boys were subjected to arduous intellectual and physical training, being expected to study—essentially learning by rote—for long hours under austere conditions. Disobedience, willfulness, and failure to perform adequately were dealt with by physical beatings administered by father and schoolmaster. The relationship between father and son generally ceased to be one of warmth and acceptance and became based, instead, upon awe—a mixture of fear and respect. Complete subservience to the father was instilled, along with the certain notion that, one day, the boy become man would assume the same role with his own sons.

Rebellion against this severe discipline appears to have been the rare exception to the rule. Acceptance of the discipline and progress in his studies made life easier for the boy, and, even as he was being punished, he was being made aware of his importance in the scheme of things and of the high status which was his to inherit. Too, gentry boys were granted increasing freedom to make contacts outside the household where their sense of personal importance was increased.

The lives of gentry girls were very different from those of boys. The girls were increasingly segregated from the outside world and even from the males of their own household. It was during this period that girls became aware of their roles as temporary members of the family. In at least some instances girls were listed in the family genealogical tables only by *nu*, the symbol for female; for at marriage they would cease to be members of their fathers' families and become members of their husbands' families.

This blow to the girl's self-esteem was compensated for, in many cases, by the especially indulgent relationship which she had with her parents. Her mother, knowing of the difficult times which lay ahead, was likely to make the girl's life as easy as possible. The father, too, could lavish upon his daughters the affection that was not appropriate in his relationships with his sons. As a result, and in spite of the emerging definitions of unworthiness, this was often the happiest period in the girl's life.

The peasantry patterns for both boys and girls differed markedly from those of the gentry. The extensive schooling and segregation simply were not possible for the peasants, and both boys and girls were inducted early into the labors of adult life. Boys, as soon as they were able, accompanied their fathers to the fields where gradually they assumed heavier work. The girls, as was true for women also, did not work regularly in the fields but at periods of peak load they were likely to do so. Peasant women could not be isolated from contacts with outsiders as gentry women were, and peasant girls retained much more contact with male members of their households and with outsiders.

Entrance to Adulthood. The second age period lasted roughly from four years of age to about sixteen or seventeen. For peasant boys and girls, and for gentry girls, the second age period was followed relatively directly by entrance into full adulthood. Not so for gentry males. For gentry males there was a relatively long and structurally significant interstitial period which was referred to by the term, *ch'ing-nien.* This third age period for gentry males lasted until roughly age thirty, or until the young man was married.

By contrast with the preceding period, the stage of *ch'ing-nien* was a relatively easy one for gentry males. Discipline by the father was considerably relaxed and was replaced by an almost comradely, consultative relationship in which the father trained his son in the exercise of judgment. The son's academic training had by now prepared him to take the first examinations, and passing those examinations brought him higher status and considerable personal freedom. His continued schooling was likely to take place in the towns and cities where he was effectively away from direct parental supervision, and he had money to spend.

During this period the gentry male generally was introduced to the common vices of adult life—drinking, gambling, and extramarital heterosexual intercourse. His first sex experience was likely to be had either with a servant girl or with a professional prostitute. Most gentry families had female servants and there were no particular emotional barriers to the development of sex relationships with male members of the household. The strict separation of female family members and the strong incest taboos within the family only reinforced the availability of servant girls. Sexual experimentation also was likely, in the company of other Ch'ing-nien, with prostitutes in situations involving extensive drinking and gambling. Sooner or later the parents became aware of these activities and viewed them as serious threats to the stability of the family.

The parental reaction to the son's incipient dissolution was to seek for him a wife. The responsibility for so doing generally fell upon his mother who was likely to be the person most upset by the debauchery, who would have the most significant relationship with the new bride, and who acted with the full consent of her husband. The son was not likely to be consulted, for custom provided that he should not even meet his bride until the engagement. According to Chinese law, marriage as a legal contract was concluded by the heads of the bride's and groom's families, not by the young couple themselves.

Theoretically, there was supposed to be no emotional involvement between gentry males and young women but, in fact, such involvements did sometimes occur. Gentry girls were carefully chaperoned because if sexual intercourse were to occur, their chances of marrying satisfactorily would be irreparably damaged. In some areas of China cross-cousin marriages were preferred and much more contact was permitted with these girls than with unrelated girls.[17] Emotional involvement, even with a girl who was an eligible marriage partner, was a serious threat to the family and an indication that another suitable marriage should be arranged immediately. The disruption of these relation-

[17] Francis L. K. Hsu, "Observations on Cross-Cousin Marriage in China," *American Anthropologist* 47 (Jan.–March 1945), pp. 83–103.

ships was often traumatic and provides a major theme in Chinese literature. Rebellion against the wishes of the parents appears, however, to have been rare.

Full Adulthood. The next two age periods covered full maturity from marriage to some time between 30 and 40 years of age and then from 30–40 years to old age. Entrance into full adulthood was determined more by the fact of marriage than by the reaching of a particular age, for marriage was of extreme importance. Except for a small minority of religious celibates, virtually every one married. Marriage provided for children to be born, and children were essential to the fulfillment of obligations to one's ancestors and to oneself.

Gentry families usually tried to marry their daughters so as to provide useful family connections. At the minimum this meant that the man's family should have considerable landed property. Where possible, the gentry also tried to assure themselves that their daughter would be well received and well treated in her new family.

The peasants faced more extreme problems. The marriage of a son required that a gift be made to the girl's parents, which gift the girl ideally brought back to the marriage as part of her trousseau. Thus the parents of both families were supposed to make an economic contribution to the new marriage and there was considerable negotiation over the size of these contributions. If the young man's parents were very poor, however, they might be forced to keep the gift made to them by the parents of their daughter's groom in order to use it to arrange for the marriages of their own younger sons. Such a practice was considered very undesirable but appears to have been widely followed.

The situation was further complicated by a chronic shortage of marriageable girls, produced through the practices of female infanticide, prostitution, and concubinage. There are no reliable data on the extent of female infanticide but the practice is known to have existed. Levy believes that "in times of famine, drought, high taxes, and the like, it probably reached large proportions."[18] Goode emphasizes that outright infanticide may have been accompanied by more widespread neglect of daughters during times of great privation so that their death rate may have been considerably higher.[19] Table 1 presents data on sex ratios by age level in Peking about 1917, and shows dramatically the surplus of males at every age level.

Prostitution flourished on a large scale in traditional China and many peasant girls were sold into prostitution by their parents who thus escaped the costs of the girl's rearing and her marriage. Concubinage was uncommon

[18] Op. cit. p. 99.
[19] William J. Goode, *World Revolution and Family Patterns*, New York: The Free Press of Glencoe, 1963, pp. 307–9.

among the peasants, who could not afford it, but was quite common among the gentry who usually secured their concubines from peasant families. The three factors of infanticide, prostitution, and concubinage combined to produce a shortage of peasant girls, forcing many peasant males to delay the time of marriage unduly.

TABLE 1. *Sex Ratios, Peking about 1917, and from the 1953 Census of the People's Republic of China.*

(*a*) *Peking, about 1917* *

AGE GROUP	SEX RATIO
1– 5	145
6–10	138
11–15	145
16–20	185
21–25	208
26–30	224
31–35	213
36–40	161
41–45	217
46–50	167

(*b*) *China, Census of 1953* **

AGE GROUP	SEX RATIO
0	104.9
1– 2	106.2
3– 6	110.0
7–13	115.8
14–17	113.7
18–35	111.5
36–55	106.8
56 & over	86.7

* Sidney B. Gamble, *Peking, A Social Survey*, New York: George H. Doran, 1921, p. 415, as reproduced in William J. Goode, *World Revolution and Family Patterns*, New York: The Free Press of Glencoe, 1963, p. 308. Reprinted by permission of Harper and Row Publisher, Inc.

** S. Chandrasekhar, *China's Population: Census and Vital Statistics*, London and New York: Oxford University Press, 1960, p. 46. Reprinted by permission of Hong Kong University Press.

Chinese girls, including gentry girls, were married early—as soon as possible after puberty. No accurate figures on age at marriage are available, but it is significant that the present Chinese government is harshly critical of the old "feudalistic pattern of early marriage." Gentry males appear to have married at considerably older ages. Goode reports data from one clan in Canton which show the average age of the father at the time of the birth of his first living son to have been 33 years from A.D. 1150 to 1500, 31 years from 1630 to 1800, and 23 years from 1800 to 1880.[20] The average age at marriage would be slightly younger, of course but, given the emphasis on bearing sons, the difference probably would not be too great.

Marriage normally was arranged by "go-betweens" who represented the families involved, for families seldom dealt directly with outsiders. Generally these were male relatives of the patriarch who were thus trusted members of the family and yet could negotiate with the families of prospective spouses without committing the family. The procedure called for complete investigation of each family by the other and several ritual exchanges of gifts and information between them. The information exchanged included the names and birth dates of the couple, which were presented to the ancestors and which were subjected to astrological interpretation. If the interpretation was favorable, the negotiations continued. If it was unfavorable the negotiations were dropped. There is some evidence that astrologers took into account more than the stars and that if a marriage did not seem mutually advantageous, an unfavorable interpretation provided a mutually face-saving way of calling it off. If all went well, the marriage contract eventually was signed and the wedding ceremony held.

The essence of the marriage ceremony, however elaborately embellished, was the transport of the bride to the home of the groom's parents where she was introduced to the ritual worship of their ancestors. The wife thus became a member of her husband's family and her name was eligible for listing in their genealogical tables. After the ceremony the married couple were permitted to retire to spend the night together but early the next morning the bride arose before any other member of the family and ritually served tea to her mother-in-law in bed. This began a period of ritual service to the husband's family and particularly to the mother-in-law, the function of which was to take the bride, as an outsider, and to make of her a docile, effectively functioning member of her new family.

Marriage almost amounted more to the parents taking a daughter-in-law than it did to the son's taking a wife. The priority of the parents' relationship with the new bride was emphasized by the fact that the lack of affectional relationship between the new bride and groom was considered irrelevant. Indeed, should affection develop, any display of that affection before other family members was taboo. Hsu reports that newlyweds were even expected

[20] Ibid. p. 286.

to occupy the same bed for only seven days after which they were supposed to occupy separate beds in the same room. When a man's parents died, he was expected to show grief that was so great as to be barely short of suicide. If his wife died, he was "expected to show some grief, but never enough to make him forget his filial duties." [21]

Marriage usually brought about the last major change in the man's status. Not so for the woman. For her, there yet remained the birth of her first son and the retirement of her mother-in-law. The period from marriage to the birth of her first son often was the hardest period in the woman's life. She was removed from her parents, who may have treated her with affection and kindness, to the care of people who had no reason to consider her feelings at all. As an outsider she had no right to any consideration and was dominated not only by the mother-in-law but by all other family members as well. The parents, her husband, and the husband's siblings all sided against her in the case of disagreement.

About the only relief the young wife had from this domination were occasional visits back to her parental family. These may even have been used consciously to lessen the pressure. If she became pregnant, the pressure might ease somewhat in anticipation of the possible birth of a son. Her mother also might come to see her through childbirth. The bearing of sons improved the wife's position; the bearing of daughters might worsen it. In cases of exceptional mistreatment, the wife's parental family might threaten the use of force with resulting shame to the husband's family.

Occasionally wives were pushed into committing suicide. Reliable data on suicide rates are not available, but it is widely believed that, unlike the situation in the West, suicide in traditional China occurred primarily among women between the ages of 17 and 35.[22] The actual committing of suicide by harassed wives appears to have been less common than were apparently unsuccessful attempts at it. If the wife were to commit suicide, the husband's family would be shamed for its obviously excessively harsh treatment of her and they would have difficulty in securing another wife for their son. If she attempted suicide but was not successful, the husband's family might be intimidated into according her somewhat better treatment.

. . . An estimate was made in 1953 that some 70 thousand to 80 thousand women committed suicide or were killed each year because

[21] Francis L. K. Hsu, *Under the Ancestor's Shadow*, Garden City, New York: Doubleday, 1967, p. 59.
[22] Goode, op. cit. p. 309; and Levy, op. cit. p. 117.

of matrimonial difficulties. For the East China region, from January to August, 1952, over 4 thousand women were killed or committed suicide because of poor marriage relations. In one area of Kiangsu, in January–June, 1952, there were almost 40 thousand betrothals arranged by family elders, three times the number of free engagements, and about 20 thousand arranged marriages, 28 per cent more than the free marriages. In Ninghsia Province, almost 60 per cent of the marriages during the same period were reported to have been arranged by elders. In one county in Fukien, it was charged that 70 per cent of the new wives in 1953 were or had been "child wives," but in Honan 2 thousand "child wives" were reported who had not actually been married. . . .

The wife's status improved as she bore sons, as she became a smoothly functioning member of the family, and as other younger daughters-in-law were added. Strangely, according to Western thinking, there was little tendency for the daughters-in-law to gang up against the mother-in-law. Instead each young wife consolidated her own position in the family at the expense of the newcomer. Each woman took on the values inherent in the system and prepared for the day when the mother-in-law should die or retire and she would assume the responsibility for inducting other younger women into the family.

Adult life for males was somewhat less complicated. Marriage and the birth of their sons were extremely important but they were not accompanied by such drastic changes in status as were true for women. The man gradually moved into his adult life work under the increasingly gentle supervision of his father. The attitudes of fear and respect toward the father inculcated in childhood lessened somewhat and their relationship often developed considerable warmth. Not uncommonly, the father retired or died fairly early in his sons' adulthood and the eldest, at least, became the patriarch.

Old Age. The last age period began at about age 55, considerably before what we usually regard as the onset of old age. Longevity was not so great in traditional China, however, and people of 55 probably were at least as "old" as most Americans of 65 today. This was the most secure and comfortable period in the lives of both men and women. By this time the man usually was the head of the family, and his wife, rather than being an outsider, was now partner to her husband in maintaining the family intact. Furthermore, age, as such, was venerated. Oldsters, as the closest living contacts with the ancestors, received great deference from younger family members and they had first claim on the family's resources and upon all physical comforts.

The couple had made full provision for their own old age by having sons and now, as their grandchildren came along, the grandparents were free to enjoy them as they had never been free to enjoy their own children. Gradually the father turned over increasing responsibility to his sons, who shouldered the burdens but maintained complete official deference to the father. By now father and son usually saw things alike and there was a minimum of friction.

With the advent of widowhood the mother might come out from under male domination for the only time in her life. The official Confucian prescriptions required that she be subordinate to her sons, but actually she often commanded an obedience from them born of long years of affection and respect and because she was a member of an older generation due great respect.

Relative Age Roles. Not only absolute age but also relative age was very important in traditional China. Unlike our own society where after childhood the relationship between brothers is influenced little, if at all, by their relative ages, the Chinese had separate kinship terms for older and younger siblings. Moreover, it was common to use the term for "older brother" or "younger brother" rather than the brothers' given names. The term older brother was one of great respect and about the highest honor that could be bestowed upon a friend would be to refer to him as my older brother. Contrast this with the American situation in which one bestows honor on a kinsman by referring to him in non-kinship terms. Thus Americans hold out the ideal of father and son becoming "pals."

Younger siblings were expected to defer to older siblings, and the allegiance of his brothers to the eldest son was often counted upon to keep the family intact and prevent a division of property at the father's death. Normally, older sons and daughters were married before younger siblings were, and wives took their status from the relative ages of their husbands. Occasionally, when an older sibling married a much younger girl, this resulted in the older women married to his brothers being subordinated to the younger woman and created confusion and conflict.

The wives of younger brothers had a particularly difficult situation. They were dominated by virtually all other members of the family, and, being the youngest daughters-in-law, they remained under the mother-in-law's control longest and most directly. The dissatisfactions of these younger women often led them to press their husbands to seek a division of property so that they might become the highest status women in their own households.

CONCUBINAGE AND PROSTITUTION

The traditional family was basically monogamous,[23] but it was a very different sort of monogamy from that which prevails in the contemporary United States. Concubinage was fully sanctioned and, among the gentry at least, was widely practised. Yang reports that the Chinese family was like a balloon, ready to expand whenever there was wealth to inflate it. As soon as there was opportunity to employ the married sons they would remain in the father's household. Should wealth increase further, concubines and their children would be added.[24]

There are no detailed data on the extent to which concubines were taken. Hsu reports 150 cases of concubinage in a rural population of 8000.[25] In Lang's sample of 1700 high-school and college students in the 1930's, 11 per cent reported a concubine in the home while the answers of an additional 6 per cent hinted that a concubine was there.[26] Levy believes that concubinage was extremely common among the gentry but was not common among the peasantry.[27] Thus the weight of evidence and opinion supports Yang's belief that concubines were likely to be taken whenever wealth permitted.

Part of the rationale for socially sanctioned concubinage lay in the importance attached to having sons. Sons were necessary to meet one's obligations to one's ancestors and to ensure one's own future worship as an ancestor. A man without sons might adopt them but the practice was disapproved of. Men did not like to give up their sons, sons did not like to change their surnames, and adopted sons were looked down upon. Occasionally, peasant families permitted their sons to be adopted into gentry families, but the more common solution was for gentry males without sons to take concubines.

If a marriage did not produce sons the patriarch might literally demand that his son take a concubine, and even the unfortunate wife might cooperate to

[23] Instances of variation from the basic monogamy have been reported. Goode cites Van der Valk's account of the ancient custom of *chien t'iao*, according to which a man might make his nephew his heir while the boy remained his own father's heir also. Custom in ten provinces permitted such boys to take two wives, each of whom took charge of the worship of one of the two groups of ancestors. Van der Valk also reports that certain forms of polyandry were found in three different provinces. M. H. Van der Valk, *Conservatism in Modern Chinese Family Law*, Leiden: E. J. Brill, 1956, pp. 45-7, as cited in Goode, op. cit. pp. 279, 283.

[24] C. K. Yang, *The Chinese Family in the Communist Revolution*, Cambridge: The Technology Press, Massachusetts Institute of Technology, 1959, p. 9.

[25] *Under the Ancestor's Shadow*, p. 106.

[26] Olga Lang, *Chinese Family and Society*, New Haven: Yale University Press, 1946, p. 221.

[27] Op. cit. p. 98.

that end. Sometimes in such cases the wife urged that her own sister be taken as the concubine so that her position in the family would not be so threatened and to ease the adjustment to having another woman in the household. Gentry families might wish to aid such an unfortunate daughter but they did not relish having their other daughters becoming concubines. The concubines generally were secured from peasant families, often being purchased outright.

Concubinage played another important role in the Chinese family system. It offered to males some relief from their otherwise carefully ordered lives. From early boyhood, the male's structurally important relationship with his father was nearly devoid of warmth and affection; spontaneity and emotional freedom were sacrificed on the altar of filial piety. When it was time for him to marry, he took the wife selected by his parents and with whom emotional intimacy was not particularly encouraged. His relationships with his own sons —indeed with almost everyone—were structured in terms of responsibility and the subordination of personal needs to family goals. Concubines, however, were likely to be women of his own choosing with whom the relationship was romantic and erotic. Hsu found that in more than half of his cases concubines were taken where the wife had already borne sons.[28]

REPORTED CASES OF CONCUBINAGE IN A SMALL SEMI-RURAL
COMMUNITY IN SOUTHWEST CHINA
Five Cases in Which the Wife Has Given Birth to No Sons

C.S.Y.   Wife has no son. Husband used to be trader in Hankow and Hongkong; had seen Peiping. Concubine from Pao Shan, a town 300 kilometers to the southwest on the Burma Road. Concubine gave birth to three sons. Concubine used to accompany him to Hankow and Hongkong.

M.T.T.   Wife has no son. Husband is about 45; concubine was about 20. She disliked him and had affairs with other men. Later she went to Kunming and divorced him. She left her two sons with him.

M.T.T.'s
cousin   Wife has no son. Concubine gave birth to a son.

Li   He is now dead. Wife has no son. Concubine gave birth to a son and a daughter.

Y.C.Y.   He is about 40 years of age. Wife gave him no children, so he got a concubine, after which his wife chased him out of

[28] *Under the Ancestor's Shadow*, pp. 105–6.

the old home in Pin Chuan. She took charge of the old
family property. Family has a big house in West Town. He
does trading. Concubine has no son yet (several years after
marriage). He expressed to me that he had not developed
his trading on a large scale outside West Town because he
has no son, and must stay at home and concentrate on
getting a son.

Six Cases in Which the Wife Has Given Birth to One or More Sons

C.S.Y.'s
brother

Wife has 2 or 3 sons. Concubine has one son. He and his
two female companions lived in Kunming lately.

Y

He is now dead. Wife (deceased) gave birth to 3 sons.
Concubine (still living) gave birth to a son and a daughter.

Y's son

Shopkeeper in Kunming. Wife has given birth to 2 sons
and 2 daughters, all married. Concubine who stays with
him in Kunming has so far given birth to a son and 2
daughters. She is still young.

C.N.T.

One of the richest men in West Town. Wife has given
birth to a son, who is married and very prolific. The concubine is about the same age as his daughter-in-law and
has so far given birth to two children.

Ya

Old man of 73. First wife (now dead) gave birth to 4 sons
and 3 daughters, all of whom are married and have children. Second wife (now divorced for some obscure reason)
gave birth to a daughter who has a zou mei husband, and
both live with the family. It is said that a few years ago
the old man went to Pao Shan and cohabited with a widow
on a clandestine basis. The sons were worried. The old
man then asked them to get him a girl. They bought a
concubine for him from Pao Shan. She was 16 when first
married to him, and has so far given birth to a daughter.

Li, T.T.

He is a man of about 45, who was once wealthy. He now
trades tobacco for a living. His wife is 38. She gave birth
to one son and two daughters. The son is 17. Both the
son and one of the daughters are engaged. His concubine
has no offspring. She is a native of Ko Chin, a town many
miles to the southwest. His wife and children live in one
house: he and his concubine live in another.

—Francis L. K. Hsu, *Under the Ancestor's Shadow*,
New York: Columbia University Press, 1948, pp. 298–9.

The existence of large-scale prostitution in traditional China is explained in similar terms. The institution of the tea house, to which men repaired to conduct business and to gain relief from their unending obligations, was extremely common and frequently offered drinking, gambling, opium smoking, feminine companionship, and sexual intercourse. The young men who were introduced to these pastimes before marriage often continued them afterward. Yang reports that "traditional merchants as well as government officials transacted much of their business, and traditional scholars wrote some of their best lines of poetry, in whorehouses." He goes on to say that, "a recent well-known Chinese writer who used to entertain his father in houses of prostitution was praised by friends as a filial son who catered to his father's desires." [29]

Thus, concubinage and prostitution may have provided safety valves which permitted men to drain off emotions that otherwise might have threatened the stability of the family system. In that connection it is relevant to note that neither concubinage nor prostitution were disapproved of, particularly, on moral grounds. Only when they threatened the stability of the family were they regarded as harmful. A man might be censured for neglecting his wife and children in favor of his concubine, but his right to take concubines was unassailable. Similarly, visits to prostitutes were matters of concern only if family duties were neglected or if the accompanying drinking and gambling threatened to get out of hand.

The incorporation of concubinage into the family system stressed the dominant position of the wife and the priority of her children's rights. There was no formal ceremony involved in the taking of a concubine, the concubine had no recognized share in the family income, and she was assigned to work at menial tasks under the wife's supervision. She was not included among her husband's relatives, she was generally excluded from mourning deceased family members, and she could never, herself, be worshipped as an ancestor. The concubine's children were legitimate but they had only limited rights of inheritance unless the wife bore no sons. The fact that the husband often preferred the concubine often led to some jealousy between the women and among the women's children.

PATTERNS OF AUTHORITY AND AFFECTION

The traditional family was organized around the important relationships between father and son, between husband and wife, between mother-in-law and daughter-in-law, and between brothers. In general, the more important

[29] Op. cit. p. 57.

the relationship to the family the less was affection between the parties permitted to influence it.

Affection was almost irrelevant to the father-son relationship which was based upon awe, respect, and fear. These feelings directed toward the father were quite strong so that an effective, if ambivalent, bond was created between them. The father, for his part, had obligations to his sons because of his obligations to his ancestors: only if he continued the family traditions and worship through proper indoctrination of the sons could he, himself, expect eventually to join the group of revered ancestors.

The husband-wife relationship early in marriage was institutionally weak. The wife was an outsider, affection with whom might threaten the family. With the passage of time, proper indoctrination by the mother-in-law, and the birth of sons, however, the wife came to have an interest in maintaining the family that nearly equaled that of her husband. And, in spite of the fact that the marriage had been arranged for them, real affection often developed between the married pair. By the time the wife became a mother-in-law, the marriage relationship was likely to be second in strength only to the father-son relationship.

The mother-in-law–daughter-in-law relationship was quite strong but institutionally troublesome. The mother-in-law's power over the bride was nearly absolute. She could, for example, require that her son repudiate the marriage and send the girl back to her own family. There was no provision for affection to develop between the women, and the girl was likely to hate her mother-in-law. When the Chinese family system finally entered a period of rapid change, the accumulated resentments of young married women played a major role in bringing change about.

The relationship between brothers was less strong than that between father and son but was still quite strong. Younger brothers were expected to defer to their elder brothers and generally did so. The younger brothers did have the right to ask for a division of property, however, and, with urging from their wives, often did so after the father's death. The relationship between brothers and other brothers' wives was also a problem. Despite the taboo on public displays of affection, there was little sex prudery in traditional China, and the conditions of living closely together encouraged the development of sexual attractions. The relationship between a brother and his brother's wife was one of institutional avoidance but trouble did occur. Some insight into the extent and nature of the problem may be gained from the fact that the only legitimate cause for filial revolt was father–daughter-in-law incest.

Power and responsibility in the family stood generally in inverse relationship to one another. Power was based upon generation, sex, and relative age, being vested principally in males of the older generation. The patriarch was virtually all-powerful, males held power over females, and the older held power over the younger. The young had unlimited responsibility toward their elders. The indoctrination of the young was thorough, and, since each person's position in the family improved with age, there was little occasion for revolt against the system.

About the only person free enough to rebel effectively was the patriarch and he had most to gain from preserving the system intact. An occasional older male did become so fond of drinking, gambling, and extramarital sexual intercourse that he threatened to spend the family into ruin. Such dissolution, however, brought down upon the patriarch the contempt of persons outside his immediate family and might result in forcible action being taken against him by elders of the *tsu*.

All in all the family was a model of stability. The socialization of children and of daughters-in-law into the system appears to have been quite effective. Moreover, with the whole society being organized along kinship lines, there literally was no place for a potential rebel to go to escape.

There were strains within the system too. The effects of harsh treatment of sons by their fathers often were not completely overcome even in adulthood. The equal inheritance provisions tended to destroy the economic base upon which the large family depended. Finally, the extreme subordination of women made of them potential allies in any agitation for change.

DIVORCE AND REMARRIAGE

There were actually three kinds of divorce possible in traditional China: one, divorce by mutual consent; two, divorce upon the husband's initiative; three, divorce under compulsion by the authorities.

Divorce by mutual consent required the consent of the heads of the families, not of the couple themselves, and the very existence of this form of divorce emphasizes the strength of the family. Divorce was regarded as tragic, and if the patriarchs agreed to a divorce, there could be no question but what continuation of the marriage would be harmful to the families involved. In this form of divorce it was the welfare of the family that was involved, not that of the couple.

Wives could be divorced by their husbands on any one of seven grounds. They could be divorced for: (1) disobeying the husband's parents; (2) failing to have children; (3) acquiring a loathsome disease; (4) committing adultery; (5) displaying jealousy; (6) being overly talkative; or (7) stealing. In spite of these liberal grounds, however, women were not often repudiated by their husbands and the divorce rate was low. The poor could not afford divorce and remarriage, and the wealthy did not welcome it. Besides, more acceptable alternatives were available to men. Most of their recreation was taken outside the home and both feminine companionship and sexual intercourse were readily available. Men also were expected to meet their needs through the taking of concubines rather than by disrupting the marriage relationship.

. . . the position of women in the old family was never so low as many superficial observers have led us to believe. On the contrary, woman has always been the despot of the family. The authority of the mother and the mother-in-law is very well known. Even the wife is always the terror of the husband; no other country in the world can compete with China for the distinction of being the nation of hen-pecked husbands. Certainly, no other country has produced so many stories of hen-pecked husbands. The wife built up her strong position sometimes upon love, sometimes upon beauty or personality, but in most cases upon the fact that she could not be dislodged from her position: she could not be divorced! It is true that there was no law forbidding divorce; and that the Classics laid down seven conditions for divorcing a wife. Jealousy, or failure to bear sons, or even talking too much, would be sufficient to divorce her. But the same Classics also gave three conditions under which she could not be sent away: (1) if she has shared with the husband a three-year mourning for one of his parents; (2) if the husband has become rich or attained high official position since marriage; or (3) if she has no home to go back to. These conditions were very common and almost made divorce absolutely impossible.

—Hu Shih, *The Chinese Renaissance*, Chicago: The University of Chicago Press, 1943, pp. 104–5, as reprinted in Ping-ti Ho, "An Historian's View of the Chinese Family System," in Seymour Farber, *et al.*, eds., *The Family's Search for Survival*, New York: McGraw-Hill, 1965, pp. 23–4.

Divorce was particularly tragic for women. A divorced woman could only be returned to her family; there was no other place for her to go. And her repudiation, early in marriage essentially by the mother-in-law or her later divorce by her husband for cause, brought shame upon her and her family. Other families would not consider her to be a suitable marriage prospect, she was not entitled to inherit property, and she was denied the opportunity to achieve honor and respect as wife and mother-in-law.

This double standard of morality also applied to the remarriage of widows. Widowed men could remarry without restraint, and gentry males sometimes elevated a concubine to the status of wife upon the death of the first wife. The remarriage of widows was frowned upon, however, and their husbands' families could actually block a remarriage of which they did not approve. Nor could the widow take property with her into a remarriage. The only way a widow could retain a position of honor was to stay as the elderly mother in the home of her sons. The remarriage of gentry widows apparently was rare. Among the peasantry, however, economic conditions forced many remarriages.

THE TRANSITIONAL FAMILY

Major social movements tend not to have sharp beginnings and it is not possible to specify precisely when the Chinese family system began to undergo major change. The system never was completely static, of course, and change proceeded slowly throughout the 2000-odd years of apparent stability. Until around 1830, however, there was no political, military, or industrial power that could successfully break China's self-imposed isolation from the rest of the world. Marked change followed upon England's successful opening of trade with the Chinese mainland.

With the development of international trade, the Chinese coastal areas began to move in the direction of industrialization and toward the development of large-scale commercial enterprise. The impact of these developments upon the society and upon the family system was tremendous. The requirements of an industrial economy and the traditional family system were incompatible at many points.

UNIVERSALISM AND PARTICULARISM

Traditional China was structured according to highly particularistic criteria. *Particularism* refers to the distribution of opportunities and rewards according to one's membership in a series of social groups rather than according to any special qualifications or abilities which an individual possesses. In traditional China, family membership was the all-important consideration. Directly and indirectly the family controlled the system of rewards and distributed them in terms of its own normative structure. Particularly, a person's opportunities for employment—the kind of work he did—was determined largely by his position in a given family. The division of labor within the society was not, by modern standards, highly specialized and almost any adult person could be trained fairly quickly to fill almost any occupational position. This rudimentary division of labor, with ready interchangeability of personnel and most persons sharing a common core of skills, is referred to as the condition of *functional diffuseness.* Traditional China was both highly particularistic and functionally diffuse.

By contrast, the demands of a modern industrial economy are quite different. Such an economy requires the application of universalistic criteria over large areas of life and that there be a high degree of functional specificity. *Universalism* involves the assignment of opportunities on the basis of special training and skills irrespective of family and other relationships. *Functional specificity* involves a specialized division of labor in which personnel are not readily transferable from one job to another.[30]

A CONVERSATION WHICH TOOK PLACE IN 1936

"Now suppose, Yin-ching, that you have completed your studies and have become an influential official, a president of a university or something like that. One day a Mr. Chou, a remote relative of yours, presents himself and asks you to give him a job. What will you do?"

"I must get him a job," answered my friend, Chou Yin-ching.

"And if your brother wants your help?"

Yin-ching thought for a while.

"Him I must get a good job. I certainly cannot employ him as an underling; he must have something better than that."

"And suppose you have only one job and there are two candidates, your relative, Mr. Chou, and a Mr. Ch'i. What would you do then?"

"Oh, I would certainly choose my friend Mr. Ch'i. He is a very clever fellow!"

"No, Yin-ching, I don't mean Mr. Ch'i, your friend, but a Mr. Ch'i whom you don't know."

"Then I would take Mr. Chou—why should I give a job to a stranger?"

"Even if he was better qualified for the job than your relative?"

Yin-ching looked embarrassed.

"Please, don't ask me such questions," he said. "After all, I am only a student."

—Olga Lang, *Chinese Family and Society*, New Haven: Yale University Press, 1946, p. 181.

As China began to modernize and to industrialize, the particularistic requirements of the family system ran head on into the increasingly universalistic

[30] For adequate theoretical treatment of the concepts of universalism—particularism and functional diffuseness—functional specificity, see Talcott Parsons, *The Social System*, Glencoe, Illinois: The Free Press, 1951, pp. 61–3, 65–6, and *passim*.

requirements of the occupational system. The traditional norms demanded that contacts with outsiders be minimized, specified that contractual relations with outsiders were not especially binding (particularly when they conflicted with the achievement of family goals), and encouraged a widespread nepotism. The term *nepotism* refers to the practice of giving employment to kinsmen regardless of ability and was literally an obligation upon the gentry family. Western experience has indicated that factories and large-scale businesses languish when nepotism flourishes. As China industrialized, the men who ran her developing industries were faced with a dilemma. If they acted in terms of the traditional norms, their businesses suffered; if they insisted upon using universalistic criteria to determine employment they were defined as violating sacred obligations and their families suffered. In the long run it was the family system which yielded to the demands of industrialization.

THE INFLUENCE OF WESTERN IDEALS

Trade not only encouraged the industrialization of Chinese coastal areas; it also brought extensive contact with Western ideals that were subversive of the traditional order. The Western concept of treating women as near-equals with men and as full companions with men was revolutionary. The concept of individualism which elevates the well-being of individuals to a place of superiority over the welfare of the family group was equally striking. Though the institutional forms of Western religion did not make great impact, their emphasis upon the sacredness of the individual had far-reaching repercussions. Finally, the whole idea of political freedom—of individuals exercising some collective control over the conditions of their existence—formed part of the base for a new social order.

AN ALTERNATIVE WAY OF LIFE

The combination of industrialization and ideals of political freedom, individualism, and social equality provided what no influences on Chinese life had done for 2000 years—the prospect of an alternative way of living. With the growth of cities and factory employment, single persons, married couples, and nuclear families could live apart from their extended families on a permanent basis. Referring back to Zelditch's analysis: (1) the increasing separation of the kinship and occupational structures led to a weakening of parental authority; (2) income and status came to depend more upon a man's place in the occupational system than upon his family ties; (3) industrialization provided new sources of wealth potentially greater than those of the old agricultural system; and (4) people began to think of their individual interests as taking priority over their extended family obligations.[31]

No one set of influences brought about the changes which are to be described below. Nor is it possible to assign priority to one of them. It was a combination of industrialization with its application of universalistic criteria to an ever-widening sphere of life, ideals of individualism, equality and freedom, and the possibility of an alternative way of life which produced the transitional family.

EMERGING PATTERNS

The family structure of traditional China was an integrated, stable entity which could be described in considerable detail. Not so with the transitional family, for it is not clear that a new, stable form has yet emerged.[32] The process of change has been under way for at least a century and has been complicated recently by the imposition of the family policies of the communist government. How much effect and what kind of effect such policies will have is a matter of occasional furious debate and is generally unknown. What can be done here is to indicate the direction in which the family has been moving and to indicate some possible future developments.

Changing Status of Women. For the first time, women and children have become potential sources of additional income. Legally today Chinese women have full legal rights and equal rights of inheritance with men. That Chinese women often do not yet get their full legal rights only underscores the radical nature of the transformation which has taken place.

In childhood less segregation of the sexes occurs and both boys and girls appear to come more under the influence of their mothers. Formal education has been extended to almost the entire society and such education tends to be coeducational. There is less need and less desire to marry girls young and their average age at marriage appears to have been rising. The mother-in-law–daughter-in-law relationship evidently remains a source of difficulty but, with the increasing separation of the nuclear family from the extended family, is becoming less so. It would not be accurate to say that Chinese women have

[31] Morris Zelditch, Jr., "Cross Cultural Analyses of Family Structure," in Harold T. Christensen, ed., *Handbook of Marriage and the Family,* Chicago: Rand McNally, 1964, p. 496.

[32] It should be emphasized that the changes in Chinese family patterns are most typical of and may, in many cases, be confined to the urban and coastal areas which have undergone the most industrialization. The vastness of China, the numerous dialects spoken, and the limited ability of the government to impose its policies in the hinterland probably leave hundreds of millions of Chinese still living according to their traditional ways.

yet gained the near-equality of Western women, but the official ideologies are pushing them rapidly in that direction.

Development of a Youth Culture. For some 2000 years Chinese culture venerated age and assigned inferior status to youth. That situation has been changing rapidly and may now be becoming reversed.

Chinese youth and young adults have been cut loose in a very drastic sense. As they became involved in industry, they were forced, for the first time, to make decisions on their own. This produced an individualism by default, if not by design, and led to a widespread tendency to organize for political activity. The communist movement in China appears largely to be a youth movement which, because it is so articulate, assumes an importance beyond what could be justified by the number of people involved.

Peking officially discourages traditional attachments between parents and children, but members of Communist China's first families have established close private and public ties. . . .

Recent reports . . . from China . . . disclose that the first families are extending their power and influence through their children. Daughters of both the Chinese Communist leader, Mao Tse-tung, and his chief aide, Lin Piao, whose wives are already significant political figures, have emerged as influential personalities in journalism. . . .

Throughout the three-year-old Cultural Revolution in China the traditions of family life have come under increasingly severe attack. . . . A Shanghai broadcast attacked "the poisonous influence of the reactionary theory of family lineage. . . .

However, the first families of China preserve their narrow family circles and share the fruits of power with apparent disregard for the official prescriptions. Few leaders have ever seemed so vulnerable to charges of nepotism. . . .

The freeing of youth from most notions of family responsibility has produced a serious problem in relation to the aged. The old norms called for support of one's own parents but carried no responsibility for the aged in general. Now the number of aged persons in the society appears to be increasing and many of these people are in danger of being left without financial support. The Chinese communist government is thus faced with a dilemma. It wishes to substitute allegiance to the government for allegiance to the family but its very success in destroying the sense of family obligation increases the seriousness of the problem of support for the aged.

Development of Romantic Love. With urban living, a pattern of much freer association between the sexes has emerged and romantic love is threatening to replace parental arrangement as the basis for marriage. High-school and college students mingle freely, and the attractions of specific boys and girls to one another demand increasing consideration. According to Lang, there are three forms of deviation from the old pattern of arranged marriage: (1) parents arrange the marriage but ask their children's consent; (2) young people select their own mates but ask their parents' approval; and (3) the young people marry without asking parental consent.[33]

A drastic change which is an accompaniment of the institutionalization of romantic love is the appearance of sizable groups of unmarried men and women in the cities. Under the traditional norms the unmarried state for adults was regarded almost as perverted and there literally were no satisfactory social arrangements for single persons. Now, however, with the emergence of apartment living, hotels, restaurants, laundries, and the like, single persons can live quite comfortably and the old definitions of the single state are breaking down.

Increased Rates of Divorce, Suicide, and Illegitimacy. While trustworthy figures are not available, it appears that divorce rates have been increasing for some time. Under the traditional system, divorce rates were low and divorce most often involved the repudiation of the young wife by the husband's family. Revisions of the marriage laws during the present century have sought to equalize the divorce rights of husbands and wives, and most divorces now result from mutual consent or from insistence by either party to the marriage. One clue to the seriousness of the increase in divorce is found in recent educational campaigns by the communist government aimed at lowering divorce rates.

Levy reports that suicide rates apparently have been increasing also.[34] Moreover, the pattern of suicide has been changing. Whereas suicide was predominantly an alternative for young women under the traditional system, it is more often found now among middle-aged and older persons. Levy attributes the change to the greater responsibilities placed upon middle-aged people by the conditions of urban living and to the increasingly difficult position of aged parents.

Illegitimacy, in the Western sense, is almost a new problem in China. Lack of free association between the sexes and marriage at early ages, especially for

[33] Op cit. p. 123.
[34] Op. cit. p. 337.

girls, kept illegitimacy rates low during the traditional period. Too, the extramarital wanderings of males were institutionalized in the custom of concubinage. Now concubinage is under attack and it is becoming increasingly
difficult for a man to maintain a concubine either within his household or
outside it. The biggest change, however, appears to be in the premarital
behavior of young people. China never had puritanical attitudes toward sex,
such as are found in the United States, and when young people are free to
associate intimately, sexual intercourse often occurs. The communist government is now urging a more puritanical morality in an effort to reduce illegitimacy rates.

THE INFLUENCE OF THE CHINESE COMMUNIST GOVERNMENT

The policies and programs of the government of the People's Republic of
China are of continued interest and tremendous importance to the entire
world. Unfortunately the access of Westerners to China is still limited and
most of our information about what is occurring there is second-hand. There
is no question, however, that government policy is formulated in reaction to
the traditional family system as well as toward the achievement of political, economic, and military goals.

EXCERPT FROM THE MARRIAGE LAW OF THE PEOPLE'S REPUBLIC
OF CHINA. PROMULGATED BY THE CENTRAL PEOPLE'S
GOVERNMENT ON MAY 1, 1950.

Chapter One: General Principles

Article 1.

*The arbitrary and compulsory feudal marriage system, which is based
upon the superiority of man over woman and which ignores the children's interests, is abolished.*

*The New Democratic marriage system, which is based on free choice
of partners, on monogamy, on equal rights for both sexes, and on protection of the lawful interests of women and children, shall be put
into effect.*

Article 2.

*Polygamy, concubinage, child betrothal, interference with the re-
marriage of widows and the exaction of money or gifts in connection
with marriage shall be prohibited.*

Chapter Two: Contracting of Marriage

Article 3.

Marriage shall be based upon the complete willingness of the two parties. Neither party shall use compulsion and no third party shall be allowed to interfere.

Article 4.

A marriage can be contracted only after the man has reached twenty years of age and the woman has reached eighteen years of age.

Article 5.

No man or woman in any of the following instances shall be allowed to marry:

(a) Where the man and woman are lineal relatives by blood or where the man and woman are brother and sister born of the same parents or where the man and woman are half-brother and half-sister. The question of prohibiting marriage between collateral relatives by blood within the fifth degree of relationship is to be determined by custom.

(b) When one party, because of certain physical defects, is sexually impotent.

(c) Where one party is suffering from venereal disease, mental disorder, leprosy, or any other disease which is regarded by medical science as rendering the person unfit for marriage.

Article 6.

In order to contract a marriage, both the man and the woman shall register in person with the people's government of the subdistrict or village in which they reside. If the marriage is found to be in conformity with the provisions of this law, the local people's government shall, without delay, issue a marriage certificate.

If the marriage is found to be incompatible with the provisions of this law, no registration shall be granted . . .

—C. K. Yang, *The Chinese Family in the Communist Revolution*, Cambridge: The Technology Press, Massachusetts Institute of Technology, 1959, pp. 221–222.

The basic stance of the communist government is exemplified by the Marriage Law of the People's Republic of China which became effective in May, 1950, less than eight months after the establishment of the new government. The new law, which actually is a code for the regulation of many aspects of family life, establishes the following principles: (1) monogamy without concubinage; (2) free choice of spouse; (3) equal inheritance rights for both sexes; (4) protection of children's rights; and (5) divorce by mutual consent or upon insistence by either spouse. It represents a complete departure from the traditional system. Noteworthy in the law are its provisions for protection of the rights of women and children. Women are given full legal rights; Ping-ti Ho reports that it has become high fashion for a married woman to retain her own family name.[35] Children born out of wedlock have equal rights with legitimate offspring.

The communist government has made a determined effort to eliminate prostitution and points with pride to the disappearance of female infanticide. It has erratically sponsored a birth-control program designed to slow the rate of population growth and to raise the level of living. Factories turn out contraceptives and birth-control clinics are in operation.

Mrs. Hu Fang-tsu was candid and emphatic about it. "Children," she said, "are a lot of trouble. Nobody wants very many of them any more."

Mrs. Hu, 35, leader of a production team in Machiao Commune in the countryside 18 miles west of Shanghai, has one child and she and her husband have no plans to add another. . . .

Both man and wife work in the fields or at other jobs on their collective farm. Very young children can be left at nurseries during the day while parents are at work, but they need home care and feeding, and this is a burden. . . .

By their teens, children have little need of parents and parents little material need of children, for oldsters in China today rely not on their offspring for support in their old age, but on the organization to which they are attached.

. . . Mrs. Hu gave her views on children and birth control in the clean, plain but neatly furnished upstairs bed-living room of her two-room home in an apartment block near the fields in which she works. . . .

There is pressure on the young not to marry before the male is around 28 and the female around 26. Birth control pills and other contraceptive means are made available free. Vasectomies for men and sterilizations for women can be had at nominal cost in hospitals. . . .

—New York Times Service, April 22, 1971. © 1971 by The New York Times Company. Reprinted by permission.

Much public attention has been given to the reported efforts of the communist government virtually to eliminate the family as a threat to its own

[35] Op. cit. p. 26.

hold over the populace. The Marriage Law of 1950 is not consistent with such a position but seems instead to embody the highest ideals espoused by Western societies. Where the government has attacked the family system is in all of those areas formerly controlled by the *tsu*. The government's substitute for the *tsu* is the commune.

The communist government required years to consolidate its hold over major areas of China and it accompanied its control, wherever possible, by breaking up the *tsu* land holdings and redistributing them among the peasants. It then followed the land reform by organizing agricultural cooperatives designed to rationalize farm production. The government regulated the production of major crops, leaving each farmer free to raise his own garden crops. Goode reports that by the middle of 1955, there were more than 600,000 cooperatives involving 14 per cent of the farm population and that by the end of 1956, almost all peasant families were members of collectives.[36] These cooperatives appear not to have been too satisfactory. Their management appears not to have been too competent and farm production failed to meet expectations.

The cooperatives were replaced by communes. The first show-place commune was established in April 1958, and by November of that year, 99 per cent of the rural population had been grouped into communes of about 5000 households each.[37] In August 1958, 173 urban communes were formed in Honan and by 1960 urban communes were being organized on a grand scale. Up to 20 million people are said to have been involved.

The whole range of activities once covered by the family is now reduced to a narrow field in which husband, wife, and children associate together in the interstices, so to speak, of large institutions—the work group, the dining hall, the nursery—which have taken over the functions of economic coordination, housekeeping, and the rearing and education of children. The family has become an institution for producing babies and enjoying the leisure time left over from the major pursuits of every day life.

—Maurice Freedman, "The Family in China, Past and Present," *Pacific Affairs*, 31 (Winter 1961–62), p. 334, as reprinted in Ping-ti Ho, "An Historian's View of the Chinese Family System," in Seymour Farber, *et al.*, eds., *The Family's Search for Survival*, New York: McGraw-Hill, 1965, p. 26.

---

[36] Op. cit. p. 299.
[37] Ibid.

The new communes were bigger than the old collectives and involved the collectivization of much more of daily living. In addition to agricultural production, they were to have charge of such tasks as banking and the building of dams and steel mills. Common dining rooms were provided, nurseries were established for the care of children, and women were expected to play a full role in the occupational system. Universal primary education was offered to children, inexpensive weddings and funerals were provided, and homes for the aged were established.

Western attitudes toward these communes—particularly those attitudes expressed in the public press—were quite negative. They recalled to Americans the earlier Russian experiments with communes and were widely interpreted as an attack on the family institution—as an attempt to eliminate the family, as we know it, from Chinese society. Actually, it appears that nothing so drastic was intended. Many Westerners also predicted that the communes were bound to fail; an oversimplified prediction to say the least.

In sober retrospect, the communes appear to have been designed to replace the network of authority and loyalty which was part of the extended family system and the clan organization, but not to replace the family itself. The communists complain—and their complaints are not without some foundation—that the old system was completely corrupt and that it led to the degradation of all but the small group of gentry families who held power. They point to the fact that the allegedly universalistic examination system was actually under the control of the gentry; they point to the rampant nepotism which kept positions of wealth, power, and prestige within the gentry group; they point to the infanticide, prostitution, and sale of women as degrading. And they present themselves as truly representing the interests of all of the people against the tyranny waged through the traditional family system. They have sought to free women and children from that tyranny and to redistribute wealth in the society.

That the communists have encountered many serious problems also is certain. Chandrasekhar reports that the People's Government estimates that between 3 million and 20 million bandits, landlords, warlords, reactionaries, counter-revolutionaries, and other "enemies of the people" have been "liquidated." [38] There are many evidences that the communes have been badly run and that there is much public dissatisfaction with them. The plight of many aged people and the rising divorce and illegitimacy rates also have forced the communists to retreat somewhat from their ideal of completely independent womanhood and from their attacks on the doctrine of filial piety.

It is extremely difficult to evaluate the policies of the present Chinese gov-

[38] Op. cit. p. 61.

ernment without bias and quite hazardous to predict what the future may hold. The most able assessment to date may be that of Goode who offers the following predictions.[39] First, Goode believes that the commune, or some variant of it, will not disappear over the next several decades in spite of the many problems associated with it. Second, China has begun successfully to surmount the barriers blocking industrialization. It has made great strides already and will make even more rapid progress in the future. Third, the Chinese are attempting to destroy the traditional family but not the family itself. The family will remain as a primary economic and social unit. And, fourth, with the achievement of greater economic and political stability there will be a swing back toward a more definite sex division of labor and toward the family as a primary unit of identification.

SUMMARY

Study of the Chinese family system has both theoretical and practical implications. First, it serves as a model of extended, patriarchal, patrilineal systems, of which there are many in the world. Second, after at least 2000 years of relative stability that system is now undergoing rapid change. And, finally, China not only is the most populous nation in the world but she also poses a grave political, economic, and military threat to the Western world.

The traditional Chinese family described in this chapter was most characteristic of the Ch'ing dynasty. To understand it one must distinguish between the gentry who were about one-fifth of the population, and whose customs and ideals were universally admired and widely imitated throughout the society, and the vast peasantry who lived close to the minimum subsistence level and for whom little elaboration of social patterns was possible.

The traditional family was patriarchal, patrilineal, patrilocal, and monogamous. Ideally, it involved six generations living together and went nine generations without a division of property. Actually, few families contained more than three or four generations and the modal family may actually have been the stem family. The practice of ancestor worship and the doctrine of filial piety probably kept the family from changing to a simple conjugal system.

The tsu, or clan, was composed of all persons of a given surname tracing descent from a common ancestor. The tsu served as a buffer between the extended family and the larger society and performed educational, welfare, religious, and judicial functions.

Traditional Chinese society was rigidly structured according to age and sex.

[39] Op. cit. pp. 306–7.

Old age was highly esteemed and males dominated females. Role prescriptions for each family member at each stage in life were laid down in great detail.

Gentry boys and girls were segregated early in childhood. Boys were remanded to the strict discipline of fathers and tutors while girls were affectionately indulged by both parents. As they grew in responsibility, boys' lots improved while girls could look forward only to harsh treatment at the hands of their husbands' families.

Marriages were arranged by parents without the consent of the young people being required. The man's status changed little at marriage, but the bride began a period of ritual servitude to the husband's family, the function of which was to properly socialize her into her new family. The mother-in-law treated the young girl harshly, and the resulting antagonisms between them were a major source of strain in the traditional family.

The husband continued to grow in responsibility and personal freedom; the wife's status improved as she bore sons. As they moved into old age the relationship between them became quite strong and they received complete deference from their children.

Escape from the order and responsibility of every day life was provided for males through the practice of concubinage and through widespread commercial prostitution. Since concubines usually were chosen by the men involved, there often was rivalry between the concubine and her children and the wife and her children. Concubines sometimes were elevated to the status of wife, and the children of concubines were legitimate.

Divorce was uncommon during the traditional period and was regarded as undesirable. Divorce might occur with the mutual consent of the families involved or the husband might divorce his wife on any one of seven specified grounds. Remarriage was common among men but very difficult for women. Similarly, widowers generally remarried but the remarriage of widows was strongly disapproved.

Extensive social changes began early in the 1800's. As China began to industrialize, the particularistic and functionally diffuse character of the family system came into conflict with the universalistic and functionally specific requirements of the occupational system. Western ideals of individualism, equality, and political freedom also helped to subvert the traditional system. The actual transition of the family system finally was made possible by the development of urban institutions, which made an alternative way of life possible.

The character of the transitional family is not fully established. There is an unmistakable trend toward the conjugal form of family organization based upon romantic love and with more equality between the sexes. Divorce rates and illegitimacy rates have risen. With the rebellion of youth against the traditional system, care of the aged has become a major problem.

The communistic government which came into power in 1949 has supported these changes and has attacked the traditional system as feudalistic. It has virtually eliminated female infanticide, has outlawed concubinage, and is attempting to stamp out prostitution. It has sponsored birth-control programs and demands full equality for women and protection of the rights of children.

The most controversial of the communist innovations are the communes which were established on a large scale between 1958 and 1960. Westerners often interpret the communes as an attempt to destroy the family. In reality, the communes are intended as a substitute for the *tsu* and for the extended family but not for the conjugal unit upon which the communist government already depends. In spite of their disappointing performance so far, the communes seem destined to continue indefinitely. With increasing economic and political stability, the conjugal family also seems destined to receive more official support.

SUGGESTED READINGS

Freedman, Maurice, ed., *Family and Kinship in Chinese Society*, Stanford: Stanford University Press, 1970. An excellent collection of papers focusing upon the traditional Chinese kinship system, particularly as it exists in rural areas.

Goode, William J., "China," in *World Revolution and Family Patterns*, New York: The Free Press of Glencoe, 1963, pp. 270–320. A comprehensive analysis of changes in the Chinese family system over the past half century, with emphasis on the influence of the People's Republic of China.

Hill, Reuben, and König, René, eds., *Families in East and West: Socialization Process and Kinship Ties*, Paris and The Hague: Mouton, 1970. A collection of papers presented to the Ninth International Family Research Seminar in Tokyo. Emphasizes the categories and methodologies employed by Eastern and Western scholars in analyzing family relationships. Two of the articles focus specifically on Chinese family patterns.

Ho, Ping-ti, "An Historian's View of the Chinese Family System," in Seymour Farber, Piero Mustacchi, and Roger H. L. Wilson, eds., *Man and Civilization: The Family's Search for Survival*, New York: McGraw-Hill Book Company, 1965, pp. 15–30. A brief but penetrating account which puts both traditional and contemporary family patterns into historical perspective. Contradicts many widely held beliefs.

Meijer, M. J., *Marriage Law and Policy: In the Chinese People's Republic*, Hong Kong: Hong Kong University Press, 1971. A distinguished lawyer and sinologist shows how the marriage law of 1950 has been used to destroy the old "feudal" institutions and to build, in their stead, a new political morality.

"Special Issues on Marriage and the Family," *Chinese Sociology and Anthropology* 1 (Fall 1968) (Winter 1968–69). Translations of articles from Chinese publications. Most of the articles emphasize the commitment of the Chinese leadership to "destroy the old and establish the new" in family relationships. There are explicit role models of proper and improper marriage partners, and ideal and errant youth.

Yang, C. K., *The Chinese Family in the Communist Revolution*, Cambridge, Mass.: The Technology Press, Massachusetts Institute of Technology, 1959. The most comprehensive study available of the impact of the communist regime upon the Chinese family system. Stresses the strains inherent in the classical system and the more general process of change which predates communist control.

FILMS

Born Chinese: A Study of the Chinese Character (*Time-Life* Films, 43 West 16th Street, New York, 10011), 57 minutes. Shows the daily life of the Lung family, Hong Kong refugees from Red China. The camera studies their daily routine and analyzes the motives behind their behavior. No Westerners are seen.

Peiping Family (available through Audio-Visual Services, The Pennsylvania State University, University Park, Pa.), 21 minutes. Daily life in middle-class Chinese family; struggle of an American-educated man and his wife to educate their large family. Celebration of grandfather's birthday; visit to Temple of Heaven.

Sampan Family (available through Audio-Visual Services, The Pennsylvania State University, University Park, Pa.), 16 minutes. Story of Ling family who make their living on one of the thousands of small river boats filling the harbors and waterways of China.

QUESTIONS AND PROJECTS

1. Distinguish between the gentry and the peasantry. Why were the gentry patterns so important in traditional China?
2. Describe the "ideal" gentry family, using the concepts of family structure presented in Chapter 2. How did the "real" gentry patterns differ from the ideal? How did the peasantry patterns differ from the gentry patterns?
3. Explain the inheritance patterns in the traditional family. How was "ceremonial primogeniture" important? How was the division of property provided for? How often did it occur?
4. What was the *tsu* and what was its relationship to the extended family? What specific functions did the *tsu* perform?
5. Describe the infancy and childhood periods in the lives of gentry boys and girls. In what way did the relationship between boys and their fathers become a source of strain in the family?
6. Who were the interested parties in arranging a marriage? What was the essence of the marriage ceremony?

7. Describe the relationship between mother-in-law and daughter-in-law. How do you account for the harsh treatment accorded the daughter-in-law?
8. What was the significance of relative age in the traditional family?
9. What functions were served by the practice of concubinage? How was the stability of the family system linked to extramarital sexual activity on the part of males?
10. What regulations governed divorce in the traditional family? Explain how the practice of divorce by mutual consent actually reflected the strength of the family. How common was divorce in traditional China?
11. What forces finally led to disruption of the traditional family system? Assess the roles of industrialization, ideals of individualism and equality, and of the possibility of an alternative way of life in promoting the change.
12. Describe, as completely and accurately as you can, the family system of transitional China.
13. What has been the influence of the People's Republic of China upon the family system? Describe how the communes are consistent with the government's family policy. What is likely to be the future of the family in China?

5 | *Utopian Family Experiments*

In remote valleys and canyons or cluttered city apartment houses, thousands of young adults, seeking economic advantages, social revolution, love, pot, God or themselves, are creating a new life style in America.

Whether the arrangement is called a commune, a colony, a cooperative, an affinity group or a family, these young adults have some form of sharing in common, and they reject the traditional style of living that groups people together largely because of blood or legal relationships. . . .

Nearly 2000 communes in 34 states have been turned up by a *New York Times* inquiry seeking to determine how many permanent communal living arrangements of significant size could be found in the country, why they existed and who lived in them. . . .

Several generalizations about the new lifestyle were found, including the following:

—No accurate count exists largely because official agencies—except the police who watch urban communes and collectives for narcotics—generally ignore the development. In addition most are quiet and sometimes secretive, and thus go unnoticed by neighbors.

—The average size of a communal group ranges from 5 to 15 persons, usually in their late teens or early 20's, but increasing numbers of groups whose members are over 30 are being reported.

—All involve sharing space and finance and most go beyond this to share common work, goals or ideas. Others share themselves.

—Despite general fears . . . few successful group living arrangements are built around narcotics or promiscuous sexual relations, although both exist in some degree or other. But these attractions are too readily available outside the group to provide the basic cement.

—Although communal living experiments are common throughout American history . . . , few of the modern experiments have studied these historical roots. They regard themselves less as an experiment than as . . . "a path from things as they are to things as they should be." . . .

Probably the largest single group of communal living groups, and the type accounting for the rapid growth of the experiments are those built near colleges and universities. Surrounding nearly every major college and university are houses in which the walls have been knocked down to make community rooms where students can live as one family.

". . . It's an attempt to be truly human beings in the way we've always been taught to believe human beings were supposed to live with one another—with love and understanding."

There are more practical reasons, too. A group of three, six or 10 people sharing the rent can considerably reduce the cost of living for a student.[1]

F OR some ten years now, there has been serious discussion in America of whether the family is outmoded. The quotation above reflects the concern. Academicians and popular writers, in addition to young people, are proposing "alternatives" to conventional family living including communal living groups and "multilateral marriage."[2]

As *The New York Times* survey indicated, few proponents of today's experiments in non-family living have bothered to study the history of such attempts. Utopian family experiments have been going on for a very long time. Plato, for example, proposed to eliminate the family, as we know it, in *The Republic*. Many other such efforts have held, in common, the view that pathologies in the larger society are linked to the family system and that elimination of vices such as selfishness, jealousy, and discrimination requires elimination of the family.[3]

We may be able to understand the contemporary American situation better if we put it in broader perspective. To do that, we will examine three other major attempts of groups and societies to eliminate the family. Then we will return to the current scene.

THE ONEIDA COMMUNITY

The story of the Oneida Community is inextricably linked with the personality and the religious beliefs of John Humphrey Noyes. Noyes, of an old

[1] Bill Kovach, "Communal Living Becoming a Factor in the U. S.," *The New York Times*, January 3, 1971. © 1971 The New York Times Company. Reprinted by permission.

[2] See Herbert A. Otto, ed., *The Family in Search of a Future*, New York: Appleton-Century-Crofts, 1970; and Arlene S. Skolnick, and Jerome H. Skolnick, eds., *Family in Transition: Rethinking Marriage, Sexuality, Child Rearing, and Family Organization*, Boston: Little, Brown and Co., 1971.

[3] See, for example, R. H. S. Crossman, *Plato Today*, New York: Oxford University Press, 1959; R. V. Hine, *California's Utopian Colonies*, New York: Huntington Library, 1962; and G. B. Lockwood, *The New Harmony Movement*, New York: D. Appleton Company, 1905.

New England family, graduated from Dartmouth and began the practice of law. He underwent religious conversion at a revival meeting, gave up law, and entered the seminary, where the zealousness that was to characterize his later years became evident. He decided that the doctrine of repentance for sinning was completely wrong and that man should strive, instead, to live a perfect life here on earth. Noyes narrowly escaped being expelled from the seminary, and soon after he began to preach his license was revoked.

Noyes continued to preach and to develop his doctrine of *perfectionism*. Gradually he gathered a group of believers about him at his home in Putney, Vermont, and this group became, in 1846, the Putney Community—a group who lived together in the first stages of what came to be called *complex marriage*.

The true and detailed origins of complex marriage may never be known. It was part of a larger "Bible communism" that involved a complete sharing of wealth, the elimination of all private property, and the principle that every adult male in the society should have sexual privileges with every adult female and vice versa. The Putney Community started when Noyes arranged for his two sisters to marry two of the men in the group. Folsom reports that the actual sexual communism began when Noyes became highly attracted to one of the women in the group and began to have sex relations with her after first consulting with his own wife and with the woman's husband.[4]

Unquestionably, Noyes was a complicated man. His charismatic leadership made men loyal to him and attracted women both sexually and otherwise. He is reputed to have fathered at least eleven children by various women. At the same time, Noyes was a deeply religious man who genuinely eschewed lust and personal selfishness. Such men usually are not easily tolerated by those around them, and, in 1848, Noyes and his little band were driven out of Putney.

The group re-established itself in central New York state on the banks of the Oneida Creek, where it was to exist as the Oneida Community for approximately thirty years. The group grew in size to about 300 people and, after a difficult start, prospered financially. Unlike most of the other utopian American communities which emphasized farming, Oneida developed a sizable industrial base. One of the members invented a steel trap which was very widely used, and shortly before the community broke up they embarked upon the manufacture of silverware. The silverware business was extremely profitable and continued after the break-up of the community as the well-known company, Oneida, Limited.

[4] Joseph K. Folsom, *The Family and Democratic Society*, New York: John Wiley and Sons, 1943, p. 143.

COMPLEX MARRIAGE

According to the principle of complex marriage, all men should naturally love all women and all women should naturally love all men. Romantic love and monogamy were seen as both cause and effect of selfishness and jealousy, selfishness and jealousy being barriers to leading the perfect life.

Consistent with these beliefs, the Oneidans practiced a form of group marriage or sexual communism in which any man in the group had the right to seek sexual relations with any woman. Women were completely free either to accept or reject any specific proposal. If a man wished to initiate a relationship he was supposed to convey his request to the woman through a Central Committee. An older woman member of the Committee relayed the proposal to the woman, making it easy for her to respond either way without embarrassment. What little evidence there is on the point makes it seem that women seldom refused. The man then appeared at the woman's room at bedtime and retired to his own room again before going to sleep. Such an elaborate procedure may have been used only when a new relationship was begun and probably, after the first visit, matters were more informally handled by the couples involved.

The absence of any right to demand sexual privileges is said by some writers to have resulted in Oneida men and women remaining more attentive to and considerate of one another than is usually true in more conventional situations. For given couples to develop romantic attachments to one another, however, was regarded as unseemly and there is some evidence that sanctions occasionally were applied; the couple might be chided about their relationship and one member of the couple might be sent out of the community for a time.

The Oneidans distinguished sharply between the right to sex relationships and the right to reproduction. The community agreed that during the first twenty years of its existence there should be no childbearing. After the community was firmly established and child-care facilities were provided, a committee was appointed to determine which men and women in the group should reproduce. Though modern notions of eugenics did not yet exist, Noyes had been influenced by the writings of Galton and Darwin and called his planned parenthood program *stirpiculture*.

Eventually some 53 women and 38 men were selected to become parents and 58 children were born into the community. For the most part the parents were the authorized ones but apparently a few unauthorized women were highly desirous of having children and managed to become pregnant.

The birth-control technique used by the Oneidans casts interesting light on their concept of appropriate sex relationships. They practised the technique of coitus reservatus, in which intercourse is continued without the male reaching the point of ejaculation. This technique has been used in various areas of the world, particularly India, and has occasionally been highly regarded. It calls for a high degree of control on the part of the man, however; enough so that there is doubt of its feasibility for whole populations. Moreover, it inevitably alters the character of the sex relationship, replacing the explosive sexual climax with a diffuse and suffuse lower-key pleasure. The combination of free sexual access with intentional toning down of the erotic seems consistent with the deeply religious nature of the Oneida Community.

Associated with this concept of appropriate sex relationships was the "principle of ascendance" according to which men learned the appropriate techniques of control by having their early sex experiences only with older, experienced women—often those beyond menopause who were not in danger of becoming pregnant. Similarly, it was deemed proper for young, inexperienced women to be taught the intricacies of sex only by older, experienced men who were "properly spiritual" and would not be carried away.

THE PRINCIPLE OF ASCENDANCY

Oneidans entirely reject the idea that love is an inevitable and uncontrollable fatality, which must have its own course. They believe the whole matter of love and its expression should be subject to enlightened self-control, and should be managed for the greatest good. In the Community it is under the special supervision of the fathers and mothers, who are guided in their management by certain principles, which have been worked out and are well understood in the Community. One is termed the principle of the Ascending Fellowship. It is regarded as better, in the early stages of passional experience, for the young of both sexes to associate in love with persons older than themselves, and if possible with those who are spiritual and have been some time in the school of self-control, and who are thus able to make love safe and edifying. This is only another form of the popular principle of contrasts. It is well understood by physiologists that it is undesirable for persons of similar characters and temperaments to mate together. Communists have discovered that it is undesirable for two inexperienced and unspiritual persons to rush into fellowship with each other; that it is far better for both to associate with persons of mature character and sound sense.

—*Handbook of the Oneida Community*, p. 39, as reproduced in William M. Kephart, "Experimental Family Organization: An Historico-Cultural Report on the Oneida Community," *Marriage and Family Living* 25 (Aug. 1963), p. 270.

Unfortunately, little is known about how well the system worked in practice. The Oneidans appear not to have talked much about their sex relationships and most of the early documents left by members of the community later were burned by officers of Oneida, Limited, to prevent possible embarrassment to living descendants. Apparently, the birth-control technique was quite effective. There was, however, grumbling about the system on the part of younger men during the latter part of the community's existence and this may have been one of the factors leading to the community's breakup. It may have been responsible, also, for John Humphrey Noyes's leaving the community and going to Canada, where he died. There are unsubstantiated rumors that some of the young women were under "the age of consent" and that Noyes believed that he might be prosecuted for statutory rape.

Complex marriage also removed the child-rearing function rather completely from the parents. When children attained the age of 15 months, they were removed from the direct care of their mothers and housed together in the children's wing of the great mansion house which, by that time, had been built and in which the members of the community lived. The children had a visiting period with their mothers once each day. As was true with adult relationships, all adults were supposed naturally to love all children and all children to love all adults. The relationship to children was not impersonal or distant, but one in which adults were supposed to show warmth and affection for all children irrespective of their parenthood.

Students of the Oneida Community have tended to place considerable emphasis on the structure of the mansion house, itself, in determining the social patterns within the group. While each adult had his own room and while there was a separate wing for the children, there were common dining, recreation, and general living areas. The seeking of privacy was discouraged and true communal living was expected. What records exist generally indicate that life in the mansion house was pleasant and that there was a high degree of sharing of interests and activities.

The Oneidans' communistic practices extended throughout the economic sphere, were buttressed by a somewhat ascetic morality, and were accompanied by a lively interest in the arts. Private property was done away with altogether. Not only was the community property jointly held, but even clothing and personal effects were furnished from a central supply. Sexual attractiveness was not emphasized. The women wore their hair short and wore loose fitting trousers that extended to the feet under their knee-length dresses. Even the children held their toys in common. There was one brief period when the small children in the nursery were provided with their own dolls but this was soon discovered to be encouraging attitudes of personal selfishness and the privately owned dolls were ritually destroyed.

Effort was made to reinforce the inherent dignity of all work, and status distinctions among those who worked at different tasks were played down. Whenever possible, people were rotated from one job to another so that permanent status distinctions would not appear. Yet the Oneidans managed their enterprises well and the community prospered.

Another paradox appeared in that dancing and card playing, which were defined as healthy social activities, were encouraged while alleged personal vices such as smoking, drinking coffee, and the use of alcoholic beverages were strictly prohibited. The community also sponsored musical and other cultural programs which outsiders from the surrounding area were permitted to attend. Except for these occasions, contacts between members of the community and outsiders were kept to a minimum.

THE BREAKUP OF THE COMMUNITY

Even as the community prospered, its radical ways produced pressures, both from within and without, that proved to be its undoing. What priority should be assigned to the various factors cannot be said for sure. But by 1880, barely thirty years after its beginning, the community had broken up.

As nearly as can be determined, most individual members of the community were well thought of by outsiders. Even as a group they appeared to have the reputation of being sober, hard-working, religious people who bothered no one. But the community's concept of complex marriage was too radical for surrounding communities to take. Rumors grew of sexual orgies, to say nothing of "free love" and the breeding of human beings "like cattle." The prospect of older men having sex relationships with young girls not only outraged the public morality but appeared also to be in violation of the laws against statutory rape. The pressure grew greater and greater until, by 1879, the community was forced to give up complex marriage and return to official monogamy.

Some of this same pressure came from within the community, which was not entirely successful in indoctrinating its young people with their parents' values. Some of the children were quite sensitive to the taunts of outsiders who referred to them as "bastards" and "Christ boys." To their parents' dismay some of the younger people also assumed the romantic and monogamous attitudes of outsiders. The rebellion of some of the younger men against the principle of ascendance was mentioned earlier.

The fate of the community also was linked to the leadership of John

Humphrey Noyes. Like many other charismatic leaders, he gave unstintingly of himself for the community's welfare but, like many other charismatic leaders also, he failed to provide adequately for his own succession. Power in the community was vested in its elders, with the balance of power often being held by Noyes himself. The younger generation was not trained to leadership and became, instead, a divisive force within the community. In 1877, John Humphrey Noyes resigned as leader of the colony and was replaced by one of his sons. In 1879 Noyes left for Canada and soon afterward the community dissolved.

Of the many utopian experiments within the United States, Oneida was the most successful. For thirty years and among some 300 people the family, as we know it, virtually ceased to exist. It is significant, however, that the experiment did not last through the raising of even one generation.

The Soviet Family Experiment

In turning our attention to the great family experiment in the Soviet Union, we jump from consideration of an isolated, short-lived experiment among some 300 people to analysis of a social system with a long history and involving some 200 million people composed of several major ethnic groups and as many as 175 separate nationalities.[5]

The major cultural division in prerevolutionary Russia was between the Slavic peoples who were concentrated in European Russia and the non-Slavic peoples who were located in the Caucasus, central Asia, the Steppes, and Siberia. The Slavs composed about four-fifths of the population and had a family pattern which loosely associated the conjugal family with a larger bilateral kindred. This stood in contrast to the Kayakh family which was a large, patrilineal, extended family, firmly attached to a larger clan group and governed by Moslem law. The situation was further complicated by the fact that there were significant differences in family patterns between the urban minority (about 30 per cent of the population) and the vast peasant masses in the hinterlands.

The dominant, bilateral, conjugal family was large by modern standards, tending toward an extended family system. Particularly among the wealthier segments of the population there was strict patriarchal control associated with the ownership of large tracts of land. The power of these elite families traced directly from the Czar and was supported by the powerful Eastern Orthodox

[5] Kent Geiger and Alex Inkeles, "The Family in the U.S.S.R.," *Marriage and Family Living* 16 (Nov. 1954), p. 397.

Church. It was against the concentration of power in these three places that the Bolshevik Revolution of 1917 was directed.

EARLY SOVIET POLICY

The new Soviet regime, in only its second month, issued decrees regulating marriage and divorce. One decree replaced religious marriage with civil marriage, and another decree made divorce available at the request of one or both parties to a marriage. The next year, 1918, a more comprehensive code supplemented these decrees with the stipulation that, "birth itself shall be the basis of the family. No differentiation whatsoever shall be made between relationships by birth, whether in or out of wedlock." [6] The code provided, further, that neither parents nor children should have any rights to one another's property and that their obligations to support one another should be conditioned upon "destitution and the inability to work." Thus, from the very beginning the Soviet regime adopted policies which attacked the very foundations of the family: the church was denied the power to solemnize marriages; divorce was made easy; all penalties attached to illegitimacy were removed; the legal obligations of parents and children to one another were minimized; and the family inheritance of property was attacked.

The most radical policies, however, were still to come. A new Code on Domestic Relations was enacted by the largest Soviet state in 1926, and was soon adopted by all of the other Soviet republics. The new code did not even require the registration of marriages, declaring only that registration offered the best proof that a marriage existed. The courts were also empowered to recognize marriages where there was "the fact of cohabitation, combined with a common household, evidence of marital relations before third parties or in personal correspondence and other documents, mutual financial support, the raising of children in common if supported by circumstantial evidence, and the like." [7] In brief, none of the rights and obligations of spouses, parents, or children were to depend upon whether a marriage had been registered. Legal statuses derived from the facts of cohabitation and the production of children, not from the performance of a ceremony or the registration of a marriage.

The code of 1926 was equally drastic in its provision for divorce. The couple jointly, or either spouse separately, could request the dissolution of a

[6] Vladimir Gsovski, "Family and Inheritance in Soviet Law," in Alex Inkeles and Kent Geiger, eds., *Soviet Society: A Book of Readings*, Boston: Houghton Mifflin, 1961, p. 531.

[7] Ibid. p. 532.

marriage without giving any reasons for their dissatisfaction. There was no trial or other judicial procedure. Divorces simply were registered in the fashion that marriages were registered. If the divorce was registered by one party only, the other party was notified to appear at the Registry, not to contest the dissolution but to acknowledge it. If he failed to appear, he was notified of the divorce by mail.

Laws relating to sexual behavior were conspicuous, early in the regime, by their absence. One of the few laws in this area legalized abortion in 1920. Other laws dropped adultery, bigamy, and incest from the list of punishable offenses. The prevailing attitude was that there should be no barriers to free sex relationships; that there should be no reactionary bourgeois morality. Contraceptive devices were made readily available and all stigma was removed from illegitimacy.

The conclusion is inescapable that the Soviets sought to destroy the family. Gsovsky quotes Professor Brandenburgsky in an explanation of the Soviet Code on Domestic Relations:

Until Socialism is achieved the individual family is inescapable. . . . We undoubtedly are approaching public upbringing of the children, free labor schools, the widest social security at the expense of the State. If at present we maintain the duty of mutual support within the family, we do it because the State cannot yet, for the time being, replace the family in this respect. . . . The family creating a series of rights and duties between the spouses, the parents and children, will certainly disappear in the course of time and will be replaced by governmental organization of public education and social security.[8]

Perhaps the most explicit Bolshevik spokesman on marriage and the family was Friedrich Engels, who wrote that "the modern monogamous family is founded on the open or disguised domestic slavery of women."[9] Engels equated marriage with prostitution and foresaw the complete demise of the family in the new Socialist state.

THE EFFECTS OF THE SOVIET POLICIES

It did not take long for the effects of the new policies to become evident. There can be no question but what the traditional family system was greatly altered and that the family itself was weakened. Some of the accompanying changes were consistent with socialist ideology and were approved by the

[8] Op. cit. p. 533.
[9] The Origin of the Family, Private Property, and the State, Chicago: Charles H. Kerr and Company, 1902, p. 89.

government; some unanticipated consequences, however, wrought havoc and eventually forced reversal of the earlier policies.

The Emancipation of Women. The Soviet leaders sought complete equality between men and women. "Bourgeois marriage" had involved the subjugation of women and the subjugation of any group was forbidden by socialist morality. Moreover, if women could be induced to rebel against marriage, the threat to the new regime posed by the family would be removed. Too, the Soviet Union needed workers. If all women could be persuaded to work outside the home, the work force would be doubled and industrialization would proceed much faster.

. . . No nation can be free when half of the population is enslaved in the kitchen.

—Lenin.

The marriage laws removed all of the legal disabilities attaching to woman's status. At marriage the woman was permitted to adopt the husband's surname, or he could take her surname, or each was permitted to retain his own surname. Their place of residence had to be fixed by mutual consent. If the husband moved to another location the wife was under no obligation to follow him. Neither the husband nor the wife was liable for the other's support unless one of them was incapacitated; then the other partner was liable, irrespective of sex. The husband and wife were equally liable for their children and they had equal rights of divorce.

Discrimination in employment was prohibited and women streamed into factories. They performed hard manual labor, they worked at clerical tasks and, as their educational levels increased, they moved into the professions. By 1935, it is estimated that two-thirds of all able-bodied women of working age were employed, compared with about two-fifths in the United States.[10] By 1940, the percentage of all workers who were women was 38 per cent in the Soviet Union compared with 31 per cent in Germany and only 24 per cent in the United States. By that time, 75 per cent of the medical students, 50 per cent of the education students, and 23 per cent of the engineering students in Russia were women.[11] The peak employment of women in the

[10] Folsom, op. cit. p. 199.
[11] Mildred Fairchild, "The Status of the Family in the Soviet Union Today," *American Sociological Review* 2 (Oct. 1937), pp. 624–5.

U.S.S.R. was reached during World War II when 53 per cent of all workers were women. Since that time the proportion has stabilized at just under 50 per cent.[12]

That the new regime was quite successful in raising the status of women is indisputable. It may well be that the status of women, relative to that of men, is higher in the Soviet Union today than anywhere else in the Western world. Some writers have pointed out that this literal equality may mean imposing a heavier burden on women since they must carry most of the reproductive burden along with the work function.[13] Women's roles in the United States will be analyzed in a later chapter of this book.

Rise in the Divorce Rate. The unavailability of systematic data makes it impossible to specify the rise in the divorce rate precisely, but there is no question that the increase was enough to alarm the Soviet leadership. Accounts were published of marriages contracted only for convenience—for example, to qualify for rooms and apartments in the crowded cities—and immediately followed by divorce. Another widely circulated story concerned a maiden schoolteacher unable to find a husband, who offered to pay a sizable sum to a woman friend if she would locate a husband for her. The scheming friend, already married, arranged for her own husband to divorce her and marry the schoolteacher. As soon as she received the money, the husband was then supposed to divorce the schoolteacher. In attacking such practices, the Soviet press gleefully pointed out that the husband, in this case, decided that he preferred the school teacher and remained married to her.

It was reported in *Izvestia* that the divorce rate in Moscow in 1934 was 37 divorces per 100 marriages and that in the first half of 1935 the rate climbed to 38.3 divorces per 100 marriages. These figures are believed to be about 50 per cent higher than those which prevailed during the latter part of the Czarist period. The regime became quite concerned about the divorce rate, both as a symptom of the decay of socialist morality and as a contributor to the falling birth rate.

Fall in the Birth Rate. The precipitous fall in the birth rate was believed to be a function of legalized abortion and the rising divorce rate. Timasheff reports that 154,000 abortions were performed in Moscow in 1934 while only 57,000 children were actually born in the city. In 1935, there were 155,000

---

[12] H. Kent Geiger, *The Family in Soviet Russia*, Cambridge, Mass.: Harvard University Press, 1968, p. 178.

[13] For a discussion of the distribution of the work and reproduction functions and of various concepts of equality for women, see Clifford Kirkpatrick, *The Family: As Process and Institution*, New York: The Ronald Press, 1963, Chs. 7 and 17.

abortions to 70,000 live births.[14] Writing for the year 1927, Alice Field claims that 60 per cent of the abortions were done for "social" rather than medical reasons.[15] The alarmed government restricted abortion again in 1936, and the Moscow birth rate for the first half of 1937 doubled over that for the same period during the preceding year.

Rise of Hooliganism. In its effort to destroy the family, the government sought not only to make wives independent of their husbands but also to take much of the socialization of children out of the hands of parents. Universal primary education was instituted and the educational level of the general population was raised markedly. Part of the schooling consisted of systematic indoctrination in Socialist ideology and this indoctrination was carried out even more vigorously in the youth organizations such as Komsomol and the Pioneers.

Education during the revolutionary years stressed the development of complete loyalty to the state and attacked religion and the family as sources of counterrevolutionary sentiments and corrupt capitalist beliefs. The authority of the parents was undermined and, for a time, children actually were encouraged to report counterrevolutionary sentiments on the part of their parents to the authorities.

TABLE 1. *Mode of Interpreting Soviet Regime to Children of Anti-Regime Parents as Reported by Children and Parents.*

POSITION OF RESPONDENT IN FAMILY	MODE OF INTERPRETING REGIME			TOTAL
	OVERTLY ANTI-REGIME	NON-COMMITTAL	FAVORABLE TO REGIME	
Child	71%	19%	10%	100% (N=94)
Parent	47%	47%	6%	100% (N=51)

Source: Kent Geiger, "Winning Over the Youth," in Alex Inkeles and Kent Geiger, eds., *Soviet Society: A Book of Readings,* Boston: Houghton Mifflin, 1961, p. 554.

Table 1 presents data gathered from Soviet political refugees which indicate that a substantial proportion of the parents who were hostile to the regime refrained from communicating their attitudes openly to their children. More than half of these anti-regime parents view themselves as having expressed themselves noncommittally or as being favorable to the government's policies.

[14] Nicholas S. Timasheff, "The Attempt To Abolish the Family in Russia," in Norman W. Bell and Ezra F. Vogel, eds., *A Modern Introduction to the Family,* The Free Press of Glencoe, Illinois, 1960, p. 58.

[15] Alice Field, *Protection of Women and Children in Soviet Russia,* New York: Dutton, 1932, p. 83.

Nearly 30 per cent of the children saw their parents as being less than forth-right. How much open spying developed within families is difficult to say, but we do know that one effect of the disruption of family patterns was a rapid increase in what we call juvenile delinquency and what in Russia is called hooliganism.

By 1929, hooliganism was recognized as a major problem, and between 1929 and 1935 the official rate of youthful crime almost doubled. Adolescent gangs were reported to roam the cities making vicious unprovoked attacks upon helpless citizens. Vandalism, stealing, robbery, rape, and even murder occurred with increasing frequency.

During the early 1930's the government began to rethink its family policies. Universal primary education and the raising of the status of women had brought some very beneficial results. But they had been accompanied by wide-spread increases in almost every form of pathology associated with family life. To cope with these unanticipated problems, the regime reversed itself drastically.

REVISED FAMILY POLICY

What might be called the second stage in the Russian family revolution began in the middle 1930's and extended into the 1950's. This was a period of reaction against the radicalism of the post-revolutionary phase. A law out-lawing homosexuality for example, was passed in 1934 and, in 1935, another law made parents responsible for the delinquent acts of their children. Major recodifications occurred in 1936 and again in 1944.[16]

After 1944, only officially registered marriages were recognized as legal marriages. Common law marriage was outlawed and illegitimacy, although that word was not used, was re-established. The fathers of illegitimate children were not liable for their support, and such children had no right to inherit from their fathers.

Requirements for obtaining a divorce became increasingly strict until divorce in the Soviet Union became much more difficult to get than in the United States. The divorce might be petitioned for by either partner, but both had to be summoned to court and the specific grounds for divorce proved to the court's satisfaction. Even then, the People's Court could not grant the divorce, but sought reconciliation of the couple. If that failed, the suit had to be filed again in a higher court. That court might or might not grant the di-

[16] See Rudolph Schlesinger, ed., *Changing Attitudes in Soviet Russia: The Family in the U.S.S.R.*, London: Routledge and Kegan Paul, 1949.

vorce, depending upon whether it judged the divorce to be in the interest of the state. The whole process was also quite expensive.

Such measures were characteristic of the period through World War II and until after the death of Joseph Stalin. Then, in the 1950's, the pendulum began to swing the other way again. Abortion was made legal, again, in 1955, apparently largely to stamp out the flourishing illegal abortion practices that existed.

The extreme difficulty in securing divorces came under attack for encouraging people to enter informal liaisons without having been divorced from their former partners. Legal recodification came in 1965 when the lower People's Courts were authorized to grant divorces. Subsequently, even court hearings were done away with in cases where neither partner objected and where there were no minor children involved. In recent years, 85 per cent of Russian divorces have been granted by filling out a form at the Registry, with the divorce becoming final after three months.[17]

The Soviet Union's divorce rate has more than doubled in the past eight years. Last year there were probably at least 700,000 divorces, in a country reckoned to have between 60 and 70 million families. . . .

Ease of divorce is regarded as a factor in the emancipation of women and as basic to communist social practice.

If a Soviet couple are not happy together, they can obtain a divorce by mutual consent after a period of three months to think it over and payment of a sum equivalent to about a third of a month's wages for a moderately well-paid industrial worker. They do not need to go to court unless one partner objects or questions of children and property are involved. . . .

Not only is the divorce rate rising, but the marriage rate is falling, too. . . .

Communism is often believed to be anti-family but even in Russia it is recognized that there is still really no substitute for a good family as an incubator of good citizens and that divorce is bad for the children.

—Dispatch of *The Times*, London,
January 7, 1970.

The Russians also are trying to make marriage more attractive. Although only the civil registration of marriage is recognized, great effort is made to

[17] Edwin A. Roberts, Jr., *Russia Today*, Silver Spring, Maryland: The National Observer, 1967, p. 153.

make the registration a solemn affair. The Registry offices are large, attractive, and well furnished. The date for the registration of a marriage must be set in advance, and parents and friends are invited to witness the ceremony. Attractive certificates of the registration are issued and even wedding rings may be used.

In addition to revising its regulations concerning marriage and divorce, the Soviet Union has continued to support the practice of mothers working and has sought to encourage large families. Pregnant women who are working in factories are given paid leaves of two months before the baby is born and two months afterward. In addition they are given free medical care and some baby clothing. Both factories and collective farms maintain nurseries where mothers may leave their babies while they are working, and the mothers receive time off every three hours to nurse their infants. The state also operates kindergartens for children between the ages of three and eight, where the children receive three full meals and medical care.

While the Chinese are postponing marriage to control the population level, the Russians were bluntly told this week to marry at an earlier age to produce more children. Bachelors were denounced for not doing their part. . . .

For some years the authorities have adopted a laissez-faire policy in population matters. For those who wish few or no children, abortion has been made legal and cheap and some birth-control devices are available. Those who like large families receive lump-sum and monthly payments after the birth of a fourth child, and mothers of 10 children or more are declared mother-heroines. . . .

Literaturnaya Gazeta . . . followed up with an attack on the institution of bachelorhood, virtually accusing single young men of being traitors to Soviet society. An article said that, "part of a person's wage is intended for the support of children . . . the bachelor simply robs others who are married and do support children."

Bachelors already pay a special tax of 6 per cent of income.

—*The New York Times*, April 25, 1971.

The policy of encouraging large families operates through a series of monetary subsidies paid to mothers as the number of children increases. The payments begin with the birth of the third child, when the mother receives a payment of 200 rubles. The amount increases with the birth of each additional child until 2500 rubles are paid for the eleventh and all subsequent children. In addition, the mother receives 40 rubles per month for the fourth child and up to 150 rubles per month for the eleventh child. These monthly payments are made from the time the child is a year old until he reaches the age of five. Obviously, since the payments end at age five, couples cannot expect to produce children for a profit, but the payments do provide some incentive. The average Soviet worker has a net income of only about 650 rubles per month; thus the subsidies range from 6 per cent to about 25 per cent of other net income.[18]

The modal family form in the Soviet Union today appears to be a two-generation conjugal family in both urban and rural areas. The birth rate continues to decline under the impact of urbanization and industrialization. A three-generation unit also appears to be relatively common. This unit involves one or more grandparents living with the parents and children and with the grandparents assuming many of the household and child-care duties of the working mother.[19] This arrangement nicely relieves the state of much responsibility for the care of both children and oldsters. Such extended units also are advantageous in the cities where housing is allotted on the basis of family size.

FINAL EVALUATION OF THE SOVIET EXPERIMENT

The Russian attempt to do away with the family is the largest such effort ever made. Unlike the communist Chinese who, from the beginning, sought to destroy only the extended family, the Russians tried to do away with the family altogether. Significantly, again, this radical effort did not last for more than a generation. The revolution occurred in 1917 and by the early 1930's the ground was being laid for strengthening the family once again.

The early revolutionary leaders saw a threat to socialist ideology in the family itself. They viewed the family as an inherently reactionary institution which could be used only in the service of capitalistic exploitation of the masses. And the traditional family was a major obstacle to the consolidation of power by the new regime. By the 1930's, however, the Soviet leaders realized that the generation growing to adulthood had never experienced the old ways and presented no threat to the regime. Indeed they discovered that the family could be used to indoctrinate youth with socialism just as it had earlier promoted loyalty to the Czarist government.

The family in the Soviet Union today appears to be remarkably similar to the family in the United States, having many of the same strengths and the

[18] Geiger and Inkeles, "The Family in the U.S.S.R.," p. 401.

[19] Kent Geiger, "The Soviet Family," in Meyer F. Nimkoff, ed., *Comparative Family Systems*, Boston: Houghton Mifflin, 1965, pp. 306–7.

same problems. The great Soviet effort to eliminate the family has ended and few direct results of the effort remain.

THE KIBBUTZ

The American utopian communities were very small, the Russian experiment was on a grand scale, and the kibbutzim fall in between. There are over 200 kibbutzim in Israel involving some 85,000 members.[20] These 227 kibbutzim are organized into three major federations, one of which—Marxist in ideology and Soviet in inclination—has been most carefully studied. The kibbutz patterns to be described in this section represent the most completely collectivized and the most antireligious of the kibbutzim.[21]

The kibbutz is a form of agricultural collective. In it virtually all property is collectively owned, work is collectively organized, consumption is collectively organized, there are communal living arrangements, and even the rearing of children is assumed by the group as a whole. The original settlers of the kibbutzim were middle-class European intellectuals who migrated to Israel and who made of physical labor the highest vocational goal. Rather than aspiring to upward social mobility, these pioneers deliberately sought to create a socialist enterprise in which all persons would experience the deep satisfaction to be derived from working the soil.

The history of the kibbutzim dates back to the 1880's when a group of Russian Jews established the first agricultural collectives in what, at that time, was Palestine. Between 1882 and 1903, some 25,000 Jews migrated to Palestine. Forty thousand more came between 1904 and the start of World War I. After World War I, Palestine became a mandate of Great Britain and the migration continued. By 1931 some 116,000 more immigrants arrived. Persecution of the Jews under Hitler brought 225,000 more between 1932 and 1939. And in 1948, the State of Israel came into being.[22] By 1936 there were 47 kibbutzim in Palestine, by 1948 there were 149, and in 1954 the number reached 227.

The kibbutzim range in size from 40 to 50 members to more than 1000

---

[20] *The New York Times*, Nov. 23, 1969.

[21] The description of kibbutz patterns in this section leans heavily on the published reports of two scholars who have studied them first-hand. See Melford E. Spiro, "Is the Family Universal?—The Israeli Case," in Norman W. Bell and Ezra F. Vogel, eds., *A Modern Introduction to the Family*, New York: The Free Press, 1968, pp. 68–79; and Yonina Talmon, "The Family in a Revolutionary Movement—the Case of the Kibbutz in Israel," in Meyer F. Nimkoff, ed., *Comparative Family Systems*, Boston: Houghton Mifflin, 1965, pp. 259–86.

[22] Raphael Patai, *Israel Between East and West: A Study in Human Relations*, Westport, Conn.: Greenwood Publishing Corp., 1970, pp. 59–72.

members in the more established villages. The pattern is for a nucleus of original settlers to be joined by other groups who have received some training in kibbutz life and organization from the youth movement. The settlers have tended to be young, with men outnumbering women by a substantial margin. Each collective is operated as though it were a single large household. A general assembly is the governing body, aided by a secretariat and a series of committees.

Living conditions in the kibbutz are austere. One of their prime goals has been the reclamation of increasingly arid and barren land on the Israeli frontier, necessitating not only a joint economic effort but a low living standard on the part of members. All income of the members, from whatever sources, is paid into the common treasury which, in turn, provides a small personal allowance to each member. Clothing is provided from the central supply. The members live in small rooms—sometimes several persons to a room—in which there is a minimum of furniture and no conveniences. Bathrooms and showers are centrally located and jointly used.

There is a complete playing down of differences between persons and between the sexes. All work is regarded as noble and rewarding, with physical labor in the fields being the most noble of all. To the extent to which status differences do exist, administrative and clerical personnel have lower, not higher, status. In the early stages of kibbutz development, women wore masculine clothes and there was no use of makeup or other personal adornment. Women were equally entitled with men to work in the fields and women did, and still do, military service. There is no segregation of the sexes and men and women often share the same sleeping rooms.

Actually some division of labor by sex emerged quite early. Certain of the heavier agricultural tasks simply could not be handled by women, and women disproportionately became involved in the collective's service enterprises—the nurseries, schools, kitchens, dining rooms, and laundries. Increasingly, too, women have come to wear dresses instead of, or along with, shirts and trousers.

The most distinguishing feature of the kibbutz, for our purposes, has been its attitude toward the family and the practices which it evolved to implement that attitude. Talmon hypothesizes that "there is a certain fundamental incompatibility between commitment to a radical revolutionary ideology and intense collective identification on the one hand and family solidarity on the other." [23] The kibbutz has considered itself to be an effort to revolutionize the structure of society and it considers family ties as incompatible with that goal.

---

[23] Op. cit. pp. 260–61.

Family and kinship are based upon ties between the generations and upon the passing of tradition from one generation to the next. Revolutionary movements seek to break the ties with the past. Thus, from the beginning, the kibbutz was antifamilistic. It sought to eliminate the family as an institution and as a social group.

KIBBUTZ MORALITY

The kibbutz completely rejected the morality of middle-class European society. That society's values of chastity and life-long sexual fidelity, combined with a double standard for men and women and widespread premarital and extramarital intercourse, were seen as "bourgeois" and hypocritical. The kibbutz taught that sex relationships should reflect the physical needs and the emotional relationship between the persons involved. There were to be no barriers to premarital sexual intercourse and both sex relationships and marriage should continue only so long as there was a deep emotional relationship. Kibbutz members were seen as free men and women entitled to form and dissolve relationships at will.

The average American is likely to view such liberal norms as an invitation to license. On the contrary, kibbutz morality was restrained and almost ascetic. In most kibbutzim there was very little promiscuity and a disavowal of the erotic. Nudity was accepted, men and women often slept in the same room without erotic complications, showers were shared, and there was little overt preoccupation with sex. Part of the explanation appears to lie in the conservative family backgrounds of most kibbutz members; ideologically liberal, they remained behaviorally tied to the standards of their upbringing. Important, too, was the pervasive commitment to renunciation of physical comfort and pleasure that characterized the kibbutz.

It appears that sexual relationships among youth of high-school age generally were frowned upon. After that, however, young people were free to become involved without censure. No special notice was taken of these relationships and no sanction was given to them. After a period of some experimentation, most youth settled down to one partner and became monogamous. At some point in their relationships they were likely to request that they become a "couple" and have a separate room assigned to them.

MARRIAGE

Marriage, since it implied the development of an ominous solidarity within the kibbutz was given little support. The couple simply applied for a room and moved into it with no fanfare. In many kibbutzim, the concentration upon the development of productive facilities resulted in there being a shortage of sleeping rooms and, in some instances, the couple might have to wait for months for a room to become available. If the shortage was severe they might also have to accept sharing the room occasionally with another person. There were no restrictions upon the right of separation and divorce.

Marriage was accompanied by no discernible shift in status either for the man or for the woman. Wives could keep their maiden names and usually did so. Husbands and wives were not allowed to work at the same jobs and often did not even have the same day off. For some time, radios and electric utensils were not permitted in the rooms, to discourage couples from spending much time there. Virtually all free time was supposed to be spent in the public rooms and areas in interaction with all other members of the collective.

There was a studied avoidance of any public acknowledgment of the relationship. The husband and wife often did not even eat together but ate with other members of the group as if to reinforce their primary loyalty to the kibbutz. The word, marriage, was not used. Instead, they "became a couple." The man referred to his wife as "my young woman" or called her by her given name, and vice versa. The public display of affection was considered to be in bad taste and aroused feelings of shame in the participants. Ordinarily a wedding ceremony was held at the time of the birth of the first child, but only because the state required it for the legitimization of the offspring.

FAMILY AND PARENTAL ROLES

There was no basis for the husband to dominate the wife in marriage. Each remained on the kibbutz rolls as a separate person and each continued to receive his own personal allowance. The husband shared equally in what little housework was required to keep their room in order and both parents assumed responsibility for their children. Anniversaries and birthdays, which would have placed unseemly emphasis on family relationships, ordinarily were not celebrated.

Child-rearing was separated as completely as possible from the marriage relationship. New-born infants went directly from the hospital to the nursery. From birth they lived in special children's houses where they ate, slept, and studied. This arrangement had at least two special advantages. First, it permitted the children to have a much higher standard of living than that of their parents. In spite of the antifamilistic ideology, children were the means to perpetuation of the collectivist ideology and were highly valued; regardless of what privations their parents might undergo, children received the best of food, clothing, and medical care. The separate child care arrangements also left mothers free to continue their productive work in the community and reduced the number of persons required specifically to care for children.

Children generally spent some time each day with their parents, usually the afternoon and early evening hours. Parents also went to the nursery to put their young children to sleep each night. Saturdays and holidays also brought families together. Emotional relationships between parents and their young children were surprisingly close. The relationship was nonauthoritarian, discipline being the function of the persons who supervised the children's upbringing rather than that of the parents. Spiro believes that the attachment of young kibbutz children to their parents was greater than in our own society.[24] The parents provided security and love and played a crucial role in the psychological development of the child.

The relationship between all adults and children was a warm, rewarding one and emphasis was placed upon the fact that the children belonged to the whole community. Children were likely to refer to their parents by their given names instead of by kinship terms while adults referred to all children as "son" and "daughter."

In the children's houses, each age group had its own section. The nurses and teachers were primary sources of indoctrination with the history, norms, and values of the kibbutz. The peer group itself became a primary reference group.[25] Several writers have pointed out that the relationship among the members of each age group became much like that among brothers and sisters in a conjugal family. The psychological character of this bond is reflected in the fact that, as they grow to adulthood, these age groups are voluntarily and almost completely exogamous. There are no barriers to marriage within the group but the young men and women react to one another as though they truly were brothers and sisters.

Thus, in its unique way, the kibbutz went as far as either the Oneida Community or the Soviet Union in attempting to do away with the family. The experiment with the kibbutzim is more recent than either of the others; it is still going on today. Moreover, some of the kibbutzim already have lasted longer than either of the other experiments did. Some kibbutz-born children already are adults and, themselves, full-fledged kibbutz members. But the kibbutzim are changing rapidly. The revolutionary fervor of the 1930's and 1940's is fading. As it fades, the kibbutzim are having to accord a more prominent place to the conjugal family.

---

[24] "Is the Family Universal?—the Israeli Case," p. 70.
[25] A reference group for the individual is one whose norms he takes as his own.

EMERGING KIBBUTZ PATTERNS

As economic conditions in the kibbutzim improve, there is more emphasis upon adequate living standards. People are not so completely absorbed in work as they were and seek to have some personal possessions. The private living quarters begin to reflect the personal tastes of their inhabitants and to become more adequately furnished. Radios in the private quarters become common and kitchen facilities appear. Many families have some "good" clothes which are cared for at home and which are treated as private possessions.[26] Afternoon tea in the family quarters becomes common and some families eat part or all of their meals "at home." Children spend more time with their parents even going so far as to sleep in the parents' quarters.

Part of what is happening here is the result of a generalized process of differentiation occurring within the kibbutz. The kibbutzim are no longer peopled just by the original pioneers; groups of varying backgrounds and ages have been added. Relationships between the subgroups become complicated by intellectual, religious, political, and economic differences.[27] Hostility develops and social distance widens. With the appearance of differences within the group, the family comes to be assigned a place among the subgroups.

Differentiation within the family itself plays a major role. As long as the kibbutz was peopled predominantly by young persons and gained its recruits primarily through immigration, it did not have to cope with the whole range of family ties. As the kibbutz birth rate rose, the phenomenon of generational ties emerged. As parents grow old and children grow to adulthood these ties become more numerous and more complex. Such ties are reflected in changes in the living quarters. The typical private living quarters may now be a semi-detached flat instead of a room. Where grandparents are present, they may be housed in separate buildings or they may have quarters adjoining those of their children. The ties also are reflected in terminological changes. Parents are more likely to address offspring as "my son" and "my daughter" and the terms "my man" and "my woman" are taking on connotations usually associated with the terms "husband" and "wife."

The relationships among the sabras,[28] as they grow into adulthood, also are significantly different from those which prevailed among their parents. There

[26] Eva Rosenfeld, "Institutional Change in the Kibbutz," *Social Problems* 5 (Fall 1957), pp. 110–36.
[27] Melford E. Spiro, "The Sabras and Zionism: A Study in Personality and Ideology," *Social Problems* 5 (Fall 1957), pp. 100–110.
[28] Children born in the kibbutz.

is less de-eroticization than formerly. Women are dressing to appear more attractive and there is more public display of affection by couples. The sex norms have become more conservative. While there still is no taboo on pre-marital intercourse, promiscuity is strongly discouraged, liaisons tend to be short and to precede marriage immediately, and increasingly couples are de-laying sex relationships until marriage. Marriage ceremonies, before beginning life together, are becoming common, and wives increasingly take their hus-band's names. Divorce is becoming rare.

> . . . most of [the kibbutzim], after twenty years, have mellowed some-what as frontier outposts, more resembling—with guest houses now and lobbies with postcard racks and souvenir shops—sedate tourist re-treats. The American stayed overnight in one kibbutz called Kfar Blum in upper Galilee, near the Lebanese border, which was originally settled in the Forties by expatriate American Jews. Arriving on a Sun-day afternoon, he found youths playing soccer in bathing suits on a grassy lawn beside a swimming pool, and after registering, he walked over the grounds until suppertime, on the neat-mown lawns under mimosas and cedars, with bicycles occasionally flickering past on the walkways, mothers pushing children in strollers, a child's gleeful cack-ling coming from one screened back porch. At dinner, a large group of tourists from England sat at a long table near him, wearing Bermuda shorts and yarmulkes and singing Jewish hymns. The plump woman who was waiting on tables this evening brought the American a salad, and when he declined it, she lifted her eyebrows, "So—you're so healthy you don't need the vitamins? . . .
>
> —Marshall Frady, "In Israel: An American Innocent in the Middle East, Part III," *Harper's Magazine*, 242 (January 1971), p. 72.

In short, the antifamilism of the kibbutz movement seems largely to have ended. For a while the kibbutz appeared to have functioned without the family because the community itself functioned as a family. Spiro emphasizes the fact that kibbutz members perceived one another as kin.[29] Now the struc-ture of the family is re-appearing.

THE CONTEMPORARY AMERICAN SCENE

The connections between political, economic, and family changes are diffi-cult to disentangle, but there is some indication that the preoccupation of

[29] Is the Family Universal?—the Israeli Case, pp. 70–71.

American college youth today with developing alternatives to conventional family living has been influenced by the Chinese, Russian, and Israeli experiences. More recently, the hippie phenomenon, the general permissiveness of modern society, and a prolonged period of financial prosperity that permits many people to live without worrying about the future have had something to do with it. There are other factors that we cannot go into here.

We should, however, make some estimate of the impact of the communal living movement upon American society. The impact already is greater than that of the last such movement in the United States which occurred during the 1930's. In the thirties, there were several radical proposals. *Term marriage* would have permitted a couple to marry for five years with an option for renewing for another ten years. If they then elected to stay together they would be permanently married. *Trial* marriage would have permitted a couple to live together for a period of one year to see whether they were suited to one another. *Companionate marriage* would have made it possible for marriages to remain childless and would have accepted divorce by mutual consent.[30] These were radical proposals, but they were not taken seriously by many people and they are almost forgotten today.

Today's communal living experiments may involve around 20,000 people; no reliable figures are available. Even if this guess is off by as many as 10,000 people, it would not make much difference. The number is relatively large, and the people involved are tactically important beyond their numbers; they are predominantly young, well educated, and potential leaders. They could represent the shape of the future. They could achieve what Oneida, the Russians, and the Kibbutzniks did not.

On the other hand, there are few signs, yet, of significant long-term change. The communal movement is only about a decade old, and many such movements in the past have endured for at least a generation. Second, although the total number of people involved in the movement is large, most of the individual groups are quite small and without stable organization. Many members remain with the group for only a few months to a year or two. The absence of a firm ideological base contributes to this transiency.

Many of today's communes are not even particularly radical compared to past attempts. The drug influence has been over-emphasized and already appears to be waning. Moreover, many members are surprisingly monogamous. The members who are past about age 25 often are married and function, within the commune, as nuclear family units. Finally, the participants are overwhelmingly youthful. They have not yet confronted the problems of

[30] Benjamin B. Lindsey, *The Companionate Marriage*, New York: Boni and Liveright, 1927.

child-bearing, child-rearing, and aging. As today's members become parents and middle-aged, we will get some indication of how stable the movement is.

We can only conclude that the evidence is not yet in. Proponents on either side of the issue can make a good case. History offers some clues. We turn to those in the next chapter.

Summary

The United States is witnessing a search for alternatives to conventional family living. Many such experiments have been tried before.

The Oneida Community was founded in 1848 by John Humphrey Noyes, with whose life and teachings the community is inseparably linked. Noyes preached "perfectionism" in life here on earth and saw monogamous marriage and private property as barriers to the unselfishness required for fulfillment of the perfectionist doctrine. His system of "complex marriage" was based on the assumption that all men should love all women and vice versa. Young men were initiated into sex relationships by older women and young women were taught by older men, according to the principle of ascendance, the proper spiritual techniques for making love and avoiding the complications of pregnancy. Only persons approved by a central committee were entitled to become parents. Children were reared, apart from their parents, in a separate wing of the mansion house.

The community prospered financially but encountered resistance from the surrounding society. Children of the community were ridiculed by outsiders and there were rumors of impending legal prosecution of the adults. Some of the children failed to accept completely the teachings of the community. In 1877, Noyes resigned as leader of the community and by 1880 it had broken up.

The Soviet family experiment followed the Bolshevik revolution in 1917, and barely lasted into the 1930's. The Soviets sought to do away with the family as a corrupt bourgeois institution. Marriage and divorce became simple matters of registration with a government bureau, and even registration was not required. Abortion was made legal, birth control was encouraged, and children were urged to break ties with parents who evidenced counterrevolutionary tendencies.

By the middle 1930's a reverse trend had set in. Rising divorce rates, falling birth rates, personal irresponsibility, and rampant juvenile delinquency were by-products which the Soviets had not counted on. A series of laws from 1936 to 1944 re-emphasized the solemnity and permanence of marriage and made divorce very difficult. The equality of women was upheld and a series of allowances were provided to parents of large families. The Soviet Union now sees a stable family system as a bulwark of socialism.

The kibbutzim are agricultural collectives in Israel. Communistic in ideology, they sought to eliminate the family as a competing source of identification. All production and consumption were collectivized and all recognition of kinship ties was discouraged. Marriage virtually was done away with, couples simply applying for a room when they wished to make their relationships permanent. Such relationships also could be dissolved at will. When children were born they were reared in groups apart, only visiting with their parents at prescribed times.

Time has seen changes in the kibbutzim. Marriage has become somewhat regularized, more adequate quarters are provided for families, and more functions are being transferred to the home. Extended family relationships are being formed and contact with kin outside of the kibbutz is increasing.

Attempts to eliminate the family are relatively few, small, and short-lived. The large-scale Soviet experiment did not last for more than a generation.

The contemporary communal living experiment appears to have been influenced, ideologically, by the Chinese, Russian, and kibbutz experiments. It is far too early to predict the outcome of this latest effort.

SUGGESTED READINGS

Ald, Roy, *The Youth Communes*, New York: Tower Publications, 1970. One of the very few comprehensive analyses of the new communal movement. Its general thrust casts doubt on their viability.

Carden, Maren Lockwood, *Oneida: Utopian Community to Modern Corporation*, Baltimore: The Johns Hopkins Press, 1969. A detailed analysis of the Oneida experiment and its transformation into a modern industrial corporation.

Geiger, H. Kent, *The Family in Soviet Russia*, Cambridge, Mass.: Harvard University Press, 1968. The Soviet family experiment is analyzed in terms of Marxist theory and is brought up to date. From the Russian Research Center at Harvard University.

Leon, Dan, *The Kibbutz: A New Way of Life*, Oxford, Eng.: Pergamon Press, 1969. An insider's view of one of the four national federations of kibbutzim. Traces the movement up to about the Six-Day War of 1967.

Robertson, Constance Noyes, ed., *Oneida Community: An Autobiography, 1851–1876*, Syracuse: Syracuse University Press, 1970. A granddaughter of John Humphrey Noyes tells the history of the community based upon the community's files and its newspapers. A sympathetic and interesting account.

Samuel, Edwin, *The Structure of Society in Israel*, New York: Random House, 1969. Places the kibbutz in the context of other Israeli institutions and in historical perspective.

Sorlin, Pierre, *The Soviet People and Their Society*, New York: Frederick A. Praeger, 1969. A history of the Soviet Union from 1917 to the present. Places the family experiment in broad institutional and historical context.

FILMS

Serafima Kotova (National Council of American-Soviet Friendship, Inc., 156 Fifth Avenue, New York, N. Y. 10010), 20 minutes. Pictorial story of a Soviet woman, made an orphan in World War II. Mrs. Kotova works in a textile mill, where she is now a forelady. She is also a Deputy of the Supreme Soviet of the Soviet Federation. Film shows her relationships with her husband and her young son.

A *Great Family on a Collective Farm* (National Council of American-Soviet Friendship, Inc., 156 Fifth Avenue, New York 10010), 20 minutes. The daily life of a family with 6 children and 30 grandchildren on a prosperous collective farm. Methods of payment to farmers and collective social services are discussed.

QUESTIONS AND PROJECTS

1. Approximately how many communes are there in the United States today? What is the average size of those communes?
2. Describe the role of John Humphrey Noyes in the development and maintenance of the Oneida Community. What is meant by the statement, "Noyes was a charismatic leader"?
3. What was the doctrine of "perfectionism"? How was it relevant to the establishment of the Oneida Community?
4. Describe the institution of "complex marriage"; the operation of the "principle of ascendance"; the program of "stirpiculture."
5. What factors led to the breakup of the Oneida Community? What are the implications of the Oneida experience for family sociology?
6. When did the Soviet family experiment begin? How long did it last?
7. Why was the Soviet regime opposed to the family? What steps did it take to eliminate the family?
8. What were the effects of the Soviet family legislation of the 1920's on divorce rates and birth rates? upon the status of women? upon juvenile delinquency?
9. What legislative countermeasures were taken from 1936 to 1944? Describe the procedure required for securing a divorce in the Soviet Union today.
10. Sketch briefly the history of the kibbutzim in Israel. What is a kibbutz? Describe the economic organization, the level of living, and the ideology of the kibbutz.
11. Describe the patterns of sexual morality in the kibbutz. Was there anything paradoxical in sexual standards and sexual behavior? What? How do you explain it? What changes in moral standards have been occurring in recent years?

12. Describe the relationship of "couples" early in the kibbutz. Describe the child-rearing practices. What specific techniques were used to de-emphasize kinship?
13. What has been the long-term kibbutz experience in attempting to do away with the family? What trends appear likely in the kibbutz in the future?
14. Evaluate the communal living experiment in the United States today in terms of its probable endurance. What factors suggest that it will endure? that it will not?

Part | II

HISTORICAL PERSPECTIVE

6 | The Development of Western Family Organization: I

. . . Nowhere is this more evident than in the change in the nature of the family. In the traditional world, work and home life were one, and the family was both an economic and a social unit. Not only that, but it was the setting for almost all the other social functions as well—welfare, recreation, education and religious instruction.

The modern world has witnessed the separation of the family, as an institution, from most of these functions. There is, more radically, a separation of family from occupation, whether it be the breakup of the family farm, the family business, the family enterprise or the family tradition, such as medicine, law, carpentry, fishing. Education has been taken over almost entirely by the schools, recreation primarily by commercial enterprises, welfare by the government or by social institutions. The family is now focused largely on fulfilling psychological and emotional needs. . . .

The change in the nature of the family—historically the most crucial of all human institutions—has had a contradictory effect on a person's sense of individualism. In a psychological sense, as the ties with a family have weakened or been cut altogether, the feeling of individualism has been enhanced. To the classic question of identity—"Who are you?"—a traditional person would answer: "I am the son of my father." But today a person says, "I am I. I come out of myself, and in choice and action I make myself." The great thrust of the American character—the urge, the compulsion to strike out on one's own, to cut away from the father and even to surpass him—has been one of the richest of the sources of dynamism in in American life. . . .[1]

IN our analysis of the Chinese family system, we found that change was very slow until about a hundred years ago—so slow that we could use a single model to describe the family over a period of 2000 years. Not so with the family system of the West. We can trace our family system back 3000 years

[1] Daniel Bell, "Toward A Communal Society," *Life Magazine* 62 (May 12, 1967), p. 114.

or so, and, in the process, can learn a great deal about how the American family functions today. During that 3000 years the focus of our interest shifts many times and the family system changes from a strongly patriarchal, patrilineal, patrilocal, polygynous one to a nearly equalitarian, monogamous, bilateral, conjugal one. Change has been rapid and continuous. We will begin with the ancient Hebrews, Greeks, and Romans and briefly trace the evolution of the Western family to its contemporary American form.

The Ancient Hebrew Family System

We begin with the ancient Hebrews because their family system is the earliest direct antecedent of our own system, about which there is comprehensive and reliable knowledge. The earliest Hebrew records go back as far as written language itself, approximately 4000 years. Not surprisingly the earliest records are fragmentary and difficult to interpret. By the dawn of history proper, the Hebrews were a nomadic desert people with a pastoral economy. They roamed the countryside seeking adequate pasture for their herds and flocks and maintaining an elaborate kinship organization. Beyond the family itself, there was a *sib*, which was a group of kinsmen related through males (a patrilineal descent group), and a *clan*, which included the wives of the men as well. Several related clans made up a *tribe*, and twelve tribes constituted the nation of Israel.[2]

By about the twelfth century before Christ, the Hebrews began to develop agriculture and to give up their nomadic existence in favor of settling in villages and towns. As they did so, the old tribal organization was gradually replaced by a more centralized organization around a king.

During the nomadic period, the Hebrew family was patriarchal, patrilineal, patrilocal, polygynous, and extended. There is evidence of a quite different form of organization before the dawn of recorded history,[3] and the patriarchy was considerably modified as settled agriculture developed.

[2] Stuart A. Queen and Robert W. Habenstein, *The Family in Various Cultures*, Philadelphia: J. B. Lippincott Company, 1967, pp. 143–4.

[3] Some scholars believe that the Hebrew family once was both matrilineal and matrilocal. The generations of Esau are traced, in Genesis, through his wives rather than through himself, and Leah and Rachel are referred to as the women who did "build the house of Israel." The incest taboos permitted the marriage of half brothers and sisters where the common parent was the father but not where the common parent was the mother. Certain of the patriarchs and their wives are also known to have lived with their wives' fathers over long periods of time. See Queen and Habenstein, ibid. p. 143; and Panos D. Bardis, "Family Forms and Variations Historically Considered," in Harold T. Christensen, ed., *Handbook of Marriage and the Family*, Chicago: Rand McNally, 1964, p. 416.

PATRIARCHY

The Hebrew family was quite a strong patriarchy, with the authority of the father being nearly absolute. All women were held under the rigid control of one or more males, the only exception being that of a widowed mother. The sons were trained in respect and obedience to their mother, whereas other women were considered to be their property.[4] The husband could put his wife to death if he discovered her in adultery, but not for any other reason. All of this implies a low status for women, and their status was indeed low. Yet, there is little evidence that Hebrew women were abused. On the contrary, wives appear to have been highly regarded and often to have wielded a great deal of power. Marriages often were made to cement ties between two extended families, and the wife's family retained an interest in her welfare.

The father had even greater power over his children. The familiar story of Abraham's near-sacrifice of Isaac indicates that he held, literally, the power of life and death. Hebrew children were expected to be obedient to and respectful of their parents, and the Mosaic law specifically provided that persistently disobedient children should be put to death. That there was some limitation on the father's power is indicated by the fact that a stubborn or gluttonous son was to be stoned to death by his fellow Israelites after the father had testified against him; but he was not to be killed by the father himself.[5]

The father could marry off his children at will and was permitted to sell their labor. Theoretically, the young persons' consent to a marriage was required, but it appears seldom to have been refused. The father's power again was restricted in that he was forbidden to make his daughter a prostitute [6] and could not sell his children to foreigners (non-Hebrews). The offense of Joseph's brothers in selling him was twofold: first, they usurped the prerogative of the patriarch; and, second, they sold him to foreigners.

POLYGYNY

The Hebrews practised both polygyny and concubinage. Several wives appear to have been common among the patriarchs and kings, with additional concubines being taken from among servant and slave girls. One rationaliza-

---

[4] Willystine Goodsell, A History of Marriage and the Family, New York: The MacMillan Company, 1939, p. 54.
[5] Deuteronomy 21:18–21.
[6] Leviticus 19:29.

tion for the practice of concubinage was the high value placed upon having sons. Barren wives might give their female servants to their husbands as concubines, claiming the concubines' children as their own. The concubines were treated well and sometimes were raised to the status of wife, particularly after a wife died. The children of concubines could inherit, though not so much as the children of the wives.

Polygyny was not without its problems, though it did not yield completely to monogamy until the Middle Ages. Some jealousy developed among wives and concubines and it was common for each wife and her children to have a separate dwelling.[7] Sororal polygyny helped to keep antagonisms in check. The vast majority of the Hebrews must have been monogamous, of course. Beyond the biological facts of the sex ratio, the custom of bride price restricted polygyny to the relatively well-to-do.

BETROTHAL AND MARRIAGE

According to Talmudic law, the minimum ages for marriage were thirteen for boys and twelve for girls. Fathers could betroth their children at younger ages but the nuptials could not take place until they became of age. In earliest times betrothal and marriage were not distinct. Betrothal was regarded as the beginning of marriage, even though the marriage was not consummated until later,[8] and sometimes nuptials were not even held.

Gradually, betrothal became distinct from marriage and, when the parties were of age, one year commonly elapsed between betrothal and marriage. Betrothal took two forms: the transfer of money or the preparation of a written instrument. *Kaseph* involved the man giving a coin to the woman and saying, "Be thou consecrated to me." Kaseph is believed to be a symbol of earlier explicit wife purchase among the Hebrews. The other ceremony, *kiddushin*, involved the man's giving the woman a document which probably read, "I do hereby betroth thee according to the law of Moses and Israel." Two witnesses were required in either case, and a benediction was given either by the bride's father or by a rabbi.

The marriage ceremony (nuptials) was a completely private family affair in which the bride was transported to the groom's house to receive the benediction. The presence of a rabbi was not required, but ten witnesses were necessary. By the first century B.C., the *ketubah*, or marriage contract, came to be a document separate from the betrothal agreement. In addition to the mar-

---

[7] Genesis 31:33.
[8] Sexual intercourse with another person after betrothal was regarded as adultery and was punished as such.

riage vows, the ketubah stated the bride price, or *mohar*, and specified that it had been paid; it enumerated the property which the bride brought to the marriage (the dowry); it defined the mode of inheritance in case no children were born to the marriage; and it specified the wife's right to support from her husband and his obligation to have sexual intercourse regularly with her.[9]

Marriage was extremely highly valued among the ancient Hebrews and to remain celibate was regarded as a religious crime. There are a number of reasons for the high value place upon marriage. First, marriage was regarded as a family matter. Marriage was designed to produce sons so that a man's house "should not die out of Israel"; it was not regarded primarily as a means of producing personal satisfactions for the man and woman involved. Second, marriage was seen as a more acceptable alternative than illicit sexual activity.[10] Third, the Hebrews were keepers of herds and flocks, and children, especially sons, were economic assets to their fathers.

The importance attached to having sons was institutionalized in the levirate. If a man died without having sons, the widow was expected to marry the deceased husband's brother. The first son born to the brother and the widow was then regarded as the offspring of the deceased brother. Since the Hebrews were polygynous, the levirate was possible even if the brother was already married. The only way that the brother could escape the duty of the levirate was to humiliate himself through the custom of *chalitza*, according to which the widow loosened the brother's shoe, spat in his face, and accused him of failing to do his duty to his brother—all this in a public ceremony. The levirate prevailed among the Hebrews well into the Middle Ages.[11]

DESCENT AND INHERITANCE

By the time of the patriarchs, patrilineal descent and inheritance were well established among the Hebrews. During the earliest period there was some-

[9] The husband's obligation to have regular sexual intercourse with each of his wives placed a practical limitation upon the number of wives a man could take. Both husband and wife could be fined if they failed in their marital duties toward each other. More important than the right to sexual satisfaction was the great importance attached to having children. If sexual intercourse were not had regularly, the production of children would be threatened.

[10] Sexual attitudes among the Hebrews were characterized by considerable prudery and by a preoccupation with avoiding prostitution and perversion. Nudity was regarded as shameful; only foreign women were ever acceptable as prostitutes; and sodomy was considered repulsive, yet may have been widely practised. Students will recall the story of Lot and the destruction of the cities of Sodom and Gomorrah.

[11] The crime of Onan (onanism), which is widely regarded today as masturbation, was actually Onan's refusal to impregnate his brother's widow. In his relations with the widow, Onan practised coitus interruptus.

thing very close to complete primogeniture. The eldest son received the father's blessing and inherited almost all of the father's property.[12] Students will remember the story of Rebekah's and Jacob's treachery in inducing the nearly blind Isaac to give the blessing to Jacob instead of to his older brother, Esau. During this period daughters did not inherit.

Somewhat later, as agriculture developed, it was provided that the eldest son should receive a double portion, with all of the other sons inheriting equally.[13] If there was no son, property passed to the daughters, and if there were no children the property passed to brothers or uncles.[14] Sometimes if there were no sons the patriarch would marry his daughter to one of his male slaves and make the slave his heir.[15] The property thus passed from patriarch to grandson with the slave serving as intermediary.

Further clues to the importance of maternal kin among the Hebrews and to a possible earlier matrilineal stage are found in the incest taboos. The prohibited relationships extended to both consanguineal and affinal [16] kin. The prohibited relationships did not extend very far, for marriage between first cousins and between step-brothers and step-sisters was permitted.

DIVORCE

Until nearly the time of Christ, the Hebrew husband had almost unlimited power to divorce his wife, while she had no right to divorce him. The Mosaic law provided, simply, that the husband should hand his wife a bill of divorcement stating, "Be thou divorced from me," and send her out of the house.[17]

Over the centuries, resistance developed to the husband's power to thus repudiate his wife and, by the time of Christ, the public authorities would accept divorce only on certain specified grounds: adultery, indecency, refusal to cohabit, barrenness, change of religion, refusal to observe the ritual laws, and insulting the husband. Gradually the wife also was provided with rights of divorce. By the Roman period she could divorce her husband for: impotence,

---

[12] Bardis, op. cit. p. 419.

[13] Deuteronomy 21:15-18.

[14] Numbers 27:1-11.

[15] The extended family group often was quite large. In addition to the patriarch, his wives and concubines, their unmarried children, married sons and their wives and children, there often were servants and slaves, and sometimes even nonrelatives who had placed themselves under the authority and protection of the patriarch. Servants and slaves usually were well treated—almost as family members. Consequently, making a son-in-law and heir of a slave did not seem too unusual.

[16] Affinal kin (affinity) are those related through marriage rather than through parenthood.

[17] Deuteronomy 24:1-2.

change of religion, refusal to support her, commission of a serious crime, extreme dissolution on the part of the husband, and affliction with a loathsome disease (leprosy). Significantly, the wife could not divorce her husband for adultery. Later, the rabbis also secured the power forcibly to separate couples either for adultery or for barrenness.

Women who were unjustly divorced by their husbands did not suffer greatly. For one thing they became free agents. They were no longer under the power of either their fathers or their husbands. They were also entitled to return of their dowries, which provided them with economic livelihood. If they were divorced for cause, however—and the causes were, by modern standards, trivial—then the divorced wives lost their dowries and suffered loss of status as well.

THE GRADUAL DEVELOPMENT OF PUBLIC CONTROL

The traditional Hebrew family was an organization of great strength and unity. It existed in a social context where there were no other elaborately developed institutions. Political power was held largely by the patriarchs; the economy was rudimentary; even religion was primarily a family matter. The patriarch served as priest at worship and presided over the various ceremonial activities.[18] There was not yet a separate class of rabbis. Under these conditions the family performed many functions for its members and appears to have been a strong and stable unit.

Gradually, with the development of settled agriculture, other sources of power arose to challenge the family's control of its affairs. In the eighth century B.C., Israel was conquered by the Assyrians. Then in the sixth century B.C. came the Babylonian conquest, and eventually Israel fell under the power of Rome. The public authorities, as they expanded their control over the society, undertook increasing regulation of marriage and family matters.

Gradually, too, a separate class of religious functionaries—the rabbis—emerged. At first the rabbis did not challenge the power of the patriarchs. But gradually they interpreted the scriptures to limit the power of husbands over wives and of fathers over their children. A body of rabbinical law emerged which became the foundation for marriage and family life.

The changes brought about by the public authorities and the rabbis may be illustrated by the transformation of the custom of wife purchase and the accompanying changes in the status of women. In earliest times, husbands

---

[18] There is some possibility that, in prehistory, the Hebrews were ancestor worshippers. The graven images referred to in the Old Testament are thought by some to be symbols of ancestors. Moreover, the family burial ground was regarded as a sacred place.

apparently purchased their wives outright—almost as they would purchase cattle. Gradually the bride price became compensation to the girl's father for loss of her services and a guarantee of her good treatment. The bride price might be paid either in service or in money. Jacob, it will be remembered, worked for Laban for fourteen years in order to marry Leah and Rachel. The money cost often was 50 shekels. During this period women were regarded as chattels.

The rabbis sought to protect women through the development of the ketubah, or marriage contract. Betrothal and marriage became differentiated, and the money which traded hands at betrothal was reduced to a single, symbolic copper coin. Instead, the ketubah spelled out the economic interests and rights of both families. As the rabbis took control of marriages, the parties became less the two families and more the particular man and woman involved. The ketubah listed the amount of the bride price, which was gradually transformed into a *dower* right—a sum of money or property which was to be held for the wife in the event of the husband's death or her unjust divorce. The dowry too—essentially the wife's family's economic contribution to the marriage—was listed. The husband was given life use (usufruct) of the dowry but, again, the wife retained an interest in it and might have it returned to her if she was divorced by her husband. The balance of power between the husband and wife shifted, and women came to be considered as legal persons with legal rights as well as responsibilities.

The Hebrew family remained a strong unit right up until the time of Christ; but the patriarchy of old was increasingly restricted under the influence of outside authority. And, in the meantime, the seat of European civilization and the source of political power shifted to Greece and Rome.

The Ancient Greek Family System

The detailed origins of Greek culture, like those of the Hebrews, are lost in antiquity. It is believed that the mainland of Greece was settled first by voyagers from Crete, around 1600 B.C. These settlers were invaded successively by the Ionians, a blue-eyed, fair-haired people from the north, by the nomadic Achaeans, and by the also nomadic Dorians. By the seventh century B.C. these three groups had become a series of self-governing city-states, bearing a largely common culture. During the fifth century B.C. the Greek city-states went to war with and defeated the Persian Empire to the east, and Greece reached its zenith. A series of civil wars between the city-states finally weakened the empire, and by 146 B.C. Greece had become just a Roman province.

Description of the family system of ancient Greece is complicated both by continuous social change and by major differences in the patterns of Athens and Sparta. During the earliest (Homeric) period, Greece's economy was mainly agricultural and its family system reflected that economic base. The family was a strong patriarchy in which divorce and other forms of family pathology were quite uncommon. Beyond the extended family there existed the *gens*, a clan consisting of all of the extended families which traced descent from a common ancestor. The gens established the legitimacy of children born within it, sought to prevent the alienation of land from its constituent units, and saw to it that legitimate heirs were provided. The Greeks early became organized into city-states and the dominant family patterns became those of the cities of Athens and Sparta. During the "golden age" of Greece its family system was an urban one, evolved from its patriarchal land-oriented precursor.

The Athenian and Spartan patterns present major variations on the general theme of ancient Greek culture. Athens was an aristocratic state in which the cultivation of knowledge was highly regarded. Most of the Greek contributions to philosophy, literature, architecture, and engineering originated here. The Athenians also emphasized the development of athletic skills, but Sparta made virtually a fetish of these. The Spartans were exceedingly militaristic, emphasizing the production of warriors and the development of courage. Spartan boys at the age of seven generally left their parental homes to live in military-style barracks, where they underwent arduous physical training and where they continued to live during most of their adult lives. The separation of husbands and wives entailed by this kind of existence produced very different relationships between the sexes than obtained in Athens. Spartan women were much freer, much more aggressive, and much more nearly equal with their husbands.

In the ensuing description of Greek family patterns, the emphasis will be upon the common core of culture shared by rural and urban, Athenian and Spartan groups alike. Where variations appear, we shall try to point them out.

PATRIARCHY

The Greek father, like his Hebrew counterpart, was exceedingly powerful. Unlike the Hebrew patriarch, however, the Greek father did not hold power in his own right. Instead, his power derived from his position as trustee of the family estates and from his role as priest in the family worship of ancestors. Membership in the Greek family was based upon being eligible to worship the ancestors and coming under the control of the family head.

During the early agricultural period there is evidence that women had relatively high status—that they were virtually the equals of their husbands. However, their status worsened very early and, by the "golden age," women were little better off than slaves.

Athenian men dominated women almost completely. Their women generally were defined as being biologically, intellectually, and emotionally inferior to men. They were minors having no legal status, were poorly educated, and were inadequate companions to their learned husbands. Mature men of about thirty years of age often were married to adolescent girls just a few years past puberty. Once married, women were confined to the women's apartments in the house and were unable to leave the house without the husband's permission. On the streets they had to be veiled and to be accompanied by a slave who acted as chaperone. When the husband had guests, women never were permitted to eat with them. The husband held power of life and death over his wife only in the event of adultery. If he discovered them in the act, the husband could kill both the wife and her lover without penalty. If he did not kill the wife immediately, he was permitted only to beat her and confine her to the house.

Spartan wives during the early period also occupied a very inferior position and were treated without sentiment. There was almost no wedding ceremonial. The bride was taken forcibly to the groom's house,[19] where a female servant cut her hair in ragged boyish style, dressed her in men's clothing and shoes, and left her in the dark to await her husband. The husband visited her for sexual purposes and little else. Even in their sex relationship, the emphasis was upon the production of heirs and not upon physical and emotional satisfaction. For companionship and pleasure the husband turned to a special class of women who were provided for the purpose.

The father's power over his children was even more extreme. In the early period he could expose his infants, could sell their labor, and could bestow them in marriage without their consent. Some writers have maintained that the father had full authority to determine whether any given child lived or died[20] and this may have been so. It seems likely, however, that the father's right to expose an infant was linked to the Grecian emphasis on the produc-

[19] There are many references in Greek literature to "wife capture" and there has been much speculation whether this was not the prevailing means of mate selection in the prehistoric era. The Spartan ceremonial just described, and the Athenian custom of carrying a bride, feigning resistance, over the threshold are sometimes interpreted as symbolic of the earlier wife capture. There is no way to tell, of course, whether a general practice of wife capture ever existed.

[20] Manuel C. Elmer, *The Sociology of the Family*, Boston: Ginn and Company, 1945, p. 80.

tion of healthy children who could inherit property and carry on the family line. Exposure seems to have been limited mainly to illegitimate children and to deformed or sickly children. There is also indication that girls were more likely to be exposed than boys. Girls could not serve in the military, and their marriage, during the later period, carried heavy dowry obligations.

During the early period, the Greek father could sell both sons and daughters. Although this is not certain, it is generally believed today that he was not empowered to sell them into genuine slavery but could sell them into indentured servitude while they were growing to adulthood. Even this power was restricted as Greek civilization developed.

In the early period, too, sons remained under the father's control for as long as the father lived. The father did have the power to "emancipate" the son through a ceremony which excluded the son from worship of the family ancestors and released him from paternal authority. Sons were highly valued, however, and emancipation was rare. Later on it became common to emancipate the son when he reached maturity.

INHERITANCE AND DESCENT

The system of patrilineal descent was tied to the practice of ancestor worship.[21] Only men could carry on the worship of the ancestors, so descent was traced through males only. This extreme form of patrilineal descent in which relationship is traced only through males is known as *agnation*. Primogeniture existed with landed property, all of the family estates being inherited by the oldest son. The younger sons left home with the movable property; daughters did not inherit at all.

Great emphasis was placed upon the provision of legitimate heirs. If a man produced daughters but no sons, his daughter was required to marry the father's brother. Since the Greeks were monogamous, this sometimes meant that the brother had to divorce his wife in order to marry his niece. Or the father might give the daughter in marriage to some other man on condition that the couple's first son be given to him as his own.[22]

Spartan inheritance laws were more liberal. Women were permitted to inherit land as well as movable property, and one of the effects of Greece's series of wars was increasingly to concentrate property in the hands of women.

[21] As with the Hebrews, it is believed that the Greeks may have practised matrilineal descent in prehistoric times.

[22] In the more liberal Sparta, older men who were childless sometimes encouraged their younger wives to have intercourse with younger men so that they might become pregnant.

MARRIAGE

Marriage was regarded as a sacred obligation. It was the means to continued worship of the ancestors and it provided for the inheritance of the family property. Celibacy was regarded as a legal offense; both Athens and Sparta passed laws punishing those who remained single.

During the Homeric period marriage was a simple affair. The groom made "gifts" to the bride's father—a not very subtle form of bride price—and the girl was handed over to her husband. At this stage, the wife ordinarily brought no property to the marriage.

As Greece developed, the arrangements became more elaborate. Betrothal and marriage became separated. The betrothal was a business contract between the parents, setting forth the bride price which was to be paid and the dowry which the woman was to bring to the marriage. The husband was permitted to administer the wife's dowry but it was returned to her at the husband's death or in the event of her unjust divorce.

The Athenian wedding ceremony was an extravagant religious affair which began with ritual preparations by the bride and groom. The principal ceremonies occurred either in the bride's home or in a temple. There was a ritual eating of sesame-seed cakes to ensure the fertility of the marriage, the bride's father offered sacrifices to the gods of marriage, and he handed his daughter over to her husband by releasing her from his own power and from the worship of his ancestors. Then there was an elaborate parade to the groom's home, more ritual eating, and the commending of the bride to the husband's ancestors. It is important to note that no special religious functionaries participated. The fathers acted as priests; marriage was a private family affair.

Harlots we keep for the sake of pleasure only, concubines for daily service, but wives for bearing us legitimate children and acting as loyal guardians of our households.

—Demosthenes

CONCUBINAGE AND PROSTITUTION

The Greeks were firmly monogamous [23] but supplemented monogamy with institutionalized concubinage and widespread prostitution. Concubines were

[23] Bardis reports that both polygyny and polyandry may have existed in prehistoric times. Op. cit. pp. 423-4.

taken by wealthy men generally from among the family slaves or from among women who had been captured in war. The concubines had lower status even than wives and were not permitted to worship the family ancestors. Their children were not true family members and could not inherit property.

Perhaps the best known women of ancient Greece are the *hetaerae*. The *hetaerae*—trained from childhood in knowledge, the arts, and social graces—were captured women of noble birth from other peoples or were Greek girls who had survived exposure and who were then reared to be the social and sexual companions of wealthy men. These women were remarkably free in their daily activities, were highly regarded, and often wielded power and influence. Their status stands in marked contrast to that of wives who were poorly educated and lacking in social graces.

For the poorer Greeks, there was a large class of ordinary prostitutes. Again these were exposed girls from poor families or captured women. The city-states licensed the houses of prostitution and heavily taxed the prostitutes' income. The taxing was less a matter of morality than of financing the state.

DIVORCE

If divorce existed at all during the earliest period, it was very rare. Even during Homeric times the indissolubility of marriage was emphasized. Gradually, however, the husband's right to repudiate his wife emerged. He had only to state his displeasure with her in the presence of witnesses. Such repudiations apparently were rare both because they were strongly disapproved and because they necessitated the husband's returning the wife's dowry. On either of two grounds—adultery or barrenness—the husband was regarded as justified in divorcing his wife. Gradually the law came to demand annulment in the event of flagrant adultery on the part of the wife.

At least during the period of urbanization, the wife also had limited rights of divorce. She could not, however, divorce her husband for adultery no matter how flagrant or continuous such behavior might be. Only if his actions involved physical cruelty to her or gross neglect of his family was she entitled to seek divorce. Even then she had to seek permission from the public authorities, which she could not do unless her husband permitted her to leave the house to do so.

The Roman Family System

According to legend, Rome was founded in 753 B.C. Little is known of this period, except that Rome was a village occupied by Latin-speaking tribes.

Gradually these tribes increased in military power and conquered the whole of what today is Italy. They adopted the Greek alphabet and created the Roman Empire.

The development of the Roman family system is even more markedly progressive than that which occurred among the Hebrews and the Greeks. For purposes of convenience, it is conventional to divide Roman history into two main periods: from 753 B.C. until the close of the Punic Wars in 202 B.C., and from 202 B.C. until the fall of the Empire in the third century A.D.

BEFORE THE PUNIC WARS

The early Roman family was the strongest patriarchy of which we have any knowledge. Descent was patrilineal. Marriage was monogamous, and a three-generation extended family was common.

Patriarchy. The family was a large, strong and stable unit. It performed many functions for its members and those functions were concentrated in the hands of the patriarch, the *pater familias.* The father was priest in the practice of ancestor worship, he was the only "legal" person in the family, and he held sole ownership of all real and movable property.

The father's power over his children was called *potestas* and extended throughout his lifetime; some of the most famous Roman generals were still under the *potestas* of their fathers and were unable to control their own property or earnings. Newborn infants were brought before their fathers to determine whether they should live or die. If the father decided to expose them, they were left in the open countryside either to die or to be taken as slaves to some other family. The father also had the power to sell his children into slavery, to banish them from the country, or to kill them. Before he could kill them, he was obligated to consult with the adult males of his *gens*, but, after doing so and in spite of their recommendations, he was free to do as he wished.

The father could both marry off and have his children divorced without their consent and even against their will. Even married sons and their sons remained under the patriarch's power. The only escape from *potestas* for the son, until the father's death, was through emancipation, a mock sale which freed the son to become a *pater familias* himself. Sons were highly valued, however, and emancipation ceremonies were rare.

Daughters also fell under *potestas* and, at marriage, simply were transferred to the *manus* (hand) of their husbands. Theoretically, no Roman woman was ever a free agent. The husband was empowered to name, in his will, a guardian for his wife after his own death. Since women were not legal persons, the husband was responsible for any crimes his wife might commit and he could punish her accordingly. If she caused him financial loss he could sell her labor to pay it. After consulting with the adult males of both his *gens* and his wife's, he could kill her. If she committed adultery, he could kill her immediately.

Paradoxically, Roman women had generally high status. They were the respected mistresses of their households, they were free to come and go as they wished, and they were the social and intellectual companions of their husbands. Their status is symbolized by the phrase which they customarily uttered upon being carried over the threshold by their new husbands: "Where thou art lord, I am lady." In the home, the Roman woman was located not in women's apartments but in the atrium, the central room of the house.

Descent and Inheritance. The *familia* was a unit of the *gens*, a patrilineal descent group. Like the Greeks, the Romans practiced *agnation*, tracing descent through males only. The *gens* was composed of all *familia* which traced descent from a common ancestor. In the very earliest times the *gens* held property, provided guardians for dependent or defective members, conducted religious services, maintained burial grounds, and even passed resolutions which were binding upon its members.

In ancient Rome, there was no place for unattached persons. Everyone belonged to a household and came under the control of the family head. At the death of the *pater familias* each adult son inherited an equal share of the estate and set up his own *familia*. Later on, the widow and the daughters who lived at home and were under *potestas* came to receive equal shares with the sons. Such daughters then had to have the consent of the *gens* in order to marry and they were not permitted to sell or otherwise dispose of their shares of the estate.

Marriage. Marriage was as important to the early Romans as it had been to the Hebrews and Greeks before them. The emphasis upon ancestor worship and continuing the family line made of marriage both a patriotic and a religious duty. Single persons were heavily taxed, and widowed and divorced persons were urged to remarry. Girls, particularly, were married young. Often men of twenty-five were married to girls of fifteen. Marriage forms and ceremonies varied according to the social status of the participants. The highest status group were the patricians, or Roman citizens. Then came the plebians and, finally, the slaves.

Betrothal appears to have been common among the patricians, although it was not so binding as among the Greeks and Hebrews. Breaking of such an engagement, while disapproved of, could be done by either family without penalty. It was not unusual to betroth girls of ten or twelve, and if such girls were subsequently to engage in sexual intercourse they were considered to be guilty of adultery.

The major function of the betrothal was the setting of the girl's dowry, which, with the passage of time, tended to become increasingly large. The dowry ordinarily was controlled by the husband, who received the income from it but was not permitted actually to own it or dispose of it. At his death, or upon divorce, the dowry was returned to the girl's family.

There were two basic forms of marriage: *matrimonium justum* and *matrimonium nonjustum*. Until 445 B.C., *matrimonium justum* could be entered into only by two Roman citizens; after that, it could be arranged between a citizen and a plebian. *Matrimonium nonjustum* was arranged between a citizen and a noncitizen. *Matrimonium justum* carried with it both *potestas* and *manus* and the children born to such a union were Roman citizens. *Matrimonium nonjustum* carried neither *potestas* nor *manus* and the children could not become citizens.

Beyond the two basic forms of marriage, there were three different ways of celebrating marriage with *manus*. The first of these, *confarreatio*, was an elaborate religious ceremony presided over by priests and ten witnesses. The bride was carried in elaborate procession to the groom's home, where a sheep was slain and there was a ritual eating of sacred cake. This form of ceremony was most common among the patricians or citizens. A second type of ceremony, *coemptio*, rested solely on the consent of the parties to the marriage (the parents of the bride and groom) and consisted of a mock sale of the bride instead of a religious ceremony. The passing of a small coin symbolized the woman's being brought under *manus*. The least highly regarded custom was that of *usus* (use), where the marriage actually grew out of cohabitation. If the man and woman lived together for a full year without the woman being gone from the man's home for three consecutive days, she was automatically brought under *manus*. This form was most common among the plebians.

Although the Romans were strictly monogamous, *matrimonium nonjustum* constituted a form of concubinage. It was a socially sanctioned relationship between two people who could not legally marry according to *matrimonium justum*, in which the woman had very low status and the offspring were not recognized as members of the man's family.

Divorce. Apparently the Roman husband was always entitled to divorce his wife for adultery, the preparation of poisons, or wine drinking.[24] Divorce

---

[24] This is the first instance in Western history of a man being unable to divorce his wife for barrenness. Although child-bearing was very highly regarded, a man suffered severe economic penalties for divorcing his wife because she was childless.

was severely discouraged during the early centuries, however, and must have been very uncommon. Before a man could repudiate his wife, even when she had committed the specified acts, he had to consult with the adult males of both *gentes*. The breaking of a marriage entered into by *confarreatio* was even more difficult. The couple had to endure a *diffarreatio* ceremony to which all of those who had attended the wedding were invited.

Divorce was a private affair between the families involved and generally was not interfered with by the public authorities. As the centuries progressed, divorce became more common and a distinction between just and unjust divorce emerged. The case of Spurius Carvilius Ruga about 230 B.C. often is cited as the first instance in Rome of a man divorcing his wife for other than the three specified causes.[25] This man was compelled to forfeit half of his property to the goddess Ceres and to turn over the other half to his divorced wife.[26] In general it appears that a man who divorced his wife without cause was required to return her dowry.

AFTER THE PUNIC WARS

There was not, of course, a sharp change in Roman family patterns in 202 B.C. Change had been occurring over the centuries and was greatly aggravated by the effects of Rome's long wars with Carthage. The most immediate effect was to take Roman men off to war and to leave their wives, by default, in unprecedented freedom and in positions of increasing power. The wives were no longer under the *potestas* of their fathers and their husbands were away. Women were forced to take over the management of family estates and, in many cases, managed them quite well. Inevitably a shift in the power relations between the sexes occurred. Roman men, when, and if, they returned home, found many wives unwilling to submit to *manus*.

These changes were closely associated with vastly increased family wealth. Rome emerged victorious over Carthage and went on to subjugate the entire Mediterranean region. As she did so, the wealth of the provinces was siphoned away to Rome and a vast number of servants and slaves was accumulated. As family wealth increased, the size of daughters' dowries increased proportionately, and daughters came to inherit more property from their fathers. Fathers became more and more reluctant to see this property going to the husbands and, after the second Punic War, the practice of marriage without *manus* became common. Theoretically, this left the wife under the *potestas* of her father but, practically, it worked to free women from direct male con-

[25] Goodsell, op. cit. p. 126.
[26] Ibid. pp. 126–7. See also footnote 24.. Spurius Carvilius' wife was childless.

trol. Many women became quite wealthy in their own right. Moreover, as large numbers of Greek scholars were brought to Rome, some women became learned and active in public affairs. As they did so, changes in other marriage and family practices took place.

Men who marry wives that are much their superiors in riches often become, before they are aware of it, not the husbands of their wives, but the slaves of their marriage portion.

—Plutarch

Potestas, in general, declined. The civil authorities increased in number and power and gradually freed the property of adult sons from the control of their fathers. Caesar gave to sons the right to dispose of property which they had acquired in their military careers. The power of the father over children was restricted also. Infant exposure, never common, still was permitted but the power of life and death over children was taken away. Only very poor parents were permitted to sell their children's labor, and public officials assumed jurisdiction over children who committed legal offenses. Daughters, as we have seen, indirectly escaped from *potestas* through marriage without *manus*.

Change in the marriage ideals was not striking. Marriage still was highly regarded and marriages on the whole remained stable. There was, however, a steady erosion of the foundations of marriage which led to conspicuous increase in various forms of pathology. Marriage had always been, in Rome, a private family matter resting on the consent of the two families involved. It remained so but, with time, the consent of the husband and wife became more prominent. The specific customs of *confarreatio, coemptio,* and *usus* all but disappeared. The formal trappings of the wedding, in the form of an elaborate torchlight parade and banquet, remained, but much of the substance withered away.

What erosion of marriage ideals took place occurred most conspicuously at the very top of the socio-economic order. Within a rapidly increasing leisure class, marriage ceased to be a sacred obligation and became primarily a matter of personal satisfaction and economic convenience. Both men and women married for financial gain or they married not at all. *Matrimonium nonjustum* degenerated into men taking mistresses much in the fashion of this practice in modern society. Prostitution also increased markedly. The drop in the marriage rate became a matter of grave concern, and, by the time of Christ, legislation was passed penalizing the unmarried. Single adults were disqualified from receiving inheritances unless they married within a prescribed period.

The birth rate also fell. Apparently abortion was widely practised, and the exposure of infants reached scandalous proportions. To correct this situation, laws were passed taxing the inheritances of childless couples at 50 per cent of the inheritance. The laws exempted children by adoption, however, and it became fashionable to adopt adult children for the purpose of receiving inheritances. Both the couples doing the adopting and the adopted entered such relationships according to calculated advantage. The state grew more concerned and the birth rate continued to fall.

Divorce, too, became quite common. Divorce, like marriage, was a private matter, and divorce by mutual consent became possible simply by transferring a bill of divorcement in the presence of seven witnesses. There are no rates of divorce available, of course, so we can judge their increase only by the amount of public concern. This concern is reflected in the following statements by famous men:

Tertullian: The fruit of marriage is divorce.
Juvenal: Some women divorce their husbands before the marriage garlands have faded.
Seneca: Women no longer measure time in terms of the administrations of Roman consuls, but by the number of their husbands.

The famous Julian Law, in 17 B.C., provided that a woman guilty of adultery should be deprived of half her dowry and one-third of her property and be banished to a desert island. Ironically, one of the women punished under this law was Julia, daughter of the Emperor Augustus who had the law passed. The same law deprived an adulterous husband of half of his property and of all his wife's dowry and banished him from Rome.

What had begun several hundred years before as a strong and stable family system had become a symbol of social disorganization and personal degeneracy. While Roman officials were attempting to cope, unsuccessfully, with the decay of Roman society, another set of influences that were to be major ones for more than 1500 years were taking shape. Those influences were to be found in a small heretical sect—the Christians.

THE INFLUENCE OF CHRISTIANITY

This section is headed "the influence of Christianity" because the Christians did not have nor did they develop a family system as such. They were not a nation, nor even an ethnic group. They began as a small sect within Judaism and gradually made converts from among the Romans, Greeks, traditional Hebrews, and others. Rome remained as the center of political power in Europe, and the Christians, as they gained in strength and numbers, contested with the Roman government for control of marriage and family matters.

The new religion spread slowly in Rome, for it challenged, both directly and indirectly, the power of the state. From the beginning the Christians taught that the power of the church was superior to that of the state. The Christians refused to celebrate the emperor's birthday, they would not offer sacrifices to the spirits of departed emperors, and they discouraged their members and converts from serving in the Roman armies. Whereas the emperors were passing laws to penalize celibacy, the Christians taught that the virgin state was a more exalted one than marriage. As a result of such teachings, the Christians were persecuted by the authorities and by much of the general populace. One group of authors offers the observation that Christians were about as popular in ancient Rome as communists are in the contemporary United States.[27]

The first teachings of the Christian church must be seen both in the context of religious history and in terms of the prevailing morality in Rome. In some ways the Christians sought to resurrect the stern morality of earlier Hebrew, Greek, and Roman periods. For their concept of the relationship between the mind and the body, the spirit and the flesh, they went back to the Persian philosophy of dualism which was some 2000 years old. They saw the demands of the spirit and the flesh as being mutually opposed and believed in the necessity for suppressing the demands of the flesh. Rome appeared to be catering almost completely to the flesh. Divorce, celibacy, infanticide, prostitution, childlessness, and worldliness were common. The Christian policies were formed both from tradition and in reaction against the prevailing conditions in Rome.

The church did not immediately take clear-cut positions on marriage and divorce. It did not develop its own wedding ceremonies. It continued to accept the Roman ideas of marriage and divorce as private matters and sought to express its ideals within the framework of Roman law and customs. Thus it embarked upon a policy which is followed, even today, of working through established institutions rather than attempting to supplant them. Until the fourth century A.D., the state was clearly the dominant influence. By A.D. 311,

27 Queen and Habenstein, op. cit. p. 182.

the Christians had grown too numerous and too powerful to be suppressed. Finally in 313, Christianity became an officially tolerated religion of Rome.

ATTITUDES AND POLICIES CONCERNING MARRIAGE

It is ironic that the Christian church should have drastically lowered the status of marriage, and yet this is so. Under Christian influence, marriage and the family were more lowly regarded than ever before or since in Western history. The Christians began by attacking the more blatant evils of Rome—adultery, abortion, infanticide, and child exposure.[28] But, in so doing, they became victims of a conception of marriage as a purely sexual union—as a slightly more desirable alternative than fornication. Exactly how such a conception developed and how far it went has ever since been a matter of debate among theologians. Certainly some of the early church fathers held lofty views of marriage. But over the centuries the dominant view became that which is represented by some of the writings of St. Paul. Paul's statement that "it is better to marry than to burn" is widely quoted.[29] The Christians did not actually condemn marriage, for Christ himself had given his approval to it. What they did was to regard the highest state as that of virginity; next came celibacy after marriage; then marriage; and, finally, fornication.

For I would that all men were even as I myself. But every man hath his proper gift of God, one after this manner and another after that. I say therefore to the unmarried and widows, It is good for them if they abide even as I. But if they cannot contain, let them marry: for it is better to marry than to burn.

—St. Paul, I Corinthians 7:7–9.

Sexual intercourse even in marriage was considered to be a necessary evil rather than a source of pleasure. It was necessary for the purpose of producing children and the virgins idealized by the church. At the fourth Council of Carthage, in A.D. 398, it was declared that bride and groom should abstain

---

[28] Roman law continued to permit the exposure of infants and the selling of children of destitute parents.

[29] This statement also is widely misinterpreted. Some people have concluded that Paul offered marriage as an alternative to condemnation to the fires of hell. Actually the phrase "to burn" referred to the fires of passion, and Paul's statement should be interpreted to say that those who cannot abstain from illicit sexual intercourse should marry.

from intercourse on their wedding night out of respect for the benediction. Later the period was extended to three nights. The couple could avoid the obligation by paying a moderate fee to the church.

In the encouragement of celibacy, marriage gradually was denied to priests and nuns. By A.D. 402, priests were required to remain single. For a while, the church also encouraged married couples who had borne children to reassume the celibate state in marriage. The resulting friction was so great, however, that the policy was modified to include only those marriages where the husband and wife agreed on the desirability of celibacy. Second marriages also were condemned. An early Christian manual stated that "a second marriage is wicked, a third one indicative of unbridled lust, and one after the third, synonymous with fornication." [30]

The church disapproved violently of the latter-day Roman practice of permitting first cousins to marry and gradually created a whole series of "prohibited relationships" within which people might not marry. Relatives by blood (consanguinity) were taboo within seven degrees of kinship. Relatives by affinity (marriage) likewise were prohibited within seven degrees. Even persons who presided together as godfathers and godmothers at baptisms and confirmations were considered to be related (spiritual affinity) and were forbidden to marry. A glance back at Figure 3 in Chapter 2 will show how drastic these prohibitions were. Within a few generations almost everyone in the villages and towns of the day would be related within the prohibited degrees. For a thousand years, however, efforts were made to check upon such relationships, and, in the 13th century, the obligatory publishing of the banns in the churches was designed to give those who knew of impediments to a marriage a chance to speak. By their very nature these prohibitions were not really enforceable and they gave rise to a series of problems which we will describe later.

Christianity had no marriage ceremonies of its own for centuries. It accepted, first, the Roman customs of betrothal and private nonreligious wedding ceremonies, and, later on, it similarly accepted the customs of the Teutonic invaders from the north. What the church did do was to urge the couple to seek the blessing of a priest after the nuptials had been performed. Not until perhaps the ninth century was marriage within the church firmly established.

The reaction against marriage was harshest in the early centuries of the Christian era and gradually softened over the years. The sacred nature of marriage was emphasized increasingly as the church gained control, and, by the twelfth century, marriage was defined as one of the seven sacraments.

30 Quoted in Bardis, op. cit. p. 442.

THE STATUS OF WOMEN

The early Christian attitude toward women again was paradoxical. On the one hand men and women were conceived of as being equal in the sight of God, both being possessed of divine souls. Virgins were especially highly regarded and were given an important role to play in the church. As "brides of Christ" they were assigned duties of caring for the sick and for needy widows and orphans, of visiting prisoners and otherwise administering relief programs. Widows, too, who forsook remarriage had high status and were employed in charitable activities.

But I would have you know, that the head of every man is Christ; and the head of the woman is the man; and the head of Christ is God. Every man praying or prophesying, having his head covered, dishonoreth his head. But every woman praying or propheysing with her head unveiled dishonoreth her head; for it is one and the same thing as if she were shaven. For if a woman is not veiled, let her also be shorn: but if it is a shame to a woman to be shorn or shaven, let her be veiled. For a man indeed ought not to have his head veiled, forasmuch as he is the image and glory of God: but the woman of the man: for neither was the man created for the woman but the woman for the man: for this cause ought the woman to have a sign of authority on her head. . . .

—Jerome, *Letter XXII*, Wright Edition, Harvard University Press, p. 57.

On the other hand, the idea of the inferiority of women was pronounced. Women were assumed to represent the evils of sex and to be the unwholesome tempters of men. Tertullian symbolizes this view with the following statement:

You are the devil's gateway: You are the unsealer of that forbidden tree: You are the first deserter of the divine law: You are she who persuaded him whom the devil was not valiant enough to attack. You destroyed so easily God's image, man. On account of your desert—that is, death—even the Son of God had to die. [31]

[31] Tertullian, *On the Apparel of Women*, Book I, Chapter I, Ante-Nicene Fathers, Vol. 4, p. 14, as quoted in Queen and Habenstein, op. cit. p. 186.

It seems ironic, in view of the aggressive sexuality of men in most societies, that Christianity should have placed responsibility for carnal desires upon women, but all women everywhere were considered to be tainted with the sin of Eve. They were admonished to confine themselves to their homes in housework and prayer. Women were not permitted to teach the new religion or to perform baptisms. The idea of women representing the evils of sex is one which has come down to us today and it was to be a thousand years before the situation of women in the church would improve appreciably.

DIVORCE

The Christian attitude toward divorce required many centuries to crystallize. As in other areas, there was a split within the church. Christ had seemed to sanction divorce where adultery had been committed. In general, however, the sentiment was against divorce: "What therefore God hath joined together, let not man put asunder." [32]

By A.D. 140 the church permitted divorce only on grounds of idolatry, apostasy, covetousness, and fornication. Over the next century or two, the policy wavered back and forth but tended toward increasingly strict regulation of divorce; the church moved slowly because of the difficulty of enforcing its edicts in the face of the less restrictive policies of the Roman government. In A.D. 314 the Council of Arles affirmed the general principle of the indissolubility of marriage but did not make it mandatory. Finally, at the Council of Carthage in A.D. 407 the church took an irreversible stand against divorce.

Perhaps nowhere else have differences in policy on the part of church and government caused so much difficulty. The later Roman emperors, influenced by Christianity, vacillated in their regulation of divorce. The civil laws wavered back and forth but generally took a more lax view of divorce than did the church. Finally, in the twelfth century, civil law was brought into complete conformity with canon law and absolute divorce almost disappeared from Europe.

The German-English Family System of the Middle Ages

The Roman Empire finally succumbed to conquest about the end of the fourth century. For about two hundred years various portions of the empire were overrun by a series of loosely federated tribes ranging from the Vandals, Visigoths, Lombards, East Goths, Alemanni, and Burgundians in the south to the Angles, Saxons, Frisians, and Jutes in the north. Eventually Great

[32] Matthew 19:6.

Britain was invaded by the Angles, Saxons, and Jutes, carrying the cultural stream which was to be transported to America.

Our knowledge of this period is not nearly so complete nor reliable as we would like. The word, barbarian, which is customarily attached to the Teutonic tribes connotes, among other things, a lack of and disrespect for learning that produced few written records. What we shall try to do here is not to analyze the family system of any one tribe in detail but to indicate the general character of the peoples among whom Christianity spread up until the time of the Renaissance.[33]

INHERITANCE AND DESCENT

The kinship system of the Germanic and English peoples was a considerable departure from the earlier patri-lineages of the Hebrews, Greeks, and Romans. Both sets of peoples (the Anglo-Saxons in England and the Saxons and Frisians on the Continent) practised double descent. Relationship was traced both through the father's line and through the mother's line, with each person being a member of two separate kin groups. These extended kin groups were called the *maegth* in Britain and the *sippe* on the Continent. In each case membership in the kin group was traced from the grandchildren of a common set of ancestors.

The *sippe* occupied a position between the individual household and the state, as it developed, comparable to the position of the *tsu* in traditional China. The state depended upon the *sippe* to enforce the law among its members, and the *sippe* wielded large power over households and even over individuals.

Membership in the *sippe* was by blood or adoption. Illegitimate children had no rights of inheritance; wives remained members of their own *sippes* after marriage. The father admitted each child to the *sippe* at its birth. The child was brought to him before it had tasted food either to be accepted or to be condemned to exposure. Although the father could not kill children who had tasted food, infanticide and exposure were permissible at least until the eleventh century.

Among these warlike peoples, membership in a kin group was the primary means of individual protection. If an individual was killed, his kin either avenged his death or extracted payment (*wergild*) from the slayer's kin. If he killed someone else, then his paternal kin paid two-thirds of the *wergild* and his maternal kin paid one-third. A major function of the *sippe* was to restrain

[33] This section follows closely Goodsell, op. cit. pp. 189–210.

its landless male members from aggressive behavior which would place liability on the whole *sippe*.

In spite of the system of double descent, property generally was passed from father to son in the male line. Wives and daughters were not prohibited from inheriting, however, and sometimes did so. In later centuries, the wife's inheritance rights became increasingly fixed through the dower.

PATRIARCHY

The father's power over his children was not so great as among the ancients. Fathers could punish their children vigorously, but the laws of the Jutes, for example, provided that he should not break their bones. Among the Anglo-Saxons children could be sold into slavery until they became seven years old, and among the Germanic peoples both wives and children could be sold in time of famine. The power of the *sippe* always was available to protect wives and children from abuse beyond permissible limits.

Among the Anglo-Saxons, fathers could give their young daughters in marriage without the girls' consent, at least until the eleventh century. They could also commit sons and daughters to monasteries and nunneries. Girls whose entrance into a convent often was accompanied by a substantial gift to the church were not entitled to seek release from the convent even at adulthood.

The rights of sons exceeded those of daughters. While fathers generally had the usufruct of their children's property, the Anglo-Saxon father could not claim his son's earnings. Moreover, the father's power over his sons was drastically restricted when the sons reached majority, most commonly at twelve years of age.

The husband's power over his wife was limited by the fact that she remained a member of her own *sippe*. Her *sippe* remained responsible for any crimes which she might commit and the *sippe* also collected her *wergild* in the event that harm was done to her. Short of doing her severe bodily injury, however, the husband was expected to chastise her for misdeeds. A man who failed to punish an unruly wife might himself be punished by his neighbors.

BETROTHAL AND MARRIAGE

By the late Middle Ages, betrothal and the nuptials had become quite distinct among the Germanic peoples. The betrothal, called *beweddung*, originated in an agreement between the groom and the bride's father for a bride price of cattle, money, or arms. Gradually, however, the interval between *beweddung* and *gifta* (marriage) lengthened until it became common to betroth children and even infants.[34] With child betrothal, only a token sum was paid to the father as a kind of deposit on the full bride price. Eventually it became common to pay the money to the bride herself and, still later, the payment took the form of a ring—the precursor of the modern engagement ring. The bride price also was transformed from an actual payment to the bride's father into a dower right in the husband's property in the event that the husband should die before she did. This dower right often amounted to half of the husband's property. *Beweddung* was regarded as the first step in marriage and subsequent sexual intercourse on the part of the girl was severely punished.

"Nowadays young people develop more quickly than they did in my day," says the most Rev. Geoffrey Francis Fisher, 83, the former Archbishop of Canterbury. In a new book, Touching on Christian Truth, Dr. Fisher proposes to help the young avoid the sin of fornication by reviving the ancient rite of betrothal. "It would have to take place with the full consent of the two families," he wrote. "It would, in fact, be a sacramental act, made, as indeed marriage itself is, essentially by the two persons themselves. After that, sexual intercourse between them would not be regarded as, in the moral sense, fornication." Marriage and children would follow when and if the two parties felt ready for it.

—Reprinted by permission from *Time*, The Weekly Newsmagazine; copyright Time, Inc., 1971.

Gifta, the marriage ceremony itself, was a private family matter involving the bride's being turned over to her new husband by her father. In some cases the father also handed over a hat, sword, and mantle, which were the husband's symbols of authority over the wife. Goodsell also reports that in some tribes the groom then stepped on the bride's foot as a means of reinforcing the symbols.[35] It is important to emphasize that no religious officials were involved. The girl's father simply transferred power over her to the husband. After the tenth century, the girl sometimes selected another male relative to give her away or she gave herself in marriage. This giving of oneself in marriage, *self-gifta*, later evolved into common-law marriage.

[34] George E. Howard, A *History of Matrimonial Institutions*, Chicago: University of Chicago Press, 1904, Vol. I, pp. 258–72.
[35] Op. cit. p. 200.

Between the seventh and tenth centuries, the financial negotiations for marriage were complicated by the developing custom of the "morning gift." On the morning after the bridal night, the husband gave his wife a small gift which symbolized his satisfaction with her. This gift cemented the marriage bargain and the husband could no longer send the wife back to her family. By the tenth century the giving of the morning gift had become obligatory and the morning gift had become of far greater value than the bride price. Gradually, bride price and morning gift became one in the provision of a dower interest in the husband's property.

These marriage customs were little influenced by the spreading Christian church. As it had among the Romans, the church accepted the native customs for many centuries. The church worked principally through emphasizing the sacred character of marriage and urging the couple to seek the blessing of a priest following *gifta*. Attending mass on the day following *gifta* became common, and, by the tenth century, *gifta* was often performed just outside the church entrance and in the presence of the priest. The presence of a priest was not necessary, however; marriage remained a private matter based upon the consent of the contracting parties.

DIVORCE

The Germanic peoples, like the ancients, had early permitted the repudiation of wives by their husbands. As this power became restricted, the influence of Rome was felt in the appearance of divorce by mutual consent—mutual consent, with the advantages lying clearly with the husband. Adultery on the part of the woman, for example, not only was cause for divorce but produced such moral outrage that the woman might be driven through the village and beaten to death. Men ordinarily could not be divorced for adultery. A man caught in the act of adultery might be killed, not on moral grounds but for violating the property rights of another man!

The church, it will be recalled, had established the doctrine of the indissolubility of marriage by the fifth century. For another 500 years, however, it continued to compromise with secular customs. Divorce by mutual consent was recognized and even remarriage was permitted. Often the bishops demanded that their consent be secured before remarriage occurred. The church even gave slight encouragement to divorce in cases where one of the partners had converted to Christianity but the other had not.

During these 500 years the church consolidated its power and steadily assumed control over divorce until, by the tenth century, it had wrested control completely away from the civil authorities. The bishops' courts came to hear all divorce cases and canon law replaced civil law. Canon law permitted two remedies to discontented couples: *divortium a vinculo matrimonii;* and *divortium a mensa et thoro.*

Divortium a vinculo matrimonii, which means "divorce from the bonds of matrimony" was not divorce as we know it, but annulment—an ecclesiastical declaration that a valid marriage had never existed in the first place. There were ample grounds upon which annulment might be sought, for the church prohibited marriage within seven degrees for both consanguinity and affinity and between those who had been religious sponsors for a child. A large proportion of any local population was related within the prohibited degrees. As if this were not enough, annulment also was permitted where either the husband or wife had entered into a previous verbal contract of marriage in words of the present tense. By the very nature of such a contract, no records were available and the whole procedure was subject to great abuse.

Divortium a mensa et thoro, literally divorce from bed and board, was not absolute divorce either. It was separation permitted and enforced by the church. The parties remained legally married to one another and escaped none of the obligations of marriage other than cohabitation. *Divortium a mensa et thoro* was permitted on three grounds: adultery, cruelty, and apostasy (heresy).

With the promulgation of the regulation permitting *divortium a vinculo matrimonii,* the church had opened Pandora's box. Most couples, if they were determined enough, could find grounds upon which annulment might be secured. Moreover, the church itself often was a not too reluctant partner in fraud. Annulments were granted to wealthy personages upon the payment of substantial sums of money, and special dispensations permitting marriage within the prohibited degrees were available for the proper consideration.[36]

To understand this situation, one must be aware that the church was not only a religious institution but also an increasingly powerful political institution. In its contest with civil authorities over matters of morals, the church wielded economic power with good effect. It missed few opportunities to increase its wealth or its holdings in land. Be that as it may, the church had established definitions that were to create problems for centuries to come.

SUMMARY

Knowledge of its history is essential to adequate understanding of the modern American family system. So far, we have traced the history of Western family organization from the ancient Hebrews through the German-English family system of the middle ages.

[36] Howard, op. cit. Vol. II, pp. 56–9.

The ancient Hebrew family, associated with a pastoral economy, was patriarchal, patrilineal, patrilocal, polygynous, and extended. Kin groups beyond the extended family included the patrilineal *sib*, the clan, and the tribe. The patriarch had almost absolute power, being permitted to destroy his children and even his wife if he discovered her in adultery. The father could marry off his children at will and could sell them into slavery. Among women, only widowed mothers were free from the direct control of males. Patriarchs and kings had both multiple wives and concubines.

The minimum ages for marriage were thirteen for boys and twelve for girls, although childhood betrothal was common. Betrothal took two forms: *kaseph*, which involved the transfer of money; and *kiddushin* which required the preparation of a written instrument. Marriage was a completely private family affair which required no participation by rabbis. Marriage was carefully solemnized, however, and included signing of the *ketubah*, or marriage deed.

Marriage was highly valued as a means of producing sons so that a man's house "should not die out of Israel." The marriage regulations included the practice of levirate. During the early period there was complete primogeniture; later on, the eldest son received a double portion of the inheritance. Daughters inherited only if there were no sons.

During the early period, the patriarch had almost unlimited right to divorce his wife, being required only to hand her a bill of divorcement. The wife had no right of divorce at all. Gradually the husband's right of divorce was restricted and the wife gained the right to divorce her husband for specified causes. Later still, the rabbis gained the power forcibly to separate couples for either barrenness or adultery. The history of the Hebrew family is essentially one of movement from private to public control.

The family system of ancient Greece also was patriarchal, patrilineal, patrilocal, and extended. The Greeks, however, were monogamous. Beyond the extended family there was the *gens*, which consisted of all extended families tracing descent from a common ancestor. The Greeks became more urbanized than the Hebrews and varying patterns developed in the city-states of Athens and Sparta.

The extreme power of the Greek father stemmed from his position as trustee of the family estates and from his role as priest in the practice of ancestor worship. Membership in the Greek family derived from the worship of its ancestors and coming under the power of the patriarch. Athenian women had extremely low status, being defined as inherently inferior to men. As among the Hebrews, the husband had power of life and death over the wife only in the event of adultery. Women were confined to the women's apartments in the house and could leave the house, under chaperone, only with the husbands' permission. The father could expose infants, sell the labor of his children, or bestow them in marriage. The emancipation of adult sons, rare at first, later became common.

The Greeks traced descent through males only, the system known as *agnation*. There was primogeniture in the inheritance of landed property, younger sons leaving the family home and daughters not inheriting at all. In Sparta, daughters did inherit and, with the expansion of the Greek empire, many women became wealthy and powerful.

Marriage, a sacred obligation, provided for the inheritance of family estates and for continued ancestor worship. Celibacy was punished by law. Betrothal was a business contract between the parents setting forth the bride price and the dowry. Marriage was an extravagant religious affair but no religious functionaries other than the two fathers participated.

The Greeks had both institutionalized concubinage and various forms of prostitution. Concubines, usually taken from among family slaves, had even lower status than wives; their children were not regarded as family members and could not inherit. Some of the highest-status women in ancient Greece were the *hetaerae*, the socially gifted, intellectually and artistically inclined, social and sexual companions of wealthy men. For the poorer classes, there was a large group of ordinary prostitutes.

Divorce was rare or nonexistent during the earliest period, but gradually the right of a husband to repudiate his wife emerged. Later on, the wife gained limited rights of divorce but could never divorce her husband for adultery.

Before the Punic Wars, the Roman family was a strong, solidary unit. It was the most complete patriarchy ever known. After consulting his *gens*, the father could kill his children; after consulting both his *gens*, and hers, a husband could kill his wife. He could kill her immediately if he discovered her in adultery. The power of a father over his children was called *potestas*; that of a husband over his wife was called *manus*. Offspring remained under *potestas* for as long as the father lived.

There were two principal marriage forms, *matrimonium justum* and *matrimonium nonjustum*, and three ways of celebrating marriage, *confarreatio, coemptio,* and *usus*. In spite of the extreme patriarchy, Roman women had high status. As among the Greeks and Hebrews, divorce was rare in the early period. The Roman husband apparently always had the right to repudiate his wife for specified causes, however, and gradually divorce became more common.

Roman civilization began to disintegrate after the Punic Wars, and the family system with it. Roman women, left to manage the family properties, had become quite powerful, and marriage without *manus* became common.

Potestas declined. Celibacy, childlessness, divorce, and abortion became common. Although the authorities sought to reverse these trends, they were powerless to do so.

The early Christians contended with the Roman authorities for control over family matters, ultimately winning out. In many ways the early Christian policies were a reaction against prevailing conditions in Rome; nevertheless, some effects were to lower the status of marriage, to define sex as inherently evil, and to lower drastically the status of women. For centuries, the Christians accepted the pagan marriage customs, but they discouraged remarriages and gradually developed the doctrine of marital indissolubility. The church also greatly extended the prohibited relationships within which people might not marry.

When Rome was overrun from the north, Christianity accepted and worked within the Teutonic customs just as it had with the earlier Roman practices. The Germanic and English peoples practised double descent, with the extended kin groups being called the *sippe* and the *maegth*. In the absence of strong central government, the *sippe* exercised broad protective functions for individuals, extracting *wergild* in the event of their injury or death.

Like their predecessors, the Germanic and English peoples were patriarchal, but the system of double descent protected wives from too great abuse. The power of the father over his children also was limited.

Betrothal among the Germans was called *beweddung,* and private marriage, called *gifta,* was deeply entrenched. Like the ancients, the Germanic and English peoples had a double standard of morality, favoring males; wives might be divorced for adultery but husbands could not be. Gradually the church succeeded in doing away with absolute divorce altogether, permitting only *divortium a vinculo matrimonii* (annulment) and *divortium a mensa et thoro* (separation).

SUGGESTED READINGS

Bardis, Panos D., "Family Forms and Variations Historically Considered," in Harold T. Christensen, ed., *Handbook of Marriage and the Family*, Chicago: Rand McNally, 1964, pp. 403–61. Describes the Hebrew, Greek, Roman, and early Christian families.

Bardis, Panos D., *The Family in Changing Civilizations*, New York: Associated Educational Services Corporation, 1967. A collection of Bardis' previously published articles covering theories of family change, ancient family systems, and modern family systems.

Cross, Earle B., "The Hebrew Family in Biblical Times," in Jeffrey K. Hadden, and Marie L. Borgatta, eds., *Marriage and the Family*, Itasca, Illinois: F. E. Peacock Publishers, Inc., 1969, pp. 60–73. A series of brief selections from the author's book-length study of the Hebrew family.

Goodsell, Willystine, A *History of Marriage and the Family*, New York: The Macmillan Company, 1939. Traces the development of Western family organization from the time of the ancient Hebrews to the early twentieth century.

Johnston, Harold W., "The Roman Family," in Jeffrey K. Hadden, and Marie L. Borgatta, eds., *Marriage and the Family*, Itasca, Illinois: F. E. Peacock Publishers, Inc., 1969, pp. 73–81. A brief selection, emphasizing the system of agnation, from the author's book-length study of the Roman family.

Lewinsohn, Richard, A *History of Sexual Customs* (trans. by Alexander Mayce), Greenwich, Conn.: Fawcett Publications, Inc. 1958. A fascinating study by a physician and historian of the range of sexual attitudes and customs throughout history.

Nash, Arnold S., "Ancient Past and Living Present," in Howard Becker and Reuben Hill, eds., *Family, Marriage, and Parenthood*, Boston: D. C. Heath, 1955, pp. 84–103. A well-informed, brief history of the Western family from the ancient Hebrews up through the early Christian period.

Queen, Stuart A., and Habenstein, Robert W., *The Family in Various Cultures*, Philadelphia: J. B. Lippincott, 1967. Contains eight chapters on the development of Western family organization which provide an expanded treatment of the materials covered in this chapter.

Sussman, Marvin B., Cates, Judith N., and Smith, David T., *The Family and Inheritance*, New York: Russell Sage Foundation, 1970. A report of research conducted by two sociologists and an attorney on how family inheritance works in the contemporary United States.

FILMS

Bar Mitzvah (National Film Board of Canada, Mackenzie Building, Toronto), 15 minutes. A careful portrayal of the ceremonies in which a Jewish youth confirms his faith. An honored estate, Bar Mitzvah, the coming of age, follows several years of study of the Hebrew language, scriptures, and customs.

QUESTIONS AND PROJECTS

1. Describe the form and content of the ancient Hebrew patriarchy. Were there any restrictions on the power of the father over his children? Of the husband over his wife? What were they?
2. Define: *kaseph; kiddushin; ketubah*. How was marriage regarded among the Hebrews? What was the purpose of marriage? How were polygyny and concubinage consistent with the prevailing conception of marriage?
3. Trace the gradual evolution of Hebrew patterns of marriage, divorce, and inheritance from the earliest period to the time of Christ.
4. How did the Greek patriarchy differ from the Hebrew one? What was the source of the patriarch's power? Describe the status of women.
5. What is the kinship system known as "agnation"?

6. What was the Greek attitude toward marriage? Reconcile the existence of the *hetaerae* with the Greek attitude toward marriage.

7. What was the history of divorce among the Greeks? Was there any double standard operative in the divorce norms?

8. Detail the progressive character of Roman family patterns. Describe any parallels to the Hebrew and Greek family experiences.

9. Define: *matrimonium justum; potestas; manus; confarreatio; coemptio; usus; diffarreatio.*

10. Explain why the early Christians took the positions which they did on the nature of marriage, sex, and the status of women. What were the attitudes of the church on divorce and remarriage?

11. Describe the kinship system of the Anglo-Saxon and Teutonic peoples during the Middle Ages. What was the *sippe* or *maegth*? What role did it play in the society?

12. Define: *beweddung; gifta; self-gifta; wergild; divortium a vinculo matrimonii.*

13. In addition to the family, the ancient Hebrews recognized three other social units that were basically kinship units. What were they? What was the relationship of each of them to the family?

14. What was the *levirate*? How was the custom of the *levirate* consistent with the nature of the Hebrew system of marriage?

15. Compare and contrast the marriage and family patterns of Athens and Sparta. How do you account for the differences?

16. What were the two basic forms of marriage among the ancient Romans? What were their implications for *potestas* and *manus*? What forms of the marriage ceremony were related to each?

17. What were the bases for the struggles between the Roman authorities and the early Christians? What economic and political factors were involved? How was the struggle resolved?

7 | The Development of Western Family Organization: II

THE IMPACT OF FEUDALISM

HERE we depart again from the analysis of family systems, as such, to consider the influence of developments in other institutional spheres upon family patterns. We have already traced some of the influences of the religious institutions from about the time of Christ to the tenth or twelfth century. Now we must incorporate the influences of major changes in the economy. Following this, we will return to the influence of the church during the late Middle Ages and through the Reformation.

Feudalism developed first on the Continent, where the countryside was divided into large and small estates accumulated and held through military power. Kings, unable to exert direct control over their holdings, bestowed vast portions of land upon nobles, who constituted a landed aristocracy paying tribute to the king and contributing armies to his service. In turn, the nobles farmed their holdings with the labor of a multitude of serfs who literally were bound to the soil and who served in the nobles' armies. In addition there were free men, or yeomen, who owned their own farms and who occasionally became quite prosperous. Finally, there was a growing class of artisans and tradesmen who lived in the towns. It was a more rigidly and elaborately stratified society than had existed since the Roman Empire and it rested firmly on a military foundation. This feudal economy was, for the most part, transferred to England with the Norman invasion, where it was dominant until about the time of the Reformation.

Feudalism had major impact upon inheritance, marriage, and the status of women. Moreover, these changes were not discrete, but were intricately interwoven. They all stemmed, perhaps, from the necessity to hold estates intact and to keep the estates under the control of male heirs who could protect them against plunder.

The practices of *unogeniture* and *entail* became firmly established. Uno-geniture means simply that the estate tends to be transmitted intact to one of the sons. Primogeniture seems to have been the most common form, but ultimogeniture also was found.[1] Entail involved the lands being inalienably settled upon a man and his straight-line descendants. Thus, great emphasis was placed upon "heirs of the body," and as long as a man had sons, no other relatives could inherit his land.

Younger sons and widows were not especially well provided for. Occasionally younger sons were permitted to inherit recently acquired lands which were not considered to be part of the traditional estate, but, by the fourteenth century, even that practice had given way to providing younger sons with life interests in the income from rents and trusts. Wives had only their dower interests in the husband's property and this was defined as not to include the man's dwelling-house, which must go instead to his heir.

It should come as no surprise that feudalism operated to deprive women again of much of the status which they had begun to recoup during the early Middle Ages. That the husband became the only legal person is illustrated by Glanvill's statement that "husband and wife were one person and that person was the husband." The husband had the ownership of the wife's dowry for as long as the marriage survived and had a life interest in it even after her death. If the husband died first, the wife might have great difficulty in acquiring control of her dower. For a woman to hold land outright, if just for her lifetime, threatened the lord's interest in it: she might marry a man who would alienate the land, or the land might be wrested from her by force. Consequently, when a man died the lord acquired control of the destiny of the widow almost as he did of the land. The widow had to secure the consent of the lord to a proposed remarriage, or the lord might actually marry the widow off to a knight of his choice who would protect his interest in the land.

The plight of children under feudalism was even more difficult than that of women. Discipline was harsh, with physical beatings the approved way of securing obedience and respect. It became quite common for children to be sent away from home to be trained by other families who would instill discipline and virtue without sentiment. When the father died, his small children came under the power of the lord, who had complete power to arrange their marriages or to sell that right to some other person if he did not wish to avail himself of it.

---

[1] Morris Zelditch, Jr., "Family, Marriage, and Kinship," in Robert E. L. Faris, ed., *Handbook of Modern Sociology*, Chicago: Rand McNally, 1964, p. 721.

The arranging of marriages became a matter of coldly calculating bargaining in which children were used as pawns in building estates. Although marriages could not be consummated until the boy reached 14 and the girl 12, much younger children were involved in marriage agreements. Queen and Habenstein quote Coke as writing that a nine-year-old widow should have her dower, "of what age soever her husband be, albeit he were but four years old."[2] Children of seven could legally contract marriage.

THE INFLUENCE OF CHIVALRY

As feudalism matured, the standards of living of the upper classes improved greatly. The familiar feudal castle appeared to serve as home, fortress, and social center. Boys and men were trained in the arts of warfare while girls and women learned the domestic arts of spinning, sewing, and weaving. There was even some cultivation of knowledge—sometimes directly and sometimes through the stories and songs of wandering troubadours.

All of this was accompanied by subtle and not so subtle changes in the relations between men and women. Medieval ladies began to acquire power when their husbands went to war just as Roman matrons before them had done. Left in charge of the castles and retinues of servants, many women developed both competence and assurance in the management of their affairs. Too, it was possible for women to inherit property. If a man died without heirs of the body his widow might become wealthy and powerful.

Ladies of leisure, isolated in their castles, gradually became preoccupied with manners and etiquette. How much sheer boredom had to do with it, we cannot say. Then there was the fact that women could not act directly in their own behalf; a woman wronged could only seek recourse through some man who might champion her cause. A man might champion his own wife's cause, but not out of sentiment. Marriage between them had been arranged on economic grounds and its primary purpose was to provide heirs to keep the estates intact. Since there was not provision for men and women to seek the satisfaction of emotional needs in marriage, both sexes sought to satisfy those needs outside of marriage in a pattern of extramarital intrigue which has since come to be called chivalry.

Chivalry appears to have been a two-sided thing. On the one hand it was lusty and sensual. There was a great deal of overt sex-seeking, with little regard for the feelings or reputations of the persons involved or their families.

[2] Stuart A. Queen and Robert W. Habenstein, *The Family in Various Cultures*, Philadelphia: J. B. Lippincott, 1967, p. 235.

On the other hand, chivalry fostered an idealization of love and the partner, which had no counterpart in the ancient world. In short, chivalry produced the concept of romantic love. Romantic love and marriage were widely regarded as incompatible with one another, but the ideal of seeking continued, intense satisfaction in the person of a member of the opposite sex was created as a legacy to be passed on to future generations.

How widespread chivalry became in the later Middle Ages is unknown. Probably it was confined to the upper classes, serving only as an ideal for the great mass of men and women who worked their modest holdings or at their trades in the towns. Much less is known of the actual family behavior of people in the Middle Ages than of the ideal standards which the age set for them.

Church Policy Through the Reformation

After the tenth century the church vigorously contested the concept of marriage as a private matter, not requiring the participation of the clergy. As long as the father gave the bride in marriage, the clergy did not complain openly; but when it became common for other laymen to do it, the clergy demanded that only a priest should give a woman in marriage. Laymen who bestowed a bride in marriage were threatened with excommunication. Much of the Continent, however, and most of England was not prepared to surrender the concept of marriage as a private affair. One result of the church's stand was the spread of "clandestine" marriage.

The old custom of *self-gifta* had evolved into the assumed right of a man and woman to marry each other simply by stating their vows to one another "in words of the present tense," with or without witnesses. As the church more violently opposed this custom, it became common for the vows to be said in secret and often without witnesses.

The church was caught in a dilemma. If it refused to recognize such marriages, it would drive the participants away from the church and condemn their children to illegitimacy. If it recognized the marriages, it would abdicate its power to regulate marriage and family life.

During the twelfth century, Peter the Lombard attempted to find a way out of the dilemma by declaring that vows stated in words of the present tense (I take thee) produced a marriage but that vows spoken in words of the future tense (I *will* take thee) did not.[3] The result was chaos. Clandestine

[3] Willystine Goodsell, A *History of Marriage and the Family*, New York: The Macmillan Company, 1939, p. 260.

marriages were held to be as binding as those which were formally performed in the church. Moreover, in neither English nor German is there any very clear distinction between the present and future tenses. If a man says "I will," to a woman does it mean that he will right now or at some time in the future? [4]

The church's logic was supported by a distinction which it created between "legal" and "valid" marriages. Legal marriages were those which met the formal requirements of the church. Marriages which occurred without church sanction, although illegal, were still recognized as valid. The church discouraged marriage in words of the present tense by requiring severe penance of those who were so married, but to no avail.

The number of clandestine marriages increased rapidly and there were wholesale abuses. Some children were held to be validly married while other couples who had been living together for years were declared not to be married. Unscrupulous men were able to escape from marriages where there were no witnesses. Between the thirteenth and sixteenth centuries, abuse of clandestine marriage became so common as to constitute a major public scandal.

In 1215, Pope Innocent III decreed that the banns must be read in the church three times before a marriage ceremony could be performed, but the decree was not rigidly enforced. Finally, at the Council of Trent in A.D. 1563, it was declared that, in the future, valid marriages must be celebrated in the presence of a priest and two or three witnesses. The Council also decreed that the publishing of the banns should be enforced. Even then, however, the church failed to make publication of the banns a condition of valid marriage, and high-status persons continued to secure their licences without the banns having been read.

In at least two other areas the church was plagued by scandal. First, there were the continuing abuses centering on *divortium a vinculo matrimonii*. It had proved impossible to enforce kinship restrictions within seven degrees, and Innocent III, in 1215, specified that the prohibited relationships should extend only to the fourth degree. Still the prohibitions were erratically applied. In some instances, spiritual affinity was held to impose restrictions to four or seven degrees, while in other cases, persons consanguineally related within three degrees were given dispensation to marry. Even more irksome was the fact that persons of sufficient wealth and influence continued to secure annulments when less fortunate persons could not do so.

[4] A common form of Protestant marriage ceremony in use in the United States at the present time uses the phrase "I will" rather than the phrase "I do."

. . . In a 12,500-word encyclical called Sacerdotalis Caelibatus (Priestly Celibacy), the Pope decreed that the present ban on marriage "should today continue to be firmly linked to the ecclesiastical ministry."

One by one, [Pope Paul VI] took up the objections to celibacy—that it is contrary to human nature, that there is no Scriptural basis for it, that its observance has become almost impossible—and rejected them all. . . . "Priestly celibacy," he declared, "has been guarded by the church for centuries as a brilliant jewel, and retains its value undiminished even in our time."

The encyclical referred to the recent wave of priests who have left the church to marry as "lamentable," and proposed rigorous new methods of choosing and training candidates for the cassock, including more psychological guidance. . . .

—Reprinted by permission from *Time,* The Weekly Newsmagazine; copyright Time Inc., 1967.

Another scandal revolved around the requirement for a celibate priesthood. Enforcement of the requirement was lax and there were continuous rumors of licentious behavior by priests. On the Continent, some priests took women, had children by them, and then married the women just before they died in order that the children might inherit their property.[5] The church even taxed clergy for the privilege of keeping concubines.[6]

THE REFORMATION

A crisis was reached at the end of the fifteenth century in a widespread revolt against the abuses with which the church was plagued. Martin Luther served as a symbol of the revolt, and it probably was he who was most influential in reintroducing the concept of civil marriage. Luther held the married state in very high regard and objected strenuously to clandestine marriage, to the abuses associated with clerical celibacy, and to fraud in the granting both of special dispensations to marry and annulments. Consequently, he took the position that marriage was not a sacrament but rather was a civil contract which was blessed by God. It followed from this, of course, that mar-

---

[5] O. E. Feucht, ed., *Sex and the Church,* St. Louis: Concordia, 1961, p. 63, as quoted in Panos D. Bardis, "Family Forms and Variations Historically Considered," in Harold T. Christensen, ed., *Handbook of Marriage and the Family,* Chicago: Rand McNally, 1964, p. 451.

[6] Una B. Sait, *New Horizons for the Family,* New York: The Macmillan Company, 1938, p. 155, as quoted in Bardis, ibid. p. 451.

riage and divorce should be regulated by the state, not by the church. Luther himself in 1525 married a nun who had fled from a convent.

The church became fragmented into Catholic and Protestant factions, and the civil authorities gradually assumed legal control of marriage and family matters. The performance of the marriage ceremony proper was left to the church for at least another generation, with civil ceremonies not becoming common until much later. Nor was there any immediate change in the prohibition of absolute divorce; with the restriction on fraudulent annulments, marriage actually became more binding than before.

One early effect of the Reformation was the removal of most of the impediments to marriage established by the church. Prohibitions for spiritual affinity were done away with altogether and even barriers due to consanguinity were removed beyond the third degree. Interestingly, and significant for modern-day America, the Protestant churches continued to forbid marriages between Christians and non-Christians—so-called "mixed marriages."

Ironically, the Reformation helped to preserve one of the very evils against which it was directed. The Church of England continued to recognize marriage in words of the present tense as valid until the eighteenth century. The canon law and the civil law were in conflict, for while canon law declared the children of such marriages to be legitimate, the civil law held that they could not be legitimated even by the subsequent religious marriage of their parents. The church gained the power to force a subsequent religious marriage and could jail, with government aid, persons who refused to do so. Be that as it may, the stage was set for the transport of the concept of common law marriage to America.

The English Family: the Sixteenth Century to the Eighteenth Century

After the feudal period the class structure began to undergo modification as a consequence of the diversification of occupations, the increasing physical mobility of the population, increasing settlement in cities and towns, and the development of trade. Ties to the land were not quite so universal as before: the top three classes—nobles, freeholders, and yeomen—still deriving their income from land, constituting only about one-fifth of the population. The remaining four-fifths of the population was composed of professionals, tradesmen, craftsmen, and laborers—people who sold their labor for a living.

The English family remained basically patriarchal, though not so rigidly as before. As late as 1663 a man was legally entitled to beat his wife. Wealthy men remained as the heads of large households, holding authority over kin and non-kin alike who resided within them. On a smaller scale the same thing applied to craftsmen, tradesmen, and farmers. Marriages still were arranged by parents, but there were the beginnings of free choice based upon romantic love. Children began to go to school in greater numbers, but the majority were still placed in apprenticeship or loaned out to other families to learn discipline and the social graces.

MARRIAGE

There are no reliable figures to indicate what proportions of the population followed what marriage customs, but at least three general practices were followed: the arrangement of child marriages, clandestine marriages, and private marriages.

The socially most acceptable and probably majority practice was that of child betrothal and marriage. Queen and Habenstein, report the marriage of a boy three years old,[7] and Goodsell refers to a widow of nine.[8] These child brides and grooms continued to live with their own parents generally until they reached twelve and fourteen years old. Their marriages were arranged frankly on the basis of financial considerations to ensure the welfare of parents and to provide for the preferred inheritance of property.

Women . . . are only children of a larger growth; they have an entertaining tattle and sometimes wit, but for solid reasoning good-sense, I never knew in my life one that had it, or who reasoned or acted consequentially for four-and-twenty hours together. . . . A man of sense only trifles with them, plays with them, humors and flatters them, as he does with a sprightly, forward child; but he neither consults them about nor trusts them with serious matters, though he often makes them believe that he does both, which is the thing in the world that they are proud of; . . .

—E. G. Johnson, ed., *The Best Letters of Lord Chesterfield*, 9th edition, pp. 91–2, as quoted in Willystine Goodsell, *A History of Marriage and the Family*, New York: The Macmillan Company, 1939, p. 323.

Clandestine marriages continued to be a problem and even increased in number during the seventeenth and eighteenth centuries. Certain rectors of

[7] Op. cit. p. 256.
[8] Op. cit. p. 329.

the Church of England discovered that marrying people without licences could be a very profitable sideline and engaged in the practice on a large scale. Even more notorious were the so-called "fleet marriages" performed by clergymen who had been imprisoned for debt. These enterprising gentlemen sometimes even arranged to have offices outside the prison, where they performed large numbers of illegal marriages for persons who were of age. After several unsuccessful attempts to do away with such marriages, the Hardwicke Act finally was passed in 1573. This law required that all marriages should be performed before two witnesses by an Anglican clergyman after the publication of banns or the securing of a licence from the bishop. Registers of marriages had to be kept, and destroying or falsifying a register was made punishable by death.

Private marriages apparently were an attempt to escape the expenses and publicity associated with public marriages. The couple secured a licence instead of having the banns published and were married quietly by clerics who, again, found the business profitable.

DESCENT AND INHERITANCE

Inheritance laws changed but little from medieval times. Primogeniture and entail were widely followed with landed property, younger brothers generally leaving the family home to make their own way. Daughters ordinarily inherited only in the absence of sons. Wives had a dower right in their husbands' property which amounted to life use of one-third of his property if there were children and one-half of his property if there were not.

One sign of the times was the increased number of men and women who lived apart from any group of kin. During the Middle Ages, the church had maintained monasteries, nunneries, hospitals, and the like, to which unattached persons repaired as the *sippe* or *maegth* declined in importance. Now, with the role of the church greatly restricted, laws were passed making families financially responsible for their indigent members. Where the families were not able to provide care and support, the obligation was now defined as a public responsibility. The Poor Laws of 1597 saw government entrance into a field which formerly had been exclusively the prerogative of the family.[9]

DIVORCE

There was little change either in the laws or customs with regard to separation and divorce. Divorce became legally possible, though the Roman Catholic

[9] Kenneth W. Eckhardt, "Family Responsibility and Legal Norms," *Journal of Marriage and the Family* 32 (Feb. 1970), pp. 105–9.

church still insisted on the indissolubility of marriage. Divorce cases were heard in the bishops' courts on grounds of adultery, impotence, refusal to co-habit, and cruelty. Apparently, few divorces were granted.

Somewhat later on, powerful and wealthy people sometimes were granted divorces by special act of Parliament. Great stigma, however, was attached to divorce on the grounds available and few persons endured the ordeal. The most significant development lay in the fact that the groundwork was being laid for more liberal divorce practice in the future.

The Family in the American Colonies

Even as the family practices described in the preceding section were devel-oping, they were being transported, in modified form, to what was to become the United States of America. As the settlement of the New World proceeded, however, adaptation to the conditions of immigration and to both the physical and social environment of the new country produced a family system that was unlike, in many ways, its English genitor. A specifically American family system came into being.

The conditions of immigration precluded what little chance there might have been for the establishment of any form of clan organization in America. The *sippe* and the *maegth* were in decline on the Continent and in England anyway, so the migrants might not have been disposed to resurrect them even had conditions been favorable. But they were not favorable. The immigrants generally came, not in extended family groups but in nuclear families and as single persons. Particularly in the southern colonies, there were large numbers of unattached men. Consequently the basic social units of the New World were two: the nuclear family and the household.

There are no data to indicate what proportion of all households contained persons in addition to members of the nuclear family but probably it was quite large. In Puritan New England, where the population early gathered in towns, the household often contained either wage-earning or indentured servants. As sons grew to adulthood and married, the laws of inheritance favored the eldest son, particularly, bringing his bride to the home of his parents. Adopting the English precedent, the New England colonies followed, for a while, the modi-fied form of primogeniture in which the eldest son received a double portion. Settlement in the southern colonies was more often on isolated farms and plantations, the very self-sufficiency of which encouraged the development of large households. At the center of the social structure were the plantation owners and operators who accumulated a large number of indentured servants and Negro slaves; and beyond this elite were an undetermined number of ordinary farmers and "poor whites."

In all the colonies the size of the household was increased by the emphasis upon marriage and the production of large families. From England came the tradition of accumulating property and transmitting it intact to one's heirs; the frontier and farming made economic assets of children; and marriage was generally regarded as protection against vice and immorality. So important was this last that the New England colonies in particular discouraged adults from remaining single and imposed restrictions upon those who did. In some areas of Pennsylvania, single men paid double taxes, and in Hartford "the selfish luxury of solitary living" was taxed twenty shillings per week.[10] In many areas single persons of either sex were required to live with families who were licensed for the purpose and who would be responsible for their morals. This meant that many families had unmarried adult relatives living with them.

Related to the large size of colonial families was the fact that many, perhaps most, of them performed almost every necessary service for their members. With help, the men and boys built the house they lived in. Farm buildings, tools, implements, and furniture similarly were provided. Most families provided at least a portion of their own food, with the women processing and storing it. Thread was spun, cloth was woven, clothing was sewn, candles were poured, soap was made, and so on. The family was nearly an independent economic unit. The family was a primary educational agency, with at least the skills of farming or trade and those of housewifery being taught at home. Even where there were private or public schools, some of the education in the three R's often was done at home. Not only was the family an educational unit but it was a primary religious unit. In the north the orientation was Puritan and in the south it was Anglican, but in both cases the family was a solidary religious unit organized around the father, who directed reading of the scriptures, family prayers, and hymn singing. The colonial family today is often looked back upon as a splendid example of a strong, stable, multifunctional family.[11]

It may not be amiss to point out that the conditions of life in the early years, and especially in New England, were hard. Shelter was crude, living in

---

[10] Trumbull, *Blue Laws True and False*, 1876, p. 258, as cited in Goodsell, p. 368.

[11] See Gillian Lindt Gollin, "Family Surrogates in Colonial America: The Moravian Experiment," *Journal of Marriage and the Family* 31 (Nov. 1969), pp. 650–8; also Herman R. Lantz, Margaret Britton, Raymond Schmitt, and Eloise C. Snyder, "Pre-Industrial Patterns in the Colonial Family in America: A Content Analysis of Colonial Magazines," *American Sociological Review* 33 (June 1968), pp. 413–26.

sod huts and even caves being found. Food was scarce, medicine rare, and the mortality rates exceedingly high. The remarriage of widows and widowers was a phenomenon of major importance, and families of from 10 to 25 children often resulted in half, or less, that number growing to adulthood.[12]

PATRIARCHY

The system of law which was brought to the colonies was essentially the English common law which had emerged during the late Middle Ages and the Renaissance. Over the centuries the settling of disputes without clear precedent or explicit legislation had given way to the accumulation of court decisions and a body of parliamentary law. According to these precedents, both women and children were held under the power of the husband.

Women held no property unless it was specifically given them by their husbands for their personal use; even the wife's personal property and clothing belonged to the husband. On the other hand, husbands were legally responsible for their wives, were obligated for their support, and were even responsible for the wife's debts incurred both before and after marriage.[13] A wife also had the right to a dower interest in the husband's real property which could not be sold or disposed of without her concurrence.[14] If the husband died first, the wife gained control of her own property. If the wife died first, the husband was granted a "courtesy interest" in her property for the rest of his life.

The question of whether unmarried women could own land early arose. In New England, generally, the practice was discouraged. In the middle and southern colonies, however, women often held land in their own names.

HINTS FOR YOUNG MARRIED WOMEN, 1788

. . . *Never let your brow be clouded with resentment! Never triumph in revenge! Who is it that you afflict? The man upon earth that should be dearest to you! Upon whom all your future hopes of happi-*

---

[12] Benjamin Franklin was one of 17 children. Bossard remarks that families of 20 to 25 children "were not rare enough to occasion comment." See James H. S. Bossard and Eleanor S. Boll, *The Sociology of Child Development*, New York: Harper, 1960, p. 611.

[13] The fact that the husband was responsible for his wife's debts incurred before marriage led, in scattered locations, to the custom of "smock marriages" in which the couple would be married in the open countryside, with the bride clad only in a slip. This ceremony was supposed to symbolize the wife's coming to her husband unencumbered and to free him from the obligation to pay any debts which she might owe.

[14] This dower right is recognized even today in the requirement that signatures of both the husband and wife appear on any transfer of real estate. Otherwise, if the husband died, the wife might reclaim her dower interest in the property.

ness must depend. Poor the conquest, when your dearest friend must suffer; and ungenerous must be the heart that can rejoice in such a victory.

Let your tears persuade—these speak the most irresistible language with which you can assail the heart of man; but even these sweet fountains of sensibility must not flow too often, lest they degenerate into weakness, and we lose our husband's esteem and affection by the very methods which were given to us to ensure them. Study every little attention in your person, manners, and dress that you find pleasing. Never be negligent in your appearance because you expect nobody but your husband. He is the first person whom you should endeavor to oblige. Always make your home agreeable to him; receive him with ease, good humor, and cheerfulness—but be cautious how you inquire too minutely into his engagements abroad. Betray neither suspicion nor jealousy. Appear always gay and happy in his presence. Be particularly attentive to his favorite friends, even if they intrude upon you. A welcome reception will at all times counterbalance indifferent fare. Treat his relations with respect and attention; ask their advice in your household affairs, and always follow it when you can consistently with propriety.

Treat your husband with the most unreserved confidence in everything that regards yourself, but never betray your friends' letters or secrets to him. This he cannot, and indeed ought not, to expect. If you do not use him to it, he will never desire it. Be careful never to intrude upon his studies or his pleasure; be always glad to see him, but do not be laughed at as a fond and foolish wife. Confine your endearment to your own fireside. Do not let the young envy you, nor the old abuse you for a weakness which upon reflection you must yourself condemn. . . .

—*Wilmington Sentinel and General Advertiser*, June 18, 1788.

The over-all status of women varied widely from north to south. In New England, the early Christian notions of the inferiority and the carnal nature of women were prominent. It was thought proper for women to be bound closely to their homes and to be permitted out only to attend religious services. In the south, on the other hand, women were scarce during the early decades and came to have high status. The plantation economy also encouraged a high status for upper-class women by providing servants and slaves to do the menial labor and freeing women to develop manners and social graces. The feudal practice of elevating women to unrealistically high status resulted in an American form of chivalry.

American men generally were not permitted to beat their wives, as they had been able to do in England, and could not even tongue-lash them too freely. The notion of "cruelty" as grounds for legal action against the spouse emerged early and protected both husband and wife from too great abuse by the other.

The power of the father over his children was great, but not so great as it had been in the past. He was the sole legal guardian of the children and was empowered to make many decisions concerning them. Laws in Massachusetts and Connecticut even provided that persistently disobedient children might be put to death. There is no indication of children actually having been slain under these laws, but the influence of the old Hebrew traditions is clearly there.

Parents frequently sought to arrange marriages for their children, and, under the common law, boys could be married at fourteen and girls at twelve. Furthermore, a young man could not call upon or court a young woman without specifically securing her father's consent. With all this, child marriages appear to have been uncommon, young people were granted considerable freedom, and girls could refuse to marry the young men their fathers had selected for them.

COURTSHIP, BETROTHAL, AND MARRIAGE

The contradictory conditions of rigid control and considerable premarital freedom applied to relationships between young people. On the one hand, a young man had to secure the consent of a girl's father before he could call on her. But on the other hand, young men and women were permitted to travel to and from dances unescorted and even to travel from town to town together. Towns often were far apart and the journey often took more than one day. There is evidence, too, of young couples frequenting taverns together.

The word "courtship," which oldsters insist upon using to describe premarital relationships even today, had definite meaning. Young men were not supposed to pay particular attention to a girl unless and until they had the prospect of marriage in mind. When the young man approached the father for permission to court his daughter, it was quite appropriate for the father to inquire "whether his intentions were honorable." If considerable freedom was granted the young couple, it was also expected that they should not delay marriage for long.

One of the most intriguing of colonial courtship customs was that of bundling. This practice which apparently was imported from Europe occurred to some degree in New Amsterdam and the New England colonies. It permitted the courting couple to retire to bed together fully clothed, or almost so, to carry on the courtship under the covers.[15] The custom was the more remarkable when one considers that the northern attitude toward sex was harsh and disapproving and that persons guilty of fornication might be compelled to marry, or be fined, whipped, or forced to stand in the stocks. Where a child was born within seven months of the time of marriage, the couple also were forced to make public confession of having had premarital intercourse.

Defenders of the practice claim that it was quite innocent: the couple were fully clothed; there often was a bundling board between them; and the girl's parents often were asleep in the same room. More cynical persons agree with the observation of Washington Irving that, "To this sagacious custom, therefore, do I chiefly attribute the unparalleled increase of the . . . Yankee tribe; for it is a certain fact, well authenticated by court records and parish registers, that wherever the practice of bundling prevailed, there was an amazing number of sturdy brats annually born unto the state, without the license of the law, or the benefit of clergy." [16] Assuming that the endocrinological makeup of men and women then was comparable to what it is now, we might conclude that the custom was more compatible with the expectation of short courtships than of longer ones.

There is evidence, too, that bundling was more common among lower-economic groups and was an adjustment to frontier conditions. The New England winters were cold, and firewood, oil for lamps, and candles were in short supply. Bundling may have been a device for permitting the couple to carry on their "conversations" after the family retired and without wasting fuel and light. The custom appears to have faded as living conditions improved.

Again in New England, formal betrothal, called *precontract*, and analogous to the Anglo-Saxon *beweddung*, existed. Precontract required parental consent and was solemnized before two witnesses. Its essence was a promise to marry in the future and was often followed by the preaching of a sermon. *Precontract* changed both the legal and the social status of the couple. Since they were "almost married," the couple were more likely to begin sexual intercourse, and the laws punishing fornication were softened for them, the penalties prescribed generally being half those imposed upon other couples.

In all the colonies the arrangement of marriage often hinged frankly upon economic considerations. Single living for adults was discouraged, and both

---

[15] For a light-hearted account of the origins, incidence, and practice of bundling, see Henry R. Stiles, *Bundling: Its Origin, Progress, and Decline in America*, New York: Book Collector's Association, 1934.

[16] Washington Irving, *Diedrich Knickerbocker's A History of New York*, New York: Putnam, 1880, p. 210.

men and women found it socially and economically advantageous to marry. Calhoun stresses the fact that romantic inclinations were often subordinated to financial advantages and that parents haggled openly over the man's wealth and the woman's dowry.[17]

The financial bargaining appeared most unabashedly among widows and widowers. With the prevailing high death rates, men and women often found themselves in the position of seeking mates for a second or even a third time. Widows with children actually were somewhat preferred marriage partners. The children provided a labor force and the widows often owned property in their own right, or at least had a life interest in the property left to them by their first husbands. Goodsell describes several cases of ruthless bargaining between widows and widowers and emphasizes how promptly they remarried.[18] One colonist proposed marriage to a woman just after the funeral of his first wife, and the remarriages of persons widowed for only a few weeks appears to have been common.[19]

Rich widows are the only secondhand goods that sell at first-class prices.

—Benjamin Franklin

Although there are no reliable data available, marriage for most persons apparently occurred quite early. The legal minimum ages for marriage were 14 for boys and 12 for girls. Moreover, girls of 20 were looked upon as old maids.

The colonies were very careful to hedge marriage with legal restrictions. In general, they required that: (1) parental consent be secured, (2) notice of intention to marry be given, (3) the marriage ceremony be performed by an authorized officiant, and (4) the marriage be officially registered.

Since each colony had its own laws, there was no strict uniformity from one colony to another. Before long, however, virtually all the colonies made provision either for the publication of banns or the securing of a licence. The banns were either posted or read on three successive Sundays at the church or meeting-house. As an alternative, most of the colonies permitted the securing of a licence from the governor or from one of the courts. Then, as now, excep-

[17] Arthur W. Calhoun, *A Social History of the American Family From Colonial Times to the Present*, New York: Barnes and Noble, 1945, Vol. I, pp. 56–9.

[18] Op. cit. pp. 374–7.

[19] Queen and Habenstein, op. cit. p. 275.

tions were made for certain religious groups, such as the Quakers, who were permitted to post notice of impending marriage according to their traditional customs and without the securing of a licence or the reading of banns.

In only one colony, New York, was it specifically provided that failure to post banns or secure a licence rendered a marriage void. All of the other colonies provided punishment for disobeying the law but they did not invalidate illegal marriages. In New York, too, failure to have a marriage performed by a licensed officiant rendered the marriage invalid; in other colonies lesser penalties were provided.

Deep distrust, in New England, of the established church resulted in ministers generally being prohibited from performing marriage ceremonies. All ceremonies had to be performed by justices of the peace or by magistrates. In the south, where the Church of England became firmly established, the opposite situation prevailed; only religious ceremonies were permitted. The middle colonies generally followed a middle course, accepting both religious and civil marriages.[20] Although the groups authorized to perform marriages varied, all of the colonies carefully regulated performance of the marriage ceremony.

The registration of marriages was equally carefully controlled. In the more closely settled areas of the north, the town clerk usually was required to register marriages, births, and deaths. Failure to register a marriage within a prescribed period resulted in the imposition of a heavy fine. Parish ministers often were responsible for the registration of marriages in the south, gradually being replaced by elected officials. In the middle colonies, intermediate arrangements prevailed.

Almost from the beginning, and in spite of such careful regulations, the custom of self-marriage crept into the colonies. As we have seen, self-marriage in words of the present tense was firmly established in Europe. In the American colonies the practice emerged mostly in the rural South and on the frontier. In those areas, ministers, and civil officials too, were scarce. The ministers often were circuit riders who visited isolated communities very infrequently. In the interim, when a couple wished to marry they might simply say their vows at a gathering of friends and neighbors and proceed to live together as man and wife until a preacher appeared to formalize the relationship. In some cases, by the time a minister became available the couple were so thoroughly habituated to the marital state that a religious ceremony seemed

---

[20] Maryland was an exception. To this day Maryland permits only religious ceremonies. Other states which have adopted the same practice are Delaware and West Virginia. In Delaware the only civil official authorized to perform a wedding ceremony is the mayor of Wilmington.

unnecessary. In more isolated sections even the saying of marriage vows before witnesses was omitted. The colonial laws generally did not declare such marriages to be invalid and subsequent court decisions generally upheld them. Thus, what we today call common-law marriage came into the United States.

The colonies also sought to regulate the process of mate selection. Minimum ages for marriage and the necessity for parental consent already have been discussed. Prohibitions for relationships within specified degrees of consanguinity and affinity were established. Queen and Habenstein report that in some instances there were 30 classes of kinsmen who were forbidden as mates.[21] Reference back to Figure 3 in Chapter 2 will indicate that such prohibitions extend out to approximately first cousins. In some states in the United States today first cousins are permitted to marry; in others they are forbidden to do so. Persons in New England who married within the prohibited degrees sometimes were punished by being required to wear a large "I" (for incest) sewn prominently on their clothing.

Prohibitions on interracial marriages had appeared before 1700. Bardis reports that Chester County, Pennsylvania, prohibited Negro-white marriages in 1698 and that Massachusetts forbade Negro-white and mulatto-white marriages in 1705.[22] White-Indian marriages also were widely forbidden. The southern colonies generally forbade all interracial marriages.

DIVORCE

The New England Puritan rebellion against the Church of England included the recognition of absolute divorce. Practices varied from one colony to another. Massachusetts first granted jurisdiction over divorces to the Court of Assistants but transferred it to the Governor and Council before 1700. In many cases divorce suits were heard by the colonial legislatures, each divorce requiring a separate act of the legislature. Only Connecticut administered divorce proceedings solely through the courts.

The grounds upon which divorce might be secured also varied from colony to colony. In general in New England, however, the grounds were fairly liberal and discriminated in favor of men. Men could divorce their wives for adultery, for desertion, and for cruelty. Women, on the other hand, were not entitled to divorce on grounds of adultery alone; only if it was accompanied by desertion or failure to provide was the husband's adultery grounds for divorce. Some

[21] Op. cit. p. 294.
[22] Bardis, op. cit. p. 452.

of the New England colonies provided that the woman might be granted alimony if she was unjustly divorced by her husband.

There are few comprehensive data available on the incidence of divorce in these early days, but Calhoun presents some illustrative figures.[23] Between 1639 and 1692, in Massachusetts, 25 divorces were granted. From 1692 to 1739 there are no pertinent records. During the next 20 years, from 1739 to 1760, there were only three divorces, two separations from bed and board, and two annulments. The year 1760 appears to have marked a turning point. Over the next 26 years, 75 divorces, seven separations from bed and board, and five annulments were granted.

Interestingly, throughout this period, more suits for divorce were brought by women than by men. Our brief survey of the history of Western family organization has shown that the divorce rules have almost always favored men. Yet the first time that figures become available we find more divorces being granted to women. Would this also have been true among the ancient and medieval periods or was this a distinctively American innovation? There are at least two plausible explanations. One is that, although the general condition is one of male domination, the family is everywhere more central to the lives of women and, in spite of legal disabilities, women more often seek relief from intolerable circumstances. Another possibility, tracing from the chivalric period, is that men more often permit their wives the face-saving alternative of being the active seeker of the divorce even when they themselves wish the marriage to be terminated.

The middle and southern colonies were not so liberal in their attitudes toward divorce. The Church of England became firmly established in the south, and the church did not recognize absolute divorce; it permitted only separation from bed and board for adultery and cruelty. The southern colonies became even more conservative because, although they accepted the church, they refused to establish church courts in the new world. The result was that no organization was empowered to hear divorce suits and neither absolute divorce nor legal separation were granted in the southern colonies.[24] Some couples separated anyway, of course, and some southern courts heard requests for alimony from persons thus separated.

The middle colonies generally followed divorce policies closer to those of the southern colonies than to those of the New England colonies. Very few absolute divorces were granted in New York or Pennsylvania. The middle colonies

[23] Op. cit. Vol. II, pp. 332–66.

[24] It was not until 1949 that the last southern state, South Carolina, finally began to grant absolute divorces.

generally failed to grant jurisdiction over divorce to the courts, and what few suits there were, were heard by the legislatures.

THE COLONIAL ATTITUDES TOWARD SEX

Attitudes toward sex and the prevailing morality have been dealt with tangentially in our discussions of earlier periods, but this is the first time they have been singled out for separate treatment. In part this is due to the incompleteness of our knowledge of earlier societies. But not entirely. We single out sex and morality here because the attitudes established during the colonial period can be traced directly to the present day. The contemporary American family system cannot be completely understood without understanding its strong and contradictory traditions in the area of sexual behavior.

An unmarried couple was found guilty of fornication Friday under a 1790 law that had been a dead letter for more than 170 years.

[The couple] were found guilty on three counts—one for each of the three illegitimate children [the woman] had borne when the charge was filed in 1967. Officials said she had had a fourth child since then.

Municipal Judge Ervan F. Kushner ordered the filing of the fornication charge . . . when [the woman] filed a non-support charge against [the man].

"I saw a crime being committed when a single woman walked into my court pregnant," Kushner said.

—United Press International, June 15, 1969.

Colonial New England took its attitudes toward sex from the Hebrew-Christian tradition. Sex was considered to be inherently evil and all sexual activity other than that required for procreation within marriage was defined as sinful. The colonies went to great lengths to discourage and punish premarital and extramarital sexual activity. Yet there were overtones of interest in sex which belied the official norms.

Premarital sex relationships were punishable by fines, whipping, and/or being forced to marry. The offenders might also be forced to stand in the stocks and to be branded on the cheek. The woman who bore a child out of wedlock might also be imprisoned. Even married couples who bore a child within seven months of the time of marriage were punished. After the birth of the infant, the couple were required to make public confession of their sin before the entire congregation of the church. Bardis reports that church attendance increased substantially for such events and that the sensationalism may actually have promoted sexual immorality.[25]

Most New England colonies actually permitted adulterers to be put to death and some death sentences were meted out. More commonly the punishment was whipping, branding, and being required to wear the scarlet letter A, for "adulterer." Women often were more strictly punished than men, but one unfortunately eager sea captain was forced to stand in the stocks for the "crime" of kissing his wife in public and on Sunday after returning home from a three-year voyage.

All of this in the very region in which bundling was practised. Queen, and Habenstein present data indicating that between 1726 and 1780, in one Massachusetts county, 160 married couples, 31 wives, and 523 single women were punished for sex offenses.[26] In one Groton church, approximately one-third of the parents of first-born children confessed to having had premarital intercourse.

Some teen-agers, with their parents' approval, have revived the co-lonial form of courtship known as bundling. The youngsters say that there is nothing wrong with it since it is strictly supervised.

"It's a form of togetherness which allows two people to be alone," Miss Dolores Smyth said. Miss Smyth, president of the Pottsdown Society to Bring Back Bundling to America, said that the members expected some criticism.

"But we expect to prove that bundling is not only an innocent form of courtship, but one which preserves morals while allowing a close relationship between couples," she added. Eighteen teen-agers have joined the society. All must have the approval of their parents to join. . . .

—*The New York Times*, August 31, 1969.

The situation in the South was quite different. The development there of a landed aristocracy, combined with an early shortage of women and then with an abundance of Negro women slaves, to produce a glaring double standard—one standard for men and another for women.

Legal provisions in the south were less strict than those in the north. The

[25] Op. cit. p. 456.
[26] Op. cit. pp. 285–6. See also Emil Oberholzer, Jr., *Delinquent Saints: Disciplinary Action in the Early Congregational Churches of Massachusetts*, New York: Columbia University Press, 1956.

laws generally did prohibit both fornication and adultery, and punishments including fines and whipping sometimes were provided. No stocks were used, however; there were no scarlet letters; and physical punishment was carefully restricted. More important, the laws were not systematically enforced.

Upper-class women occupied a very special position. A chivalry not completely unlike that of medieval England was shown toward them; they were pampered, humored, and catered to. Unlike the medieval ladies, however, upper-class southern women were carefully guarded against sexual involvement before marriage and against extramarital affairs after marriage. The fiction was maintained, and it often may have become a self-fulfilling prophecy [27] that genteel women generally viewed sex in terms of duty rather than in terms of personal fulfillment.

Upper-class men, by contrast, appear to have enjoyed great sexual freedom both before marriage and while married. If they were the victims of their own expectations concerning upper-class women, it was also expected that they would meet their sexual needs wherever they could. With a large dependent population of Negro women available, there was widespread violation of the miscegenation statutes. Many white men apparently used Negro and mulatto women at their convenience but there also were numerous semi-permanent liaisons in which the men acknowledged their illegitimate offspring and accorded special favors and status to their mistresses.

The double standard operated between men and women and also between Negroes and whites. The keeping of mistresses by wealthy white men was so open that at least two state governors saw no need to conceal their extramarital relationships. Censure actually would fall upon the wife if she failed to accept the situation graciously. And, at the same time that white men openly exploited Negro women, any hint of sexual interest in a white woman by a Negro man was sufficient cause for him to be put to death. The hostilities and fears engendered by this situation continue to plague Negro-white relationships to the present day.

THE TRANSITION TO THE PRESENT

In many ways it is a far cry from colonial days to twentieth-century America. From the original thirteen colonies huddled on the eastern seaboard, we have

---

[27] Sociologists use the phrase, self-fulfilling prophecy, to refer to a *"false* definition of the situation evoking a new behavior which makes the originally false conception come *true.* The specious validity of the self-fulfilling prophecy perpetuates a reign of error. For the prophet will cite the actual course of events as proof that he was right from the very beginning." See Robert K. Merton, *Social Theory and Social Structure,* Glencoe, Illinois: The Free Press, 1957, p. 423.

become a nation of 50 states and 210 million people. Whereas, at the time of the first United States Census in 1790, the population was 95 per cent rural, in 1970 it was 75 per cent urban. A volume larger than this one could be written on the changes in family patterns which have accompanied the development of this country.[28] To some extent the remainder of this book does contrast the family structure of today with that of colonial times. But it is also true that the basic outlines of American family patterns had been laid down by the time the United States emerged as an independent nation. It remains, in the closing section of this chapter, to indicate a few of the major forces operating to transform the colonial family into that of the 1970's.

THE INFLUENCE OF THE FRONTIER

Even in colonial days, there was relatively little elaboration of kinship structure. The household had largely replaced the clan, and even the extended family, as the basic unit of society. Households were large both in northern communities and on southern plantations. Ties to the land and a tendency toward primogeniture encouraged the formation of stem families; and unmarried kin often had no choice but to attach themselves to existing households. Even then, however, nuclear family units often were entire household units. The influence of the frontier operated to sever ties from both kin and land and to increase the isolation of the nuclear family.

Following the Revolution, the growing population spread westward, first across the Appalachians, then to the Mississippi, and finally to the Pacific Ocean. The migrants were, as they usually are, predominantly young people. Young men took their nuclear families with them or they sought wives and built families after they had left the settled communities of the east for the isolation and self-sufficiency of the frontier. The grand-parental generation most often was left behind; it had its ties, and the settlement of the frontier was arduous work.

The effects of this migration upon family structure hardly could have been imagined. First, it was accompanied by the further decline of patriarchal control. Throughout history strong patriarchies have been associated with extended families. Children growing up on the frontier could never know the direct authority of their grandfathers and consequently never learned to expect

---

[28] See the three-volume work by Calhoun, op. cit.; Michael Gordon, "The Ideal Husband as Depicted in the Nineteenth Century Marriage Manual," *The Family Coordinator* 18 (July 1969), pp. 226–31; and Michael Gordon and M. Charles Bernstein, "Mate Choice and Domestic Life in the Nineteenth-Century Marriage Manual," *Journal of Marriage and the Family* 32 (Nov. 1970), pp. 665–74.

to control their own future grandchildren. True, they still saw their father as the person of final authority in the family and it was to be many years before women gained real legal equality with men. But the isolation and rigor of life on the frontier produced a hardy breed of women without whom the country could not have been won and who had a *de facto* equality with men. The future could only bring an increasing democratization of relationships within the family.

Equally drastic were the effects upon patterns of inheritance. Extended patriarchal families historically were associated with ties to the land and with a favored inheritance status for the eldest son. As extended families broke up and spread over the countryside, parents resorted to disposing of their property by will. Instead of being held intact for future generations, the property was broken up and sold. As the colonies became the United States of America, the democratic ideology upon which they were founded refused to sanction inherited inequality among siblings and the various state constitutions outlawed the practice of entail. The tradition developed that all children, girls included, should inherit equally from their parents.

The immortality of the old extended family system was waning. In its place, there gradually emerged a conjugal family system without much family tradition and without either economic or sentimental ties to a wide array of kin.

THE EFFECTS OF LARGE-SCALE IMMIGRATION

The United States population grew both through natural increase—the excess of births over deaths—and through immigration, chiefly from Europe. Up to now we have dealt only with the dominant English tradition. But the number of migrants from other areas of Europe and Africa far exceeded those from England for most of two centuries. The United States became a relatively heterogeneous nation with heterogeneous family patterns.

Little attention is paid, ordinarily, to the fact that the largest migration to America, before 1800, was of Negro slaves. The exact size of this migration will never be known. The number probably falls between 10 and 20 million people. By contrast, the number of migrants from all of Europe during the same period was not over 5 million. The conditions of Negro slavery before the Civil War and the varied conditions ever since have produced family patterns which are both like and unlike their white counterparts. At the present time, there are approximately 22 million people in the United States who are defined as Negro. The distinctive family patterns of this largest American minority will be treated in detail in a later chapter of this book.

After 1800 the mass migration from Europe to the United States got under way. During the nineteenth century approximately 19 million people came, chiefly from northwestern Europe—Great Britain, Ireland, Germany, and France. Beginning about 1890, the countries of origin of the migrants shifted from northwest Europe to southern and eastern Europe. Between 1890 and 1930, an additional 22 million people came, this time mostly from Italy, Austria-Hungary, and Russia. In the year 1930, there were more than 14 million foreign-born persons living in the United States. Since that time a restrictive immigration policy has drastically limited the number of migrants and the number and proportion of foreign-born in the population have been declining.

The peak migration between 1890 and 1920 differed from earlier ones in several ways. First the migrants were not so often farmers. Second, they found the country largely settled and, rather than spreading out over the countryside, they tended to create ethnic enclaves in the larger eastern cities. Third, a large proportion of the immigrants was Roman Catholic.

These new migrants were not altogether hospitably received. They reacted to prejudice and discrimination by turning inward upon themselves, preserving their traditional languages and customs. Their family patterns varied by nationality and religion and, within these, by economic status. For generations they somewhat resisted assimilation into the mainstream of American life. They became, in some ways, sources of the preservation of old world family patterns in the new world. In the 1970's they are not nearly so conspicuous as they were a generation earlier. But even today they provide significant variations on the major American family theme.

URBANIZATION AND INDUSTRIALIZATION

In the United States, urbanization and industrialization developed together and promoted broad social change. Industrialization got under way shortly after 1800 as the factory system replaced the old system of home production. Cities grew up around the new factories and there were several direct effects on family organization. First, the family ceased to be a principal unit of production, becoming transformed into basically a consumption unit. Instead of father, mother, and children working together in an integrated economic enterprise, the father now went out of the home each day to earn the family's living. Business and industry became structured according to increasingly universalistic standards, while the family remained a haven of particularism.

Second, the prospect of factory employment freed young adults and unmarried men and women from direct dependence upon their families. As their wages made them financially independent, the authority of the head of the household weakened further. Urbanization also brought the development of such specialized commercial establishments as hotels and rooming houses, restaurants, bakeries, grocery stores, and laundries, making it possible for many persons to live apart from families altogether. This situation had special significance for women who no longer had to marry in order to have a place to live and who no longer had to stay married simply because there was no alternative. The divorce rate began to rise.

Finally, children ceased to be economic assets and became liabilities instead. Although there was a period of the use and abuse of child labor, legal regulation gradually removed children from the job market. At the same time, formal educational requirements were increasing, lengthening the period of dependence upon parental support. Living space in the cities was crowded and expensive; child-care was demanding. The birth rate began to fall.

And so we come to the contemporary American family. To compress 3000 years of history into two chapters obviously produces tremendous oversimplification. We have sought not to present a detailed history of the Western family but to trace certain threads which are most directly relevant to understanding the family system of today. Some "meaning" has been both implicit and explicit in this discussion. A few sociologists have confronted this problem of meaning more directly and have formulated comprehensive theories of family structure and family change. Before turning to description and analysis of the modern American family, we will examine three of these theoretical analyses.

SUMMARY

The emergence of feudalism placed a premium on the ability to bear arms and lowered the status of women again, almost to that of chattels who went with the land. Primogeniture and entail emerged to hold estates intact; marriages were calculatingly arranged for children in order to build the family estates. With the prolonged absence of their husbands, upper-class women gained both leisure time and *de facto* power, and the romantic tradition of chivalry appeared. Romantic love became a primary value but it was widely considered to be incompatible with marriage.

After the tenth century the church wrested control of marriage from laymen but, in so doing, encouraged the spread of clandestine marriage according to which persons married themselves simply by speaking their vows in words of the present tense. The church's attempt to uproot clandestine marriages by creating a distinction between legal and valid marriages was a dismal failure. The church became further plagued by scandals surrounding the requirement for a celibate priesthood and by widespread abuse of the granting of annulments.

The Reformation produced a definition of marriage as a civil contract and re-created absolute divorce. Most of the impediments to marriage were removed. The English family from the sixteenth century to the eighteenth century changed but little. The importance of the *sippe* continued to decline.

The family system which emerged in the American colonies was organized around the nuclear family and the larger household. It was a stable family system in which early marriage was urged and in which the family performed almost every conceivable service for its members. It was clearly a patriarchal system in which all of the wife's property belonged to the husband and women were not even the legal guardians of their own children. The wife's dower interest in her husband's property was clearly established, however, and the husband was responsible for his wife's support.

The common-law minimum ages for marriage were fourteen for boys and twelve for girls. Consent of the girl's father was required for courtship, but considerable freedom was granted to courting couples and girls were permitted to reject specific suitors. Bundling existed for a while in several of the northern colonies; in New England, a formal betrothal, called precontract, existed. Marriage was based upon economic considerations and there was much haggling over dower and dowry.

The colonies generally required that parental consent to a proposed marriage be secured, adequate notice of intention to marry be given, the marriage ceremony be performed by an authorized officiant, and the marriage be properly recorded. The northern colonies generally favored civil marriage while the southern colonies favored religious ceremonies. The northern colonies also permitted divorce; the southern colonies did not. In spite of the efforts to prevent it, self-marriage crept into the colonies and evolved into what we today call common-law marriage.

Colonial attitudes toward sex were confused and inconsistent. In New England, attitudes were harshly repressive and violations were severely punished. In the south, by contrast, there was a marked double standard exalting virginity and faithfulness for upper-class women and sanctioning premarital and extramarital adventures for men. The double standard also operated between Negroes and whites, favoring the exploitation of Negro women by white men.

With the passage of time, the influence of the frontier and widespread geographical mobility further weakened the patriarchal tradition and broke up the pattern of family estates. Equal inheritance by all children was encouraged. Heterogeneity of family patterns was fostered by large-scale immigration until about 1930; somewhat distinctive Negro and ethnic family patterns appeared.

Finally, industrialization and urbanization transformed the family into a small consumption unit. Work and home became separated and alternatives to family living became feasible.

SUGGESTED READINGS

Aries, Philippe (trans. by Robert Baldick), *Centuries of Childhood: A Social History of Family Life*, New York: Alfred A. Knopf, 1962. Traces the emergence of the modern conception of parenthood and childhood over the past four centuries. Emphasizes the situations in pre-nineteenth century France and England.

Calhoun, Arthur W., *A Social History of the American Family from Colonial Times to the Present*, New York: Barnes and Noble, 1945. A new edition of an original three-volume comprehensive history of the development of the American family up through the first decade of the twentieth century.

Demos, John, *A Little Commonwealth: Family Life in Plymouth Colony*, New York: Oxford University Press, 1970. An historian writes of the Pilgrim family; of roles and relationships over the life-cycle.

Gordon, Michael, and Bernstein, M. Charles, "Mate Choice and Domestic Life in the Nineteenth-Century Marriage Manual," *Journal of Marriage and the Family* 32 (November 1970), pp. 665–74. Emphasizes the diversity of family patterns and the absence of romantic love as an important factor in mate choice.

Howard, George E., *A History of Matrimonial Institutions*, Chicago: University of Chicago Press, 1904. A three-volume work covering the development of matrimonial institutions in England and the United States.

Lantz, Herman R., Britton, Margaret, Schmitt, Raymond, and Snyder, Eloise C., "Pre-Industrial Patterns in the Colonial Family in America: A Content Analysis of Colonial Magazines," *American Sociological Review* 33 (June, 1968), pp. 413-26. Emphasizes the prevalence of male authority along with evidence that women wielded a great deal of power indirectly.

Schermerhorn, Richard A., "Family Carry-overs of Western Christendom," in Howard Becker and Reuben Hill, eds., *Family, Marriage, and Parenthood*, Boston: D. C. Heath, 1955, pp. 104–30. A brief history of the European family from the Middle Ages up until the time of the colonization of America.

Stiles, Henry R., *Bundling: Its Origin, Progress, and Decline in America*, New York: Book Collectors' Association, 1934. A quaint and humorous account which apparently was written around 1870 but not commercially published until 1934.

Sullerot, Evelyne (trans. by Margaret S. Archer), *Woman, Society and Change*, New York: McGraw-Hill, 1971. An account, by a French scholar, of the changing status of women in society. Recent historical changes are emphasized.

FILMS

Early Marriage (Churchill-Wexler Films, 801 N. Seward St., Los Angeles), 24 minutes. Ancient and modern marriage customs are shown. These are contrasted with the "run away" marriage. Various elements which contribute to the probable success or failure, especially among teenagers, are discussed in a counseling and classroom setting.

From Father to Son (National Film Board of Canada, Mackenzie Building, Toronto), 25 minutes. A story about the descendants of French-Canadian prisoners who first settled on strip farms along the St. Lawrence River. The film concerns a family with 13 children, representing the eighth and ninth generations to live on the ancestral farm.

Our Changing Family Life (McGraw-Hill Book Company, Text-Film Division, 330 West 42nd St., New York 10036), 22 minutes. A farm family in 1880 is shown as an economically, culturally, and emotionally integrated unit. Three generations live under one roof. Religion, recreation, and the sharing of work play important roles in holding the family together. Since 1880, industrial expansion, urbanization, and the political and economic emancipation of women have radically changed the pattern of family life. The farm family has become less important as an economic and social unit. The roles of husband and wife have changed, and companionship has become more important in marriage.

The Decision (National Film Board of Canada, Mackenzie Building, Toronto), 30 minutes. Under the pressures of rising prices, competitive markets, and higher production costs, more and more farmers are being forced to abandon their traditional view of farming as a way of life for one that places it on the level of business. In this film, we see how a father and son—the father holding to old ways, the son favoring the new—resolve difficulties in such a way as to enable them to keep abreast of developments in agriculture.

QUESTIONS AND PROJECTS

1. Define the concepts of *unogeniture* and *entail*. How did these practices operate during the Middle Ages?
2. What was the basis for the church's distinction between "legal" marriages and "valid" marriages? What problem was the distinction meant to solve? How did it work?
3. Describe the nature of the English family system from the sixteenth through the eighteenth centuries. What was the nature of marriage? How was the system of descent and inheritance consistent with the nature of marriage?
4. What was the practice of *bundling*? What was the practice of *pre-contract* in the American colonies? Can you see any relationship between the two?
5. How did divorce practices vary among the colonies? What were the most

common grounds for divorce? What substitute for divorce was used in the southern colonies?

6. What were the influences of feudalism on family life? Of chivalry?

7. What major problems, in the regulation of family matters, plagued the church during the Middle Ages? How did the Reformation attempt to deal with these problems? How successful were the attempts?

8. Describe the family system which developed in the American colonies. What variations existed from north to south? What were the varying attitudes toward sex and morality in the colonies?

9. With what safeguards did the colonists surround marriage? Were they able to forestall the development of *self-gifta* in America?

10. How did the influence of the frontier encourage emphasis on the nuclear family in the United States? How did large-scale immigration increase the heterogeneity of United States family patterns? What were the general effects of urbanization and industrialization upon the family in the United States?

Part | III

THEORETICAL PERSPECTIVE

8 | Theories of Family Structure and Family Change

The United States, as well as the other countries of western Christendom, will reach the final phases of a great family crisis between now and the last of this century. By that time the social consequences of this crisis will approach a maximum. This crisis will be identical in nature to the two previous crises in Greece and Rome. The results will be much more drastic in the United States because, being the most extreme and inexperienced of the aggregates of western civilization, it will take its first real "sickness" most violently.

Efforts to meet this situation in the United States will probably be very exaggerated. We will probably try all the "remedies" suggested or tried in Greek and Roman civilization, profiting perhaps but little from the mistakes already made in those periods. The violence and abruptness of the changes will probably be extreme indeed . . .[1]

. . . Prior to modern times the power and prestige of the family was due to seven functions it performed: . . .

These seven functions—economic, status giving, educational, religious, recreational, protective, and affectional—may be thought of as bonds that tied the members of a family together. If one asks why do the various members of a family stay together instead of each going his way, the answer is that they are tied together by these functions. If they didn't exist, it is not easy to see that there would be any family.

The dilemma of the modern family is caused by the loss of many of these functions in recent times. . . . at least six of the seven family functions have been reduced as family activities in recent times, and it may be claimed that only one remains as vigorous and extensive as in prior eras.[2]

. . . I do not regard differentiation as synonymous with decline. Historically one of the very critical events of the development of modern industry in its early phases was the separation of the productive unit from the household. In traditional

---

[1] Carle C. Zimmerman, *Family and Civilization*, New York: Harper and Brothers, 1947, p. 798. Reprinted by permission of Harper & Row, Publisher, Inc.
[2] William F. Ogburn, "The Changing Family," *The Family* 19 (July 1938), pp. 139-43.

agriculture they are fused together as one unit. In the farm family, the household is a producer of agricultural commodities, and also a residential consumer household in urban centers. When we use the word "family" to designate the stage before differentiation has taken place, as in the farm family, and use the same word to designate one of the two outcomes of the process of differentiation, we must say, "Of course, the family has lost its function." There is a certain logical absurdity in this. Anything that lives has certain functions, even though they may have declined. I think that the question of whether or not the family has declined in the functional sense of not doing its job must be judged in the context of its contemporary relation to other things because it is often exceedingly desirable that differentiations of this sort be made. . .[3]

T HESE three quotations are from three well-known American sociologists who have developed general theories of family structure and family change. Each man has taken the raw facts of history and contemporary existence, examined and systematized them, and arranged them into a comprehensive explanation of the nature of our family system. It goes without saying that their interpretations are not completely consistent with one another. Zimmerman sees imminent catastrophe unless present family and societal trends are halted; Ogburn perceives a family system stripped of most of the functions it once had; and Parsons believes that the modern family is well adapted to the larger society in which it functions. Obviously they cannot all be correct. Our purpose here, however, is not to decide which of them is right but to examine constructively and critically the theoretical arguments which have led them to their respective conclusions. In the end we shall find that it is impossible to *prove* the validity of one interpretation over the others. Here, as elsewhere, science provides neither final answers nor an unerring guide to social action. We should find that each of these three theories has some utility in explaining some of the facts of history and of current existence. And, in the process, we should become familiar with some of the complexities with which future theorists of family structure will have to deal.

A major theme running through this book is that there are complex, pervasive, and subtle interrelations between the family system and other institutional structures. This is hardly a startling notion among sociologists. It represents, instead, a systematic way of organizing data and interpreting them. This approach often is called using an institutional frame of reference.[4]

[3] Talcott Parsons, Panel discussion on "The Forces of Change," in Seymour M. Farber, Piero Mustacchi, and Roger H. L. Wilson, eds., *Man and Civilization: The Family's Search for Survival*, New York: McGraw-Hill Book Company, 1965, p. 56.

[4] For those students who have not encountered the concept before, a frame of reference is simply a series of facts and interpretations of fact which are used as a basis for further study. See John Sirjamaki, "The Institutional Approach," in Harold T. Christensen, ed., *Handbook of Marriage and the Family*, Chicago: Rand McNally, 1964, pp. 33–50.

Among family sociologists who have used the institutional frame of reference, not many have had the temerity to develop sweeping theoretical systems. Perhaps this is because they are too aware of the difficulties involved and are unwilling to produce interpretations which they know beforehand will prove inadequate. Most scholars have been content to point out some of the empirical interrelations between family structure and social structure, as we have done in Chapters 2 and 3 of this book, and to explore the general problem of the degree to which the family is an active or a passive agent in social change.[5]

When the family is conceived of as an active or causal agent in social change, one simply reasons that changes in the family system precede in time and help to bring about changes in other aspects of the social structure. Ideally, of course, the determination of whether changes in the family produce changes in the larger society derives from examination of the data themselves. Few people, however, including sociologists, can be completely neutral and objective about the family and there is some fear that occasionally we are inclined to assign a causal role to family changes out of ideological and personal commitment to the importance of the family.

It probably is accurate to say that the family has more often been conceived to be a passive agent in social change—to adapt to changes in other areas of society rather than to cause changes in other areas. The economic and political institutions are widely believed to change more rapidly than the family does, and social change can be produced only by institutions that are themselves changing. Actually it is oversimplification to say that most scholars treat the family as an active *or* a passive agent in social change. Most sociologists see changes in the family system as both cause *and* effect of changes in other institutional structures.

There have been a few major attempts to formulate comprehensive interpretations of the relation between the family system and other social institutions. The three theories selected for analysis in this chapter might be labeled, respectively, a cyclical theory, a progressivist theory, and a structure-function theory.[6]

[5] For a recent and able analysis of the family as an active and passive agent in social change, see Meyer F. Nimkoff, *Comparative Family Systems*, Boston: Houghton Mifflin, 1965, Ch. 3 and 4.

[6] Recently, sociologists of the family, like other sociologists, have concentrated on developing consistent conceptual approaches to family data, and "theories of the middle range" rather than all-embracing "grand theories." For accounts of efforts to develop conceptual approaches, see Harold T. Christensen, ed., op. cit. Chs. 2–5; and F. Ivan Nye, and Felix M. Berardo, eds., *Emerging Conceptual Frameworks in Family Analysis* (New York: Macmillan, 1966).

Many middle range theories are discussed throughout this book. Included among these

A Cyclical Theory

The best-known advocate in American sociology of a cyclical theory of family structure and family change undoubtedly is Carle C. Zimmerman. Zimmerman developed his theory most carefully and fully in his book, *Family and Civilization*,[7] and that book is the major source for the following discussion. *Family and Civilization* is an erudite tome of more than 800 pages and covering nearly 4000 years of history. Inevitably, something is lost in assessing Zimmerman's thesis in a few pages, as we must do.

First of all, Zimmerman regards the study of family organization in preliterate societies as largely irrelevant to the experience of what he calls the "high civilizations." [8] He states that "primitive" peoples probably come from a different universe of societies, that they are not predecessors of our own society, and that they do not represent an earlier stage of development of civilized society.[9] By contrast, he believes that "the range of principles" [10] which determines our family behavior operates among the great societies of the world. He includes in this universe the Mediterranean and European civilizations including America and Australia, and those of Asia. The major part of his analysis draws upon data from the Western tradition beginning with ancient Greece, progressing through Rome, and then coming forward through the Middle Ages to twentieth-century America.

Zimmerman assumes that there is a close connection between the nature of the family organization and the nature of the larger society. He assumes, also, that changes in the one are closely associated with corresponding changes in the other. Family and civilization are thought to cause changes in one another, the family being viewed both as a major cause of general social change and as being changed by alterations in the larger society. In addition to the family, two other institutions—the church and government—are sources of social change and vie with the family for control over family relations.

---

are: Robert O. Blood and Donald M. Wolfe's theory of marital decision-making in *Husbands and Wives: The Dynamics of Married Living* (The Free Press of Glencoe, Illinois, 1960); Bernard Farber's theory of orderly replacement in *Family: Organization and Interaction* (San Francisco: Chandler, 1964); and Robert F. Winch's theory of complementary needs in mate selection in *Mate Selection: A Study of Complementary Needs* (New York: Harper and Brothers, 1958).

[7] Op. cit. Zimmerman's thesis was anticipated, in Europe, by Frederic LePlay. See Pierre Guillaume Frederic LePlay, *Les Ouvriers europeens*, Paris, 1879.

[8] Ibid. pp. 90–91.

[9] Ibid. p. 92.

[10] Ibid. p. 93.

Throughout Western history, Zimmerman finds that there have been three main family types—the trustee family, the domestic family, and the atomistic family.[11] These three family types are defined according to the amount of power vested in the family, the width of its field of action, and the amount of social control which it exercises.

THE TRUSTEE FAMILY

The trustee family derives its name from the fact that living members of the family are not considered to be *the family* but only the living trustees of its name, its property, and its blood. The family itself is considered to be immortal. An extreme degree of familism is found; there is virtually no concept of individual rights and all questions of individual welfare are subordinated to the welfare of the family group.

The trustee family has great power over its individual members, often amounting to power of life and death. The authority of the husband and father is not absolute authority, however, but is power delegated to him in his role as trustee and for the specific purpose of carrying out family responsibilities. Families are organized into *gentes*, and these combined families make up the state. There is little in the way of organized power outside the family and what little government there is does not interfere in family matters.

Membership in the family generally is based upon formal action, new members being either accepted or rejected by the group. Absolute divorce virtually does not exist. What does exist is the right to repudiate a spouse (wife) who fails to support the integration of the group.

THE DOMESTIC FAMILY

The domestic family is an intermediate type which evolves from the trustee family. As the state gains power, the control of the family over its members is weakened. The state does not replace the family but comes to share power with it, restricting the right of the family to punish its members and creating a concept of individual rights to be maintained against family authority. The *gens* tends to disappear.

The family remains a strong unit, maintaining a balance between the forces of familism and those of individualism. Conceptions of absolute divorce emerge, but divorce is uncommon. The characteristic device for alleviating difficult marital conditions is legal separation, *divortium a mensa et thoro.*

[11] Zimmerman explicitly states that these are ideal family types rather than empirical family types (p. 120).

THE ATOMISTIC FAMILY

The atomistic family represents the other extreme. Familism is replaced by individualism. The power and scope of authority of the family are reduced to an absolute minimum and the state becomes essentially an organization of individuals. If self-sacrifice in favor of group goals is the prevailing ethic in the trustee family, an unabashed hedonism characterizes the atomistic family. Marriage becomes a civil contract instead of a sacrament and, with its sacred nature eliminated, is often broken by divorce. The sacredness now attached to the individual person results in the blurring of distinctions between legitimate and illegitimate children; whereas the trustee family tends to destroy illegitimate children as a threat to itself, the state declares illegitimate children to have full rights in the atomistic family system. Other evidence of rampant individualism are to be found in feministic movements, childlessness, youth problems, and most of the other pathologies which are associated with family life. The atomistic family loses the capacity to carry out necessary family functions and it cannot satisfy the growing demands of individualism.

THE CYCLE OF CHANGE

Zimmerman traces the history of Western society from approximately 1500 B.C. to the present. Social change, he says, has proceeded according to a more or less deterministic pattern, with the family system and the level of civilization in mutual cause-and-effect interaction. Up to the present time change has proceeded blindly, without human control or guidance. Unless man comes to comprehend the nature of social change and determines to control it, it will continue to operate blindly and the decay of the great civilizations of the past will be repeated in the decay of our own society.

Change is alleged to occur in giant historical swings or cycles which, for Western society, are summarized in Figure 1. According to Zimmerman, the first of these cycles of which we have adequate record embraced the rise and fall of ancient Greek civilization. Greek civilization grew and declined from the fifteenth through the 3rd century B.C. Even as Greek civilization was decaying, Roman civilization was gaining strength. Roman society then achieved greatness and declined by the 4th century of the Christian era. During the so-called Dark Ages there was no great Western civilization. By the twelfth century the trustee family had emerged again and the greatness of the Renaissance was foreshadowed. The present finds Western society, particularly in America, again in a terminal phase. Unless human intelligence is brought to bear—and soon—our society will suffer the fate of Greece and Rome.

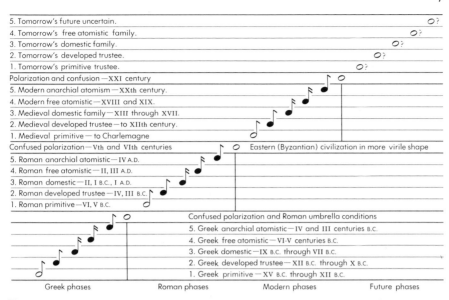

5. Tomorrow's future uncertain.				O?
4. Tomorrow's free atomistic family.				O?
3. Tomorrow's domestic family.				O?
2. Tomorrow's developed trustee.				O?
1. Tomorrow's primitive trustee.				O?

Polarization and confusion — XXI century
5. Modern anarchial atomism — XXth century.
4. Modern free atomistic — XVIII and XIX.
3. Medieval domestic family — XIII through XVII.
2. Medieval developed trustee — to XIIth century.
1. Medieval primitive — to Charlemagne
Confused polarization — Vth and VIth centuries   Eastern (Byzantian) civilization in more virile shape
5. Roman anarchial atomistic — IV A.D.
4. Roman free atomistic — II, III A.D.
3. Roman domestic — II, I B.C., I A.D.
2. Roman developed trustee — IV, III B.C.
1. Roman primitive — VI, V B.C.

Confused polarization and Roman umbrella conditions
5. Greek anarchial atomistic — IV and III centuries B.C.
4. Greek free atomistic — VI-V centuries B.C.
3. Greek domestic — IX B.C. through VII B.C.
2. Greek developed trustee — XII B.C. through X B.C.
1. Greek primitive — XV B.C. through XII B.C.

| Greek phases | Roman phases | Modern phases | Future phases |

FIGURE 1. *The chain reaction pattern in cultural determinism for the Western family system since 1500 B.C.*

Source: Carle C. Zimmerman, *The Family of Tomorrow: The Cultural Crisis and the Way Out,* New York: Harper and Brothers, 1949, p. 218. Reprinted by permission of Harper & Row, Publisher, Inc.

The great cycles of change in Greek, Roman, and medieval civilizations have followed a common pattern. Each has emerged in a relatively primitive state. Order and stability were achieved through the family which gradually emerged as the trustee type. Under the trustee family each civilization moved toward greatness. The authoritarian character of the trustee family, however, inevitably led to the limitation of its power by the state and the church. The trustee family gradually evolved into the domestic type which, with its balance between individualism and familism, permitted each civilization to attain true greatness. The changes already set in motion, however, led the state to assume greater control of family matters until the domestic family was replaced by the atomistic one. In each case, the atomistic family was associated with moral degeneration. Goals of self-sacrifice and creativity in every field of human endeavor gave way under the demands of relentless hedonism.

The cycle of change gets under way because the trustee family carries within itself the seeds of its own destruction. While its primitive code of justice produces an orderly society, promotes the accumulation of wealth, and emphasizes productive work, its unchecked authority over its members leads to abuses;

wives may be unjustly repudiated, children may be exposed or subjected to despotic control, and the rights of individuals generally may be suppressed. There allegedly is a tendency, too, for disputes to break out between families. Religious and governmental powers emerge to mediate between families and to offer protection to individual family members. The autocratic trustee family is thus humanized. As the society develops, the power of the extended kin group continues to diminish and the domestic family emerges.

The domestic family is the most common type in civilized societies and offers the greatest potential for greatness. It becomes the modal family type in the society because of forces operating both inside and outside the family. It arises from the desire for more equitable treatment on the part of family members and from the influences of government and religion. Unlike the trustee family, it does not carry the seeds of its own destruction; it continues to be acted upon from the outside. The state continues to accumulate power to itself and religion takes charge of morality. These institutions further restrict the power of the family and give increased sanction to the rights of individuals. There is a general cultural determinism operative which creates an increasingly antifamilistic attitude, and the atomistic family develops.

The atomistic family is both cause and effect of decay in social life. In its later stages, there appear elimination of the real meaning of the marriage ceremony, widespread adultery, acceptance of sexual perversions, easy divorce, childlessness, and delinquency. Concepts of loyalty and self-sacrifice wane; personal selfishness replaces them. Under these conditions the family cannot carry out its basic functions. Neither can the growing demands for individual freedom and personal satisfactions be met. Nor is there anything in the atomistic family which might produce a swing back toward familism. The experience of the past has been that the decay continues until eventually a new trustee family emerges out of the darkness.

THE LESSON OF HISTORY

Zimmerman's is a voice crying out of the wilderness. The United States is destined to experience the last stages of a great family crisis by the end of the present century. By now, however, we can understand the forces which have been operating and we have the power to alter the course of social change. The initiative must be seized by government—which is the only agency powerful enough to do it—to bring about a resurgence of familism. We must swing back toward the domestic family and toward the personal and national greatness which are associated with it. The morality to be reinstituted is to be found in the teachings of the church, which has always made virtues of familism and self-sacrifice but which in recent centuries has lost much of its power and influence.

Speaking to Midwest news editors in Kansas City, President Nixon referred to federal buildings in Washington and said: "Sometimes when I see those pillars, I think of seeing them on the Acropolis in Greece. I think of seeing them also in the Forum in Rome. . . . I think of what happened to Greece and Rome, and you see what is left—only the pillars. What has happened, of course, is that great civilizations of the past, as they have become wealthy, as they have lost their will to live, to improve, they then have become subject to the decadence that eventually destroys the civilization. The United States is now reaching that period."

To be sure, Nixon quickly went on to express his confidence that the nation has the "vitality, courage and strength" to remain morally and spiritually healthy. . . .

—Reprinted by permission from *Time*, The Weekly Newsmagazine; copyright Time, Inc., 1971.

Although he does not say so, we might hazard the guess that Zimmerman is pessimistic. He presents us with an analysis of the blind working of fate and then offers us a way out. The very force with which his causal analysis is developed makes it appear unlikely that our civilization will handle the crisis more effectively than earlier civilizations did.[12]

FINAL CRITIQUE

When Zimmerman's major work on the sociology of the family was published in 1947 it attracted considerable attention. Even today it is required reading for all students in the field. But although Zimmerman's cyclical analysis is provocative, it has found few adherents. The fraternity of professional social scientists has embraced it somewhat less than enthusiastically. Following are a few interpretations of the theory which are widely shared.

One cannot fail to be impressed by the apparent erudition of the analysis. It embraces nearly 4000 years of history and varied civilizations, in detail, and with flourish and assurance. One of the problems with such an erudite analysis,

---

[12] For a recent reaffirmation of this basic position, see Carle C. Zimmerman, "The Atomistic Family—Fact or Fiction," *Journal of Comparative Family Studies* 1 (Autumn 1970), pp. 5–16.

however, is that lesser mortals cannot be certain that Zimmerman's data are adequate and reliable, and that they have the meaning which Zimmerman attributes to them. While no one questions the integrity of the analysis, there are those who are reluctant to accept it as adequately proven.

A second problem derives from the exclusion of all data from preliterate societies. Zimmerman takes advantage of our ignorance of social origins when he maintains that preliterate societies are inherently different from civilized ones. It cannot be proved that he is wrong but neither can it be proved that he is correct.

Finally, it should be said that Zimmerman is not entirely alone in his views of the cyclical nature of social change. Periodically, historians have produced cyclical theories and, in sociology, Zimmerman's mentor and colleague, Pitirim Sorokin, has developed a more elaborate parallel analysis which does not focus particularly on the family.[13] Undoubtedly the prevailing bias of the twentieth century is to view change as unending and without specific direction. Zimmerman may be wrong. But it also is possible that our preconceived notions of the mutability of everything may be blinding us to some permanence, some regularity in human experience, that actually exists.

A Progressivist Theory

William F. Ogburn's publications in sociology spanned more than three decades. The first of his major works, for our purposes, was published in 1922,[14] and the last in 1955,[15] not too long before his death. It is a mark of the stature of the man that his thinking about the nature of social change did not remain constant over his lifetime but changed in response to professional evaluations of his earlier works and as his own thinking matured. This very intellectual growth, however, makes the presentation of his analysis of family change more difficult; for what began as a sweeping theory of social change had become much more tentative and much more eclectic[16] before his death. In presenting Ogburn's theory we will present his original formulations first, for in them are to be found his major contributions to sociological theory, and then trace his thinking through his later publications.

Ogburn belonged to what Zimmerman referred to as the "passive school"

[13] Pitirim A. Sorokin, *Social and Cultural Dynamics*, 4 vols., New York: American Book Company, 1937.

[14] *Social Change*, New York: Viking Press, 1922.

[15] *Technology and the Changing Family*, Boston: Houghton Mifflin, 1955.

[16] An eclectic theory is one which combines elements from two or more existing theories into a new and presumably more useful one.

of family sociologists. He viewed the family not as an active causal agent in social change but as being acted upon from the outside, as passively adapting itself to changes in the larger society. Looking outside the family for the primary source of social change, Ogburn found it in the increasing rate of invention in a technologically oriented society.

The range of data used by Ogburn was much narrower than Zimmerman's. He confined his analyses of the family essentially to the American scene, using the pre-industrial family as an informal baseline and tracing the changes which occurred during the nineteenth and twentieth centuries. Not surprisingly, his analysis was somewhat culture-bound.

MATERIAL AND NONMATERIAL CULTURE

A sharp distinction between material culture (factories, machines, means of transportation, engineering achievements, munitions, clothing, and so on) and nonmaterial culture (values, attitudes, customs, institutions, etc.) was central to Ogburn's thinking.[17] He stressed particularly the different ways in which material and nonmaterial culture change. Change in material culture, he said, tends to be cumulative and directional while change in nonmaterial culture is not characterized by any such regularity.

The difference between material inventions and customs lies in the fact that there are generally agreed-upon standards in the society which are used to evaluate inventions. Thus, an engine may be evaluated in terms of the horsepower it produces, the fuel it consumes, its weight, its cost, and its durability. With the standards agreed upon, a better engine soon is produced. Because it is a better engine, it is adopted, a still better engine then is produced, and so on. Change in the area of material culture is rapid and accelerates with the passage of time.

In the area of nonmaterial culture, on the other hand, there are few universally accepted standards of worth. Societies, and groups within societies, who use the same internal-cumbustion engines disagree violently over the merits of their respective political and economic systems. Or in the area of the arts, who is to determine the merits of Brahms over Mozart or Picasso over Gainsborough? As a consequence of such lack of agreement, change in customs and institutions tends to be both slow and without continuing direction. And in the uneven rates of change between material and nonmaterial culture are to be found the sources of culture lag.

---

[17] *Social Change*, pp. 66–79, 200–213.

CULTURE LAG

The culture-lag hypothesis holds that rapid change in one part of the culture requires that corresponding adjustments be made in other related parts of the culture. Such adjustments, however, are frequently made only after a time lag of months, years, or decades. The intervening period is one of maladjustment or disorganization. During this period of cultural lag, the attitudes, habits, and customs passed down from previous generations seem to have lost their effectiveness and there is widespread personal and group distress.

Ogburn maintained that change may originate in either material or nonmaterial culture and that change in either requires corresponding change in the other. Most often, however, he viewed change as originating in material invention and the necessity for adjustment occurring in the nonmaterial, adaptive culture.

A primary illustration of the operation of cultural lag is to be found in the family. Before the development of industrialization, the family was in fairly satisfactory adjustment to agricultural conditions. It possessed economic, educational, recreational, religious, and protective functions along with its biological functions. Marriage was a business arrangement and divorce was a very serious matter. With the development of the factory system, production was taken out of the home. Women who formerly played an important economic role in the family now found themselves either forced to go out of the home to work or to accept an essentially nonproductive economic role. If they did go to work, problems in the management of household and children arose; if they did not go to work, their estimates of their own worth often suffered. Children, too, encountered adjustment problems in the new milieu. They were transformed from economic assets into liabilities. There were not proper places for them to play and their supervision became onerous for parents and children alike.

Related developments in material culture also played a disorganizing role. The invention of the automobile, for example, offered to adolescents the opportunity to escape their parents' supervision and to gain complete anonymity in a matter of minutes. The old norms governing courtship could not operate effectively in the new situation. Parents found it increasingly difficult even to know the boys with whom their daughters associated. A lengthy period of heterosexual association, dating, grew up, and neither parents nor young people knew how to cope with its complications. These are examples of what Ogburn called culture lag and social disorganization.

FAMILY DEFUNCTIONALIZATION

The major empirical documentation of Ogburn's thesis that developments in technology have largely stripped the American family of its traditional functions is to be found in a comprehensive report prepared for President Hoover's Research Committee on Social Trends and published in 1934.[18] In that report, Ogburn discussed seven major functions that the family possessed before modern times and the changes which occurred in them with rapid advances in technology.

The Economic Function. In colonial times the home was literally a factory, producing virtually all that the family consumed. A man sought in his wife, not only a companion but also a business partner. Children, too, contributed to the productive activities. Gradually, however, productive activities were assumed by other agencies and lost to the family. The production of tools and furniture was lost early. Gradually the production of medicines and soaps was lost. By the 1930's most families had given up the baking of bread, home canning, and the sewing of clothing. The transfer of these tasks reduced the wife's economic importance to the family, and increased numbers of women sought employment outside the home.

The nature of the family dwelling changed accordingly. The number and proportion of multifamily dwellings in the cities increased rapidly. The new dwellings were smaller than their predecessors and much of their routine maintenance was assumed by janitors and other hired employees. The development of gas and electricity for domestic power simplified the storing and preparation of food. Even so, the number of restaurants and delicatessens increased rapidly and more and more meals were taken outside the home.

Men increasingly worked outside the home. And, although women continued to put in long hours at "housework," the definition of woman's economic contribution suffered; the phrase "just a housewife," with its unflattering connotations, came into use. Children ceased to have much economic value, and home economists began to figure how many dollars it cost to raise each child to adulthood.

The Protective Function. Traditionally, the family protected its members from bodily harm by outsiders and provided them with economic security

---

[18] William F. Ogburn and Clark Tibbitts, "The Family and Its Functions," Report of the President's Research Committee on Social Trends, *Recent Social Trends in the United States,* New York: McGraw-Hill Book Company, 1934, pp. 661–708.

through childhood, in times of injury, illness, and unemployment, and in old age. In recent decades, much of this protective activity has been assumed by public organizations and by the state. In the matter of health care, for example, the increased use of physicians, the expansion of hospital facilities, and the rapid spread of accident insurance, hospitalization insurance, and workman's compensation have tended to replace family nursing care. Mentally ill and mentally deficient family members also are increasingly cared for in hospitals.

The family shotgun and even the family dog as sources of protection against intruders have been replaced largely by an army of police, sheriffs, detectives, guards, and the like. Protection against fires is provided by public fire departments.

Protection against dependency has been transferred largely to the government. Aid to Families and Dependent Children, social security, medicare, unemployment insurance, work-study programs, and the like are more recent versions of government programs already emerging on the scene when Ogburn wrote.

The Religious Function. In earlier days, the family was a close-knit religious group. Marriage itself was considered to be a sacrament and the production of children a divine obligation. The family was primarily responsible for the establishment and maintenance of ethical standards. Even the teaching of the scriptures was a family responsibility; family prayers, the saying of grace, the reading of Bible passages, and hymn-singing were common customs.

Now religion has been largely removed from the home and located in the church. Family prayers have become quite uncommon and even the saying of grace is disappearing. Marriage has become as much a secular as a sacred matter, and the having of children is becoming a matter of rational planning. Parents send their children to church to learn appropriate moral and ethical behavior.

The Recreational Function. There has been a tremendous absolute increase in the time devoted to recreational pursuits and in the recreation facilities available to cater to these needs. The taffy-pull, the popping of popcorn, and group-singing are perhaps the stereotypes of the old pattern of family-centered recreation. Now even these homely forms of recreation have been removed, for the most part, to the church, the school, the company social program, and to the community at large. More spectacular is the growth of commercialized recreation. The spectator sports of baseball, football, basketball, hockey, horse-racing, tennis, and golf amuse hundreds of thousands and, now with television, perhaps millions of people at a time. Active participant recreation ranging from amusement parks, to swimming pools, night clubs, and so on takes people away from their families more often than it involves the whole family group. During the 1950's, some people saw a return to family-style recreation in the gluing of whole families to the television set in the living room. But as television becomes more widely diffused, the scattering of the family before different sets in different rooms, where each can watch his favorite shows, seems to be an increasingly common pattern.

The Educational Function. Formal education was not elaborate during colonial days. While there was some teaching of the "three R's," such academic training was minimal and even some of it was done at the family fireside. The past two centuries have seen both a tremendous elaboration of formal academic training and the transfer of various kinds of training from the home. Almost all children are in school by the age of five or six, and kindergartens and nursery schools may take them by the age of three. Paid teachers increasingly teach everything from how to tie shoes and button clothes to table manners and appropriate social behavior. And not only does the schooling start earlier but it takes up more of the day and lasts longer. A complete high school education is now the norm, and college and postgraduate work are increasingly common.

To some extent the educational system has become a competitor with the family. Not that there is conscious competition; but the modern school system has its own standards of what children should be and become, standards that are not always consistent with those of the parents. With the advent of the federal government's antipoverty program in the mid-1960's, the public educational system became a primary instrument to be used to wean poor children from the values and attitudes of their parents.

The Status-Conferring Function. Membership in a given family traditionally defined each person's place in the community. In small communities, the fact that a young person was Tim Swenson's son or Tony D'Amato's daughter specified pretty clearly how far they should be expected to go in school, what kind of work they would do when they got out, whom they would (or could) marry, what part of town they would live in, and so on.

In the modern metropolis this function appears to have been reduced to a bare minimum. Contact with neighbors may be avoided, with few people in the vicinity knowing in detail what the husband does for a living. His status as a person stems largely from his job and may literally be shed when he leaves the office or plant. His wife's status may be defined largely in terms of what organizations she participates in and may vary from one organization to another. The children compete under the universalistic standards of the school system. Indirectly, the family's way of life is still determined somewhat by the husband's income and by the value system adhered to by members of his occupation, but the direct participation of the family in defining each member's role in the community is much less than it used to be.

FAMILY DISORGANIZATION

According to Ogburn, a certain amount of disorganization inevitably resulted from the loss of these family functions. One of the primary symptoms of this disorganization was the rapid increase in the number of broken homes. Since 1880, the number of divorces per 1000 population has increased roughly about 3 per cent per year. Broken homes signify unhappy men and women whose expectations of harmonious marital life have been frustrated in the defunctionalized family. Divorce produces problems, not only for the parents but also for their children, who must suffer emotional conflict, loss of a parent, and often financial privation. Frequently associated symptoms of social disorganization include illicit sexual activity, family desertion, and juvenile delinquency.

It should be noted that Ogburn did not pursue the analysis of family disorganization beyond this point. He saw the family having its remaining functions strengthened, as we will see in a moment, and he was social scientist enough not to fall victim to the temptation to equate the defunctionalization of the family with imminent catastrophe. Ogburn's analysis, however, had great appeal for many lay writers who did not share his scientific caution, and the popular press during the 1920's and 1930's extended his thesis to predict complete family disorganization and even the disappearance of the family as a social institution. Thus, the idea that the family was "breaking down" became firmly implanted in the public mind.

STRENGTHENED FUNCTIONS

In addition to the institutional functions, which Ogburn said it has been losing, the family performs certain personality functions for its members. These personality functions operate at two levels: in the relationship between husband and wife and in the relationship between parents and children. In the old multifunctional family these functions were not especially conspicuous. The arduous conditions of life, the detailed division of labor within the family, and the emphasis on economic productivity did not encourage great concern with the quality of the emotional relationship between the spouses. The relevant considerations in evaluating a prospect for a husband were whether he owned property, was hard-working, sober, God-fearing, and just. Women were supposed to be good housekeepers, morally upright, strong, and equipped to bear and rear children. Assuming these qualities, the differences between one person and another were minimized; one did not expect great and continued emotional satisfaction in marriage. Similarly, children were trained to be industrious, obedient, and mannerly. Considerations of whether they were well adjusted and happy were virtually nonexistent.

As the family ceased to be a productive unit and was freed from many of its traditional responsibilities, husbands, wives, and parents were also freed to cultivate their relationships with one another. Couples became concerned with the happiness of their marriages, seeking personal growth and fulfillment. Parents sought not only food, clothing, and shelter for their offspring but increasingly emphasized their social and emotional development. Thus, according to Ogburn, the family has fewer functions today but may be performing those few functions as well or better than it did in the past.

CRITIQUE

The great strength of Ogburn's analysis probably lay not so much in his theoretical formulations as in his description of the changed relationship between the family and other institutional structures. He documented, as no one else has done, the increased participation of government, commercial enterprises, education, and so on, in what were once private, family affairs. The accuracy of Ogburn's facts is unquestioned, and other writers on the family have borrowed heavily from him.

Ogburn also alerted a generation to the importance of technology as a source of social change. If Ogburn overemphasized the role of material invention in his early writing, his later formulations ascribed causal influence to nonmaterial factors—ideologies, values, birth control, etc.—as well.[19] He never wavered from his belief that technology was a prime mover in social change, but he broadened his scheme to allow more influence from other aspects of culture.

One problem in attempting to attribute meaning to recent changes in family functions derives from Ogburn's use of the American colonial family as the baseline from which to measure change. If we are not careful, we can easily assume that the functions of the colonial family are the *sine qua non* of the family and that retreat from those basic functions represents breakdown. Actually we know that the colonial family was simply one historical variant of the Western family, adapted to the agricultural conditions which then prevailed. If Ogburn's description of recent changes is accurate, his

[19] *Technology and the Changing Family*, op. cit. Ch. 1 and 2.

implicit conclusions about whether or not the family is doing its job are much more tenuous.[20]

Other sociologists also have been somewhat critical of the concepts of culture lag and social disorganization. The charge has been made that these are normative concepts, containing hidden value judgments, and that change in nonmaterial culture does not always lag behind material culture. Fashions in women's clothes, popular music, teen-age jargon, and fads in children's toys may be pointed out as elements of nonmaterial culture which change erratically and extremely rapidly. Even in long-range terms, material culture may lag behind. Educational research, for example, long ago demonstrated the value of movable furniture in the school classroom. Yet, in most school rooms the furniture remains bolted firmly to the floor.

Ogburn's analysis is a less gloomy one than Zimmerman's. Yet one cannot help but sense in it a certain nostalgia for the good old days of yesteryear and a minor foreboding about the future.[21] The small, unstable family of today seems but a pale shadow of the early American farm family. To some degree, such conclusions derive inevitably from the mode of analysis used. The analysis which follows interprets these same phenomena quite differently.

A STRUCTURE-FUNCTION THEORY

The structure-function approach to analysis of the family system is a less historical one than either of the two just discussed. It also focuses less on family change and more on the integration between the family and other institutions—particularly with the occupational system. It views the family in the structural terms developed in Chapters 2 and 3 of this book and analyzes the functions which this particular structural unit performs in modern industrial society.

Structure-function analysis is one of the dominant theoretical orientations in modern sociology. It is so pervasive that identification of it with one or a

[20] There is also a widespread tendency to idealize the colonial family. The stereotype of that family as brimming with satisfaction for all family members and uncomplicated by conflicts and frustrations has been labeled by William J. Goode as "the classical family of Western nostalgia." See his *After Divorce*, Glencoe, Illinois: The Free Press, 1956, p. 3; and *World Revolution and Family Patterns*, New York: The Free Press of Glencoe, 1963, pp. 6–7.

[21] Other writers, building upon Ogburn's work, have dropped the more value-laden aspects of his theory and have emphasized the family's role in translating change in the larger society into the socialization process. See William Goode's concept of "the mediating function," in *The Family*, Englewood Cliffs, New Jersey: Prentice-Hall, 1964, pp. 2–3. See also Clark Vincent's concept of "the adaptive function," in "Familia Spongia: The Adaptive Function," *Journal of Marriage and the Family* 28 (Feb. 1966), pp. 29–36.

few writers is bound to be misleading.[22] The most comprehensive and systematic application of structure-function theory to the family probably has been made by Talcott Parsons, upon whose writings the present discussion is based.[23] Parsons's analysis will be presented briefly and selectively as was done with the cyclical and progressivist theories.

STRUCTURAL ISOLATION

The analysis begins with emphasis on the fact that the American family system is an open, multilineal, conjugal system.[24] The nuclear family is more than ordinarily isolated from larger groups of kin, isolation being built into the very structure of the family. There are, for example, no larger kinship units which are recognized even to the point of having names given to them and which cut across nuclear families. There is no clan, lineage, or other kin group to which the individual remains attached. Each pair of nuclear families (see Figure 2) is linked by only one member whom they share in common. Ego is the common member of his families of orientation and procreation, his spouse shares the same family of procreation with ego but not the same family of orientation, and so on for each other member of the family. At marriage, each person is partially removed from one kinship unit (nuclear family) and creates one new family.

This "poverty" of kinship organization is reflected in an accompanying poverty of kinship terms. We really have only the term "family," which usually refers to the nuclear family, and the term "relatives," which does not refer to a kinship unit as such but which encompasses all of the other *people* to whom a person is regarded as related. The monogamous character of the system is shown by the fact that the terms "mother," "father," "husband," and "wife" apply to only one person at a time. No terminological distinctions are made on the basis of birth order, all brothers and all sisters being called

[22] Jesse R. Pitts, "The Structural-Functional Approach," in Harold T. Christensen, ed., op. cit. pp. 51–124.

[23] Parsons's most comprehensive work on the family is one written with Robert F. Bales, *Family, Socialization and Interaction Process*, Glencoe, Illinois: The Free Press, 1955. The summation of his views, on which the present discussion rests, is found in Talcott Parsons, "The Social Structure of the Family," in Ruth N. Anshen, ed., *The Family: Its Function and Destiny*, New York: Harper and Brothers, 1959, pp. 241–74. See also Talcott Parsons, "Age and Sex in the Social Structure of the United States," *American Sociological Review* 7 (Oct. 1942), pp. 604–16; and Hyman Rodman, "Talcott Parsons' View of the Changing American Family," in Hyman Rodman, ed., *Marriage, Family, and Society*, New York: Random House, 1965, pp. 262–86.

[24] "The Social Structure of the Family," op. cit. p. 242.

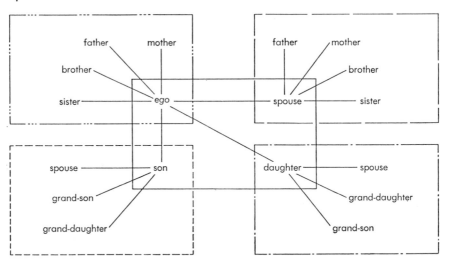

FIGURE 2. *Five overlapping nuclear families. Each pair of nuclear families shares only one common member.*

by the same term. Contrast this with the Chinese large-family system in which older and younger brothers are called by separate kinship terms.

Furthermore, our kinship terminology generally ceases to make meaningful distinctions among relatives beyond the second or third degree.[25] As one traces relationship outward from ego (refer to Fig. 3, Chap. 2), separate kinship terms stop at the levels of cousin, grandparent, and grandchild. From there on we indicate degree of relationship by using numerical prefixes—first cousin, second cousin, etc.—or by using the prefix "great"—great grandfather, great great grandfather—and so on.

AN OPEN, MULTILINEAL SYSTEM

The structural isolation of the nuclear family does not end with the facts that we have an endless overlapping of nuclear families and a poverty of kinship units and kinship terms. There is also the influence of what Parsons refers to as the "open" and "multilineal" nature of the kinship system.

In the terms presented in Chapter 2, our kinship system is technically a bi-

[25] For illustrations of the research use to which kinship terminology and terms of address may be put, see Lionel S. Lewis, "Terms of Address for Parents and Some Clues About Social Relationships in the American Family," *Family Life Coordinator* 14 (April 1965), pp. 43–46; and Jay D. Schvaneveldt, "The Nuclear and Extended Family as Reflected in Autobiographical Dedications: A Comparative Study," *Journal of Marriage and the Family* 28 (Nov. 1966), pp. 495–7.

lateral one. Parsons prefers the term multilineal, however, to emphasize the fact that no kin groups based on lines of descent tend to develop. Each generation selects its mates from outside the proscribed circle of relatives and without consideration for the cementing of ties with kin of earlier generations. Thus there are no preferred marriage partners defined in terms of family relationships. Any given nuclear family which is the product of the merging of two family lines is likely to merge with still different family lines at each succeeding generation.

Moreover, there are strict norms which militate against any favoritism being shown to either the husband's or the wife's family line. At the marital level this is shown by the ingenious arrangements worked out by young married couples and their parents to guarantee equal attention on both sides. Thus, if the young couple has dinner with one set of parents on one weekend, they must dine the next weekend with the other parents, or at least work out the equivalent thereto. If Thanksgiving is spent at one parental home, Christmas must be spent at the other, and so on. The norms, although not always verbalized, are so clear that all three couples ordinarily know when the rules are being violated and corrective action is taken. From the viewpoint of the parents, the same impartiality must be shown to their several children. If a gift is made to one offspring and his or her spouse, a corresponding gift must be made to the other.

A generally unanticipated but structurally significant consequence of these equal-treatment norms is gradually to increase the social distance between the generations and to isolate the separate nuclear families. Eventually the young married couple begins to form a solidary unit against the expectations of both parental families. Whereas, in the beginning, each spouse may subtly (or not so subtly) wish to favor relationships with his own parents, finally husband and wife band together to decide that they "want to spend their holidays at home this year," or that they "shouldn't see quite so much of either set of parents." In similar fashion the parents are likely to decide that they won't go to visit the one son and his wife this weekend because, if they do, they will have to visit each of their other children on succeeding weekends.

The openness of the system is especially evident from the vantage point of the grandchildren, who have no terminological means to distinguish between maternal and paternal grandparents and who are discouraged from showing any favoritism toward either side of the family. Grandparents ordinarily are distinguished only by surname—that is, Grandfather O'Brien from Grandfather Schmidt. With so little basis for making distinctions, grandchildren tend not to grow "too close" to either set of grandparents and, as they grow to adulthood, are likely to lose most significant contact with both.

The older generation also operates under strictures with regard to inheritance patterns. The wife's interest in her husband's property is protected by her dower right, and minor children also are protected. Beyond these minimum provisions, however, the law presumes in favor of equal inheritance by all children, older and younger, and male and female. Parents are expected to leave equal amounts of property to each of their children but not to leave too much to any of them. The stereotypes which earlier surrounded the names of John D. Rockefeller and Henry Ford are a case in point. Both men gained some reputation for being stingy and selfish—largely because they amassed extensive property and passed it on to their children. The establishment of the Ford and Rockefeller foundations, which have redistributed a substantial amount of the accumulated wealth in ways our society deems appropriate, has markedly enhanced the reputations of both families.

The equal inheritance norms and the bias against the hereditary transmission of excessive wealth tend to remove the family's ties to the land and further to isolate successive generations. At the death of the parents, their home is likely to be sold and the proceeds distributed among the heirs. Not even the eldest son has reason to locate geographically near his parents, and none of the children has any financial incentive to curry special favor with them or to seek to carry on family traditions.

EMPHASIS ON THE CONJUGAL UNIT

Parsons describes marriage as the structural keystone of our kinship system. Unlike the situation faced by people in most societies, people in our society have no kinship unit in which they retain membership throughout life. Instead, at marriage, they undergo fairly drastic separation from their families of orientation and assume loyalties to their spouses and children which outweigh loyalties to parents and siblings. Moreover, the rule of residence is basically neolocal. Young married couples are expected to take up residence apart from the location (and the influence) of both parental families.

Consistent with the structural and geographical isolation of the conjugal family unit, parents are not expected to play a significant role in mate selection. In societies having large-family systems, parents do typically participate in the selection of mates for their offspring because the new spouse will become a member of their household and kinship units; the parents and other family members have a large stake in the person selected. In our case, however, adjustment between the spouses is paramount and relationships with other kin are largely irrelevant. As will be seen in a few moments, integration of the couple into a larger kin group may even be dysfunctional.[26]

In the same vein, the fact that the conjugal unit is both structurally and geographically isolated from other kin groups encourages an emphasis on romantic love as the basis for marriage and as the primary reason for staying married. Large kin groups typically discourage the flowering of romantic love because the development of intense attraction between spouses would threaten the priority of their loyalties to parents and to the group. Where the large kin group is absent, however, romantic love serves as a kind of substitute for a network of detailed role prescriptions. When a husband and wife in our society come into conflict, there is no omnipresent group of kin urging them to moderate their differences and solve their disagreements. The emotional attraction between them is the functionally equivalent substitute therefor.

The fact that the conjugal unit is small also permits the married pair to structure their roles in relation to each other in a variety of ways. Romantic love as the basis for marriage provides a strong bond while, at the same time, making a variety of role relationships possible.

INTEGRATION WITH THE OCCUPATIONAL SYSTEM

According to structure-function analysis, the workings of the family system cannot be understood without reference to the ties between the family and the occupational system. When the interrelations of these two are analyzed, it appears that much of what other writers have interpreted as symptoms of family disorganization are not that at all. Much of this alleged disorganization represents, instead, a rather effective adaptation to the requirements of an industrial economy.

The status of the family in American society is overwhelmingly bound up with the occupation of the husband through the income, prestige, and style of life which derive from it. If one had to construct a picture of what any family is like from the answer to a single question, the most useful question

[26] In structure-function analysis, society is viewed as a dynamic system of interconnected parts. In analyzing this system, one repeatedly asks the question, "What are the consequences of each part of the system for every other part and for the system as a whole?" The term *function* is used to refer to such consequences. The term *dysfunction* refers to negative consequences—to situations in which the effect of one part of the system on other parts is harmful to the system. See Marion J. Levy, Jr., *The Structure of Society*, Princeton: Princeton University Press, 1952, pp. 76–83; and Robert K. Merton, *Social Theory and Social Structure*, Glencoe, Illinois: The Free Press, 1957, pp. 46–52.

probably would be, "What does the husband do for a living?" His occupation, and the perquisites that go with it, heavily influence where a family will live, their values and aspirations, how they are regarded by others, their material possessions, the nature of the children's educations, and so on.

In pre-industrial economies, there often is a direct integration between family and occupational system. The father works in or around the home and other family members assist him in his productive activities. With the appearance of the factory system, such direct integration no longer is possible. The husband must go outside the home to earn a living. In the universalistic atmosphere of the business world, he must not be restricted by the particularistic criteria which govern relationships within the family. Similarly, relationships within the family cannot be structured according to the universalistic criteria operative in the economy. This dilemma is resolved through the segregation of familial and occupational roles.[27] The world of the family and the world of the job are fairly completely separated.

Normally, only one member of the family—the husband and father—plays a fully competitive role in the occupational system. Such a situation is required in order to protect the marriage relationship, which rests solely on continuance of romantic love, against the destructive competition which might result if the wife followed an occupation with the same vigor as her husband. Thus, even though married women are working outside the home in increasing numbers, the proportion of women employed in the highest-ranking occupations has not increased significantly in over a generation. Most women work at lower-paid, even temporary, jobs and clearly subordinate their own occupational ambitions to those of their husbands.

The segregation of occupational and familial roles serves to isolate the nuclear family and protect it against destructive internal rivalries. It also permits both the social and geographical mobility which is required by the system. Whereas in an agricultural economy the requirements of the system are met by having the son remain on the farm and at the same social level as his father, the requirements of an industrial economy are quite different. Sons can play successful competitive roles in the economy only by moving with their jobs, by acquiring technical skills, and by developing new attitudes and values.

The modern family is adapted to a situation in which scientists, engineers, and managers play more significant roles in the economy than do farmers.

[27] For accounts of how family and occupational roles impinge upon one another, see Joan Aldous, "Occupational Characteristics and Males' Role Performance in the Family," *Journal of Marriage and the Family* 31 (Nov. 1969), pp. 707-12; and John Scanzoni, "Occupation and Family Differentiation," *The Sociological Quarterly* 8 (Spring 1967), pp. 187-98.

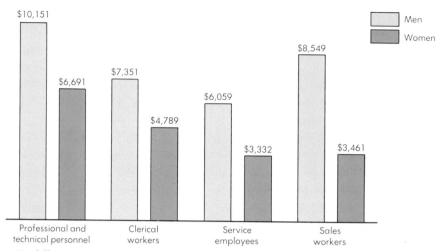

For full-time, year-round workers, 1968.
Source: Women's Bureau, U.S. Department of Labor

FIGURE 3. *Women Earn Less Than Men*

University educations, rather than home apprenticeships, are required to prepare people for these new occupations. Moreover, young men, once trained,
cannot return to the bosom of their families and expect to put their training
to best use. Many of the parents live in the small towns and open areas, while
most of the technical jobs (and the rewarding ones) are to be found in the
metropolitan centers from New York to Houston to Seattle. Furthermore,
even the boy from New York who is trained as physicist or engineer is likely
to find that his occupation requires him to move to distant sections of the
country.

Social mobility, too, is involved. The young man who would rise in the
business, professional, or scientific worlds must leave not only the family home-
stead but also its way of living. Higher education is the means to an occupation which requires that one think, feel, and act differently from one's parents.
Most college students are familiar with their own tendencies to lapse back
into familiar ways when they return home for vacations, and are astonished
by how different they are when they return to the university milieu. So it is in
larger canvas. The isolation of the nuclear family unit permits the young married pair to follow the demands of the husband's job and, at the same time,
to create a way of life for themselves that is attuned to the job and different
from the way of life of either set of parents.

In functional terms, the structure of our family system is such as to favor a
breaking of family ties at any point where the continuance of those ties would

prejudice participation in the occupational system. The major break comes at the point where the young man completes his technical training and prepares to enter the occupational world. At that point, he appropriately "falls in love" with a girl in whom his parents have no special interest and moves away with her to further his career. The love relationship between them provides a strong bond and yet permits the continual adaptation of family roles to fit the demands of the husband's job.

The subordination of family obligations to those of the occupation continues in marriage. So long as the segregation of marital and occupational roles remains effective and the marital relationship supports the husband in his job, the couple remain "in love." If, however, the wife competes unduly with her husband or if the values, attitudes, social graces, and so on, of the husband and wife do not develop apace, the couple "fall out of love." Their rationalizations may be that they are no longer interested in the same things, that they have grown apart, and so on. Actually the stage is set for them to part so that each may find another spouse whose interests will be more in harmony with his own. Thus, even marital disruption is not seen as pathology but as a means of re-adjusting family roles to meet the requirements of the occupational system. If one presses it far enough he may be moved to make the opposite value judgment on divorce from that implicit in the cyclical and progressivist theories. Divorce occasionally becomes useful instead of harmful.

CRITIQUE

Alone among the three theories presented, the structure-function theory does not interpret recent changes in family patterns as reflecting breakdown or disorganization. On the contrary, Parsons is quite explicit about the process of differentiation which operates in society to produce the increasing specialization of institutions and other units "so that certain functions formerly carried out by one unit are taken over by other specialized units, while the original unit concentrates upon fewer functions. . . ." [28] The freeing of the family from the many tasks which it performed previously may actually enable it to perform its remaining tasks more successfully. As an agency for meeting the continuing affectional and personality needs of both adults and children, the modern family may be well adapted to the requirements of an industrial society.

Although our discussion of the theory has not indicated it, Parsons makes it clear that the isolated nuclear family is found most extensively among white, urban, middle-class Americans. Some of the significant variations from this

[28] Hyman Rodman, "Talcott Parsons' View of the Changing American Family," *Merrill-Palmer Quarterly* 11 (July 1965), p. 210.

middle-class model were mentioned at the end of Chapter 7 and will be treated at length in Chapter 10. The isolated nuclear family is presented as the prototypical American family. It is the family portrayed and admired through the mass media—TV, the movies, radio, and so on. It is probably the most common family type in America today and is increasingly emulated by Americans of all social classes.

Parsons's emphasis on the apparent isolation of the nuclear family has caused some difficulty. The theory assumes, but does not prove, that nuclear families are both socially and physically more isolated than they were during the pre-industrial era. Empirical data have been amassed in recent years that cast some doubt upon this assumption, which data will be presented in Chapter 11, "The Kin Network." However, Parsons maintains, and his point appears valid, that the theory and data are not necessarily contradictory. The explanatory power of the concept of isolation lies principally in the context of anthropological comparisons with other societies and not in the context of the history of our own society.[29] One of our tasks in subsequent chapters of this book is to show how the structural biases of the kinship system are and are not reflected in actual family behavior.

Finally, it should be clear that there is much less explicit emphasis on social change in this theory than in either of the other two. Change is dealt with only by implication. It is implied or assumed that Western family structure was more elaborate before industrialization and that the small, isolated, conjugal family represents an adaptation to modern conditions. But the process of change itself is left unspecified. Some sociologists have been critical of the entire mode of structure-function analysis on precisely this point. They maintain—and structure-function theorists stoutly deny—that the emphasis on the interpenetration of parts of the social system and the whole notion of the system tending toward equilibrium lead to an essentially static conception of society; that by nature structure-function theory is ill adapted to the analysis of social change.[30]

Thus we have three comprehensive, systematic attempts to interpret the nature of the modern family system and its interrelations with the larger society. Their value for us lies in the perspective which they provide for the weighing of data to be presented in subsequent chapters.

---

[29] Talcott Parsons, "The Normal American Family," in Seymour M. Farber, Piero Mustacchi, and Roger H. L. Wilson, eds., *Man and Civilization: The Family's Search for Survival*, New York: McGraw-Hill Book Company, 1965, p. 35.

[30] Students who wish to follow the running debate should consult Harry C. Bredemeier, "The Methodology of Functionalism," *American Sociological Review* 20 (April 1955), pp. 173–80; Bernard Barber, "Structural-Functional Analysis: Some Problems and Mis-

SUMMARY

There are relatively few comprehensive theories of family structure and family change. Most analyses have treated the family either as a causal agent, bringing about change in the larger society, or, more often, as a passive agent, adapting to changes in other aspects of the social structure. This chapter summarizes three theories of family structure and family change—a cyclical theory, a progressivist theory, and a structure-function theory.

Carle Zimmerman bases his analysis on the examination of data from Western civilization, from the ancient Greeks to modern America. Throughout history he finds that there have been three recurring family types—the trustee family, the domestic family, and the atomistic family. Change, he finds, has occurred in giant historical cycles. As each great society emerges out of primordial darkness, its institutions are relatively undifferentiated and the trustee family prevails. The trustee family completely subordinates individuals to its needs, and gradually outside power develops to restrict its abuses. The domestic family, associated with a society's greatest achievements, is an intermediate type in which familism and individualism are in balance. The forces of change, once set in motion, however, continue and the atomistic family form eventuates. The insatiable demands of rampant individualism lead to societal decay and the civilization gives way to another in which the trustee family is likely to be found.

Unless man learns the lesson of history, Zimmerman believes that our society faces complete decay. If he will heed the signs, there still is time to alter our family system back to the idealistic type.

The progressivist theory is based upon data from the Western family from colonial times to the present. In it Ogburn finds technological developments as the prime causes of social change and features the family as passively adjusting to outside changes. Changes in nonmaterial culture lag behind changes in material culture, however, producing at least temporary social disorganization. Ogburn documents the fact that many functions—economic, protective, religious, recreational, educational, and status—formerly performed by the

---

understandings," *American Sociological Review* 21 (April 1956), pp. 129–35; Walter Buckley, "Structural-Functional Analysis in Modern Sociology," in Howard Becker and Alvin Boskoff, eds., *Modern Sociological Theory in Continuity and Change,* New York: Dryden Press, 1957, pp. 236–59; Kingsley Davis, "The Myth of Functional Analysis as a Special Method in Sociology and Anthropology," *American Sociological Review* 24 (Dec. 1959), pp. 752–72; Francesca Cancian, "Functional Analysis of Change," *American Sociological Review* 25 (Dec. 1960), pp. 818–27; and Ronald P. Dore, "Function and Cause," *American Sociological Review* 26 (Dec. 1961), pp. 843–53.

family have been at least partly removed from the home. He associates rising divorce rates and other forms of family pathology with this loss of functions. The two functions remaining to the family—affectional and personality functions—are more important than they used to be.

The structure-function theory focuses on the integration of the family system with the occupational system. An isolated, nuclear family system is described in which there are no effective larger kinship groups and in which normative prescriptions encourage the minimizing of ties with the parental generation. Marriage is the structural keystone of the system, and because the marital unit is not incorporated into a larger kin group, marriage is based upon romantic love.

The particularism of the family system becomes consistent with the universalism of the occupational system through the segregation of roles, which permits only one family member, the husband, to be a full participant in the occupational system. The husband's success in the occupational world requires that the nuclear family be both geographically and socially mobile.

Provision is made for family ties to give way at every point where they would conflict with the requirements of the husband's job. The young man leaves his parental family at the point where he enters the occupational system, and if his wife ceases to support his occupational advancement, they are likely to divorce and find more satisfactory partners. This theory interprets our small, relatively unstable family system as being well adapted to the requirements of an industrial economy.

SUGGESTED READINGS

Duncan, Otis Dudley, ed., *William Ogburn on Culture and Social Change*, Chicago: University of Chicago Press, 1964. A collection of Ogburn's writings, including selections on the concept of culture lag.

Ogburn, William F., and Nimkoff, Meyer F., *Technology and the Changing Family*, Boston: Houghton Mifflin, 1955. Ogburn's mature analysis of the role of technology in bringing about the defunctionalization of the family.

Parsons, Talcott, and Bales, Robert F., *Family, Socialization, and Interaction Process*, Glencoe, Illinois: The Free Press, 1955. Parson's major theoretical work on the family. For the serious student.

Rodman, Hyman, "Talcott Parsons' View of the Changing American Family," in Hyman Rodman, ed., *Marriage, Family, and Society*, New York: Random House, 1965, pp. 262–86. An excellent interpretive analysis of all of Parsons's major views on the American family.

Scanzoni, John H., *Opportunity and the Family*, New York: The Free Press, 1970. Report of a large-scale research project that lends systematic support to the dependence of family cohesion upon the husband's successful participation in the occupational system.

Veroff, Joseph, and Feld, Sheila, *Marriage and Work in America: A Study of Motives and Roles*, New York: Van Nostrand Reinhold Company, 1970. Research in which two psychologists examine motives for affiliation, achievement, and power as these operate in work and family relationships. Emphasizes, again, the interpenetration of work roles and family roles.

Zimmerman, Carle C., *Family and Civilization*, New York: Harper and Brother, 1947. Zimmerman's most important work on the relation between family change and social change. An impressive and controversial analysis.

FILMS

Hazel and David (National Film Board of Canada, Mackenzie Building, Toronto), 29 minutes. A study of what may happen when a husband insulates his family from his job. David feels that what happens at work should not be allowed to bother his family. Hence, when his job is in doubt, his wife discovers it by accident. In the subsequent discussion there is some promise of improved communication in the family.

Our Changing Family Life (McGraw-Hill Book Company, Text-Film Division, 330 West 42nd St., New York 10036), 22 minutes. A farm family in 1880 is shown as an economically, culturally, and emotionally integrated unit. Three generations live under one roof. Religion, recreation, and the sharing of work play important roles in holding the family together. Since 1880, industrial expansion, urbanization, and the political and economic emancipation of women have radically changed the pattern of family life. The farm family has become less important as an economic and social unit. The roles of husband and wife have changed and companionship has become more important in marriage.

The Decision (National Film Board of Canada, Mackenzie Building, Toronto), 30 minutes. Under the pressures of rising prices, competitive markets, and rising production costs, more and more farmers are being forced to abandon their traditional view of farming as a way of life for one that places it on the level of business. In this film, we see how a father and son—the father holding to old ways, the son favoring the new—resolve difficulties in such a way as to enable them to keep abreast of developments in agriculture.

QUESTIONS AND PROJECTS

1. What is meant by the family as an "active agent" in social change? A "passive agent"? In which role do sociologists more often see the family?
2. Define: the trustee family; the domestic family; the atomistic family.
3. Describe Zimmerman's theory of social and family change. Make explicit the interaction between family and society at each stage.
4. What, according to Zimmerman, is the significance of this pattern of social change for contemporary American society? Does Zimmerman propose a solution. What is it?

5. Evaluate this cyclical theory of change. To what degree can the theory be verified? To what degree can it be refuted?
6. Distinguish between material and nonmaterial culture. How is this distinction central to Ogburn's analysis of social change?
7. Define the concept of culture lag and give illustrations of its operation. What criticisms of this concept have been offered by other sociologists?
8. What time period and what cultural area does Ogburn's analysis cover? Does this scope influence the direction in which he sees society moving?
9. Describe the major functions which the family performed during colonial days and the subsequent defunctionalization that has occurred. How has this defunctionalization "disorganized" the family?
10. What structural features of the American kinship system contribute to the isolation of the nuclear family? Include in your answer the nature of existing kinship units, kinship terminology, and normative pressures operating on each generation.
11. How is marriage "the structural keystone of our family system"? How is marriage based upon romantic love consistent with such a system?
12. How does the segregation of familial and occupational roles help to maintain the system? To which set of roles, occupational or familial, does our society assign priority? How do the demands of familial roles yield to those of occupational roles?

Part | IV

THE SOCIOLOGY OF THE FAMILY

9 | *The Middle-Class Family Model*

As any young executive in a big, national corporation quickly learns, it is almost impossible to succeed in business without really moving. Companies have found that there is no more challenging way to broaden a promising man's horizon or to give him an opportunity to grow. These days, the rate at which they are shuffling their young executives about the country is positively dizzying.

On the way to becoming assistant secretary to Humble Oil & Refining Company, Charles Goodyear, 33, has moved six times in eleven years. Until he landed in the head office in Houston a year ago, his nine-year-old son had never finished a single grade in the same school in which he began it. Johnson Wax moved Ed Furey, 30, from Racine, Wisconsin, to New York to Chicago, where he is regional office and warehouse manager, all in the past ten months. . . . Last year Union Carbide moved 1200 of its executives, compared with 600 only five years ago.

Since each change brings with it a promotion—or a promise of one—corporate nomads tend to be cheerful movers. Their children, at least until they become teen-agers, prove highly flexible. Wives, too, for the most part, enter into the arrangement with zest. Gloria Bradfield . . . has moved her household ten times in the past nine years. During that time, the Bradfields have bought one house, built two others, and had three children. "We're not as eager to move as we once were," says Mrs. Bradfield, but she still sees virtues in the nomadic life. "It's sort of like New Years," she explains, "getting a chance to start all over again. I'd hate to get in a rut."

. . . many big companies these days go out of their way to make the uprooting as painless as possible. They not only pay all moving costs . . . but frequently pick up the tab for new drapes. Many even buy up an executive's old house if he has difficulty getting the price he wants in a hurry. But even with company backing, the search for a new house is a pins-and-needles operation for the whole family. . . .[1]

[1] Reprinted by permission from *Time*, The Weekly Newsmagazine; copyright Time, Inc. 1967.

THIS is a very new phenomenon, and a geographically limited one. Over most of the world today, people are born, grow up, marry, reproduce, and die all within a few miles of a given location. The pattern in middle-class America, however, has been changing rapidly. By the early part of this century it had become common enough for people to move about the country that many a conversation opened with, "Where are you from?" In this way, the conversationists could acknowledge the increasing mobility in the society and still place one another on certain dimensions that would give structure to their relationship. To a degree this still is true. But increasingly we encounter the situation described above where people almost have no geographical roots, where they move from city to city and region to region as a part of advancing with the husband's job. The family home is not a particular structure on a given block in a certain town but is more a set of relationships, goals, and needs among its members. The family's house can be changed almost as readily as its bath towels.

Much more is involved, of course, than simply moving from place to place. The geographical mobility is a means to the far more important goals of increasing one's income, raising one's prestige in company and community, and altering one's style of life. Family life is a far different thing in this context than it was down on the farm. If the large farm family is the "family of Western nostalgia," the mobile family described above may well be the family of the future.

. . . "Togetherness" is the order of the day, with competence no longer strictly a masculine attribute nor tenderness strictly a woman's. The result is a family which is small and flexible, which relies on outside institutions for many of its needs, which deepens the emotional resources within its membership, and which can, as a result, travel light and intact. "The hope is," writes Dr. Paul Lemkau of the New York City Mental Hygiene Bureau, "that stronger relationships in the family will help to substitute for some of the ancient attachments to places and things." . . .

—Alvin Schorr, "Families on Wheels," *Harper's Magazine*, Jan. 1958, p. 74. By permission of the author.

Whether the family patterns to be described in this chapter are typical, it is impossible to say. What is to be described is not one integrated pattern which characterizes a specific group but a series of trends—a theme, perhaps—

which is emerging and which is spreading to ever larger segments of the society. Its patterns are the ones held up to us as models by government agencies, churches, and schools. Its patterns are described in typical American novels and are displayed on movie and TV screens, and in magazines. Its patterns are "ideal" patterns for much of the nonwhite, non-Anglo, non-Protestant, non-middle-class segment of the population, much as the gentry family patterns served as an ideal in traditional China. In twentieth-century America, however, an increasing proportion of the population is achieving the ideal.

What we are dealing with here is, to some extent also, an ideal type. It may not describe the exact way most families live or even the way that any one family lives. But if this is not empirical reality it represents only a very slight extension of that reality, a sharpening, as it were, of typical patterns that may enable us to see those patterns more clearly. The middle-class family lies very close to the heart of the American family system. To comprehend it is to open the way to comprehension of the larger system.

EMERGING PATTERNS IN THE AMERICAN FAMILY

One way to describe the middle-class family model is to present the system of moral principles, social norms, or rules and regulations according to which it is structured. Lee Burchinal has provided us with the core of such a list under the label "emerging patterns" in the American family.[2] These patterns do not apply to all American families—patterns vary among regional, ethnic, and youth subcultures. They are an attempt to strike an average, and increasingly characterize all families in the society. We present our interpretation of them here as the core of the normative system of the middle-class family.

EQUAL STATUS FOR WOMEN

Earlier chapters in this book have shown that woman's climb toward equal status with men has been long, slow, and uncertain. The end has not yet been reached. Middle-class people, however, are ideologically committed to the equality of the sexes in marriage and in the market place. This commitment is strongly buttressed in the law. Marriage is defined as a means to personal

[2] Lee G. Burchinal, "The Rural Family of the Future," in James H. Copp, ed., *Our Changing Rural Society: Perspectives and Trends*, Ames, Iowa: Iowa State University Press, 1964, pp. 161–8.

fulfillment for both partners and involves no subjugation of the woman to the man's interests and needs. Marriage is no longer seen as the ultimate source of satisfaction for many women.

FLEXIBLE DIVISION OF TASKS

Equal status of the sexes is reflected in rejection of the stereotyped notions of men's work and women's work. The household division of labor is supposed to be based upon the personal preferences of the particular couple rather than involving an arbitrary division of tasks. The division of labor within the home also is supposed to take the wife's working outside the home into account. As wives bring home the bacon, husbands are expected to participate more fully in housework and child care.

MORE EQUALITY FOR CHILDREN

Children no longer are economic assets to their parents, they are fewer in number, and the imposition of discipline has ceased to be an end in itself. The differential status and power positions of parents and children are minimized in order that the personal and social development of the children may be furthered. Parent-child relationships should be characterized by affection and by increased participation of children in family decision-making.

PERSON-CENTERED MATE SELECTION

Improvements in the level of living have freed adolescents from the labor market, increased their leisure, and encouraged casual association between the sexes. Youth are expected to use their freedom to meet and evaluate prospective marriage partners. Ultimately, they are supposed to choose on the basis of love and companionship rather than in terms of family background, religion, and other traditional criteria.

PREMARITAL SEXUAL PERMISSIVENESS

Over the past 50 years, startling change in sexual norms has occurred. Both men and women have come to have the right to the enjoyment of sex. Moreover, these rights extend into the premarital period when the level of participation is expected to increase according to the level of emotional involvement.

With dating beginning quite early, relatively serious involvements also occur early and increases in petting activities have been pronounced over the past several decades. Now, increasing numbers of parents and offspring alike sanction sexual intercourse in relationships where a high degree of affection is present.

FOCUS ON THE NUCLEAR FAMILY

Industrialization, urbanization, and geographical mobility have discouraged emphasis upon the extended family and have caused people to concentrate on the conjugal unit. The traditional functions of child-bearing, socialization, and economic cooperation continue to be performed, but there is more emphasis upon sexual and companionship functions. There also is more attention given to articulation of family patterns with other social systems, particularly the occupational system. Family patterns are expected to facilitate participation in the occupational system and to yield whenever the two conflict.

THE PRESERVATION OF KIN TIES

Although the emphasis is upon the conjugal unit, ties with extended kin—particularly grandparents and grandchildren—are highly valued. Grandparents, when they are able, are expected to provide both financial and moral support to the young families of their offspring, and to do so in fashion that does not imply either financial or emotional dependence. In turn, the young parents and children are supposed to encourage both direct and vicarious participation of the grandparents in the life of the family. Distance often requires that much interaction be by mail and telephone, supplemented by occasional visits. As the grandparents grow older and more dependent, the younger family members are expected to increase both the amounts and types of their support.

THE PROFESSIONALIZATION OF MARITAL AND PARENTAL ROLES

Greater demands have led to professionalization of both parental and marital roles for both partners, but particularly for the wife. No longer are wives supposed to rely upon folk knowledge as a basis for performing their roles. Instead, they are expected to utilize professional help to develop their competence. Classes in preparation for marriage, childbirth, and parenthood are standard fare. In addition, the reading of women's magazines and consultations with specialists in medical clinics, schools, and counseling offices are accepted ways of increasing competence in the performance of marital and parental roles.

THE USE OF INTERPERSONAL CRITERIA OF SUCCESS

The permanence of marriage or the stability of family relationships have virtually ceased to be ends in themselves. Marriages are expected to promote the personal growth and wellbeing of the partners. When this does not happen, professional help should be sought to discover the source of the difficulty. Both partners should work to eliminate the problems but, if they are unable to do so, divorce is preferable to continuation of an unhappy marriage.

Similarly, parent-child relations are expected to be rewarding to the members of both generations. When problems are encountered, their causes should be rationally sought and mutually beneficial solutions, rather than those based upon the imposition of authority, should be pursued. Marriage and parenthood are intended to be for the satisfaction they bring to the participants.

The Family Life Cycle

The concept of "family life cycle" came out of rural sociology in the early 1930's[3] to take into account the changes in family structure, composition, and behavior that accompany the inevitable progression from birth to death. Families, like individuals, have a life cycle which arbitrarily may be said to begin with marriage, to proceed through the bearing of children, to be hectic and busy as the children grow to adulthood, to contract again with the marriage of the children and, finally, to terminate in the death of the parents.

Many scholars have contributed to the development of family life-cycle analysis. Major credit for quantifying the concept and using demographic data to describe its operation in American society must go to Paul C. Glick of the U.S. Bureau of the Census.[4] Evelyn Duvall has made most systematic use of

[3] See Pitirim A. Sorokin, Carle C. Zimmerman, and C. J. Galpin, A *Systematic Source Book in Rural Sociology*, Minneapolis: University of Minnesota Press, Vol. II, 1931, p. 31.

[4] Paul C. Glick, "The Family Cycle," *American Sociological Review* 12 (April 1947),

the concept in describing the variation in family patterns over the cycle,[5] Reuben Hill has furthered the use of life cycle as a theoretical orientation in family sociology,[6] and Rodgers and Magrabi and Marshall have further specified the concept for research purposes.[7]

Our purpose here is not to explore life-cycle analysis at length but to use the descriptions especially of Glick and Duvall to show how the family life cycle has changed over the past three-quarters of a century and what the implications of these changes are for families in general and for the middle-class family model in particular. It may be that most people do not gain adequate perspective on the family life cycle until they themselves approach death; certainly it is true that most college and university students, preoccupied as they are with mate selection, fail to perceive adequately the complexity of the stages that follow.

Figure 1 presents the most commonly used eight-stage family life cycle showing the length in years of each stage. The first stage involves the young married couple who have not yet produced children. Couples currently remain in this stage for an average of two years. The second stage abitrarily is said to last from the birth of the first child until that same child is two and one-half years old. The "families with pre-school children" stage lasts another three and one-half years, until the oldest child reaches six years of age. Stage IV, "families with school children," lasts seven years as does the "families with teenagers" stage. Thus, the two stages in which parents have children in school last almost twice as long as the three preceding stages added together! The period during which the children marry and leave home lasts an average of eight years.

The length of stages VII and VIII will come as a surprise and perhaps as something of a shock to many students. The period during which husband and wife remain together after the children are gone and until the husband's retirement averages 15 years, seven times as long as they were together before their first child was born. How myopic are the mate selection emphases in American society which emphasize adjustment during the first years and com-

---

pp. 164–74; and Paul C. Glick, "The Life Cycle of the Family," *Marriage and Family Living* 17 (Feb. 1955), pp. 3–9.

[5] Evelyn M. Duvall, *Family Development*, Philadelphia: J. B. Lippincott Company, 1962.

[6] Reuben Hill and Donald A. Hansen, "The Identification of Conceptual Frameworks Utilized in Family Study," *Marriage and Family Living* 22 (Nov. 1960), pp. 299–311.

[7] Frances A. Magrabi and William H. Marshall, "Family Developmental Tasks: A Research Model," *Journal of Marriage and the Family* 27 (Nov. 1965), pp. 454–8; Roy H. Rodgers, *Improvements in the Construction and Analysis of Family Life Cycle Categories*, 1962 copyright by Roy H. Rodgers.

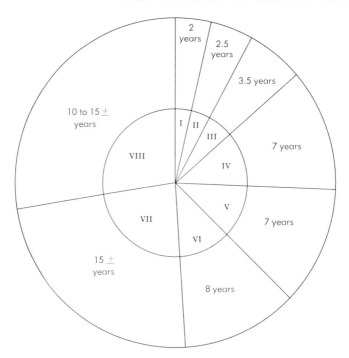

I BEGINNING FAMILIES (married couple without children).
II CHILDBEARING FAMILIES (oldest child birth—30 months).
III FAMILIES WITH PRESCHOOL CHILDREN (oldest child 30 months—6 years).
IV FAMILIES WITH SCHOOL CHILDREN (oldest child 6–13 years).
V FAMILIES WITH TEENAGERS (oldest child 13–20 years).
VI FAMILIES AS LAUNCHING CENTERS (first child gone to last child leaving home).
VII FAMILIES IN THE MIDDLE YEARS (empty nest to retirement).
VIII AGING FAMILIES (retirement to death of both spouses).

FIGURE 1. *The family life cycle by length of time in each of eight stages.*

Source: Reprinted by permission from *Family Development* by Evelyn Duvall, published by J. B. Lippincott Company. Copyright © 1971, 1962, 1957 by J. B. Lippincott Company.

pletely ignore the demands of most of the years that the couple will actually live together! After the husband's retirement it is from 10 to 15 years, approximately, until the death of the last partner. The husband who outlives his wife —and most husbands don't outlive their wives—outlives her by an average of about 7.5 years. Usually the wife outlives her husband and survives him by nearly 16 years.[8] Perhaps marital preparation for women should include preparation for prolonged widowhood.

[8] Duvall, op. cit. p. 15. Refined data on the length of the various stages in the family life cycle may be found in Paul C. Glick, and Robert Parke, Jr., "New Approaches in

Table 1 presents data on changes in the family cycle since 1890 and projects those changes forward to 1980. The data are presented separately for husband and wife, showing their median ages at the time of marriage, at the birth of their last child, at the marriage of their last child, and at the death of the first spouse. Both men and women marry younger today, child-bearing is completed earlier, and both are considerably younger at the time their last child leaves home. The length of time they have together after their children are gone has increased most of all.

TABLE 1. *Ages of Husband and Wife at Critical Stages in the Family Life Cycle in the United States, 1890, 1940, 1950, 1960, 1980*

STAGE OF THE FAMILY LIFE CYCLE	1890	1940	1950	1960 (AVERAGES)	1980 (PROJECTIONS)
Median age of wife at:					
First marriage	22.0	21.5	20.1	20.1	19.21
Birth of last child	31.9	27.1	26.1	25.9	26-28
Marriage of last child	55.3	50.0	47.6	47.1	47-49
Death of husband	53.3	60.9	61.4	63.5	65-67
Median age of husband at:					
First marriage	26.1	24.3	22.8	22.3	21-23
Birth of last child	36.0	29.9	28.8	28.0	28-30
Marriage of last child	59.4	52.8	50.3	49.1	50-52
Death of wife	57.4	63.6	64.1	65.5	68-70

Source: Paul C. Glick, "The Life Cycle of the Family," *Marriage and Family Living* 17, (February 1955), pp. 3–9; Paul C. Glick, *American Families* (New York: John Wiley and Sons, 1957); Paul C. Glick and Robert Parke, Jr., "New Approaches in Studying the Life Cycle of the Family," *Demography* 2 (1965): 187–202; and averages for 1960 and projections for 1980 derived from Bureau of the Census data with methods similar to those used for earlier years; see also Robert Parke, Jr., and Paul C. Glick, "Prospective Changes in Marriage and Family," *Journal of Marriage and the Family* 29 (May 1967): 249–56, as reproduced in Evelyn M. Duvall, *Family Development*, Philadelphia: J. B. Lippincott Company, 1971, p. 407.

The family of today, and especially the middle-class family, is a very different thing from the family of yesteryear. Just a few generations ago, men married in their middle twenties and often had been buried before their last child left home. Women married only slightly earlier and often were worn, tired, and

Studying the Life Cycle of the Family," *Demography*, Vol. 2, 1965, 187–202. These data, based upon birth cohorts of women, support the present analysis but indicate a possible trend toward a somewhat longer childbearing period.

widowed before their children were grown. Now most parents are on their own again before they reach fifty years of age and, at fifty, appear younger, healthier, and more active than people of thirty-five to forty did fifty years ago. The increased longevity of the United States population has increased the overlap of generations in the family tremendously. Grandparents often live to see their grandchildren grown and married. In the process, the relationships between parents and their grown children have changed and family relationships generally have become more complicated.

GEOGRAPHICAL MOBILITY

Approximately one family in every five in the United States moves each year. Not that the same families move year after year, of course; some families set up a household at the time of marriage and remain there for the rest of their lives. And some families of migratory workers are on the move constantly. Our thesis here is that for a vast intermediate segment of the population, occasional changes of house and community occur as part of the husband's quest for occupational advancement and as the family seeks to find a congenial atmosphere in which to fulfill itself and rear its children.

Census data on mobility are revealing at this point. Mobility is highest among the young adult age groups and declines steadily as people get older. In Table 2 it can be seen that over 40 per cent of males between 20 and 24 years of age moved to a different house over a one-year period. Over half those who moved, moved to another house within the same county, but 8 per cent moved to another county and 9 per cent moved to another state. Between the ages of 25 and 29, some 36 per cent moved in the one-year period; between 30 and 34 years, nearly 25 per cent moved; between 35 and 44, 16 per cent moved; and between 45 and 64 years, the figure still was over 10 per cent.

When mobility is stated by income, we find that the greatest mobility is to be found at the middle income levels. Pedersen reports that, for the period 1955–60, 42 per cent of families with incomes under $2000 and 39 per cent of those with incomes over $15,000 moved; 50 per cent of those with incomes between $4000 and $6000 moved. Moreover, families with household heads under 25 years of age and incomes between $5000 and $6000 have mobility rates of 90 per cent. Between 25 and 29 years, the highest mobility rates are found among those with incomes between $7000 and $10,000. Between 30 and 34 years the highest mobility rates are found among those with incomes over $15,000.[9]

[9] Harald A. Pedersen, "Family Mobility—Rural and Urban," in Iowa State University Center for Agricultural and Economic Development, *Family Mobility in Our Dynamic Society*, Ames, Iowa: Iowa State University Press, 1965, p. 63.

TABLE 2. *Mobility of the United States Population During a Single Year,*
March, 1968-March, 1969.

| | | PER CENTS* | | |
	DID NOT MOVE	MOVED WITHIN THE COUNTY	MOVED TO DIFFERENT COUNTY	MOVED TO DIFFERENT STATE
Males	80.4	11.9	3.3	3.4
Females	81.6	11.5	3.1	3.3
Males between				
20–24 yrs.	53.6	24.1	7.9	9.2
25–29	62.3	21.6	6.2	7.6
30–34	73.9	16.2	4.3	3.9
35–44	83.0	9.9	3.0	3.1
45–64	89.3	6.9	2.0	1.5
65 & over	92.5	4.9	1.6	1.0

* Per cents do not total 100 because some persons were abroad and not included in computations.

Source: Computed from U. S. Bureau of the Census, *Statistical Abstract of the United States: 1970* (Washington, D. C.), p. 33.

These figures indicate a growing pattern of geographical mobility in the United States which is characteristic of young college-educated men and their families who form the technical and management base of the nation's large corporations. The process was illustrated in the quotation that opened this chapter. In addition to the figures given there, General Electric Company found, when it compared a group of its 35-year-old executives with a comparable group of its 45-year-old executives that 42 per cent of the older group and 58 per cent of the younger group had been moved at least once. Another indication is found in the changes of address reported to *Fortune*, a magazine oriented to the business executive community. In 1953, 1954, and 1955, 14.8 per cent, 16.6 per cent, and 17.4 per cent of its subscribers reported that they had moved. Long-distance moving companies also state that the largest single group of their clients are corporation people being transferred from one location to another.[10]

Such "organization men" typically move across the country from suburb to suburb, moving physically but taking much the same way of life with them from place to place. As Whyte puts it, "With each transfer the *décor*, the architecture, the faces, and the names may change; the people, the conversa-

[10] William H. Whyte, Jr., *The Organization Man*, Garden City, New York: Doubleday and Company, 1956, pp. 298–305.

tion, and the values do not—and sometimes the *décor* and the architecture don't either." [11] These transients most commonly inhabit the suburbs because living there is the proper thing to do for those who are "on the way up," because in the suburbs they find other people of similar socio-economic status, tastes, and values, and because the suburbs are supposed to be good for family living—good places in which to rear children.[12] Among such people, what we have chosen to call the middle-class family model is most highly developed.[13] Let us look now at some ways in which middle-class youth are socialized to prepare them for this kind of life, and then at some of the characteristic processes that operate in the lives of middle-class couples and between middle-class parents and their children.

ANTICIPATORY SOCIALIZATION

So far in this chapter we have emphasized the pervasiveness of the family style of life of a highly mobile, consumption-oriented middle class. In this section we continue to develop the idea of a middle-class family model, widely lived and even more widely imitated throughout the larger society. We focus

[11] Op. cit. p. 305. Lack of stress accompanying such moves was shown in a recent study of 100 middle-class families with a history of frequent moves on short notice. See Judson R. Landis and Louis Stoetzer, "An Exploratory Study of Middle-Class Migrant Families," *Journal of Marriage and the Family* 28 (Feb. 1966), pp. 51–3.

[12] The processes involved in residential mobility and suburbanization have been studied at length. See Wendell Bell, "Social Choice, Life Styles, and Suburban Residence," in William A. Dobriner, ed., *The Suburban Community*, New York: Putnam, 1958, pp. 225–47; Lee G. Burchinal and Ward W. Bauder, "Adjustments to the New Institutional Environment," in Iowa State University Center for Agricultural and Economic Development, op. cit. pp. 197–222; Edgar W. Butler, Georges Sabagh, and Maurice D. Van Arsdol, Jr., "Demographic and Social Psychological Factors in Residential Mobility," *Sociology and Social Research* 48 (Jan. 1964), pp. 139–54; Sylvia F. Fava, "Contrasts in Neighboring: New York City and a Suburban County," in William A. Dobriner, ed., op. cit. pp. 122–31; Arnold S. Feldman and Charles Tilly, "The Interaction of Social and Physical Space," *American Sociological Review* 35 (Dec. 1960), pp. 877–84; William F. Kenkel, "The Family Moving Decision Process," in Iowa State University Center for Agricultural and Economic Development, op. cit. pp. 178–93; Gerald R. Leslie and Arthur H. Richardson, "Life-Cycle, Career Pattern, and the Decision To Move," *American Sociological Review* 26 (Dec. 1961), pp. 894–902; Ernest R. Mowrer, "The Family in Suburbia," in William A. Dobriner, ed., op. cit. pp. 147–64; and Peter H. Rossi, *Why Families Move*, Glencoe, Illinois: The Free Press, 1955.

[13] The emphasis on the corporate way of life in this and the succeeding discussion should not obscure the fact that, although the large corporation may provide the best example of the points we are trying to make, the same basic processes operate in a much larger and increasing segment of the society. Few would argue, for example, that universities are as highly bureaucratized as most corporations. Even so-called independent professional people —physicians, lawyers, accountants, and so on—and small business men find that their lives are quite similar to those of the so-called organization men.

here on some of the ways in which the experiences of children and adolescents prepare them to live the middle-class family model even more fully than their parents do.

Riesman and Roseborough in discussing the relationship between the family life cycle and consumer behavior agree with our thesis that the middle-class model is being accepted by an ever-expanding segment of the population. As they phrase it, there has been a general lowering of barriers going on between age groups, between the sexes, among regions of the country, and among social classes. As this happens a fairly uniform middle-majority life style is becoming a major American theme with variations.[14]

Empirical support for this position is provided by Katona and his associates at the University of Michigan Survey Research Center. Katona refers to the United States as a "mass consumption society," emphasizing the fact that, in 1961, two out of every five American families belonged to the "discretionary income group" having incomes between $6000 and $15,000 per year.[15] The use of the $6000–$15,000 range was appropriate in 1961, but is already badly out of date. More current figures, using $10,000 and up as representing the discretionary income group, are shown in Figure 2.

The discretionary income group is not wealthy in the traditional sense, but they generally are people who have significant amounts of money left over after the basic necessities of life are provided for. This "left-over" income may be saved or it may be used to provide whatever luxuries are consistent with a given family's particular style of life. Katona points out that between 1929 and 1961 the number of families in the United States increased by 55 per cent and national income increased by nearly 160 per cent, but, even after adjusting for differences in price levels, the number of families with incomes between $6000 and $15,000 increased by 400 per cent![16] He also states that families with heads between 35 and 54 years of age and incomes between $5000 and $10,000 were only 25 per cent of all families in 1951, but the same age group with incomes between $6000 and $15,000 in 1961 contained 49 per cent of all families. Thus a vast and increasing segment of the population qualifies financially for inclusion in the middle class.

The middle-class theme, according to Riesman and Roseborough, is symbolized by the almost universal possession of, or seeking after, a common set of

[14] David Riesman and Howard Roseborough, "Careers and Consumer Behavior," in Lincoln H. Clark, ed., Consumer Behavior, Volume II: The Life Cycle and Consumer Behavior, New York: New York University Press, 1955, pp. 1–2.

[15] George Katona, The Mass Consumption Society, New York: McGraw-Hill Book Company, 1964, p. 9.

[16] Ibid. pp. 13–14.

FIGURE 2. *Distribution of Family Units and Their Income, by Income Groups,*
    1968

Source: U. S. Bureau of the Census, *Statistical Abstract of the United States:* 1970
(Washington, D. C.), pp. 322–3.

material possessions—automobile or automobiles, furniture, television, radios,
refrigerator-freezer, and standard brands of food and clothing. These possessions they call the "standard package" [17] which almost all middle-class families
possess and which they can easily transport with them as they move about the
country and up the occupational ladder.

There are variations on the package, of course. Differences in region of the
country, ethnic group, occupation, and life style are revealed by slight variations within the package. More striking than the variations, however, is the
homogenization of taste and style over the country. Riesman and Roseborough cite Lynes's discovery that Sears no longer puts out regional catalogs
because essentially the same tastes prevail all over the country. One might
cite also the fact that foods such as chow mein, pizza, stroganoff, and shish
kabob are served almost everywhere and in communities where nothing is
known of the origin of these dishes. Perhaps the most startling evidence of all
is provided by the emerging popularity of trading houses and possessions over

[17] Riesman and Roseborough, op. cit.

long vacation periods. A family in Cape Cod or New York City arranges by mail, and sight unseen, to trade houses for the summer with a family from San Francisco or Tucson. Moreover, it works. Each wife leaves the linens in the drawers, the china in the cupboards, and even the soap and bathroom tissue. The alternate family moves in and almost within hours is as settled as they were at home. Often the greatest problem lies in finding "where she keeps the bottle opener." What better evidence could there be for the existence of a widely common middle-class way of life?

The key to the universality of the standard package is to be found in the preparation of children and adolescents to want and expect to possess it when they reach adulthood. The process begins early in life when, via television and the movies, children learn what the components of the package are and witness their parents' desires to own them. The children are undergoing what sociologists call "anticipatory socialization," a process of role-playing and fantasy which leads them to anticipate the conditions of adulthood and to respond to those conditions in a predetermined way.[18]

The special significance of the concept of anticipatory socialization for our purposes lies in the fact that children are thus prepared to live in ways that their parents have not really lived. In fact, they are prepared to live as no one has yet lived. They are prepared not only to expect the standard package of today but to anticipate the additions that will be made to it from ten to twenty years in the future.

This anticipatory socialization continues throughout childhood and adolescence. The typical middle-class school often is more modern than the homes from which the children come. As they move on into college, many young people live either in fraternity or sorority houses, in modern dormitories, or in apartments that may be even more lavishly appointed than the Greek houses. That their parents may have to scrimp and save in order to maintain their offspring in such luxury probably makes less impression on the young people than the fact that this is the way to live. Thus, college living conditions help to prepare young people not only to live better than their parents do but to begin to do so much earlier in life.

It seems probable that most of the middle-class parents who have collected the components comprising the standard package have required many years

[18] Robert K. Merton and Alice S. Kitt, "Contributions to the Theory of Reference-Group Behavior," in Robert K. Merton and Paul S. Lazarsfeld, eds., *Continuities in Social Research: Studies in the Scope and Method of "The American Soldier,"* Glencoe, Illinois: The Free Press, 1950, pp. 87–9. See also Roy G. Francis, "Family Strategy in Middle Class Suburbia," *Sociological Inquiry* 3 (Spring 1963), pp. 157–64.

to do so. In the environment in which they grew up, one became prepared to save for many years to acquire the amenities. Their children, however, having had most of the package for most of their lives and, having had their tastes further upgraded in adolescence, are not so often disposed to wait. They do not wait for marriage, but often marry before the man is established in an occupation and while they are essentially without material possessions. Once married, and even though their incomes are quite adequate by most standards, they are likely to use installment buying to spend beyond their incomes and more quickly acquire the complete package. They begin marriage almost at the economic and status level it has taken their parents twenty to thirty years to achieve.[19]

The clamorous demands of youthful activists, which have shaken the universities and unsettled the political parties, are spreading to the world of business. A new generation—confident, iconoclastic and thoroughly professional—has entered the nation's corporations. . . . The younger men who have grown up in an era of affluence and clearly enjoyed the luxuries of suburbia, claim to reject traditional incentives.

What, then, do the young managers want? Very largely, they want almost instant responsibility, a chance for individual expression or . . . "opportunity for impact." . . . Today's young businessman is a member of the committed generation who insists on meaning and a sense of social responsibility in both his job and his life. . . .

For all their idealism, young men want—and get—record salaries. "The young employee is more rapacious these days," says . . . a vice-president of California's Security Pacific National Bank. "The fact that his boss worked 20 years to get where he is does not move him."

Many young managers finding that they can get more and more money by changing jobs, do so with startling frequency. Dr. Edgar Schein of the MIT Sloan School of Management estimates that companies lose half of their new college graduates within the first three to

[19] As this is being written, a middle-class youth counterculture is conspicuous around most college campuses. This counterculture specifically rejects the middle-class family model and its standard package of possessions, declaring them to be outmoded and irrelevant in today's world. This counterculture, however, is likely to go the way of its bohemeian, beat, and hippie predecessors; after a few years of defiance, its members will re-enter the mainstream of American life.

If, by chance, the author is wrong in this hypothesis, it still won't make much difference. If today's counterculture representatives remain committed to it, they will simply suffer downward social mobility while black and other minority youth, along with poor white youth, will go to college, work hard, and become conspicuous representatives of a new middle class.

five years of employment. Graduates of 15 years ago often regarded a job, like a marriage, as being for life; today's young men are more inclined to equate it with an affair—good until something more fetching comes along. . . .

—Reprinted by permission from *Time*, The Weekly Newsmagazine; copyright Time, Inc., 1969.

In their analysis, Riesman and Roseborough also emphasize the role of the corporation in regulating the family's consumption pattern and in helping to produce tensions between the husband and wife. The family consumption pattern is regulated indirectly by the need to gauge one's possessions to one's status level, neither understating it nor overstating it. Thus the proper automobile for a junior executive may be a new Chevrolet Impala, Plymouth Fury, or comparable car. If one's immediate superior drives an Oldsmobile 88, it may be the height of foolhardiness to purchase an Oldsmobile 98, even if one can afford it. At the same time, a promising young executive who drives a four-year-old inexpensive car may find that his superiors question his taste and judgment—in other things as well as automobiles. Nor are such restrictions confined to the husband's possessions. His wife must be careful to see that her clothing and personal adornment set her apart from the wives of her husband's subordinates, but being careful to see that she does not compete with the wives of her husband's superiors The house and neighborhood they live in, the schools their children attend, the clubs they belong to, and even the kinds of vacations they take must be adjusted to what is appropriate to their rank in the corporation. As the husband is promoted, their consumption patterns are adjusted accordingly.[20]

. . . There are signs, more subtle than revolutionary, that the corporate wife is not quite so willing to marry her husband's organization for better or for worse nor to serve docilely as the unpaid member of the team it hires.

". . . We want something more out of life than our husbands or their corporations can provide," said Nancy Hall, 23 years old, a member of the Women's Liberation Collective of the Harvard Business School Wives Club. In a much softer tone, Pat Allinson said, "Now everyone wants her own identity." . . . as Mary Moody said, "I went

[20] William H. Whyte, Jr., *Is Anybody Listening?*, New York: Simon and Schuster, 1952.

on interview trips with my husband in 1962. Some companies planned programs and made me feel I'd be conforming. It was through off-hand remarks about how the wives did things together such as bowl on Tuesday and bridge on Wednesday.

"Other companies treated me as an individual and a person. Thank heaven, my husband liked that best." . . .

. . . Among the upcoming generation of executives . . . the wives are working, "but not in the context that they are going to settle down and have babies. Joan's an artist, or Cathy is a personnel manager. I suspect many corporations will see this mode of life as a condition of attracting and holding good people."

"As people have been becoming more loyal to their professions than to their organizations, they go where the work is challenging and the environment makes work meaningful." . . .

—Marylin Bender, "Corporate Wives Studied," *The New York Times*, February 21, 1971. © 1971 by The New York Times Company. Reprinted by permission.

Some strains between husband and wife are produced by their socialization into the corporate way of life and by their upward mobility. The husband who travels on an expense account, for example, often lives much better on the road than his family can afford to live at home. He travels first class, has deluxe accommodations, eats expensive meals, and so on. In the meantime his wife, who would like very much to share his good fortune, is stuck at home caring for the children, one of whom often has a cold or is otherwise difficult to manage, and eating TV dinners or the equivalent. The wife resents her husband's privileges, or at least her inability to share in them, and, for his part, the husband must feign dislike for having to travel. And at home the husband often cannot help but compare the luxury of his travels with the hectic home existence in a too-crowded house on a too-tight budget with a harassed wife and fussy children.

When it comes to mobility up the occupational ladder, similar strains may occur. The necessity carefully to adjust one's standard of living to one's current job status demands a price from both husband and wife. Even where they could afford to do so out of private income, they must carefully avoid the purchase of a too lavish home or the appearance of prematurely putting down roots. As is more often the case, the strain of attempting to meet demands that outrun one's income is great. No man who expects to get ahead can forgo golf with the boss, membership in the country club, or expensive but proper entertainment. Moreover, the better the man's prospects, the greater may be the strain. The rising young man who feels that he cannot afford the luxuries to which his boss encourages him knows full well that the boss's judgment that he can afford them is likely to eventuate in a self-fulfilling prophecy. In the meantime, husband and wife, plagued with anxiety over how to make ends meet, are prone unwittingly to take out their frustrations the only place they can—on one another.

PARENT-CHILD INTERACTION

The nature of parent-child interaction in the middle-class family model is bound up intimately with the nature and quality of the interaction between the parents, particularly with the striving pattern in which they find themselves caught up. For, although the incomes of such young families are quite adequate by most absolute standards, they are usually inadequate in terms of the demands which the parents feel upon themselves. Pregnancy and child-bearing are not unmixed blessings, for they require substantial amounts of money which might otherwise be spent on social and occupational advancement. Nor is the problem one of money alone. Child-bearing and child-rearing consume parental time and energy. The wife especially finds herself physically tied to the household and unable to join her husband wholeheartedly in the pursuit of other goals. Since most significant activities for middle-class people are engaged in by couples, the husband's freedom is limited too.

Under these circumstances it would not be surprising if child-bearing was widely regarded as a burden. Actually the very reverse appears to be true. Middle-class people accept, perhaps more than any other group in the society, the ideas that child-bearing is to be sought after, that all children are inherently lovable, and that parent-child relationships are sources of continuous joy. The socialization of both men and women to accept these norms is so effective that middle-class parents, while literally gagging over the contents of soiled diapers, stoutly maintain how happy they are! Middle-class people, too, seem to hang on especially tenaciously to the idea that there is some vague, mysterious parental instinct which results in people having unmixed feelings of love for their children, no matter how troublesome they may be. That such a notion can be consistently adhered to in spite of evidence that some parents (usually not middle class) beat and injure their children, desert them, and even kill them suggests that there is a compulsive quality to middle-class parental love; that it is to some degree a protection against hostile impulses lurking below the surface. If this analysis is correct, there should be some very complex and ambivalent emotional interaction in middle-class families.

Parsons traces many of the features of middle-class child-rearing practices to the smallness and relative isolation of the conjugal family.[21] These conditions result in the child becoming quite dependent upon and very vulnerable to his parents. Unlike the situation in a large family system, in which the child has protection against the wrath or disapproval of a parent in the love and affection of grandparents, aunts, cousins, and so on, the middle-class American child has no one else to turn to. From birth, his life and welfare are overwhelmingly tied up with his mother. The father, a not-too-active participant during the first year or so, assumes an increasingly important position as the child grows older.

This complete dependence on the parents results in the child's becoming very sensitive to any actual or threatened withdrawal of approval by them; his need for the parents' love becomes unconditional. When the child begins to participate in the outside world, however, he finds that playmates and neighbors judge him, not according to particularistic family standards but according to the dominant universalistic standards of the larger society. He must compete for affection and approval.

He quickly learns that his parents are judged by others according to the kind of job his father has, the house they live in, the automobiles they drive, and so on. Moreover, he himself is judged by his own achievements. If he is a bright, alert youngster who accomplishes more than his fellows, he fares well. If he lags behind, he fares badly. According to Mead, American children . . . begin life with a terrific impetus toward success.[22] Before they are old enough to assess the situation critically, they become imbued with a life-long striving to excel. The American ethos proclaims that success is equivalent to virtue and success is to be achieved through hard work.[23]

The child learns not only that he must compete in the outside world for approval but also that love and approval from his parents are contingent upon

---

[21] Talcott Parsons, "The Social Structure of the Family," in Ruth N. Anshen, ed., *The Family: Its Function and Destiny*, New York: Harper and Brothers, 1959, p. 255.

[22] Margaret Mead, "Competition and Individualism," in Kingsley Davis, Harry C. Bredemeier, and Marion J. Levy, Jr., eds., *Modern American Society: Readings in the Problems of Order and Change*, New York: Rinehart and Company, 1949, pp. 35–43.

[23] Alert students will see that the success-striving middle-class person is well illustrated by Sinclair Lewis's *Babbitt* (1922). It should be remembered, however, that "babbittry" is only one form of success-striving. Not all middle-class people seek to enhance their self-esteem through the acquisition of automobiles, boats, houses, and so on. In fact, some middle-class people who are especially striving, eschew conspicuous consumption. Striving can just as readily take the form of being more knowledgeable about music or art than anyone else, of traveling widely, or giving one's time and money to charity. College professors, who are often thought to be seeking refuge from the business world and who sometimes glory in their lack of concern with material things, frequently engage in vicious competition for status among their peers. Even ministers often compete to outdo one another in their efforts at humility!

performance. For, although his parents are consciously committed to love their child regardless, they too have success needs that must be met partly through the child. Put any two middle-class mothers of young children together, for example, and some of their interaction can be predicted. They will begin to compare the accomplishments of their respective offspring. If the child of one mother began to talk earlier, then the second mother must find some achievement that her child accomplished first or performs better. The competition between the two women (and their children) often is not too carefully concealed. If the one mother and child come off badly, we might further predict that the unsuspecting husband and father is in for a bad evening! He is likely to find a quarrelsome wife who may or may not be able to tell him the source of her annoyance.

Chances are that neither the husband nor wife will be clearly aware of what is happening. For one thing, although most middle-class people are success-striving, another set of middle-class norms disapproves of too blatant striving, requiring that the competition be carried on in a seeming atmosphere of co-operation and good will. For another thing, explicit awareness of their disappointment over their child's performance might call forth hostile feelings toward the child which the parents are ill equipped to handle.

Apparently middle-class parents have difficulty showing aggression toward their children. The widespread preoccupation among them over whether children should be spanked may reflect their fear of hitting the child. Many middle-class parents use more subtle techniques of punishment which are at the same time more effective and more devastating. In one way or another and at one level or another, what they do is to threaten to withdraw love and approval. If the mother is crude and insensitive, she may literally say to her child "Mother won't love you if you do that." If she is just slightly more sophisticated, she may say "We don't do things like that in our family," implying, of course, that the child who misbehaves may be considered a depraved outsider. Middle-class mothers may thus deal a heavier blow with a softly spoken sentence or with a raising of an eyebrow than could be dealt with a strong right arm.

The effectiveness of the technique of withholding love depends upon the child's extreme dependence on the parents. Because he is so dependent, the threat that his parents might reject him is almost overwhelming. One might expect in such a situation that many children would respond with great anxiety and with direct aggression against the parents. Some children do; but more often it appears that most of the aggression is repressed and the child becomes conforming instead.

The long-term effects of these patterns on the personalities of children is a matter of some debate. A few years ago it was common in such analyses of middle-class family patterns to find that emotional conflicts existed and then to imply that these probably were more severe and disabling than the direct aggression, for example, believed to be more characteristic of lower-class family life. Research evidence, however, shows the contrary to be true.[24] Emotional illness, along with maladjustments of almost every sort, appears to be more common among the lower social classes. If middle-class child-rearing patterns do not produce gross maladjustment, however, they may still play a significant role in determining the kinds of adjustment problems that children and adults face.

Arnold Green has produced a classic analysis of this situation in which he argues that it is inevitable that middle-class parents should view their children with considerable ambivalence and should control them through the threat of withdrawal of love and approval. He maintains further that the typical middle-class boy's adjustment to this situation, by becoming outwardly submissive and conformist, makes it difficult for him to also display the aggression which is necessary for successful competition in the world of his peers. The boy is thus torn by conflict between the need to be submissive and the need to be aggressive. Whatever he does, he is likely to be torn by indecision, anxiety, and guilt in a distinctively middle-class form of neurosis. As he grows to adulthood he carries the conflict with him, becoming preoccupied with self-doubt. Whenever he behaves aggressively he feels guilty for violating the standards of his early submissive adjustment; but whenever he behaves submissively, he feels guilty over not striving to achieve.[25]

Green's analysis, in focusing upon the role of the middle-class son, implies differences in the socialization of boys and girls, which differences have been systematized by Parsons. Parsons states that middle-class children of both sexes overwhelmingly identify, in early childhood, with the mother. For the girl this identification is quite functional because the mother serves as a direct role model of what the daughter will be when she becomes adult. Most of the tasks which a wife and mother performs are quite tangible and easy for the girl to imitate. She role-plays at sweeping, ironing, cooking, and so on. She is not required to change her basic identification anywhere on the road to adulthood and Parsons believes that this may be one of the factors that accounts for girls appearing to mature, emotionally, earlier than boys do.[26]

[24] Rates of treated mental disorders are highest at lower social class levels and decline steadily as we move up the social class ladder. See August B. Hollingshead and Frederick C. Redlich, *Social Class and Mental Illness*, New York: John Wiley and Sons, 1958.

[25] Arnold Green, "The Middle-Class Male Child and Neurosis," *American Sociological Review* 11 (Feb. 1946), pp. 31–41.

[26] Op. cit. pp. 256–7.

Not that the road to successful adult functioning is completely uncompli-cated for girls. There are at least three potential sources of frustration. First, girls must discover, fairly early in life,[27] the prevailing definitions of masculine superiority. The beloved and formerly omnipotent-appearing mother is de-pendent for livelihood and security upon some man. All women are basically dependent upon men, and the girl herself must eventually attain security, not through her own initiative, but through that of her husband. The competitive disadvantages faced by women must come as a shock to the girl who has identi-fied with her mother and who tacitly believed that the route to ultimate per-sonal security lay in being like her. Parsons believes that considerable hostility may be engendered toward both men and women by this disappointment.[28] That hostility appears later in life in the beliefs that women are deceptive and not to be trusted and that men are responsible for women's subjection. It may be that some of the ambivalence of women toward sex traces to this situation.

When she reaches adolescence, the girl also discovers that the domestic atti-tudes and behaviors which have brought her approval from her mother and other adults are not similarly valued by her peers. Neither adolescent girls nor adolescent boys are especially fond of the "little mother" who cooks, sews, and cleans house. Instead, if she is to be popular, the girl must rebel against parental standards and adopt the pose of the glamor girl and the good sport. Rewards now come from compulsive conformity to the hedonistic fads and fashions of the group. Some girls do not make the transition readily and are left out of most teen-age activity. Many of the others are somewhat confused by the conflicting standards to which they are held, and lay the groundwork for continued role confusion later in life.

The third source of frustration appears as the girl moves into adulthood and marriage. Unlike her masculine counterpart, the girl does not have the op-portunity to contend directly in the struggle for status and to continue to raise her status during adult life. Instead, she essentially fixes her status and prospects as she selects her spouse. Moreover, she is normally required to make this selection at an age when the occupational potentialities of her prospective partner are yet quite unclear. If he is successful, she will be successful; if he is not, she cannot be. And even the most ardent defender of marriage based upon romantic love is unlikely to claim that it offers the girl any assurance in this particular respect.

[27] The masculine bias in American culture has been revealed by studies on the preference for male children and by the differential evaluations placed on males and females. See Simon Dinitz, Russell R. Dynes, and Alfred C. Clarke, "Preferences for Male or Female Children: Traditional or Affectional?" *Marriage and Family Living* 16 (May 1954), pp. 128–30; and John P. McKee and Alex C. Sherriffs, "The Differential Evaluation of Males and Females," *Journal of Personality* 25 (March 1957), pp. 356–71.

[28] Op. cit. p. 260.

> Women have one great advantage over men. It is commonly thought
> that if they marry they have done enough and need career no further.
> If a man marries, on the other hand, public opinion is all against him
> if he takes this view.
>
> —Rose Macaulay.

Like girls, boys tend to make a deep, early identification with the mother. Most of their intimate daily contacts are with the mother, the father being almost a background figure at first. Soon, however, boys discover that, not only are they expected to identify with the father and to assume masculine interests, but women are distinctly inferior to men.[29] To identify with the mother or to have feminine interests in home and domesticity becomes a source of shame.

Thus boys must rid themselves of a dysfunctional feminine identification. The depth of that original identification may be revealed in the resulting somewhat compulsive masculine identification and in the extreme rejection of all things feminine. Growing boys are likely to fear the label of "sissy" more than any other. They show contempt for girls, and they learn that not even the gravest personal or physical hurt should provoke them to tears, and that to become men they need to learn to fight, to smoke, to swear, and to tell dirty jokes. Before the imperious biological and social drives of adolescence begin to push the sexes toward one another again, the alienation of boys from the world of women may be fairly complete.

Middle-class parents are likely to be somewhat disturbed by their son's behavior and yet subtly to encourage it. The father's interest in his son's athletic prowess and his disapproval of domestic interest quickly communicates itself to the boy. Even the mother, while maintaining outward display of disapproval, subtly encourages her son in the same directions. After he has been fighting, making out with girls, or otherwise being mischievous, her scolding of him is likely to be tempered with the attitude that "its just like a boy." The boy hears her scolding but he also senses the expectation that he should continue to behave this way and that to do so will bring him rewards as well as punishment.[30]

[29] Scattered evidence that both men and women accept this definition is found in studies that have asked whether the person has ever wished he were of the opposite sex. Very few males ever wish that they were women, but up to one-half of women have wished that they were men. See Clifford Kirkpatrick, *The Family: As Process and Institution*, New York, Ronald Press, 1963, p. 157.

[30] See William E. Knox and Harriet J. Kupferer, "A Discontinuity in the Socialization

When the boy becomes a man and marries, he carries some of these attitudes with him. His now muted contempt for things feminine will be a source of puzzlement and hurt to his wife, and his inability to accept or express tender emotion will be a source of frustration to them both. The wife will have learned to cope with hurt by crying and otherwise seeking sympathy; the husband will have learned long ago to suppress the urge to cry by swearing and other aggressive behavior. Consequently, when the wife cries and the husband responds by swearing and stamping out of the room, each will marvel at the other's depravity.

The route to the appropriate adult identification is longer for boys because of the necessity for them to give up their feminine identification before they can assume a masculine one. Moreover, the father often provides a much less tangible role model for boys than the mother does for girls. Not only is the father away more, but it is difficult for boys to understand what their fathers do for a living. Typical middle-class occupations—technical, professional, and managerial—involve skills that are not readily transmitted to children. Consequently, boys grow up under great pressure to achieve in the occupational sphere but with little apparent preparation for so doing. The adolescent and young adult male's anxiety over his ability to make good is qualitatively different but probably at least as great as the girl's anxiety over marriage.

Summary

This chapter presents salient features of the white, Anglo-Saxon Protestant, middle-class family as a prototype of the family system in contemporary America. Focus is upon ideal-typical features of what may soon be the modal American family type.

The American family in general, and the middle-class family in particular, is structured according to an integrated set of social norms that might be called cultural configurations. These norms include prescriptions that: women should have equal status with men; there should be a flexible household division of labor; children should have a larger role in family decision-making; people should select their mates on the basis of personal qualities rather than in terms of specified background characteristics; people should live in nuclear families that adapt readily to occupational demands; ties with extended kin

---

of Males in the United States," *Merrill-Palmer Quarterly* 17 (July 1971), pp. 251–61. There is some evidence that these socialization patterns are changing in the direction of diminishing male-female differences. Male-female responses to the ink blot figures on the Rorschach Test, for example, are said to have converged over the past decade or so.

should be maintained; marital and parental roles should be professionalized; and marriages and families should promote the wellbeing of their members. These norms supply much of the moral basis upon which middle-class family life is built.

Life-cycle analysis is useful to trace changes in family organization and problems from the time of family formation at marriage to the time of its dissolution through death of the partners. While young people are likely to focus upon the early stages of the family life cycle, demographic data show that the postparental years are much more numerous. Moreover, changes over the past century have compressed the period of child-bearing and greatly lengthened the couple's life span together after their children have married. The increased life span has produced an altered pattern of relationships between parents and their adult married children.

The American population is an exceedingly mobile one, with approximately one family out of five changing place of residence each year. Mobility is highest among young adults and among middle-income groups. Much of this mobility is associated with occupational advancement and creates a relatively homogeneous style of life among a managerial-professional class all over the country.

Middle-class children and adolescents undergo a lengthy period of anticipatory socialization to prepare them to live according to the middle-class family model. They learn from their parents, the mass media, and school and college to expect to begin married life in possession of the standard package, including automobile, furniture, television, radios, refrigerator, and standard brands of food and clothing. Thus, middle-class young marrieds begin life at the social class and economic level it has taken their parents twenty or thirty years to achieve.

What might be called the corporation way of life closely regulates the family's consumption patterns and produces certain strains between husband and wife. The couple must live up to the standards expected of them, without infringing upon the perquisites of their superiors. Often this requires them to spend more than they feel they can afford in order to qualify socially for advancement within the organization. The husband's extravagant expense account living also contrasts sharply with the budget-saving measures demanded of his wife at home.

Parent-child relationships in the middle-class family are complicated by the isolation of the conjugal family, the high value placed upon children, and by emotional and financial strains upon the parents. Children are completely dependent upon their parents and quickly become very sensitive to actual or threatened rebuffs by them. For their part, the parents unwittingly extend their personal competitiveness to include their children and use the threat of withdrawal of love to secure high performance from the children. Children, thus, develop high success drives early in life. The conflict between the child's need to be dependent and his emerging success drive produces a basic ambivalence and difficulty in handling his aggressive impulses.

The girl's socialization pattern is more direct than the boy's in that her early identification with her mother provides her with an appropriate adult role model. She does encounter frustration in the discoveries that women must be subordinate to men, that nondomestic qualities are rewarded in adolescence, and in having to gamble her whole future on a young man whose potentialities are not yet evident. Boys must reject their early maternal identifications and, in the process, assume a somewhat compulsive masculinity that plagues their relationships with women. Boys also are handicapped in adopting the masculine role by the intangible nature of middle-class occupations and the lack of a clear, detailed, masculine role model.

SUGGESTED READINGS

Dobriner, William A., ed., *The Suburban Community*, New York: G. P. Putnam Sons, 1958. An excellent collection of readings on the significance of the suburban movement in the United States. Many of the articles deal directly and indirectly with changed life styles and family patterns.

Ferriss, Abbott L., *Indicators of Trends in the Status of American Women*, New York: Basic Books, 1971. The most systematic and comprehensive set of data yet compiled on the changing status of women in American society.

Goode, William J., Hopkins, Elizabeth, and McClure, Helen M., *Social Systems and Family Patterns: A Propositional Inventory*, Indianapolis: The Bobbs-Merrill Company, Inc., 1971. An immense compilation of theoretical propositions supported by research data. Propositions are cross-classified for easy use.

Heiskanen, Veronica Stolte, "The Myth of the Middle-Class Family in American Family Sociology," *The American Sociologist* 6 (February 1971), pp. 14–18. A good companion piece to this chapter. Emphasizes the diversity of American family patterns.

McKinley, Donald, *Social Class and Family Life*, New York: The Free Press of Glencoe, 1964. A theoretical analysis and report of research on variations in socialization techniques by social class. Provides insight into the nature of class variation in family patterns.

Rossi, Alice, "Naming Children in Middle-Class Families," *American Sociological Review* 30 (August 1965), pp. 499–513. A provocative article which uses the naming of children after relatives as clues to the affective structure of the middle-class American family. Concludes that the affective structure of the family is becoming more symmetrical.

Tallman, Irving, and Morgner, Ramona, "Life-Style Differences Among Urban and Suburban Blue-Collar Families," *Social Forces* 48 (March 1970), pp. 334–48. Research report on variations in life-styles as determined by social class and as determined by place of residence.

FILMS

Social Class in America (McGraw-Hill Book Company, Text-Film Division, 330 West 42nd St., New York 10036), 16 minutes. Significant contrasts are shown in the lives of three boys who come from three different social classes. The film relates the ascribed, or inherited, status of each to the wealth, occupation, residential address, and social status of his parents and shows how graduation from high school marks the beginning of increasingly different lives. Illustrates factors favoring vertical mobility in America.

Suburban Living—Six Solutions (National Film Board of Canada, Mackenzie Building, Toronto), 60 minutes. Surveys six suburbs in England, France, Holland, Sweden, and Canada. All except the Canadian example offer light, airy homes in park-like settings at rentals of about one-sixth of income. Here are six suburban neighborhoods designed to serve the needs of the whole man —suburbs and towns where the green belt enters the residential area, where there is no barrier between town park and country field.

The Cage (National Film Board of Canada, Mackenzie Building, Toronto), 27 minutes. Questions whether getting that important job and keeping up with the Joneses are worth the strain and tensions that go with them. Suggests that each man needs to find his own way out of the cage that modern living imposes upon everyone.

QUESTIONS AND PROJECTS

1. What is the significance of the middle-class family for understanding American family patterns? To what extent is the middle-class family an ideal type?
2. List the set of moral norms described under the heading of "emerging patterns" in this chapter. To what extent are they middle-class patterns? To what extent do they apply to all American families?
3. Define and describe the concept of "family life cycle." List the eight stages in the cycle and indicate the approximate length of each. What changes have occurred in the cycle over the past few generations?
4. Describe the residential mobility patterns of the United States population by age and socio-economic status. Relate these relationships to the idea of a corporate way of life.
5. Define the concept of "anticipatory socialization." How is this concept useful in analyzing the middle-class family model? What is meant by the statement that "middle-class youth are being prepared to live as no one has yet lived"?
6. What kinds of financial and emotional strains plague upwardly mobile, young, middle-class couples? Do these strains influence their relationships with their children? How?

7. Arnold Green has stated that "personality absorption" is a characteristic of middle-class parent-child relationships. What do you think he means by this? Are middle-class children especially neurotic? If there is a mild emotional conflict which is especially characteristic of middle-class boys, what is it?

8. How are middle-class youth conditioned to develop high success drives? Do they necessarily strive for financial success? What other common patterns of success striving can you describe?

9. What techniques of punishment are middle-class parents likely to use? How effective are these techniques? Why? What undesirable side-effects are they likely to produce?

10. Describe the process whereby middle-class boys achieve adult masculine identifications. Contrast this pattern with that typically followed by girls. What roadblocks does each encounter on the route to adulthood?

11. Read *The Organization Man*, by William H. Whyte, Jr. Arrange a panel discussion on the degree to which the patterns he describes are and are not characteristic of middle-class life in America.

12. Assuming that most college students have been imbued with the middle-class pattern of success striving, analyze the behavior of all the prominent groups on your campus and relate it to the satisfaction of success needs.

Racial, Ethnic, and Class Variations

The view of the black community held by many a social scientist is now familiar: a disaster area plagued by social disorganization and a host of conditions that breed emotional pathologies. It is a view based, in large measure, upon the statistics published periodically by the Bureau of the Census and the Bureau of Labor Statistics.

Last week, a new set of figures on American blacks was released—a special study by the Federal Government entitled "The Social Economic Status of Negroes in the United States, 1970." As expected, it painted a somber portrait. But by a coincidence most unexpected, the issuance of the study coincided exactly with the release of another report, this one set forth by the National Urban League. . . . And though both studies were based on the same statistics, conclusions drawn by many social scientists and those drawn by the league were worlds apart.

Thus, for example, the Government study shows that 28.9 per cent of black families are headed by females, an increase from 23.4 per cent in 1960. The familiar sociological analysis: A significant indication of continuing social deterioration and family instability. The view of the league: The assumption of instability in "matriarchal" households ignores the extended-family adaptation common in the black community—the strong kinship bonds between aunts, uncles and grandparents and the family's children. Some black sociologists go further; they argue that, in fact, roughly 70 per cent of these families actually do have a father present.

Another example: The Government study showed that, in order to obtain and maintain a median family income comparable to that of whites, both the black husband and his wife must—and often do—work. Conventional wisdom holds that this is a negative fact, since it is claimed that such families tend to be less stable than those in which the father is the sole breadwinner. But many black social scientists deny the claim, citing the prevalence of the extended-family adaptation—and they see the fact not as an indication of family deterioration but as proof of an attitude of cooperativeness and a strong work orientation in these families. . . .

On the face of it, these arguments among social scientists over statistics that, by and large, both sides accept may seem to be nothing more than an exercise in academic semantics. But for the Urban League leadership and for many black sociologists, the issue has far greater importance.

The manner in which these figures are interpreted, they feel, serves to delineate and identify the black community—in the eyes of blacks and whites alike. Statistics, heedlessly broadcast, are dangerous. And the customary negative interpretations reinforce negative generalizations, ignoring the actual and potential strengths of the black community.[1]

BLACK family patterns represent a significant departure from the middle-class family model; they also represent the largest racial or ethnic minority in America. At almost the opposite pole, debutante balls, emphasis upon ancestry, and hereditary estates represent still another pattern.

The United States is a heterogeneous land of more than 200 million people, and, although the middle-class family model is pervasive, there are millions of people who still know of it primarily through the mass media—people whose everyday family experience is structured quite differently. Our earlier survey of the history of Western family organization pointed to the contribution of large-scale immigration to the production of divergent family types in America. In this chapter we will describe a few of the major variations from the middle-class family model. In so doing, we will talk about the black family, the immigrant family, the upper-class family, and so on. Once again, students should be reminded that these are ideal types. There is no black family. There are only families whose members are black, which families differ markedly among themselves. Ideal-typical patterns are presented as models against which the reality of everyday family experience can be measured.

AMERICAN BLACK FAMILIES

American black families have a fairly long history which must be taken into account in describing their present status. It will be remembered that over ten million Negroes were brought to America before the year 1800—most of them in slavery. Distinctive family patterns emerged during the slavery period. After the Civil War, black family patterns were modified under the combined influences of interstate migration and urbanization. Finally, differentiation has accompanied upward social mobility and desegregation.

[1] Charles V. Hamilton, "Just How Unstable is the Black Family?" *The New York Times*, Aug. 1, 1971. © 1971 by The New York Times Company. Reprinted by permission.

FAMILY PATTERNS UNDER SLAVERY

The first Negroes arrived in what was to become the United States, in Virginia in 1619. These people, purchased from a Dutch ship, apparently had the same status as that of white indentured servants.[2] After they had worked to earn the amount of their purchase, they were to be released from servitude. This did happen in some cases and a class of free Negroes in the United States existed almost from the beginning. Under the economic demands for a permanent, cheap labor supply, however, permanent slavery was not long in emerging. Frazier reports that the slave status of Negroes in Virginia became fixed by law in 1670. At the time of the first United States census in 1790 there were about 700,000 slaves; before the Civil War the number had increased to almost four million.

A striking feature of black American family life from the beginning was the almost complete absence of influence from African culture. The English, as we have seen, and the Poles, Italians, and others transported many of their traditional patterns to the United States. The conditions of slavery, however, effectively prevented Negroes from doing this. Before shipment to America, members of various African tribes and cultures often were mixed to prevent the development of organized resistance among them. Then, in the New World, the process was continued in the sale and training of slaves. The newcomers had to learn a new language, adopt new habits, and assume, in some form, the customs in their new environment. The children born into this situation never learned much of their African heritage and, almost within a generation, the old ways were lost.[3]

Early sexual, marital, and family practices also were influenced by a grossly disproportionate sex ratio. Although precise data are not available, it is known that the early shipments of slaves were heavily male and not until around 1840 did the number of Negro women in the United States approach that of Negro men. Not surprisingly, many informal sexual liaisons developed first between indentured male Negroes and indentured white women and later on between slaves and indentured white women. Miscegenation may have been proportionately more frequent during those early decades than it has ever been since.

The unbalanced sex ratio undoubtedly contributed also to the casualness of sexual contact that developed between many Negro women and men. The

[2] E. Franklin Frazier, The Negro in the United States, New York: The Macmillan Company, 1957, pp. 22–26; Alphonso Pinkney, Black Americans, Englewood Cliffs, New Jersey: Prentice-Hall, Inc., 1969, p. 1.

[3] E. Franklin Frazier, The Negro Family in the United States, New York: Dryden Press, 1948, pp. 15–17.

primary factors here, of course, were the attitudes and policies of the white slave-owners. Some owners literally considered their slaves as they did livestock and sought to breed them in comparable fashion. Strong, healthy males were used as studs and the formalities of marriage often were dispensed with completely. Too, fathers were sold or traded without their wives and children, and vice versa. Under these circumstances, whatever tendency there was to seek the satisfaction of sexual hunger without assuming further obligations was greatly intensified.

It should not be assumed that conditions on the plantations were everywhere alike or that conditions were even similar for all of the slaves on a given plantation. Some slave-owners apparently treated at least some of their slaves with kindness and consideration and encouraged the development of stable family life among them. In these instances the family patterns that emerged were not significantly different from those which existed among whites and free Negroes.

On the same plantations there often were great differences between the family patterns of house-slaves and of field hands. The house-servants were exposed intimately to the ideas, sentiments, and manners of their owners; Negro women assumed much of the care and training of white children and, in the process, the family lives of owners and slaves became intertwined. The family patterns of the house-slaves often did not differ significantly from those of their owners. Often there was great social distance between house-slaves and field hands. The house-servants tended to reinforce their positions of superiority by identifying with their owners, while the field hands were cut off from such opportunities and frequently were brutalized in the process.

The field hands typically were under the supervision of an overseer whose only interest was in the production that could be secured from them and who was especially prone to treat them as chattels. The harshest effects of slavery were to be found in this context, and what has come to be considered the ideal-typical slave family was that which characterized the field hands.

It was generally among the field hands that the husband and father became a shadowy figure in the family. The field hands were most likely to be used as breeding stock, and emphasis was placed on the mother-child unit. Marriages seldom were regularized, and when families were split up there was a tendency to keep small children, at least, with their mother. Many owners reinforced the primary position of the mother and sabotaged the influence of the father by assigning to the woman the cabin in which she and her children lived and by issuing to her the rations of food.[4] Men were not encouraged to

[4] Maurice R. Davie, *Negroes in American Society*, New York: McGraw-Hill Book Company, 1949, p. 207.

assume responsibility for wives and children and many of them did not. Thus, under slavery, there emerged a distinctly mother-centered family that was to continue in modified form into the post-slavery period.

Black family life was further complicated by miscegenation. In the beginning, miscegenation was a two-way street, with intercourse between Negro men and white indentured women sometimes being encouraged by white owners who wished thereby to increase the number of their indentured servants. As the "principles" of white domination and racial integrity became fixed, however, laws were passed and were strictly enforced against unions between Negro men and white women. Although there are no precise data available, the evidence is overwhelming that relationships between white men and Negro women continued to be widespread.

Relationships between white men and Negro women ranged from the completely casual to those in which the slave was emancipated and made a legal wife. In some instances slave-mistresses were later sold, and their mulatto children with them. Often, however, the slave-mistress received special consideration and the children were treated with affection by their father. The woman sometimes was brought directly into the household and sometimes had her own small house near by. The children often were freed from slavery and occasionally were educated through college.

Nor was miscegenation confined to the plantations. There were, in cities like New Orleans, Charleston, and Mobile, large mixed-blood populations as well as free Negroes. Attractive mulatto, quadroon, and octoroon women were widely sought after by well-to-do men, with all of the varying results that characterized such relationships in rural areas. Since the children of such unions ordinarily were free, they helped to swell the ranks of free Negroes in the United States.

By 1860, there were nearly half a million free Negroes in the various states. Frazier reports that more than one-third, as compared to an estimated one-twelfth of the slave population, were probably of mixed blood.[5] Among these free Negroes still another family pattern emerged. These families sometimes were almost patriarchal, with the husband and father wielding more power and being a more influential figure than in corresponding white families. For one thing, the free Negro man often purchased his wife from slavery and, where she had children, purchased her children too. Thus we have the anomaly of slave-owning Negroes. There is even evidence of husbands selling their wives back into slavery when the marriages did not work out.[6]

On the whole, the families of free Negroes prior to the Civil War appear

[5] *The Negro in the United States*, p. 67.
[6] Frazier, *The Negro Family in the United States*, p. 139.

to have been quite stable. Their members frequently were former house-slaves who had adopted the attitudes and customs of the upper-class whites. Many free Negroes became landowners and assumed responsible places in their communities. These free Negroes began a pattern, which continues yet today, in which social class or economic status is far more closely associated with variations in family life than is the fact of race.[7]

EMANCIPATION

The effects of emancipation upon American black families were as diverse as the family forms which preceded the war. In fact, emancipation seemed mostly to sharpen trends already evident.

The families of previously free Negroes and of those who had achieved stability under slavery were not affected greatly. They continued to live much as they had lived, with the father tending to move into a position of full responsibility for the support of his family and acquiring the authority that goes with it.

Where family ties were less secure to begin with, they often broke completely under the stresses that followed emancipation. Many men who were not formally married to the women whose children they had fathered simply left their former homes to test out the limits of their newly acquired freedom. They clustered about Union army posts, they went to the cities, and they roamed aimlessly. Some women, chiefly those without children, did the same thing. Without a history of formal marriage, many of these people formed even more casual unions than had existed under slavery; among a large segment of the Negro population a sexual and marital anarchy prevailed. Legal marriages were few, desertion of wives and children was common, and there was no incentive to confine sexual activity to marriage.

The instability of much family life following emancipation further emphasized the mother-child relationship as the primary basis for family relationships. Men, and women without children, were free to come and go. But the woman with children could not be free of responsibility. She perforce had to pretty much stay in one place, she had to find some means of economic livelihood, and she had to accept men, if at all, on their own terms. To have a man even temporarily was to have some affection and some security. If having the man meant having more children, then that was the way it was. If the man disappeared, another, hopefully, might come along to take his place.

[7] The classic study by Davis and Havighurst established this fact empirically in patterns of child-rearing. See Allison Davis and Robert Havighurst, "Social Class and Color Differences in Childrearing," *American Sociological Review* 11 (Dec. 1946), pp. 698–710.

MIGRATION AND URBANIZATION

Free Negroes, even before the Civil War, were concentrated in urban areas. At the time of the first United States Census in 1790, 10 per cent of the populations of New York and Baltimore were Negro. The overwhelming majority of Negroes, however, lived in the rural South. After the war, a great trek toward southern cities, then to northern cities, and finally to the West got under way.

From 1860 to 1870 the Negro population of 14 southern cities increased by 90 per cent and the Negro population of 8 northern cities increased by 50 per cent. After this first postwar surge into urban areas, the migration slowed down somewhat and consisted chiefly of movement into southern cities. By 1910, 70 per cent of the urban Negro population still was in the South.[8]

The large-scale migration of Negroes northward got under way at the time of World War I.[9] The southern economy, by this time, was in serious decline and a major labor shortage developed in northern cities. Northern labor recruiters actually toured the south offering transportation to those who would go, and northern Negro newspapers urged their brethren to escape from southern tyranny. Frazier estimates that over one million Negroes migrated north during the war.[10] All northern cities except Pittsburgh and Kansas City increased their Negro populations by over 50 per cent. Philadelphia's Negro population increased by 59 per cent; New York's increased by 80 per cent; Chicago's by nearly 150 per cent; and Detroit's Negroes increased by over 600 per cent.[11]

The tremendous influx of Negroes into northern cities during the war changed the pattern of race relations there and created problems that plague whites and blacks today. Before the war, Chicago, for example, was considered almost a model of black-white relations.[12] Over half the Negroes in the city lived on the South Side on very amicable terms with their white neighbors.[13] Then thousands of uneducated, unskilled Negro migrants moved into the area. Homes and apartments were subdivided and then subdivided again. The dilapidated areas where rents were lowest were seized upon first, and then the human tide spilled over into adjacent middle-class areas. A huge and expanding "black belt" was exploited by unscrupulous white realtors who

[8] Frazier, *The Negro in the United States*, p. 190.

[9] Gunnar Myrdal, *An American Dilemma*, New York: Harper and Brothers, 1944, p. 193.

[10] E. Franklin Frazier, "Ethnic Family Patterns: The Negro Family in the United States," *American Journal of Sociology* 53 (May 1948), p. 436.

[11] Frazier, *The Negro in the United States*, pp. 191–2.

[12] St. Clair Drake and Horace Cayton, *Black Metropolis*, New York: Harcourt, Brace, 1945, p. 73.

[13] Robert C. Weaver, *The Negro Ghetto*, New York: Harcourt, Brace, 1948, p. 31.

frightened whites away with threats of loss of property values, and then increased rents and sale prices to incoming Negroes. The resulting tensions culminated in race riots in Chicago and in other northern cities, and a pattern of rigid residential segregation was established.

Migration to the urban North created other adjustment problems for Negroes and intensified family problems. The extreme overcrowding in residential areas made normal family life difficult. In 1930, over 40 per cent of the Negro families in New York's Harlem had from one to four lodgers living with them. And, in 1939, one single Harlem block had a population of 3871 people and was reputed to be the most crowded living area in the world. Studies done in the 1950's have shown that much irregularity of black family life and much social and personal disorganization can be traced to inadequate living quarters and the inability to find decent housing.[14]

Studies also have shown that the urbanization of Negroes has been accompanied by more family disorganization, higher proportions of broken marriages, higher proportions of families with female heads, more quasi-families, and larger numbers of unrelated members in households. While black family life in the rural south was often quite irregular, it was, at least, governed by a host of personal controls and was accommodated to the environment. Illegitimacy, for example, was not a major problem. Illegitimate children and their mothers were accepted without stigma, being incorporated into a maternal household without fuss. Little money was required to provide the minimum of food and clothing expected and the group pooled its resources to provide these. With migration north, however, the illegitimacy resulting from the continuance of casual sex contacts became a major problem. Mothers and children were stigmatized, and the failure of the father to provide produced a crisis. A vast, shifting group of homeless men, women, and children was created, dependent upon public welfare and confused in its attempts to cope with an anonymous, impersonal urban world.

It is lower-class family behavior that presents the greatest challenge to the person who tries to understand lower-class life. The following have all been considered as characteristic of the lower class: "promiscuous sexual relationships"; "illegitimate" children; "deserting" husbands and fathers; and "unmarried" mothers. These characteristics are frequently viewed in a gross manner as, simply, problems of the lower class. My own feeling is that it makes more sense to think of them as solutions of the lower class to problems that they face in the social, economic, and perhaps legal and political spheres of life. . . .

[14] Otis D. Duncan and Beverly Duncan, *The Negro Population of Chicago*, Chicago: University of Chicago Press, 1957, p. 84.

> We therefore have to stress the fact that words like "promiscuity,"
> "illegitimacy," and "desertion" are not part of the lower-class vocabu-
> lary, and that it is inaccurate to describe lower-class behavior in this
> way. These words have middle-class meanings and imply middle-class
> judgments, and it is precisely because of this that we ought not to use
> them to describe lower-class behavior—unless, of course, our intention
> is to judge this behavior in a middle-class manner in order to bolster
> a sagging middle-class ego. . . .
>
> —Hyman Rodman, "On Understanding Lower-Class Behavior,"
> *Social and Economic Studies*, 8 (1959), pp. 441–50.

The migration northward continued and, during and after World War II,
spread to the West. With few exceptions the Negroes settled in the large
central cities while the former white residents moved out to the suburbs. Between 1940 and 1950, 1,300,000 Negroes migrated to the central cities. Between
1940 and 1960, the Negro populations of Philadelphia and New York doubled,
those of Detroit and Chicago tripled, and that of Los Angeles increased by 500
per cent. By 1960, the American Negro population was over 70 per cent
urban, a far cry from the days of slavery.

CONTEMPORARY FAMILY PATTERNS

At this writing there are well over 22 million American Negroes. It stands
to reason that there are no one, two, or even three family patterns among
them. Over 70 per cent of these people live in urban areas, but "urban areas"
includes southern as well as northern cities and cities of 5000 people along
with those of five million. In addition, more than 6½ million blacks live
in non-metropolitan areas and a million live on farms.[15] That differences exist
from south to north and from rural to urban is certain. Undoubtedly there
are still other differences. But there is one dimension which is most relevant
of all to the analysis of black family patterns—the dimension of socio-economic
status. Black families vary more according to their position in the socio-
economic, the occupational, structure than according to any other variable.

As a general rule, it may be stated that Negroes are not yet fully integrated
into the American economy. In 1960, fully two-thirds of the nation's nonwhite
population lived in poverty.[16] True, the absolute levels of living of Negroes
are rising, but not nearly so fast as those of whites. Between 1950 and 1970,

[15] U. S. Bureau of the Census, *Statistical Abstract of the United States: 1970*, Washington, D. C., p. 30.
[16] *Time*, April 6, 1970, p. 94.

for example, the median income of Negroes climbed from 61 per cent of that of whites to 64 per cent of white income. More than 40 per cent of all Negroes living in rural areas earn less than $1000 per year. Even at the same educational and occupational levels, Negroes earn less than whites. Semi-skilled Negro factory workers earn only 72 per cent as much as semiskilled white workers; Negro college graduates earn less on the average than do whites with only an eighth-grade education.[17]

Black families are predominantly lower-class families among whom problems of status and morality have to yield to problems of sheer survival. At this level, the family's functioning revolves around the mother in a pattern tracing directly from slavery. Among a growing body of Negroes, greater stability has been achieved as the husband and father has achieved a secure occupational role. Finally, there is a middle-to-upper-class pattern which traces back to the free Negroes and house-servants of pre-Civil War days.

The Disorganized Matricentric Family. Among the Negroes who migrated to the cities were disproportionate numbers of unattached men and women. Some of them left "wives" and children in the South; some did not. Among many of them there was a history of sex without marriage, marriage without benefit of clergy, and "divorce" without benefit of law. Generally they were unskilled, naïve in the ways of the city, and without resources. Nor did they find, in the cities, the opportunities which they hoped awaited them.

Marriage continued typically to be a casual union based upon sexual attraction and sexual satisfaction. As long as the relationship was rewarding to both partners, it continued. When either the man or the woman found a more attractive partner or became overwhelmed by problems, however, the relationship was likely to break up. Of the two partners, the woman was likely to be the most dependable source of income. Negro men fared badly in the competition with unskilled white workers, but Negro women were in demand for menial and domestic work. Without economic leverage, the man's status in the family was low. His wife and children could do without him and the only sources of reward available to him—other women, drinking, and even the prospect of a job elsewhere—led to widespread desertion. Marital relationships were likely to be violent, both in the attractions between partners and in the fights that developed when frustration was encountered. The southern rural patterns of fighting, shooting, and stabbing created havoc in the new urban environment. As children were raised in the new milieu, violence and lawlessness became a way of life, and a disorganized, lower-class family pattern became established.

[17] Paul B. Horton and Gerald R. Leslie, *The Sociology of Social Problems*, New York: Appleton-Century-Crofts, 1965, p. 369.

The urban lower-class black family is the old matricentric family in a new setting. It still revolves around the mother and her children, with the husband and father as a peripheral, temporary member.[18] It seems destined to continue until changes in the larger society permit black men to assume the position of major breadwinner and head of the family.

The Black Proletariat Family. After the Civil War, skilled Negro workers in the South far outnumbered whites. Discriminatory practices within and outside of the developing trade unions soon eliminated Negroes from most effective competition, however, and, in both South and North, Negroes were restricted to unskilled, domestic, and personal-service jobs. During World War I, the situation began to change. The shortage of labor permitted Negroes to gain a foothold in the industrial economy. As longshoremen, steel workers, miners, and stockyard workers, they began to think of themselves as workers and to take on the value system of the stable, working-class white community. Through the churches and schools, they were exposed to norms of stable family life in which husbands are supposed to be the heads of their families, wives are supposed to devote themselves more fully to child-rearing, and children are supposed to go to school to prepare themselves for adult life.

The conditions of family life among this black proletariat are like those among the white working class, only more so. Their relatively stable incomes permit them to acquire better housing than the great mass of impoverished Negroes, but residential segregation results in their having to pay more for their housing than do whites in comparable circumstances. Consequently, more Negroes have to take in roomers to help pay the rent. In addition, more Negro wives have to work in order to supplement the husband's income.

. . . some twenty-three million American women are currently in the "work force" and . . . three out of five of them are married. This much-touted statistic creates the illusion of a nation of brisk career women who stack the breakfast dishes, park their children in nursery schools, and charge off each morning to "challenging" jobs.

But what is the case? Of the married women I know in city and suburb, not one in ten has paid employment outside her home, and few are job-hunting. . . .

---

[18] At least one author argues that the contemporary Negro urban matricentric family does not trace back to slavery conditions but is a wholly new phenomenon reflecting the conditions of urban living. See Jessie Bernard, *Marriage and Family Among Negroes*, Englewood Cliffs, New Jersey: Prentice-Hall, 1966, pp. 19–21. See also John H. Bracey, Jr., August Meier, and Elliott Rudwick, eds., *Black Matriarchy: Myth or Reality?*, Belmont, California: Wadsworth Publishing Company, 1971.

Who then are the twenty-three million? Footnotes to the statistical tables disclose—to those who trouble to read them—that a mere three million are in occupations classed as "technical or professional." Another six million work only intermittently. And most of the remaining fourteen million are in lowly, ill-paid clerical, factory, sales, or service jobs. Of those who are also mothers of young children a dismaying proportion are Negro women.

Undoubtedly they would like to earn more. And they desperately need decent day-care facilities for their young. But above all they yearn for fully employed husbands and a chance to tend their own children and kitchens instead of another woman's. The status of women is a far less burning question in these circles than the status of men.

> —Marion K. Sanders, "The New American Female: Demi-feminism Takes Over," *Harper's* Magazine, July 1965, pp. 39–40. By permission of the author.

The husband's authority in the family appears to increase in direct proportion to the adequacy and stability of his income. In some instances there is an overreaction to his former subordination and the man becomes harsh and demanding in his relationships with wife and children.[19] Although the wife's authority decreases, the tradition of female dominance remains in challenges to the husband's authority both by the wife and by her mother.

In these working-class families, fewer children are born. Although reliable figures are not available, it appears that the ideology of planned parenthood and the provision of educational opportunities for children begin to take hold. The treatment of the children varies. Where mothers must work outside the home, some neglect of children and lack of supervision of their activities are inevitable. In many cases, however, a spirit of sacrifice for the children's education is one of the most conspicuous family features.[20]

[19] Davie, op. cit. p. 213. Recent research shows great variation in the roles played by black husbands and fathers. See Joan Aldous, "Wives' Employment Status and Lower-Class Men as Husband-Fathers: Support for the Moynihan Thesis," *Journal of Marriage and the Family* 31 (Aug. 1969), pp. 469–76; Karl King, "Adolescent Perception of Power Structure in the Negro Family," *Journal of Marriage and the Family* 31 (Nov. 1969), pp. 751–55; Seymour Parker, and Robert J. Kleiner, "Social and Psychological Dimensions of the Family Role Performance of the Negro Male," *Journal of Marriage and the Family* 31 (Aug. 1969), pp. 500–506; and David Schulz, "Variations in the Father Role in Complete Families of the Negro Lower Class," *Social Science Quarterly* 49 (Dec. 1969), pp. 651–9.

[20] Hylan Lewis has cited cases where the Negro children of upwardly mobile families feel their personal needs to have been sacrificed to their parents' drive for self-improvement;

By the very nature of the thing, it is impossible to say just how many families there are in this growing Negro industrial proletariat. There are at least two significant things that may be said, however. First, the number of such families is increasing as blacks become more fully integrated into the economy. Second, the primary reference group for these families is economic, not racial. They disassociate themselves from the Negro lower class and generally they do not emulate the mulatto-based Negro middle class. As the isolation of Negro workers is broken down, their ideals and patterns of family life approximate those of other industrial workers.

The Black Bourgeoisie Family. The term, black bourgeoisie, was used by Frazier to refer to the Negro middle class and to emphasize, through that term, the emulation of the more superficial and material aspects of white, middle-class culture.[21] We use the term here, not in any invidious sense, but to refer to the Negro middle and upper classes. To date, no satisfactory differentiation between the Negro middle and upper classes has been worked out; hence the term, black bourgeoisie, to cover both.

This middle-to-upper class derives its superior status chiefly from a family heritage which results partly from its mixed ancestry. The family heritage consists principally of traditions of civilized behavior and economic stability. The relatively light skin color within the group testifies not only to mixed ancestry but also to descent from the free Negro and house-servant groups before the Civil War. It has a sizable proportion of its members in businesses catering to Negro personal services: restaurants, barber shops, funeral parlors, and the like. The core of the group, however, has a background more in the professions than in business. Hylan Lewis stresses the ownership of property, enterprise or artisanry, education, and public morality.[22]

Some light on possible distinctions between a Negro middle class and upper class is provided by analysis of the influence of occupation and skin color. Edwards considers the Negro professional group to be middle class, based upon an absolute scale in which the professions are considered to be middle-class occupations.[23] Frazier and Myrdal, however, place the Negro professional group in the upper class because of the caste structure of American society.

Hylan Lewis, "Culture, Class, and the Behavior of Low-Income Families," paper presented at Conference on Lower-Class Culture," New York, June 1963, as cited in Jessie Bernard, op. cit. p. 35.

[21] E. Franklin Frazier, *Black Bourgeoisie*, Glencoe, Illinois: The Free Press, 1957.

[22] Hylan Lewis, *Blackways of Kent*, Chapel Hill, North Carolina: University of North Carolina Press, 1955, p. 107.

[23] G. Franklin Edwards, *The Negro Professional Class*, Glencoe, Illinois: The Free Press, 1959, p. 199.

Frazier states, "The Negro upper class has its present status, primarily, because of its position in a segregated world. If members of the Negro upper class were integrated into American society, their occupations and incomes would place them in the middle class."[24]

The most distinguishing feature of the Negro upper class may be color. While not as significant a factor as it was immediately after emancipation when almost all upper-class Negroes were mulatto, the color line in Negro society still is evident.[25] All but those of fair complexion appear to be excluded from most upper-class cliques. This happens most often in the South and applies most rigidly to dark women. More recently, some very dark men have been too successful to ignore. Upper-class men select light-skinned women as wives. As Sutherland puts it, "High social standing and blackness are incompatible.[26]

With the diversity of backgrounds to be found among the Negro middle and upper class it would be surprising if there were not diverse family patterns also. We might even conceive of a continuum or scale, with the disorganized lower-class black family at one end and a stable, equalitarian, sophisticated upper-class black family at the other. In between would fall the stable working-class black family and then a whole series of types, increasingly emphasizing the characteristics which are also to be found among the white middle classes: legal marriage, conventional sex morality, stable families, equalitarian man-woman relationships, relatively few children, emphasis upon education, and striving for occupational and financial success.[27]

In describing this range of middle-class families, one can highlight the characteristics which he wishes to emphasize. He can, by judicious selection of data, focus on either stability or the divorce rate, upon authoritarianism or equalitarianism, upon crass materialism or upon the cultivation of aesthetic values. All of these would describe some segment of black middle-class families.

The most significant generalization that can be made about middle-class

---

[24] Frazier, *The Negro in the United States*, p. 291.

[25] Allison B. Davis, Burleigh B. Gardner, and Mary Gardner, *Deep South*, Chicago: University of Chicago Press, 1941, p. 248; Howard E. Freeman, David Armor, J. Michael Ross, and Thomas F. Pettigrew, "Color Gradation and Attitudes Among Middle-Income Negroes," *American Sociological Review* 31 (June 1966), pp. 365–74; Sidney Kronus, *The Black Middle Class*, Columbus, Ohio: Charles E. Merrill Publishing Company, 1971, pp. 2–5.

[26] Robert Sutherland, *Color, Class, and Personality*, Washington, D.C.: American Council on Education, 1942, p. 62.

[27] George E. Simpson and J. Milton Yinger, *Racial and Cultural Minorities*, New York: Harper and Row, 1958, p. 523.

black families, however, probably is that the factor of race is not of great significance and, even in a minor role, is of only temporary significance. Middle-class Negroes have achieved more integration into the occupational system than have even working-class Negroes. As a consequence of this integration, their family patterns increasingly are subject to the forces described in the chapter on the middle-class family model. It seems likely that neither blacks nor whites are accustomed to thinking of black families in these terms. Yet, if our thesis has any validity, many black families already are caught up in the success-seeking patterns that more fully characterize whites. To a steadily increasing degree, middle-class black family patterns approach those of the middle-class model.

THE IMMIGRANT FAMILY

During the nineteenth century, approximately 19 million people migrated to the United States from Europe. Early in the century, most of the migrants were from northwestern Europe—Great Britain, Ireland, Germany, and France. Beginning around 1890, the heavy migration began to come more from southern and eastern Europe and involved the movement of large numbers of Catholics and Jews into what had been a predominantly Protestant culture. Between 1890 and 1930, some 22 million people came to the United States mainly from Italy, Greece, Austria-Hungary, Poland, and Russia. Few of these migrants spoke English, almost all were of lower-class or peasant origin, and most of them sought to preserve the traditional family ways in their new environment.

Restrictive immigration legislation cut off most migration from Europe after the 1920's and launched the large-scale assimilation of the immigrant groups toward the American pattern. Even while this assimilation was proceeding, however, migration to the United States continued from within the western hemisphere. The most conspicuous of the new immigrant groups probably are the Puerto Ricans who, in the 1940's, began to settle in large numbers in New York City and gradually in other cities also. During the decade 1951–60, approximately 300,000 Mexican citizens migrated to the United States; since 1960 they have come at rates varying from 30,000 to 55,000 per year.[28]

Obviously, these varied immigrant groups do not all have exactly the same family traditions; nor have they adapted to the American environment in

[28] U. S. Bureau of the Census, *Statistical Abstract of the United States: 1970*, Washington, D. C., p. 93.

precisely the same way and at the same rate of speed. In some cases the differences among them may even be more significant than are their similarities.[29] There is some purpose to be served, however, by emphasizing the general features common to most of them. In this way we can show how the trend among them is toward the middle-class family model.

Most of the immigrants who came to the United States after the middle 1800's received something less than an enthusiastic reception. Set apart by differences in language, religion, and dress—and usually of low economic status—the immigrants were shunned by most residents of the United States cities into which they moved, and, themselves, reacted by clustering together in residential ethnic groups. They tended to seek out their own kind and both wittingly and unwittingly to preserve the old ways.

Early in the century, terms like "Little Italy," "Greek Town," "Polack Town," and "Ghetto" characterized urban immigrant areas. More recently there have emerged the "Spanish Harlems" and "Mexican Towns." And to a degree such areas function almost as isolated towns. In them the native language may be used instead of English. Native-language newspapers are published, ethnic stores provide the traditional foods and styles of clothing, and social organizations develop to provide common recreation and, in the process, to reinforce ethnic solidarity.

The families, almost without exception, are more patriarchal than those of the "old Americans." In Europe and south of the border, the family revolved around the husband, who was the provider.[30] He ruled the family with something ranging from benevolent despotism to outright tyranny. He controlled not only his own income but the incomes of other family members if there were any. He dominated his wife and controlled his children. When it came time for the children to marry, he helped to select their marriage partners. And, as in the old country, the norms were clearly spelled out. If the system was oppressive to some, most people knew just where they stood.

In the American environment, assimiliation, including shifts in family patterns, has tended to proceed by generations. The term, first generation, is used to describe the immigrants themselves—the young husband and wife who came to this country speaking a foreign tongue and isolated from the

[29] For accounts of varying Italian assimilation patterns, see Francis X. Femminella, "The Italian-American Family," in Meyer Barash, and Alice Scourby, eds., *Marriage and the Family: A Comparative Analysis of Contemporary Problems*, New York: Random House, 1970, pp. 127–39; and Michael Lalli, "The Italian-American Family: Assimilation and Change, 1900–1965," *The Family Coordinator* 18 (Jan. 1969), pp. 44–48.

[30] W. Lloyd Warner and Leo Srole, *The Social Systems of American Ethnic Groups*, New Haven: Yale University Press, 1945, Ch. 6.

mainstream of American culture. It was they who were likely to locate in an ethnic enclave and to begin to raise a family.

As a general rule, assimilation proceeded slowly. The husband and father had to accommodate to the larger society to some degree in order to get and to hold a job. His foreign tongue was a handicap, so he began to learn some English. Back in the ethnic settlement at the end of the working day, however, he reverted to the old language and the old ways. His wife might not even make this much concession. Bewildered by the strange ways about her and repelled by indifference or hostility from outsiders, she was more likely to seek security in the time-honored ways of her parental family. Often, she avoided learning English altogether and confined her activities to the ethnic group. As her husband's halting efforts toward assimilation created a gulf between the two of them, she often responded by clinging ever more desperately to ethnic customs. Primarily, it was she who dressed her children in the traditional way and who taught them to speak the old language.

If the first generation was resistant to change, the second generation, the children of the immigrants, could not often resist it. Even before school the children were likely to have some contacts outside the ethnic group and to learn from their more Americanized peers how funny their clothes were, how shameful it was to speak a foreign language, and how bad it was to be different.

Perhaps the primary agent of assimilation was the school. The school teachers were likely to be middle class and often were, themselves, attempting to reject their ethnic origins. The official language, of course, was English, and the school taught that to be successful, as everyone should, one must adopt middle-class ways. The schools also taught values of democracy, equalitarianism, and individualism that conflicted with the values of the parents and subverted the old form of family organization.

Children responded by refusing to speak anything but English, by protesting against being different from their peers in any way, and by adopting the attitudes of the larger society toward their parents and their ways. The parents' ways were "old-fashioned" and a barrier to the young person's need to belong.

A crisis often developed in adolescence. The young person's resistance to parental ways now approached open defiance. Whereas the parents' lower-class lives were essentially conforming and stable, their children turned to the streets to show their contempt for the adult world. With the street gang as their primary reference group, they frequently sought status in gang warfare, in delinquency, and in sexual experience. To the adult world the situation appeared to be one of complete unregulation; but among the youth the governing normative structure was quite clear. William F. Whyte shows this quite clearly in an analysis of a slum sex code which sanctioned sexual intercourse with sexually experienced girls but which strictly forbade it with virgins.[31]

Conflict often developed between parents and their emerging adult children over income and the selection of marriage partners. By parental standards, the income which young people received from employment should be turned over to the father, who would dole out an allowance to his offspring. Some young people accepted such an arrangement only eventually to rebel against it; some rebelled from the first. Parents' hopes that their children would marry within the group often were frustrated as their children found American ways and Americanized young people to be more attractive than those who clung to the ethnic traditions.

For all the complications in their young lives, many of those young people fared fairly well as they moved into marriage and the occupational world. The school had performed its acculturation function well; except for the family name (and often it was changed), few traces of ethnic status remained. While the parents generally worked at unskilled and semiskilled labor, their offspring frequently were equipped to move into the white-collar and skilled labor worlds. Their dual rejection of ethnic ways and of the low economic status of their parents led them to locate their families of procreation in non-ethnic middle-class areas. When they had children, the children were likely to be reared to seek full participation in the mass-consumption middle-class world—to live the middle-class model.

For many of the immigrant groups who came to the United States from Europe, the assimilation is virtually complete. Many of the people living the corporation way of life described in the last chapter are the third-generation immigrants just mentioned. The continuing relationships of these people with their parents will be discussed in the next chapter on the kin network. Here, suffice it to say that success in the occupational world requires them to separate their contacts with kin from contacts with friends and associates.

In one important respect the assimilation process is somewhat less complete. The religious identity of the immigrants as Catholics and Jews still separates them from much of the non-Catholic, non-Jewish world. The family implications of this religious difference will be considered in a later chapter on mate selection.

Finally, although immigration from Europe almost has ceased to alter significantly the American way of life, immigration from within the western

---

[31] William Foote Whyte, "A Slum Sex Code," *American Journal of Sociology* 49 (July 1943), pp. 24–31.

hemisphere continues on a fairly substantial scale. Many of the new immigrants, predominantly Puerto Rican and Mexican, are still in the first- and second-generation stages. It is not possible to say that their adjustment will duplicate, exactly, that of their European precursors. Indeed, there is evidence that skin color complicates the adjustment of some in these groups, likening their situation, in ways, to that of black Americans. The final unfolding of their adjustment lies in the future. But the ultimate outcome is foreshadowed in the increasing approximation of their values and attitudes to those of the middle-class model.

The Upper-Class Family

American black families and recent immigrant families both tend to cluster in the lower portion of the socio-economic structure. They provide part of an exceedingly large pool of families which accepts the middle-class family model as a goal toward which to strive. At the opposite end of the socio-economic structure—at the very top—exists a radically different kind of family pattern among a relatively small group of people who scorn middle-class ways and seek to preserve the traits that set them apart.

This upper class is the one labeled as upper-upper by W. Lloyd Warner and his associates, and reported to include only about 1 per cent of the population in those communities where it exists at all.[32] Its distinct way of life is most discernible in the old cities of the urban Northeast and the Deep South. In less bold relief it is found in some of the cities of the Midwest and Far West.

A distinguished American ancestry, income from inherited wealth, and residence in the community for several generations are criteria upon which membership in this class is based. In the East, emphasis is placed upon establishment of the family in America during the colonial period and the accumulation of the family fortune prior to the Civil War. Careers in government, business, and the professions are followed by the men, after completing their educations at Ivy League schools. The families are of old English stock and few Catholics or Jews are to be found among them. In the South, the background is either English or French. The family history is traced to pre-Civil War days and to gracious plantation living.

Cavan reports that upper-class families in eastern cities generally have established themselves in the community for eight or nine generations. In the Midwest only four or five generations in the community are sufficient to confer upper-class status, while in the Far West the time may be shorter still. The

[32] W. Lloyd Warner and Paul S. Lunt, *Social Life of a Modern Community*, New Haven: Yale University Press, 1941, p. 203.

longer the family history, the greater the emphasis placed upon illustrious fore-bears; the shorter the history, the more essential is significant accomplishment by recent generations.[33]

The structure of the upper-class family suggests the trustee family of ancient times. The present living members of the family are not regarded as *the family*, but only as its current representatives. They guard the legacy of status and wealth created by earlier generations and they are obligated to pass it on intact or enhanced to their successors in the family. This timelessness of the family is emphasized in its material possessions, in its style of life, and even in the selection of family names.

Upper-class families are not conspicuous consumers. They do not often live in spreading ranch houses, drive new Cadillacs, or indulge in the latest fads. Instead they live in ancestral family homes which are furnished with heirlooms handed down over the generations. Their automobiles are expensive but sedate—and, for the older members, often chauffeur-driven. Their wealth supports, not the making of extravagant purchases, but indulgences in charity, the sponsoring of favorite projects, and, perhaps, travel abroad.

Both given names and surnames have a significance unmatched at other class levels. The surnames of earlier branches of the family frequently are used as given names to emphasize family continuity. Henry Cabot Lodge, for example, exemplifies the ties between two of Boston's upper-class families. Similarly, Franklin Delano Roosevelt represented ties to both the Franklins and the Delanos. The names, Nathaniel, Richard, and Leverett, appear recurrently in the Saltonstall family, and there were Josiahs in four generations of the Quincy family.[34]

The integration and continuity of upper-class families also are illustrated by the existence of widespread intermarriage among them and by the existence of a large group of kin with whom fairly close ties are maintained. Cavan describes such families as nuclear families closely connected by ties of blood, marriage, history, and the current joint ownership of property.[35] The marriage of cousins once or twice removed is common enough so that kin ties pervade the whole upper-class community. Aunts, uncles, and cousins are significant members of the family, and the ties among them are reinforced by living on adjacent estates and by common interests in both real and industrial property.

[33] Ruth S. Cavan, *The American Family*, New York: Thomas Y. Crowell Company, 1963, pp. 90–94.

[34] Cleveland Amory, *The Proper Bostonians*, New York: Dutton, 1947, p. 19, as cited in Ruth S. Cavan, op. cit. p. 92. Contrast this situation with that described by Rossi for middle-class families. See Alice S. Rossi, "Naming Children in Middle-Class Families," *American Sociological Review* 30 (Aug. 1965), pp. 499–513.

[35] Op. cit.

Although upper-class families are not true extended families, there is relatively more prominence given to generational ties and the larger kin group than is true among middle-class families. The prominence of extended family relationships traces to the position of elders both as the holders of the family income and property and as the bearers of the family traditions. Older family members often control the income of younger family members, sometimes making provision, through trusts, for the distribution of wealth two or three generations in the future. Consequently, even middle-aged couples with half-grown children may remain financially dependent upon their parents. Ceremonially, the position of the elders is analogous to that of the elders in the traditional Chinese gentry family; as the closest living connections with the ancestors, they derive special status from being the bearers of the family traditions.

Technically, the descent system is bilateral, but there is a pervasive bias in favor of the husband's family. Wealth and power tend to be passed down through the male line, sons tend to follow in the occupational traditions of fathers and grandfathers, and boys are more often named for the father's relatives than for the mother's. Ironically, as is often true in extended family systems, the person around whom family activities revolve frequently is a woman. Women usually outlive their husbands, with the result that the oldest person in the family is a grandmother. Again as among the Chinese gentry, by the time a woman reaches this exalted position she has become so thoroughly socialized that she represents her husband's family almost as he himself would do.

Mate selection and marriage practices operate differently among the upper class. First there is, almost from birth, an attempt to raise young people in relative isolation from the children of other social classes. After being under the care of nurses or governesses, they are sent to private schools where they associate only with other upper-class children and where upper-class attitudes and behavior are carefully cultivated. In both school and college, sex-segregated schools often are preferred to coeducational ones. Carefully arranged relationships among small groups of men's colleges and women's colleges protect young people against "unfortunate involvement" with unsuitable persons. When the time for marriage approaches, "coming out" parties introduce eligible young men and women to each other.

Upper-class men and women appear to marry relatively late. Although national data are not available, Warner's research in Yankee City showed an average age at marriage that was three or four years older than for the general population.[36] The careful restriction of marriage partners to other members

---

[36] W. Lloyd Warner and Paul S. Lunt, op. cit. p. 423.

of the upper class provides for the relatively smooth incorporation of the couple into the larger kinship group. The young wife is required to take her place as a family member as well as a wife. In those rare instances when a man does marry outside the class, the couple—particularly the wife—may face ostracism and there may be ill-concealed hope that the marriage may break up in favor of a more appropriate one.

It cannot be emphasized too much that the primary reference group for this upper class is the class itself. It does not accept the mass-consumption mobility-oriented, middle-class model as an ideal; indeed it perpetuates its status partly through deliberate rejection of that ideal.

It does not participate fully in the trends in the American family described in the last chapter. Marriage is subordinated to perpetuation of the family traditions. Married love must compromise with the suitability of the relationship. Children are born to benefit the family; the family does not exist for the children. Conventionality in both marital and nonmarital roles is less important than in the middle-class. A certain amount of deviation in sex matters, in drinking, and so on is not so threatening as at middle-class levels, providing, of course, that this deviant behavior does not threaten the position of the family in the community.

These upper-class patterns, significant beyond the number of people involved, represent a hold-out against the middle-class model. Whether this group will be able to maintain its aloof position in the future is uncertain. There are signs of incipient breakdown.[37] The segregation of younger members of the group is a special problem. As education becomes increasingly coeducational and as young people of varied backgrounds are thrown together according to the requirements of the larger society, the pattern of a landed aristocracy may be yielding to a "jet set" which mirrors the middle-class model in exaggerated form.

SUMMARY

Although the first Negroes were brought to America as indentured servants, slavery was not long in developing. Under slavery all traces of African culture were deliberately expunged and a variable family system, reflecting the division of labor among Negroes and the policies of the white owners, emerged.

Field hands frequently were discouraged from developing stable families. Whether or not there was a deliberate policy of breeding the slaves, the primacy of the mother-child unit was stressed in the assignment of living quarters

[37] Cleveland Amory, *Who Killed Society?*, New York: Harper and Brothers, 1960. See also, Lawrence Rosen, and Robert R. Bell, "Mate Selection in the Upper Class," *The Sociological Quarterly* 7 (Spring 1966), pp. 157–66.

and food supplies. Men were more likely to be sold or traded without their families; there was little opportunity for the development of masculine responsibility.

The family patterns of house-slaves often were modeled upon those of their owners. Stability and morality were stressed; the father played a more prominent role. A father-centered family also appeared among a growing free Negro class in which miscegenation figured prominently.

Emancipation seemed generally to heighten trends already present in black families. Stable, father-centered families remained stable and the husband acquired increased responsibility. Families who were disorganized before, disintegrated further. The disorganized mother-centered family became widespread in both rural and urban areas.

After the Civil War, large-scale migration of Negroes, first to the cities, and then northward, began. The northward movement received great impetus during World War I and resulted in strict residential segregation, tremendous overcrowding in Negro areas, and the intensification of family problems. The informal norms of casual sex contact and illegitimate births created havoc in the urban situation where Negroes were deprived of their old primary group supports.

The present status of black family patterns reflects the fact that Negroes are not yet fully incorporated into the occupational system. What differences exist appear to be linked to socio-economic status rather than to race. Three contemporary types are identified: the disorganized matricentric family, the stable working-class family, and the middle- or upper-class family. An increasing proportion of Negroes is coming, vicariously or literally, under the influence of the middle-class family model.

An "immigrant problem" crystallized in the United States early in the present century. That problem reflected the migration of non-English-speaking Catholic and Jewish groups to America from about 1880 to 1920. In somewhat different form, the problem has continued since 1920 in the immigration of Puerto Rican and Mexican families.

Met with some hostility, these patriarchal, lower-class immigrant families tended to cluster in ethnic areas of American cities. There they sought to perpetuate the old ways while accommodating themselves to the new environment. As a general rule, first-generation immigrants resisted assimiliation. Their children, however, under the influence of their peers and the public schools, learned to reject their parents' "old-fashioned" ways. Conflict developed between parents and children, especially in adolescence. The second generation often married outside the ethnic group, moved away from the ethnic areas, and sought to raise its children to full participation in the middle-class family model.

At the very top of the socio-economic and status structure of American society there is a family pattern which bases its very existence on nonparticipation in the middle-class model. Concentrated in the urban Northeast and the deep south, these upper-class families derive their status from a combination of distinguished ancestry, income from inherited wealth, and long residence in the community. Rather than being conspicuous consumers, they use their wealth to solidify their status as a group apart from the larger society.

In some ways upper-class family patterns approximate an extended family model. The nuclear family is somewhat subordinate to the larger kin group, there are ties to traditional family estates, mate selection is carefully controlled, and children are raised to represent the family rather than to express their own uniqueness. Older members of the family wield considerable power, with an elderly woman often being found in the most strategic position.

Traditionally, the separation of the upper class has helped to preserve its special status. Trends in the larger society make it increasingly difficult to maintain this segregation—particularly of young people. Coeducation and widespread equalitarian values threaten to undermine the upper-class aloofness to middle-class family patterns.

SUGGESTED READINGS

Baltzell, E. Digby, *Philadelphia Gentlemen: The Making of a National Upper Class*, Glencoe, Illinois: The Free Press, 1958. A thoroughly professional study of the emergence of the American upper class in Philadelphia, Boston, and New York.

Billingsley, Andrew, *Black Families in White America*, Englewood Cliffs, New Jersey: Prentice-Hall, Inc., 1968. Offers a strong challenge to the interpretations of black family life by white sociologists. Emphasizes the strengths of black families.

Edwards, G. Franklin, *The Negro Professional Class*, Glencoe, Illinois: The Free Press, 1959. An excellent report of research on the emergence and characteristics of the enlarging Negro professional class. Contrasts with Frazier's account of the black bourgeoisie.

Gans, Herbert J., *The Urban Villagers: Group and Class in the Life of Italian-Americans*, New York: The Free Press of Glencoe, 1962. Participant observation study of a working-class group in Boston. Emphasizes the role of the family in a pattern that still differs significantly from the middle-class model.

Scanzoni, John H., *The Black Family in Modern Society*, Boston: Allyn and Bacon, Inc., 1971. A systematic and perceptive monograph based upon information gathered from 400 black households in Indianapolis.

Staples, Robert, ed., *The Black Family: Essays and Studies*, Belmont, California: Wadsworth Publishing Company, Inc., 1971. A comprehensive set of readings on many aspects of the marital and family life of black people.

Willie, Charles V., ed., *The Family Life of Black People*, Columbus, Ohio: Charles E. Merrill Publishing Company, 1970. A valuable collection of essays and research reports that puts black family patterns into proper demographic and sociological perspective.

FILMS

A Mexican-American Family (Atlantis Productions, Inc., 1252 La Granada Drive, Thousand Oaks, California 91360), 16 minutes. Provides insight into the life of a Mexican-American family: their traditions; their warmth and closeness; and their difficulties.

Crisis in Levittown (Dynamic Films, Inc., 112 West 89th St., New York), 31 minutes. Residents of a community into which a black family moves express strong and conflicting opinions in a series of filmed interviews.

Diary of a Harlem Family (Indiana University, Audio-Visual Center, Bloomington, Indiana 47401), 20 minutes. Poignant view of the plight of a Harlem family, seen through the photographs of Gordon Parks. Shows that the impotence of poverty agencies or others to help leaves the family's difficulties unsolved.

"Hey Mama" (Vaughn Obern, 501 Bay Street, Apt. B, Santa Monica, California 90405), 18 minutes. The offspring of one black woman (the "Hey Momma" of the title) are utilized in a stark documentary of lives in a Negro ghetto that might be anywhere; a powerful and enlightening view of a certain segment of black men today.

Lima Family (available through Oklahoma State University Audio-Visual Center, Stillwater, Okla.), 17 minutes. Compares the activities, culture, and standard of living of an upper-class family in Lima, Peru, with a family of similar status in the United States.

Social Class in America (McGraw-Hill Book Company, Text-Film Division, 330 West 42nd St., New York 10036), 16 minutes. Significant contrasts are shown in the lives of three boys who come from three different social classes. The film relates the ascribed, or inherited, status of each to the wealth, occupation, residential address, and social status of his parents and shows how graduation from high school marks the beginning of increasingly different lives. Illustrates factors favoring vertical mobility in America.

The Way It Is (Adelphi University, Garden City, New York 11530). A Puerto Rican family living on public assistance is followed through its daily life experiences, severe crises, and contacts with multiple community services. Shows techniques of social work intervention.

QUESTIONS AND PROJECTS

1. What is the difference between indentured servitude and slavery? How did the existence of indentured servitude influence the development of black family patterns in the United States?

2. Describe American Negro family patterns under slavery. Make explicit the different family patterns of house-servants and field hands.
3. What were the influences of emancipation upon black family patterns? How did emancipation work to increase the prominence of the matricentric family?
4. Describe the urban and northward migration of Negroes after the Civil War. What was the impact of migration upon family life? In what ways were northern cities less hospitable than the rural South had been?
5. Describe the contemporary black matricentric family; the stable working-class family; the middle- and upper-class family. Is race or class more relevant to the understanding of black family patterns?
6. Where do American Negroes stand in relation to the middle-class family model? What further changes are likely to occur over the next generation?
7. What social characteristics set European migrants to the United States after 1880 apart from earlier migrants? How were these later migrants welcomed in America? How did they respond to American definitions of them?
8. What forces worked against the assimilation of first-generation immigrants? What forces encouraged it? Show how assimilation tended to proceed through the second and third generations.
9. What differences remain today to set the descendants of these immigrants apart? How do these immigrants and their descendants stand in relation to the middle-class family model?
10. How do upper-class families stand in relation to the middle-class family model? Is social change tending to undermine the special position of this class? If so, how?
11. Describe the upper-class family system. How does it approximate an extended family system? What is the role of the nuclear family within it?
12. How does mate selection operate in the upper class? How do the patterns of mate selection fit in with the nature of the family system?

11 | *The Kin Network*

. . . Mr. Light illustrated the pattern of indirect giving used successfully by other parents in saying: "When we visit Babs and her family we take things for the grandchildren and foods which we know they can't afford. We try to do something to give them pleasure, something which we know they can't afford or won't go out to get by themselves. Here is what I mean: I once wrote a letter to Johnny asking about the cost of baby sitters. He replied with a two-page letter giving complete details perhaps thinking that I wanted to go into the business. I realized that they were having difficulty in getting out by themselves so I sent them $35, with each dollar bill in a separate envelope. I addressed it to the grand-daughter with a note, 'You can use this when your mother wants to get a baby sitter.' I did not want them to turn down invitations. I wouldn't tell them this but had to give the gift in a certain way so that they would take it.

"Our life has changed in that we are trying to do things that will mean more in the long run to them. They are very proud; they don't want to be helped. It has to be done with a certain amount of subtlety.". . .

. . . The Moodys do not approve of their son-in-law and are satisfied to have their daughter some distance from them. Mrs. Moody related: "It seems strange for a mother to say these things but after her marriage I was so heartbroken that I didn't want her near me. I never told her this. Her husband who is an engineer had an offer to go to Texas. We urged them to go. I think every mother wants her daughter nearby, but in this situation where we didn't accept her husband it was best for us that we didn't see them too often. They are now living in Texas and she will come back about once a year. It has proved very satisfactory though we do miss her and the grandchild." [1]

A theme running through this book, so far, is the trend toward some form of the conjugal family, relatively detached from the larger circle of kin. We saw it first in world-wide perspective and then as a feature of the develop-

[1] Marvin B. Sussman, "Family Continuity: Selective Factors Which Affect Relationships Between Families at Generational Levels," *Marriage and Family Living* 16 (May 1954), pp. 117–18.

ment of Western family organization. It was implicit in Zimmerman's theory of family structure and family change, somewhat more open in Ogburn's writing, and was formally stated by Talcott Parsons. Parsons argues, of course, that the isolated nuclear family is a response to the demands of an industrial economy; that only this type of family unit permits the occupational, geographical, and social mobility required by the system.

Perhaps this is a slight overstatement of Parsons's views and maybe those views, originally stated more than thirty years ago, are changing. In some of his recent writing, Parsons has stated that his concept of the isolated nuclear family does not imply that all relations to kin outside the nuclear family are broken.[2] More to the point, Parsons's model—as all good models do—has stimulated extensive research designed to test it. Over about 20 years now, a body of research has accumulated which aids us greatly to put the nuclear family more adequately in the perspective of its relationships with other kin groups.

Recognition of the continued importance of the kin network has altered significantly the approach to analysis of relationships between the married couple—particularly the young married couple—and their families of orientation. As long as the emphasis was upon the isolation of the nuclear family, relationships with other family members tended to be viewed in terms of their problem-causing potential. Thus, discussions were couched in terms of the "in-law problem," with the core of the problem being the necessity for the young married couple to free themselves emotionally and financially from dependence on either set of parents. When the focus shifts to analysis of the nuclear family in the context of a larger kin network, the normative character of the analysis changes also; one emphasizes the supportive functions of the kin group and de-emphasizes somewhat the problem aspects.

In-law problems and supportive functions of the kin group appear almost as two sides of the same coin. In this chapter, we shall look at both.

In-Law Relationships

Relationships between young married couples and their parents on both sides are an obvious source of strain in the American family system. Young people bristle at any intimation of "parental interference," and parents shake their heads sadly, or bristle in turn, at their offspring's seeming obstreperousness. Both generations quote the tired cliché that "no home is big enough for

---

[2] Talcott Parsons, "The Normal American Family," in Seymour M. Farber, Piero Mustacchi, and Roger H. L. Wilson, eds., *Man and Civilization: The Family's Search for Survival*, New York: McGraw-Hill Book Company, 1965, p. 35.

two families"; and then there are all of those mother-in-law jokes. In this section we shall look at the nature and incidence of in-law problems in American society and attempt to interpret those problems in the context of the nature of the contemporary family system.

That in-law relationships are a conspicuous problem in American marriages has been established by research. Evelyn Duvall, in what she describes as a pilot study of 5020 men and women from all over the United States and married from a few weeks to more than 40 years, found that about 75 per cent had one or more in-law problems.[3] Rockwood and Ford found that in-law conflicts loomed third as a source of marital difficulties in a sample of 364 men and women.[4] John Thomas, studying 7000 broken Roman Catholic marriages, found that in-laws were the most frequent single cause of marital breakup during the first year of marriage.[5] Finally, Judson Landis found that about 10 per cent of 409 happily married couples had not achieved satisfactory in-law relationships even after twenty years of marriage.[6]

AGE AT MARRIAGE AND IN-LAW RELATIONSHIPS

A widely quoted study has reported that the amount of difficulty couples have with their in-laws is closely related to their age at the time of marriage. Younger couples have more in-law problems; older ones not so much. This can be seen vividly in Figure 1 which relates the age of 544 wives at marriage to the quality of the adjustment to in-laws. Of those who married at age 24 or older, 63 per cent reported excellent in-law adjustment, while only 45

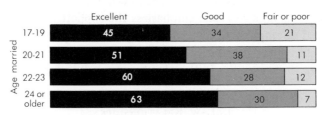

FIGURE 1. *Age of 544 wives at marriage and in-law adjustment.*

Source: Judson T. Landis and Mary G. Landis, *Building A Successful Marriage*, Englewood Cliffs, New Jersey: Prentice-Hall, Inc., 1968, p. 338.

[3] Evelyn M. Duvall, *In-Laws: Pro and Con*, New York: Association Press, 1954, pp. 187–8.

[4] Lemo D. Rockwood and Mary E. N. Ford, *Youth, Marriage, and Parenthood*, New York: John Wiley and Sons, 1945, p. 120.

[5] John L. Thomas, "Marital Failure and Duration," *Social Order* 3 (Jan. 1953), pp. 24–9.

[6] Judson T. Landis, "Adjustments After Marriage," *Marriage and Family Living* 9 (May 1947), pp. 32–4.

per cent of those who married between the ages of 17 and 19 reported excellent adjustment. Twenty-one per cent of the younger group reported fair or poor adjustment, while only 7 per cent of the older group did so.

A relationship between age and in-law difficulty was confirmed by Blood and Wolfe in a study of 909 Michigan families where they found the percentage of in-law difficulties to decline steadily as couples grew older. Fifteen per cent reported in-law disagreement during the honeymoon stage, with the percentage decreasing steadily over the rest of the life cycle.[7]

IN-LAW ADJUSTMENT AND TOTAL MARITAL ADJUSTMENT

The whole problem of the meaning of marital happiness and marital adjustment is a complicated one which will be taken up in subsequent chapters. Here, we simply wish to point out that there is a set of associations between conventional measures of marital happiness and the quality of in-law relationships. The rule which seems to hold is that better relationships with in-laws, and more quickly achieved good relationships with in-laws, are associated with higher marital happiness ratings.

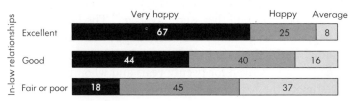

FIGURE 2. *In-law relationships and happiness in marriage.*

Source: Judson T. Landis and Mary G. Landis, *Building a Successful Marriage*, Englewood Cliffs, New Jersey: Prentice-Hall, 1963, p. 334.

Judson Landis studied two groups of couples: one group of 544 couples who were in the early years of marriage,[8] and a group of 409 couples who had been married for an average of twenty years.[9] Some of the results of the first study are shown in Figure 2. Sixty-seven per cent of those who reported excellent adjustment to in-laws also reported their marriages to be very happy. Of those who indicated fair or poor adjustment to in-laws, however, only 18 per

[7] Robert O. Blood, Jr. and Donald M. Wolfe, *Husbands and Wives: The Dynamics of Married Living*, The Free Press of Glencoe, Illinois, 1960, pp. 247–8.

[8] Judson T. Landis and Mary G. Landis, *Building A Successful Marriage*, Englewood Cliffs, New Jersey: Prentice-Hall, 1968, pp. 329–43.

[9] Judson T. Landis, "Length of Time Required To Achieve Adjustment in Marriage," *American Sociological Review* 11 (Dec. 1946), pp. 666–7.

cent reported very happy marriages. This is not to say that good in-law adjustments cause marital happiness. In-law adjustment is one part of total
marital adjustment, and the high relationships derive, in part, from correlat-
ing part of a thing with itself. It may also be that there is a halo effect operating. People whose marriages are happy may tend to overestimate the quality
of their relationships with in-laws and vice versa. The existence of these statistical associations tells us nothing about the cause-and-effect relationships
involved, but the fact of the association seems well established. People who
report good relationships with in-laws are more likely to report that their
marriages are happy than people who report poor in-law relationships.

In the study of 409 couples who had been married for approximately
twenty years, Landis found that couples who reported satisfactory in-law relationships from the beginning of marriage were more likely to report their
marriages as very happy. Fifty-two per cent of the couples with good in-law
relationships from the start of marriage said their marriages were "very
happy," 34 per cent described their marriages as "happy," and 14 per cent
reported their marriages to be of only "average" happiness. Of those couples
who had never achieved satisfactory relationships with their in-laws, 24 per
cent said their marriages were "very happy," 41 per cent said they were
"happy," and 35 per cent said they were "average." The fact that these reports
of marital happiness range only from "very happy" to "average" probably is
to be accounted for by the nature of the sample. This was a group of couples
whose marriages had survived for twenty years and who, if anything, probably
would overestimate the happiness of their marriages.

IN-LAW PROBLEMS, PRIMARILY A FEMININE PATTERN

The studies that have been done tend to pinpoint in-law problems in the
relationships between wives and their mothers-in-law and sisters-in-law. Husbands, fathers-in-law, and brothers-in-law seem to be less frequently and less
extremely involved. Figure 3, taken from Duvall's study, shows the pattern.

Duvall found that over one-third of 1337 people from whom data were
available said that the mother-in-law relationship was the most difficult. If
we exclude the 345 people who reported no in-law problems, then just about
one-half of the sample reported the mother-in-law relationship to be the most
difficult. Moreover, 90 per cent of the complaints about mothers-in-law came
from wives.[10] It is the husband's mother, more than the wife's mother, on
whom the difficulty appears to center.

[10] Op. cit. p. 187.

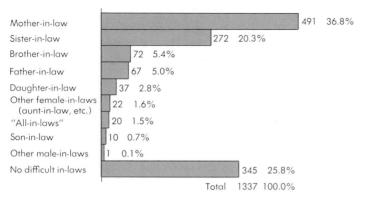

FIGURE 3. *The in-law named most difficult by 1337 persons.*

Source: Evelyn M. Duvall, *In-Laws: Pro and Con,* New York: Association Press, 1954, p. 188.

. . . In more than three-fifths of the world's societies, severe penalties follow upon the meeting of a man and his mother-in-law, and they shun each other accordingly. In northern Australia, a man who speaks to his mother-in-law must be put to death. In parts of the South Pacific, both parties would commit suicide. In Yucatan, men believe that to meet one's mother-in-law face to face would render a man sterile for life, so he may travel miles out of his way over dangerous territory to avoid being near her. Navaho men believe that they will go blind if they should see their mothers-in-law, so she is not even allowed to attend the wedding. This strenuous avoidance of son and mother-in-law has been analyzed from the point of view of the sexual potential and shame in the relationship by Freud, Margaret Mead, and many others. There is the possibility of socially disruptive pseudo-incest between parents and children-in-law, and there may also be various feelings of jealousy or outrage against the intruder who "steals" a mother's coveted son, or "defiles" the precious daughter.

In our own culture, the range of attitudes toward the mother-in-law is wide. Many people, especially women (who may be mothers-in-law themselves some day), like their mothers-in-law. Nevertheless, the mother-in-law is overwhelmingly named on all surveys as the most difficult of all relatives. Extreme avoidance is not customary but an alternative technique, the mother-in-law joke, is very common. . . .

—John M. Schlien, "Mother-in-Law: A Problem in Kinship Terminology," ETC. 19 (July 1962), pp. 161–71. Reprinted by permission from ETC: A Review of General Semantics, copyright, 1962, by the International Society for General Semantics.

These findings generally are confirmed by studies by Landis, Thomas, and Wallin. Landis, reporting on 116 husbands and 160 wives who had in-law problems, found that 42 per cent of the husbands and 50 per cent of the wives reported difficulties with their mothers-in-law. As did Duvall, Landis found the sister-in-law relationship to be the next most frequent locus of in-law problems. Only 15 per cent of the husbands and 11 per cent of the wives indicated difficulties with their fathers-in-law.[11] Thomas, studying Catholic couples, found the wife's in-laws to be involved in 48 per cent of the cases while the husband's in-laws were involved in only 38 per cent. He also reported the mother-in-law alone to be involved in 39 per cent of his cases.[12] Wallin also reported that more wives than husbands dislike their mothers-in-law.[13] The weight of the evidence is heavy; women, more than men, in the United States, experience in-law difficulty.

THE SIGNIFICANCE OF IN-LAW PROBLEMS

The particular structure of the American family system appears to produce a particular range of in-law difficulties.

First, it should be noted that what parents and their married offspring are primarily concerned about is the quality of the interpersonal relationships among them. They guard against "meddling," "interference," and "dependence." Moreover, dependence usually is defined more in emotional terms than in economic ones. To be sure, young people complain if their parents are either too niggardly or too lavish in their support of the young marriage; but the complaint generally is against the lack of love shown or the determination to control the young marriage rather than against the fact of financial support as such. As we will see in the next section, there is actually an elaborate pattern of financial support and mutual aid among different generations of the family. What makes financial support acceptable or unacceptable is the conditions under which it is given.

The apparent need of young adults to be "independent" of their parents traces back to the conditions existing within the nuclear family and the requirement that people become independent of the family of orientation at

---

[11] *Building a Successful Marriage*, p. 331.

[12] John L. Thomas, *The American Catholic Family*, Englewood Cliffs, New Jersey: Prentice-Hall, 1956, p. 235.

[13] Paul Wallin, "Sex Differences in Attitudes to In-Laws—A Test of a Theory," *American Journal of Sociology* 59 (March 1954), pp. 466–9. A recent study of 58 working-class marriages showed that husbands with less than a high-school education have as much difficulty with their mothers-in-law as their wives do. Mirra Komarovsky, *Blue-Collar Marriage*, New York: Random House, 1964, p. 259.

the time of marriage and entry into the occupational system. During childhood, both physical and emotional dependence upon the parents are relatively complete. During adolescence, the frequent adolescent revolt symbolizes the attempt to free oneself both from one's parents and from one's own need to remain in a state of child-like dependence. Not all youngsters have remained so dependent that they need to rebel, of course, and not all of those who need to rebel are able to do so. It seems fair to say that a substantial proportion of young people approach physical adulthood with their needs for emotional dependence less than completely resolved.

The hold of many young married persons on their independence is precarious. As long as this is so, they must react strongly to any actual or presumed threats to that independence. The parents are likely to have difficulties in this area too. After having had their offspring dependent upon them for ten to twenty years—after having organized their lives around their children—they often do not give up those dependent relationships without some ambivalence. Parents are reluctant to let go, and their offspring—although they stoutly deny it—are often equally reluctant. Often, some time is required for the emotional dependence of the parent-child relationship to give way to the emotional give-and-take appropriate to parent-adult offspring relationships.

Hence, the associations between age at marriage and the amount of in-law difficulty encountered. Although it is a very crude one, age probably is an index of how far young people have traveled along the road to adult independence. Those who marry before they have traveled too far must expect to complete their striving for independence after they marry; those who marry later are more likely to have this behind them.

The associations between length of time married and amount of in-law conflict are to be explained similarly. Young age, emotional dependence on parents, and newness of marriage tend to go together. With the passage of time, the dependence is resolved and in-law relationships become more harmonious. If the early conflict is too bitter, or if someone at either generational level is emotionally incapable of moving toward more adult relationships, then conflict may characterize the relationship permanently.

That in-law conflicts tend to center in the relationships among women probably is to be explained in terms of the distribution of power between the sexes. Ours is yet a somewhat male-dominated society. In such a society, women tend to compete for favor with men, and men reinforce their dominance by permitting their favor to be competed for.

Perhaps this can be illustrated by pointing out the greater emphasis placed upon "being a good wife" than upon "being a good husband" in our society. Women are far more likely to approach marriage fearing that they will not be adequate in their roles as wives than men are to fear that they will not be adequate as husbands. The wife is thrown into direct competition with the husband's mother and will be judged in terms of her ability to keep house, cook, and otherwise cater to her husband's needs; moreover, she competes with a woman with twenty or more years' experience on the job. The husband will be judged too—but not so much in terms of his performance *as a husband*. He will be judged in terms of his success in the occupational world. If a man earns a good living, does not run around with other women, and does not drink or gamble the family's livelihood away, not too much more is demanded of him as a husband.

In addition, the position of the young husband is one of sufficient power that neither his wife's parents nor his own are likely to risk an open break with him. He does have the power to move his wife (and himself) to another location where there will be no contacts at all; even in the same location he may reject the parents and leave them powerless to do anything about it. This power is illustrated by the idea that a girl marries into her husband's family. The wife's parents' claim that they have gained a son appears feeble in comparison.

The marriage of their offspring may also be inherently more threatening to mothers than to fathers in our society. Mothers' lives, more than fathers', are likely to be organized around their children. With their offspring's marriage, mothers are more likely to find themselves rendered essentially functionless; there are too many hours to fill each day and the mere continuance of her household duties affords the woman no satisfactory status. The father continues on in his occupation, which is his primary source of status, essentially without interference. His wife, however, is forced to define herself as "getting old." Since high status for women in America is associated with being young, attractive, and desirable to men, it is not surprising that many mothers strive vigorously to retain their favored relationship with their married sons.

Conflict among women in a family may also continue and be more difficult to control because of its relatively covert character. Conflict among men is likely to move rapidly to a confrontation in which the issues are resolved or some form of accommodation achieved. Women, however, if they are to compete effectively, must do it without being too obvious about it. If they force a crisis, their husbands are likely to take control and neither can win. Therefore, the hostility between mother-in-law and daughter-in-law often remains partly hidden. They compete for favor with the men in the family, using terms of endearment such as "dear" and "honey" to mask the barbs which they hurl at one another. This is a part of the feminine culture to which men have only limited access. Men often underestimate the amount of conflict among their women folk because, literally, they do not see it. One might also venture the hypothesis that men (un)wittingly ignore this conflict to some extent and thereby reinforce their own positions of dominance in the family.

In sum, there is good reason to think that much of what is called the in-law problem in America simply reflects the necessity for young adults to establish their emotional independence from their parents. Consequently, in-law conflict is most vigorous among the young and newly married. That women are frequently more involved in it than men reflects their relatively greater involvement in family matters and the subordinate role which they play in marriage.

Extended Family Relationships

Not until around 1950 were there systematic empirical data which bore directly on the question of how isolated the nuclear family really is in the United States. Theorists pointed to the breakdown of the extended family and both history and current experience seemed to bear them out.

That clan organization had disappeared as a feature of Western kinship structure was a simple fact. Moreover, many, many people could look back upon their own early experience and see how the family had changed. They remembered growing up in small cities and in the open country, with a network of grandparents, aunts, uncles, and cousins around. They could remember the family photo album and family reunions on Sunday afternoon.

The people who did the remembering, however, often were those who had moved away from their home towns, who communicated with members of their families of orientation by mail and with other kin, seldom, if at all. They seldom had more than two children, and they seemed, both to themselves and to others, to be quite alone in a sea of urban families most of whom also were quite alone. They were very conscious of the fact that grandmother was not there to baby-sit and that, in event of real emergency, there was no one around to turn to for help. In the face of such obvious evidence, it was some time before sociologists began systematically to compile data on the actual extent to which nuclear families remained embedded in a larger network of kin relationships.

MUTUAL AID AMONG KIN

Evidence on continued interaction with kin, after marriage, began to appear during the 1950's. Axelrod, reporting data from a careful sample of the Detroit area population, found that 49 per cent of the population see relatives at least once a week and an additional 25 per cent see them once a month or oftener.[14] Greer's findings in two Los Angeles census tracts almost exactly duplicate Axelrod's; [15] and Bell and Boat confirmed both sets of findings in a study in San Francisco [16] (see Table 1). Reiss's analysis of the kin relation-

TABLE 1. *Percentages of Residents of Three Metropolitan Areas, by Frequency of Interaction with Kin.*

Frequency of interaction	DETROIT high urbanism	LOS ANGELES low urbanism	SAN FRANCISCO low family status, low economic status	low family status, high economic status	high family status, low economic status	high family status, high economic status
once a week or oftener	49	49	55	33	30	45	42
once a month to once a week	25	24	21	23	28	27	24
less than once a month or data not obtained	26	27	24	44	42	28	34

Source: Data compiled from Morris Axelrod, "Urban Structure and Social Participation," *American Sociological Review* 21 (Feb. 1956), p. 16; Scott Greer, "Urbanism Reconsidered: A Comparative Study of Local Areas in a Metropolis," *American Sociological Review* 21 (Feb. 1956), p. 22; and Wendell Bell and Marion Boat, "Urban Neighborhoods and Informal Social Relations," *American Journal of Sociology* 62 (Jan. 1957), p. 394. Reprinted by permission.

ships of 161 Boston-area families produced lower figures but still showed 14 per cent interacting with kin at least once a week and 31 per cent interacting at least once a month. [17] Although this cannot be determined, it appears that Reiss's Boston sample had fewer kin in the metropolitan area than was true for any other of the samples cited. Support for this interpretation is provided by Bell and Blumberg's study of 133 migrant Negro women in Philadelphia.

[14] Morris Axelrod, "Urban Structure and Social Participation," *American Sociological Review* 21 (Feb. 1956), p. 16. See also, Aida K. Tomeh, "Informal Participation in a Metropolitan Community," *The Sociological Quarterly* 8 (Winter 1967), pp. 85–102.

[15] Scott Greer, "Urbanism Reconsidered: A Comparative Study of Local Areas in a Metropolis," *American Sociological Review* 21 (Feb. 1956), p. 22.

[16] Wendell Bell and Marion Boat, "Urban Neighborhoods and Informal Social Relations," *American Journal of Sociology* 62 (Jan. 1957), pp. 391–8.

[17] Paul J. Reiss, "The Extended Kinship System: Correlates of and Attitudes on Frequency of Interaction," *Marriage and Family Living* 24 (Nov. 1962), pp. 333–9.

In their sample, 56 per cent of whom had relatives living in Philadelphia, 46 per cent visited with close relatives at least once a week.[18]

One of the first major studies to confront this problem directly was done by Sussman in New Haven, Connecticut.[19] Sussman studied the relationships between 97 middle-class, white, Protestant, parental couples and their 195 married children living away from home. What he found did not give support to the notion of the isolated nuclear family.

First of all, Sussman found that the parents in his sample desired to extend aid to their married children and wished, in return, to remain a significant part of their children's lives. For their part, the young married couples wanted the friendly encouragement and assistance of their parents. These wishes were realized in an extensive pattern of financial aid that flowed from parents to children. In 154 of the 195 cases, the parents were giving either direct financial support or help and service. The parents were quite definite that they did not expect their children to support them in turn.[20]

Parental aid to the young married couples included financial aid in making some of their larger purchases, such as homes and automobiles, and gifts of kitchen equipment and furniture. The parents provided services, such as repairs to and painting of the home, gardening, landscaping, and baby-sitting. Ordinarily they drew the line at providing their children with a weekly or monthly check. Such support would produce or reflect a dependence that neither the parents nor their children would think appropriate.

Much of the aid extended by parents was indirect. Rather than pay the doctor's bill at the birth of a grandchild, for example, the parents might provide savings bonds, layettes, or other gifts to the grandchild himself. Similarly, parents might arrange to rent a vacation cottage that was large enough to accommodate children and grandchildren, in addition to themselves. The parents might thus bear most of the expense of a vacation which their children could not otherwise afford and without having to make a direct gift.

In one instance, Sussman found direct mutual aid between parents and married children. In 120 of the cases, parents and children took care of one another during times of illness and regardless of the distance between their homes. Most frequently this involved mothers' providing services to their daughters at childbirth. The mother might either provide direct nursing service or might care for older grandchildren during the period of confinement.

[18] Leonard Blumberg and Robert R. Bell, "Urban Migration and Kinship Ties," *Social Problems* 6 (Spring 1959), pp. 328–33.

[19] Marvin B. Sussman, *Family Continuity: A Study of Factors Which Affect Relationships Between Families at Generational Levels,* Ph.D. dissertation, Yale Univrsity, 1951.

[20] Marvin B. Sussman, "The Help Pattern in the Middle Class Family," *American Sociological Review* 15 (Feb. 1953), pp. 22–3.

There was a surprising awareness of the function of parental aid in permitting children immediately to begin living the middle-class model and to prepare themselves for continued upward mobility. In 118 of the 154 cases where a help pattern existed, the parents recognized the need for their help if the children were not to suffer a drop in socio-economic level after their marriage.[21]

Sussman's general finding of an elaborate mutual-aid network between parents and their married children was confirmed by Sharp and Axelrod in Detroit, where they found that approximately 70 per cent of all couples both give aid to and receive aid from relatives.[22] The most frequent types of help given and received were baby-sitting and help during illness. Next most common was financial aid. Help with housework also was given frequently. Other forms of aid such as giving business advice, helping to find a job, and the giving of valuable gifts also were found less often.

The distinctive contribution of the Sharp and Axelrod analysis was to show the pattern of aid according to the age of the persons involved. As we might expect, it is primarily younger women who receive baby-sitting help. In fact, help received, in each of the four major categories, declines steadily with age. Apparently, younger couples who have just begun their families are more in need of help from kin than are more established families. A surprising thing, however, is the relative constancy of aid given over the life cycle. With the one exception of aid with housework, which undoubtedly reflects the diminishing physical capacity of the older woman, the aid extended to relatives remains at rather a high level at least up to the age of retirement.

Still other studies have confirmed the existence of this network of aid among kin, particularly aid from parents to their married children. Sussman, in another study of 80 families in Cleveland, found practically all families involved in an active network of mutual aid.[23] Christopherson, Vandiver, and Krueger, studying married college students, found financial subsidies ranging from 5 to 80 per cent of their total money income being received by 38 per cent of the student families.[24]

[21] Ibid. pp. 25–7.

[22] Harry Sharp and Morris Axelrod, "Mutual Aid Among Relatives in an Urban Population," in Ronald Freedman, Amos Hawley, Werner Landecker, Gerhard Lenski, and Horace Miner, *Principles of Sociology: A Text with Readings*, New York: Holt, Rinehart, and Winston, 1956, pp. 434–5.

[23] Marvin B. Sussman, "The Isolated Nuclear Family: Fact or Fiction," *Social Problems* 6 (Spring 1959), pp. 333–40.

[24] Victor A. Christopherson, Joseph S. Vandiver, and Marie N. Krueger, "The Married College Student, 1959," *Marriage and Family Living* 22 (May 1960), pp. 126–7. For a comprehensive review of research on parental aid, see Marvin B. Sussman and Lee Burchinal, "Parental Aid to Married Children: Implications for Family Functioning," *Marriage and Family Living* 24 (Nov. 1962), pp. 320–32.

TABLE 2. *Percentage Distribution of Types of Help Given and Received, by Age of Wife.*

TYPES OF HELP	AGE OF WIFE				
	29 or younger	30–44	45–59	60 or older	Total
Received:					
Baby-sitting	67	54	20	10	46
Help during illness	60	54	41	24	50
Financial aid	53	36	18	20	34
Help with housework	32	25	24	15	26
Given:					
Baby-sitting	51	45	46	51	47
Help during illness	47	60	53	43	54
Financial aid	29	30	32	31	30
Help with housework	32	28	24	15	27

Source: Adapted from Harry Sharp and Morris Axelrod, "Mutual Aid Among Relatives in an Urban Population," in Ronald Freedman, Amos Hawley, Werner Landecker, Gerhard Lenski, and Horace Miner, *Principles of Sociology: A Text with Readings*, New York: Holt, Rinehart, and Winston, Inc., 1956, pp. 436–7.

Thus, in many locations and among a variety of samples, the same general finding obtains. Young people, at marriage, generally establish themselves apart from their parents, and both parents and children accept the idea that they should be financially independent as well. Nevertheless, a widespread, intricate pattern of support and mutual aid exists. Married children and grand-children continue to be important in the lives of parents, and young people generally welcome both the continued interest and support of their parents. Many nuclear families are not so isolated, emotionally or financially, as they appear. Rather, they are embedded in an inconspicuous kin network in which there is considerable continuity from one generation to the next.

THE CONDITIONS OF INTERGENERATIONAL CONTINUITY

In the last section, the emphasis was upon the frequency of interaction with, and mutual aid among, kin outside the family of procreation. That most families do continue to interact, particularly with the parents on both sides, appears well established. It is also clear, however, that the extent of interaction and support varies among families. Some parents and their married children remain very close; others maintain a safe distance and regulate their contacts carefully; in still other cases, there is outright alienation. In this section, we shall examine data bearing upon factors which affect the level of intergenerational continuity.

Sussman's study of the relationships between 97 middle-class New Haven parents and their 195 married children living away from home dealt not only with the extent of mutual aid but also with the social and family conditions under which intergenerational continuity flourishes.

To do this, Sussman classified each of the 195 cases according to the degree of intergenerational continuity evidenced. Four ratings were used. "High" continuity describes those cases where there was complete acceptance of each other by the parents and the married child's family. "Good" family continuity describes cases where the parents and their offspring completely accept one another, and where the parents and the offspring's spouse partially accept one another. "Fair" continuity exists where the parents and the married child's family partially accept each other. "Poor" continuity is marked by partial or complete mutual acceptance by parents and their offspring, but mutual rejection of parents and the offspring's spouse. Of the 195 cases, 122 were rated as displaying high continuity, 27 cases displayed good continuity, 25 cases had only fair continuity, and 21 cases had poor continuity.[25]

Sussman related four different factors to the level of intergenerational continuity: (1) similarity of the sociocultural backgrounds of the young married persons; (2) the type of courtship and marriage ceremony they had; (3) the type of child-rearing which they had experienced; and (4) the distance between the residences of the young married couple and the parents. The results of this analysis are summarized in Table 3 where, for purposes of simplicity, only the "high" and "poor" continuity groups are contrasted.

The findings show that when the young people married persons with ethnic, religious, social class, and educational backgrounds similar to their own, the vast majority had harmonious relationships with their in-laws and almost none had relationships marked by mutual rejection. Where the backgrounds were dissimilar, on the other hand, few managed to develop relationships of mutual acceptance, and the majority found their relationships to be strained and to be structured in terms of prevailing stereotypes of the out-group into which the young person had married.[26] This factor of sociocultural background was more highly related to intergenerational continuity than any of the other factors tested and seems to indicate that the price attached to marrying some-

25 "Family Continuity: Selective Factors Which Affect Relationships Between Families at Generational Levels," op. cit. p. 113.

26 Ibid. A recent study indicates that intergenerational continuity is associated with higher incomes and with less marital tension over religious affiliation. See Joan Aldous, "The Consequences of Intergenerational Continuity," *Journal of Marriage and the Family* 27 (Nov. 1965), pp. 462–8. Still another report suggests that integration into a kin network may be associated with lower rates of marital dissolution. See John Scanzoni, "A Reinquiry into Marital Disorganization," *Journal of Marriage and the Family* 27 (Nov. 1965), pp. 483–91.

TABLE 3. *Level of Continuity Between Parents and Their Married Offspring by Selected Social Variables.*

	LEVEL OF INTERGENERATIONAL CONTINUITY	
	High	Low
Socio-cultural background		
Similar	118	2
Dissimilar	3	21
Courtship pattern		
Traditional	115	7
Nontraditional	6	16
Childrearing pattern		
Developmental	100	8
Traditional	21	15
Location of households		
Same or near community	71	14
Distantly separated	50	9

Source: Adapted from Marvin B. Sussman, "Family Continuity: Selective Factors Which Affect Relationships Between Families at Generational Levels," *Marriage and Family Living* 16 (May 1954), pp. 115–18.

one of radically different background often includes some alienation from one or both sets of parents.

The type of courtship and marriage ceremony was measured in terms of whether there was the traditional church wedding and reception arranged by the parents and following a courtship in which the parents had ample opportunity to become acquainted with their future son-in-law or daughter-in-law. This traditional courtship and wedding was followed by high continuity in 115 cases and by low continuity in only 7 cases. Where the young people eloped or otherwise violated the expectations of parents, there were only 6 cases of high continuity compared to 16 cases of poor continuity.

The analysis of intergenerational continuity by the type of child-rearing the young person had experienced showed that so-called developmental child-rearing, where the young person was encouraged to become independent and self-reliant but to continue affectionate ties with other family members, was associated with high continuity, whereas traditional child-rearing practices— stressing strict control over the children and creation of a dependent relationship between children and parents—was associated with low continuity. Traditionally oriented parents had difficulty severing their emotional ties to their children and were likely to interfere in their offspring's marriages. Table 3 shows that of 135 developmentally reared young people, 100 had high continuity, 27 had fair or average continuity, and only 8 had low continuity.

THE INFLUENCE OF DEVELOPMENTAL CHILD-REARING

. . . Mrs. Hempstead recalled: "I was never a boss to Barbara as my sister was with her children. We always encouraged her to do the right thing but never insisted that she follow our suggestions. After Barbara was married I quit giving advice and suggestions. I realized that she was an adult and ought to be treated as such; in fact I have learned things from her such as in cooking and house repairing."

Her husband added: "We don't criticize openly. When Mrs. Hempstead goes over and sees something that needs to be done she will do it and be very careful about saying anything. Barbara will say, 'Mother don't do that,' but we know that she is very appreciative of it because she has a big job with the children. They don't object to suggestions. We are not a fighting family. We realize the closeness of the two families, and avoid criticisms. When they do something we don't like we keep our mouths shut. We came about rather naturally to this understanding."

—Marvin B. Sussman, "Family Continuity: Selective Factors Which Affect Relationships Between Families at Generational Levels," *Marriage and Family Living* 16 (May 1954), p. 117.

The analysis of residential location provided somewhat different findings. Only in this case were there no statistically significant relationships with intergenerational continuity. As can be seen in Table 3, about 84 per cent of the families living in the same or neighboring communities were characterized by high continuity; but an equally high proportion of those living in distantly separated communities had high continuity.[27] The explanation for this apparent anomaly probably lies in the fact that the location of the couple's residence is determined more by the husband's job than by the quality of the relationships with other family members. It is extremely important to emphasize that physical nearness is no guarantee of good relationships and that distance is not a great barrier to the maintenance of high intergenerational continuity.

This study illuminates at least some of the conditions which are related to good relationships between successive generations of the same family. Similar-

[27] Ibid. p. 118. An exception, where kin relationships were somewhat less important and were unrelated to the adjustment of migrants to a new community, has been reported by Berardo. See Felix M. Berardo, "Kinship Interaction and Migrant Adaptation in an Aerospace-Related Community," *Journal of Marriage and the Family* 28 (Aug. 1966), pp. 296–304; and Felix M. Berardo, "Kinship Interaction and Communications Among Space-Age Migrants," *Journal of Marriage and the Family* 29 (Aug. 1967), pp. 541–54.

ity of background between the young married pair, fairly conventional courtship and wedding with parental approval of the marriage, and affectionate but
not dependent relationships between parents and adult children all are associated with continued good relationships. The nearness of distance between
their places of residence appears to be more a function of the occupations of
the men of the family than a condition of relationships between the generations.

THE MODIFIED EXTENDED FAMILY

The data presented in the preceding sections show clearly that the nuclear
family is not so isolated as structure-function theory would lead us to believe.
Instead, we find a network of visiting, mutual aid, and emotional support
which in some ways is reminiscent of the classical extended family. Inevitably
this poses the question of whether the theory is wrong and needs to be revised.

There is not at present—and there may never be—any final answer to this
question. First, it should be reaffirmed that Parsons's emphasis on the isolation of the nuclear family was couched in structural terms; he indicated that
the structure of the American family system conduces to more occupational,
geographical, and generational isolation than do the structures of most other
family systems. He did not say that the nuclear family typically maintains no
contact with other kin. In fact, he argues that some contacts with kin are
quite consistent with the concept of the isolated nuclear family.

Another possibility is that a more isolated nuclear family may have been
characteristic of the first stages of industrialization in Western society. When
the extended family was still strong, young people may have been more con-
strained to sever ties with it completely than they are today. There may have
been no happy medium; to maintain ties at all may have been to accept subordination to parents and kin. Too, both transportation and communication
were far less efficient than they are today. A distance of even 50 miles between
the residences of the young couple and their kin may have been nearly insur-
mountable. It may have taken longer to travel that 50 miles than it takes to
travel 3000 miles today.

That there may have been more isolation of nuclear families from one to
several generations ago seems plausible. By the very nature of the thing it
is impossible to verify that plausibility empirically.

It is also plausible that recent changes in American society should have
made the continuance of intergenerational contacts easier. First, as the classical extended family has waned and the norms supporting it withered, the
threat of parental domination of young marriages may also have lessened.

Contemporary norms favoring equal status for all adult members of the family may make it easier for young people to continue relationships with their parents and yet to retain their independence.

Second, transportation and communication have improved tremendously. Air mail and inexpensive long distance telephone service have made it much easier to stay in close contact. High-speed highway and air travel have effectively lessened distances and lowered the barriers presented by distance to the maintenance of interpersonal relationships.

Third, the development of huge, diversified urban centers may have done much to reduce the need for young people to migrate far from their kin in order to put their specialized training to use. When most families lived in small communities, getting a college education and putting it to use almost necessitated migration to an urban center. In 1970, however, 73.5 per cent of the total United States population was defined as urban. Six separate states had more than four out of five inhabitants living in urban areas, and there were 30 standard metropolitan statistical areas with over a million population each.[28] In areas like New York, Philadelphia, Chicago, Los Angeles, and dozens more, almost any type of technical or professional skill may be put to use right in the area. The young couple can remain in the midst of the kin group and still seek occupational advancement.[29]

The question of whether there was a stage when the nuclear family was more isolated than it is today or whether there has been a fairly elaborate kin network all along probably will never be answered. For our purposes, it is more important that there have been recent developments in family theory which adequately take the kin network into account. The studies described in preceding sections tested the concept of the isolated nuclear family and found it inadequate to describe much of contemporary family experience. Out of this program of research has emerged the concept of the modified extended family.

The concept of the modified extended family is probably identified most closely with the name of Eugene Litwak, who showed, in a set of brilliantly conceived studies, that cohesion of the extended family in the United States is prohibited neither by occupational mobility nor by geographical mobility.[30]

[28] Paul B. Horton and Gerald R. Leslie, *The Sociology of Social Problems*, New York: Appleton-Century-Crofts, 1970, pp. 412–13.

[29] Marvin B. Sussman and Lee Burchinal, "Kin Family Network: Unheralded Structure in Current Conceptualizations of Family Functioning," *Marriage and Family Living* 24 (Aug. 1962), pp. 231–40. See also Bartolomeo J. Palisi, "Ethnic Generation and Family Structure," *Journal of Marriage and the Family* 28 (Feb. 1966), pp. 49–50.

[30] Eugene Litwak, "Occupational Mobility and Extended Family Cohesion," *American Sociological Review* 25 (Feb. 1960), pp. 9–21; Eugene Litwak, "Geographic Mobility and

He found, instead, that extended family relations can exist in a mature industrial economy and may, for bureaucratic occupations at least, actually promote occupational and geographical mobility.

Litwak describes the modified extended family as follows:

. . . the modified extended family structure . . . consists of a coalition of nuclear families in a state of partial dependence. Such partial dependence means that nuclear family members exchange significant services with each other, thus differing from the isolated nuclear family, as well as retain considerable autonomy (that is, not bound economically or geographically), therefore, differing from the classical extended family.[31]

Thus, we have a concept of extended family relationships being consistent with the occupational demands of an industrial economy.[32] We will close this

---

Extended Family Cohesion," *American Sociological Review* 25 (June 1960), pp. 385–94. See also, Eugene Litwak, and Ivan Szelenyi, "Primary Group Structures and Their Functions: Kin, Neighbors, and Friends," *American Sociological Review* 34 (Aug. 1969), pp. 465–81.

[31] Eugene Litwak, "Extended Kin Relations in an Industrial Democratic Society," in Ethel Shanas and Gordon F. Streib, eds., *Social Structure and the Family: Generational Relations*, Englewood Cliffs, New Jersey: Prentice-Hall, 1965, p. 291. For additional evidence concerning the extent and character of the modified extended family, see Bartolomeo J. Palisi, "Ethnic Generation and Family Structure," *Journal of Marriage and the Family* 28 (Feb. 1966), pp. 49–50; Bartolomeo J. Palisi, "Patterns of Social Participation in a Two-Generation Sample of Italian-Americans," *The Sociological Quarterly* 7 (Spring 1966), pp. 167–78; Robert F. Winch and Scott Greer, "Urbanism, Ethnicity, and Extended Familism," *Journal of Marriage and the Family* 30 (Feb. 1968), pp. 40–45; and Robert F. Winch, Scott Greer, and Rae Lesser Blumberg, "Ethnicity and Extended Familism in an Upper-Middle-Class Suburb," *American Sociological Review* 32 (April 1967), pp. 265–72.

[32] Although this discussion has focused upon the United States, there is abundant evidence of the existence of a modified extended family in other countries. See, for example, Everett D. Dyer, "Upward Social Mobility and Nuclear Family Integration as Perceived by the Wife in Swedish Urban Families," *Journal of Marriage and the Family* 32 (Aug. 1970), pp. 341–50; Guenther Leuschen, Robert O. Blood, Michael Lewis, Zachary Staikof, Veronica Stolte-Heiskanen, and Conor Ward, "Family Organization, Interaction and Ritual: A Cross-Cultural Study in Bulgaria, Finland, Germany and Ireland," *Journal of Marriage and the Family* 33 (Feb. 1971), pp. 228–34; James R. Mapstone, "Familistic Determinants of Property Acquisition," *Journal of Marriage and the Family* 32 (Feb. 1970), pp. 143–50; Helgi Osterreich, "Geographical Mobility and Kinship," *International Journal of Comparative Sociology* 6 (March 1965), pp. 131–44; Leonard I. Pearlin, *Class Context and Family Relations: A Cross-National Study*, Boston: Little, Brown and Company, 1971; Ralph Piddington, "The Kinship Network Among French Canadians," *International Journal of Comparative Sociology* 6 (March 1965), pp. 145–65; Colin Rosser, and Christopher Harris, *The Family and Social Change: A Study of Family and Kinship in a South Wales Town*, New York: Humanities Press, 1965; and Dorian A. Sweetser, "Intergenerational Ties in Finnish Urban Families," *American Sociological Review* 33 (April 1968), pp. 236–46.

chapter by considering social class differences, implicit norms of noninter-ference, and the support of upward social mobility through the modified extended family.

Social Class Differences. Far too little is known about social class differences in the operation of the kin network. Conceptualization of the modified ex-tended family emphasizes middle-class occupational patterns and tells us little about lower-class patterns.

Sussman did collect data in Cleveland, Ohio, from which he made com-parisons between 25 matched pairs of middle-class and lower-class families. Essentially, he found that there were class differences in the type of help and service exchanged and concluded that these differences reflected differences in life styles more than differences in willingness to participate in a mutual aid network. There was no difference in the amount of help offered during the illness of family members, but middle-class families more often extended financial aid and middle-class mothers—who less often had to work—were more often available for baby-sitting.[33]

There is some hint that the concentration of kin in a single neighborhood or community may be greater at lower-class levels and among blacks than among middle-class whites. In one area of Cleveland, in transition to becom-ing a Negro area, 67 per cent of the whites and 86 per cent of the nonwhites had relatives living in the metropolitan area. Further, 34 per cent of the whites and 60 per cent of the nonwhites had relatives living within two square miles. It seems likely that, whereas middle-class geographic mobility often involves only the nuclear family leaving the kin group, lower-class moves often involve the transfer of several related nuclear families to a new area. It is likely also that visiting kin occupies a more dominant position in the social life of lower-class families than it does among middle-class families.

Norms of Noninterference. In generations past, in-law relationships and relationships with one's own parents were plagued by problems of economic dependency and by problems of control. There was a threat inherent in young couples accepting aid or support from their parents; if the parents supported they could interfere; and if the parents supported now, they had the right to expect support, in return, in their old age.

Perhaps until the present generation in American society—and remnants are to be found yet today—there existed explicit verbal norms to the effect that young people should become economically self-sufficient at marriage.[34]

---

[33] "The Isolated Nuclear Family: Fact or Fiction," op. cit. p. 338.

[34] It should be pointed out that the existence of this verbal norm does not necessarily mean that there was any less elaborate pattern of parental support in times past than there is today. Particularly in the old-style farming economy, parental support often was elaborate

If they could not be self-sufficient, they had no right to marry. If the parents were required to continue to support their children after marriage then the children were, by definition, immature and the parents had the right to have some say about how their money was used. The price of parental support was to continue to play a child-like role.

The reverse aspect of this problem was that there was much economic dependency in old age. Before the social security system came into existence and before company retirement plans became widespread, the plight of many aging parents was serious. Unable to save enough money out of their modest incomes, their security often lay in the possibility of "moving in with" or being supported by their married children.

Under these circumstances, the giving to and accepting of help from kin was fraught with hazard. Much of the bad reputation that in-law relationships have traditionally had in the United States may have stemmed from this situation. Relationships between the generations reflected the problems of a changing economic system.

Since World War II, the economic situation has changed drastically. A large and growing proportion of parents have income protection for their old age and need no longer fear dependency upon their children. In addition, levels of living have risen to the point where many parents can subsidize offspring's marriage with no financial hardship to themselves. Under these new conditions, the norms governing parental aid to married children have changed appreciably.

By and large, today, the norms provide that parents shall not interfere in their married children's lives. To prevent there being any implication of dependency of the young people upon the parents, the subsidies must not be too obvious. The young husband might reject a check from his father or father-in-law indignantly. But when coming to visit for a weekend, the parents might load up the car with luxury foods and with furniture "that they don't need any more." Since the parents will help eat (a very small portion of) the food, and since they would just have to get rid of the furniture anyway, there is no reason

---

and continuous. At marriage, the son might move his bride into his parents' house or into a house, built for them, on the parental farm. Or, if the young couple were determined to be "independent," the father might lend them the money for a down payment on the adjoining farm and then advance money for seed, lend them equipment, and assist with the planting and harvesting of crops.

It may be that the verbal norm requiring independence at marriage emerged strongly only as the economy became industrialized and lengthy academic preparation was required for success in it. If this is correct, the independence norm may have been used as a weapon by parents who wished to discourage their sons from marrying too early and thereby hurting their chances for occupational success.

to reject the gifts, and the parents are not entitled to special consideration on the basis of them.

There does appear to be the expectation of mutual exchange in such cases, but what the parents wish, and their children are prepared to give, is emotional rather than monetary. What the parents seek is entrée to the lives of their children and especially to their grandchildren. Since the norms state that it is good for children to know and love their grandparents, the ground is laid for amiable, supportive relations between the generations.

The Support of Upward Mobility. Developers of the classical model of the isolated nuclear family argued essentially that the maintenance of ties with parents and other kin was an obstacle to occupational success. The model called for the son of a father who ate dinner in his undershirt and of a mother who disapproved of drinking and smoking, to become a sophisticated young executive.[35] Presumably he could more easily rid himself of dysfunctional attitudes and behavior and take on those appropriate to his new status if he moved away from and no longer associated regularly with his parents.

It now appears, however, that the modified extended family is not quite such a threat to upward mobility prospects.[36] Indeed, in some ways, the parents aid the mobility climb, reward their offspring for it, and themselves derive prestige from it.

The role of parents in aiding their children quickly to acquire the components of the standard package of goods and services regarded as essential to middle-class living has already been described in the chapter on the middle-class family model. Suffice it to say here that, without parental support through college and professional training, and without parental subsidization of the young marriage, the climb up the mobility ladder would be slower and less certain. This fact, while apparently not emphasized by many parents, is not lost on most young people, who appear quite willing to have their parents share vicariously, at least, in their successes.

Continued interaction with parents and other kin, after one has climbed to a higher social position, may also be rewarding both to the parents and to

[35] There were other patterns than this one, of course. But whether the son became an executive, scientist, engineer, salesman, or what-have-you, the point remains unchanged. Occupational advancement implied upward social mobility with pervasive changes from the values, attitudes, and behaviors of the parents.

[36] J. M. Bruce, "Intragenerational Occupational Mobility and Visiting With Kin and Friend," *Social Forces* 49 (Sept. 1970), pp. 117–27; Mark Hutter, "Transformation of Identity, Social Mobility and Kinship Solidarity," *Journal of Marriage and the Family* 32 (Feb. 1970), pp. 133–7; Harry K. Schwarzweller, and John F. Seggar, "Kinship Involvement: A Factor in the Adjustment of Rural Migrants," *Journal of Marriage and the Family* 29 (Nov. 1967), pp. 662–71.

their upwardly mobile offspring. To the extent to which parents identify with their children, they may continue to achieve through those children long after they themselves have climbed as high as they are going to go. Visits from their high-status offspring may also provide an opportunity to "show off" that vicarious achievement to friends and neighbors. For their part, the young people may not simply be uncomfortable in the lower status environment of their youth but they may enjoy and receive enhanced self-esteem from the homage paid to them by parents and other kin.

Implicit in this arrangement is some degree of segregation of the young people's kin relationships from their relationships with current associates. By making occasional visits "back home" and by having their parents visit them periodically, the young couple can make sure that their parents are not embarrassed by being thrown in with friends who have different attitudes and values and that, similarly, their current friends do not have to help entertain their parents. Although neither parents nor offspring wish to verbalize it, both appear to recognize that they can thus both avoid being embarrassed or ashamed.

It may even be that this is becoming less of a problem with the passage of time. The most acute embarrassment over social origins probably occurs among those who are of very low socio-economic background and who have not climbed very far. The farther they climb and the more secure they become in their new status, the less need there may be to hide their parents, like skeletons in the closet. Moreover, with the increasing affluence of parents, the virtual completion of the process of assimilation of European immigrants, and with the leveling of tastes and styles of life occurring in the larger society, the gulf between parents and their upwardly mobile children may not be so wide as it once was. There even seems to be a spreading awareness among young middle-class people-on-the-rise that most of them have similar parental backgrounds and that they need not be ashamed of those backgrounds. To the degree to which this is true, there may even be some mingling of parents with the young couples' current associates.

The modified extended family is reality to a large proportion of families today. There is every evidence that the existence of this kind of extended family unit is quite consistent with the occupational demands of a mature industrial economy.

SUMMARY

The world-wide and historical trend toward the conjugal family apparently has proceeded farthest in the United States. Here, theorists have argued, the isolated nuclear family is prototypical. Recently, however, research has shown that the American nuclear family has extensive ties in a larger kin network. Historically, the problem-causing aspects of these relationships have been emphasized. The newer emphasis on the modified extended family highlights their supportive aspects.

Research has established that both parents and their married children often encounter problems in their in-law relationships. Such problems appear to be related to age at marriage and to age in general. Couples who marry young report more in-law difficulties than those who marry when they are older. Similarly, people in the early stages of the family life cycle report more strife than those who are older. In-law adjustment also is related to total marital adjustment; those who report good marital adjustment more often report good in-law adjustment and vice versa.

In-law problems more often revolve around women than around men. Difficulties between the young bride and her mother-in-law are most common; problems with sisters-in-law come next. Husbands, fathers-in-law, and brothers-in-law are less frequently involved.

In-law problems in early marriage probably stem from conditions in the nuclear family which require adolescents and young adults to rebel against their emotional dependence upon their parents. Until the young people become secure in their independence, "meddling" by parents probably is both more common and more commonly perceived, even where it may not exist.

The concentration of in-law problems among women may be related to the dependent position of women in American society. Some accommodation between a man and his in-laws is likely to be reached quickly or an open break follows. Women, however, are not often in a position to issue ultimatums. In addition, women are under more pressure to compete with one another to prove themselves adequate in the role of housewife; men compete, but more often in their occupations than in their roles as husbands. The marriage of children also dramatizes the fact of aging to women more than it does to men.

In spite of the need for young people to become emotionally independent, research has shown an intricate network of relationships between parents and their married offspring. A large proportion of families have kin living nearby and up to half of all families may visit with kin at least once a week. Moreover, there is a pattern of mutual aid which includes the provision of help in times of illness, baby-sitting, help with housework, and so on. Financial aid more often flows from parents to children and often is substantial. This aid is carefully arranged not to interfere with the independence of either nuclear family.

Some families manage to maintain closer ties between the generations than others do. Research has shown that ties are likely to be closer when the young person marries someone of similar sociocultural background and when the courtship has been a fairly conventional one, approved by the parents. The type of child-rearing experienced by the young person also seems to be important. For the parents to maintain strict control over their offspring is negatively related to intergenerational continuity. A somewhat surprising finding is that the distance between the residences of parents and their married children does not appear to be related to the closeness of the ties between them. Residence probably depends more on the husband's job than on the closeness of kin ties.

The evidence certainly shows more contact between relatives than is implied in the concept of the isolated nuclear family. Whether Western society went through a stage when the nuclear family was more isolated than it is today may never be known. In any event, recent changes in the larger society obviously make the continuance of kin ties easier. These changes include improved transportation and communication, higher standards of living, and the development of large urban complexes within which almost any professional or technical skills can be put to good use.

The concept of the modified extended family, unhampered either by occupational or geographical mobility, is useful in describing the contemporary American family. This modified extended family apparently operates at different social class levels, includes tacit norms of noninterference, and does not hinder the upward social mobility of the younger generation.

SUGGESTED READINGS

Adams, Bert N., *Kinship in an Urban Setting*, Chicago: Markham Publishing Company, 1968. Synthesizes the literature on extended kin ties in urban America and presents the results of the author's own research in this area.

Hill, Reuben, *Family Development in Three Generations*, Cambridge, Mass.: Schenkman Publishing Co., 1970. A comprehensive report of research into trends over three generations of the same American families. Chapter three deals with interdependence among the generations.

Hill, Reuben, and König, René, eds., *Families in East and West: Socialization Process and Kinship Ties*, Paris and The Hague: Mouton, 1970. A collection of papers from the Ninth International Family Research Seminar. The largest section focuses on the relation between the family and extended kin.

Leichter, Hope J., and Mitchell, William E., *Kinship and Casework*, New York: Russell Sage Foundation, 1967. Details the kinship roles, family life cycle changes, and generational differences of a sample of Jewish families in New York City. Examines in-law conflicts in relation to kinship interaction.

Mirande, Alfred M., "The Isolated Nuclear Family Hypothesis: A Reanalysis," in John N. Edwards, ed., *The Family and Change*, New York: Alfred A. Knopf,

1969, pp. 153–63. A report of research which shows that social status and social mobility influence extended kin relationships. Finds sex differences in extended family relationships also.

Petersen, Karen Kay, "Kin Network Research: A Plea for Comparability," *Journal of Marriage and the Family* 31 (May 1969), pp. 271–80. A sophisticated methodological critique of the research that has been done on the kin network. Illustrates, vividly, the difficulties involved in trying to accumulate research findings.

Shanas, Ethel, and Streib, Gordon F., eds., *Social Structure and the Family: Generational Relations*, Englewood Cliffs, New Jersey: Prentice-Hall, 1965. An interdisciplinary symposium which focuses upon the three-generation family. Emphasizes the role relationships of older family members.

FILMS

Marriage is a Partnership (Coronet Films, Coronet Building, Chicago), 20 minutes. Analyzes the adjustments made by a young couple during the first year of marriage. Illustrates the tendency of each partner to be overdependent on his own parents. Shows the resolution of the in-law problem to be a function of the young people's attitudes.

QUESTIONS AND PROJECTS

1. What relationships exist between age at marriage and amount of in-law difficulty? How would you explain the existence of these relationships?
2. What relationships exist between in-law adjustment and total marital adjustment? How would you explain the existence of these relationships?
3. What is meant by the statement that in-law problems are primarily a feminine pattern in the United States? What relationships seem to cause the most difficulty? How do you explain this pattern?
4. What has research shown about the frequency with which urban families visit with relatives?
5. Describe the network of mutual aid which exists between parents and their married children. What kinds of goods and services are exchanged? How do these patterns vary over the life cycle?
6. What is meant by levels of intergenerational continuity? What has research shown about the relationship between intergenerational continuity and similarity of the sociocultural backgrounds of marriage partners? What implications does this have for mate selection?
7. How is type of courtship and marriage ceremony related to intergenerational continuity? How is the child-rearing pattern related to generational relationships? How do you explain these associations?
8. Why is there apparently little or no relationship between distance between residences and intergenerational continuity?
9. Define what is meant by the modified extended family. How does it differ from the classical extended family?

10. Might there have been a stage in the development of Western society when the nuclear family was more isolated than it is today? What recent changes in the United States have made it easier for families to maintain contact with other kin?

11. What social class differences do there appear to be in the nature of the kin network?

12. Explain how the modified extended family may actually promote occupational mobility.

Part | V

THE FAMILY LIFE CYCLE

| *Premarital Interaction: Dating and Love Involvement*

The phone call on Monday for a date on Saturday is going the same route as the party dress and the prom—out. In fact, the whole practice of dating seems to be disappearing.

That funny old way mom and dad did things—the nervous initial conversations on the phone, the old anticipation of the "big night," the worry over whether "he" would call is "sort of quaint," says Gil Speilberg, an Adelphi College student. And his friends shake their heads. Such things are unheard of.

The whole way of "dating" has changed. Instead of being on dates, teenagers and college students today place the emphasis upon being together . . . they tend to prefer spontaneous, informal get-togethers. Instead of emphasizing couples, they emphasize themselves, with men taking less and less of the responsibility for planning and paying.

"It's just hanging around together," says blonde Kim Lovett, 15. "You don't need to make a deal of it." She and her high school friends—boys and girls—often travel in groups, and often end up at her house on a Saturday night just talking, being together. "I don't call it a party," she says quickly, "I call it company." . . .

[Howard Brody] says most of his friends do go out on "dates," as well as groups, that the main change is just that "you don't go through that formalized thing." The relationships are more depressurized, "more a mutual thing." "You know, inside—there's more understanding. They just don't want to play a game."

"Going steady," however, is still popular and some counselors, psychologists, and parents feel that young people either go in groups or go steady, with no inbetween. "I think that the young people who go steady are more likely to have one particular boyfriend or girlfriend. There's such a tremendous feeling of loneliness, such alienation," says Dr. George Goldman, a New York psychologist. "They get much more of a sense of fulfillment from one person they know they understand and who understands them."

But the way to find that person is no longer by "dating." It is more likely to begin in a casual group at someone's house, in a casual group that goes to the movies together, to get a pizza, or even to hang around a shopping center. "In school you don't get to know anybody," says Brody . . . "so you meet at someone's house or something and that's how a lot of relationships get started."[1]

Dating behavior in the United States, at least among middle-class white youth, is changing rapidly. The changes are so recent and, as yet, are of such undetermined scope that it is difficult to say precisely just where we stand. The quotation above reflects the "cutting edge"; the one that follows reflects where American society has been and where most American youth probably still are:

. . . The "date" starts as an invitation from a young man to a girl for an evening's public entertainment, typically at his expense. . . . The entertainment offered depends upon the young man's means and aspirations, and the locality; . . . The male (the "escort") should call for the girl in a car (unless he be particularly young or poor) and should take her back in the car. . . .

"Showing the girl a good time" is the essential background for a "date," but it is not its object, as far as the man is concerned; its object is to get the girl to prove that he is worthy of love, and therefore a success. In some cases superior efficiency in dancing will elicit the necessary signs of approval; but typically, and not unexpectedly, they are elicited by talk. . . .

Since, on first "dates" the pair are normally comparative strangers to one another, a certain amount of autobiography is necessary in the hopes of establishing some common interest or experience, at the least to prove that one is worthy of the other's attention. These autobiographies, however, differ at most in emphasis, in tone of voice, from those which should accompany any American meeting between strangers. What distinguishes the "date" from other conversation is a mixture of persiflage, flattery, wit and love-making which was formerly called a "line" but which each generation dubs with a new name.

The "line" is an individual variation of a commonly accepted pattern which is considered to be representative of a facet of a man's personality. Most men are articulately self-conscious about their "lines" and can describe them with ease; they are constantly practiced and improved with ever differing partners. The object of the "line" is to entertain, amuse, and captivate the girl, but there is no deep emotional involvement; it is a game of skill.

The girl's skill consists in parrying the "line" without discouraging her partner or becoming emotionally involved herself. To the extent that she falls for the "line" she is a loser in this intricate game; but if she discourages her partner so much that he does not request a subsequent "date" in the near future she is equally a loser. To remain the winner, she must make the nicest discriminations between yielding and rigidity.

The man scores to the extent that he is able to get more favors from the girl than his rivals, real or supposed, would be able to do. [2]

[1] Penelope McMullan, "Is the Date Becoming Extinct on the Teen Scene?" *Newsday*, March 7, 1971. Copyright 1971, Newsday, Inc. Reprinted by permission.

[2] Geoffrey Gorer, *The American People: A Study in National Character*, New York: W. W. Norton and Company, 1948, pp. 114-17.

THE analysis of American dating patterns is complicated by two different things. First is the fact of change, reflected in the conflict between the two patterns described above. Second is the fact that dating and courtship behavior operate on different levels: there is conscious, goal-directed behavior about which the participants display considerable awareness; there are, also, patterns of behavior that serve functions which often go unrecognized.

DATING

Dating may well be a uniquely American contribution to the total range of marital and family behavior. In societies where parents participate extensively in the selection of marriage partners, dating, of course, is irrelevant. Dating developed spontaneously, in the United States, as an accompaniment of the process of young people selecting their own marriage partners, and, as other societies move toward a system of free mate selection, dating tends to spread among them too.

In the United States, dating as we know it probably emerged after World War I among college students and other young adults. Its specific causes cannot be isolated, but it was linked with the general process of the emancipation of women and the extension of coeducation. Both of these were accompaniments of urbanization, the emancipation of youth from direct parental control, rising standards of living, and increased leisure time. By the 1930's, dating was beginning to move downward into the high schools and was firmly established there before World War II. By the early 1940's, junior-high-school-level dating was common.

AGE AT WHICH DATING BEGINS

Parents have not always viewed dating without alarm. Even among college-age youth it has been viewed widely as a risky business, leading both to premature involvement and to unwise marriages. As the age at which dating begins moved downward, parental concern increased. Occasional stories of dating among children in elementary school, of sophisticated parties arranged by parents, and other evidences of premature growing-up led to irresponsible speculation whether there would be any end to it. Let us examine the research on when dating begins.

The beginning of dating often is not clear-cut, as for example, the onset of menstruation or graduation from junior high school; nor does it appear to be particularly related to either one. Children of five may have "girl friends" or "boy friends," indicating very early imitation of their elders. Similarly, grade-school youth may have very occasional "dates" to attend a movie or party together. To claim that dating is general at this level or that the dates of ten-year-olds have the same significance as those of sixteen-year-olds, however, is absurd. In all likelihood, many youngsters drift into a pattern of dating over a period of time, with the dates coming more and more to approximate the adult model as time goes on.

The age of earliest dating has been reported from a number of studies. Hollingshead, in a study of a midwestern community, reported that the most adventurous youngsters began to date at age 12, and that 15 per cent of the boys and 20 per cent of the girls had begun to date by age 13.[3] In Mason City, Iowa, Cameron and Kenkel found that high-school seniors had begun to date at anywhere from 11 to 18 years of age.[4] Among the earliest ages reported are those by Broderick and Fowler who found approximately 45 per cent of 10- and 11-year-old boys and 36 per cent of 10- and 11-year-old girls in one southern city already to have had at least one date.[5] At the present time it is suspected that there may be regional differences in the time at which dating begins, with southern youngsters beginning earlier than those in other sections of the country. However, the differences found may also be due to differences in the definition of what constitutes a first date.

The most definitive data on average ages at which dating begins have been provided by Lowrie, some of whose data are presented in Table 1. Lowrie collected data from 1729 juniors and seniors in high school and from two samples of college students. As Table 1 shows, the median age at first dating ranged from 14.1 to 14.9 among the high-school students, and from 14.7 to 15.7 among the college students. The higher beginning ages for college students may be accounted for in at least two ways. First, those students who eventually are headed for college may literally begin dating later than does the general population. Second, and more likely explanation, is that the college students were older at the time of reporting. Not all young people have begun to date by even age 18. Consequently, a population age 18 and under will yield lower average ages at first date than will a population age 21 and under.

[3] August B. Hollingshead, Elmtown's Youth, New York: John Wiley and Sons, 1949, pp. 224–5.

[4] William J. Cameron and William F. Kenkel, "High School Dating: A Study in Variation," Marriage and Family Living 22 (Feb. 1960), pp. 74–6.

[5] Carlfred B. Broderick and Stanley E. Fowler, "New Patterns of Relationships Between the Sexes Among Preadolescents," Marriage and Family Living 23 (Feb. 1961), p. 29. See also, Alan E. Bayer, "Early Dating and Early Marriage," Journal of Marriage and the Family 30 (Nov. 1968), pp. 628–32; and Carlfred B. Broderick and George P. Rowe, "A Scale of Preadolescent Heterosexual Development," Journal of Marriage and the Family 30 (Feb. 1968), pp. 97–101.

TABLE 1. *Median Ages at First Date, by Sex and Present Age, High School and College Samples.*

PRESENT AGE	BOYS		GIRLS	
	Number of cases	Median age	Number of cases	Median age
Sample I—High Schools				
16	204	14.12	285	14.34
17	357	14.52	495	14.58
18	209	14.88	179	14.65
Total	770		959	
Sample II—University in 1948				
18	157	15.34	261	15.00
19	195	15.35	288	15.23
20	202	15.55	206	15.37
21	279	15.66	154	15.39
Total	833		909	
Sample III—University in 1951				
18	193	15.16	218	14.69
19	298	15.10	260	14.91
20	213	15.21	190	14.90
21	166	15.13	148	14.85
Total	870		816	

Source: Adapted from Samuel H. Lowrie, "Sex Differences and Age of Initial Dating," *Social Forces* 30 (May 1952), p. 457.

Two general conclusions may be drawn from the data in Table 1. First, there appears to be no significant difference between boys and girls in the average age at which dating begins. Most persons of both sexes begin to date somewhere between their fourteenth and sixteenth birthdays. Second, the period of dating for most young people of both sexes is relatively long. Girls marry, on the average, at just over 20 years of age and boys marry, on the average, at just under 23 years of age. This means that the average period of dating is from about six to eight years. There is considerable variation in dating patterns over this time span.

NORMS GOVERNING EARLY DATING

The whole problem of the nature of the norms that regulate dating is exceedingly complex. This is true for at least two reasons. First is the fact that there are apparent differences between the way in which dating is viewed by parents and youth and differences between what youth say and what they do.

When asked, young people usually maintain that their dating values are essentially congruent with those of their parents; they view dating as an opportunity to learn to interact constructively with members of the opposite sex. Yet, boys persist in pursuing girls of whom their parents disapprove and, indeed, of whom they disapprove themselves. The sexual component in this behavior is evident in the male preoccupation with "scoring." There also are elements of defiance of the parental standards which suggest that the adolescent revolt manifests itself partly in dating behavior. Similarly, girls date boys whom they know at the time to be poor choices, but whom they find exciting and irresistible.

. . ."Dates" are public. The greater part of them . . . take place in public places; and even if there is not a witness for the final portion, as there is in "double dates," there is little expectation that what transpires will be secret. Though distorted by a certain amount of boasting, detailed accounts of past dates are among the most popular subjects of conversation with people of one's own sex and generation. As with the child recounting his triumphs in the play group or at school, it is a proper method of gaining other people's respect and admiration. . . .

—Geoffrey Gorer, *The American People: A Study in National Character*, New York: W. W. Norton and Company, 1948, pp. 118–19.

Part of the explanation for these inconsistencies is to be found in the fact that dating—even early dating—serves another, usually unstated, function for both boys and girls. It not only serves to acquaint them with members of the opposite sex, but it also provides an arena of competition within which both boys and girls compete for status—largely within their own sex group.

Young people compete not only for grades in school and for personal possessions; they also compete for success with the opposite sex. Here the norms of the peer group diverge markedly from the explicit norms propounded by parents. Boys can acquire status by dating the prettiest, most popular, most wholesome girl in the class but, among the boys, they may acquire more satisfying status by dating the girls who like to "neck" and with whom they can "make it."

Girls acquire status among the other girls by being sought after. Again, they are successful when they date the outstanding boys in the class. But the implicit youth norms state that one real test of a girl's competence is her ability to date "dangerous" boys and show that she can handle them.

Neither the girls nor the boys may be fully conscious of what they are doing. Indeed, the fact that such behavior is contrary to the formal, stated norms of the society almost requires that the fulfillment of these functions go unrecognized. Heaven knows that the parents are often confused by such apparently contradictory behavior. And to the extent to which they can understand it— by reference to their own earlier behavior—they may be even more alarmed by it. The parents' reactions and the young people's awareness both are largely irrelevant to the operation of these teen-age norms. Boys and girls go blithely on competing and receiving the rewards of the competition from their peers.

Some further insight into the functions served by early dating may be gained through analysis of the feelings that boys and girls have concerning themselves and their adequacy as dates. A number of studies show that a large proportion of each sex believe themselves to be shy, self-conscious, ill at ease, and somewhat inadequate in dating situations. In studies conducted between 1949 and 1968, the percentages of people having such feelings ranged from 22 per cent to 66 per cent among boys, and from 28 per cent to 66 per cent among girls.[6] Breed queried high-school students in a southern city to learn that about two-thirds of both boys and girls from all social class levels were "pretty scared" on their first real dates.

These anxieties concerning dating probably reflect several different factors. First, but not necessarily most important, is the newness of the dating situation and the fact that most boys and girls know that they lack the skills desired in dating partners. Second, it seems likely that both sexes experience some generalized anxiety over whether they can ever compete with older peers, siblings, and parents. Finally the direct competition for status with one's own age and sex mates makes the achievement of success in dating very important; the more important the outcome, the higher the level of anxiety generated.

The second factor that complicates analysis of the norms which govern

[6] Warren Breed, "Sex, Class and Socialization in Dating," *Marriage and Family Living* 18 (May 1956), p. 144; Carlfred B. Broderick, and Jean Weaver, "The Perceptual Context of Boy-Girl Communication," *Journal of Marriage and the Family* 30 (Nov. 1968), pp. 618–27; John R. Crist, "High School Dating as a Behavior System," *Marriage and Family Living* 15 (Feb. 1953), p. 25; and M. J. Williams, "Personal and Family Problems of High School Youth and Their Bearing Upon Family Education Needs," *Social Forces* 27 (March 1949), pp. 279–85.

dating is the fact that it covers such a long span in the social-emotional development of the individual and that it includes everything from the party date of budding teenagers to the association of couples who are about to be married. It is folly to think that precisely the same norms could operate in such different situations.

One way to approach the problem is to deal, first, with some of the salient norms governing dating early in adolescence [7] and then proceed to some of the modifications that appear as couples become older. That is the strategy which we shall follow. We have already looked at some of the unstated teen-age norms that structure dating in terms of competition for status. Let us now examine the formal, explicit norms.

A number of studies, over the years, have inquired into what characteristics young people look for in dating partners. [8] By and large, the findings of the various studies have been consistent with one another. One of the most recent efforts, and one that repeated an earlier study, queried a carefully drawn national sample of 2000 high-school boys and girls. Part of the results of that study are reproduced in Table 2.

These researchers did not actually ask what traits young people sought in dating partners but asked, instead, what traits they thought desirable in a mate. Since these were high school students, it seems reasonable to assume that their referents were as much dating partners as marriage partners.

Table 2 shows that the formal explicit norms used by teenagers are very much in accord with those used by their parents. Seven traits were judged to be very desirable by at least four out of five of the teenagers: is dependable, can be trusted; is considerate of me and others; takes pride in personal appearance and manners; shows affection; acts own age, is not childish; desires normal family life with children; and has a pleasant disposition. These qualities are quite similar to those which college students, several years older, indicate that they look for in dating and marital partners. [9]

Thus we must conclude that the norms governing early dating are multiple

[7] For a description of the "going steady" pattern in high school, see Thomas Poffenberger, "Going Steady in High School," in Ruth S. Cavan, *Marriage and the Family in the Modern World: A Book of Readings*, New York: Thomas Y. Crowell Company, 1965, pp. 112–24.

[8] Harold T. Christensen, op. cit., pp. 580–86; Harold T. Christensen, *Marriage Analysis*, New York: The Ronald Press Company, 1958, pp. 239–43; John R. Crist, op. cit. pp. 23–8; Paul H. Landis, "Research on Teen-Age Dating," *Marriage and Family Living* 22 (Aug. 1960), pp. 266–7; Samuel H. Lowrie, "Dating Theories and Student Responses," *American Sociological Review* 16 (June 1951), pp. 334–40.

[9] Lester E. Hewitt, "Student Perceptions of Traits Desired in Themselves as Dating and Marriage Partners," *Marriage and Family Living* 20 (Nov. 1958), pp. 344–9.

TABLE 2. *Percentage of Two Thousand High School Students' Rating Traits as Being Desirable in a Future Mate, 1961.*

TRAIT	VERY DESIRABLE	SOME DESIRABILITY	NOT IMPORTANT
1. Dependable, trustworthy	94%	3%	0%
2. Considerate of me and others	90	7	0
3. Takes pride in own appearance	89	8	0
4. Shows affection	85	13	0
5. Desires normal family life	82	13	2
6. Acts own age	82	16	1
7. Pleasant disposition	81	17	0
8. Clean in speech and action	77	18	1
9. Knows how to budget	69	25	2
10. Approved by my parents	65	25	6
11. Mixes well socially	55	39	3
12. Independent of parents	55	29	8
13. Has a job	52	10	26
14. Does not use liquor	49	26	14
15. Ideals like mine	49	44	3
16. Interests like mine	48	47	3
17. Knows how to cook, etc.	46	28	22
18. Popular with others	44	48	7
19. As intelligent as I	35	39	21
20. Physically attractive	31	56	11
21. Does not use tobacco	31	20	41
22. Started on career	26	32	29

Source: Adapted from R. D. Franklin and H. H. Remmers, "Youth's Attitudes Toward Courtship and Marriage," Poll No. 62, *The Purdue Opinion Panel*, Purdue University, April 1961, p. 2.

and conflicting. The formal, explicit norms reflect a conscious awareness of the relationship between early dating, later pairing-off, and marriage. Young people begin early to decide what traits they desire in marriage partners and to seek those qualities in the persons whom they date. At the same time, many young people are more or less caught up in the struggle for status and often unwittingly behave in ways that are quite inconsistent with their acknowledged goals of mate selection. The extent of this involvement probably varies from person to person, within the same person from time to time, and by such larger variables as dating desirability and social class. More will be said of this later.

DATING AND EMOTIONAL INVOLVEMENT

The route whereby students move from the tentative, uncommitted dating of the high-school period on into falling in love and getting married is both variable and complex. Some young people, for example, shortcut the whole process and marry while they are still of high-school age. The special factors operating in these very young marriages will be analyzed in a later chapter.

For the majority of both boys and girls, dating is a lengthy process which goes through several stages such as casual dating, uncommitted dating, favorite date, going steady, being pinned, and being engaged.[10] The number and sequence of stages varies from group to group and from time to time. Whatever the sequence of formal stages, however, they perhaps conceal as much as they illuminate how couples pair off actually to approach marriage. The purpose of this section is to attempt to throw some light on how this happens. To do this, we will begin with the most comprehensive and explicit—but controversial—theory of dating and courtship yet to appear in American sociology.

Waller's Theory of Dating and Courtship. Willard Waller's analyses of dating and courtship in American society are some 35 years old.[11] They were developed while he was on the staff at Pennsylvania State University, and dealt specifically with these phenomena as he observed them on the college campus. That Waller was a most insightful observer is unquestionable. Unfortunately, social research techniques were not so highly developed in the 1930's as they are today and Waller's original formulations were not carefully documented. People have been attempting to test and document his notions ever since.

Waller made, first of all, a conceptual distinction between dating and courtship. Dating, he said, allows for a period of dalliance and experimentation between the sexes. Couples are encouraged to associate under all of the conditions which, in other times and places, might lead directly into marriage. The norms governing dating, however, define it as an end in itself. Fun, rather than marriage, is the intended outcome.

Prominent in the folkways of dating is the seeking of what Waller called "thrills," physiological stimulation and the release of tension. Circumstances

---

[10] For useful analyses of the movement of high-school students through these stages, see Jerold S. Heiss, "Variations in Courtship Progress Among High School Students," *Marriage and Family Living* 22 (May 1960), pp. 165–70; Robert D. Herman, "The 'Going Steady' Complex: A Re-Examination," *Marriage and Family Living* 17 (Feb. 1955), pp. 36–40; Charles W. Hobart, "Emancipation from Parents and Courtship in Adolescents," *Pacific Sociological Review* 1 (Spring 1958), pp. 25–9; and E. A. Smith, *American Youth Culture: Group Life in Teenage Society*, New York: The Free Press of Glencoe, 1962; and James S. Wittman, Jr., "Dating Patterns of Rural and Urban Kentucky Teenagers," *The Family Coordinator* 20 (Jan. 1971), pp. 63–6.

[11] Willard Waller, "The Rating and Dating Complex," *American Sociological Review* 2 (Oct. 1937), pp. 727–34.

conducive to thrill-seeking include dancing, petting, necking, the automobile, and the amusement park. To these sources listed by Waller might be added drinking and attending the movies. A glance at the composition of most movie audiences will reveal a disproportionate number of dating couples engaging in hand holding and various forms of light necking. These functions of the movies become most explicit in some larger cities where the management thoughtfully has removed the arms between some pairs of seats so that young people may neck without cracking their ribs; and in the outdoor movie for which sobriquets such as "passion pit" require no explanation.

The thrills sought in dating are alleged to vary somewhat between the sexes. Beyond the general excitement widely sought by the young, men are inclined to seek thrills in the pleasures of sex. Women at this age are less often interested in sex for its own sake, and have been taught for most of their lives that they must resist involvement in it. Women, on the other hand, often are intensely interested in dating and in other rewards which dating brings them.

What frequently develops in dating situations is a more or less explicit bargaining relationship. The man provides the woman with satisfactions she wants from dating in the expectation that she will reward him with equivalent necking and petting on the way home.[12]

What women want from dating most often is to advance themselves in the competition for status with other girls and to form relationships with more desirable men. The achievement of these aims requires the man to spend money. He really needs an automobile if he is to take the girl to the currently fashionable dating places and if he is to take her there in a fashion that will attract the desired attention. Both the car and the dating activities cost money; and the most desirable dating activities usually cost the most money. Although to make it explicit would, in the nature of things, call forth a stout denial from both parties, the implicit assumption is that the more money the man spends (the better time he shows the girl) the more disposed the girl should be to show him affection later on.

Implicit in this kind of bargaining relationship is a certain amount of, at least latent, antagonism between the dating partners. Each seeks the best bargain which he can get and—to a degree—each distrusts the other. This

---

[12] That college students are sometimes quite aware of the nature of this bargaining relationship was well illustrated to the present author a few years ago when he was teaching at a large state university where it was common for students to take their noon meal at restaurants around the campus. Following a class discussion of Waller's theory of dating, one girl volunteered the information that she and her roommate were regularly asked for luncheon dates. They had discovered, she said, that if they did not accept more than three luncheon dates with the same boys "they didn't have to pay off!"

antagonism is illustrated by some of the characteristic stereotypes which each sex holds of the other. Thus, women often liken men to the octopus—all arms and hands seeking to intrude and overwhelm. In turn, men stereotype women as gold diggers—selfish, grasping creatures interested only in the amount of money that they can induce their dates to spend on them. These stereotypes lurk below the surface of many relationships and threaten to come out whenever either partner gets the worst of the bargain.

According to Waller, the bargaining works out equitably in a great many cases and becomes the basis for a series of commitments to be made that will transform dating into courtship and eventually lead to marriage. Often too, however, the bargaining is not equal and leads to exploitation of one partner by the other.

If the man has more bargaining power than his date he is, over a period of time, in a position to exploit her sexually. He demands increased necking and petting; the girl can either acquiesce or give up the relationship. Similarly, if the girl has superior bargaining power she can induce her date to take her wherever she wants to go whenever she wants to go and spend whatever money is necessary. Moreover, she is relatively free to concentrate on attracting men who are more desirable than her present dating partner.

Waller formalized the analysis of this competitive-exploitative dating pattern into what he called the "rating and dating complex." It is important to state, at the outset, that Waller's formulation of the rating and dating complex was primarily based upon observation of dating patterns at one university during the 1930's. That university at that time had a very high sex ratio—about six men to each woman—and, according to Waller, dating centered around campus fraternities. Waller said, "Dating is almost exclusively the privilege of fraternity men. . . ." [13] Whether Waller was correct in this, we cannot know. But it does seem apparent that Waller's analysis was confined largely to the dating patterns of this particular group.

The rating and dating complex describes the classification of students according to their desirability as dating partners, the pairing-off among them, and the resulting patterns of interaction that occur on dates. The desirability of men as dating partners is determined by such things as fraternity membership, the possession of a car, adequate spending money, being a good dancer, dressing well, and being smooth in manners and appearance. Fraternity men rank higher than nonfraternity men, and the fraternities themselves carry different amounts of status, with some fraternities ranking higher than others. Similarly, having access to an automobile is better than not having access to

[13] Waller, op. cit. p. 730.

one. Owning a new car is better than owning an old one, and a new sports car is better yet. The more the appearance and manner of the man approximate the campus ideal, the higher his status; and the more money at his disposal, the more successfully he can compete.

The traits establishing the desirability of women as dating partners are similar. Sorority membership helps, and it is better to be a member of a top sorority than of a lower ranked one. Appearance and physical beauty are more important for women than for men; the prettier and more shapely the girl, the more desirable she is as a dating partner. She, too, should be a good dresser and be able to dance well. Perhaps most important of all for women is their popularity as dates. Men compete to date the girls whom other men want to date.

One further characteristic is extremely important for both sexes. This is the possession of a good "line," the pattern of verbal banter referred to earlier in this chapter. While Geoffrey Gorer stressed the use of the "line" by the man, it appears that one of the striking features of dating interaction is the use of words by both partners to flatter, tease, and heighten the interest of the other. While the man may be expected to be the more aggressive partner, the woman, too, uses a mixture of compliments, flattery, sarcasm, and so on, to keep her partner off balance—to prevent him from knowing what her true feelings toward him are and whether she wishes to continue the relationship.[14] Each partner works to induce the other to become emotionally involved without himself becoming involved in any way. The better one's line, the higher he ranks on the dating desirability scale.

"Rating" in dating is not altogether an individual matter. Rather, it appears that there exists an informal hierarchy on the campus analogous to the social class system in the larger society. Some people by virtue of a combination of characteristics—membership in a top fraternity, lots of money, an automobile, smooth manner and dress, and a good line—rank at the very top of the dating desirability scale. Waller placed such men (and women) in a hypothetical Class A. Somewhat farther down the scale, there is a Class B, and then a Class C, Class D, and so on. At the bottom of the scale would be found those people without significant group memberships, without financial resources, and who are socially and physically unattractive.

---

[14] Assuming that the date is between people who rank about equally in other aspects of the rating and dating complex, this use of the "line" may be the chief criterion used by each partner to evaluate the other. When a young man or woman later reports to peers that the date was a "drag," or otherwise unsatisfactory, what he or she often means is that the partner was not sufficiently facile in the use of the line. A good date, on the other hand, is one whose line presents a challenge.

How many classes there are probably varies with place and time and even with one's purpose in defining them. According to Waller, however, students at Penn State in the 1930's were extremely conscious of social distinctions and of their own positions in the social hierarchy. It seems, to the present author at least, that an astute observer can see manifestations of a similar system on many campuses today.

There is a tendency for persons at each level in the hierarchy to have most of their dating experiences with members of the opposite sex whose dating desirability is comparable to their own. Thus members of certain fraternities confine most of their dating to certain sororities; the highest ranked fraternity and sorority members seek one another's company, the middle ranked Greeks associate together, and the lowest ranked groups interact by default, if not by design.[15] Similarly, people who live in residence halls may tend to date other residence-hall residents, town boys may tend to date town girls, and so on.

The rating and dating system functions most smoothly, according to Waller, when people do date at their own levels in the hierarchy. In this instance, the dating partners are likely to have approximately equal bargaining power, reducing the probability that either partner will be in a position systematically to exploit the other. Since they have equal bargaining power, each commitment to the relationship made by one partner is contingent upon a compensating commitment made by the other partner, and the relationship progresses relatively rapidly toward marriage.

There are dysfunctional aspects of the system even when people date at the same level. This dysfunctionality is felt most by people who rank low in the rating and dating complex. Being aware of their low status, and wishing for higher status, both some men and some women may prefer not to date at all rather than to have to date at levels where they can compete successfully. Undoubtedly there are many men and women who sit at home night after night because they are unwilling to accept their places in the system.

Not all dating, of course, takes place within levels of the hierarchy; occasionally people date up or down in the system. When they do, the results may be either functional, dysfunctional, or both. The person who dates downward in the hierarchy may suffer some loss of prestige for so doing but he also places himself in a better competitive position *vis-à-vis* his dating partner. Thus, the high-status male who dates a lower ranking woman is in a position to demand more sexual favors from her. If she wishes to continue the relationship, she must accede to his demands. In the same way, a high-status woman

---

[15] For an excellent account of the role of the sorority as an agent in mate selection, see John F. Scott, "The American College Sorority: Its Role in Class and Ethnic Endogamy," *American Sociological Review* 30 (Aug. 1965), pp. 514–27.

who dates a lower-status man is relieved of some of the obligation to reciprocate with necking and petting that she might otherwise feel. She can use her escort quite manipulatively to take her places while she works to establish a favorable relationship with a higher-status man.

In brief, dating outside one's own level in the rating and dating complex is conducive to exploitation of the lower-status partner. Waller formalized this idea according to what he termed the "principle of least interest." [16] The principle of least interest holds that control in a relationship redounds to the person who has the least interest in continuing the relationship. Since he has less to lose by discontinuing the relationship, he can make demands upon the other partner and insist that they be met. The partner who has more to lose by discontinuing the relationship often has no choice but to yield.

The lower-status partner who is exploited in a relationship may suffer personality damage as a result. Sooner or later he must face up to the fact that he is being exploited and revise his self-concept downward. Even if he chooses to break the relationship rather than to continue to submit to exploitation, he cannot escape the definition that he was used by the other partner.[17] It seems likely that some proportion of the "man-haters" or "woman-haters" on any campus are people who have reacted to earlier exploitation in dating by reacting defensively and thus protecting themselves against possible exploitation in the future. Their very defensiveness testifies to the existence of a low self-concept and also operates effectively to deny them the positive rewards of dating.

There is one respect in which dating outside of one's own level may prove quite functional for the individual and for the society at large. Such cross-class dating opens an avenue of upward social mobility to lower-status girls. Although the data will not be presented now, it appears that men date lower-

[16] See also James K. Skipper, Jr., and Gilbert Nass, "Dating Behavior: A Framework for Analysis and an Illustration," *Journal of Marriage and the Family* 28 (Nov. 1966), pp. 412–20.

[17] The patterns typically used by the sexes, in confronting the fact of exploitation, differ and reflect the different operation of the masculine and feminine subcultures. The man who has to face the fact that his date has been using him is more likely to go back to his peer group and share his anguish with them. His friends are likely to identify with his plight, to sympathize with him, and, in the process, to afford him considerable catharsis. He feels better for having gotten it off his chest, in finding that his buddies have had similar experiences, and in having re-established solidarity with them. His buddies, in addition to sharing his contempt for the girl, may even decide that it is their collective obligation to revenge themselves upon her.

In contrast, the girl who has been sexually exploited in a dating relationship is less often free to seek the support of her girl friends. The feminine subculture is not likely to place the blame on the boy who did the exploiting, but upon the girl who permitted it. Thus, the girl is even denied the group support which the boy has.

status women—more often than women date lower-status men—for the sexual advantages that accrue to them in such relationships. Certainly the phenomenon of college men dating town girls for this purpose is well known around many campuses.

Upon first glance, it appears that the advantages are all on the side of the male; and it is true that a great deal of sexual exploitation takes place. However, lower-status girls may more or less consciously risk such exploitation in the hope that the men will become emotionally involved and that the relationships may lead to marriage. Since the social class placement and style of life of the couple are determined largely through the man, the girl has a great deal to gain in such relationships. It is not entirely unknown, of course, for girls deliberately to become pregnant in order to make sure that the relationship leads to marriage.

In the society at large, such cross-class dating may do much to help preserve the fluidity of the social class system. If the rating and dating complex served perfectly to restrict dating to persons of the same class level, it would work to make class lines more rigid and to restrict opportunities for upward mobility. As it is, the risk of exploitation may be weighed against the chance of marrying into a higher class level.

Waller's analysis of dating and his analysis of emotional involvement are not separable. Courtship, he said, grows out of dating as one or both partners succumb to the temptation to become emotionally involved. The dating game, it will be recalled, calls for each partner to titillate the other's emotions but for both partners to resist involvement. Many relationships—particularly of younger persons—may remain at this level for some time. Each partner, however, is, to some degree, pretending greater involvement than he or she actually feels. Especially the man attempts to convince the woman that he has fallen in love with her and, by this pretense, invites her to reciprocate. Under these circumstances, either partner may actually become involved and, when he does, a different pattern of interaction ensues.

Emotional involvement tends to lead the other partner, whether deliberately or not, into being somewhat exploitative. This is consistent with the principle of least interest—he who is least interested in continuing the relation tends to control it. In the ideal situation, perhaps, the same process is going on in both partners at the same time; only neither one knows it. The artificiality of the "line" results in both partners' being kept unsure of the nature of the other's true feelings. They continue in this fashion for a while, with each fearing that he is being exploited and hoping that he is not. Tension builds between them until suddenly it comes out in a "lovers' quarrel," the essence of which is the open accusation of exploitation and the function of which is to redefine the relationship at a new level.

It should not be amiss here to point out that the young men and women who are caught up in this pattern of intrigue are the same people who consciously seek trustworthiness, consideration, dependability, and so on, in their marriage partners. When either the young man or woman is confronted with accusations of exploitation, he or she is likely to deny—to himself as well as to the partner—that such is the case. In lovers' quarrels, the cards probably are stacked in favor of both partners' making further avowals of love and serious intent.[18]

With the resolution of this crisis, each partner gains security in the relationship, and the intimacy—emotional and physical—between them increases. The relationship moves along on a fairly even keel for a while until one or both partners again become fearful of the extent of the other's involvement. Another quarrel then ensues, the relationship is redefined at a deeper level of involvement, and so on and on until it reaches the culmination of marriage. Either partner may arrive at marriage without knowing quite how he got there or whether, indeed, he intended that this should be the outcome.

Waller was not quite clear whether he believed that serious courtship was different in kind from the dalliance relationships of dating or whether he believed that the latter tends to be transformed into the former. Probably, he conceived of dating as always tending to become transformed into courtship with the development of emotional involvement. He indicated that while courtship has a marked directional trend, it can be arrested on any level or the relationship may be broken. Ordinarily, however, once the process of involvement and commitment is under way, the couple cannot return to an earlier level of involvement. In this sense, the process is irreversible.

Central to understanding of Waller's analysis of courtship is the concept of "idealization." He believed that each of the partners tends to idealize the other; that under the influence of the "line," each partner tends to create an

---

[18] An interesting question here is the degree to which the involvement leads to the quarrel which then only makes the involvement a matter of record, and the degree to which the involvement actually grows out of the quarrel and the subsequent avowal of love. It is not difficult to conceive of a situation, for example, in which the man actually has been exploiting the girl sexually. In accord with the norms of the masculine subculture, he may be somewhat aware of what he is doing. In accord with the norms of family, church, and community, however, he may prefer to avoid being too conscious of this exploitation. When the girl confronts him, in a lovers' quarrel, with her suspicions that he has been using her, what she really does is to reinforce the family and community norms. The surprised young man, in this situation, can hardly do other than to deny exploitation and to profess love. Later on, perhaps as he is returning home after the date, he may think to himself, "You know, until tonight, I never realized that I loved her." Or, if he is a bit more sophisticated, he may wonder, "I wonder if I really do love her?" If this analysis is correct, it may help to explain the lingering feelings of doubt that many young men and women have as they approach marriage.

idealized image of the other as he would like him to be. The man, already idealizing the woman, presents to her only that portion of his personality which is consistent with his idealized image of her. She, in turn, idealizes him and behaves toward him very selectively. Each reinforces the other's lack of objectivity and they tend to create a private world of their own. Here emerges whatever truth there is in the cliché that "love is blind." Waller describes love as the process of sentiment formation overcoming objectivity. The couple's absorption in one another becomes an *egoisme à deux* that borders upon *folie à deux*. Outsiders may see more clearly than the couple involved but, assuming that the relationship is a socially acceptable one, they ordinarily throw their support behind the relationship by treating them as a couple and helping to move them inexorably toward marriage.

mutual attraction, good health, and desire for home life and children in their

---

In some ways young love is far more self-centered than was the older generation's insistence on having the partner live up to one's own romantic fantasies. There is so much emphasis on experiencing the sensations induced in oneself by the partner, that the partner ends up being an accessory rather than an agent. Nowhere is this more apparent than in the dances of the young today, where each person essentially dances with himself and it often is hard to see who is dancing with whom. . . .

What this means is also apparent in the songs popular when contemporary parents were adolescents and in the songs of the youth of today. The lyrics from yesteryear tend to exult on what lovers make each other feel, what they do to each other. The lyrics of today refer to being and experiencing while being in the presence or absence of the beloved one, but the emphasis is on the person's own needs rather than on his reactions. . . .

—Povl W. Toussieng, "New Sexual Attitudes of Young People," *Sexual Behavior* (September, 1971), p. 51.

Empirical Testing of Waller's Theory. If one mark of a useful theory is its motivating others to test it, then Waller's theory of dating and courtship has been useful indeed. A long series of studies from the early 1940's right up to the present day has sought directly and indirectly to test Waller's ideas. Hill published an analysis of data collected from students at the University of Wisconsin which showed that both men and women sought such universally approved qualities as dependability, emotional maturity, pleasing disposition, mutual attraction, good health, and desire for home life and children in their future mates.[19] Several other studies showed that college students espouse norms closer to those earlier reported among high-school youth than to the competitive materialistic norms reported by Waller.[20] Himes got similar results in a study of black students.[21]

At least three studies sought to test Waller's theory directly. Christensen at Purdue,[22] Smih at Penn State,[23] and Blood at the University of Michigan[24] all did questionnaire studies in which students picked from preconstructed lists those traits which they looked for in dating and marital partners. All three researchers reported that their findings failed to bear out Waller's thesis.

Smith reported that students at Penn State, 15 years after Waller's study, were still aware of a rating and dating complex but that many of the materialistic qualities that afforded prestige earlier were no longer effective. The sex ratio had dropped in the interim and there appeared to be less exploitation. Students particularly did not like to admit that group pressures might take precedence over individual likes or dislikes. Finally, Smith pointed out that most students did not distinguish dating from courtship and engagement. The rating and dating complex did appear to be more operative during the precourtship period than after.

Blood found that the items listed in Waller's rating and dating complex were not the most generally supported criteria for dating popularity at the University of Michigan in the early 1950's. Instead, he found that men and women, Greeks and non-Greeks, and underclassmen as well as upperclassmen valued the date's being pleasant and cheerful, having a sense of humor, being a good sport, being natural, being considerate, and being neat in appearance.

[19] Reuben Hill, "Campus Norms in Mate Selection," *Journal of Home Economics* 37 (Nov. 1945), pp. 554–8; John W. Hudson, and Lura F. Henze, "Campus Values in Mate Selection: A Replication," *Journal of Marriage and the Family* 31 (Nov. 1969), pp. 772–5; and Marvin R. Koller, "Some Changes in Courtship Behavior in Three Generations of Ohio Women," *American Sociological Review* 16 (June 1951), pp. 366–70.

[20] Harold T. Christensen, *Marriage Analysis*, New York: The Ronald Press Company, 1958, p. 260; Eleanor Smith and J. H. G. Monane, "Courtship Values in a Youth Sample," *American Sociological Review* 18 (Dec. 1953), pp. 635–40; Marvin B. Sussman, and H. C. Yeager, Jr., "Mate Selection Among Negro and White College Students," *Sociology and Social Research* 35 (Sept.-Oct. 1950), pp. 46–9.

[21] Joseph S. Himes, Jr., "Mate Selection Among Negro College Students," *Sociology and Social Research* 33 (Jan.-Feb. 1949), pp. 204–11.

[22] *Marriage Analysis*, pp. 240–41, 258–63.

[23] William M. Smith, Jr., "Rating and Dating: A Restudy," *Marriage and Family Living* 14 (Nov. 1952), pp. 312–17.

[24] Robert O. Blood, Jr., "A Retest of Waller's Rating Complex," *Marriage and Family Living* 17 (Feb. 1955), pp. 41–7.

Blood also reported, however, that there is considerable diversity in campus values on dating. Women students were inconsistent, for example, in saying that for the male to own a car, be a fraternity member, and be prominent in activities were important to other women on campus but not to them.[25] Similarly, "willingness to neck" was "seen as part of the male rating complex by more than twice as many men as in the expressed preferences of the women." However, 71 per cent of the women believed that willingness to neck was conducive to dating popularity.

Especially interesting, for our purposes, is Blood's analysis of the difference in dating preferences between Greek and independent students on the campus. A portion of his results is shown in Table 3. This table shows six items that are quite similar to the original items in Waller's rating and dating complex and which receive significantly more support from Greeks than from independents. Blood found that there was a "free-floating" set of values on the campus that was believed to be part of a general campus scale of values by a larger proportion of students than subscribed to them in their actual dating behavior. This free-floating complex was made up largely of Waller-type items and more frequently sanctioned by Greeks than by independents. He states: "This means that the 'free-floating Waller complex' is not simply a hangover from the past but rather a reflection of the contemporary dating behavior of the most conspicuous organized groups on campus—the social fraternities and sororities. In this sense, the Waller complex is not floating in thin air but is reinforced by the actual dating patterns of the Greek members of the student body." [26]

Thus, the refutations by Blood and Smith of Waller's competitive-materialistic rating and dating complex appear to show that our basic thesis of there being multiple sets of norms governing dating is well founded. In this case, the distinction is not only one of the relative awareness of the different value systems but also of variation among different social groups. It should come as no surprise to sociology students to find that there may be significant variations in dating values by such socioeconomic-related characteristics as fraternity and sorority membership.

As early as the 1940's, data were being gathered which showed a definite relationship between dating and social class. Hollingshead, for example, dis-

[25] Robert O. Blood, Jr., "Uniformities and Diversities in Campus Dating Preferences," *Marriage and Family Living* 18 (Feb. 1956), p. 38.

[26] Ibid. p. 41. It should also be pointed out that Blood emphasized that the norms of the Waller complex are less extensively followed than they are verbalized even by fraternity and sorority members.

TABLE 3. *Significant Differences Between Greek and Independent Students in Perceived Campus Norms and Personal Preferences in Casual Dating.*

	PER CENT OF RESPONDENTS CHOOSING ITEM	
	Perceived campus norms	Personal preferences in casual dating
A. *Female Roles*		
1. "Is popular with opposite sex"		
Independent men	75.9 *	55.2
Fraternity men	94.6 *	54.1
Total men	83.2	54.7
2. "Is affectionate"		
Independent men	79.3 *	75.9
Fraternity men	91.9 *	83.8
Total men	84.2	78.9
3. "Is good looking, attractive"		
Independent men	91.4 *	82.5
Fraternity men	100.0 *	89.2
Total men	94.7	85.1
B. *Male Roles*		
4. "Belongs to a fraternity"		
Independent women	26.8 *	6.2 *
Sorority women	45.9 *	27.0 *
Total women	32.1	11.9
5. "Goes to popular places"		
Independent women	53.7	28.9 *
Sorority women	70.3	64.9 *
Total women	57.9	38.8
C. *General Role* (regardless of sex)		
6. "Is willing to drink socially"		
Independent students	ca. 48	36.3 *
Greeks	ca. 53	57.7 *
Total students	ca. 50	43.7

* Vertically adjacent items with asterisks differ significantly from one another at the 0.05 level or better.

Source: Adapted from Robert O. Blood, Jr., "Uniformities and Diversities in Campus Dating Preferences," *Marriage and Family Living* 18 (Feb. 1956), p. 40.

covered that dating among the high-school students of a midwestern community was highly related to the social class of their parents.[27] Turning to more recent studies and to the college campus, Levine and Sussman found that there is a relationship between family income, the amount of dating students do, and their opportunities to be pledged to fraternities; as might be

[27] August B. Hollingshead, *Elmtown's Youth*, New York: John Wiley and Sons, 1949.

expected from Blood's findings just reported, the fraternity pledges have higher family incomes and date more.[28]

Rogers and Havens, studying 725 students at Iowa State College in 1960, followed Waller's lead and had 11 judges rank various campus residences by prestige.[29] The judges agreed that prestige differences did exist on the campus and were easily able to pick out the high and low prestige groups. These researchers also secured data on the actual dating patterns of students rather than on attitudes toward dating, as Blood, Smith, and Christensen had done. What they found was that both men and women tend to date at their own prestige levels. Moreover, this prestige endogamy persisted at all levels—from casual dating through pinning to formal engagement.

More recently, Larson and Leslie have shown that campus dating is governed by a status hierarchy which reflects the social class system of the larger community. Both casual and serious dating are more common within given levels of the hierarchy.[30]

The evidence indicates that college-level dating, like that among high-school students, is structured in terms of multiple sets of norms.[31] Parts of Waller's formulations have been validated in subsequent research; much dating occurs within prestige categories which reflect the larger social class system. There is also evidence of competition, exploitation, and the influence of materialistic, superficial values.

At the same time, the majority of young people disapprove of the intrusion of such influences into their relationships and consciously strive to structure those relationships in terms of a set of values that should be far more functional for future family life. We might hazard the hypothesis that 30 years ago dating was far more confined to the upper-status groups on campus than it is today and that, as dating has spread over a larger proportion of the population, it has ceased to be as separable from the processes of mate selection as Waller portrayed it. Dating, courtship, and mate selection merge into one another so inconspicuously that the term courtship has virtually gone out of our vocabulary. Now mate selection tends to be structured in terms of stages

28 Gene N. Levine and Leila A. Sussman, "Social Class and Sociability," *American Journal of Sociology* 64 (Jan. 1960), pp. 391–9.

29 Everett M. Rogers and A. Eugene Havens, "Prestige Rating and Mate Selection on a College Campus," *Marriage and Family Living* 22 (Feb. 1960), pp. 55–9.

30 Richard F. Larson and Gerald R. Leslie, "Prestige Influences in Serious Dating Relationships of University Students," *Social Forces* 47 (Dec. 1968), pp. 195–202.

31 Something of the complexity of youth culture norms, at the high-school level, has been shown by Snyder. See Eldon E. Snyder, "Socioeconomic Variations, Values, and Social Participation Among High School Students," *Journal of Marriage and the Family* 28 (May 1966), pp. 174–6. Undoubtedly, the situation is at least equally complex at the college level.

in the dating process—casual dating, steady dating, being pinned, and formal engagement.[32]

THE DEVELOPMENT OF LOVE RELATIONSHIPS

One view of the development of love relationships was given in the account of Waller's theory of dating. Waller tended to view love as deriving from the efforts of each partner to involve the other, without becoming involved himself. Love, he said, emerges when sentiment formation overcomes objectivity. Inherent in the development of love, he said further, was the process of idealization. Without being aware of it, each partner strives to be like the dating partner's idealized image of him. Thus, each assumes, during courtship, a stature and nobility that otherwise are not characteristic of him. What he is not able to achieve in actual behavior, the partner completes in his imagination.

This conception of love views it as nonrational, or even irrational. The partners find themselves caught up in a powerful flow of emotion and are swept along toward marriage. The further they travel the less able they are to exercise critical judgment concerning themselves and their relationship. By the time they reach marriage they are hopelessly caught up in their fantasies and, as a consequence, the early stages of marital adjustment involve the necessity to reorient the relationship on a reality level. Love, in this view, is a powerful force pushing people toward marriage. The unreality of it also poses later adjustment difficulties for them.

Other views of love have been proposed and some research bearing upon the development of love has been conducted.[33] William Kolb took issue with those who would de-romanticize dating and courtship by arguing that love provides protection against the development of completely endogamous norms of mate selection.[34] If people did simply marry in accordance with the norms handed down by their parental generation, he said, the result would be an extreme conventionality, and would stifle further personality growth or creativity in interpersonal relationships.

[32] See Jack Delora, "Social Systems of Dating on a College Campus," *Marriage and Family Living* 25 (Feb. 1963), pp. 81–4.

[33] Margaret E. Donnelly, "Toward a Theory of Courtship," *Marriage and Family Living* 25 (Aug. 1963), pp. 290–93; and Glenn M. Vernon and Robert L. Stewart, "Empathy as a Process in the Dating Situation," *American Sociological Review* 22 (Feb. 1957), pp. 48–52.

[34] William H. L. Kolb, "Family Sociology, Marriage Education, and the Romantic Complex," *Social Forces* 29 (Oct. 1950), pp. 65–72.

> . . . such aspects as persons' names may even be seen as redundant.
> It tells another person more to know he or she is in the presence of
> someone who likes sunsets and Bob Dylan than to know what the
> partner's name is. [They] proceed to point out that this may also
> reflect a "semiconscious search for the elusive essence of masculinity
> or femininity in one's partner." They stress that one can only infer
> this from watching which partners are chosen to become really serious
> about, because each sex in everything else "feels freer now to have
> attitudes, interests and tastes which were formerly the exclusive prop-
> erty of one sex or the other." The press and many elders today tend
> to view this as a striving for a "unisex," but the evidence militates
> against such a goal being sought. The word, therefore, probably re-
> flects the discomfort of the older generation. . . .
>
> —Povl W. Toussieng, "New Sexual Attitudes of Young People,"
> *Sexual Behavior* (Sept. 1971), p. 52.

Hugo Biegel also rose to the defense of romantic love, claiming that it is
an expression "of a socio-psychological process that aims at the reconciliation
of basic human needs with frustrating social conditions." [35] He pointed out,
further, that romantic love is not only not harmful, but that it has done much
to raise the status of women and promote equality between the sexes. Love,
in a society where there are few institutional supports for the permanency of
marriage, aids and assists couples to adjust to the inevitable frustrations encountered in their relationships.

A quite different approach to the nature of heterosexual love in modern
society was taken by Nelson Foote, who views love as that relationship between two people which is most conducive to the optimum development of
both. [36] He sees the family ideally as affording to each person the opportunity
continuously to develop increasing competency in interpersonal relationships. [37] He argues against the idea of romantic love as an unstable emotion
based upon idealization, and contends that people commit themselves to one
another on the basis of real possibilities which can emerge in marriage with
proper trust and cultivation.

Perhaps the most impressive conceptualization of the sociological signifi-

---

[35] Hugo G. Biegel, "Romantic Love," *American Sociological Review* 16 (June 1951),
p. 326.

[36] Nelson N. Foote, "Love," *Psychiatry* 16 (Aug. 1953), pp. 245–51.

[37] Nelson N. Foote and Leonard S. Cottrell, Jr., *Identity and Interpersonal Competence:
A New Direction in Family Research*, Chicago: University of Chicago Press, 1955.

cance of love has been made by William Goode.[38] He notes that definitions of love are notoriously open to attack because value judgments are implicit in most of them. Most of us, however, have had the experience of love just as we have experienced other emotions, such as disgust, melancholy, and hate.

. . . All societies recognize that there are occasional violent emotional attachments between persons of opposite sex, but our present American culture is practically the only one which has attempted to capitalize these and make them the basis for marriage. Most groups regard them as unfortunate and point out the victims of such attachments as horrible examples. Their rarity in most societies suggests that they are psychological abnormalities to which our own culture has attached an extraordinary value just as other cultures have attached extreme values to other abnormalities. The hero of the modern American movie is always a romantic lover just as the hero of the old Arab epic is always an epileptic. A cynic might suspect that in any ordinary population the percentage of individuals with a capacity for romantic love of the Hollywood type was about as large as that of persons able to throw genuine epileptic fits. However, given a little social encouragement, either one can be adequately imitated without the performer admitting even to himself that the performance is not genuine.

—Ralph Linton, *The Study of Man*, New York: D. Appleton-Century Company, 1936, p. 175.

Societies vary, says Goode, according to the degree to which they institutionalize love. In some societies love is treated as an aberration, while in other societies it is given such approval that it is almost shameful to marry without it. Traditional China illustrates the first approach, while middle-class America illustrates the second.

In all societies, according to Goode, love is potentially disruptive of the larger social structure. Unless it is controlled and channeled in some way, it may lead to unions that would weaken the stratification and lineage patterns. To be effective the control must be exercised before love appears, and societies impose such control through child betrothal and marriage, rigid definition of classes of eligible spouses, the isolation of young people from ineligibles, institutionalized chaperonage, and even through formally free courtship practices.

Our own society may be taken as an example of this last pattern. We literally encourage the development of love play among youngsters and depend

[38] William J. Goode, "The Theoretical Importance of Love," *American Sociological Review* 24 (Feb. 1959), pp. 38-47.

upon the influence of parents and the peer group to narrow gradually the individual's choice to a "socially acceptable" member of the opposite sex. Parents "seek to control love relationships by influencing the informal social contacts of their children: moving to appropriate neighborhoods and schools, giving parties and helping to make out invitation lists, by making their children aware that certain individuals have ineligibility traits (race, religion, manners, tastes, clothing, and so on). Since youngsters fall in love with those with whom they associate, control over informal relationships also controls substantially the focus of affection." [39]

Considerable research has been done on the development of love relationships among college students. These studies estimate the effects of romanticism on love relationships, assess the trauma involved in the breaking of love relationships, and assess the degree to which people are madly in love at the time of marriage.

Charles Hobart used a romanticism scale to secure data from a sample of students at a west coast, sectarian, coeducational college. He found that the romanticism of males tended to increase as the men moved from no favorite date, to favorite date, to going steady, and to becoming engaged. Among women, however, no such trend appeared.[40] The failure of women to show increases in romanticism was interpreted to mean that, in late adolescence, they were still less emancipated from their families of orientation than were the men.

Other analyses of data from the same college sample showed that there is some tendency for both men and women to experience disillusionment as they move from courtship into marriage. The tendency was more pronounced among men than among women. Hobart was not able to establish a definite relationship between romanticism and subsequent disillusionment, but he did find indications that such a relationship may exist.[41] Thus, Hobart did find tendencies toward romanticism among men and he did find both men and women experiencing some disillusionment early in marriage. To this degree, his research gives general support to Waller's formulations.

Dean attempted to cast further light on the development of romanticism

[39] Ibid. p. 45.

[40] Charles W. Hobart, "The Incidence of Romanticism During Courtship," *Social Forces* 36 (May 1958), pp. 362–7. See also Eugene J. Kanin, Karen R. Davidson, and Sonia R. Scheck, "A Research Note on Male-Female Differentials in the Experience of Heterosexual Love," *The Journal of Sex Research* 6 (Feb. 1970), pp. 64–72; and David H. Knox, Jr., and Michael J. Sporakowski, "Attitudes of College Students Toward Love," *Journal of Marriage and the Family* 30 (Nov. 1968), pp. 638–42.

[41] Charles W. Hobart, "Disillusionment in Marriage, and Romanticism," *Marriage and Family Living* 20 (May 1958), pp. 156–62.

in courtship by relating it to emotional maturity or immaturity among a sample of college women. He found no relationship between romanticism and emotional maturity, but he did find that women of lower social status show more romanticism than women of higher social status.[42]

Data on a sample of 399 University of Minnesota students' love affairs were provided by Kirkpatrick and Caplow, who found that both men and women showed more movement toward love in their recent relationships as compared with their earlier ones.[43] They also found that men tended to be more jealous than women, and that they were more likely to feel trapped in their relationships with their partners.

One of the most interesting parts of this study provided data on the breaking of serious love affairs: some 230 broken love affairs for men, and 414 broken affairs for women.[44] Nearly half of the men and 38 per cent of the women reported that mutual loss of interest was the chief cause of the break. In 45 per cent of the male reports, however, and in 48 per cent of the female reports, the relationship broke because one of the partners had become interested in some other person. These data are shown in Table 4.

TABLE 4. *Causes of Breakup of Love Affairs of University of Minnesota Students.*

CAUSE FOR BREAKUP	MALE RESPONSES (N=230)	FEMALE RESPONSES (N=414)
Parents	5.2%	8.6%
Friends	3.1	5.8
Subject's interest in another person	15.1	32.2
Partner's interest in another person	29.7	15.3
Mutual loss of interest	46.9	38.1
Total	100.0	100.0

Source: Clifford Kirkpatrick and Theodore Caplow, "Courtship in a Group of Minnesota Students," *American Journal of Sociology* 51 (Sept. 1945), p. 123. Reprinted by permission of The University of Chicago Press.

The students' reported reactions to these broken love affairs were quite varied. Reactions of bitterness, being hurt, angry, remorseful, and crushed

[42] Dwight G. Dean, "Romanticism and Emotional Maturity: A Preliminary Study," *Marriage and Family Living* 23 (Feb. 1961), pp. 44-5.

[43] Clifford Kirkpatrick and Theodore Caplow, "Courtship in a Group of Minnesota Students," *American Journal of Sociology* 51 (Sept. 1945), pp. 114-25.

[44] For further analysis of the nature of these breaks, see Clifford Kirkpatrick and Theodore Caplow, "Emotional Trends in the Courtship Experience of College Students as Expressed by Graphs With Some Observations on Methodological Implications," *American Sociological Review* 10 (Oct. 1945), pp. 619-26.

were reported. Most interestingly, however, over 70 per cent of the men and 66 per cent of the women reported that their reactions ranged from indifference through mixed regret and relief to satisfaction and happiness. Another estimate of the relative trauma involved is presented by the data in Table 5. Just about half of both men and women reported that it took them no time

TABLE 5. *Time Required for Minnesota Students To Adjust to the Breakup of Love Affairs.*

	PER CENT REPLYING	
ESTIMATE	Males (N=230)	Females (N=414)
None	51.4	49.4
Several weeks	33.6	19.5
Several months	7.7	19.5
A year	5.0	6.3
Several years	2.3	5.3
Total	100.0	100.0

Source: Clifford Kirkpatrick and Theodore Caplow, "Courtship in a Group of Minnesota Students," *American Journal of Sociology* 51 (Sept. 1945), p. 125. Reprinted by permission of The University of Chicago Press.

at all to readjust to the breaking of the relationship. Thirty-four per cent of the men and 20 per cent of the women said it took several weeks; 7 per cent of the men and 12 per cent of the women said it took a year or longer. Apparently, for the majority of persons there is no great trauma involved in the breaking of premarital love affairs; for a minority there are feelings of bitterness and hurt which last for quite a long time.

One final bit of evidence on the nature of love involvement before marriage is provided by the monumental study of 1000 engaged couples by Ernest Burgess and Paul Wallin.[45] These authors believe that there is some idealization in love affairs but that it is not universal and that, where it exists, it is not usually extreme. In support of this position, they present data on how much in love couples say they are at the time of marriage and on whether they have ever had doubts about whether they wanted to marry their fiancés.

Two hundred twenty-six of the engaged couples who were interviewed— and had filled out questionnaires—provided the data in Table 6. Something less than one-fourth of the men and women described themselves as being head over heels in love, the one answer that should reflect extreme idealiza-

[45] Ernest W. Burgess and Paul Wallin, *Engagement and Marriage*, Chicago: J. B. Lippincott Company, 1953.

TABLE 6. *Percentages of 226 Men and Women Reporting Specified Love for Engagement Partner.*

EXTENT OF LOVE	MEN	WOMEN
Head over heels	23.5	24.8
Very much so	70.4	68.1
Somewhat or mildly	6.2	7.1
Total	100.1	100.0

Source: Ernest W. Burgess and Paul Wallin, *Engagement and Marriage*, Chicago: J. B. Lippincott Company, 1953, p. 170.

tion. Approximately 70 per cent said that they were "very much" in love. Forty-one per cent of the men and 48 per cent of the women also indicated that, at some time, they had felt hesitation about marrying their fiancés.

Research has not yet provided any final answers on the nature of love involvement in the United States before marriage. Neither has it indicated how functional or dysfunctional love is for subsequent marriage adjustment. In all likelihood, love involvement is quite variable, ranging from being completely overwhelmed to those cases in which the existence of love is rationalized only because of the public expectation that it should exist. The effects of love on marriage probably are no less variable.

SUMMARY

Dating emerged in the United States shortly after World War I. Before World War II, it had spread downward to the junior-high-school level. Most boys and girls begin dating between 14 and 16 years of age and continue it until they marry, six to eight years later. In dating, young people both seek to learn constructively about the opposite sex and compete for status. In their early dating experiences, particularly, they are plagued by feelings of inadequacy.

Several studies have shown that high-school-age youth, when queried about their preferences in dating partners, select traits that are very much in accord with their parents' values: dependability; honesty; consideration of others; neatness; maturity; affectionate; and desire for normal family life. Similar values are expressed by college students who are several years older.

The most comprehensive and explicit theory of dating and emotional involvement was formulated to apply to university students during the 1930's. In that theory, Waller distinguished between dating, which he described as a

dalliance relationship, and serious courtship. Dating, he said, was characterized by a questing after thrills, for which each partner bargained with the
other. Males were perceived to be interested in necking and petting, while
women are more interested in being sought after as dating partners. So long
as the partners have approximately equal bargaining power, the process is
alleged to work out well.

Bargaining, however, leads easily into exploitation whenever the pair are
unequally matched. Men tend to exploit women sexually, and women use
men to squire them around in the search for more attractive dates.

Students are classified, informally, according to their desirability as dating
partners. Waller called this pattern the "rating and dating complex" and
specified the traits that produce high status. They include fraternity or
sorority membership, dressing well and being smooth in manners, and being
a good dancer. Physical attractiveness is important for women and having a
car and spending money is important for men. Among members of both sexes
the possession of a good "line"—a pattern of verbal banter designed to titillate
the other—is important.

People tend to date at their own levels in the rating and dating hierarchy,
but sometimes they do not. When they don't, the lower-status person is likely
to be exploited, sometimes with unfavorable personality consequences. Such
cross-class dating, however, also opens the possibility of making a desirable
marriage to lower-status girls who are willing to accept the gamble. This may
be an important mechanism in the promotion of upward social mobility.

Courtship, said Waller, grows out of dating when the partners begin to
succumb to one another's blandishments. This involvement may be uneven
and be accompanied by temporary exploitation of the more involved partner,
according to the "principle of least interest." The balance between the partners tends to be restored through a series of lovers' quarrels which produce
increasing commitment to the relationship and lead toward marriage. Involvement is accompanied by idealization of each partner by the other; sentiment
formation overcomes objectivity.

Waller's analysis has led a whole series of scholars to attempt to test various
portions of it. Questionnaire studies in various sections of the country and
among both black and white students have shown explicit verbal standards
closer to those of high-school students and parents than to those of Waller's
rating and dating complex. These studies also showed, however, that contemporary students do not distinguish dating from courtship and engagement,
and that the rating and dating complex appears to be more operative during
the precourtship period. The studies further showed great diversity in dating
values and some approximation to the rating and dating complex among fra-

ternity and sorority members. Other studies have linked the rating and dating complex to the operation of the social class system in the larger society.

Theories of romantic love have indicated ways in which it is both functional and dysfunctional for the larger social system. It poses a threat to the society's endogamous norms and follows idealization with disillusionment. At the same time, it prevents the mate selection system from becoming overly rigid.

Research has verified the existence of romanticism during courtship, finding more of it among men than among women. There also appears to be some disillusionment with the movement into marriage. At the same time, most couples profess themselves not to be unrealistically in love with one another at the time of marriage. People approach marriage by different routes and with different degrees of involvement. The nature of their early marital adjustments undoubtedly varies accordingly.

SUGGESTED READINGS

Bell, Robert R., *Marriage and Family Interaction,* Homewood, Illinois: The Dorsey Press, 1971, Ch. 4 and 5. Sociologically sophisticated analyses of dating, courtship, and love in the context of preparation for marriage.

Burchinal, Lee G., "The Premarital Dyad and Love Involvement," in Harold T. Christensen, ed., *Handbook of Marriage and the Family,* Chicago: Rand McNally, 1964, pp. 623–74. Comprehensive summary of our knowledge of dating, courtship, and mate selection.

Hill, Reuben, and Aldous, Joan, "Socialization for Marriage and Parenthood," in David A. Goslin, ed., *Handbook of Socialization Theory and Research,* Chicago: Rand McNally, 1969, pp. 885–950. An excellent summary of the state of theory and research. Contains sections on dating, going steady, and engagement.

Hollingshead, August B., *Elmtown's Youth: The Impact of Social Classes on Adolescents,* New York: John Wiley and Sons, 1949. Study of 735 adolescents in a midwestern town. The formation of cliques and dating are analyzed in terms of social class.

Lantz, Herman R., and Snyder, Eloise C., *Marriage: An Examination of the Man-Woman Relationship,* New York: John Wiley and Sons, 1969, Ch. 6, 7, 9, 10. These chapters on the nature of heterosexual love and dating and courtship in middle-class American society are perceptive and constructive. Especially useful for young persons approaching marriage.

Waller, Willard, and Hill, Reuben, *The Family: A Dynamic Interpretation,* New York: Dryden Press, 1951. A revision of Waller's original textbook on the family. Chapters 8, 9, and 10 present Waller's analysis of dating and courtship.

FILMS

Anatomy of a Teenage Courtship (Coronet Films, 65 E. South Water Street, Chicago 60601), 24 minutes. Reveals the pressures, fears, indecisions and emotions a teenage couple experience before their engagement.

Is This Love? (McGraw-Hill Book Company, Text-Film Division, 330 West 42nd St., New York 10036), 14 minutes. Contrasts the romances of two college roommates. One girl, impulsive and emotional, is resentful of any persuasion to delay her marriage. The other girl hesitates to consider marriage until she has solid proof of her love through successive stages of dating, courtship, going steady, and engagement.

Joe and Roxy (National Film Board of Canada, Mackenzie Building, Toronto), 30 minutes. Touches upon problems facing today's teenagers: going steady, planning for a secure future, and seeing education in proper perspective. Shows how the inadequate home lives of Joe and Roxy fail them during adolescent adjustment.

When Should I Marry? (McGraw-Hill Book Company, Text-Film Division, 330 West 42nd St., New York 10036), 19 minutes. A young couple, eager to marry but urged by their parents to delay, ask a minister's advice. He describes the experiences of two other couples who married at an early age. From this description, he is able to summarize some practical points that should be of help to all young people in answering the question of when to marry.

QUESTIONS AND PROJECTS

1. To what factors do you attribute the existence of dating in American society? Evaluate the argument that people begin dating at younger ages all the time.
2. At what ages do boys and girls generally begin to date? How long is the dating period before marriage?
3. Describe the formal, explicit norms that govern early dating. Is there another implicit set of dating norms which brings parents and youth into conflict? How does that set of norms work? What are its functions?
4. Outline Waller's theory of rating and dating. Upon what evidence was the theory based? What has research shown about the operation of the rating and dating complex on campuses today?
5. How does bargaining in dating relationships lead to exploitation? Be specific about the influence of differences in rating and about the use of the "line."
6. What are the effects of being exploited upon dating partners? Are there any positive effects which stem from cross-class dating and accompanying exploitation?
7. How did Waller distinguish between dating and courtship? How does courtship begin? Through what processes, according to Waller, does it lead to marriage?
8. Describe Goode's arguments on the significance of love for the social structure. What useful functions does love serve? What problems of control does it pose?

9. According to Waller, how does idealization develop in courtship? What does research evidence show about idealization in courtship? What proportion of couples appear to be madly in love at the time of marriage?

10. How do young people react to broken love affairs? What are the most common causes of the breaking of these relationships? How long does readjustment take?

11. Suppose you wanted to determine how influential rating and dating is on your campus. How would you go about it? Would a questionnaire study be likely to get at it? Why, or why not?

12. Arrange a panel discussion on the nature and functions of heterosexual love in American society. Notice where the panel places the emphasis. Is it upon the social functions of love? On the psychodynamics of love? On what kind of love relationship provides a suitable basis for marriage?

13 | *Premarital Interaction:*
Sexual Involvement

For many young people, boys and increasingly for girls, the mere fact of engaging in sex is a boost for self-esteem. This is an old story for young men. They gain stature among their fellows for having had sex, sometimes called "scoring" with a female. Lying is common, but better than admitting to having failed. Even if not found out, the young man who has failed to score may experience a diminishing of his self-esteem. This accounts, in part, for the desperate attempts of some young men to make it. The young woman involved may be genuinely puzzled or even frightened by his frantic behavior. She, in turn, may have her self-esteem tied to not having sex, or at least not too soon. One may legitimately wonder if sex has anything to do with the situation at all, or whether it is simply the arena for testing worth or mettle, akin in this respect to the gladiators on the football field. . . .[1]

It should be understood that this does not necessarily mean a denial of being a male or a female. The anatomical facts very much become a part of the total experience, but not the center of attention. For one thing, sharing a situation with a person of the other sex gives a feeling of completeness to the situation, just like the overwhelmingly loud music and other accessories add to the feeling of total experience. In other words, experiencing one's own anatomy directly is what counts, rather than experiencing it via the partner's reactions. Because this obviates the seduction of the partner, there is less need to stress the differences in sex roles, many of which in this context become artificial. For example, sexual conquest of the female by the male, a required ritual for many in the older generation, is unnecessary when consummation of a sexual relationship depends exclusively on whether both partners happen to feel like it at the same time. . . .[2]

[1] John L. Schimel, "Self-Esteem and Sex," *Sexual Behavior*, (July 1971), p. 5.
[2] Povl W. Toussieng, "New Sexual Attitudes of Young People," *Sexual Behavior* (Sept. 1971), p. 52.

Tʜᴇsᴇ two quotations, from articles written by psychiatrists in 1971, reflect the conflict and change occurring in premarital sexual norms. The first quotation describes patterns that have been common in the United States for some time, and which still have many adherents. The second quotation describes a new pattern that is emerging as part of the youth counterculture.

Tʜᴇ Cᴜʟᴛᴜʀᴀʟ Bᴀᴄᴋɢʀᴏᴜɴᴅ

It will be recalled, from Chapter 2, that most of the world's societies do not make sex itself the focus of regulation of sexual behavior; rather, they regulate sex as one part of the larger regulation of marriage, reproduction, kinship determination, and the ascription of social status. Moreover, most societies do not prohibit all sex relationships outside of marriage. The United States is one of only about 5 per cent of known societies whose formal norms traditionally have completely restricted sexual relationships to marriage.

Western society has a long history of the disapproval of sexual involvement before marriage. Not incidentally, the continuous proscription of such relationships testifies to the fact that premarital intercourse as a social problem did not begin in the 20th century. The ancient Hebrews punished sexual intercourse that occurred after betrothal as adultery. The Romans did likewise. With the advent of Christianity, sex itself came to be defined as evil. Sex in marriage was considered as a necessary evil, and sex before marriage was held to be a grave sin. These attitudes were carried forward through the Dark Ages and Middle Ages, and were complicated by the idealization of heterosexual relationships that emerged during the chivalric period. A dualistic conception of the nature of women, in relation to sex, developed. On the one hand, women were held to be the evil tempters of men; on the other hand, they generally were idolized as they offered to men the most precious of all gifts.

These conflicting attitudes were brought by the colonists to America—along with a certain bawdiness that persisted from the ancient wedding ceremonies through the ballads of medieval minstrels to the practice of bundling in New England. Colonial New England both condemned premarital relationships harshly and took an almost morbid interest in them. Fornicators were punished with branding, imprisonment, fines, public confessions, and being required to marry. In spite of this, the few data available indicate that premarital intercourse and premarital pregnancy were widespread. In the southern colonies, somewhat less harsh penalties were provided and a clear double standard was evident. Upper-class men were almost expected to have premarital intercourse, while upper-class women were carefully guarded against it.

Since colonial days, the various states have continued to take a dim view of virtually all forms of sexual activity except for so-called "normal" intercourse in marriage. Contrary to popular belief, however, state laws regulating sexual behavior are by no means uniform. As one authority on domestic relations law put it, "One of the most remarkable features of American sex offense laws is their wide disparity in types of sexual behavior prohibited and their extraordinary variation in penalties imposed for similar offenses." [3] After pointing out that contemporary American law has gone far beyond that of Tudor England in proscribing various sexual acts, Ploscowe emphasizes that a bare majority of states prohibit fornication and that the penalties attached in those states where it is prohibited vary from a ten-dollar fine in Rhode Island to a three-year prison term in Arizona. Adultery is more widely prohibited and the penalties prescribed are more severe, but again there is wide variation from one state to another.

Of special significance here are the laws governing statutory rape which prohibit sex relations with girls under stated ages even when they consent to and actively seek such activity. The age of consent is most frequently 16 or 18, but is as low as 7 in one state and is 21 in at least one state. Most authorities believe that the statutory rape laws need revision and should adjust the age of consent downward, for most convictions involve girls of 15, 16, and 17 years of age who are active participants in relationships with young men of comparable ages.[4]

Not surprisingly, the widespread legal prohibitions of premarital sex behavior are reflected in public attitudes of condemnation. Nor are these attitudes confined to the general public. Hudson found that high-school textbooks on marriage and the family treat sex as though young people were unaware of the sexual aspects of life, and that where they do deal with kissing, necking, and petting, put the emphasis on control and sublimation.[5] At the college

[3] Morris Ploscowe, "Sex Offenses: The American Legal Context," *Law and Contemporary Problems* 25 (Spring 1960), pp. 217–24; see also Stanton Wheeler, "Sex Offenses: A Sociological Critique," ibid. pp. 258–78.

[4] See Harriet F. Pilpel and Theodora Zavin, *Your Marriage and the Law*, New York: Rinehart and Company, 1952; Morris Ploscowe, *Sex and the Law*, Englewood Cliffs, New Jersey: Prentice-Hall, 1951; and Robert V. Sherman, *Sex and the Statutory Law*, New York: Oceana Publications, 1949.

[5] John W. Hudson, *A Content Analysis of Selected Family Life Education Textbooks Used at the Secondary Level*, Ph.D. dissertation, Ohio State University, 1956. See also A. E. Bayer and F. Ivan Nye, "Family Life Education in Florida Public High Schools," paper read before National Council on Family Relations, Denver, 1963; G. A. Christensen, *An Analysis of Selected Issues in Family Life Education*, 1958, Ph.D. dissertation, Michigan State University, 1958; Edward Z. Dager, Glenn A. Harper, and Robert N. Whitehurst, "Family Life Education in Public High Schools: A Survey Report on Indiana," *Marriage*

level, Reiss found that authors also take a negative attitude toward premarital sex.[6] He concludes that they tend to neglect and misinterpret much of the empirical evidence, assuming that premarital intercourse is almost always lustful, promiscuous, and devoid of affection.

There seems to be no question but what the prevailing attitudes in American society have been quite negative toward sexual expression in general and toward premarital sexual involvement in particular. Our purpose, in this chapter, is neither to reinforce these attitudes nor to refute them. It is, instead, to present the available data on premarital sexual involvement, to assess the sociological significance of existing patterns of involvement, and to try to interpret the meaning of varying patterns of involvement in the life histories of young men and women.

THE INCIDENCE OF PREMARITAL SEX INVOLVEMENT

The scientific study of human sex behavior began between 50 and 80 years ago. The first studies were made in Europe and, while of great theoretical significance, were methodologically not very sophisticated. Systematic sex research, involving the use of instruments and stressing the use of statistical techniques, originated in the United States during the second decade of the present century.[7] The first of these studies appeared during World War I.[8] Between the two world wars, a number of monographs appeared[9] and, after

---

and *Family Living* 24 (Nov. 1962), pp. 365–70; Robert A. Harper and Frances R. Harper, "Are Educators Afraid of Sex?", *Marriage and Family Living* 19 (Aug. 1957), pp. 240–46; Richard K. Kerckhoff, "Family Life Education in America," in Harold T. Christensen, ed., *Handbook of Marriage and the Family*, Chicago: Rand McNally, 1964, pp. 881–911; Lester A. Kirkendall, "Values and Premarital Intercourse—Implications for Parent Education," *Marriage and Family Living* 22 (Nov. 1960), pp. 317–24; and Donald S. Longworth, "Certification of Teachers of Family Living: A Proposal," *Marriage and Family Living* 14 (May 1952), pp. 103–4.

[6] Ira L. Reiss, "The Treatment of Pre-Marital Coitus in 'Marriage and the Family' Texts," *Social Problems* 4 (April 1957), pp. 334–8.

[7] Winston W. Ehrmann, "The Variety and Meaning of Premarital Heterosexual Experiences for the College Student," *Journal of the National Association of Women Deans and Counselors* 26 (Jan. 1963), pp. 22–8.

[8] M. J. Exner, *Problems and Principles of Sex Education: A Study of 948 College Men*, New York: Association Press, 1915.

[9] Dorothy D. Bromley and Florence H. Britten, *Youth and Sex: A Study of 1300 College Students*, New York: Harper and Brothers, 1938; Katherine B. Davis, *Factors in the Sex Life of Twenty-two Hundred Women*, New York: Harper and Brothers, 1929; Gilbert V. Hamilton, *A Research in Marriage*, New York: Boni, 1929; and Lewis M. Terman, *Psychological Factors in Marital Happiness*, New York: McGraw-Hill Book Company, 1938.

World War II, the monumental studies of the Institute for Sex Research—the so-called Kinsey reports—received nation-wide attention.[10]

To much of the general public it appears that our knowledge of human sex behavior stems exclusively from the Kinsey reports and that the trustworthiness of that knowledge depends on the validity of the Kinsey findings. As has been indicated above, this simply is not true. There were more than half a dozen major studies made before the Institute for Sex Research began its work. The special significance of the Kinsey studies derives from their size and scope. The study of male sex behavior was based upon full case histories from 5300 white males of varying educational background, and the female study was based upon case histories of 5940 white females. The published reports based upon these samples contain more data on sex behavior than all of the other published works combined.

As if this were not enough, there have been a number of other significant studies published in recent years. Freedman followed a carefully drawn random sample of women from an eastern woman's college through the four years of their college experience.[11] Bell and Chaskes,[12] and Christensen and Gregg[13] studied matched groups of students in 1958 and again in 1968. Robinson, King, Dudley, and Clune studied University of Georgia students.[14] Peretti studied unmarried people in two midwestern cities[15]; and, finally, Luckey and Nass surveyed 2230 college students in five countries.[16]

In sum, the amount of evidence on premarital sexual behavior is impressive. An accumulation of evidence over a period of about 50 years yields a remarkably consistent picture of what young people are like sexually.

[10] Alfred C. Kinsey, Wardell B. Pomeroy, and Clyde E. Martin, *Sexual Behavior in the Human Male*, Philadelphia: W. B. Saunders Company, 1948; Alfred C. Kinsey, Wardell B. Pomeroy, Clyde E. Martin, and Paul H. Gebhard, *Sexual Behavior in the Human Female*, Philadelphia: W. B. Saunders Company, 1953.

[11] Mervin B. Freedman, *The College Experience*, San Francisco: Jossey-Bass, 1967.

[12] Robert R. Bell and Jay B. Chaskes, "Premarital Sexual Experience Among Coeds, 1958 and 1968," *Journal of Marriage and the Family* 32 (Feb. 1970), pp. 81–4.

[13] Harold T. Christensen and Christina F. Gregg, "Changing Sex Norms in America and Scandinavia," *Journal of Marriage and the Family* 32 (Nov. 1970), pp. 616–27.

[14] Ira E. Robinson, Karl King, Charles J. Dudley, and Francis J. Clune, "Change in Sexual Behavior and Attitudes of College Students," *The Family Coordinator* 17 (April 1968), pp. 119–23.

[15] Peter O. Peretti, "Premarital Sexual Behavior Between Females and Males of Two Middle-Sized Midwestern Cities," *The Journal of Sex Research* 5 (Aug. 1969), pp. 218–25.

[16] Eleanore B. Luckey and Gilbert D. Nass, "A Comparison of Sexual Attitudes and Behavior in an International Sample," *Journal of Marriage and the Family* 31 (May 1969), pp. 364–79.

PRE-ADOLESCENT SEX PLAY

Strictly speaking, pre-adolescent sex play is not a part of premarital sexual involvement. Much of this behavior is not explicitly heterosexual and, qualitatively, much of it is very different from the types of behavior that will appear later on. On the other hand, the extent of pre-adolescent sex behavior completely refutes the widely held notion that imperious sexual urges do not exist in childhood. From the prevalence of such behavior, there is every reason to think that all efforts simply to prohibit sex play will meet with failure. In addition, even though childhood sexual experimentation seems far removed from true premarital behavior, early sex play is accompanied by the development of attitudes and values in relation to sex, and to man-woman relationships generally, that will significantly influence the course of future relationships.

Because such behavior often is solitary and because adult memories of early childhood behavior are scanty, there are few precise figures on pre-adolescent sex play. What is of overwhelming importance, however, is that some boys and girls display signs of sexual arousal almost from birth and that substantial numbers of both sexes are involved in explicitly sexual behavior before they attain puberty. Kinsey reports that approximately 10 per cent of boys are engaging in some kind of sex play by age five and more than 35 per cent by age ten. Some 57 per cent of older boys and men recall some kind of sex play before adolescence.[16] In his female sample, Kinsey found that 4 per cent of the women reported that they were responding sexually by five years of age, 16 per cent by age ten, and 27 per cent before they reached adolescence. Fully 14 per cent of the girls had reached orgasm by age 13.[17]

Two implications of these figures are worth pointing out at this point. First, almost all human sex behavior is characterized by great variability. While nearly three-fifths of boys may engage in sex play before puberty, another two-fifths do not. Similarly, a fourth of all girls may experience sexual arousal before puberty, but the other three-fourths do not. Personal bias and one's purpose in making the analysis determine which figures are emphasized. Whatever the kind of sex behavior being discussed and whatever the ages of the persons involved, it is well to remember that most statements of what people are like, sexually, require elaborate and careful qualification.

[16] *Sexual Behavior in the Human Male*, pp. 162–5.

[17] *Sexual Behavior in the Human Female*, pp. 103–5; For a review of the available data on pre-adolescent sex behavior and development of the thesis that heterosexual development is determined by family experiences, see Carlfred B. Broderick, "Sexual Behavior Among Pre-adolescents," *The Journal of Social Issues* 22 (April 1966), pp. 6–21.

The second implication has to do with male-female differences. Even in pre-adolescence, boys, on the average, are more active sexually than girls. With the single exception of marital intercourse, where the figures must be equal, males tend to be more active than females in every form of sexual activity. Full consideration of the reasons for this difference would take us beyond the scope of the present discussion. Suffice it to say that both biological and cultural factors probably are involved. Some writers emphasize the fact that males in virtually all animal species are more aggressive sexually and that men respond more directly to hormonal and seminal influences.[18] On the cultural level, it is obvious that women undergo more repressive sexual conditioning than men do. In any event, the more active and aggressive sexuality of men influences heterosexual relationships throughout life.

Prepubertal sex play among both sexes is of many different sorts: solitary sex play or masturbation, sex play with members of the opposite sex, and play with members of the same sex. Homosexual play is of relevance to our analysis only to illustrate that before the expression of sexual drives is channeled by cultural expectations, it tends to be about as common as heterosexual play. Among pre-adolescent boys, homosexual play actually is more common, occurs more frequently, and is more specific than heterosexual play.[19] Kinsey attributes this to the greater accessibility of boys to other boys than to girls, to young boys' disdain for girls, and to the greater curiosity of boys about their genitalia. The incidence of girls who experienced homosexual play before adolescence, 33 per cent,[20] actually exceeded the proportion who reported sexual arousal before adolescence and illustrates another fundamental fact about female sex behavior: it need not reflect, or even be accompanied by, sexual arousal. At these early ages, the motivations often were those of simple nonerotic curiosity. Only a minority of either boys or girls carry their homosexual experimentation into either adolescence or adulthood.

The age at which masturbation begins is partly a matter of definition. Kinsey reports that while there is a great deal of incidental touching of the genitalia during both solitary and social play, most of this is not masturbation in the strict sense. Apparently about 20 per cent of boys begin to masturbate by age 12.[21] Just before adolescence and during early adolescence, the proportion rises rapidly until something over 90 per cent of all males participate.

[18] See the discussions in Robert O. Blood, Jr., *Marriage*, New York: The Free Press of Glencoe, 1969, pp. 131–2; and William M. Kephart, *The Family, Society, and the Individual*, Boston: Houghton Mifflin, 1966, pp. 23–6.

[19] *Sexual Behavior in the Human Male*, p. 168.

[20] *Sexual Behavior in the Human Female*, p. 114.

[21] Ibid p. 173.

Masturbation is the most common source of first ejaculation among males and remains the commonest source of sexual outlet during early adolescence.

Interestingly, about three-fourths of all boys hear about masturbation from other boys before experimenting with it; only 28 per cent of Kinsey's male subjects discovered masturbation on their own.[22] Girls, on the other hand, do not discuss their sexual experiences as males do. Of the female respondents who began to masturbate before adolescence, a full 70 per cent discovered it through manipulation of their own genitalia.

Some 12 per cent of Kinsey's female sample had masturbated to orgasm by age 12. By age 15, the figure had climbed to 20 per cent. An interesting comparison, here, although it goes beyond pre-adolescent experience, is that the total incidence of female masturbation reaches only 62 per cent as compared with over 90 per cent among males. Moreover, the proportion of males who masturbate is highest during the late teens and declines thereafter, while the proportion of females who masturbate continues to increase right up to middle age.[23] Masturbation is also the technique through which the highest proportion of women, relatively, are able to achieve orgasm. Of the 62 per cent of women who ultimately masturbate, 58 per cent also reach orgasm. No other technique, including marital coitus, produces such a high proportion of orgasmic response.

Of most direct relevance to the concern of this chapter is pre-adolescent heterosexual play and its implications for sociosexual development. Kinsey found evidence of such play in about 40 per cent of his male histories. He also found something else of great significance in the understanding of male sex behavior: the type and amount of sexual activity is very much related to educational level. In this case, the pre-adolescent play of boys who subsequently went on to college tended to be limited to one or two experiences and not to involve attempts at intercourse. Among lower-status boys who did not go beyond the eighth grade, however, pre-adolescent play often was influenced by older boys or girls and, in three-fourths of the cases, involved attempts at intercourse.

About 30 per cent of Kinsey's female sample recalled pre-adolescent heterosexual play.[24] A most significant thing about such play is that much of it is

---

[22] Ibid. p. 138.

[23] Ibid. p. 173.

[24] *Sexual Behavior in the Human Female*, p. 107. Some caution should be used in the interpretation of these statistics. The 30 per cent of girls who experienced heterosexual play cannot be added to the 33 per cent who participated in homosexual play, for only 48 per cent of the sample recalled any sociosexual play before adolescence. This simply means that 15 per cent had sex play with boys only, 18 per cent had it with girls only, and 15 per cent had it with both boys and girls.

not clearly separated from other forms of play in which children imitate adult behavior, and much of it is not overtly erotic. The "doctor" games and "mother and father" games that are typical often are carried through without sexual arousal on the part of any of the participants. Such nonerotic play shades off, of course, into frankly sexual play and attempts at intercourse.

Both anthropological evidence and evidence from our own society establish, without a doubt, that sexual awareness is not limited to adolescents and adults. Some children—even very young children—have quite active sex lives. On the other hand, a good deal of what adults interpret as sexual interest among children involves attempts to imitate adult behavior and an only partly erotic generalized curiosity. Adults read sexuality into some child behavior that children do not perceive as such.

HETEROSEXUAL PETTING

While some preadolescent behavior is explicitly sexual and some is not, male sex play in adolescence becomes pointed to sexual arousal and satisfaction. An increasing proportion of boys begin to seek petting with their dating partners. That petting and dating are associated is shown by the fact that the proportion of males petting has increased closely in accord with the spread of dating over the past 40 years. Moreover, the age at which petting begins has tended to drop even as the age at which dating begins has dropped. In Kinsey's total sample of older and younger males, 88 per cent engaged in some sort of petting before marriage. In 28 per cent of this population the petting was extensive enough to produce orgasm in the male. Petting in the younger generation, however, has increased to include about 95 per cent of all males, with over 50 per cent petting to sexual climax.[25]

The statistics also show that the incidence and nature of petting among males are closely related to educational level. Some 84 per cent of grade-school-level males engage in petting, but this activity, among them, tends to be desultory and a very brief prelude to coitus. Ninety-two per cent of high-school- and college-level males are involved, with the figure being still higher among the younger generation. Furthermore, their petting tends to involve intensive erotic play which may continue for hours and yet never arrive at coitus. "Orgasm as a product of petting occurs among 16 per cent of the males of the grade school level, 32 per cent of the males of the high school level, and over 61 per cent of the college-bred males who are not married by the age of 30." [26]

[25] *Sexual Behavior in the Human Male*, p. 533.
[26] Ibid. p. 537.

The available statistics on petting among females are not strictly comparable to those available for males. Generally the figures show the proportion of women who become involved to be related to age and to the behavior of the men involved. Approximately 40 per cent of Kinsey's female sample had petting experience by 15 years of age, between 69 and 95 per cent had experience by age 18 and almost 100 per cent of the women participated in petting before marriage.[27] That women sometimes participate to please their male companions is shown by the fact that only 80 per cent of the sample reported that they had ever been erotically aroused in petting. Thirty-nine per cent of the women had responded to orgasm on at least one occasion.

That petting is frequently involved in dating is suggested by the number of partners with whom the women had petted. Among the women who were already married, only 10 per cent had limited themselves to a single partner before marriage. Nearly one-third (32 per cent) had had from two to five partners, and another fourth (23 per cent) had petted with from six to ten men. Thirty-five per cent had had more than ten partners.[28] This relative promiscuity does not appear in most other forms of female sexual activity.

At first glance, it appears that petting among women is related to educational level just as it is among men. Closer examination shows, however, that this apparent relationship is a function of different average ages at marriage among different educational groups. The higher educated women marry later. If we take the proportions who had petted to orgasm before marriage, we find almost exactly the same proportions among the various educational groups.

As among men, there has been considerable generational change. Among women who had been born before 1900, 80 per cent had some petting experience before they were 35 years old; among those born between 1900 and 1910, the figure was 91 per cent; and among those born between 1910 and 1929, the figure was 99 per cent. Petting to orgasm showed the same progression, the percentages being 26 per cent, 44 per cent, and 53 per cent.[29] The period of crucial change in this regard appears to have been during and after the First World War. The group which came to adulthood during this period showed more change from preceding generations than later generations have shown from this one.

A final significant set of relationships exists between religiosity and premarital petting experience. Kinsey failed to find any significant differences among Protestant, Catholic, and Jewish groups. However, when each of these groups was broken down into devout, moderate, and inactive groups, associa-

[27] *Sexual Behavior in the Human Female*, p. 233.
[28] Ibid. p. 239.
[29] Ibid. p. 243.

tions did appear. The modest correlation between any petting experience and religiosity is illustrated by the fact that 96 per cent of less devout, unmarried Protestants were involved, but only 85 per cent of the devout group was involved. Where orgasm is involved, the differences are much greater. By age thirty-five, 39 per cent of inactive Protestants were involved as compared with 23 per cent of devout Protestants. Among Catholics, for whom data are available only for younger groups, the figures are 40 per cent for inactive women age 25, and 22 per cent for devout women. Since no devout classification was used for Jewish women, it should be reported that religious moderates generally showed slightly lower percentages reaching orgasm than among the religiously inactive.[30] Kinsey concludes that religion may not be too effective in preventing women from engaging in some petting activity but it definitely limits how far they will go.

The conclusion seems unavoidable that there is a great deal of petting activity associated with dating. Practically all men and women become involved, to some degree, before they are married. Moreover, there is no longer any question about the specifically sexual nature of this activity; more than 40 per cent of young women today and 50 per cent of young men carry some of their petting activity to the point of sexual climax. Some petting, of course, serves as a prelude to premarital intercourse.

PREMARITAL INTERCOURSE

The normative prohibitions of sexual expression in American society may well be strongest in the area of premarital intercourse. This, and the fact that most sociosexual research has been done on college campuses where premarital coitus is a continuing issue, probably accounts for the fact that this subject has been thoroughly researched from 1915 right up to the present day.

Tables 1 and 2 present very brief summaries of the findings of major studies of the incidence of premarital intercourse among college students, mixed high-school and college groups, and persons some of whom were single and some of whom were married at time of study. A complete explanation of the material in the "sample" columns of the tables will be found at the bottom of Table 2.

Several things in these tables deserve special mention. First, of course, is the expected finding that all of the figures for men are higher than those for women. This is consistent with our earlier generalization that men tend to be sexually more active. Second is the tendency for the percentages to be higher in more recent studies. This tendency is readily apparent in Table 1, but to see it in Table 2 one must look carefully at the age and marital status of the

[30] Ibid, p. 278.

TABLE 1. *Incidence of Premarital Intercourse of Males as Reported by Various Investigators.*

INVESTIGATOR	DATE	SAMPLE *	INCIDENCE %
Exner	1915	518 college students (Western sample), S	36
Peck & Wells	1923	180 college level, 23, S & M	35
Peck & Wells	1925	230 college level, 23, S & M	37
Hamilton	1929	100 college level, M	54
Bromley & Britten	1938	470 college students (questionnaire), 16–23, S	51
Bromley & Britten	1938	122 college students (interview), 16–23, S	52
Peterson	1938	419 college students, S	55
Terman	1938	760 college and high school level, 28, M	61
Porterfield & Salley	1946	285 college students, 18–30, S	32
Finger	1947	111 college students, 17–23, S	45
Hohman & Schaffner	1947	1000 college level, 21–28, S	68
Kinsey *et al.*	1948	2308 college level, 20, S & M	44
Kinsey *et al.*	1948	761 college level, 25, S & M	64
Kinsey *et al.*	1948	202 college level, 20, S & M	68
Ross	1950	95 college students, 21, S	51
Gilbert Youth Research	1951	—— college students, 17–22, S	56
Burgess & Wallin	1953	580 college and high-school level, 26, M	68
Landis & Landis	1953	600 college students, S & M	41
Ehrmann	1959	274 college students (nonveterans), 18–21, S	57
Ehrmann	1959	302 college students, veterans), 20–26, S	73
Ehrmann	1959	50 college students (interview), 19–24, S	68
Robinson, King, et. al.	1968	129 college students	65
Luckey & Nass	1969	670 college students, S	58
Peretti	1969	117 college students and 181 non-college, 17–24, S	48
Christensen & Gregg	1970	245 midwestern college students, S	50

* See explanation below Table 2.

Source: Adapted from Winston W. Ehrmann, *Premarital Dating Behavior*, New York: Holt, Rinehart, and Winston, Inc., 1959, p. 33.

subjects at the time of reporting. For obvious reasons, studies of older and married persons yield higher percentages. This is related to the third point, which is that these percentages generally indicate the proportions of the subjects who had had coitus *by the time of study*, not the proportions who have coitus before marriage. Only for married subjects should the figures be taken to represent total involvement in sexual intercourse before marriage. Finally, the variation in percentages even among comparable groups should not be

TABLE 2. *Incidence of Premarital Intercourse of Females as Reported by Various Investigators.*

INVESTIGATOR	DATE	SAMPLE *	INCIDENCE %
Davis	1929	1200 college level, 37, S	11
Davis	1929	1000 college and high-school level, 26, M	7
Hamilton	1929	100 college level, M	35
Dickinson & Beam	1934	500 college and high-school level, 27, S	12
Bromley & Britten	1938	618 college students (questionnaire), 16–23, S	25
Bromley & Britten	1938	154 college students (interview), 16–23 S	26
Terman	1938	777 college and high-school level, 25, M	37
Landis et al.	1940	109 high-school and college level, 18–30, S	23
Landis et al.	1940	44 high-school and college level, 22, M	27
Porterfield & Salley	1946	328 college students, 18–20, S	9
Gilbert Youth Research	1951	—— college students, 17–22, S	25
Kinsey et al.	1953	3303 college level, 15, S & M	2
Kinsey et al.	1953	2070 college level, 20, S & M	20
Kinsey et al.	1953	487 college level, 25, S & M	39
Burgess & Wallin	1953	604 college and high-school level, 24, M	47
Landis & Landis	1953	1000 college students, S & M	9
Reevy	1954	139 college students, 18–23, S	7
Ehrmann	1959	265 college students, 18–22, S	13
Ehrmann	1959	50 college students (interview), 18–22, S	14
Freedman	1965	49 college seniors (interview), S & M	22
Robinson, King, et. al.	1968	115 college students	29
Luckey & Nass	1969	728 college students, S	43
Peretti	1969	160 college students and 207 non-college, 17-24, S	21
Christensen & Gregg	1970	238 midwestern college students, S	34

* Since the descriptive remarks under the heading "Sample" are brief, they are very incomplete. The number of subjects are the actual number, or an approximation, who furnished information on this particular item. "College student" merely indicates that all subjects in the sample were in college at the time of study. "College level" or "college and high-school level" signifies that the subjects went to these points in their education and that some, many, or all were no longer in school at the time of investigation. A single figure after the educational status identification is the mean age, or an approximation, of single persons at the time of study or of married persons at the time of marriage. That the subjects were single, married, or mixed single and married at the time of study are indicated by "S," "M," or "S & M." An age range, such as 17–22, represents either the age distribution of all individuals or of the great majority in the sample."

Source: Adapted from Winston W. Ehrmann, *Premarital Dating Behavior*, New York: Holt, Rinehart, and Winston, Inc., 1959, p. 34.

overlooked. While the studies establish the fact of considerable premarital coitus beyond all doubt, the methodological problems involved in studying sex behavior are formidable and the possibility of substantial error in individual studies exists.[31] Beyond this, however, we should expect to find variation from one group to another. This is in accord both with the general principle of wide variation in sex behavior stated earlier, and with empirical evidence. In the study by Bromley and Britten, for example, which included students from 46 different colleges, the proportions of girls who had had intercourse varied from 9 per cent to 36 per cent.[32]

For the most comprehensive statistics on the incidence of premarital intercourse, we again return to the Kinsey studies. Kinsey's findings for males will be presented first, followed by those for females.

Premarital intercourse by males is closely related to educational level. Just as high-school and college males are more active in heterosexual petting, they are less likely to carry their activities to coitus. Among men who went on to college, only 67 per cent had intercourse before marriage; among those who did not go beyond high school, the figure was 84 per cent; and among those who stopped with grade school, the proportion climbed to 98 per cent.[33] It appears that, at lower social levels, coitus is considered to be the "normal" way to pursue sexual interest and most males become involved during their teens. At upper levels, however, where higher value is placed upon virginity, petting serves as a functionally equivalent substitute for coitus.

A somewhat surprising finding is that the position of premarital coitus in the lives of males appears not to have changed significantly over the last

[31] Discussions of the confidence to be placed in specific studies of sex behavior often generate as much heat as light. The Kinsey studies particularly have been criticized for a biological bias, for their sampling procedures, and for their use of volunteer subjects. See Purnell H. Benson and Evelyn Bently, "Sources of Sampling Bias in Sex Studies," *Public Opinion Quarterly* 21 (Fall 1957), pp. 388–94; John A. Clausen, "Biological Bias and Methodological Limitations in the Kinsey Studies," *Social Problems* 1 (April 1954), pp. 126–33; William G. Cochran, Frederick Mosteller, and John W. Tukey, "Statistical Problems of the Kinsey Report," *Journal of the American Statistical Association* 48 (Dec. 1953), pp. 673–716; Judson T. Landis, "The Women Kinsey Studied," *Social Problems* 1 (April 1954), pp. 139–42. On the other hand, it must be pointed out that the Kinsey studies are methodologically far superior to many social science studies whose findings are accepted without question. For an excellent discussion of societal resistances to the acceptance of sex research, see Winston W. Ehrmann, "Marital and Nonmarital Sexual Behavior," op. cit. pp. 616–20.

[32] As cited in Winston W. Ehrmann, *Premarital Dating Behavior*, op. cit. p. 35.

[33] *Sexual Behavior in the Human Male*, p. 552. For a perceptive analysis of the pressures on men in relation to premarital intercourse, see Irving B. Tebor, "Male Virgins: Conflicts and Group Support in American Culture," *Family Life Coordinator* 9 (March–June 1961), pp. 40–42.

generation. Men are not having more premarital intercourse now than formerly. The only significant change here is that less of what coitus is had now appears to be had with prostitutes. Males at the upper social levels, particularly, are more likely today to have their sex relationships with women from their own social levels, women whom they may ultimately marry.

The major changes that have occurred in the incidence of premarital intercourse are to be found among women. Among women who were born before 1900, the percentage who had premarital coitus was less than half what it was among women born in any subsequent decade. Of women still unmarried at age 25, for example, 14 per cent of the older generation had had coitus while 36 per cent of those born during the next decade had done so.[34] The major change apparently occurred among those women who reached adulthood at or shortly after World War I. The change occurred at all social and educational levels and, along with the corresponding increase in heterosexual petting, represents the major change in American sexual patterns during the present century.

In Kinsey's total female sample, approximately 50 per cent had intercourse before they were married. The factor most related to the incidence of premarital intercourse was age at marriage; girls who married earlier were likely to begin having premarital intercourse earlier, and those who married later began having intercourse later. A large proportion of the intercourse was confined to the year or two just before marriage, and a good proportion of that was had with the fiancé only. Of the women who were already married at time of interview, 46 per cent had had intercourse with the fiancé only. Forty-one per cent had it with the fiancé and other men; 13 per cent had had it with some other man but not with the fiancé.[35]

Again we find a relationship between religious background and the likelihood of premarital intercourse. Religiously inactive women were much more likely to become involved than were the religiously devout. Among women who had not married by 35 years of age, over 60 per cent of inactive Protestants and Jews, and 55 per cent of inactive Catholics, were involved. The corresponding figures for the devout were about 30 per cent for Protestants and 24 per cent for Catholics.[36] Differences within each of the three major

[34] *Sexual Behavior in the Human Female*, p. 298.

[35] Ibid., p. 292–3.

[36] Ibid. p. 304. These general findings have been confirmed in other studies. See Richard R. Clayton, "Religious Orthodoxy and Premarital Sex," *Social Forces* 47 (June 1969), pp. 469–74; Jerry D. Cardwell, "The Relationship Between Religious Commitment and Premarital Sexual Permissiveness: A Five Dimensional Analysis," *Sociological Analysis* 30 (Summer 1969), pp. 72–81; Jean Dedman, "The Relationship Between Religious Attitude and Attitude Toward Premarital Sex Relations," *Marriage and Family Living* 21 (May

religious groups generally were greater than the differences between the devout of different faiths and between the inactive of different faiths.

Thus, research confirms the existence of a substantial amount of premarital sexual involvement, often beginning in childhood and being transformed in late adolescence into widespread, nearly universal, heterosexual petting. For up to half of all women and more than half of all men, there is also some coital experience before marriage. These are some of the raw facts of premarital sex behavior. In this form, however, the facts do not tell us enough about the significance of such behavior for interpersonal relationships or for the family as a social institution. The Kinsey studies, upon which we have drawn so far, have a heavy biological emphasis. To analyze some of the social factors in premarital sex behavior, we now turn to another range of studies.

The Sociology of Premarital Sex Involvement

The Kinsey statistics are not without explicit social significance. We have already seen, for example, the consistent relationship, among males, between educational level and the amount and type of sexual experience. No comparable associations exist among women but, among them, age at marriage is closely related to premarital sex behavior. In both sexes, religiosity, as reflected in church attendance, exercises a restraining influence on premarital sex involvement. Finally, major change in premarital sex behavior occurring about the time of World War I has been substantiated. Heterosexual petting before marriage has become nearly universal, and the premarital coitus which men have is now more often had with women of their own social levels than with professional prostitutes.

One of the most interesting studies of premarital sex behavior, sociologically, was done by Winston Ehrmann at the University of Florida. Studying a total of 1157 students, he collected invaluable data on the influence of social class upon the development of sex relationships and upon the relation between sex behavior and the development of love in the relationship.

1959), pp. 171–6; Eugene J. Kanin, and David H. Howard, "Postmarital Consequences of Premarital Sex Adjustments," *American Sociological Review* 23 (Oct. 1958), pp. 556–62; Frank Lindenfield, "A Note on Social Mobility, Religiosity, and Students' Attitudes Toward Premarital Sexual Relations," *American Sociological Review* 25 (Feb. 1960), pp. 81–4; Howard J. Ruppel, Jr., "Religiosity and Premarital Sexual Permissiveness: A Response to the Reiss-Heltsley Debate," *Journal of Marriage and the Family* 32 (Nov. 1970), pp. 647–55; Alfred J. Prince and Gordon Shipman, "Attitudes of College Students Toward Premarital Sex Experience," *Family Life Coordinator* 6 (June 1958), pp. 57–60; and Gordon Shipman, "The Psychodynamics of Sex Education," *The Family Coordinator* 17 (Jan. 1968), pp. 3–12.

CROSS-CLASS DATING AND SEXUAL INVOLVEMENT

The significance of cross-class dating for premarital relationships in general was discussed in the last chapter. There we saw that such relationships are conducive to exploitation of the lower-status partner. It was also recognized that lower-status girls may accept such relationships on the chance that they will lead to marriage.

Ehrmann classified his respondents according to whether they belonged to the same social class, a higher class, or a lower class than their dating partners. It is significant that only a few of his subjects had any difficulty in classifying their dating partners by this method. The patterns of social class dating are shown in Table 3. First, it should be noted that six out of ten men and seven out of ten women dated persons of the same social class only. This is in accord with the analyses of Waller and Reiss. In addition, most crossers of class lines dated persons from their own social class as well as others. A

TABLE 3. *Dating Patterns, by Social Class, of University of Florida Students.*

DATES WITH COMPANIONS OF THESE SOCIAL CLASSES	MALES (N=533)	FEMALES (N=263)
Same only	61%	69%
Lower only	2	2
Higher only	2	1
Same and lower	16	5
Same and higher	7	13
Both	12	10
	100	100

Source: Adapted from Winston W. Ehrmann, *Premarital Dating Behavior*, New York: Holt, Rinehart, and Winston, Inc., 1959, p. 144.

total of 96 per cent of the men and 97 per cent of the women dated some persons of the same social class. Thirty per cent of the men, but only 17 per cent of the women dated persons from a lower social class. Twenty-one per cent of the men and 24 per cent of the women dated upward.

Some of the influence of relative social class upon sexual involvement is shown in Table 4, which shows the social class of the companions with whom the subjects had had the most advanced sex behavior. To make these ratings, Ehrmann classified sex behaviors along a continuum ranging from no physical

TABLE 4. *Social Class of Companion with Whom Subject Had the Most Advanced Heterosexual Behavior*

ACTIVITY WITH COMPANIONS OF THESE SOCIAL CLASSES	MALES (N=553)	FEMALES (N=263)
Same only	69%	79%
Lower only	14	3
Higher only	3	5
Same and lower	9	3
Same and higher	2	7
Both	3	3
	100	100

Source: Adapted from Winston W. Ehrmann, *Premarital Dating Behavior*, New York: Holt, Rinehart, and Winston, Inc., 1959, p. 145.

contact or holding of hands only, through necking and the fondling of genitals, to sexual intercourse. The differences between men and women here are striking. Although seven out of ten men and eight out of ten women went farther with companions of their own social class, the male class-crossers tend to have their more intimate behavior with women of a lower social class or of the same and a lower class while the female crossers have theirs with men of the same and a higher social class. Twenty-six per cent of the men, but only 9 per cent of the women have their most intimate experiences with a lower-status person. Fifteen per cent of the women, but only 8 per cent of the men have their most intimate experiences with persons of a higher class.

Ehrmann's findings in this area were anticipated by Kanin and Howard, who secured data from 177 already married women on a midwestern university campus. These researchers found no relationship between the husband's social class position and premarital intercourse, but they did find a relationship between the comparative social class of the husband and wife and premarital intercourse. The incidence of premarital intercourse was highest where the husband came from a higher social class than his wife, was intermediate where they were of the same social class, and was lowest where the husband's social origin was lower than his wife's.[37]

These findings on the influence of relative social class upon sexual involvement make it quite clear that premarital sexual involvement is a social as well as a physical process and that it is closely connected with the system of dating and mate selection.

[37] Eugene J. Kanin and David H. Howard, op. cit. p. 558.

LOVE AND SEXUAL INVOLVEMENT

Ehrmann also studied the relation between sexual involvement and love involvement. This portion of his research was based on extensive interviews with 50 men and 50 women randomly selected from his larger sample. Dating relationships were broken down into those with acquaintances, friends, and lovers. All of the men and women had dated with friends and acquaintances, but only 45 men and 42 women reported that they had been in love. Each of the respondents was classified according to "lifetime sexual behavior," referring to the most intimate sex behavior which he or she had ever experienced, and according to "personal code," referring to the most intimate behavior considered permissible with an acquaintance, friend, or lover. Part of the results of this analysis are presented in Table 5.

The first finding of note is that far more men had had sexual intercourse with friends and acquaintances (56 and 60 per cent) than had done so with women they loved (24 per cent). When the personal code is considered, the same pattern holds; far more men consider coitus acceptable with friends and acquaintances than with lovers. In addition, the discrepancy between lifetime behavior and personal code is small in the case of friends and acquaintances, but large in the case of lovers. Thus, men adhere to a far more conservative standard of behavior with women they love than with those whom they do not. Moreover, their actual behavior with women they love is more conservative still.

When we look at the data on women's behavior, we find that the percentages who have had coitus are lower than among the men in the sample. The *pattern* among women is reversed from that among men. Very few women have had intercourse with friends or acquaintances, but more have done so with men whom they loved. Nor is there a major difference anywhere among the women between lifetime behavior and personal code. Women believe that intimacy is more acceptable in love relationships and their behavior closely parallels their standards.[38]

In summary, men are more liberal than women in every way. Men become more conservative when in love, however, and women become more liberal. Nevertheless, the proportion of men who are willing to have intercourse with the woman they love is still twice as large as those who do so and three times

---

[38] Winston W. Ehrmann, "Premarital Sexual Behavior and Sex Codes of Conduct with Acquaintances, Friends, and Lovers," *Social Forces* 38 (Dec. 1959), pp. 160–61. See also Robert L. Karen, "Some Variables Affecting Sexual Attitudes, Behavior, and Inconsistency," *Marriage and Family Living* 21 (Aug. 1959), pp. 235–9.

TABLE 5. *Lifetime Sexual Behavior and Personal Code of Sex Conduct of 100 Single College Students with Acquaintances, Friends, and Lovers.*

NUMBER	STAGES OF BEHAVIOR AND CODES (per cent)			
	Light petting	Heavy petting	Coitus	Total
MALES				
With Acquaintances:				
(50) Lifetime behavior	28	16	56	100
(50) Personal code	28	12	60	100
With Friends:				
(50) Lifetime behavior	22	18	60	100
(50) Personal code	20	8	72	100
With Lovers:				
(45) Lifetime behavior	36	40	24	100
(45) Personal code	24	29	47	100
FEMALES				
With Acquaintances:				
(50) Lifetime behavior	92	6	2	100
(50) Personal code	92	4	4	100
With Friends:				
(50) Lifetime behavior	82	12	6	100
(50) Personal code	84	10	6	100
With Lovers:				
(42) Lifetime behavior	42	41	17	100
(42) Personal code	46	40	14	100

Source: Winston W. Ehrmann, "Premarital Sexual Behavior and Sex Codes of Conduct with Acquaintances, Friends, and Lovers," *Social Forces* 38 (Dec. 1959), p. 161.

as large as the number of women who are willing to do so. Being in love decreases for men and increases for women the proportion who are willing to have coitus and who actually do so. Being in love not only decreases the incidence of coitus among men and increases it among women, but it also brings the standards of the sexes closer together.

Perhaps as important as the figures on sexual intercourse are those on heavy petting among persons who are in love. Forty per cent of the women believe intimacies at this level to be acceptable and 30 per cent of the men believe that heavy petting should suffice. Fewer than half of the women and one-fourth of the men would restrict behavior with a loved one to the level of light petting.

PREMARITAL SEX STANDARDS

The questions which Ehrmann's research raises about the relationships between sexual behavior and sexual standards have been extended by Reiss, who has done an extensive analysis of premarital sexual standards, and changes in those standards, in America.[39]

Reiss, first of all, conceives of two types of sex behavior that shade into one another on a continuum. The one type he calls body-centered; the other type he calls person-centered. Body-centered relationships emphasize the physical part of sex; person-centered relationships emphasize the particular person with whom the experience is had. Sexual standards, he says, tend to lead either to body-centered unaffectionate sex behavior or to person-centered affectionate behavior.

There are four principal sexual standards in existence in America today. They are:

1. Double Standard: Premarital intercourse is considered right for men but wrong for women.

2. Permissiveness Without Affection: Premarital intercourse is considered right for both men and women whenever there is physical attraction, regardless of whether affection is present.

3. Permissiveness with Affection: Premarital intercourse is considered right for both men and women providing strong affection is present.

4. Abstinence: Premarital intercourse is considered wrong for both men and women, regardless of circumstances.

Reiss avoids being trapped into stating which of these standards is right and which is wrong. Instead, he examines each standard to determine the degree to which it is consistent with our other societal values and in terms of the consequences of adherence to it.

The double standard is the dominant informal standard in Western society. In earlier chapters, we saw that this standard is widely associated with male dominance and that, in Western society, it has survived from ancient times right down to the present day. Logically, however, it involves a paradox. If all men are to have sexual experience and all women are to remain chaste, with whom are the men to have intercourse? Historically, this "virginity paradox" has been partially solved by the creation of a special class of women with whom intercourse was sanctioned, leaving most women virginal. Professional prostitutes constituted the core of this class of women, but lower-class

[39] Ira L. Reiss, *Premarital Sexual Standards in America*, Glencoe, Illinois: The Free Press, 1960.

women, women of different religions, ethnic, and racial groups, and women identifiable as "bad" women also were included.[40] The paradox is rendered sharper, however, by the fact that virtually all women in the society are considered to be appropriate sexual targets by some groups of men.

In some ways the double standard conflicts with other widely held values in American society, and in some ways it is quite consistent with other values. In addition to the paradox just cited, the double standard conflicts with our notions of justice and equal treatment; it assigns full responsibility and blame for sexual activity to the female partner. On the other hand, the double standard works to reinforce the traditional male domination in Western society, strengthening the role of the husband as head of the family, breadwinner, and protector of women.

The body-centered sex relationships encouraged by the double standard receive most explicit approval under the permissiveness without affection standard. In spite of recent equalitarian and rational trends in American society, Reiss believes this one to have the smallest number of adherents of any of the standards listed. It may be most widely accepted among certain extreme lower-class groups in which there is little marital stability, little regular employment, and few restrictions on coitus. It is sanctioned by some elements of the youth counterculture who believe, on intellectual grounds, that sexual intercourse is as natural and necessary as eating and sleeping and that sex is justified by the prospect of physical pleasure alone.

In some ways, according to Reiss, the permissiveness without affection standard is logically integrated with other aspects of American culture. Because it treats the sexes alike, it does not conflict with our ideas of justice. Moreover, it does not define sex as bad and it does not lead to a virginity paradox. In general, however, this standard is poorly integrated with the rest of the culture and is not likely to become widespread. It violates our conceptions of the value of virginity and of sexual intercourse; it conflicts with all of our major religious traditions; it challenges the traditional subordination

[40] The Western tendency to classify women into "good women" and "bad women" apparently has at least two roots. First, in point of time, was the ancient tendency to use foreign women and lower-class women as concubines and prostitutes. Later, Christianity was influential in further defining sex as evil and creating the image of the sacred virgin.

In modern times, there is a pervasive tendency for double-standard men to make the distinction between good and bad women in terms of whether or not they will have intercourse. A woman who will is, by definition, bad. One of the functions of dating is to permit the male to test his partner to see whether, indeed, she is not a bad woman. If he succeeds— even after months or years of trying—then his suspicions as to her character are confirmed and he is justified in seducing her. By yielding, the woman likely removes herself from the list of potential marriage partners. Double-standard men usually want to marry asexual good women in the images they hold of their mothers and sisters.

of women; and it encourages body-centered relationships that are not likely to lead to marriage.

The permissiveness with affection standard is alleged to be more popular than permissiveness without affection but less popular than the double standard. Sexual intercourse is not defined as an end in itself; it is likely to be person-centered and an expression of the partners' feelings for one another. This standard may be most popular among educated, middle-class people; at least research verifies its existence among various groups of college students. It does not condone promiscuity but, since it insists upon strong affection or love between the partners, is actually a somewhat conservative single standard.

Reiss believes that acceptance of this standard has become much more widespread over the past century. Those parts of the culture with which this standard is in conflict—female subordination, the value attached to virginity, and traditional religion—are also changing. The standard continues to be opposed, in spite of its essential conservatism, however, by almost all official spokesmen for the larger society.[41]

The formal, single standard of abstinence was brought into Western culture by Christianity and imposed upon the Hebrews, Greeks, and Romans, all of whom had double standards. The new single standard held that coitus was too important and too valuable to be performed outside the marriage relationship. There are no precise figures on the degree of adherence to this standard before the present century, but recent data show both adherence to and deviation from it. Adherence varies by social class. About one-third of college-educated men remain virgin until marriage, but only about 2 per cent of grade-school-educated men do so. Among women, social class factors are less in evidence and age at marriage is more important; about 50 per cent have intercourse before marriage. Short of intercourse, necking and petting are virtually universal. Reiss indicates that many of the men and women who adhere to the formal standard of abstinence are "technical virgins" or "promiscuous virgins." On the other hand, the abstinence standard still has a strong hold on a large number of young people. They derive security from adherence to it and define premarital sex behavior as cheap and immoral.[42]

Reiss believes that the double standard in American society clearly is weakening. As it weakens, it forces young people toward a choice between the abstinence standard or a permissive standard for both men and women. While a full return to the abstinence standard seems to be a theoretical possibility, the widespread acceptance of necking and petting has undermined it, probably to the point of no return. Moreover, the spread of contraceptive

<hr/>

41 *Premarital Sexual Standards in America*, 117–45.

42 Ibid. pp. 195–217.

knowledge and trends toward equality for women encourage the spread of permissive standards. There is little evidence, however, of any large trend toward permissiveness without affection or body-centered coitus. Among college-level persons, at least, there is little evidence of greater acceptance of any type of premarital coitus over the past 40 years. Moreover, what acceptance there is appears generally to be conditioned upon the movement of the relationship toward marriage.

Announced about 10 or 15 years ago, the sexual revolution has yet to take place. . . . the Institute for Sex Research at Indiana University . . . has just completed a new study, begun in 1967, in the course of which 1200 randomly selected college students were interviewed. Comparing the findings with those obtained in its study 20 years ago, the institute reports increasing liberalism in sexual practices but stresses that these changes have been gradual. . . . Most close students of the sexual scene seem to agree that the trend toward greater permissiveness probably began back in the nineteen-twenties, and has been continuing since. . . .

The sexual changes one notes on the advanced campuses are of two kinds. First, there is a greater readiness to establish quasi-marital pairings, many of which end in marriage; these are without question far more common than in the past, and are more often taken for granted. Second, there is a trend, among a very small but conspicuous number of students, toward extremely casual sexuality, sometimes undertaken in the name of sexual liberation. To the clinician, these casual relationships seem to be more miserable than not—compulsive, driven, shallow, often entered into in order to ward off depression or emotional isolation. The middle-class inhibitions persist, and the attempt at sexual freedom seems a desperate maneuver to overcome them. We have a long way to go before the sexually free are sexually free. . . .

—Joseph Adelson, "What Generation Gap?" *The New York Times Magazine*, January 18, 1970, p. 34. © 1970 by The New York Times Company. Reprinted by permission.

An excellent and very recent study bearing upon this whole matter was done by Freedman among recent graduates of an Eastern women's college. This study is noteworthy because the researcher secured both test and interview data from whole classes of students and from careful random samples of those same classes. His results, therefore, cannot be said to contain volunteer error.[43]

[43] Mervin B. Freedman, op. cit.

The test data were secured from three classes of students who were tested shortly after entering college and again toward the end of their senior year. The interview sample was drawn from one of the classes and was interviewed several times a year beginning with the freshman year, as part of a longitudinal study of personality development during the college years. Of the 51 women in the interview sample who graduated with their class, only two refused to continue the interviews beyond the freshman year. The data reported here are based principally upon the interviews with the remaining 49 women.

TABLE 6. *The Sexual Experience of a Random Sample of College Senior Women* (N=49).

LIMITED EXPERIENCE	RESTRICTED PETTING	EXTENSIVE PETTING	INTERCOURSE CONFINED TO SERIOUS RELATIONS	UNINHIBITED BEHAVIOR
N 5	13	20	8 *	3
% 10	27	41	16	6

* Included in this figure are two women who had engaged in intercourse with a man with whom they were not intimately involved emotionally. They had not had intercourse with other men, however.

Source: Mervin B. Freedman, "The Sexual Behavior of American College Women: An Empirical Study and an Historical Survey," *Merrill-Palmer Quarterly* 11 (Jan. 1965), p. 36.

The women were classified according to their experience in sexual behavior (Table 6). Those who were classified as having had "limited experience" had not gone beyond kissing. "Restricted petting" means petting above the waist only. "Extensive petting" includes genital involvement, but not intercourse. "Intercourse confined to serious relationships" means that intercourse had been had in a relationship involving emotional intimacy; in most cases only one man had been involved, never more than two. "Uninhibited behavior" means that intercourse had not been confined to relationships where there was emotional intimacy. As can be seen from Table 6, the largest group of women fell into the extensive petting category. The two petting categories covered more than two-thirds of the women. The figure of 22 per cent of the women having had intercourse is quite consistent with the findings of both Ehrmann and Kinsey.

In responding to test items that dealt with their feelings about their sex behavior, most of the women indicated that they were content with the status quo. If anything, the more negative responses came from the women in the limited experience and restricted petting categories, who displayed some desire for more experience.[44] None of these women showed any inclination

[44] Another study of 250 female and 160 male college students found that one-third of the women and three-fourths of the men wished that they had been more intimate in their dating relationships. See Robert R. Bell and Leonard Blumberg, "Courtship Stages and Intimacy Attitudes," *Family Life Coordinator* 8 (March 1960), p. 62.

to seek sexual experience as such, however. What they sought was a deep relationship with some man in the context of which sexual participation would become acceptable.

Taking just the 22 per cent who had had intercourse, all reported the experience to be pleasurable, none acknowledged feelings of guilt, and none felt that they had transgressed basic moral or religious codes.[45] The 4 women, out of the 11, who felt some dissatisfaction with sexual matters were not involved in serious relationships with men whom they hoped to marry. Two were in the uninhibited category and the other two were regretful because their relationships with the men involved had turned out badly.

The study also sought to get at the sex codes adhered to by the women. In general, the standard which they used to judge the behavior of others was fairly liberal. Extensive petting in the context of a love relationship was considered appropriate, and affairs, if they were not promiscuous, were not condemned. The women's personal codes, however, were more conservative; the great majority wished to avoid premarital intercourse.

The values underlying the conservative personal codes were, in general, not the traditional ones. Few women attached any great value to virginity as such, few sought support from religious teachings, and few were concerned about general social attitudes of disapproval. Their reasons for not wishing to become involved tended to be stated in personal and interpersonal terms. Some mentioned fear of pregnancy, some were afraid of guilt or loss of self-respect that might be damaging to their relationships with the men involved, some wanted to retain their virginity because they thought that it was important to good marriage relationships, and so on. The researcher's opinion was that these stated reasons reflected a sense of caution and inhibition that is a deep-

---

[45] The problem of guilt feelings over premarital sex behavior is a very knotty one. How much misgiving or apprehension does there have to be before guilt exists? "Guilt" in the Freedman study apparently refers to a fairly pervasive phenomenon, and his results probably should be interpreted to mean that none of the girls were deeply upset over their behavior. Burgess and Wallin's finding that over 90 per cent of their engaged couples who had had intercourse reported that it had strengthened their relationship is consistent with Freedman's findings. See Ernest W. Burgess and Paul Wallin, *Engagement and Marriage*, Philadelphia: J. B. Lippincott Company, 1953, pp. 371–2. That apprehension, at some level, over premarital sex experience is common is indicated by Bell and Blumberg's study. These researchers found that a little over one-third of the women who had gone steady and done any petting expressed guilt over their behavior. Of those who had had intercourse during engagement, 41 per cent of both men and women reported some feelings of guilt. Another study showed 35 per cent of college girls believe intercourse during engagement is very wrong and another 48 per cent believe it to be generally wrong. See Robert R. Bell and Jack V. Buerkle, "Mother and Daughter Attitudes to Premarital Sexual Behavior," *Marriage and Family Living* 23 (Nov. 1961), p. 391. See also Robert R. Bell, "Parent-Child Conflict in Sexual Values," *The Journal of Social Issues* 22 (April 1966), pp. 34–44.

seated middle-class characteristic and that the women were only dimly aware of the complex sentiments that actually motivated their behavior.

The combination of the women's fairly conservative behavior and their conservative personal standards does not lend much support to the idea that American sexual behavior is changing drastically.[46] Something of a revolution in the premarital association between the sexes did take place early in the century, and a gradual trend toward more permissiveness has continued since that time. Freedman states that "non-virginity among college women probably doubled or trebled in the years following World War I, starting from a base of quite low incidence. That increase apparently became stabilized by about 1930. Since that time the incidence of premarital intercourse appears to have risen gradually, particularly among couples who are in love."[47]

THE RELATION OF PREMARITAL SEX BEHAVIOR TO MARITAL ADJUSTMENT

Possibly no other area in the study of the family is so loaded with value judgments and conflicting interpretations as the effects of premarital intercourse upon subsequent adjustment. Partisan views often prevail over serious attempts to understand the evidence. Let us see what research shows.

The early studies of marital adjustment generally showed a negative relationship between premarital intercourse and marital happiness or marital adjustment. Lewis Terman's study of 792 California couples during the 1930's showed a slightly higher frequency of marital happiness among couples who had not had intercourse before marriage, a slightly lower frequency for those

---

[46] See Shirley Angrist, "Communication About Birth Control: An Exploratory Study of Freshman Girls' Information and Attitudes," *Journal of Marriage and the Family* 28 (Aug. 1966), pp. 284–6; Jack O. Balswick and James A. Anderson, "Role Definition in the Unarranged Date," *Journal of Marriage and the Family* 31 (Nov. 1969), pp. 776–8; Danny E. Harrison, Walter H. Bennett, and Gerald Globetti, "Attitudes of Rural Youth Toward Premarital Sexual Permissiveness," *Journal of Marriage and the Family* 31 (Nov. 1969), pp. 783–7; Gilbert R. Kaats and Keith E. Davis, "The Dynamics of Sexual Behavior of College Students," *Journal of Marriage and the Family* 32 (Aug. 1970), pp. 390–99; Alfred Mirande, "Reference Group Theory and Adolescent Sexual Behavior," *Journal of Marriage and the Family* 30 (Nov. 1968), pp. 572–7; Hallowell Pope and Dean D. Knudson, "Premarital Sexual Norms and Social Change," *Journal of Marriage and the Family* 27 (Aug. 1965), pp. 314–23; John R. Stratton and Stephan P. Spitzer, "Sexual Permissiveness and Self Evaluation: A Question of Substance and a Question of Method," *Journal of Marriage and the Family* 29 (Aug. 1967), pp. 434–41; and Jetse Sprey, "On the Institutionalization of Sexuality," *Journal of Marriage and the Family* 31 (Aug. 1969), pp. 432–40.

[47] "The Sexual Behavior of American College Women," op. cit., p. 46. Comparable conclusions have emerged from a recent careful study of the sexual behavior of young people in Great Britain. See M. Schofield, *The Sexual Behavior of Young People*, London: Longmans, Green, 1965.

who had had coitus with the future spouse only, and a lower frequency yet for those who had had intercourse with the future spouse and others.[48] This finding generally was supported by Locke's comparison of happily married couples with divorced couples. Few women in either of Locke's groups would admit to premarital intercourse, but a larger percentage of the divorced than of the happily married men reported that they had had premarital intercourse with women other than their wives.[49]

The negative effects of premarital intercourse probably are especially marked when pregnancy results. The report of the Institute for Sex Research on pregnancy, birth, and abortion showed that approximately one-fifth of the unmarried women who have intercourse become pregnant. Some 94 per cent of those pregnancies, where the mother does not marry before the birth, terminate either in induced abortion or spontaneous abortion, and in only 6 per cent of the cases are the pregnancies carried to term. Some 16 per cent of the women who become pregnant before marriage subsequently get married before the child is born.[50] Christensen studied marriages in Utah and Indiana which occurred after the woman became pregnant and found that approximately one-fifth of all first children had been conceived before the marriage of the parents.[51] Subsequent study of these same couples showed that the divorce rate was twice as high among them as among couples where the woman was not pregnant at marriage.[52]

Perhaps the most systematic inquiry into the effects of premarital intercourse upon the subsequent adjustment of the couple was made by Burgess and Wallin in their study of 1000 engaged couples from 1937 to 1939 and the

[48] Lewis M. Terman, et al., *Psychological Factors in Marital Happiness*, New York: McGraw-Hill Book Company, 1938, Ch. 12.

[49] Harvey J. Locke, *Predicting Adjustment in Marriage: A Comparison of a Divorced and a Happy Married Group*, New York: Henry Holt and Company, 1951, p. 133. The pattern found in the Terman and Locke studies was confirmed recently in David F. Shope, and Carlfred B. Broderick, "Level of Sexual Experience and Predicted Adjustment in Marriage," *Journal of Marriage and the Family* 29 (Aug. 1967), pp. 424–7.

[50] Paul H. Gebhard, Wardell B. Pomeroy, Clyde E. Martin, and Cornelia V. Christenson, *Pregnancy, Birth, and Abortion*, New York: Harper and Brothers, and Paul B. Hoeber, 1958, pp. 39, 54, 57.

[51] Harold T. Christensen, "Studies in Child Spacing: I—Premarital Pregnancy as Measured by the Spacing of the First Birth from Marriage," *American Sociological Review* 18 (Feb. 1953), pp. 53–9. For a discussion of the social issues involved in pregnancy among unwed teenagers, see Clark E. Vincent, "Teen-Age Unwed Mothers in American Society," *The Journal of Social Issues*, 22 (April 1966), pp. 22–3.

[52] Harold T. Christensen and Hanna H. Meissner, "Studies in Child Spacing: II—Premarital Pregnancy as a Factor in Divorce," *American Sociological Review* 18 (Dec. 1953), pp. 641–4; and Harold T. Christensen and Bette B. Rubinstein, "Premarital Pregnancy and Divorce: A Follow-up Study by the Interview Method," *Marriage and Family Living* 18 (May 1956), pp. 114–23.

restudy of 666 of those couples after they had been married from three to five years. Comprehensive interview data were secured from only 226 of the couples and it is upon that section of the sample that Burgess and Wallin base their analysis.

Figure 1 compares engagement success scores of the 88 couples who had had intercourse with those of the 138 couples who had not. The higher the success scores, the better the adjustment according to the criteria used. Inspection of the figure reveals that, for both men and women, the proportions falling in the higher success categories is greater among those who had not had intercourse. When the average success scores of those who had had intercourse are compared with the average success scores of those who had not had intercourse, however, the differences are small, only 8 points for men and 6 points for women.

These data show that there is a small but consistent difference in engagement success scores in favor of those who had not had intercourse. Burgess and Wallin emphasize, however, that this does not prove that premarital intercourse has a negative effect on adjustment. To prove this would require that measures of adjustment be gathered both before and after intercourse occurred. The associations shown in Figure 1 may only mean that the couples who have intercourse are different to begin with; they may be less conventional people who are likely both to have premarital intercourse and to make slightly lower scores on conventional measures of engagement success.

Burgess and Wallin also related couples' premarital sex histories to their subsequent over-all adjustment in marriage. They found that men and women who did not have premarital intercourse had the higher probability of marital success. Couples in which the husband or wife had premarital intercourse with spouse and others had the lowest probability. Between these two extremes, the evidence was not altogether consistent; they could not show whether the chances of marital success are better for persons who had intercourse only with their future spouses than for those who restricted their sex relations to other persons. In summarizing their conclusions on the effects of premarital intercourse, they quote Terman with approval:

Premarital strictness in regard to sex may or may not be the *cause* of the greater happiness. It [marital happiness] may, instead, merely tend to select the persons who by ideals and personality have greater natural aptitude for successful marital adjustment, while laxness before marriage may tend to select those with less of this aptitude. The relatively small prediction weights warranted by our data on sex experience prior to marriage are in striking contrast with the importance attached by moralists to premarital chastity.[53]

[53] Terman, op. cit. p. 329.

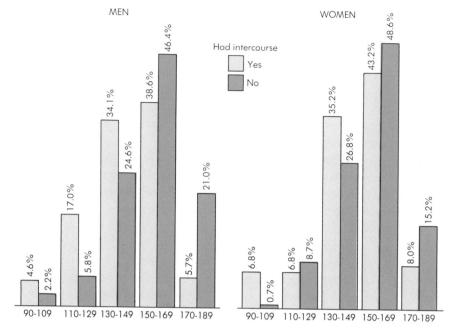

FIGURE 1. *Engagement success scores of 226 men and women classified by whether they had intercourse with their engagement partners.*

Source: Ernest W. Burgess and Paul Wallin, *Engagement and Marriage*, Philadelphia: J. B. Lippincott Company, 1953, p. 355.

In addition to the studies of the relation between premarital intercourse and general marital adjustment, several studies have focused on the relation between premarital coitus and the subsequent sex adjustment in marriage. And again we find a series of complex associations that do not lend themselves to easy interpretation.

Kanin and Howard studied the relationship between premarital intercourse and adjustment during the honeymoon period. In addition to discovering that couples who had been having intercourse were far less likely (47 per cent vs. 87 per cent) to bother with the formality of a regular wedding trip, they found certain associations with marital sex adjustment. About 71 per cent of the women who had premarital intercourse with their husbands reported satisfying sex relations on their wedding nights as contrasted with only 47 per cent of the women who had not had prior intercourse.[54] As in the Burgess and Wallin study, it is not possible to say whether these effects are due to the premarital sex experience or to the selective factors which determine whether or not one has premarital sex experience.

[54] Op. cit. p. 560.

Paradoxically, more of the women who had premarital intercourse also reported some sexual difficulties early in marriage (75 per cent vs. 43 per cent). Kanin and Howard believe that this probably is due to the higher expectations that women with sexual experience have for marital sex adjustment. This interpretation is strengthened by the fact that although more of the experienced women reported sexual difficulties, 87 per cent of them, compared to 31.5 per cent of the inexperienced, also reported that their marital sex experiences were satisfying.

Finally, these researchers found that whether or not the woman experienced orgasm in premarital coitus was important. Only 28 per cent of the women with orgasm experience in coitus reported sexual difficulties in marriage while 47 per cent of the women who failed to have orgasm in premarital coitus reported marital sex difficulties. When the wives were asked about the influence of their premarital sexual activity on marital sex adjustment, more of those with experience in coitus reported beneficial effects; 58 per cent of those with coitus reported beneficial effects, 54 per cent of those with heavy petting experience reported good effects, and only 34 per cent of those who restricted their petting to above the waist reported that it helped their marital adjustment. It should not be overlooked that 42 per cent of those who had premarital coitus stated that it had not helped their marital sex adjustment.[55] Which figure one chooses to emphasize may again reflect one's own personal bias.

Burgess and Wallin, too, related the likelihood of achieving orgasm in marriage to premarital sex experience. Their findings suggest the possible operation of a selective factor which may predispose the sexually most responsive women to have premarital intercourse both with their future spouses and with other men. The lowest frequencies of marital orgasm were had by wives who had not had premarital coitus. Women who had premarital intercourse with the husband only had somewhat higher frequencies of marital orgasm, and those who had premarital intercourse with the husband and others had the highest frequencies of marital orgasm.

The most comprehensive data on the relation between premarital orgasm experience and orgasm in marriage come from the Kinsey research. According to these authors, no factor showed a higher relationship with the frequency of marital orgasm than the presence or absence of premarital orgasm experience.[56] Forty-four per cent of the women with no premarital orgasm experience did not have orgasm during the first year of marriage; among those with limited premarital orgasm experience, 19 per cent failed to have orgasm during

[55] Ibid. pp. 560-1.
[56] Sexual Behavior in the Human Female, p. 385.

the first year of marriage; and of the women who had orgasm at least 25 times before marriage, only 13 per cent failed to achieve it during the first year of marriage. Where the premarital orgasm was had in coitus, rather than in petting or masturbation, the associations were even more striking. Only 3 per cent of the women who had orgasm 25 or more times in premarital coitus failed to have it during the first year of marriage.

Kinsey also found that it is the type of premarital experience which is associated with marital orgasm. Premarital coitus with orgasm was positively related to orgasm experience in marriage, but if the premarital coitus had not resulted in orgasm, the reverse was true. Among women who had failed to reach orgasm in premarital intercourse, between 38 and 56 per cent failed to reach orgasm during the first year of marriage. Even after 10 years of marriage, between 11 and 30 per cent of the premaritally unresponsive women were not able to achieve orgasm with their husbands. If premarital coitus aids marital sex adjustment, apparently it does so only if the premarital coitus leads to orgasm. Premarital intercourse which is not satisfying may produce trauma that interferes with subsequent marital sex adjustment.

To complicate the situation even further, the Kinsey researchers also found that women who have premarital intercourse apparently are more likely to have extramarital intercourse after they are married. Of the women who had not had premarital coitus, only 13 per cent had had extramarital coitus by the time they were interviewed. Among those who had premarital coitus, fully 29 per cent also had experienced extramarital intercourse. Whatever selective and/or experiential factors operate to produce correlations between premarital intercourse and good sex adjustment in marriage apparently operate to increase the likelihood of extramarital sexual involvement also.

The Dynamics of Premarital Sexual Involvement

Few responsible people question seriously the general validity of the findings cited in earlier sections of this chapter. There are those who refuse to accept the Kinsey findings, and some of the public press plays on the alleged unreliability of the findings of scientific studies.[57] The description of American premarital sex behavior, however, does not depend upon any one or even a few studies. There are literally dozens of studies which show the wide range of variation in behavior to be expected in any complex society but which also yield a consistent picture of widespread premarital sexual involvement. Moreover, comparative evidence from other societies makes it exceedingly unlikely that an institutionalized dating pattern, extending through adolescence and

[57] See Leo P. Chall, "The Reception of the Kinsey Report in the Periodicals of the United States: 1947–1949," in Jerome Himelhoch and Sylvia F. Fava, eds., op. cit. pp. 364–77.

into adulthood, could exist without such complications. It is not enough, however, simply to establish the fact of such involvement. There remains the task of attaching meaning to the statistical findings. Some of this has been described in the earlier discussion. In this section, we shall try to describe some of the typical ways in which young people incorporate sex involvement into their lives.

For purposes of convenience, let us talk about typical male sexual involvement first. Our statistics indicate that by the time men approach marriage most of them have been interested in sex for a long time. Although these facts ordinarily are concealed from their parents, their girl friends, and even from one another, most of them have been seeking physical and emotional satisfaction through masturbation. About 80 per cent of them started masturbating by the time they were 15 years old and most have continued this activity with regularity ever since; regularity means that about 50 per cent of them masturbate at least three times a week.

Masturbation is a relatively private activity and not often overtly social; the boy usually is alone. Covertly or vicariously, however, masturbation even from a very early age is usually social and heterosexual. For boys, as they masturbate, typically imagine themselves in sex play with some female. Whatever the boys daydream about, they actually are rehearsing attitudes and emotions for real relationships with girls and women later on. It is commonplace by now that masturbation itself produces no particular physical or emotional harm. The fantasies that boys have about themselves, about women, and about what exists between men and women, however, have major significance for their later relationships. Although there are no statistics on this, there is ample evidence that some boys' fantasies focus on what they should do *to* women, while some fantasies emphasize what they will do *with* women. The distinction is important. In the first case, the boys are tending toward an exploitative, hurtful use of sex, while, in the second case, they are tending toward a pattern that will be maximally rewarding both to them and to their women partners.

Many boys also begin their overt sexual interaction with girls at an early age. Using such devices as "playing doctor," many little boys are divesting little girls of their panties and are rehearsing the manipulation of the female genitalia by the time they are from five to eight years old. By the time they reach puberty at about 12 or 13, 70 per cent of all boys have had some experience in sex play and some 37 per cent have reached orgasm with the help of their girl companions. This leads, in early adolescence, into necking and petting. By the time of college graduation, nearly 90 per cent of all men have had experience in heavy petting and about 25 per cent of them have had orgasm and ejaculation either through their own arousal at their fondling of their companions or through reciprocal petting by the women involved. Again by the time of graduation from college, about one-half of the men have had full sexual intercourse with one or more women.

Now, let's consider the same situation for women. One of the really basic facts about American sex behavior is that women are not so actively involved or involved in such large numbers as men. The reasons for this difference are not wholly clear. That there are biological differences between men and women is clear enough, but how those differences lead to different sex involvement is not so clear. Most informed thinking on the subject recognizes that the internal nature of the female genitals may help account for the relative slowness of girls to take up sexual activity, but assigns the major role in their reluctance to the concerted suppression of sexual interest by a society which fears the social consequences that might result from too much sexual interest on the part of young females. In any event, women do not become as involved in any form of sex activity as men, up until they are married and begin marital intercourse.

Some girls begin masturbation in infancy, as some boys do. By the time of puberty, about 12 per cent of girls have masturbated, and by age 20, the figure has climbed to about one-third. Some girls, once they begin, continue masturbation regularly, as most boys do. But many experiment with it infrequently, and for short periods, and then give it up again. Girls do not fantasy as much as boys do, perhaps because they are systematically discouraged from developing erotic interests. We might hypothesize that girls, in masturbation, are responding more directly to physical need than is the case with boys. In any event, the vast majority of women who masturbate are able thus to achieve sexual climax—something some of them will find more difficult in their relationships with men.

Since petting takes two people, many girls gain heterosexual experience before marriage also. By age 18, some 80 per cent of college girls have had petting experience and, before marriage, some 37 per cent of them have petted to the point of orgasm. And here lies a very significant fact about female premarital sex behavior. The factor most related to the kind and amount of premarital sex behavior among women is the age at which they marry. It seems to work this way. Females are thoroughly conditioned against sex involvement while they are young. All of the pressures are against it, and, although there are occasional failures, the indoctrination is pretty effective. After puberty, however, conflicting forces begin to operate. Girls begin to experience some real physical push toward sex experience and the society at large begins reluctantly to sanction it. Most girls marry quite young (half of them before they are 21 years of age) before this reorientation toward sex has had time to go too far.

One excellent study of college-student sex behavior, done by two women incidentally, showed this very well and cast considerable light on the meaning of sex participation, or the lack of it, among college women. Some of the results of that study, for both men and women, are shown in Table 7. Of 872 junior and senior women, these authors classified 12 per cent as being "Victorian Virginals" (innocent and unawakened). Presumably, these were girls who had not yet begun to react against the childhood taboos against sexual interest. Another 24 per cent were classified as "Wait for Marriage" (innocent but awake). These girls had had enough experience in necking and petting to be aware of their own sex needs and capacities, but were firmly committed to avoiding sexual intercourse before marriage. Another 38 per cent of the girls were called "Technical Virgins" (not gone wrong yet). They recognized that they could not go on avoiding intercourse indefinitely, and that, if marriage were too long delayed, it would happen.

Approximately 25 per cent of the women in this study had already had intercourse. Of these, the largest single group ("Loving") were either in love

TABLE 7. *Sexual Patterns of 872 Women College Students and 592 Men College Students, 1930's.*

Virginal Women		75%
Innocent and Unawakened	12 %	
Wait for Marriage	24	
Technical Virgins	37½	
Homosexually Inclined	1½	
Nonvirginal Women		25%
Loving	11 %	
Experimenters	9	
Sowers of Wild Oats	3½	
Homosexually Inclined	½	
Remorseful	½	
Married	½	
Uninitiated Men (including 4% homosexual variants)		48%
Nonvirginal Men		52%
Hot Bloods	21 %	
Pragmatists	14	
Discriminating	7	
Romantics	7	
Homosexual Variants	3	

Source: Adapted from Dorothy D. Bromley and Florence H. Britten, *Youth and Sex: A Study of 1300 College Students*, New York: Harper and Brothers, 1938, p. 289. Reprinted by permission of Harper & Row, Publishers.

with the men involved or thought they were. In a very real sense, they may be technical virgins who didn't get married soon enough. This conclusion is strengthened by the fact that more than two-fifths of the inexperienced girls said that if they were in love and unable to marry, they would not hesitate to have intercourse.

The "Experimenters" were a somewhat more heterogeneous group. Most of them apparently had started out as "Loving," but, for one reason or another, the relationship had not led to marriage. A minority had begun their experience in intercourse self-consciously and motivated by curiosity and determination to use sex in the pursuit of further personality development. Bromley and Britten characterize the "Experimenters" as intelligent, intellectually inclined, often from liberal homes, and, occasionally, radically inclined. In terms of Reiss's sexual standards, they include advocates of both permissiveness with affection and permissiveness without affection. Almost all of the "Experimenters" were looking forward to marriage and slightly over half of them hoped for sexual fidelity in marriage.

While the "Experimenters" were quite selective in their sex relationships, the 3.5 per cent of the sample who were classified as "Sowers of Wild Oats" were not. These girls were the only ones in the sample who seemed to fit the popular stereotype of the bad girl. Their early sex experiences often had been motivated by feelings of personal inadequacy and they felt that they had little else to offer. Often they were antagonistic to men—viewing sex as a contest—and their recklessness in sex often was associated with drinking. Permissiveness without affection was their theme, although most of them hoped to marry and have children.[58]

A conceptual distinction which aids in the interpretation of these data is that between premarital and nonmarital behavior. So far, we have used the word, premarital, to refer to all sex behavior before marriage. But not all sex behavior before marriage occurs in anticipation of marriage. Perhaps if all sex experience occurred between people who were about to marry, there would be much less public concern about it. In premarital relationships the people are in love with one another, or think they are, and there is much more to their relationship than sex. They are interested in one another's total welfare and they use sex to contribute to their individual and mutual well-being. Such relationships tend to be person-centered in contrast to the body-centered relationships that are more characteristic of nonmarital behavior. In nonmarital sex behavior the emphasis is upon physical satisfaction and the other person involved is relatively unimportant.

[58] Dorothy D. Bromley and Florence H. Britten, *Youth and Sex: A Study of 1300 College Students*, New York: Harper and Brothers, 1938.

In these terms, it seems clear that the orientation of most women to sex definitely is premarital. Whether or not they eventually have intercourse before marriage, most women accept sex only as a part of continuing, meaningful relationships which they expect to lead to marriage. Few women are willing to seek after sex as a value in itself. The orientations of men, however, are often quite different.

Many middle-class boys, even before graduation from grade school, have acquired two sets of attitudes which encourage them toward nonmarital sex behavior. First is an ambivalent set of attitudes toward women. This dualistic conception, which goes far back into our cultural history, divides women into two classes: good women, identified essentially with mother and sisters, and other people's sisters from among whom one eventually will choose a marriage partner; and bad women, those potentially panting harlots whose chief purpose in life is to have sex with men. These are the women whose unclothed likenesses appear on the rest-room walls of public buildings, surrounded by a lettered set of obscene suggestions. Many males, while they may not be fully aware of it, tend to divide women into those who will and those who won't; those whom one should enjoy and those who are taboo.

The second set of attitudes is related to the first and pertains directly to sex. Boys are encouraged to learn that they are inherently sex-seeking beings, that sexual satisfaction is a primary value in life, and that as wide a variety of females as possible should be tested to determine if they are not, indeed, bad women.

These attitudes, along with others, form part of a masculine subculture which exercises an imperious force in most boys' lives and which most girls— because there is no truly feminine equivalent of it—seldom understand. The most prominent symbol of the masculine subculture among boys and young men probably is the bull session.

Although other things are discussed and other functions are served, the primary functions of young male bull sessions are three. First, they provide all participants with opportunity to participate vicariously in, and to receive erotic arousal from, one another's sex lives. A typical procedure is for each boy in turn to tell of a sexual exploit, embellishing it with exciting detail. As the session progresses, each narrator tries to top his predecessor, making himself appear more experienced, more successful, and more of a man than the others. This, then, is the second function; to permit each boy to enhance his own conception of himself as a male, at the expense of the others.

It might be appropriate here to point out that the primary ingredient in most bull sessions really is "bull." An honest boy in a bull session is about as hard to find as the proverbial camel being passed through the eye of a needle.

Honesty is not one of the functions of the bull session. Honesty would seriously hamper the first function of providing erotic stimulation, for most of the boys have neither as many nor as exciting experiences as they report to the group. With frequent, intense participation in bull sessions, however, the experiences which are fabricated take on reality for the teller until, after a while, he is not sure himself where experience leaves off and fantasy begins. Each boy is likely to be somewhat aware that he, himself, has not been wholly honest but, unfortunately, his insight does not enable him to be equally critical of his fellows' accounts. One result is that, even while he is enhancing his ego by exaggerating his own experiences, he is acquiring an uncomfortable sense of inadequacy by listening to and believing the wilder tales of his companions.

Thus the bull session's third function is brought into being. On the fringe of the bull session are likely to be one or more wide-eyed innocents. These are the most honest boys whose inability to get into the swing of things makes them the logical scapegoats for the accumulating fears of inadequacy being experienced by other members of the group. One of the ringleaders is likely to turn and say something like, "Hey, look at Joe. I'll bet he has never had any." Everyone then jumps on Joe and, by making him feel terribly inexperienced, they relieve somewhat their own feelings of inadequacy. The end result of all of this is to leave each boy with the idea that everybody else is making out better than he is and that not only should he get his share, but he is not much of a man if he doesn't.

Remember that these are not especially depraved young men. Many are nice middle-class boys who still have difficulty believing that their mothers enjoy going to bed with their fathers and who will defend their sisters against any unscrupulous male who tries to make it with them. But the pressure on these young men is great. While they are dating young women and trying to get to know them as people, they have to cope with more than their own natural sex urges and those of their dates. In addition, they are haunted by the need to acquire trophies to have for their own satisfaction and to be able to share in future bull sessions.

Now it may be instructive to look at the bottom half of Table 7. About half of Bromley and Britten's sample of college men had not yet had intercourse. Of these, some 80 per cent reported that ideals, fears, or a mixture of the two, had kept them from becoming involved. The significant groups among the other half, who had had intercourse, included the "Hot Bloods," the "Pragmatists," the "Discriminating," and the "Romantics."

Forty per cent of the experienced men, and 20 per cent of the total sample, were classified as "Hot Bloods." These men, more than the other types, were characterized by the "hunter's instinct." They were impulsive, reckless, and irresponsible. A large proportion of them adhered self-consciously to a double sex standard. Often among the most popular men on campus, they were inclined to be quite egocentric. Their approach to sex was largely in nonmarital terms.

The "Pragmatists" constituted 14 per cent of the total sample and 27 per cent of the experienced men. They are described as being less promiscuous than the "Hot Bloods," with a shrewd eye for their own interests and an awareness of the practical results of their behavior. They were less likely to espouse a double standard and analyzed sex as they did other aspects of their lives. They took a practical attitude toward life and played their cards close to the vest.

The "Discriminating" and the "Romantics" comprised smaller groups. The "Discriminating" are described as personally fastidious and biding their time until they achieve a sex relationship with a proper blend of aesthetic, intellectual, and sensual qualities. Body-centered relationships were repulsive to them and only the larger relationship with the girl made sex acceptable.

The "Romantics" were the most idealistic of all of the experienced groups; their code, in the terms of the 1960's, permitted permissiveness with affection only. It is significant that only this 7 per cent of the total male sample conceived of sex in terms similar to those held by most women.

Although the Bromley and Britten study is relatively old now, there is no reason to think its findings any less applicable today. And it illustrates well some of the complexities of sexual interaction before marriage. It is perhaps fair to say that few girls find nonmarital sex acceptable and that a majority of men seek it. As couples approach marriage, it may well be that men are likely to give up some of their exploitative attitudes and also to conceive of sex in premarital terms. Research shows, however, that aggression continues to intrude into many serious relationships.

The problem of sexual aggression in premarital relationships was studied by Kanin and Kirkpatrick among 291 women students at a midwestern university. These researchers distinguished among five different degrees of erotic aggressiveness: attempts at necking; petting above the waist; petting below the waist; sexual intercourse; and attempts at sexual intercourse with violence or threats of violence. A total of 56 per cent of the women reported that they had been offended at least once, at some level, during the academic year. Moreover, 21 per cent were offended by forceful attempts at intercourse, and 6 per cent by aggressively forceful attempts at intercourse that involved threats or the infliction of pain.[59]

[59] Clifford Kirkpatrick and Eugene Kanin, "Male Sex Aggression on a University Campus," *American Sociological Review* 22 (Feb. 1957), pp. 52–8. See also Eugene J.

A most significant finding was that there was a significant association between offensiveness at a mild level of erotic intimacy with casual dating relationships and offensiveness at more intimate levels with "pinned" and engaged relationships. Apparently the development of an emotional relationship between the man and woman is no real protection against sexual aggression. Offenses at the petting levels tended on the average to be repeated twice and, in half the cases, attempts at intercourse were repeated. Only when attempted intercourse was accompanied by threats or violence did it appear that the relationships were likely to be broken off.

In less than 6 per cent of the offenses were the matters reported to parents or academic authorities. The women were more inclined to reason with and rebuke the offender and were more likely to keep secret the offenses at advanced intimacy levels. Thus, there appears, in spite of the availability of institutional services, to be little protection for women against sexual aggression. In a companion study of offenses at the high-school level, Kanin found that female proneness to sex aggression was related to the absence of older male siblings.[60] Presumably, girls with older brothers are more likely to have some insight into the masculine subculture and are consequently more able to prevent aggression from occurring.

SUMMARY

Western society has a long history of disapproval of sexual involvement before marriage. Premarital intercourse generally is prohibited by law, and both the lay and professional publics have tended to ignore the problem and to distract attention from it. Nevertheless, the scientific study of human sex behavior began nearly 80 years ago and data have been accumulating ever since.

The data show that some boys and girls display sexual interest from a very early age and that substantial numbers of both sexes become involved in sex play before puberty. Boys are more active than girls and this differential in favor of more male participation continues throughout life in most forms of sexual activity.

Most pre-adolescent sex play takes the form of masturbation. Some of this activity, and particularly the associated heterosexual play, is motivated as much out of curiosity as out of definite erotic interest. Beginning early in ad-

---

Kanin, "Male Sex Aggression and Three Psychiatric Hypotheses," *The Journal of Sex Research* 1 (Nov. 1905), pp. 221-31.

[60] Eugene J. Kanin, "Male Aggression in Dating-Courtship Relations," *American Journal of Sociology* 63 (Sept. 1957), pp. 197-204. See also Eugene J. Kanin, "Selected Dyadic Aspects of Male Sex Aggression," *The Journal of Sex Research* 5 (Feb. 1969), pp. 12-28.

olescence, however, heterosexual petting becomes prominent and the goals are explicitly sexual arousal and satisfaction. Recent generations are more active in petting, suggesting a connection between the increase and the spread of adolescent dating. Among men, the incidence of petting is positively associated with educational level, and among women it is inversely related to church attendance.

The data on premarital intercourse also show relationships with educational level and religiosity. The incidence of premarital coitus among men has not changed significantly over the past few generations, but an increasing proportion of women have become involved. The major change occurred around the time of World War I with gradual increases since then. Much of this behavior occurs just before marriage and in anticipation of marriage. Nearly half of the women involved have intercourse with the future spouse only.

Studies of college students' sex behavior confirm the fact that students tend to date at their own class levels and that dating downward in the class structure is associated with more advanced forms of sexual activity. These studies also show that men are more likely to seek intercourse in casual relationships than in serious ones. For women the reverse is true; they become more accepting of sex as the relationship progresses toward marriage. The majority of both sexes sanction heavy petting among couples who are in love.

There appear to be four formal standards of premarital sex behavior in America: abstinence, the double standard, permissiveness with affection, and permissiveness without affection. Of the four, the double standard, which is fraught with inconsistencies, may be the most widespread. The abstinence standard, while widely admired, is even more widely thought to be unrealistic. Permissiveness without affection seems not to have much support except in the youth counterculture and at lower social levels. In recent decades there appears to have been some trend at middle- and upper-status levels toward acceptance of permissiveness with affection, toward making sexual involvement conditional upon serious love involvement rather than simply upon marriage.

The most recent studies of sexual involvement and sexual attitudes among college students show them generally to be rather conservative and quite concerned about the consequences of their behavior. They reject, however, prohibitions based upon authority and upon traditional morality. Most are rather content with their own sexual patterns, with some tendency for the least involved to report the greatest dissatisfaction.

Early studies of the relationship between premarital intercourse and subsequent marital adjustment showed a slight negative relationship. Whether the relationship was a causal one or whether simply a statistical association is unknown. More recent studies have produced conflicting findings. Studies of the relation between premarital intercourse and marital sex adjustment suggest that those who participate in premarital coitus receive more sexual satisfaction in marriage but that they also have higher expectations of the marital sex relationship. Again, whether the associations are causal is unknown.

There are some negative associations also. Those who have coitus before marriage but do not achieve orgasm are much less likely to achieve orgasm in the marital relationship. The probability of extramarital relationships also is significantly higher among those who have premarital intercourse.

Analysis of the dynamics of premarital sex involvement is furthered by a distinction between premarital and nonmarital sex behavior. Premarital involvement anticipates marriage and includes consideration of the well-being of the partner, while nonmarital involvement is an end in itself, is likely to be body-centered, and is egocentric in character. The socialization process, at least for most middle-class persons, produces some acceptance of premarital sex among women, but generally disavows nonmarital sex behavior. Men, in contrast, frequently are taught to seek sex in nonmarital terms. This leads to complications in the relationships between the sexes and frequently produces, as a by-product, some male sex aggression even in serious relationships. Those women who are most aware of the existence and norms of the masculine subculture seem best able to protect themselves against aggression.

SUGGESTED READINGS

Bell, Robert R., *Premarital Sex in a Changing Society*, Englewood Cliffs, New Jersey: Prentice-Hall, Inc., 1966. The most systematic account available of what sociologists have learned about premarital sex behavior.

Ehrmann, Winston, "Marital and Non-Marital Sexual Behavior," in Christensen, Harold T., ed., *Handbook of Marriage and the Family*, Chicago: Rand McNally, 1964, pp. 585–622. Includes an excellent summary of the state of our knowledge concerning premarital sex behavior.

Gagnon, John H., and Simon, William, *The Sexual Scene*, Chicago: Aldine Publishing Company, 1970. A collection of articles that appeared originally in *Trans-Action* magazine. Includes articles on changing premarital sex behavior, and on hippie morality.

Kirkendall, Lester A., *Premarital Intercourse and Interpersonal Relationships*, New York: Julian Press, 1961. A report of research on the nature and effects of the sexual involvements of 200 college level men. Propounds a humanistic ethic.

Reiss, Ira L., *The Social Context of Premarital Sexual Permissiveness*, New York: Holt, Rinehart and Winston, 1967. Includes data on sexual attitudes from a national probability sample of the American population.

Sagarin, Edward, ed., "Sex and the Contemporary Scene," *Annals of the American Academy of Political and Social Science*, 376 (March 1968). Special issue of a respected journal which takes stock of changes in sex behavior occurring in America. Includes an article on the de-polarization of sex roles.

Schur, Edwin M., ed., *The Family and the Sexual Revolution: Selected Readings*, Bloomington, Indiana: Indiana University Press, 1964. A recent collection of readings focusing upon sex standards, women's roles, and birth control.

FILMS

How Much Affection? (McGraw-Hill Book Company, Text-Film Division, 330 West 42nd St., New York 10036), 20 minutes. How much affection should there be between a couple who are going steady? How far can young people go in petting and still stay within the bounds of social mores and personal standards? The carefully presented drama of this film sets the stage for frank and constructive discussion of these and related questions.

Social-Sex Attitudes in Adolescence (McGraw-Hill Book Company, Text-Film Division, 330 West 42nd St., New York 10036), 20 minutes. How different home backgrounds affect attitudes and life adjustments of adolescents; describes a wide range of normal behavior.

Teenage Pregnancy (Sterling Educational Films, 241 East 34th Street, New York 10016), 14 minutes. The discovery that a teenage daughter is pregnant causes upheaval in a family. The frantic mother desperately tries to restore unity to her family.

QUESTIONS AND PROJECTS

1. What does research show about the involvement of pre-adolescent boys and girls in sex play? What generalizations can be made? What variation exists? Is all such play exclusively erotic?

2. What appears to be the relation between dating and sexual involvement? What variations are there by educational level? By religiosity? What generational changes have occurred?

3. What is the general incidence of premarital intercourse in the United States? What variation exists by educational level? What is the pattern of generational change? How is age at marriage a factor?

4. How is comparative social class related to the extent of premarital sex involvement? Can you reconcile this with research findings concerning dating interaction in general?

5. How are the sex codes of college men related to the development of emotional involvement? Compare this with the attitudes obtaining among college women. Does the disparity between male and female standards become larger or smaller as a couple approaches marriage?

6. Name and describe the four major premarital sex standards operative in the United States. How is each both consistent and inconsistent with other widely

held values? How widely held is each of the four standards? Which are in ascendance and which in decline?

7. What does the most recent research show about the standards adhered to by college women? What values seem to underlie the women's personal codes?

8. What does research show about the relation between premarital coitus and general marital adjustment? Between premarital coitus and marital sex adjustment? Explain the difficulty involved in distinguishing correlation from causation in these findings.

9. Distinguish between premarital and nonmarital sex behavior. How is the distinction important?

10. How does the masculine subculture condition boys toward the pursuit of nonmarital sex? What proportion of girls can accept sex in nonmarital terms?

11. How widespread is male sex aggression in dating relationships? Is aggression confined to casual relationships? To relationships with lower-class partners? In what ways do girls handle male sex aggression?

12. Arrange a panel discussion of the masculine and feminine subcultures specifically in relation to premarital sex behavior. Notice the lack of understanding and the misunderstanding that occur between the male and female participants. Are such discussions likely to be helpful in future dating?

14 | *Mate Selection*

The family is the oldest institution of the human race. Other institutions have always depended on it and I think people will go right on doing this. But if we would take a look at the modern world we would realize that people today are taking extraordinary risks. Young people are marrying across wide expanses of the world, choosing partners of other classes, other religions, other races. And people who are taking these risks ought to realize that they are doing something different but that they take the risk because they feel it is worth it—because they care about differences, because they care about contrast, because they care about intensity. Such relationships do have greater intensity, but they are also more hazardous. If you are not going to marry the boy next door—and if you do you may die of boredom—then you have got to work much harder.[1]

ALL societies have mechanisms for controlling who gets married to whom. In this chapter, we will look systematically at the ways in which mates are sorted out in American society.

HOMOGAMY

Marriage based upon romantic love is the norm in American society and is spreading rapidly to other areas of the world. No society, however, leaves the process of falling in love solely to the whims of the young. The general process of societal regulation of mate selection is subsumed under the concepts of endogamy and exogamy; people are required to select their spouses from within certain groups and are forbidden to choose them from certain other groups. These norms may be formalized into law, in which case they are quite obvious, or they may be largely implicit and may be studied only through analysis of who actually marries whom in the society.

[1] Margaret Mead, "We Must Learn to See What's Really New," *Life Magazine* (Aug. 1968), p. 34. © Time, Inc. 1968.

Comparatively speaking, American society has few exogamous norms. The incest taboos extend outward roughly to the first-cousin relationship, but there are no clans or other kinship structures within which mate selection is prohibited. Endogamous norms are more pervasive. It will be recalled from earlier chapters that Christianity has a long history of forbidding marriage with outsiders. Early in colonial days, interracial marriage also was forbidden. In few other respects are there civil or ecclesiastical laws requiring people to marry within their own groups. There is, however, evidence of a widespread tendency for people to marry others who are like themselves in ways that are not subject to formal regulation. This general tendency for like to marry like is called homogamy.

Literally hundreds of studies have been done of the operation of homogamy in American society. They embrace homogamy by age and marital status, by social status, by religion, by ethnic affiliation, by race, and by a host of other social and personal characteristics. Only a small portion of this research can be presented here.

AGE AND MARITAL STATUS

Legal requirements concerning age at marriage extend only to determining that parties to the marriage should be old enough to give valid consent. The minimum ages for marriage, with parental consent, under the old English common law were 14 for boys and 12 for girls. Virtually all of the American states subsequently passed legislation setting the minimum ages for marriage with and without parental consent.[2] The most common provisions permit men of 21 and women of 18 to marry without parental consent. With parental consent, the most common minimum ages are 18 for men and 16 for women. In a few jurisdictions both men and women must be 21 in order to marry without parental consent and, in a few others, 12-year-olds may marry with parental consent.

In many states the courts may grant special permission for underage couples to marry when it is determined that the girl is pregnant. There were over 155,000 girls between the ages of 14 and 17 married in the United States in 1968.[3] The long-time historical trend in age at marriage in the United States appears to be downward. In 1890, for example, the median ages at marriage

---

[2] The United States Constitution provides that all powers not expressly granted to the federal government should be reserved to the states. Since there is no section of the constitution dealing directly with domestic relations, family law generally is state law. Each of the 50 states and the District of Columbia has its own domestic relations law, and the laws vary widely from one jurisdiction to another.

[3] National Center for Health Statistics, *Monthly Vital Statistics Report*, Feb. 11, 1971.

were 26.1 for men and 22.0 for women. By 1950, these average ages at marriage had dropped to 22.8 for men and 20.3 for women. In 1969, the median ages were 22.4 and 20.6.

Obviously, most Americans marry young. What is just as impressive, however, is the very narrow age range within which most people marry. Sixty per cent of all first marriages occur within a four- or five-year period and 75 per cent of them occur within three or four years on either side of age 21.[4] Apparently, the mechanisms that operate to get people married in American society work with remarkable efficiency around the times of graduation from high school and college.

That homogamy operates in age at marriage is indicated by the relative ages of brides and grooms. On the average, brides are 2½ years younger than their grooms and in 10 per cent of all cases the bride and groom are of the same age. In three-fourths of all cases, brides are younger than their grooms, and in one case out of seven the bride is older than the groom.

> A legislative move to overturn the nation's lowest legal marrying ages was defeated in the state Senate today. . . . As a result, girls of 13 and boys of 14 can still marry in New Hampshire—with parental and court consent.
>
> [One senator] argued that passage of the bill to raise the age three years would "close the one viable option to those involved in premarital pregnancy." He was supported by [another senator] who warned that if the age were raised young men would not marry the girls they made pregnant.
>
> [Still another senator], who argued for reform, said modern society was too complex for youths of 13 and 14 to make a success of marriage.
>
> —United Press International, June 5, 1969.

Homogamy, by age, holds for all of the subgroups in the population that have been studied. Hollingshead compared the age relationships of Negro couples and white couples in both first marriages and remarriages (Table 1). In all four types of marriages and within both races, the correlations were high.

---

[4] John Mogey, "Age at First Marriage," in Alvin W. Gouldner and S. M. Miller, eds., *Applied Sociology: Opportunities and Problems*, New York: The Free Press, 1965, pp. 248–59.

TABLE 1. *Correlation Between the Ages of Husbands and Wives at Time of Marriage by Type of Marriage and by Race.*

MARRIAGE TYPE	WHITES	NEGROES
First marriage for both spouses	0.74 *	0.69
First marriage for husband, second for wife	0.64	0.73
Second marriage for husband, first for wife	0.78	0.84
Second marriage for both spouses	0.77	0.84

* A correlation of 1.00 would indicate perfect correspondence between the ages of husbands and wives.

Source: August B. Hollingshead, "Age Relationships and Marriage," *American Sociological Review* 16 (Aug. 1951), p. 497.

Glick verified the operation of age homogamy at different occupational levels ranging from professionals to laborers.[5]

The age-homogamy norms are themselves a function of age; they operate most strongly at youthful ages and become less effective as people grow older. At age 20, men marry women of median age 19—only one year's difference. By age 25 there is three years' difference, by age 30 there is nearly five years' difference, and by age 60, there is almost ten years' difference.[6] Women, of course, typically choose husbands who are older than themselves, but the pattern fluctuates widely with the age of the woman. Girls who marry at age 15 choose men almost five years their seniors. By age 20 the difference has dropped to less than three years, and by age 30 there is less than one year's difference (Table 2). Beyond age 30 the difference begins to increase again. After age 30, women tend to marry men who are from two to four years older than they are.

Age, of course, also is related to whether people are marrying for the first time or not. Bowerman studied these relationships in Seattle and reached the following conclusions. First, single persons who are selected as marriage partners are younger, on the average, than persons who have been previously married; among the previously married, widows who are selected as marriage partners are older than divorcées. These generalizations hold regardless of the age, sex, and previous marital status of the person doing the choosing. Second, as men get older they marry increasingly younger women. The age differences are least when men marry widows. As women get older, on the other hand,

[5] Paul C. Glick and Emanuel Landau, "Age as a Factor in Marriage," *American Sociological Review* 15 (Aug. 1950), pp. 517–29.

[6] Paul H. Jacobson, *American Marriage and Divorce*, New York: Rinehart and Company, 1959, pp. 63–4.

TABLE 2. *Median Age of Bride and Groom by Age of Spouse at First Marriage of Both, for 21 Reporting States: 1953.*

AGE OF BRIDE	MEDIAN AGE OF GROOM	AGE OF GROOM	MEDIAN AGE OF BRIDE
15 years	19.7	18 years	18.1
16 years	20.1	19 years	18.5
17 years	20.6	20 years	19.0
18 years	21.3	21 years	19.4
19 years	21.9	22 years	20.2
20 years	22.7	23 years	20.7
21 years	23.3	24 years	21.2
22 years	24.2	25 years	21.7
23 years	24.9	26 years	22.2
24 years	25.7	27 years	22.7
25 years	26.6	28 years	23.3
26 years	27.4	29 years	23.9
27 years	28.3	30 years	24.6
28 years	29.1	31 years	25.0
29 years	30.0	32 years	26.1
30 years	30.8	33 years	26.7
31 years	32.0	34 years	27.5

Source: Paul C. Glick, *American Families,* New York: John Wiley and Sons, 1957, p. 123.

they marry men who are more nearly their own age, the age differences being greatest when they marry widowers. Finally, those who are remarrying do not differ significantly in the age difference from their mates from those who are marrying for the first time. [7]

In summary, these data show that homogamy does operate by age, but that the effectiveness of the norms varies by age and the associated previous marital status. There are several possible explanations for this situation. First, age differences undoubtedly seem greater to the young; at age 20, a difference of two years may loom larger than a difference of five years at age 40. Second, the range of association with persons of different ages probably becomes greater as one grows older. Third, the opportunities for selecting a mate at one's own age level become more restricted with increasing age; most of one's age mates already are married. If one wishes to marry at all one may have to be more flexible in one's age requirements for a spouse. The competitive situations of men and women differ here. Although this easily can be overemphasized, the initiative in mate-seeking tends to rest with men, and men seek physical attractiveness in women. As men get older, frequently their economic status

[7] Charles E. Bowerman, "Age Relationships at Marriage, by Marital Status and Age at Marriage," *Marriage and Family Living* 18 (Aug. 1956), pp. 231-3.

improves and they are able to attract younger women. As women get older, however, they face a declining market situation and have to accept marriage with older men or with men their own ages who have been married before.

Age Relationships and Marital Success. A number of studies has demonstrated that age at marriage is related to the happiness or adjustment subsequently achieved. The early Burgess and Cottrell study of the prediction of marital success found that the highest adjustment scores were made by men and women who were from 28 to 30 years old at the time of marriage. Intermediate scores were made by those who married in their mid-twenties and the lowest scores were made by men who married earlier than age 22 and women who married before age 19.[8] Terman's study of California couples also found that men who married before age 22 and women who married under age 20 were less likely to achieve marital happiness.[9] More recent studies by Landis confirmed these findings but tended to set the critical ages somewhat lower: in one study of 409 marriages the critical age was 20 for both men and women; in a study of 544 marriages the critical age was 20 for men and 18 for women.[10]

The same general findings obtain when divorce rates are related to age at marriage. Locke's comparison of divorced and happily married couples found that the divorced men and women had married younger than their happily married counterparts. A much larger proportion of the divorced men had married before age 21 and, of the women, before age 18.[11] A study by Landis, of the marriages of the parents of 3000 college students, found that the divorce rate decreased steadily as the age at marriage increased.[12] One of the most comprehensive studies was done by Monahan, who tabulated data on 52,722 marriages and 8040 divorces in Iowa. This study confirmed the fact that very youthful marriages are more likely to end in divorce and that they break up sooner than other marriages.[13] Monahan de-emphasized the influence of age after the age of legal majority, however, and laid the unfavorable experience of many very young marriages to factors other than age itself.

The general logic underlying these findings, of course, is that age is related

[8] Ernest W. Burgess and Leonard S. Cottrell, Jr., *Predicting Success or Failure in Marriage*, New York: Prentice-Hall, 1939.

[9] Lewis M. Terman, *Psychological Factors in Marital Happiness*, New York: McGraw-Hill Book Company, 1938.

[10] Judson T. Landis and Mary G. Landis, *Building a Successful Marriage*, Englewood Cliffs, N. J.: Prentice-Hall, 1968, p. 122.

[11] Harvey J. Locke, *Predicting Adjustment in Marriage: A Comparison of a Divorced and a Happily Married Group*, New York: Henry Holt and Company, 1951, pp. 101–2.

[12] Op. cit. p. 129.

[13] Thomas P. Monahan, "Does Age at Marriage Matter in Divorce?" *Social Forces* 32 (Oct. 1953), pp. 81–7.

to emotional and social maturity;[14] persons who marry after age 20, at least, are less likely to be rebelling against parental authority, are less likely to be forced into marriage by pregnancy,[15] are less likely to be broken up by the parents or others, and encounter fewer financial hardships. That many marriages of high-school-age youth do encounter these special problems seems inescapable.

The findings on youthful marriages have led, in the United States, to an exaggerated impression of the trend toward them and to a widespread public reaction against them. Many people are of the belief that marriages among 17- and 18-year-olds are increasing rapidly; they also incline to the belief that such marriages are doomed to failure.

The trend toward youthful marriages has been assessed by Burchinal, who found that the number and proportion of marriages in which at least one partner was 18 years of age or younger increased steadily from 1910 to 1950. The increases occurred among both males and females and among Negroes and whites. Among nonwhite girls, the greatest increases occurred between 1910 and 1930, while among white girls the largest increase occurred between 1940 and 1950. Emphasis is placed upon the marriage of young girls because roughly five times as many girls as boys are married by age 18.[16]

Contrary to widely held belief, however, youthful marriage rates have not increased since 1950. The rates have remained stable or may even have de-

[14] Lee G. Burchinal, "Adolescent Role Deprivation and High School Age Marriage," *Marriage and Family Living* 21 (Nov. 1959), pp. 378–84; J. Ross Eshleman, "Mental Health and Marital Integration in Young Marriages," *Journal of Marriage and the Family* 27 (May 1965), pp. 255–62; Floyd M. Martinson, "Ego Deficiency as a Factor in Marriage," *American Sociological Review* 20 (April 1955), pp. 161–4; Floyd M. Martinson, "Ego Deficiency as a Factor in Marriage—A Male Sample," *Marriage and Family Living* 21 (Feb. 1959), pp. 48–52; and J. Joel Moss and Ruby Gingles, "The Relationship of Personality to the Incidence of Early Marriage," *Marriage and Family Living* 21 (Nov. 1959), pp. 373–7.

[15] Of all girls who marry while still in high school, from one-third to one-half are pregnant. Half to three-fourths of the high-school-age boys who marry are involved in premarital pregnancies. See Lee G. Burchinal, "Comparison of Factors Related to Adjustment in Pregnancy-Provoked and Non-Pregnancy-Provoked Youthful Marriages," *Midwest Sociologist* 21 (July 1959), pp. 92–6; Rachel M. Inselberg, "Marital Problems and Satisfaction in High School Marriages," *Marriage and Family Living* 24 (Feb. 1962), pp. 74–7; and Martin L. Norris, "Teenage Marriages: Facts and Figures," paper presented at Indiana Council on Family Relations, March 24, 1962.

[16] Lee G. Burchinal, "Trends and Prospects for Young Marriages in the United States," *Journal of Marriage and the Family* 27 (May 1965), pp. 243–4. See also Karl E. Bauman, "The Relationship Between Age at First Marriage, School Dropout, and Marital Instability: An Analysis of the Glick Effect," *Journal of Marriage and the Family* 29 (Nov. 1967), pp. 672–80; and Lolagene Coombs, R. Freedman, J. Friedman, and W. F. Pratt, "Premarital Pregnancy and Status Before and After Marriage," *American Journal of Sociology* 75 (March 1970), pp. 800–820.

clined slightly. This stability suggests that the end of the long-time downward trend in the average age at marriage may almost have been reached.

Part of the public attention being given to young marriages today may be accounted for by the fact that the public schools are changing their policies, somewhat, in dealing with such marriages. Before World War II, young people who married while still in high school were dropped from school almost automatically. Many schools, either formally or informally, still have such policies. An increasing number, however, are attempting to make provisions to keep such youngsters in school.[17]

The divorce rate among high-school-age marriages is estimated at from two to four times that among marriages begun by persons after the age of 20.[18] Burchinal found that 5.7 per cent of persons married and aged 18, in 1960, were either divorced or separated.[19] Part of the high divorce rate among very young marriages is to be accounted for by the fact that young marriages are concentrated among high divorce-rate groups: those of low educational levels, low socio-economic levels, and those who are premaritally pregnant. Even when the influence of these factors is partialled out, however, the disadvantage remains. Those who marry very young appear more likely to marry out of dysfunctional emotional needs and to encounter a disproportionate set of "outside" problems.

At least one writer has criticized the widespread condemnation of young marriages. Doress argues that such criticism ignores the large number of apparently successful young marriages and questions whether couples who marry in their late twenties and early thirties may not have developed individual patterns of living that are scarcely affected by marriage. The stability of these later marriages, he says, may be largely due to the fact that they do not involve the deep commitments of young marriages. There may be less welding, less joining together, less *egoisme à deux*.[20]

[17] See Wayne J. Anderson and Sander M. Latts, "High School Marriages and School Policies in Minnesota," *Journal of Marriage and the Family* 27 (May 1965), pp. 266–70; Glenn C. Atkyns, "School Administrative Policy Related to Motherhood, Pregnancy, and Marriage," *The Family Coordinator* 17 (April 1968), pp. 69–73; James W. Gladden, "Trends in High School Marriages and Public School Policy in the United States," *The Family Coordinator* 17 (Oct. 1968), pp. 279–87; Vladimir de Lissovoy and Mary Ellen Hitchcock, "High School Marriages in Pennsylvania," *Journal of Marriage and the Family* 27 (May 1965), pp. 263–5; June M. Henton, "The Effects of Married High-School Students on Their Unmarried Class-Mates," *Journal of Marriage and the Family* 26 (Feb. 1964), pp. 87–8; Wilson Ivins, "Student Marriages in New Mexico Secondary Schools: Practices and Policies," *Marriage and Family Living* 22 (Feb. 1960).

[18] Monahan, op. cit.

[19] "Trends and Prospects for Young Marriages in the United States," op. cit. p. 250.

[20] Irving Doress, "The Problem of Early Marriage," *The Bulletin on Family Development* 2 (Spring 1961), pp. 20–23.

Unquestionably the normative disapproval of young marriages has much to do with their high failure rate. If society were to support such young marriages with enthusiasm, the present negative effects of emotional immaturity might be largely overcome. To say this does not change things, however. There are few signs that American society will become more accepting of youthful marriages in the near future. The norms provide that girls should marry somewhere around 20 years of age and boys approximately two years later. The society is more tolerant of marriages occurring after these ages than it is of marriages occurring earlier.

SOCIAL STATUS

Some of the data presented in the last two chapters showed both that people tend to date at their own status levels and that dating outside one's own status level is associated with sexual involvement, exploitation, and the hope of marriage on the part of the lower-status partner. These data should lead us to expect both status homogamy and status heterogamy in marriage; and, indeed, this is what we find.

Early studies established that status endogamy is widespread. Burgess and Wallin found that their 1000 engaged couples had tended to select persons of similar family background.[21] Richard Centers, using a national sample, found that both men and women marry persons from their same occupational level more often than they marry persons from any other one occupational stratum. He also found, however, that fewer than 50 per cent of people marry within their own occupational level and that, despite the endogamous tendency, more men of each occupational level are married to women of strata other than their own than are married to women of it.[22] In New Haven, Connecticut, Hollingshead discovered that both men and women tend to marry persons who come from the same class of residential area and from the same educational level.[23] Sundal and McCormick confirmed Centers's findings on marriage within occupational levels in the city of Madison, Wisconsin.[24]

Not all of the evidence clearly supports the operation of status endogamy, however. Hunt, using data on marriages occurring in Norwood, Massachusetts,

---

[21] Ernest W. Burgess and Paul Wallin, "Homogamy in Social Characteristics," *American Journal of Sociology* 49 (Sept. 1943), pp. 117–24.

[22] Richard Centers, "Marital Selection and Occupational Strata," *American Journal of Sociology* 54 (May 1949), pp. 530–35.

[23] August B. Hollingshead, "Cultural Factors in the Selection of Marriage Mates," *American Sociological Review* 15 (Oct. 1950), pp. 619–27.

[24] A. Philip Sundal and Thomas C. McCormick, "Age at Marriage and Mate Selection: Madison, Wisconsin, 1937–1943," *American Sociological Review* 16 (Feb. 1951), pp. 37–48.

failed to find much evidence for status endogamy in the selection of husbands by women.[25] Only women from the lowest status levels made mostly endogamous marriages. At all other status levels there was no uniform tendency for the selection of partners from any status level.

Leslie and Richardson attempted to throw light on the operation of status endogamy by studying a group of students who married while they were in college. These researchers reasoned that, while status endogamy may operate in the larger society, it might not be so effective in a group virtually all of whom were middle class. They reasoned further that, if parents tend to pressure their offspring toward endogamous marriages, such pressure might be less effective when students marry while they are away at college and subject to the democratic norms that are conspicuous on most campuses. They found only a slight tendency toward homogamy among those students who married someone whom they had known at home before attending college and none at all among couples who met and married while on the campus.[26] They concluded that the campus situation, by encouraging the association of persons of diverse backgrounds and through its formal democratic norms, appears to favor heterogamous pairings. Direct group pressures operating at the time of marriage appear to be at least as influential as homogamy-oriented norms internalized earlier in life.

Coombs, studying married couples at the University of Utah, supported the idea that campus norms may favor status heterogamy while community norms favor status endogamy. He found that the incidence of status homogamy was much higher when both parties to the couple lived at home during courtship than when neither lived at home. Eighty-three per cent of the relationships were homogamous when both lived at home, and only 61 per cent were homogamous when neither lived at home.[27]

Data such as these suggest the possibility that status homogamy might be declining with the passage of time, at least in some segments of the population. Unfortunately there are few data available to test this possibility and the data that are available are somewhat equivocal. Hollingshead's New Haven study

---

[25] T. C. Hunt, "Occupational Status and Marriage Selection," *American Sociological Review* 5 (Aug. 1940), pp. 495-504. See the discussion in Lee G. Burchinal, "The Premarital Dyad and Love Involvement," in Harold T. Christensen, ed., *Handbook of Marriage and the Family*, Chicago: Rand McNally and Company, 1964, p. 653.

[26] Gerald R. Leslie and Arthur H. Richardson, "Family Versus Campus Influences in Relation to Mate Selection," *Social Problems* 4 (Oct. 1956), pp. 117-21. At least one study indicates that some apparent homogamy may develop as a function of interaction between the couple. See Eloise C. Snyder, "Attitudes: A Study of Homogamy and Marital Selectivity," *Journal of Marriage and the Family* 26 (Aug. 1964), pp. 332-6.

[27] Robert H. Coombs, "Reinforcement of Values in the Parental Home as a Factor in Mate Selection," *Marriage and Family Living* 24 (May 1962), pp. 155-7.

showed status homogamy to be equally present in all three major religious groups in 1950. Dinitz, Banks, and Pasamanick attempted to get at this problem directly by studying 2706 couples who secured marriage licenses in Columbus, Ohio, in the years 1933, 1939, 1949, and 1957–58. What they found was that there had been declines at the two extremes. There were fewer maximally homogamous marriages and fewer widely heterogamous marriages with the passage of time. There was also a tendency for people to select marital partners from a somewhat broader socio-economic spectrum within the middle range.[28] This could be consistent with the data on college marriages cited above, of course. There might be both increasing disapproval of widely exogamous marriages and somewhat greater freedom of mate selection permitted within the middle range.

The Mating Gradient. Just as the data on patterns of dating and premarital sex involvement led us to expect both status homogamy and status heterogamy in marriage, they should also lead us to expect that certain patterns would exist in heterogamous marriages. The dating data showed that men more often date below their social levels while women more often date above theirs. In fact, there seems to be a tendency for men to wish to marry at their own levels or below on an exceedingly wide range of characteristics. That men tend to marry down in terms of age was shown in the preceding section. Early studies also demonstrated that men tend to marry down both in terms of education and I.Q. This tendency for men to marry downward has been labeled the mating gradient.

Most of the various studies on status homogamy have shown, clearly, the operation of the mating gradient. In Centers's national sample, Hollingshead's New Haven sample, and Sundal and McCormick's Madison, Wisconsin, sample, men married downward more frequently than they married up. The data suggest further that, except at the very top and bottom levels, men have a wider range of mate choice than women do.[29]

An interesting implication of the operation of the mating gradient is that it appears to work to keep substantial numbers of the highest status women and the lowest status men from marrying. Women whose families exist at the

---

[28] Simon Dinitz, Franklin Banks, and Benjamin Pasamanick, "Mate Selection and Social Class: Changes During the Past Quarter Century," *Marriage and Family Living* 22 (Nov. 1960), pp. 348–51.

[29] Some of the formidable methodological difficulties in getting a definitive test of the operation of the mating gradient are analyzed in the following series of articles: Zick Rubin, "Do American Women Marry Up?" *American Sociological Review* 33 (Oct. 1968), pp. 750–60; John F. Scott, "A Comment on 'Do American Women Marry Up?'" *American Sociological Review* 34 (Oct. 1969), pp. 725–8; J. David Martin, "A Comment on Whether American Women Do Marry Up," *American Sociological Review* 35 (April 1970), pp. 327–8.

highest socio-economic levels have a smaller pool of potential mates to begin with, because it is not generally acceptable for them to marry downward. In addition, these high-status women must compete for the high-status men, not only against one another, but also against women from other status levels. To the extent that high-status men marry downward, they may leave high-status women without partners. Among men, the reverse situation obtains. The lowest-status men generally are not eligible to marry higher-status women; yet higher-status men may select their spouses out of the pool of lower-status women. Thus, unmarried women may be, disproportionately, high-status women, and unmarried men may be, disproportionately, low-status men.

RACIAL BACKGROUND

Nowhere are the homogamy norms more widely held to, or more rigorously enforced, than in the area of race. Over the past twenty years, the courts have been tending to strike down laws forbidding miscegenation and intermarriage and, in 1967, the United States Supreme Court declared Virginia's law unconstitutional, thereby nullifying similar statutes or constitutional provisions in the 16 other states that still had them.

Although persons of different racial backgrounds may now legally marry in a majority of jurisdictions, the intermarriage rate is still so low as virtually to defy reliable measurement. Studies of intermarriage rates in various states and cities in the period up to 1960 showed rates of one-half to one and one-half per cent.[30] Then in 1960, for the first time, the United States Census yielded data on the race of husband and wife for all married couples in the United States. Some of the results are shown in Table 3.

There were 163,800 couples, 0.4 per cent of the total 40,491,000 married couples in the United States, who reported themselves to be of different races. White-Negro marriages were the largest group comprising some 31 per cent of all intermarriages. There were some 25,900 marriages of white husbands to Negro wives, and 25,500 marriages of black husbands to white wives.

Fifty-five per cent of the mixed marriages involved white-"other" (nonwhite except Negro) combinations. Three out of five of these were white-Japanese, or white-American Indian. Smaller numbers of Chinese, Filipinos, Hawaiians, and Eskimos were involved.

[30] See Larry D. Barnett, "Interracial Marriage in California," *Marriage and Family Living* 25 (Nov. 1963), pp. 424–7; John H. Burma, "Interethnic Marriages in Los Angeles, 1948–1959," *Social Forces* 42 (Dec. 1963), pp. 156–65; and Joseph Golden, "Characteristics of the Negro-White Intermarried in Philadelphia," *American Sociological Review* 18 (April 1953), pp. 177–83.

TABLE 3. *Married Couples, By Race of Husband
and Wife: United States, 1960.*

RACE OF HUSBAND	ALL MARRIED COUPLES	RACE OF WIFE		
		WHITE	NEGRO	OTHER
Total	40,490,998	37,132,013	3,061,342	297,643
White	37,152,907	37,071,672	25,913	55,322
Negro	3,063,673	25,496	3,033,122	5,055
Other	274,418	34,845	2,307	237,266

Source: U. S. Bureau of the Census, *U. S. Census of Population: 1960*, Subject Reports, Marital Status, Final Report PC (2)-4E, table 10; as reported in Hugh Carter, and Paul C. Glick, *Marriage and Divorce: A Social and Economic Study*, Cambridge, Mass.: Harvard University Press, 1970, p. 117.

These data indicate little increase in interracial marriage rates up to 1960. What is of great interest, however, is whether, with the liberalizing of race relationships recently, the rates have tended to climb since 1960. Unfortunately, the data available are very fragmentary. A comprehensive study of such marriages in upstate New York showed a sharp increase from 1959 to 1964,[31] and a study of the very racially mixed state of Hawaii also showed increases from 1956–57 to 1967–68 of at least 15 per cent.[32]

In spite of the smallness of the number of people involved—or, perhaps, because of it—there is an almost morbid curiosity about the kinds of people who violate such a strongly held norm. Several studies have sought to specify some of the social and emotional characteristics of the racially intermarried.

Several recent studies have verified that interracial marriages more often involve nonwhite men and white women than vice versa.[33] Golden found that 58.5 per cent of Negro-white marriages in Philadelphia were of this combination, and Pavela found the corresponding percentage among Indiana interracial marriages to be 72.6. These figures probably do not mean that white men do not form sexual associations with nonwhite women, but only that such relationships do not tend to lead to marriage. White women, in contrast,

[31] Thomas P. Monahan, "Interracial Marriage in the United States: Some Data on Upstate New York," *International Journal of Sociology of the Family* 1 (March 1971), pp. 94–105.

[32] Robert C. Schmitt, "Recent Trends in Hawaiian Interracial Marriage Rates by Occupation," *Journal of Marriage and the Family* 33 (May 1971), pp. 373–4.

[33] John H. Burma, "Research Note on the Measurement of Interracial Marriage," *American Journal of Sociology* 57 (May 1952), pp. 587–9; Joseph Golden, op. cit. p. 178; Thomas P. Monahan, op. cit.; and Todd H. Pavela, "An Exploratory Study of Negro-White Intermarriage in Indiana," *Journal of Marriage and the Family* 26 (May 1964), pp. 209–11.

have more bargaining power when they enter interracial relationships and are more able to get the men to marry them.

The same studies found that the persons who enter interracial marriages tend to be older at the time of marriage than are those who enter racially homogamous marriages. In Philadelphia, the average age at marriage for all spouses, Negro and white, was 28; in Los Angeles, the median age of whites marrying Negroes was 39 years, and, in Indiana, the average ages were lower but were still higher than in racially homogamous marriages. There is some evidence that these higher ages at marriage are associated with the persons' having previously been married. More than one-third of the Negro grooms interviewed in Philadelphia and almost one-fourth of the brides had been previously divorced. In Indiana, Pavela found that 29 per cent of Negro brides and 25 per cent of Negro grooms had been divorced; the corresponding percentages among the white brides and grooms were 18 per cent and 21 per cent.

The personal and emotional characteristics of those who intermarry are much more difficult to get at. Because they are relatively so few and in blatant violation of such strong norms, it is widely believed that interracial marriages must be highly selective in terms of personal characteristics. Both Golden and Pavela demonstrated that families and friends of both races tend to exert strong pressures against such marriages.[34]

The study going into the problem of personal characteristics in greatest depth may be that of Freeman, who studied interracially married and interracially dating couples in Hawaii.[35] All of his respondents described early feelings of rejection, frequently tracing back to parent-child relationships. All of the respondents also reported poor social adjustment in grade school and high school. The backgrounds of felt rejection produced feelings of frustration and hostility toward the individuals' ethnic groups. They desired to escape identification with the ethnic group and turned toward deviant behavior in the attempt to do so. Exposure to other ethnic groups led to idealization of opposite-sex members of those groups, dating, and, often, marriage. Many of

[34] Joseph Golden, "Patterns of Negro-White Intermarriage," *American Sociological Review* 19 (April 1954), pp. 144–7; and Todd H. Pavela, op. cit. p. 210.

[35] Linton Freeman, "Homogamy in Interethnic Mate Selection," *Sociology and Social Research* 39 (July–Aug. 1955), pp. 369–77. The unique situation in Hawaii has been studied extensively. See, for example, Paul H. Besanceney, "On Reporting Rates of Intermarriage," *American Journal of Sociology* 70 (May 1965), pp. 717–21; Andrew W. Lind, *An Island Community: Ecological Succession in Hawaii*, Chicago: University of Chicago Press, 1938; Andrew W. Lind, "Interracial Marriage as Affecting Divorce in Hawaii," *Sociology and Social Research* 49 (Oct. 1964), pp. 17–26; Thomas P. Monahan, "Interracial Marriage and Divorce in the State of Hawaii," *Eugenics Quarterly* 13 (March 1966), pp. 40–47; and Robert C. Schmitt, "Demographic Correlates of Interracial Marriage in Hawaii," *Population Index* 30 (July 1964), pp. 312–13.

the interethnic dating relationships were short-lived and, when marriage occurred, adjustment was a long, difficult process in which the rebelliousness of one or both spouses abated.

> Almost one person in five responding to a nationwide poll released Sunday said they had dated inter-racially, but nearly half said they were still troubled by the question of sex and marriage between races. The poll was conducted by Louis Harris and Associates. . . .
>
> "One simply cannot say that half the country is tolerant and the other half intolerant," Harris said. "The most overtly bigoted responses were few, but even among those who professed tolerance, doubts emerged."
>
> The magazine said the poll showed an acceptance that inter-racial dating was inevitable. "And most young people—particularly the young, the affluent, the better educated—have no quarrel with the trend, at least in theory," . . .
>
> But when actual problems of inter-racial dating were discussed . . . an ambivalence developed that could lead persons to agree to such seemingly diverse statements as "if all men are created equal, it shouldn't make any difference who goes out with whom," and "any white girl who goes out with a black man is going to ruin her reputation."
>
> —United Press International, May 25, 1971

Although Freeman's analysis is impressive and his general conclusions are widely shared, Burchinal argues that interracial marriages may occur disproportionately among a very different class of youth.[36] In cities and especially among university students and professional people, he says, racial equalitarianism and integration are widely supported. Interracial dating occurs with increasing frequency and interracial marriage becomes increasingly likely.

In support of this general argument, Blood and Nicholson found that acquaintances with students from other nations were almost universal on the University of Michigan campus and that almost half of the women had dated foreign students. Of those women who had not dated foreign students, most said that they would if they were asked.[37] Moreover, international dating did

[36] Lee G. Burchinal, "The Premarital Dyad and Love Involvement," in Harold T. Christensen, ed., *Handbook of Marriage and the Family*, Chicago: Rand McNally, 1964, p. 648.

[37] Robert O. Blood, Jr. and Samuel O. Nicholson, "The Attitudes of American Men and Women Students Toward International Dating," *Marriage and Family Living* 24 (Feb. 1962), pp. 35–41.

not appear to be related either to rebellion or to any crusade against prejudice. The women reported satisfaction with their experiences, their women friends were sympathetic, and their parents and American boy friends typically were neutral. [38]

Burchinal believes that some of the old barriers to interracial dating and marriage are rapidly disappearing and that research should indicate what changes in the norms are occurring. He points out, as illustrated in the paragraph above, that we know more about international dating experiences than we do about the interracial dating experiences of American youth.

Racial Heterogamy and Marital Success. It is not surprising that the strong United States norms against racial intermarriage should be accompanied by beliefs that such marriages are fraught with special hazards and are more likely to fail than are racially homogamous marriages. One college textbook puts it this way: ". . . Interracial marriages present a more serious problem. Though biologically unobjectionable, they are usually inadvisable on social and cultural grounds. This is especially true if racial prejudice is strong, for the newlyweds not only have to adjust their own differences growing out of separate backgrounds but they also need to buck the currents of public opinion and social stigma. There are the children to consider and the social handicaps they will be under. The problem in both of these types of marriages [international and interracial] is that of prejudice plus cultural differences. Where these are nonexistent or only slight there isn't much of a problem, but where they are considerable the problem is correspondingly great." [39]

This admonition to young people is more carefully qualified than many; but the message of special danger comes through loud and clear. Fortunately data are now beginning to be assembled upon some of the strengths and problems of interracial marriage. So far, the data show the situation to be anything but simple.

One perceptive study was made of marriages between American service men and Japanese women early in the 1950's. At the time of the study, the couples were living in the Chicago, Illinois, area; 30 men and 15 of their wives completed lengthy, separate interviews. Based upon his data, Strauss challenges the assumption that Oriental-Caucasian marriages are subject to greater strains than the ordinary marriage. He contends that, as in other marriages, the strains that occur in mixed marriages are patterned and relatively

[38] Robert O. Blood, Jr. and Samuel O. Nicholson, "International Dating Experiences of American Women Students," *Marriage and Family Living* 24 (May 1962), pp. 129–36. See also, Harrop A. Freeman and Ruth Freeman, "Dating Between American and Foreign College Students," *Journal of Sex Research* 2 (Nov. 1966), pp. 207–14.

[39] Harold T. Christensen, *Marriage Analysis: Foundations for Successful Family Life*, second edition, © copyright 1958, The Ronald Press Company, New York, p. 287.

predictable. Some Japanese-American marriages, he says, are likely to be quite stable and to involve fewer strains than many American marriages. [40]

It's not only in Vietnam that Americans are acquiring Oriental wives in considerable numbers. They're doing the same thing in other Asian countries to which they are assigned. For example, in the fiscal year 1969–70 the following numbers of wives were brought home to the U. S.—2833 Koreans, 933 Thais and 1773 Japanese. And for the first six months of 1970–71, the figures are 1948 Koreans, 739 Thais and 924 Japanese.

Strauss's husbands were mostly semiskilled or skilled laborers, professional soldiers, or white-collar workers; as a group they were not upwardly mobile. Some had married without their parents' knowledge but most had received either enthusiastic or grudging approval. Their wives had married at an average age of 22, were usually urban working girls, and their marriages to Americans frequently were opposed by their parents. Early in their marriages, the couples faced the usual adjustment problems of content and timing having to do with food, sex, play, work, finances, and so on. In addition, they faced special problems of learning how to communicate, of handling the women's parents, and of becoming parents. By the time of interview several years later, however, differences of age, class, religion, and education did not appear to cause strain.

Strauss found that there were strains in these marriages still. Some of the strains were more serious and some of them less so than in most American marriages.

The strains involved in leaving the parental family were different from typical in-law problems in American society but not automatically more or less severe. Few women had much guilt, shame, or stress over having left their parents or Japan. There was some nostalgia to see their parents and country again, and a very few of the wives were attempting to get their husbands to return to Japan.

Few couples experienced strong institutional pressures. They had few organizational affiliations and were not usually deeply religious. A few brides had become Catholic, thus avoiding possible sharp differences between themselves and their husbands. Much of their recreation took place in their own

[40] Anselm L. Strauss, "Strain and Harmony in American-Japanese War-Bride Marriages," *Marriage and Family Living* 16 (May 1954), pp. 99–106.

homes or those of friends. Their problems in this area seemed to be fewer and less conspicuous than in many American marriages.

There was a fairly complete separation of the world of home and the world of work. The women appeared satisfied with their husbands' incomes and did not pressure them toward achievement; similarly, the husbands did not expect their wives to have careers, although some of them worked, and did not wish them to become mobility conscious. These couples seemed satisfied on steady, modest incomes.

Relationships with the husbands' families generally were good and the in-laws often played an important role in helping the young bride learn American ways. When in-law conflict did develop, there was severe strain as in comparable American marriages. Relationships with friends also appeared good but highly selective; much peer-group interaction was had with other interracially married couples. It would be interesting to speculate on the degree to which this pairing-off of interracially married couples reflected common interests and the degree to which it resulted from rejection by other couples.[41]

Presumably, the strains involved in Oriental-Caucasian marriages may be less than those in Negro-white marriages. Data on Negro-white marriages also reveal the situation to be complicated.

At least three in depth studies of Negro-white marriages have been completed since about 1950: one in New York, one in Philadelphia, and one in Indianapolis.[42] The number of couples was small: 22, 50, and 9, respectively. All couples were carefully interviewed. Although there were differences of location and although the interviews were done over a ten-year time span, the three studies present a rather consistent picture of what such marriages are like.

[41] For further background on the nature and incidence of international intermarriage see Larry D. Barnett, "Research on International and Interracial Marriages," *Marriage and Family Living* 25 (Feb. 1963), pp. 105–7; John Biesanz and L. M. Smith, "Adjustment of Inter-Ethnic Marriages on the Isthmus of Panama," *American Sociological Review* 16 (Dec. 1951), pp. 819–22; C. K. Cheng and Douglas S. Yamamura, "Interracial Marriage and Divorce in Hawaii," *Social Forces* 36 (Oct. 1957), pp. 77–84; Chester L. Hunt and Richard W. Coller, "Intermarriage and Cultural Change: A Study of Philippine-American Marriages," *Social Forces* 35 (March 1957), pp. 223–30; Yukiho Kumura, "War Brides in Hawaii and Their In-Laws," *American Journal of Sociology* 63 (July 1957), pp. 70–6; Robert C. Schmitt, "Interracial Marriage and Occupational Status in Hawaii," *American Sociological Review* 28 (Oct. 1963), pp. 809–10; and Gerald J. Schnepp and Agnes Masako Yui, "Cultural and Marital Adjustment of Japanese War Brides," *American Journal of Sociology* 61 (July 1955), pp. 48–50.

[42] Joseph Golden, "Patterns of Negro-White Intermarriage," op. cit.; Todd H. Pavela, op. cit.; and Charles E. Smith, *Negro-White Intermarriage, Metropolitan New York—A Qualitative Case Analysis*, Columbia University Teachers College, 1961.

The evidence suggests that many people who enter intermarriages are relatively isolated from their families to begin with. Often, the family of the white partner, at least, does not know of the courtship, which tends to be carried on with some secrecy. In some cases, the secrecy in relation to the white parents is continued after the marriage. Golden found that some white spouses avoided contacts with their parents and with former white friends. On the other hand, not all white parents oppose the marriages. Pavela found both some opposition and some support among the white parents. Both Golden and Pavela found that there was much less opposition from the Negro parents; acceptance or rejection of the white partner was more likely to be based upon his or her personal characteristics than upon the mere fact of race.

No couple, in any of the studies cited, was completely ostracized by members of both races. They tended to live in borderline Negro-white residential areas, with more couples living in all-Negro areas than in all-white areas. Their relations with their neighbors usually were amicable but not intimate. Their friends were more often Negro than white; relatively few had extensive contacts with other interracially married couples. Some of Smith's New York couples even reported that they probably had more social contacts than similar white or Negro couples.

Many of the couples did report special difficulties. The problem of being stared at in public places was emphasized by the New York couples and was reported, also, by the Philadelphia couples. Some of the white spouses had lost jobs when their employers learned of their marriages; others concealed the fact from employers and fellow employees. Some couples were discriminated against in securing housing, a problem sometimes solved by sending the white partner to inspect the property and sign the lease. In general, the problems encountered by interracial couples were those typically met by Negro couples.

Over half the Philadelphia and Indianapolis couples had children, and none of the New York couples had decided against having children. If these couples had fewer children than average, this fact may be related to their older average age at marriage. Relatively little discrimination against the children was experienced at the hands of Negroes, but virtually all parents acknowledged that their children would have to be raised as Negroes. Many couples longed for the day when racial prejudice would not be a problem.

Golden, who gathered data on the length of time the couples had been married, reported that 34 couples out of 50 had been married five years or longer. He concluded that these marriages have a good chance of survival. Pavela's conclusion is consistent with Burchinal's analysis of the changing nature of interracial marriage. He says: "In many respects, the Negro-white marriages studied contradict the picture of such marriages in the public mind or even in much sociological literature. It would appear that such intermarriage now occurs between persons who are, by and large, economically, educationally, and culturally equal and who have a strong emotional attachment, be it rationalization or real. The external pressures faced by interracial couples are often great but certainly do not appear to be overwhelming.[43]

RELIGIOUS AFFILIATION

The norms supporting religious homogamy in the United States have long been thought to be extremely strong—only slightly less strong than those supporting racial homogamy. In 1950 in New Haven, Connecticut, for example, Hollingshead reported that 97 per cent of Jewish marriages, 94 per cent of Catholic marriages, and 74 per cent of Protestant marriages were religiously homogamous.[44] Other studies have challenged the existence of this extreme religious endogamy, however, and have shown, in the process, that even the computation of rates of religious homogamy is very complicated.

Thomas, for example, gathered data for Catholic dioceses in different sections of the country and reported mixed-marriage rates ranging from 10 per cent in El Paso to 70 per cent in Raleigh and Charleston.[45] The mixed-marriage rate for one-half of the Catholic dioceses in the United States was about 30 per cent. For the state of Connecticut, Thomas estimates that the rate probably is about 50 per cent.

If taken at face value, the figures reported by Hollingshead for New Haven and by Thomas for all of Connecticut appear to be in serious conflict. Part of the discrepancy is to be accounted for by the fact that these are not comparable rates. The rate reported by Hollingshead is a mixed-marriage rate for individuals while Thomas's rate is a rate for marriages. A *mixed-marriage rate for individuals* refers to the percentage of married persons (in any category) who enter mixed marriages; a *mixed-marriage rate for marriages*, in contrast,

---

[43] See Thomas P. Monahan, "Are Interracial Marriages Really Less Stable?" *Social Forces* 48 (June 1970), pp. 461–73; Thomas P. Monahan, "Interracial Marriage and Divorce in Kansas and the Question of Instability of Mixed Marriages," *Journal of Comparative Family Studies* 2 (Spring 1971), pp. 107–20; and Robert C. Schmitt, "Age and Race Differences in Divorce in Hawaii," *Journal of Marriage and the Family* 31 (Feb. 1969), pp. 48–50.

[44] Op. cit.

[45] John L. Thomas, "The Factor of Religion in the Selection of Marriage Mates," *American Sociological Review* 16 (Aug. 1951), pp. 487–91.

TABLE 3. *Sample Transformations of the Two Rates of Mixed Marriage.*

MIXED MARRIAGE RATE FOR MARRIAGES	MIXED MARRIAGE RATE FOR INDIVIDUALS
0.0	0.0
10.0	5.3
20.0	11.1
33.3	20.0
40.0	25.0
50.0	33.3
57.1	40.0
60.0	42.9
66.7	50.0
75.0	60.0
80.0	66.7
88.9	80.0
94.7	90.0
100.0	100.0

Source: Hyman Rodman, "Technical Note on Two Rates of Mixed Marriage," *American Sociological Review* 30 (Oct. 1965), p. 778.

refers to the percentage of marriages (in any category) that are mixed.[46] Making Thomas's figures comparable to Hollingshead's, his rate for Connecticut turns out to be 33.3 per cent.

Even after the data are rendered comparable, Thomas's point that the New Haven data are not representative appears to be well taken. Burchinal and Chancellor found individual mixed-marriage rates in Iowa to range from 9 per cent to 24 per cent.[47] In New York City, Heiss found 18 per cent of Jews, 21 per cent of Catholics, and 34 per cent of Protestants to be intermarried.[48] Finally, Rodman's computations, based upon data from the *Cur-*

[46] The importance of distinguishing between mixed marriage rates for individuals and for marriages has been pointed out by Rodman, who also provided the following illustration. If there are six homogamous Catholic marriages and four mixed marriages, the mixed-marriage rate can be either 40 per cent or 25 per cent. Four of the ten marriages are mixed, but only one out of four of the Catholics is involved in a mixed marriage. Hyman Rodman, Technical Note on Two Rates of Mixed Marriage," *American Sociological Review* 30 (Oct. 1965), pp. 776-8.

[47] Lee G. Burchinal and Loren E. Chancellor, "Ages at Marriage, Occupations of Grooms, and Interreligious Marriage Rates," *Social Forces* 40 (May 1962), pp. 348–54. There have been numerous other studies of the incidence of interfaith marriages in various groups. See, for example, Donald H. Bouma, "Religiously Mixed Marriages: Denominational Consequences in the Christian Reformed Church," *Marriage and Family Living* 25 (Nov. 1963), pp. 428–32; and David M. Heer, "The Trend of Interfaith Marriages in Canada: 1922-1957," *American Sociological Review* 27 (April 1962), pp. 245–50.

[48] Jerold S. Heiss, "Premarital Characteristics of the Religiously Intermarried in an Urban Area," *American Sociological Review* 25 (Feb. 1960), pp. 47–55.

rent Population Reports yield individual mixed-marriage rates of 3.7 per cent for Jews, 4.5 per cent for Protestants, and 12.1 per cent for Catholics.[49]

These varied figures on mixed-marriage rates mean several things. First, the rates by themselves are of little value unless a clear distinction is made between individual rates and rates for marriages. Second, there is a considerable amount of mixed religious marriage in spite of the traditionally strong norms against it. Finally, the variation in mixed-marriage rates from group to group and region to region needs to be accounted for.

One of the factors most closely associated with religious intermarriage rates is the proportion that the religious group is of the community; the larger the proportion which the group is of the total community, the lower the intermarriage rate, and vice versa.[50] In Iowa, for example, a correlation of .66 was found between the proportion of Catholics in county populations and the proportion of homogamous Catholic marriages.[51] This general finding has been borne out by studies using data from the *Official Catholic Directory* [52] and from the Dominion Bureau of Statistics in Canada.[53]

Interreligious marriages also tend to vary inversely with the cohesiveness of the ethnic group; the more integrated the ethnic group, the lower the intermarriage rate. Research shows that the ethnic bonds tend to weaken first, with marriages occurring across nationality lines but still within each of the three major religious groups.[54] One study of Polish and Italian residents of Buffalo showed in-group marriages among the Poles falling from 79 per cent to 35 per cent between 1930 and 1960 and in-group Italian marriages falling from 71 per cent to 27 per cent. The decreases were particularly great after 1940.[55] There are relatively few data on the increase in interreligious marriage

---

[49] *Current Population Reports*, "Religion Reported by the Civilian Population of the United States: March, 1957," Series P-20, No. 79, Washington, D. C.: U.S. Bureau of the Census, 1958, as reported in Hyman Rodman, op. cit. p. 777.

[50] For a summary of research on factors associated with intermarriage, see Larry D. Barnett, "Research on Interreligious Dating and Marriage," *Marriage and Family Living* 24 (May 1962), pp. 191–4.

[51] Lee G. Burchinal and Loren E. Chancellor, "Proportions of Catholics, Urbanism, and Mixed-Catholic Marriage Rates Among Iowa Counties," *Social Problems* 9 (Spring 1962), pp. 359–65.

[52] Harvey J. Locke, Georges Sabagh, and Mary Margaret Thomes, "Inter-faith Marriages," *Social Problems* 4 (April 1957), pp. 329–33.

[53] David M. Heer, op. cit.

[54] Ruby Jo Reeves Kennedy, "Single or Triple Melting Pot? Intermarriage Trends in New Haven, 1870–1940," *American Journal of Sociology* 49 (Jan. 1944), pp. 331–9. See also Simon Marcson, "Predicting Intermarriage," *Sociology and Social Research*, 37 (Jan.–Feb. 1953), pp. 151–6.

[55] B. R. Bugelski, "Assimilation Through Intermarriage," *Social Forces* 40 (Dec. 1961), pp. 148–53.

rates over-all, but one study of members of the United Lutheran Church in America showed a mixed marriage rate of 46 per cent during the period from 1936 to 1940, 47 per cent from 1941 to 1945, and 58 per cent from 1946 to 1950.[56] There have also been a number of studies showing increasingly widespread acceptance of interreligious dating and marriage. Studies of the attitudes of college students show that at least 50 per cent would accept a mixed marriage,[57] and one study showed 97 per cent of the students to approve of interreligious dating.[58]

A study of religiously intermarried New York City residents, by Heiss, casts some light on the influence of early family experiences. He found that Catholics who intermarried were more likely to have nonreligious parents, expressed greater dissatisfaction with their parents when young, reported greater early strife with their parents, and were more emancipated from their parents at the time of marriage. The relationships for the Protestant intermarried were smaller, but in the same direction. None of the relationships held for Jews except for the strength of their family ties while young and at the time of marriage.[59]

Religious Heterogamy and Marital Success. As with racial intermarriages, religious intermarriages are widely believed to be associated with marital failure. A number of studies of the divorce rates of mixed and nonmixed religious marriages appear to bear this out.

Studies made up to the time of World War II generally showed divorce rates to be lowest among Catholics and Jews, somewhat higher among Protestants, higher still in mixed marriages, and highest of all where there was no religious affiliation.[60] Just after World War II, a study of 4108 mixed and nonmixed marriages of the parents of Michigan college students yielded similar

---

[56] James H. S. Bossard and Harold C. Letts, "Mixed Marriages Involving Lutherans—A Research Report," *Marriage and Family Living* 18 (Nov. 1956) pp. 308–10.

[57] See Lee G. Burchinal, "Membership Groups and Attitudes Toward Cross-Religious Dating and Marriage," *Marriage and Family Living* 22 (Aug. 1960), pp. 248–53; Victor A. Christopherson and James Walters, "Responses of Protestants, Catholics, and Jews Concerning Marriage and Family Life," *Sociology and Social Research* 43 (Sept.–Oct. 1958), pp. 16–22; and Judson T. Landis, "Religiousness, Family Relationships, and Family Values in Protestant, Catholic, and Jewish Families," *Marriage and Family Living* 22 (Nov. 1960), pp. 341–7.

[58] Alfred J. Prince, "Attitudes of College Students Toward Inter-Faith Marriage," *Family Life Coordinator* 5 (Sept. 1956), pp. 11–23.

[59] Op. cit. For a recent analysis of Jewish intermarriages in one American community, see Sidney Goldstein and Calvin Goldscheider, "Social and Demographic Aspects of Jewish Intermarriages," *Social Problems* 13 (Spring 1966), pp. 386–99.

[60] Howard M. Bell, *Youth Tell Their Story*, Washington, D.C.: American Council on Education, 1938; and H. Ashley Weeks, "Differential Divorce Rates by Occupation," *Social Forces* 21 (March 1943), p. 336.

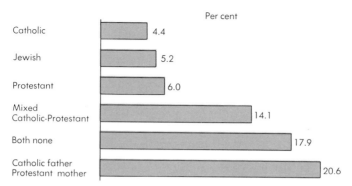

FIGURE 1. *Religious affiliation and percentage of marriages broken by divorce or separation, 4108 parents of college students.*

Source: Judson T. Landis and Mary G. Landis, *Building a Successful Marriage*, Englewood Cliffs, New Jersey: Prentice-Hall, © 1968, p. 192. Reprinted by permission of Prentice-Hall, Inc.

findings. Catholic, Jewish, and Protestant couples all had quite low divorce and separation rates (see Figure 1). The divorce and separation rates in mixed Catholic-Protestant marriages were over twice as high. The rates were highest of all where the mixed marriages involved Catholic fathers married to Protestant mothers.[61]

The most definitive study, to date, of divorce rates in interfaith marriages was done for the whole state of Iowa, using data for a seven-year period from 1953 through 1959. This study, which imposed controls for both age and social status, partly confirms the results of earlier, less rigorous studies and partly calls their findings into question. It did show the divorce rate in homogamous Catholic marriages to be lower than in marriages where Catholics were married to denominationally affiliated Protestants. The size of the differences, however, was considerably reduced, and there were no significant differences according to whether the Catholic spouse in the mixed marriages was husband or wife. The researchers concluded that the smaller differences found in this study did not justify generalizations of considerably greater marital difficulties facing Catholics who marry outside their faith, providing the person they marry is identified with a Protestant denomination.[62]

[61] Judson T. Landis, "Marriages of Mixed and Non-mixed Religious Faith," *American Sociological Review* 14 (June 1949), pp. 401–7.

[62] Lee G. Burchinal and Loren E. Chancellor, "Survival Rates Among Religiously Homogamous and Interreligious Marriages," *Social Forces* 41 (May 1963), pp. 353–62. See also Thomas P. Monahan and Loren E. Chancellor, "Statistical Aspects of Marriage and Divorce by Religious Denomination in Iowa," *Eugenics Quarterly* 2 (Sept. 1955), pp. 162–73.

A special contribution of this study was the computation of marital survival rates for many types of religiously homogamous and religiously heterogamous marriages. Several factors stand out in the data presented in Table 4. First,

TABLE 4. *Rank Order of Marital Survival Rates, by Religious Affiliation Types.*

RELIGIOUS AFFILIATION TYPES	MARITAL SURVIVAL RATES
Homogamous Catholic	96.2
Mixed Presbyterian	94.6
Homogamous Lutheran	94.1
Residual specified Protestant	94.0
Mixed Lutheran	93.0
Mixed Methodist	92.9
Homogamous Methodist	91.4
Homogamous Presbyterian	91.0
Catholic-Lutheran	90.5
Mixed Baptist	90.0
Catholic-Presbyterian	89.8
Homogamous Baptist	89.8
Catholic-residual specified Protestant	89.1
Homogamous Protestant	86.2
Catholic-Methodist	83.8
Mixed unspecified Protestant	82.7
Catholic-Baptist	81.6
Catholic-interreligious	77.6
Homogamous unspecified Protestant	35.0
Catholic-unspecified Protestant	28.7
Total Population	87.6

Source: Lee Burchinal and Loren Chancellor, "Survival Rates Among Religiously Homogamous and Interreligious Marriages," *Social Forces* 41 (May 1963), p. 360.

the survival rates almost form a continuum without sharp breaks until the last two categories are reached.[63] Second, while homogamous Catholic marriages had the highest survival rate, a number of other homogamous and mixed marriage types had survival rates nearly as high. Third, many of the survival rates ranged within a single percentage point of one another. Fourth, the lower-middle segment of the table includes homogamous Protestant marriages, marriages of Catholics with Methodists or Baptists, and the total for all interreligious marriages.

Of particular interest is the fact that Presbyterians, Methodists, and Baptists married to other Protestants had higher marital survival rates than mem-

[63] The data reported for the last two categories probably are unreliable. Analysis of this point would take us beyond the scope of the present discussion. Interested students are referred to the original report, pp. 359–60.

bers of those same denominations who were homogamously married. Moreover, the full data indicated that the observed marital survival rates were influenced more by age at marriage and social status than by the mere fact of religious differences. Marital survival rates were consistently higher among marriages involving older brides and couples marrying at higher status levels.

In summary, we must conclude that, in spite of the apparently higher divorce rates among some types of mixed marriages, the data are somewhat equivocal. Some authors have gone further and argued that the frequent admonitions in the literature concerning the hazards of mixed marriages reflect a widespread bias against such marriages as much as they reflect data on divorce rates. Vernon, for example, states that family-life educators should be taken to task for persisting in presenting only one side of the question on the frequency of divorce associated with religiously homogamous or heterogamous marriages. The statistics on the proportion of each type of each marriage which endure are ignored, he says, in the usual presentation of data to students.[64] Vincent makes a similar point and, in addition, claims that existing data on divorce rates could as easily be used to indicate that the problem is not so much one of intermarriage as it is the persistence of religious differences.[65]

At best, divorce rates are a very crude index of marital success or failure. We cannot even assume that all of the marriages which result in divorce are unhappy marriages. In some segments of the population, divorce may be sought whenever the advantages in it appear to outweigh those involved in remaining married. At the other extreme, divorce may not be acceptable in some groups no matter how great the unhappiness. No one knows what proportion of religiously homogamous marriages may survive simply because the church condemns divorce. Confident generalizations of qualitative differences between homogamous and heterogamous marriages probably should be based upon actual studies of marital interaction.

A number of studies comparing adjustment in religiously homogamous and heterogamous marriages have been made and, again, the evidence is far from one-sided. One part of Heiss's study of intermarried couples in New York City, for example, included comparisons between matched samples of intermarried and intramarried couples. The findings generally showed intermarried Catholics to be more dissatisfied, to worry more about marriage, to be in poorer mental health, to have fewer children, and to have more problems

---

[64] Glenn M. Vernon, "Bias in Professional Publications Concerning Interfaith Marriages," *Religious Education* 55 (July–Aug. 1960), pp. 261–4.

[65] Clark E. Vincent, "Interfaith Marriages: Problem or Symptom?," in Marvin B. Sussman, ed., *Sourcebook in Marriage and the Family*, Boston: Houghton Mifflin, 1963, pp. 349–59.

with the children they have. Differences between intermarried and intramarried Jews were somewhat smaller and less consistent, but Heiss concluded that intermarried Catholics and Jews may carry something of an additional burden. The pressures on intermarried Protestants were seen as not quite so great.[66]

Two other studies present the other side of the picture. In a study of 194 interfaith marriages, Prince found that nearly half of the spouses were themselves the offspring of interfaith marriages. Moreover, more than half of the spouses reported themselves to be either very much satisfied or entirely satisfied with their marriages. Fewer than 10 per cent reported any degree of dissatisfaction.[67]

Dyer and Luckey made carefully controlled comparisons among the marriages of 522 former University of Minnesota students and concluded that there was no significant relation between religious affiliation and marital happiness ratings. This was true in both denominationally homogamous and heterogamous marriages. In testing the relationship of personality variables and marital happiness, again no differences were found. The researchers pointed out that these were young couples who had hardly embarked upon parenthood and who might encounter difficulties later on. On the other hand, they believe that their results may reflect a trend in the United States to accept and deal with heterogamous marriages more adequately.[68]

RESIDENTIAL PROPINQUITY

Some 35 years ago, sociologists discovered that not only are there widespread tendencies toward homogamy but also that a large proportion of people select their marriage partners from among those who live very near to them geographically. This tendency to select partners from those near at hand usually is called residential propinquity.

The first study of propinquity, made in Philadelphia, showed that one-sixth of 5000 consecutive pairs applying for marriage licenses lived within one city block of each other. One-third of the couples lived within five blocks of each other, and over half lived within 20 blocks.[69] Bossard concluded that the pro-

---

[66] Jerold S. Heiss, "Interfaith Marriage and Marital Outcome," *Marriage and Family Living* 23 (Aug. 1961), pp. 228–33.

[67] Alfred J. Prince, "A Study of 194 Cross-Religion Marriages," *Family Life Coordinator* 11 (Jan. 1962), pp. 3–7.

[68] Dorothy T. Dyer and Eleanore B. Luckey, "Religious Affiliation and Selected Personality Scores as They Relate to Marital Happiness of a Minnesota College Sample," *Marriage and Family Living* 23 (Feb. 1961), pp. 46–7.

[69] James H. S. Bossard, "Residential Propinquity as a Factor in Marriage Selection," *American Journal of Sociology* 38 (Sept. 1932), pp. 219–24.

portion of marriages decreases steadily and markedly as the distance between contracting parties increases.

Over the next 20 years or so, several other studies verified the fact that people select marriage partners disproportionately from those who live nearby, but they did not substantiate the *steady* decrease in marriages with increasing distance that Bossard had hypothesized.[70] Rather than concentrate on the specific proportions of couples selecting mates from within one-block, five-block, and ten-block distances, these researchers have tended to focus on whether the general findings would hold up in increasingly controlled studies and upon developing theoretical explanations for the operation of residential propinquity.

The propinquity studies have assumed, of course, that distance is related to mate selection through the opportunities that people have to meet and become acquainted. Clarke tested this assumption in Columbus, Ohio, by securing the addresses of the partners at the time of their first date as well as at the time of marriage. He found that nearly half of the sample had changed addresses between first date and application for a marriage license. Some couples moved closer to one another and some moved farther away, with the result that the proportion residing within 16 city blocks remained approximately the same.[71] He did find that the proportions reporting the same address or living within four city blocks increased by the time of applying for the license (see Table 5).

Having thus established that propinquity does not emerge simply from courtship interaction, we turn to two major theoretical interpretations. Katz and Hill, after considering the evidence from all the major propinquity studies, propound a norm-interaction theory. Briefly, that theory holds that: (1) Mate selection is normatively regulated; (2) within eligible groups of potential spouses, the probability of marriage varies directly with the probability of interaction; and (3) the probability of interaction is governed by distance and by the segregation of racial, religious, economic, and other groups

[70] Ray H. Abrams, "Residential Propinquity as a Factor in Marriage Selection: Fifty Year Trends in Philadelphia," *American Sociological Review* 8 (June 1943), pp. 288–94; Alfred C. Clarke, "An Examination of the Operation of Residential Propinquity as a Factor in Mate Selection," *American Sociological Review* 17 (Feb. 1952), pp. 17–22; Alan C. Kerckhoff, "Notes and Comments on the Meaning of Residential Propinquity as a Factor in Mate Selection," *Social Forces* 34 (March 1956), pp. 207–13; Marvin R. Koller, "Residential Propinquity of White Mates at Marriage in Relation to Age and Occupation of Males. Columbus, Ohio, 1938 and 1946," *American Sociological Review* 13 (Oct. 1948), pp. 613–16; Joseph R. Marches and Gus Turbeville, "The Effect of Residential Propinquity on Marriage Selection," *American Journal of Sociology* 58 (May 1953), pp. 592–5.

[71] Op. cit.

TABLE 5. *Residential Propinquity of White Couples at Time of First Date, Engagement, and Application for Marriage License, Columbus, Ohio.*

BLOCKS BETWEEN RESIDENCES	AT FIRST DATE		AT ENGAGEMENT		AT APPLICATION	
	Number	Per cent	Number	Per cent	Number	Per cent
Same Address	9	3.2	8	2.8	31	9.8
Within:						
4	70	24.9	73	25.3	95	30.0
8	105	37.3	108	37.4	126	39.8
12	132	46.9	135	46.7	149	47.1
16	153	54.4	154	53.2	169	53.4
20	172	61.2	172	59.4	190	60.6
24	182	64.7	187	64.6	209	66.0
28	197	70.0	199	68.8	221	69.8
32	215	76.4	216	74.8	236	74.5
36	227	80.7	229	79.3	249	78.6
40	239	85.0	241	83.5	262	82.7
44	251	89.3	249	86.3	274	86.5
48	258	91.8	256	88.7	281	88.7
52	262	93.2	265	91.8	290	91.5
56	267	95.0	273	94.6	298	94.0
60	271	96.4	278	96.3	303	95.6
64	277	98.5	283	98.0	308	97.2
68	278	98.8	285	98.7	311	98.2
72	280	99.6	287	99.4	313	98.8
76	281	100.0	288	99.7	314	99.1
80	281	100.0	289	100.0	315	99.4
84	281	100.0	289	100.0	316	99.7
88	281	100.0	289	100.0	317	100.0

Source: Alfred C. Clarke, "An Examination of the Operation of Residential Propinquity as a Factor in Mate Selection," *American Sociological Review* 17 (Feb. 1952), p. 18.

in the community.[72] According to this theory, groups that are most segregated residentially will tend to be the most propinquitous; and where the homogamy norms are strong there will tend to be more propinquity.

This norm-interaction theory is very useful in explaining the variations in propinquity that have been found in the various studies. Catton and Smircich, using data from Seattle, however, find that the most useful model is one which interprets distance gradients as reflecting an economy of time and energy rather than competition between near and remote courtship opportunities or the operation of normative factors.[73] They suggest that the number

[72] See Alvin M. Katz and Reuben Hill, "Residential Propinquity and Marital Selection: A Review of Theory, Method, and Fact," *Marriage and Family Living* 20 (Feb. 1958), pp. 27–35.

[73] William R. Catton, Jr. and R. J. Smircich, "A Comparison of Mathematical Models for the Effect of Residential Propinquity on Mate Selection," *American Sociological Review* 29 (Aug. 1964), pp. 522–9.

of "meaningful" mate-selection opportunities that most people have are rather few; most people simply do not become intimately acquainted with many eligible persons of opposite sex. The probability that any one person of opposite sex will be included among that small number probably depends upon the time and energy costs in traveling.

The Catton and Smircich theory has not been adequately tested as yet. It is important, however, because it implies that normative factors in mate selection may not be as important as we think. It holds, instead, that propinquity may lead to homogamous marriages and that the familiarity of homogamous marriages leads to the development of homogamy norms.

THE THEORY OF COMPLEMENTARY NEEDS

The preceding discussion of the operation of homogamous norms in mate selection was confined to homogamy in *social* characteristics because it is in the area of social matchmaking that the concept appears to have most utility. This does not mean that there are no homogamous tendencies in the area of *personal* characteristics, for there are. Early studies showed similarity between husbands and wives in physical traits, attractiveness, intellectual ability, attitudes, and temperament. More recently, Schellenberg studied the similarity in values among engaged and married couples and found more similarity than in a group of artificially paired couples.[74] Kerckhoff and Davis, studying consensus on family values, found it to increase as dating couples moved toward more permanent relationships.[75]

The evidence in favor of homogamy in personal characteristics is not nearly so convincing, however, as that demonstrating homogamy in social characteristics. There were, even among the early studies, some which suggested that people may choose marriage partners who have traits opposite from their own. Kretschmer found such a pairing of opposites among 170 married couples, and Gray found the mating of complementary types rather than the mating of homogamous personality types.[76]

---

[74] James A. Schellenberg, "Homogamy in Personal Values and the Field of Eligibles," *Social Forces* 39 (Dec. 1960), pp. 157–62. For similar findings with regard to empathy, see Norman Goodman, and Richard Ofshe, "Empathy, Communication Efficiency, and Marital Status," *Journal of Marriage and the Family* 30 (Nov. 1968), pp. 597–603.

[75] Alan C. Kerckhoff and Keith E. Davis, "Value Consensus and Need Complementarity in Mate Selection," *American Sociological Review* 27 (June 1962), pp. 295–303. Snyder found, however, that homogamy in self, social, and total adjustment, and in IQ, existed among 20 couples prior to their selection of one another as marital partners. See Eloise C. Snyder, "Marital Selectivity in Self-Adjustment, Social Adjustment, and I.Q.," *Journal of Marriage and the Family* 28 (May 1966), pp. 188–9.

[76] This literature is summarized in Clifford Kirkpatrick, *The Family: As Process and Institution*, New York: The Ronald Press Company, 1963, pp. 335–6.

The formulation of a comprehensive theory of mate selection in terms of complementary personality needs and the partial testing of that theory were accomplished by Robert Winch and his associates.[77] This theory holds, first, that all human behavior is oriented toward the gratification of needs. Certain important needs become organized in the personality and give pattern to behavior. Not all of these needs are always conscious, so people are aware of some of their needs, only partly aware of others, and completely unaware of some.

Needs are learned in the process of personality development and, so, become subject to normative regulation. They must be expressed within the general endogamous and exogamous norms of the group. The endogamous and exogamous norms define, for each person, his "field of eligibles"—those persons from among whom he is permitted to select a mate.

Building upon these assumptions, Winch then describes how love and mate selection operate in middle-class America. Love he defines as the positive emotion expressed by one person in a relationship in which the second person meets certain important needs of the first or manifests or appears to manifest personal qualities highly valued by the first. In mate selection, then, each person selects, from within his or her field of eligibles, that person who gives greatest promise of providing him with maximum need gratification. The partners' need patterns, consequently, will be complementary rather than similar. The complementariness, further, was hypothesized to be of either of two kinds. First, the needs being gratified for the one spouse may be different in kind from the needs being gratified for the second spouse. Or, second, the needs being gratified for the one spouse may differ in degree or intensity from those being gratified for the other.

The research which sought to verify or refute these hypotheses was a very complex pattern of research upon a very limited sample. Lengthy need interviews and case history interviews were supplemented through the use of projective testing. Ratings of personality needs were then based upon content analysis of the need interview and case history materials, summarized and evaluated at conferences of the team of investigators.

[77] The research to be summarized here appeared in a series of journal articles. See Thomas Ktsanes, "Mate Selection on the Basis of Personality Type: A Study Utilizing an Empirical Typology of Personality," *American Sociological Review* 20 (Oct. 1955), pp. 547–51; Robert F. Winch, "The Theory of Complementary Needs in Mate Selection: A Test of One Kind of Complementariness," *American Sociological Review* 20 (Feb. 1955), pp. 52–6; Robert F. Winch, "The Theory of Complementary Needs in Mate Selection: Final Results on the Test of the General Hypothesis," *American Sociological Review* 20 (Oct. 1955), pp. 552–5; Robert F. Winch, Thomas Ktsanes, and Virginia Ktsanes, "Empirical Elaboration of the Theory of Complementary Needs in Mate Selection," *Journal of Abnormal and Social Psychology* 51 (Nov. 1955), pp. 508–13.

The sample from whom these data were secured were only 25 native-born, undergraduate, recently married, childless couples at Northwestern University. The data were subjected to elaborate statistical analysis.

PESONALITY NEEDS TESTED FOR COMPLEMENTARINESS

1. abasement	8. nurturance
2. achievement	9. recognition
3. approach	10. status aspiration
4. autonomy	11. status striving
5. deference	12. succorance
6. dominance	13. anxiety
7. hostility	14. emotionality

15. vicariousness

The actual analyses of the data were too technical to be reported here. Suffice it to say that the results generally supported the hypotheses. An early test, for example, supported the notion that the assertive-receptive dimension is important in mate selection; high assertives had tended to marry high receptives. Similarly, it was found that when the same traits in husband and wife were correlated (abasement with abasement, hostility with hostility, dominance with dominance, and so on) the relationships were generally negative. In the conceptual language of the previous section, they found little evidence of personality homogamy. When the husbands' hostility scores were correlated with the wives' abasement scores, by contrast, the relationship was positive; their needs in this respect tended to be complementary.

The research was too complex for the results not to have required careful qualification. Winch acknowledged that the results were not quite as compelling as they might have been. He concluded, however, that the bulk of the data supported the theory of complementary needs. Moreover, that portion of the results which did not clearly support the theory of complementary needs did not support the idea of homogamy in personal needs either; they simply showed little relationship among the variables.

The theory of complementary needs in mate selection has attracted considerable attention in American sociology. If subsequent research should establish its validity, it would contribute a great deal to our knowledge of mate selection. It is not surprising that, although the original research is scarcely ten years old, there have already been several attempts to test the theory further.

At least five studies have attempted to test Winch's findings directly, using the Edwards Personal Preference Schedule to measure personality needs and to get at complementariness in the relationship. One study used as subjects 60 college couples who either were regular dating partners or were engaged,[78] one used 36 unmarried couples and 64 married couples,[79] one used an accidental sample of 50 relatively well adjusted married couples,[80] one used 62 couples who were either dating, going steady, or engaged,[81] and the fifth used 258 Swedish couples who had published the banns.[82] In all five studies, the results were essentially negative; no real support was found for the theory of complementary needs.

It should be pointed out that these studies were not strictly comparable to Winch's study. The research instruments and procedures differed. Moreover, the samples in all six studies were small and highly selective. On the basis of this pattern of research, the theory of complementary needs cannot be said to have been either adequately established or adequately refuted. Perhaps the most valuable contribution of the theory so far has been to lead to attempts to improve the theory itself.

Rosow has pointed out that Winch's formulation of the theory of complementary needs undoubtedly is oversimplified. He maintains that there are at least four kinds of complementarity that affect marital cohesion: (1) the relations strictly between the couple, as studied by Winch; (2) the relations which involve either partner acting for the couple in interaction with outsiders; (3) relations between the couple, as a couple, in interaction with outsiders; and (4) relations in which each partner separately seeks, within the marriage, to balance satisfactions or frustrations encountered outside the family. He points out, too, that needs exist, not as isolated traits, but as organized patterns and that the importance of these various need patterns in an individual's life may change over time.[83]

---

[78] Charles E. Bowerman and Barbara R. Day, "A Test of the Theory of Complementary Needs as Applied to Couples During Courtship," *American Sociological Review* 21 (Oct. 1956), pp. 602–5.

[79] James A. Schellenberg and Lawrence S. Bee, "A Re-examination of the Theory of Complementary Needs in Mate Selection," *Marriage and Family Living* 22 (Aug. 1960), pp. 227–32.

[80] John A. Blazer, "Complementary Needs and Marital Happiness," *Marriage and Family Living* 25 (Feb. 1963), pp. 89–95.

[81] Jerold S. Heiss and Michael Gordon, "Need Patterns and the Mutual Satisfaction of Dating and Engaged Couples," *Journal of Marriage and the Family* 26 (Aug. 1964), pp. 337–9.

[82] Jan Trost, "Some Data on Mate Selection: Complementarity," *Journal of Marriage and the Family* 29 (Nov. 1967), pp. 730–8.

[83] Irving Rosow, "Issues in the Concept of Need-Complementarity," *Sociometry* 20 (Sept. 1957), pp. 216–33. See also, Jan Trost, "Some Data on Mate Selection: Homogamy

Udry has suggested, further, that we react to others on the basis of our *perceptions* of them and that perception may or may not coincide with measured personality traits. He found empirically that mates' perceptions of one another tend to exaggerate personality differences between the sexes and that the perceptions involve a substantial projection of their own traits. One implication of his work is that an adequate theory of complementary needs will need to be more complex than the existing theory.[84]

Finally, Bolton has introduced some much-needed balance into the development of theories of mate selection by arguing that, while both the homogamy and complementary theories have utility, mate selection must be studied not only in terms of variables brought by the partners to the courtship situation but also in terms of the process by which their relationship moves toward marriage. There are many turning points and commitments leading to marriage.

A Developmental Approach to Mate Selection

In this context, the development of a courtship is viewed as not being mechanically predetermined by either social or personality variables. Instead, the outcome is the end product of a long series of interactions characterized by advances and retreats, by changing definitions of the situation, and by the resolution of tensions between the couple. Bolton describes five different types of developmental processes:[85]

Type I: *Personality meshing developmental processes.* The predominant characteristic of this type is the mutual perception of personality "fit," with the chief functions of interaction being those of bringing into meshing the existing personality orientations of the two parties and providing the qualities of experience which serve as indexes of a marriageable relation. Couples tend to be homogamous in background and values but complementary in personality needs and organization. Attraction is felt early, the developmental tempos of the pair are in close rhythm, and interactions increase in frequency to the saturation point, with erotic interaction, empathy, and idealization important. These relations, then, correspond fairly closely to romantic expectations.

---

and Perceived Homogamy," *Journal of Marriage and the Family* 29 (Nov. 1967), pp. 739–55; and Ellen S. Karp, Julie H. Jackson, and David Lester, "Ideal-Self Fulfillment in Mate Selection: A Corollary to the Complementary Need Theory of Mate Selection," *Journal of Marriage and the Family* 32 (May 1970), pp. 269–72.

[84] J. Richard Udry, "Complementarity in Mate Selection: A Perceptual Approach," *Marriage and Family Living* 25 (Aug. 1963), pp. 281–9.

[85] Charles D. Bolton, "Mate Selection as the Development of a Relationship," *Marriage and Family Living* 23 (Aug. 1961), pp. 234–40.

Type II: *Identity clarification developmental processes.* The central theme is the focus of interaction upon the clarification or change of one or both individuals' identities. Though the two individuals may differ initially about values, interaction brings about increasing agreement along with a role pattern tending to be equalitarian. The assumption of compatibility either is made early or emerges implicitly out of interaction about identity problems. . . . Identity problems are precipitated by interaction such as through generation of conflict with parents or threat to defenses against intimate involvement. The relation cannot progress to marriage until the identity problems are resolved. The importance of interpersonal strategies is great; turning points are frequent; and a texture of shared understandings of considerable depth is built up. More than in any other type there is a withdrawal into the relationship and away from outside influences.

Type III: *Relation centered developmental processes.* The central theme is the building up of images of the other, amorous identifications and bonds which lead the couple to the decision that theirs is a viable relationship for marriage. Personalities do not spontaneously mesh; their "fit" remains in doubt through a large portion of the premarital period. Adjustments, shared understandings, and commitments are consciously built up, though they may not have much depth. There is an initial superficial commitment, and then one or both parties begin having questions, and the central theme becomes the viability of the relation. There are more ups and downs, breaks, rivals, incongruities of definition, and outside pressures to maintain the relation than in any other type.

Type IV: *Pressure and intrapersonal centered developmental processes.* The two parties are rather similar and traditional in background, and both dislike conflict. But their personalities decidedly do not mesh. One party uses direct, frontal pressure while the other depends upon subtle manipulation, with one being relatively free of blocks while the other has personality barriers to forming intimate involvements. Several themes emerge: (1) one member, being under an expediency pressure to marry, falls in love quickly and pressures the other for marriage, but the resisting or apathetic member blocks; (2) a concentration directly upon questions of marriageability and upon securing commitments; (3) a dependence of one or both members more upon the relationship per se than upon one another; and (4) a great importance of fantasy for one or both members. Identity problems are avoided except at crisis points—and then interaction halts short of efforts at resolution—and even amorous identifications tend to be built up primarily in intrapersonal processes. The marked lack of congruity of definitions is met by fantasy and tactical maneuvering. There is an emphasis upon formality, romanticism, and role playing, with an avoidance of the directly erotic. Often crucial developments come by correspondence, where the inhibited member feels freer and ambiguity is harder to maintain.

Type V: *Expediency centered developmental processes.* The relation centers on a strongly felt pressure to marry on the part of one or both members, this need occurring in the context of a basic personality problem or identity crisis. Where this pressure characterizes only one partner, the other is inexperienced in heterosexual relationships, highly suggestible, or apathetic toward his interpersonal fate. If expediency exists at the outset, the process is short; if it emerges after a casual relation is in progress, there are a series of sharp turning points and tactical maneuvers through which the relationship quickly moves toward marriage. Personality "fit" and mutuality of values are only superficially considered, though some fantasy is important for providing the trappings of a romantic atmosphere.

Whether these five types cover all of the processes whereby dating partners are selected as future spouses, their very construction displays a broad and perceptive knowledge of personality structure and of courtship processes. They indicate the importance of personal, interpersonal, and situational variables within the general context imposed by the operation of social homogamy.

Bolton carries this developmental analysis further by describing a series of "escalators" that tend to carry dating couples along toward marriage. These escalators refer to the fact that, once the person takes the first step in developing a relationship, the involvement acquires a built-in momentum that carries the couple along toward marriage. Students should note the compatibility of this concept of escalators with Willard Waller's conception of how couples are carried along toward marriage by lovers' quarrels.

Institutionalized escalators are illustrated by the romantic fantasy pattern and the dating-going steady-pinned-engaged-married pattern, reinforced by the sanctions of the couple's immediate associates. Five types of these escalators may be identified. First, the "involvement escalator" comes into operation as the person finds that his educational and career plans, his religious and moral identity, and even his daily schedule become involved in the relationship with the dating partner. Second, a "commitment escalator" operates both through the sequence of formal, publicly announced commitments and through the changes in definition of self that accompany those announcements. Third, there is what might be called an "addiction escalator." According to this concept, there is a tendency for the person to avoid the psychological withdrawal symptoms that would accompany the loss of sexual, affectional, or prestige relations. Fourth, there is a "fantasy escalator" in which the person seeks to hold onto the relationship as a symbol of whatever fantasy surrounds the involvement. Fifth, and finally, an "idealization escalator" comes into operation as the person's self-esteem becomes bound up with his romanticized conception of the partner.

Perhaps still other escalators exist. In any event, it seems obvious that the developmental approach to mate selection adds significantly to our understanding of it. We do not, as yet, have an adequate, comprehensive theory of mate selection. The general principle of homogamy operates to imperfectly sort out potential mates into groups of eligibles and ineligibles. Theoretically, the group of eligibles, for most persons, is quite large. Practically, however, the propinquity factor operates to keep the working group of eligibles rather small. Within the working field of eligibles some selection in terms of homogamous and complementary personality needs undoubtedly occurs. We have not, as yet, succeeded in perceiving the full complexity of this process. Finally, the entire set of factors operates in something less than completely deterministic fashion. The dynamics of each relationship, as it develops, either realize or reject the potential inherent in the more general selection process.

Finally, it should at least be questioned whether we do not over-rationalize the whole process of mate selection. Our emphasis upon free marital choice seems to imply that one chooses a mate as rationally as one buys a garden tool or a tube of toothpaste. At the same time, it seems apparent that, at about a certain age, strong cultural pressures are generated for people to find mates and they do just that—telling themselves, all the while, how carefully their choices are being made. Some writers have suggested that, while the percentage of marriages that are purely of the "supply and demand" variety may be small, possibly most marriages embody some element of chance.[86]

SUMMARY

Homogamy, the tendency for like to marry like, reflects the operation of endogamous norms in the United States. The existence of homogamy has been verified for a number of social characteristics, including age, marital status, social status, race, religion, and ethnic background.

Most Americans marry young and marry persons of nearly their own age. The age-homogamy norms become less effective in remarriages than in first marriages. A number of studies show that age at marriage is related to marital success, with those marrying very young having poorer chances of achieving marital happiness. The number and proportion of marriages of high-school-age youth increased from 1910 to 1950 but the rate has not increased significantly since that time. The divorce rate among such young marriages is estimated at from two to four times that among persons who marry after 20 years of age. The high divorce rate is related to low educational levels, low economic levels, premarital pregnancies, and possibly to personality difficulties. Whether young marriages that remain intact are of higher or lower quality than other marriages is unknown.

Status homogamy appears to operate by occupational level, educational

86 Ibid.; and William M. Kephart, "Some Knowns and Unknowns in Family Research: A Sociological Critique," *Marriage and Family Living* 19 (Feb. 1957), pp. 7-15.

level, and class of residential area. When status homogamy does not hold, however, the general pattern is for men to marry downward. This "mating gradient" may tend to leave very high-status women and very low-status men disproportionately among the unmarried. There is some evidence that status homogamy may be declining with the passage of time.

Traditionally, the norms requiring racial endogamy have been very strong. Perhaps no more than 1 per cent of all marriages are interracial marriages although the intermarriage rate may be increasing. There is great interest in that small proportion of the population which does intermarry.

Studies show that the spouses in interracial marriages tend to be older than those entering homogamous marriages, that they are more likely to have been married before, and that they may have histories of feeling rejected by parents and their own racial group. On the other hand, the spread of equalitarian norms in the society may be leading certain groups to contemplate interracial dating and marriage without the historically associated conditions of rebellion and noncomformity.

Interracial marriages are widely believed to be doomed to failure. Studies of war-bride marriages and Negro-white marriages do not bear out the belief, however. Instead, the studies show that strains in interracial marriages are patterned and predictable just as they are in racially homogamous marriages. The sources of strain in Negro-white marriages include some isolation from parental families, particularly the white family, and having to raise their children as Negro. Discrimination may be encountered in housing, employment, and in public places. Most of the marriages studied, however, appear to be as stable as other marriages.

Studies of religious homogamy have shown wide variation in intermarriage rates. In general, the larger the proportion a religious group is of the community, the lower its intermarriage rate and vice versa. Intermarriage also tends to vary inversely with the cohesion of the ethnic group. Few studies have been made of the actual increases in intermarriage rates, but studies do show very widespread attitudes of acceptance of such marriages.

Research shows divorce rates to be higher in marriages where Catholics marry non-Catholics than in homogamous Catholic marriages. The differences appear to be smaller than generally believed, however, and do not extend to cover all types of religious mixed marriages. Marital survival rates appear to be influenced more by associated factors of age and social status than by religious differences. Actual studies of adjustment in interfaith marriages have produced conflicting findings. Some studies show special problems of adjustment stemming from religious differences and some do not. It may be that the society is becoming increasingly accepting of interfaith marriages.

The term, residential propinquity, refers to the tendency of persons to select marriage partners who live very near to them geographically. Propinquity has been shown to operate at the time of first date and at the time of marriage. Theories proposing to explain the operation of propinquity have emphasized residential segregation, homogamous norms, the relation between distance and the likelihood of interaction, and the sheer time and energy costs involved in traveling.

The evidence for homogamy in personal characteristics is not so strong as that showing homogamy in social characteristics. In fact, there is some evidence that people seek marital partners who complement themselves in terms of personality needs. A comprehensive theory of mate selection in terms of complementary needs has been formulated and has received some empirical support; subsequent testing has failed to confirm the original findings, however. Efforts to develop further the theory continue. Full understanding of mate selection requires that relationships be viewed developmentally in addition to the perspective provided by the operation of homogamy, propinquity, and the theory of complementary needs. The development of courtship is not completely predetermined but involves a series of advances and retreats, changing definitions of the situation, and commitments as the relationship proceeds toward marriage. Once a relationship is begun, there are a series of institutionalized escalators that help to move it along.

Finally, it must be said that mate selection is, as yet, not fully explained. There appear to be fortuitous factors operating. Perhaps few instances of mate selection can be ascribed wholly to chance, but some chance elements may enter into most relationships.

SUGGESTED READINGS

Berman, Louis A., *Jews and Intermarriage: A Study in Personality and Culture*, New York: Thomas Yoseloff, 1968. A comprehensive summary of research, and an analysis of the problems confronting Jewish-Gentile marriages.

Cahnman, Werner J., ed., *Intermarriage and Jewish Life in America*, New York: Herzl Press, 1962. A collection of readings dealing with the history, present status, and implications of intermarriage.

Carter, Hugh, and Glick, Paul C., *Marriage and Divorce: A Social and Economic Study*, Cambridge, Mass.: Harvard University Press, 1970. A rich compilation of data, from federal sources, on marriage patterns in the United States.

Gordon, Milton M., *Assimilation in American Life: The Role of Race, Religion and National Origins*, New York: Oxford University Press, 1964. Brilliant theoretical analysis of the assimilation of racial, ethnic, and religious groups. Deals with problems and processes of intermarriage.

Lenski, Gerhard, *The Religious Factor: A Sociological Study of Religion's Impact on Politics, Economics, and Family Life*, Garden City, New York: Doubleday and Company, 1961. Comprehensive report of research which, among other things, indicates that subculture differences among the major religious groups may be increasing rather than declining.

Vernon, Glenn M., *The Sociology of Religion*, New York: The McGraw-Hill Book Company, 1962. Good introductory treatment of the sociological analysis of religious phenomena. One section deals with the interrelation between religion and other social institutions, including the family.

Winch, Robert F., *Mate Selection: A Study of Complementary Needs*, New York: Harper and Brothers, 1958. Theoretical development of the concept of complementary needs and a report of research testing its applicability.

FILMS

Choosing Your Marriage Partner (Coronet Films, Coronet Building, Chicago), 13 minutes. Young man tries to decide which of two girls to marry. Considers such factors as emotional maturity, family background, philosophy of life, and harmony of personalities.

It Takes All Kinds (McGraw-Hill Book Company, Text-Film Division, 330 West 42nd St., New York 10036), 20 minutes. Analysis of personality is seen as an important step in choosing the right marriage partner. Shows a series of young people, each disclosing the essential pattern of his or her personality in reacting to an identical tense situation.

Mixed Marriages (*Time-Life* Films, 43 West 16th Street, New York 10011), 30 minutes. The problems of five interracial marriages—all seeking different solutions—are analyzed. Problems of adjusting to parental families, and of raising children, are emphasized.

This Charming Couple (McGraw-Hill Book Company, Text-Film Division, 330 West 42nd St., New York 10036), 19 minutes. Focuses on a frequent cause of broken marriages—false ideas of romantic love. Follows the courtship of two young people who refuse to evaluate each other's good qualities and shortcomings in a realistic, adult fashion. Because they are in love with "love" and not with each other, their marriage is doomed to fail.

QUESTIONS AND PROJECTS

1. What is meant by the concept of homogamy? How is the operation of homogamous norms related to rules of endogamy and exogamy?
2. What is the pattern of homogamy by age? How is it related to marital status?
3. What trends have been and are evident in relation to very youthful marriages in the United States? What factors are related to the success or failure of such marriages? Can you see any elements of a self-fulfilling prophecy operating in the higher failure rate of youthful marriages?
4. Does homogamy operate by status levels in the society? What is the evidence? Is there any evidence that status homogamy may be weakening?
5. What is meant by "the mating gradient"? How does it work? What influence

does it have on determining what groups are likely to remain among the unmarried?

6. How much interracial marriage is there in the United States? How rapidly is the rate increasing?

7. What are the consequences of interracial marriages? Are these consequences in accord with traditional stereotypes? What do we know about the personality needs of those who intermarry? What, if any, social change may be occurring here?

8. How much religious homogamy is there in the United States? What factors are related to intermarriage rates? Is intermarriage increasing? How do you know? What do studies show of attitudes toward intermarriage in the United States?

9. What is the relation between religious homogamy or heterogamy and divorce rates? Is the relationship a simple one? What does research show about the relationship between marital happiness and interfaith marriage?

10. Define the term, residential propinquity. How does propinquity operate in mate selection? What explanations have been proposed for the operation of residential propinquity?

11. Explain the theory of complementary needs in mate selection. What does research show concerning it? Is further development of the theory needed? What additional factors may need to be taken into account?

12. How may mate selection be conceived of as a developmental process? Relate this concept of mate selection to Waller's theory of dating and courtship.

15 | *Marital Adjustment*

. . . Now marriage is, in actual fact, just a way of living. We don't expect life to be all sunshine and roses, or even beer and skittles. But somehow we do expect marriage to be that way. People who are accustomed to bickering with everyone else are shocked when they find that they bicker with their wives. Women who have found everything somewhat disappointing are surprised and pained when marriage proves itself no exception. Most of the complaints about the institution of holy matrimony arise not because it is worse than the rest of life, but because it is not incomparably better.

There are reasons for this almost universal feeling of disillusionment about marriage. One is that we are taught to expect too much from it. . . . But even if we have become profoundly cynical about marriage in general we are apt to be disillusioned about our own, because most of us marry while we are in love. . . . The sexual excitement, the uncertainties and novelties of the new relationship, actually lift us out of ourselves for a time. With the best will in the world we cannot during the falling-in-love stage show ourselves to our beloved as we really are, nor see her in her everyday personality. We are quite genuinely not our everyday selves at this period. We are more intense, more vital than usual. Moreover we see ourselves through the eyes of our beloved. Unconsciously we match our feeling about ourselves with the glorified impression she has formed of us.

This excited state of mind cannot endure the protracted association of marriage. The thrilling sexual tension which normally keeps engaged couples in a state of fervid and delighted expectation abates with frequent, satisfying intercourse. The element of uncertainty is dissipated—and there is no doubt that a goal we have not yet won is more intriguing than one which is wholly ours. . . . Sooner or later, when flamboyant anticipations of betrothal give way to the sober satisfactions of marriage, we lapse back into our ordinary selves. Fortunately, we can surpass ourselves during emotional crises without seriously depleting our reserves. We can run from a bear very fast indeed, but if we made that speed habitual we would soon collapse entirely. Walking is the most practicable gait for common use, and marriage too must be paced at the rate of our usual temperament. This inevitable change of pace is what we call disillusionment. Our disillusionment does not proceed wholly, or perhaps even primarily, from the unromantic facts we learn about our partner in the course of daily observation. It comes largely from our bored recognition of the same old self within our own breast. Our own newfound charm and prowess and glamour evaporate when we can no longer read them in a worshipping gaze, when we are no longer stimulated by the desire for conquest. . . .[1]

THE last few chapters have shown that the routes whereby couples approach marriage are multiple and varied. It seems likely that some persons do exercise a large amount of rationality in their selection of spouses and that they approach marriage with somewhat realistic expectations. At the other extreme are to be found couples who are caught up in overwhelming emotional attraction for one another. Some of these relationships develop essentially without exploitation and involve intense idealization of each partner by the other. In others, one partner is clearly dominant, with the disadvantaged partner more or less successfully concealing the already present pain which the relationship produces. Some couples literally are trapped into marriage by pregnancy. Some appear to result primarily from the pressures exerted by parents and friends, and the lack of a better alternative. Some defy explanation.

We cannot even list all of the qualities of relationships and all of the courtship processes that lead people into marriage. It does seem obvious, however, that the nature of the adjustments required early in marriage are related to the nature of the relationships upon which marriages are based; the adjustment of a pair of 22-year-old college graduates who have parental approval and adequate finances and who have selected the most promising prospect from a carefully defined field of eligibles, certainly will differ from that of high-school students trapped by pregnancy. Moreover, the adjustment of an aggressive, unattractive 25-year-old bride and a previously divorced man will differ from both. Processes of marital adjustment are unlikely to be fewer or simpler than those of courtship.

No one has yet succeeded in developing a fully adequate theory of marital adjustment. In fact there is scarcely a satisfactory definition of what constitutes marital adjustment. In this chapter, we will look first at what may be somewhat common patterns of interaction in early marriage and then subject the concept of marital adjustment to critical scrutiny. In the following chapter, we will consider the specifically sexual adjustments in marriage, family planning, reproduction, and patterns of child-rearing.

---

[1] John Levy and Ruth Munroe, *The Happy Family*, New York: Alfred A. Knopf, 1948, pp. 65-7.

The Dynamics of Marital Adjustment

Marriage may or may not involve a drastic change in the living arrangements of the married pair. Clarke, for example, found that 10 per cent of the couples he studied reported themselves as having the same address on the marriage-license application form.[2] Some of this might be accounted for by couples reporting the address to which they were moving rather than where they had previously been living. Other evidence, however, suggests strongly that some of these couples already were living together. The proportion of couples reporting the same address has been found to increase directly with the ages of the partners, and it makes sense that older couples are more likely to be living together than younger ones. It has also been found that black couples are more likely than white couples to report the same address.[3]

Other evidence indicates that whether the couple already are having sexual intercourse influences some of their early marital adjustments. Kanin and Howard found that couples who were having premarital intercourse were less likely to take wedding trips, were less likely to practise contraception early in marriage, and were more likely to report both sexual satisfaction and aspiration toward better sexual adjustment in marriage.[4]

HONEYMOON INTERACTION

For most couples, marriage does represent a sharp break with conditions of prior living. The marriage ceremony gives full sanction to whatever relationship already exists between the pair and, often, propels them into a twenty-four-hour-a-day physical and emotional intimacy for which they are not wholly prepared. Marriages seldom are scheduled to coincide with the couple's readiness for full intimacy but are arranged, instead, in terms of less relevant criteria such as the time of graduation from college, attaining the minimum legal age for marriage, being released from military service, having the harvest in, and so on. It should not be surprising if the sudden transition occasioned by the performance of the wedding ceremony were accompanied by both bliss and strain in the lives of most young couples.

Perhaps the most perceptive analysis of the nature of early marital adjust-

[2] Alfred C. Clarke, "An Examination of the Operation of Residential Propinquity as a Factor in Mate Selection," *American Sociological Review* 17 (Feb. 1952), pp. 17-22.

[3] Alan C. Kerckhoff, "Notes and Comments on the Meaning of Residential Propinquity as a Factor in Mate Selection," *Social Forces* 34 (March 1956), pp. 207-13.

[4] Eugene J. Kanin and David H. Howard, "Postmarital Consequences of Premarital Sex Adjustments," *American Sociological Review* 23 (Oct. 1958), pp. 556-62.

ment among middle-class young couples has come from the pen of Willard Waller. It cannot be said, for obvious reasons, that Waller accurately described the adjustment processes operating in all young marriages, but something approaching some of the conditions he describes may well appear in most of them.[5]

Waller describes the early weeks of marriage as being suffused with an erotically tinged euphoria. To whatever degree idealization has developed during courtship, each partner carries into marriage a romanticized conception of what the other is really like. Each has been living somewhat beyond himself—on Cloud nine as it were. It seems wonderful to be marrying such an extraordinary person as the partner appears to be and, if the partner is so exceptional, then one must also be rather special in order to merit such a partner.

Many forces operate in the premarital period to enhance the egos and general sense of well-being of the couple. To have found a partner at all represents some success in the competition for mates. To have found such an ideal partner produces something akin to a mild, continuing intoxication. Then as the sex relationship progresses, there is the overwhelming desire for complete fulfillment. As with other forms of fulfillment, the anticipation, the fantasy, and the accompanying feelings probably are as important as the achievement itself. We might even hypothesize that the drive toward full physical and emotional intimacy continues in most premarital relationships, regardless of the actual level of sexual involvement. Finally, the approval and vicarious participation of family and friends in the relationship brings with it psychic rewards. One's position has shifted a little closer to the center of the universe and one experiences emotions that surely are denied to most ordinary people.

This heady euphoria tends to continue into the early weeks of marriage. Moreover, it is reinforced by the excitement of being in a new married status, acquiring new possessions, moving into new quarters, and establishing new routines. According to Waller, this has an almost narcotic effect. It anesthetizes each partner against the too early and too violent intrusion upon his pre-existing habit patterns of the nonmeshing habits of the partner. Thus, a man who is fussy about his food can eat the undercooked eggs prepared by his new bride without suffering the gastrointestinal spasms they would otherwise produce. Similarly, the young wife who finds that her husband wears his underwear for three days and then throws it under the bed is not immediately overcome with revulsion. Locked in one another's arms, in their continuing

---

[5] The following discussion draws heavily on Willard Waller and Reuben Hill, *The Family: A Dynamic Interpretation*, New York: Dryden Press, 1951, pp. 253–321.

fantasies, in their new status, and in the special interest and approval of others, most couples experience—whether or not they take a wedding trip— an initial blissful adjustment which merits the sentimental term, honeymoon.

Honeymoons not seldom end worse than they began, and to recover from them may take quite a long time.

—Arnold Bennett.

Even during this early period, however, the couple begin to move toward a *modus vivendi.* Our system does not provide rigidly structured roles into which the husband and wife must fit, but depends upon the emotional attraction between them to see them through the development of reciprocal roles which are appropriate to their special situation and which will enhance their social and economic status. There are large areas of appropriate role behavior which must be defined in a short period of time.

Paradoxically, what might be called the honeymoon period also is characterized by unusual sensitivity of each spouse to the behavior of the other. The euphoria is accompanied by, or alternates with, periods of excessive hurt and shock at actual or alleged slights. If idealization frequently accompanies courtship, so does doubt—of self, of partner, and of the quality of the relationship. To the degree to which love serves as a rationalization of the movement toward marriage, the partner who has these feelings may react violently to their confirmation early in the marriage. The first time, for example, that the husband comes home from work too tired to go out with his wife, it may constitute irrefutable proof that he does not love her. The first time that the wife crawls into bed and goes promptly to sleep may signal to the husband that he should have heeded his doubts about getting married in the first place.

"*Love is an ideal thing, marriage a real thing; a confusion of the real with the ideal never goes unpunished.*"

—Goethe

The opportunities for rebuffs and slights to be experienced in early marriage are legion. Moreover, marriage forces upon people an intimacy which is not all erotic and which may have been unparalleled in their earlier lives. Husbands cannot escape confrontation with the paraphernalia attending management of menstruation or with hair curlers and the ritual washing of lingerie. Wives must handle the dirty socks and underwear and clean up the bathroom which has been turned into a swamp during their husbands' daily showers. Both sexes must contend with messy toothpaste tubes and catsup bottles—rendered that way by inconsiderate partners.

Waller defined the honeymoon as being that period in the psychic adjustment of the couple while illusion lasts. Eventually, he thought, the opposition between idealization and euphoria on the one hand and the intrusion of humdrum reality on the other has to yield in favor of reality. Inherent in this process is some degree of disillusionment, both with the partner and with oneself. If the partner proves not to be so different from others as was believed, then the special desirability that was imputed to oneself must be illusory also. The shattering of dreams is always painful and the onset of disillusionment in marriage sets the stage for conflict.

There is some empirical support for the idea of generalized disillusionment early in marriage. Hobart reports a study of 258 couples ranging from "favorite date" to "married" at a West Coast college. He found strong evidence of disillusionment in the transition from engagement to marriage. The data indicated more disillusionment among men than among women and also showed more tendency among men for the disillusionment to be associated with prior romanticism.[6] What is particularly striking is the implication that disillusionment may occur early in marriage even where there has not been excessive unreality in courtship.

Indirect evidence of disillusionment in early marriage also is provided by separation and divorce rates, and by contemplated separation rates. Landis, studying 544 college couples who had been married about two years, found that one-fifth of them had considered separation.[7] In Oregon, Johannis found that one-third of 54 college couples married three years had considered separation. For the country as a whole, there are more divorces during the first year of marriage than in any year after the fourth year. Moreover, the highest divorce rates by duration of marriage occur during the second and third years of marriage.[8] Undoubtedly many of these couples have separated after only a few months of living together. While these rates do not automatically

---

[6] Charles W. Hobart, "Disillusionment in Marriage, and Romanticism," *Marriage and Family Living* 20 (May 1958), pp. 156–62; Peter C. Pineo, "Development Patterns in Marriage," *The Family Coordinator* 18 (April 1969), pp. 135–40.

[7] Judson T. Landis, "On the Campus," *Survey Midmonthly* 84 (Jan. 1948), pp. 17–19.

[8] Theodore B. Johannis, Jr., "The Marital Adjustment of a Sample of Married College Students," *Family Life Coordinator* 4 (June 1956), p. 29.

testify to disillusionment as such, they certainly do indicate that many couples undergo severe stress in the early months and years of marriage.

When and where disillusionment occurs, it appears likely that conflict will develop in the relationship. No one enjoys being hurt and, in this case, the marriage partner is not only the most available target but is also, by a perverse but very common sort of logic, responsible for one's plight. What is more natural than to seize any opportunity to leap to the attack?

THE EMERGENCE OF CONFLICT

The incidents that appear to set off marital conflict more often than not are trivial. The same undercooked eggs that one gamely ate before now become intolerable. The messy catsup bottle, the messy bathroom, lack of enthusiasm for going to the movies or making love—all produce rage. Often, of course, the partner is undergoing comparable frustrations and easily meets rage with rage. Even when the other partner is not disposed to quarrel, he or she seldom is prepared to withstand continual hostile attacks from the other. Whatever doubts and anxieties surround oneself and the relationship become the focus of attention. Without intending to, and without wanting to, many young couples test their relationships severely.

At middle-class levels, conflict usually is waged with words. Couples quarrel. But conflict is conflict whether it is fought with words or with empty beer bottles. The use of beer bottles by middle-class couples obviously would result in the involvement of police and lawyers and very shortly lead to separation or divorce. What is not so often recognized is that words, especially in the mouths of articulate people, may produce wounds that go even deeper and which require even longer to heal.

Waller and Hill get at the potential destructiveness of quarreling by shrewdly fathoming its basic nature. They point out that ordinarily people in general, and spouses in particular, handle quite carefully the little fictions, rationalizations, and half-truths according to which people order their lives and protect their self-concepts.[9] A woman may know, and her husband may know, that she is not very attractive. Usually, however, she emphasizes her good points, such as wavy hair or well-shaped legs. Her husband, too, em-

---

[9] Willard Waller and Reuben Hill, op. cit. p. 301. See also, Wells Goodrich, Robert G. Ryder, and Harold L. Raush, "Patterns of Newlywed Marriage," *Journal of Marriage and the Family* 30 (Aug. 1968), pp. 383–91; Robert G. Ryder, John S. Kafka, and David H. Olson, "Separating and Joining Influences in Courtship and Early Marriage," *American Journal of Orthopsychiatry* 41 (April 1971), pp. 450–64; and Jetse Sprey, "The Family as a System in Conflict," *Journal of Marriage and the Family* 31 (Nov. 1969), pp. 699–706.

phasizes her good features. There is a tacit conspiracy in which each protects the other and both protect the relationship. For so long as they are getting along well, it works just fine. Even in marriage each partner is able to preserve some of the adoration so carefully cultivated in courtship.

"The music at a wedding procession always reminds me of soldiers going into battle."

—Heinrich Heine

When conflict develops in the relationship this tends to break down. Each partner is hurt and wishes to inflict hurt in turn. How better to do it than to attack where the other is vulnerable. In middle-class marriages, for example, the husband's occupational success is all-important. As pointed out in an earlier chapter, the degree to which he is a success depends upon many factors, not the least of which is his wife's ability to play her role as hostess and companion. Even if she is extraordinarily adroit at furthering her husband's career, usually she plays down her role and basks in the husband's success. When he comes home at night to tell her how astutely he put over a program, she tells him what a wonderful executive he is. Not until they come into serious conflict will she point out to him that much of his success depends upon the friendship that she has so carefully cultivated with the boss and the boss's wife. Only then will she tell him that most people think of him as only an average boy who was fortunate to marry such a talented woman.

The example could be multiplied hundreds of times and could be turned against the husband and wife equally. The point is that, under extreme provocation, each partner sets out to destroy the little fictions that are so important to maintaining the self-concept. And in these bitter attacks upon one another, they may soon destroy the basis upon which their relationship is built. In the illustration, the husband who has been so confronted by his wife will find it difficult to share his successes with her in full enthusiasm again. Once it has been said, neither of them can assume the full pretense that operated before. If he is to adjust benignly, the husband may come to seek approval more from his coworkers. In that case, his marriage suffers only by attrition. In more obviously destructive forms, the husband may come to cherish the adoration bestowed upon him by a secretary at the office, a girl he picked up in a bar, or even the attentive ear of the bartender.

TYPES OF OVERT CONFLICT

There are many ways to conceptualize conflict. One way is to describe it in terms of acute, progressive, or habituated forms.

Acute conflict is most characteristic during the early married period and stems from the many undefined situations which exist at that time. Its function is to permit the couple to work out a *modus operandi*, a joint pattern of life in which the frustrations that accompany early disillusionment have been worked through. The question, of course, is whether adequate accommodation will be achieved before the destructive results of quarreling have destroyed the foundation upon which the accommodation must rest. As the particular problems that a young couple face are resolved, acute conflict tends to disappear from the marriage. It may reappear, however, whenever any basic change in conditions produces a new undefined situation. If acute conflict has subsided by then, for example, it may reappear when the first child is born and continue until techniques for handling the accompanying changes are worked out. Similarly, a promotion, a move to another city, the marriage of one's children, and having to care for one's aged parents all may provoke new outbursts of acute conflict.

Acute conflict involves relatively intense explosions of hostility with a great deal of emotional involvement on the part of both spouses. It is the kind of conflict illustrated above in which each party sets out to inflict maximum damage upon the other. Its potential for disruption of the relationship is great. Apparently most couples resolve most basic issues before too much damage is done. And having eliminated most acute conflict from a marriage apparently improves the chances that subsequent outbursts of it will also be handled successfully. Some marriages do break down, however, after 10, 20, or 30 years of marriage. Some of these probably have proved to be ultimate victims of the inability to resolve acute conflict.

Unless couples learn rather quickly to resolve the conflicts that grow out of differences in values, habits, expectations, and the like, the probability appears great that the conflict will take a directional form; it will tend to become progressive. When acute conflict is not resolved, each quarrel leaves a residue of hard feeling between the couple and an area in which they cannot communicate effectively. Then each time that a quarrel develops, there is not only the new issue to solve but the hard feelings and unresolved issues from earlier quarrels tend to become involved too. The conflict spirals, with the areas of disagreement becoming wider and the feelings more bitter. Very much of this may produce estrangement—a condition in which the partners regard themselves as permanently alienated. Unless the couple is irrevocably committed to the permanence of marriage, movement toward separation and/or divorce may follow.

The tendency for acute conflict quickly to become progressive may help to explain the rather large number of marriages which result in separation during the very first year. What is not known is whether marriages that remain intact involve less conflict. At the present state of our knowledge, it appears likely that most of the marriages that survive do show less conflict; it also appears likely that some of the intact marriages continue in spite of marked estrangement between the spouses.

In the "best" of marriages, there may be little apparent conflict after the initial adjustments are worked out. In the "worst" of marriages, husband-wife interaction, except for conflict, virtually may not exist. Most marriages probably fall somewhere in between. In most areas they have worked out a reasonably satisfactory adjustment, but there also remain areas where they have reached only tentative compromises or where they cannot agree. Illustrative of areas where this may happen are the areas of in-law relationships and money management. In spite of our equal treatment norms, either spouse may be unable to accept his or her in-laws completely. He may avoid contact with them and may lash out at the spouse whenever he or she is tactless enough to force the issue. Similarly, after the grocery budget, insurance payments, and all of the rest have been worked out, one spouse may consistently overspend or underspend as compared to the partner's expectations. The situation may generally be kept under control, with open conflict emerging only at the time the bank statement is received or when the couple run out of money before the end of the month.

Such areas of conflict which crop up again and again in a marriage, with a stable accommodation never quite being achieved, may be labeled habituated conflict. Habituated conflict differs from acute conflict in that there is not the same emotional investment in it; it is less explosive. In early marriage, when a husband sleeps on the living room sofa all of a Sunday afternoon it may throw his wife into an unreasoning rage. After a stable level of adjustment has been reached, he may continue to nap on the sofa and his wife may mutter with some disgust that he is a lazy slob, but neither she nor he is likely to be greatly upset by it. Habituated conflict also differs from progressive conflict in that it does not tend to become worse. The wife may even reach the point where she is able to refer to her husband as a lazy slob with some slight overtones of affection.

Marriages may vary widely in the amount of habituated conflict in them and in the amount of such conflict that they can tolerate. In some there may be very little, while in others there may be little else. The dynamics of marital accommodation may be as variable as the personality structures of husbands and wives, as the interests which they do and do not share, and as the patterns of interaction which led them into marriage.

COVERT CONFLICT

So far, we have dealt with marital conflict as though it were synonymous with open fighting. We have assumed that quarreling is as normal a process in marriage as it is in the rest of life and that most couples learn to handle quarreling in marriage in a fashion comparable to the ways in which they learn to control it in other relationships. To conceive of marital conflict in such limited terms, however, probably is to miss some of the most significant and devastating ways in which people struggle against one another.

Throughout this book we have given credence to the assumption that behavior occurs at varying levels of awareness. Some behavior may best be understood by considering it as fully conscious and rational. In other instances, people act in ways that do not make sense unless one is willing to assume that certain actual functions of the behavior are quite different from the apparent ones. We saw how this operates in dating and mate selection. Now we observe it in marriage.

The frequency and pervasiveness of covert conflict in marriage are difficult to estimate. By definition it is hidden and cannot be observed directly. Only through psychotherapeutic evaluation can it often be definitely established. Yet there is widespread agreement that there is a whole series of what might be termed "emotional withholdings" in many relationships that reveal undercover hostility. Some would go so far as to say that some conflict is inherent in all relationships and that, if a couple do not at least occasionally disagree openly, one is sure to find evidences of unknowing sabotage in the relationship.

Perhaps the most widely recognized forms of emotional withholding in marriage are in the sexual area. Lack of sexual responsiveness in wives and impotence in husbands are the most obvious examples. This is not to say that there may not be occasional instances of this sort where there are organic problems or that there may not be deep-seated psychological factors operating in other cases. The incidence of apparent frigidity and impotence is far greater than can be accounted for in these terms, however. What better way for a spouse, who cannot show his hostility openly, to hurt his partner than to fail to respond to him or her sexually.

Short of actual frigidity or impotence, husbands and wives even more commonly contest with one another by being "too tired" to be interested in sex. The amount and seriousness of such conflict is difficult to estimate because often there are legitimate reasons for being too tired. All fatigue cannot be interpreted to represent covert conflict. However, whenever the fatigue is recurrent and cannot be accounted for medically, there is a strong presumption of problems in the relationship. On the basis of impressionistic evidence and the testimony of psychotherapists, such conflict is widespread.

There are other forms of withholding—ways of making one's partner suffer without appearing to do so. The spouse who is hypochondriacal often unwittingly uses his illness to control his partner and to deny the partner the full joy of living; the ill one must be cared for and catered to but cannot be expected to be a satisfying sex partner and companion. At less extreme levels, the whole range of psychosomatic symptoms—rashes, allergies, headaches, ulcers, obesity, almost any unexplained symptom—may represent marital conflict. In very minor form, such problems may plague all marriages.

One problem here is that one cannot always be certain that the psychosomatic symptoms trace to problems in the marriage. Among men, the underlying problems may derive more from conditions at work than at home. For women they may stem from frustrations encountered outside the home; and among both sexes, they may be tied to problems with parents or children. Given the central role which marriage plays in the life of American adults and the interpenetration of family with the occupational and community spheres, however, it seems plausible that many such conditions either reflect or cause problems in the marriage.

Mental hygienists usually affirm that covert conflict is potentially more damaging to people and to relationships than is open fighting. When people quarrel they are at least aware that they have a problem. The chances are good that they will find some sort of solution to the problem. When the problem is masked as something else, however, it may take its toll without the source of the difficulty ever being discovered. The loss of efficiency and personal satisfaction stemming from covert conflict may be greater, in some ways, than open conflict which leads to marital dissolution.

On the other hand it may be that some marriages become stabilized around a pattern of covert conflict. There is at least the possibility that the personal and social costs of organizing some marriages around an ulcer or migraine headaches may be less than the costs of confronting those couples with the essentially neurotic character of their interaction. Few reasonable people would deny that countless numbers of ulcerous parents have had outwardly successful marriages and raised apparently healthy, successful children.

THE ROLE OF INSIGHT

This brings up the whole question of what factors are linked with the successful resolution of marital conflict. And, in all candor, it must be acknowledged that, even though we can describe typical processes of conflict, we know little about the ways in which conflicts are limited or eliminated, or why some couples apparently do it better than others.

One factor which is important—but which, unfortunately, operates in very complex fashion—is the kind and amount of insight which each partner develops into his own behavior and that of his spouse. Some people appear to be totally incapable of comprehending underlying motivations for either their own or others' behavior, while other people shrewdly anticipate one another and quickly recognize what the long-term consequences of given courses of action are likely to be. The possession of this capacity for insight is not an all-or-none matter. Probably people can be ranged along a continuum according to how insightful they are. Differences among them are differences of degree rather than differences in kind.

"An occasionally lucky guess as to what makes a wife tick is the best a man can hope for. And even then, no sooner has he learned how to cope with the tick than she tocks."

—Ogden Nash

In general, insight probably works to increase harmony in marriage. Many of the attacks which marital partners make upon one another are motivated out of hurt or fear. When one realizes that one's partner is only retaliating for injury done to him or is afraid that he will be rejected, it becomes much easier to react in ways that will lessen the hurt and fear rather than to leap to the attack oneself. Once the process of understanding instead of hurting becomes established, the interaction takes on spiral form. Here we have the reverse of progressive conflict. An insightful and constructive response from one partner calls forth an equally constructive response from the other partner, and so on and on. It may be that there are critical points early in most marriages where the interaction takes on spiral form. If it tends to spiral negatively, estrangement soon results. If it spirals as a function of insight development, the areas of sharing may rapidly be enlarged.

This assumes, of course, that both partners show some insight development. In some cases undoubtedly they do. It is plausible, however, to think that many couples are unequal in their capacities for insight just as they are unequal in other regards. What happens when they are unequal in insight is less certain and leads to less optimistic conclusions.

If both partners are somewhat insightful, then it may be that the partner who is more insightful is in a position to control the relationship. By anticipating a bit more quickly and a bit more accurately, he may be able to influence the partner more than he, himself, is influenced. Theoretically, that power may be exercised either in the interests of both partners and the relationship or it may be used to profit the one partner at the expense of the other.[10] Some exploitation of the less insightful partner may be a frequent occurrence.

In some instances the partners' capacities for insight may differ markedly. Waller and Hill point out that this situation may actually lead to the domination of the more insightful spouse by the less insightful one. Particularly if the less insightful spouse is a rigid person to begin with, he or she may continue the conflict regardless of the ultimate harm that is likely to be done to the relationship. The more insightful spouse, foreseeing the outcome, may yield rather than destroy the relationship or his partner. This is not a very comforting thought to those who believe that the possession of insight is accompanied by power.

There has also been speculation on the quality of marriages in which the more insightful partner is dominated by the less insightful one. The speculation stems from doubt that a perceptive person can endure continued domination and continue to invest himself fully in the marriage. What appears plausible is that the insightful partner may gradually withdraw emotionally from the relationship. Outwardly the marriage may be quite stable but emotionally it may be hollow.

Perhaps because of the abstractness of the concept of insight, there is relatively little research bearing directly upon these problems. A project by Luckey did show that satisfaction in marriage is related to the wife's accurate perception of her husband's self-concept, but that satisfaction was not related to the accuracy of the husband's perception of his wife's self-concept. She suggests that this difference between the sexes may reflect the fact that wives are re-

---

[10] For evidence that altruism on the part of both partners is not always associated with good marital adjustment, see Jack V. Buerkle, Theodore R. Anderson, and Robin F. Badgley, "Altruism, Role Conflict and Marital Adjustment: A Factor Analysis of Marital Interaction," *Marriage and Family Living* 23 (Feb. 1961), pp. 20–26.

quired to make the greater adjustments in marriage.[11] Her findings are in accord with the widely accepted generalization that subordinate persons and groups tend to be more insightful than those who are able to control through the open use of power.

At least two studies have failed to establish any relation between the possession of insight and marital adjustment. Corsini, studying 20 volunteer couples at the University of Chicago, concluded that there is no evidence that happiness in marriage is a function of understanding the mate.[12] Udry, Nelson, and Nelson studied 34 couples married from one to ten years and found that the degree of agreement between husband and wife was not associated with frequency of interaction or length of time married. In addition, there was no relationship between "understanding" and either the frequency of interaction or the length of time married. The couples with the least "togetherness" could predict the responses of their spouses as well as those who spent the most time together, and those married for only a short time could predict their spouses' reactions as well as those who had been married for years.[13]

ESTIMATES OF MARITAL HAPPINESS

Consideration of the dynamics of marital interaction, in noting that some conflict normally develops in early marriage, may lead to the interpretation that marital adjustment is seldom very satisfactory. It would be surprising, however, if this were the case, for the American ethos places great emphasis upon the achievement of success in various aspects of life. If the majority of people were not moved to define their marriages as being successful, serious strain would be placed upon the system and would be felt by the persons involved.

A number of studies have sought to determine the proportions of various samples of people who define themselves as being happily married. The results of several of these studies are summarized in Table 1.

These studies of marital happiness ratings took place over a period of approximately 30 years from the mid-1930's to the mid-1960's. The results secured were remarkably consistent over that period of time. Burgess and

[11] Eleanore B. Luckey, "Marital Satisfaction and Congruent Self-Spouse Concepts," *Social Forces* 39 (Dec. 1960), pp. 153-7.

[12] Raymond Corsini, "Understanding and Similarity in Marriage," *Journal of Abnormal and Social Psychology* 52 (May 1956), pp. 327-32.

[13] J. Richard Udry, Harold A. Nelson, and Ruth Nelson, "An Empirical Investigation of Some Widely Held Beliefs About Marital Interaction," *Marriage and Family Living* 23 (Nov. 1961), pp. 388-90.

TABLE 1. *Marriage Happiness Ratings Reported in Selected Studies*
(Percentage Distribution)

	MARRIAGE HAPPINESS RATING		
SELECTED STUDY	VERY HAPPY	PRETTY HAPPY	NOT TOO HAPPY
1738 Respondents from ten metropolitan areas	60	36	3
360 Illinois Men	76	23	1
1865 Married U. S. Respondents	68	29	3
792 California Couples	85	9	5
526 Illinois Couples	63	14	22

Source: Susan R. Orden and Norman M. Bradburn, "Dimensions of Marriage Happiness," *American Journal of Sociology* 73 (May 1968), p. 717.

Cottrell's 526 Illinois couples had been married an average of just over three years. Over 60 per cent described their marriages as happy, while only one couple out of five would admit to being unhappy.[14] Terman's study of 792 middle-class California couples reported even higher percentages of happy marriages.[15]

The most recent of these studies was that of Orden and Bradburn, done in 1965, which collected information from 781 husbands and 957 wives. Table 1 shows their findings on marital happiness, along with those of the other four studies similarly classified into three categories. Orden and Bradburn found 60 per cent of their respondents saying they were very happy and only 3 per cent admitting to being not too happy.[16]

Even allowing for the possible operation of a halo effect—for people to report more happiness than they actually experience—these figures still are impressive. They strongly suggest that, early in marriage at least, the majority of couples find their marriages to be pretty satisfactory. At middle-class levels where the emphasis upon success is greatest, the proportions are even higher.

THE MEASUREMENT OF MARITAL ADJUSTMENT

Sociologists have not been content with simple estimates of marital happiness and have long sought to objectify their findings by developing measures

[14] Ernest W. Burgess and Leonard S. Cottrell, Jr., *Predicting Success or Failure in Marriage*, New York: Prentice-Hall, 1939, p. 32.

[15] Lewis M. Terman, *Psychological Factors in Marital Happiness*, New York: McGraw-Hill Book Company, 1938, p. 78.

[16] Susan R. Orden and Norman M. Bradburn, "Dimensions of Marriage Happiness," *American Journal of Sociology* 73 (May 1968), pp. 715–31.

of marital adjustment. In the process, much has been learned about marital adjustment and the value problems inherent in various concepts of marital adjustment have emerged strongly.

Perhaps the earliest comprehensive study of marital adjustment was that of Burgess and Cottrell. These authors, who developed a scale to permit the prediction of marital success, distributed lengthy questionnaires to nearly 7000 couples and received 526 completed questionnaires from Illinois couples who had been married from one to six years.

The questionnaires contained items which appeared to have some relevance to adjustment in marriage, items on the premarital backgrounds of the husband and the wife, and items on their postmarital attitudes and experiences. Each couple was asked to rate the happiness of their marriage. Then an index of marital adjustment was constructed from the answers to 27 items on the questionnaire. In constructing this index, or scale, of marital adjustment, Burgess and Cottrell assumed that a well-adjusted marriage is one in which: (1) the husband and wife are in essential agreement on matters that might be critical issues in their relationship; (2) they share common interests and joint activities; (3) they share demonstrations of affection and mutual confidences; (4) they have few complaints about the marriage; and (5) they are not bothered with feelings of loneliness, irritability, and miserableness. Scores on the marital adjustment scale correlated satisfactorily with the marital happiness ratings. From then on in the research, individual items were tested to determine how well they were correlated with total marital adjustment scores.

A large number of social background factors proved to be associated with marital adjustment. Some of the more significant include the following:

(1) The greater the similarity in family backgrounds, the larger was the proportion of couples in the very high adjustment class.
   (a) The husband's family background appeared more closely related to adjustment than did the wife's family background.
   (b) The economic and social status of the parents seemed less important for marital success than did other factors.
   (c) Rural backgrounds for persons who migrated to the city were found to be more favorable than a childhood spent in either town or city.
   (d) Differences in educational background or religious affiliation showed no relation to marital adjustment. Church attendance, however, was associated with marital success.
(2) The domestic happiness of the parents was correlated with the marital adjustment of their children.
   (a) Closeness of attachment and absence of conflict between parents and son showed a small positive relationship to marital adjustment.
   (b) Size of family also was more important for the adjustment of the

husband than for that of the wife. Two- to five-child families were more favorable than only-child families.

(3)   Several factors relating to the couple's social type were found to be related to marital adjustment.

    (a)   Marriage between 28 and 30 years of age for men was found to be favorable. Very early marriages were unfavorable.

    (b)   Marriage success scores were positively associated with increased educational achievement for both spouses.

    (c)   Continuing to go to Sunday School until age 19 was associated with marital success. Marriage taking place in a church also was favorable.

    (d)   Having several friends of both sexes and belonging to organizations was associated with good adjustment.

    (e)   Residence in a suburb was more favorable than residence in an apartment or rooming-house area.

    (f)   The longer the period of intimate association before marriage, the greater were the chances for marital success.

    (g)   Security and stability of occupation were more important than income level.

    (h)   The desire for children was associated with good adjustment.[17]

Burgess and Cottrell emphasized that the correlations between single items and marital success scores were very low. To be used for predictive purposes, a large number of items had to be combined in a marriage prediction scale. They did develop such a scale, which has been used in further research and which has had limited clinical application.

Probably the greatest significance of the Burgess and Cottrell research is to be found in the general concept of marital adjustment that emerged from it. Good adjustment—defined in terms of husband-wife agreement, common interests and activities, sharing of affection and confidences, few complaints, and absence of loneliness—was found to be associated with similarity of the couple's background, happiness in the parental family, and a fairly conventional adjustment in other areas of life.

At the same time that the Burgess and Cottrell research was under way, a group of psychologists under the direction of Lewis Terman was searching for personality factors associated with marital adjustment. They had questionnaires filled out by 792 middle- and upper-middle-class urban California couples who had been married, on the average, about 11 years. Precautions were taken to make sure that there was no collaboration between husbands and wives in filling out the questionnaires.

Terman derived total marital happiness scores from the answers to questions on common interests, agreements and disagreements, method of handling dis-

---

[17] Ernest W. Burgess and Leonard S. Cottrell, Jr., op. cit.

agreements, frequency of regretting marriage, whether one would marry the same person again, contemplation of divorce or separation, rating of marital happiness, length of unhappiness, and number of complaints about the marriage. Then a group of 300 happily married couples and 150 unhappily married couples from the total sample were equated for age, number of years married, schooling, and occupational status. These groups were used to test the general idea that a large proportion of incompatible marriages are so because of a predisposition to unhappiness in one or both of the spouses.

In all, 132 items were found to discriminate between happily married and unhappily married persons. Following is a summary portrait of the husbands and wives:

Husbands
    Happy: emotionally stable, cooperative, equalitarian in ideals, extroverted, responsible, methodical, and conservative.
    Unhappy: moody, neurotic, feel inferior and insecure, domineering and radical.
Wives
    Happy: kindly, cooperative, methodical, meticulous, conservative, conventional, self-assured, and optimistic.
    Unhappy: emotionally unstable, feel inferior, rivalrous, overactive, radical, and egoistic.[18]

Terman does not claim that all unhappy marriages can be explained in terms of basic personality problems, but he does believe that such factors play a large causal role.

Terman also used a large number of social background factor items from the Burgess and Cottrell research, and included items on premarital sex experience which they had omitted entirely. Some of the general findings in these areas were:

(1) For men to marry under age 22 and for women to marry under 20 was slightly unfavorable. Relationships where the husband was ten or more years older or younger than his wife were slightly favorable.

(2) Wives of husbands of inferior mental ability tended to be unhappy while their husbands were happy. Markedly superior husbands tended to be unhappy, but their wives were happy. Both spouses had the best chances for marital happiness where husband and wife were equal in ability or the husband was slightly superior.

(3) There was an association between length of acquaintance and length of engagement and marital success.

(4) Marital happiness was correlated with happiness of the parents' marriages.

[18] Lewis M. Terman, op. cit. Ch. 7.

(5) Happiness was associated with attachment to and lack of conflict with parents.

(6) Childhood happiness and firm but not harsh discipline were found to be favorable.

(7) A number of items relating to sex education, attitudes, and premarital experience were favorable for marital happiness.

  (a) Frank parental responses to sex curiosity, without evasion.

  (b) Indifference to or pleasant anticipation of the sex relationship on the part of the male. Passionate longing or aversion were unfavorable.

  (c) "No petting" before marriage, for the wife, appeared somewhat favorable.

  (d) Wife's admission of present or past desire to be of the opposite sex was unfavorable.

  (e) For husbands, premarital intercourse with wife was not unfavorable. Wives who had premarital intercourse with men other than the husband had low happiness scores.

(8) Some items relating to marital sex experience also were associated with marital happiness.

  (a) Happiness ratings of wives who found their first sex experiences disgusting were lower than those of wives who found them enjoyable.

  (b) Husbands who were above average in sexual desire had lower happiness ratings while wives who were above average in desire had higher happiness ratings.

  (c) Where the spouses were equal or the wife was slightly less passionate, the happiness ratings of both spouses were highest.

  (d) Wife's orgasm capacity was highly correlated with happiness scores of both spouses.

In spite of the relationships found, Terman concluded that happiness could be predicted almost as well from personality and background factors as from those factors and the sex factors combined. Most sexual maladjustment was seen as stemming from personality and background factors, with little unhappiness resulting from any biological sexual incompatibility.

The Burgess and Cottrell, and the Terman studies were done in different parts of the United States and used different samples and different techniques of data collection. One emphasized the role of background factors and one emphasized personality and sexual factors. Their results, however, were surprisingly consistent with one another. Where their items were similar, their findings also were similar. In general, they found that mature, stable, conventional, conforming people who come from untroubled family backgrounds scored high on their criteria of marital success and happiness.

A number of investigators have sought to test the Burgess and Cottrell, and the Terman findings and to improve the possibilities of predicting marital success. Kelley used Terman's background and personality items with 300 unmarried couples whom he then checked for adjustment after two years of marriage.[19] King used the Burgess and Cottrell items with a southern Negro sample,[20] and Stroup used them with a random sample from the telephone directory in Akron, Ohio.[21] Locke used items from both early studies in comparing happily married with divorced couples in Indiana,[22] and Karlsson did a similar study in Sweden.[23] Although these studies used different samples and varied their techniques from those of the original researches, the general pattern of findings was highly confirmatory.

The most comprehensive study of marital prediction and marital adjustment to date was made by Burgess and Wallin as a follow-up to the study of Burgess and Cottrell and in response to recognized limitations in the two early studies. Those studies were not truly predictive studies because the adjustment and prediction scales were built upon study of couples who were already married.

Burgess and Wallin secured completed questionnaires from 1000 engaged couples in the Chicago area; almost one-fourth of the couples also were interviewed extensively. Attempts were then made to collect marital adjustment data from those same couples after they had been married for at least three years. Some couples had not married, some already were divorced, and some could not be located, but marital adjustment questionnaires were secured from 666 of the original couples.

Rather than a single composite index of marital success, multiple indices were used. These included permanence (attitudes toward separation or divorce), marital happiness, general satisfaction, specific satisfactions and dissatisfactions with different aspects of the marriage and the spouse, consensus

[19] E. Lowell Kelley, "Concerning the Validity of Terman's Weights for Predicting Marital Happiness," *Psychological Bulletin* 36 (1939), pp. 202–3.

[20] Charles E. King, "The Burgess-Cottrell Method of Measuring Marital Adjustment Applied to a Non-white Southern Urban Population," *Marriage and Family Living* 14 (Nov. 1952), pp. 280–85.

[21] Atlee L. Stroup, "Predicting Marital Success or Failure in an Urban Population," *American Sociological Review* 18 (Oct. 1953), pp. 558–62. King's and Stroup's interest in the utility of the Burgess and Cottrell scale with persons of different social class backgrounds was extended in Julius Roth and Robert F. Peck, "Social Class and Social Mobility Factors Related to Marital Adjustment," *American Sociological Review* 16 (Aug. 1951), pp. 478–87.

[22] Harvey J. Locke, *Predicting Adjustment in Marriage: A Comparison of a Divorced and a Happily Married Group*, New York: Henry Holt and Company, 1951. See also James L. Hawkins, "The Locke Marital Adjustment Test and Social Desirability," *Journal of Marriage and the Family* 28 (May 1966), pp. 193–5.

[23] Georg Karlsson, *Adaptability and Communication in Marriage: A Swedish Predictive Study of Marital Satisfaction*, Uppsala: Almqvist and Wiksells, 1951.

about family matters, love for mate and of self by mate, sexual satisfaction, companionship, and compatibility of personality and temperament.

For purposes of predicting marital success, three separate groups of pre-marital items were used: (1) social background items similar to those used in the Burgess and Cottrell study, (2) personality items similar to those used by Terman, and (3) a group of items about the couple's engagement history. A group of "contingency" items also was used, in which the couple were asked to anticipate such conditions of their marriage as whether the wife would work, the number of children they expected to have and where they would live. The general findings were quite consistent with those of the Burgess and Cottrell, and Terman studies.

An index of engagement success was constructed and proved to be the best single predictor of subsequent marital adjustment scores. Apparently a better guess about marital adjustment can be made on the basis of how a couple gets along during engagement than on the basis of any combination of background or personality factors. The level of predictive ability achieved by Burgess and Wallin was not significantly different from that attained in the earlier study.[24]

A variety of recent studies have sought to extend our measurement of marital adjustment.[25] Buerkle and Badgley, for example, constructed a battery

---

[24] Ernest W. Burgess and Paul Wallin, *Engagement and Marriage*, Philadelphia: J. B. Lippincott Company, 1953. Several investigators have done follow-up work to this study. Purnell Benson has demonstrated that some common interests are favorable for marital success and some are not. See Purnell Benson, "The Interests of Happily Married Couples," *Marriage and Family Living* 14 (Nov. 1952), pp. 276–80; Purnell Benson, "Familism and Marital Success," *Social Forces* 33 (March 1955), pp. 277–80; and Purnell Benson, "The Common Interest Myth in Marriage," *Social Problems* 3 (July 1955), pp. 27–34. Bowerman attempted to develop a Guttman-type scale for the prediction of marital success; see Charles E. Bowerman, "Adjustment in Marriage: Over-all and In Specific Areas," *Sociology and Social Research* 41 (March-April 1957), pp. 257–63. The use of multiple predictors was investigated in Raymond J. Corsini, "Multiple Predictors of Marital Happiness," *Marriage and Family Living* 18 (Aug. 1956), pp. 240–42. Keeley studied the relation between value convergence between the spouses and marital success; Benjamin J. Keeley, "Value Convergence and Marital Relations," *Marriage and Family Living* 17 (Nov. 1955), pp. 342–5. The utility of a concept of creativity in predicting marital success was explored in Eugene Litwak, Gloria Count, and Edward M. Haydon, "Group Structure and Interpersonal Creativity as Factors which Reduce Errors in the Prediction of Marital Adjustment," *Social Forces* 38 (May 1960), pp. 308–15. Locke and others have done work toward development of a short-form marital-prediction test. See Nathan Hurvitz, "The Significance of Discrepancies Between the Scores of Spouses on a Marital Adjustment Scale," *Alpha Kappa Deltan* 29 (Spring 1959), pp. 45–7; Harvey J. Locke and Karl M. Wallace, "Short Marital-Adjustment and Prediction Tests: Their Reliability and Validity," *Marriage and Family Living* 21 (Aug. 1959), pp. 251–5; and Harvey J. Locke and Robert C. Williamson, "Marriage Adjustment: A Factor Analysis Study," *American Sociological Review* 23 (Oct. 1958), pp. 562–9.

[25] Millard J. Bienvenu, Sr., "Measurement of Marital Communication," *The Family Coordinator* 19 (Jan. 1970), pp. 26–31; James L. Hawkins, "The Locke Marital Adjust-

of items to get at the process of role-taking in marital interaction which measured new dimensions of adjustment and indicated the need for further conceptual analysis.[26] Work on indirect measures of marital adjustment that would eliminate the tendency for persons to overstate their marital happiness has been reported by Kirkpatrick, Taves, and Frumkin.[27] Finally, a different approach to the measurement of marital adjustment has been tried by Farber, who used a consensus index and a role-tension index.[28]

One further set of studies which deserves mention here has sought to relate marital satisfaction to the ways in which spouses perceive themselves, one another, and their parents. Luckey has reported that better adjusted persons are characterized by agreement of: (1) perception in regard to self and the perception of self by spouse, (2) perception of self and the parent of the same sex, (3) perception of spouse and parent of the opposite sex, and (4) perception of one's ideal mate and of one's spouse.[29] Other findings which generally support these have been reported by Stuckert and by Katz and associates.[30]

The effort to develop useful measures of marital adjustment and to perfect scales for the prediction of marital success goes on. In the more recent studies there is evidence of an attempt not only to improve the process of measurement but also to arrive at a more adequate concept of the nature of marital adjustment. Scholars are becoming more sensitive to what are essentially ethi-

---

ment Test and Social Desirability," *Journal of Marriage and the Family* 28 (May 1966), pp. 193–5; and Michael J. Sporakowski, "Marital Preparedness, Predictions and Adjustment," *The Family Coordinator* 17 (July 1968), pp. 155–61.

[26] Jack V. Buerkle and Robin F. Badgley, "Couple Role-Taking: The Yale Marital Interaction Battery," *Marriage and Family Living* 21 (Feb. 1959), pp. 53–8. See also Jack V. Buerkle, "Self-Attitudes and Marital Adjustment," *Merrill-Palmer Quarterly* 6 (Jan. 1960), pp. 114–24.

[27] Robert M. Frumkin, "The Kirkpatrick Scale of Family Interests as an Instrument for the Indirect Assessment of Marital Adjustment," *Marriage and Family Living* 15 (Feb. 1953), pp. 35–7; Clifford Kirkpatrick, "Community of Interest and the Measurement of Marriage Adjustment," *Family* 18 (1937), pp. 133–7; Marvin J. Taves, "A Direct vs. an Indirect Approach in Measuring Marital Adjustment," *American Sociological Review* 13 (Oct. 1948), pp. 538–41.

[28] Bernard Farber, "An Index of Marital Integration," *Sociometry* 20 (June 1957), pp. 117–18.

[29] Eleanore B. Luckey, "Marital Satisfaction and Its Association with Congruence of Perception," *Marriage and Family Living* 22 (Feb. 1960), pp. 49–54; Eleanor B. Luckey, "Perceptional Congruence of Self and Family Concepts as Related to Marital Interaction," *Sociometry* 3 (Sept. 1961), pp. 234–40.

[30] Irwin Katz, Judith Goldston, Melvin Cohen, and Solomon Stuckers, "Need Satisfaction, Perception, and Cooperative Interactions in Married Couples," *Marriage and Family Living* 25 (May 1963), pp. 209–13; and Robert P. Stuckert, "Role Perception and Marital Satisfaction—A Configurational Approach," *Marriage and Family Living* 25 (Nov. 1963), pp. 415–19.

cal implications of a general concept of marriage adjustment unwittingly carried forward from the early studies. That concept of marital adjustment emphasizes the prosaic nature of ordinary human beings who are tacitly urged toward making conventional, conforming, stable marriages by carefully selecting their partners from within their own race, nationality, religion, and social class. Thus, the very existence of sociological norms governing mate selection, it is suggested, have come to be used to reinforce an anti-individualistic, anti-personal-freedom bias in middle-class American society.

CRITIQUE OF THE CONCEPT OF MARITAL ADJUSTMENT

Perhaps the most effective critic of the general concept of marital success implicit in the marital adjustment studies has been William Kolb. Kolb, in two provocative papers,[31] has developed a thesis worthy of careful examination and has anticipated an emerging pattern of research on types of marital adjustment.

The basic thesis is that there are implicit value judgments in the criteria used to define successful marriage. These value judgments lend support to a family structure which is in basic conflict with democratic values and with ideals of personal growth and freedom. Moreover, the family structure which results from the use of these criteria is one which is unsatisfactory even in terms of the stated goals of insuring conventionality and stability.

Kolb presents a composite picture of the "successful" marriages emerging from the marital adjustment studies. First, he says, the spouses in such marriages describe themselves as being happy. Second, the spouses agree on what decisions need to be made within the family. Third, the couple agree on

---

[31] William L. Kolb, "Sociologically Established Family Norms and Democratic Values," *Social Forces* 26 (May 1948), pp. 451–6; and William L. Kolb, "Family Sociology, Marriage Education, and the Romantic Complex: A Critique," *Social Forces* 29 (Oct. 1950), pp. 65–72. See also Vernon H. Edmonds, "Marital Conventionalization: Definition and Measurement," *Journal of Marriage and the Family* 29 (Nov. 1967), pp. 681–8; James L. Hawkins and Kathryn Johnsen, "Perception of Behavioral Conformity, Imputation of Consensus, and Marital Satisfaction," *Journal of Marriage and the Family* 31 (Aug. 1969), pp. 507–11; Mary W. Hicks, and Marilyn Platt, "Marital Happiness and Stability: A Review of the Research in the Sixties," *Journal of Marriage and the Family* 32 (Nov. 1970), pp. 553–74; Richard H. Klemer, "Self Esteem and College Dating Experience as Factors in Mate Selection and Marital Happiness," *Journal of Marriage and the Family* 33 (Feb. 1971), pp. 183–87; Edwin L. Lively, "Toward Concept Clarification: The Case of Marital Interaction," *Journal of Marriage and the Family* 31 (Feb. 1969), pp. 108–14; Alexander B. Taylor, "Role Perception, Empathy, and Marriage Adjustment," *Sociology and Social Research* 52 (Oct. 1967), pp. 22–34; and Robert N. Whitehurst, "Premarital Reference Group Orientations and Marriage Adjustment," *Journal of Marriage and the Family* 30 (Aug. 1968), pp. 397–401.

leisure-time preferences and engage in their outside interests together. Fourth, there is affection and confidence between them. Finally, the couple are satisfied with their marriage. In addition, there is the expectation that the marriage will be permanent, that it will conform to the expectations of the community, and that it will involve a high degree of interdependence between husband and wife.

A major problem with this concept of marital adjustment is that it does not specify what the people are happy about, what they are adjusted to, what goals are at the center of family stability, or what value content is at the center of family integration. In some cases, Kolb says, these factors will be associated with other goals that we value and in some cases they will not.

A dual image of the "happy," "adjusted" middle-class family emerges from the literature. Which of the two images fits a given family may depend upon the vantage point from which it is viewed. In Kolb's words:

One [image] is that of a family characterized by absence of conflict, the prevalence of accommodative habits, mutual affection, the middle-class paraphernalia of status, i.e., an owned home, radios, bathtubs, and automobiles, social conservatism and conformity, discreet and cautious extra-marital adventures, and the unending struggle for success. . . . The other image contains the above characteristics as easily observable phenomena, but emphasizes the structure of this family as the breeding ground of neurosis and conflict. It pictures the role of the middle-class wife as empty, stultifying, and confused; the role of the husband as that of the individual subjected to all the pressures of the struggle for success; and the role of the child as determined by the ambivalent attitudes of his parents toward one another and toward him.[32]

It should be remembered that this grim portrayal is of couples who would do well on marriage adjustment scales; it is not meant to describe outwardly unhappy relationships. It criticizes the whole concept of marital adjustment as being essentially negative—as defining the goals of marriage in terms of absence of conflict and accommodation to the status quo rather than in terms of the achievement of any positive goals. No matter how much "adjustment," "happiness," and "integration," such marriages are seen as stunting the personal growth and development of the marriage partners. Without defining personality growth—which is an extremely difficult idea to define adequately —it is argued that personality growth "cannot mean the extreme concentration upon status and economic struggle which is characteristic of the middle class family."

Kolb does not argue that the existing concept of marital adjustment should be discarded entirely. He knows full well the role which the normative regula-

[32] "Sociologically Established Family Norms and Democratic Values," op. cit. p. 454.

tion of mate selection and marital interaction play in maintaining order and stability in the society. He does appear to propose that goals of new experience and personality development should be part of the test of a "happy" marriage. He also concludes that major changes in the social, political, and economic structure of American society may be necessary before such marriages will become a reality.

Two Provocative Analyses of Marital Adjustment

It may well be that most family sociologists share some of William Kolb's dissatisfaction with the conventional concept of marital adjustment. Professionally, most of them know that the image of middle-class couples existing in a state of almost cow-like contentment is far too simple. It fails to encompass the richness of love and hate, exultation and sorrow, boredom and excitement that are part of the lives of even the most outwardly drab persons. On the personal level, many sociologists and others are repulsed by the idea of there being so little to life. Yet, efforts to develop a more vital concept of marital adjustment are few and far between. Few among us show any flair for conceiving of marriage in any but conventional terms. The purpose of this concluding section is to look briefly at two analyses of marital adjustment that are unconventional enough to be somewhat frightening in their implications but which also give the impression of having been based upon perceptive study of real, live people.

What are to be presented here are two typologies of marital adjustment that have stemmed from research. Neither of the two research projects was methodologically very rigorous. Neither of the authors would argue that he was dealing with a representative sample, that his methods were foolproof, or that his findings can be generalized even to all middle-class couples. Each did, however, gather a body of data systematically and then exercise a fertile mind in ordering those data and developing a composite picture of what the marriages studied were like. To say the least, the findings provide food for thought.

Carolyn (Levy) Cline and her students at the University of Kansas City conducted 112 interviews with people married from one to 46 years. All were at least high-school graduates, most were white, and they were estimated to vary from upper-lower to upper-middle class. The respondents were classified according to basic themes which the investigators observed running through the interviews. The themes are not mutually exclusive and more than one theme sometimes was apparent in a given marriage. Five themes around which these 112 marriages appeared to be organized were labeled: (1) mass-produced marriages; (2) inside-out romantic complex marriages; (3) I've grown accustomed to my fate marriages; (4) marriage makes estranged bed-fellows; and (5) she and empathy marriages.[33]

We can do no better than to describe these five types of marriages in Cline's words:

Mass-produced Marriages. The "mass-produced marriage" refers to the marriage of those who seem to marry because that is what is done and seem likely to stay married because that is what is done. They refer to their spouses more nearly as room-mates of the other sex rather than partners in the intimacy of marriage. They seem to view unhappy marriages with little more than a mild curiosity and explain happiness or unhappiness in terms such as, "If people would just do what they're supposed to do, everything would be all right." They use themselves as the yardstick and, being conformists themselves—often without being aware of conforming—almost by definition are apt to have fewer problems of which they are aware. They seem not to verbalize or recognize problem areas.

Perhaps it will more clearly state the case if we designate this theme of mass-produced marriage as mass-producing marriage, for such may be the products, members of masses, not individuals. We might call them "omni-directed." For the omni-directed there are many alternatives, but all of them seem so similar. All the mass media, offering so many variations of choices seem still to offer, all of them, essentially the same thing. And more than that, the whole society seems to the omni-directed to be in agreement on that same thing. The omni-directed, then, do not have, like Riesman's other-directed, a sensitive radar mechanism to follow a varying lead of others. Instead, they see themselves as following "all"—since the mass media say to them, "Everybody's doing whatever you're doing."

These omni-directed (or automatons of the mass-mesmerizing media) often may appear to be the well integrated, upright citizens who "get things done" and are always "Johnny on the spot." But omni-directed action must be differentiated from autonomous action. Living in a world where there are many alternatives does not mean that the individual, even when aware of them, is able to implement alternatives in his own decision-making process.

Inside-out Romantic Complex Marriages. Although the "inside-out romantic complex" theme was not as prevalent as the "mass produced" in these interviews, it might account for many of the marriages in that group. It differs from the "mass-producing" marriages in that the individuals are aware of and are, at least verbally, attempting to deal with the stereotypes of marriage as conveyed by the mass-mesmerizing media. Many respondents, and most poignantly, the teenagers said, "We want to prove we can make it work." They not only did not mention "love" or any of its grammatical relatives as a reason for getting married, but also they attempted to show a picture of themselves as being "not romantic" adolescents. This stance can be summed up by the

---

[33] Carolyn (Levy) Cline, "Five Variations on the Marriage Theme: Types of Marriage Formation," *The Bulletin on Family Development* 3 (Spring 1962), pp. 10–13.

statement, "What Hollywood, we won't." This is tantamount to the partners in the marriage saying, "We are not going to ask that our marriage be the all and end all of being; we are not going to be led down that primrose path to divorce. We, on the other hand, are going to imitate the going version of adult (middle-age and routinized) marriage behavior and ask, and settle for, a marriage of accommodation along the competitive lives of a push-pull arrangement (whether 50/50, 60/40, or 90/30) and thereby show that we are responsible individuals and have our feet on the ground."

I've Grown Accustomed to My Fate Marriages. [This] theme is typified by the woman who after twenty years of wondering why her husband wished to remain married to her and finally ended up divorcing him said, "I think he wanted a Mother, and that was not the kind of love I had to offer. I don't know what it is, but things happen to me that don't seem to happen to other people. I've had an awful lot of trouble; I guess some people are just born luckier than others. I'm one of the unlucky ones." Another wife said, "At first I kept saying, 'Well, it'll be different after we get more used to one another.' But it didn't. I kept hoping he'd change, or I would, but we didn't. Now it doesn't seem to matter much."

These are people who distrust themselves as choosers. Perhaps they even "will to lose." They feel themselves to be pawns in a completely deterministic life. Everyone else is a pawn too and even the knights and kings and queens move in their directed ways.

Marriage Makes Estranged Bedfellows. [This] theme is illustrated in the following quotations:

A wife reported, "During the first years we had sex so often I would have been ashamed for anyone to know how often. We still do more than other people who are 'old married couples.' The only time we don't argue is in bed."

Another wife said, "I cried a lot during the first year. Nothing was the way I expected. In bed it was just matter-of-fact. Still is. But I don't cry anymore."

And a husband stated estrangement directly. "Sometimes it's like living with a stranger—without the excitement. But she never did really enjoy it— and I can get my kicks elsewhere, if you know what I mean."

While in these interviews no effort was made to probe sexual compatibility and incompatibility, the theme of estrangement either assuaged or reinforced in sexual relations appears not to be uncommon.

She and Empathy Marriages. [This] category . . . is most nearly opposite to that of the "mass-produced" marriage theme. And, just as the mass-produced theme seems to be most frequently found in these interviews, this romantic emphasis upon understanding and insight is rarely found. People in this category seem (1) acutely aware of the state of their marriage (especially the women, and even more poignantly so, the teen-aged women), and (2) ready to act to do something about the marriage. More women than men fall into this category and, also, more romanticists. One wife said:

"The best thing about our marriage is that we can talk. We always could— and get through to each other."

Her husband said, "It's relaxing with her—sometimes I think about other women—prettier, smarter, maybe—and think, wouldn't it be fun—but then I think, fun okay but what else? Of course I feel guilty too."

Another wife said, "I was very much in love with him when we were married, couldn't get enough of him. Loved him more than he did me. But I could see he felt kind of smothered. It hurt me, but I learned to handle it." [34]

The emphasis in this research was on the development of types of marital adjustment, so no figures are given on how many couples fell into each of the five categories. It does seem clear that the mass-produced and inside-out romantic complex marriages were the most common and that the she and empathy marriages—those that would most closely fit the American middle-class ideal of what marriage should be like—were the least numerous.

The author takes pains to point out that the validity of these five themes has not been established. She maintains, however, that the results are highly suggestive of a direction which future research on early marital adjustment might take. The outcome of mass-produced marriages, she says, may be predictable after the first few months of marriage. The inside-out romantic complex operating early in a marriage may indicate a mass-producing marriage in the future. Unsatisfactory relationships at the beginning of a marriage may suggest a future phrased in terms of "I've become accustomed to my fate." Estrangement, it appears, may develop either early in marriage or later on. Among the most significant of the author's suggestions is the possibility that romanticism early in a marriage may be predictive of a warm empathic relationship later on. Romanticism, it is implied, may not be simply a sign of emotional immaturity but may be associated with achievement of the finest which marriage has to offer.

The second classification of marriages to be presented here derives from a unique study of 437 persons between 35 and 55 years of age. Although single, divorced, and widowed persons were interviewed also, the portion of the analysis to be reported here is based upon couples who had been married for at least ten years and who had never seriously considered separation or divorce. The authors describe these couples as upper-middle class, highly educated, widely traveled, articulate, financially successful people who had been exposed to a variety of emancipating experiences. None of the subjects was deemed to display signs of gross emotional maladjustment.[35]

[34] Ibid.

[35] John F. Cuber and Peggy B. Harroff, "The More Total View: Relationships Among Men and Women of the Upper Middle Class," *Marriage and Family Living* 25 (May 1963), pp. 140-45.

As Carolyn Cline did, Cuber and Harroff presented descriptions of five general themes pervading marriage relationships:

Conflict-Habituated Relationships. In this husband-wife configuration there is much tension and conflict—although largely "controlled." At worst, there is some private quarreling, nagging, and "throwing up the past" of which members of the immediate family, and more rarely even close friends and relatives, have some awareness. At best, the couple is discreet and polite, "genteel about it" when in the company of others, but rarely succeeds completely in concealing it from the children—although the illusion is common among them that they do. The essence, however, is that there is awareness by both husband and wife that incompatibility is pervasive, conflict is ever-potential, and an atmosphere of equilibrated tension permeates their lives together. These relationships are sometimes said to be "dead" or "gone" but there is a more subtle valence here—a very active one. So central is the necessity for channeling conflict and bridling hostility that these imperatives structure the togetherness. Some psychiatrists have gone so far as to suggest that it is precisely the conflict and the habituated need to do psychological battle with one another which constitutes the cohesive factor which ensures continuity of the marriage. Possibly so, but from a less psychiatric point of view, the overt and manifest fact of habituated attention to handling tension, keeping it chained, and concealing it, becomes the overriding life force. And it can, and does for some, last for a lifetime.

Devitalized Relationships. Here the relationship is essentially devoid of zest. There is typically no serious tension or conflict and there may be aspects of the marriage which are actively satisfying, such as mutual interest in children, property, or family tradition. But the interplay between the pair is apathetic, lifeless. There is no serious threat to the marriage. It will likely continue indefinitely, despite its numbness. It continues, and conflict does not occur in part because of the inertia of "the habit cage." Continuity is further ensured by the absence of any engaging alternatives, "all things considered." Perpetuation is also reinforced, sometimes rather decisively, by legal and ecclesiastical requirements and expectations. These people quickly explain that "there are other things in life," which are worthy of sustained human effort. But the relationship *between the pair* is essentially devoid of vital meaning, essentially empty, by comparison to what it was when the mating began and what was then considered to be its *raison d'être*.

This kind of relationship is exceedingly common. Many persons in this circumstance do not accurately appraise their position because they frequently make comparisons with other pairs, many of whom are similar to themselves. This fosters the illusion that "marriage is like this—except for a few odd balls or pretenders who claim otherwise."

While these relationships lack vitality, there is "*something* there." There are occasional periods of sharing at least of something, if only memory. Formalities can have meanings. Anniversaries can be celebrated, even if a little grimly, for what they once commemorated. As one said, "Tomorrow we are celebrating the anniversary of our anniversary." Even clearly substandard sexual expression is said by some to be better than nothing, or better than a clandestine substitute. A "good man" or "good mother for the kids" may "with a little affection and occasional companionship now and then, get you by."

Passive-Congenial Relationships. This configuration seems roughly about as prevalent as the preceding one. There is little suggestion of disillusionment or compulsion to make believe to anyone. Existing modes of association are comfortably adequate—no stronger words fit the facts. There is little conflict. They tip-toe rather gingerly over and around a residue of subtle resentments and frustrations. In their better moods they remind us that "there are many common interests" which they both enjoy. When they get specific about these common interests it typically comes out that the interests are neither very vital things nor do they involve participation and sharings which could not almost as well be carried out in one-sex associations or with comparative strangers. "We both like classical music"; "We agree completely on religious and political matters"; "We both love the country and our quaint exurban neighbors"; "We are both lawyers."

We get the strong feeling when talking with these people that they would have said the same things when they were first married—or even before. When discussing their decisions to marry, some of them gave the same rationales for that decision that they do now for their present relationship, some twenty or thirty years later. This is why we have said that they seem to be passively content, not disillusioned even though, as compared to the next type, they show so little vitality and so little evidence that the spouse is important— much less indispensable—to the satisfactions which they say they enjoy.

Vital Relationships. It is hard to escape the word, vitality, here—vibrant and exciting sharing of some important life experience. Sex immediately comes to mind, but the vitality need not surround the sexual focus or any aspect of it. It may emanate from work, association in some creative enterprise, child rearing, or even hobby participation. The clue that the *relationship is vital* and significant derives from the *feelings of importance about it* and *that that importance is shared.* Other things are readily sacrificed to it. It is apparent, even sometimes to the superficial observer, that these people are living for something which is exciting; it consumes their interest and effort, and the particular man or woman who shares it is the indispensable ingredient in the meaning which it has.

Total Relationships. The total relationship is like the vital relationship with the important addition that it is *multi-faceted.* This kind of man-woman relationship is rare in marriage or out, but it does exist and undoubtedly could exist more often than it does were men and women free of various impediments. One will occasionally find relationships in which *all* important aspects of life are mutually shared and enthusiastically participated in. It is as if neither partner had a truly private existence. Cynics and the disillusioned scoff at this, calling it "romance" and usually offering an anecdote or two concerning some such "idyllic" relationship which later lost its totality, if not its vitality too. This should not be taken to mean, however, even if accurately interpreted and reported, that the relationship had not been total at the prior time. Or it may simply be evidence of the failure of the observer to be more discriminating in the first place.

Relationships are not *made* vital, much less total, by asserting them to be so, by striving to make them so, or by deceiving the neighbors that they are so. This is not to deny, however, that the total relationship is particularly precarious; precisely because it is multi-faceted, it is multi-vulnerable as circumstances change. [36]

Cuber and Harroff do not indicate how many relationships fell into each of these five types, but the implication is clear that the vast majority of their sample couples ranged from conflict-habituated to passive-congenial. They state that total relationships are rare; the frequency of vital relationships presumably is somewhat greater. Like Cline, these authors make no claim for the ultimate validity of their five types. In fact, they explicitly state that their findings should not be generalized beyond the particular upper-middle-class segment of the society from which the sample couples came.

In one sense, the findings of these two studies are quite sobering; they suggest that the majority of American marriages may be routinized and unexciting. On the other hand, they suggest that the marriages which rank high on marital adjustment scales may include many mass-produced, passive-congenial relationships. If Cline, Cuber, and Harroff are guilty of presenting a pessimistic picture of marital adjustment, perhaps it is because they set their aspirations high.

SUMMARY

The early weeks of marriage often are suffused with an erotically tinged euphoria that provides some protection for each partner while the initial adjustments are being worked out. In adjustment terms, this may be called the honeymoon period. Under the pressure of 24-hour-a-day living, however, whatever idealization exists tends to break down. Extraordinary sensitivity to the moods of the partner tends to bring the honeymoon to an end and permits the entry of some conflict into the relationship.

Middle-class couples tend to fight with words, which they use with devastating effect. Instead of protecting the partner as they have done in the past, each spouse becomes hurt and sets out to inflict pain in return. Overt conflict in marriage may be classified into three basic types. First there is explosive acute conflict, the function of which is to enable the couple to work out a

[36] Ibid. pp. 142-3.

modus vivendi. If acute conflicts are not resolved satisfactorily, they tend to cumulate in a worsening spiral; the conflict has become progressive. Even after most of the basic issues in a marriage have been solved, some touchy areas remain and become the source of intermittent, habituated conflict.

Conflict may also be hidden or covert. In this case, couples who are not fully aware of their resentments may resort to emotional withholdings such as frigidity, impotence, physical illness, or may develop other unexplained symptoms, one result of which is to sabotage the relationship with the spouse. Mental hygienists emphasize that covert conflict is especially dangerous because its true nature is disguised.

The capacity for insightful understanding of the spouse generally should be an aid in adjustment. Whether insight will be used for the benefit of the partner or to control him, however, is not predetermined. Where the spouses are greatly unequal in insight, the relationship may even be controlled by the less insightful partner whose very insensitivity makes him a formidable antagonist.

Most couples, when asked about the happiness of their marriages, do not emphasize the conflict in them but report their marriages to be relatively happy. One-fifth or less report their marriages to be unhappy. Even when more formal measuring devices are used, the pattern holds. Most middle-class Americans report satisfactory marriages.

A general concept of marital adjustment has emerged out of research designed to predict and measure adjustment. In general, well-adjusted marriages are described as being relatively free of conflict, the husband and wife are in relative agreement on major issues, they enjoy the same leisure interests and participate in them together, and they show affection for one another. Well-adjusted spouses are described as mature, stable, conventional, conforming people who themselves come from untroubled family backgrounds.

This concept of marital adjustment has been criticized for containing implicit value judgments. It is maintained that these value judgments support a family structure which is in conflict with our basic democratic values of personal growth and freedom. What traditionally have been defined as successful marriages may emphasize stability and conventionality at the expense of vitality in the husband-wife relationship and may stunt the emotional growth of children.

A satisfactory alternative concept of marital adjustment has yet to be developed. Two provocative, but not very rigorous, recent studies have produced typologies of marriages which suggest that the average "successful" marriage may be devoid of zest. While these studies are less optimistic than the early marital adjustment studies, they also find evidence of the existence of a minority of marriages which are deeply satisfying to the people involved and which contribute to the full joy of living.

SUGGESTED READINGS

Bowerman, Charles E., "Prediction Studies," in Harold T. Christensen, ed., *Handbook of Marriage and the Family*, Chicago: Rand McNally, 1964. Excellent summary and critique of the major marital prediction and marital adjustment studies.

Burgess, Ernest W., and Wallin, Paul, *Engagement and Marriage*, Philadelphia: J. B. Lippincott Company, 1953. The most comprehensive of the marriage-adjustment studies.

Christensen, Harold T., and Johnsen, Kathryn P., *Marriage and the Family*, New York: The Ronald Press, 1971. Part IV of this sophisticated textbook presents an insightful and scholarly analysis of marital interaction.

Eshleman, J. Ross, ed., *Perspectives in Marriage and the Family: Text and Readings*, Boston: Allyn and Bacon, Inc., 1969. Chapter 8 offers a judicious selection of readings on husband-wife interaction in the early years of marriage.

Klemer, Richard H., *Marriage and Family Relationships*, New York: Harper and Row, 1970. Designed as a textbook for functional courses on marriage, this excellent book contains several chapters focusing on problems of early marital adjustment.

Lantz, Herman R., and Snyder, Eloise C., *Marriage: An Examination of the Man-Woman Relationship*, New York: John Wiley and Sons, Inc., 1969. Chapters 13–18 offer an unusually readable and penetrating analysis of the factors involved in adjustment in young marriages.

Thomas, John L., *The American Catholic Family*, Englewood Cliffs, New Jersey: Prentice-Hall, 1956. Treats the Catholic family as a minority system in American society. Oriented toward the maintenance of that system as a distinct system.

FILMS

Being in Love (NET Film Service, Indiana University, Bloomington, Ind.). Film opens with two brothers meeting in a restaurant. One brother plans to divorce his wife to marry a woman he has met in business. Psychotherapist discusses the possibilities of success for such a second marriage and questions whether the man is mature in his attitude.

In Time of Trouble (McGraw-Hill Book Company, Text-Film Division, 330 West 42nd St., New York 10036), 14 minutes. The story of a couple whose happy marriage is jeopardized by a lack of understanding of each other's needs. The advisability of seeking outside help is stressed.

Jealousy (McGraw-Hill Book Company, Text-Film Division, 330 West 42nd St., New York 10036), 16 minutes. Incidents from the life of a young married couple demonstrate the unfortunate results of a treacherous imagination and lack of faith and understanding in a marriage relationship. Stresses the importance of continuous self-appraisal, and indicates that a basic change of attitude often is necessary to combat jealousy.

Marriage Problems (NET Film Service, Indiana University, Bloomington, Ind.). Conversation between two sisters, one recently married and the other about to have her second child. Neither is happily married. Psychotherapist points out that young couples often are the victims of their own unrealistic expectations.

Weddings (*Time-Life* Films, 43 West 16th Street, New York 10011), 45 minutes. Shows that weddings all over the world have a ritual element. All have some kind of party attached to them. Weddings tend to be charged with fertility symbols (like confetti) that nobody really understands. They all cost big money—for the celebration itself and for gifts.

Who's Boss? (McGraw-Hill Book Company, Text-Film Division, 330 West 42nd St., New York 10036) 16 minutes. Compromises and adjustments are necessary in maintaining a happy marriage relationship. Emphasizes the need to think of oneself as a member of a partnership first and as an individual secondarily. Shows how patience, love, and understanding help achieve a good balance where neither is boss, but both are partners.

QUESTIONS AND PROJECTS

1. As distinguished from the wedding trip, how can the honeymoon be defined in terms of the emotional dynamics that are characteristic of it?
2. What factors operate during the honeymoon to bring about some disillusionment with self and partner? What objective evidence is there for such disillusionment?
3. Describe three major types of overt conflict in marriage. What is the significance of each for subsequent adjustment? Contrast overt with covert marital conflict. Give examples of, and estimate the significance of, covert conflict.
4. How may the possession of insight into self and spouse influence marital adjustment? May the possession of insight be related to the power structure that develops in the marriage? How may the less insightful partner come to dominate a marriage?
5. How do most middle-class people rate the happiness of their marriages? What proportions acknowledge that their marriages are unhappy?
6. Describe the methodology of the early Burgess and Cottrell study of marital adjustment. What concept of marital adjustment was used? Summarize the findings relating social background factors to marital adjustment.
7. Compare and contrast Terman's study of marital happiness with the Burgess and Cottrell study of marital adjustment. How did the findings of the two studies compare?
8. How did the Burgess and Wallin study differ most significantly from the two earlier ones? In this study, what was the best single predictor of marital success?
9. What criticism has been offered of the general concept of marital adjustment deriving from the marriage prediction studies? How valid do you think this criticism is? Why?

10. Recall the typologies of marital adjustment developed in the two studies reported in the last section of this chapter. Do you see these as giving cause for optimism or pessimism? Why?

11. Suppose you wanted to reconcile some of the apparent contradictions in research findings on marital adjustment. What methods or techniques could you devise to get at what marriages are really like? How confident are you that you could do better than has already been done?

12. Arrange a panel discussion among married students in the class. Select a moderator who can draw out of these students their concepts of marital adjustment. Have them react to the various concepts of marital adjustment developed in this chapter. See whether a typology of marital adjustment makes sense for these students.

16 | *Sex Adjustment,*
Child-bearing, and
Child-rearing

Shepard and Linnette Erhart got married in a field near the old mill where they had been living together for 18 months. . . . A small group of close friends and relatives gathered in the field for the wedding. . . . Everyone spent the night in the mill and the next morning the newlyweds set off in a Volkswagen loaded with camping equipment. . . . "Sure," said Shepard, . . . "we took a honeymoon but it wasn't some archaic kind of thing where we travelled to an isolated island to sleep together for the first time. . . . That would be absurd. . . ."

Christine and Henry Greene were quite another story. Twenty-year old Christine was so flustered she forgot to wear her corsage. . . . "I had never even been out of New York," she remarked as she sipped a rum punch in the lounge at Cove Haven, a resort exclusively devoted to honeymoon couples . . . in the Poconos. She wore a name tag on her collar, a plastic party hat on her head, and leis around her neck. . . . "The whole thing," she continued . . . , "was really frightening. I guess it really was terrible. . . . I was so embarrassed. . . . But, on the other hand," she went on . . . , "it was so beautiful and all. Your honeymoon is supposed to be the most perfect time of your life."[1]

I have a daughter who was born in 1949, and a son born in 1951, and then in 1953 we had another daughter and finally we had our youngest, a boy, in 1955. [Do you want more?] Heavens, no! I am 34 and my husband is getting close to 40. I like to be young with my children and enjoy them, and since we got married so darned young I want time alone later. My husband's in complete agreement with me. With the high cost of education and the necessity of having a child go to college we would be foolish to have more. I used a diaphragm before and after our children were born until I started using the pill (about three years ago). I hated the diaphragm and so did my husband—it was messy and miserable. I'm so glad

---

[1] Lacey Fosburgh, "New Fashions in Honeymoons: Hip, Super Hip, and Super Square," *The New York Times*, June 13, 1971. © 1971 by The New York Times Company. Reprinted by permission.

we have the pill. We both have complete faith in it. It is such a convenient thing to pop a pill in your mouth every morning. I'm completely sold on it.[2]

MORE than four out of every ten couples in the United States produce a child during the first year of marriage. Ultimately, about 90 per cent of all married couples have children. The average age of the wife at the time of the birth of her first child is about 22.7 years; she produces three children on the average; and is finished with her childbearing by about the age of 30. During about the first ten years, the physical facts of sex, contraception, and reproduction are very prominent in marriage. After that, the center of attention frequently has shifted to the children that have been produced.

The areas of sexual adjustment, family planning, and childbearing are by no means discrete. As the following discussion will show, they are intricately interrelated. Since we must begin somewhere, we will start with the general process of sexual adjustment.

SEXUAL ADJUSTMENT

The vast majority of couples marry young and with drastically different amounts of premarital sex experience on the part of the husband and wife. It is nearly twice as likely that the husbands will have had intercourse before marriage, and the number of times which men have had orgasm is about seven times as great.

As was shown in the chapter on premarital sexual involvement, most couples are moving toward some kind of common pattern by the time of marriage. Their interest in, and readiness for sex relationships in marriage, however, usually are not equal. The pattern which develops tends to be something of a compromise with varying satisfactions and frustrations for each partner.

FREQUENCY OF INTERCOURSE AND SEXUAL ADJUSTMENT

According to the Kinsey research, and supported by the findings of the 1965 National Fertility Study, married couples in their teens have intercourse

[2] Lee Rainwater, *Family Design: Marital Sexuality, Family Size, and Contraception*, Chicago: Aldine Publishing Company, 1965, p. 17.

nearly three times per week on the average.[3] This frequency drops, with age, to about twice a week at age 30, one and one-half times per week at age 40, once a week by age 50, and to once about every 12 days by age 60.[4] These are average figures, of course, and conceal a wide range of variation among couples. Fourteen per cent of the teenaged wives had intercourse as often as once a day, and 5 per cent of the 30-year-old married women did so.

As significant as the raw figures on frequency of coitus are the discrepancies between the median figures reported by men and by women (see Table 1).

TABLE 1. *Reports of Frequency of Marital Intercourse at Various Ages*

AGE GROUP	MEDIAN FREQUENCIES PER WEEK (KINSEY STUDY)		MEAN FREQUENCIES PER MONTH (1965 NATIONAL FERTILITY STUDY)
	MEN	WOMEN	
16–20	2.6	2.8	10.3
21–25	2.3	2.5	8.1
26–30	2.0	2.1	7.3
31–35	1.8	1.9	6.7
36–40	1.6	1.5	5.9
41–45	1.3	1.2	5.1
46–50	0.9	0.9	
51–55	0.7	0.8	
56–60	0.6	0.4	

Source: Alfred C. Kinsey, Wardell B. Pomeroy, Clyde E. Martin, and Paul H. Gebhard, *Sexual Behavior in the Human Female*, Philadelphia: W. B. Saunders Company, 1953, p. 77; and Leslie A. Westoff, and Charles F. Westoff, *From Now to Zero: Fertility, Contraception and Abortion in America*, Boston: Little, Brown and Co., 1971, p. 24.

The median figures reported by the men tend to be slightly lower than those reported by the women, suggesting the possibility of relative satiation on the part of the women and deprivation on the part of the men. Women, who would prefer less sexual intercourse, may overestimate the actual frequency

[3] The frequencies used here are median frequencies—the midpoints of the various distributions. The median is used because it is less affected by extreme cases near the ends of the distributions. If arithmetic mean figures were used, they would be slightly higher than those reported here.

[4] Alfred C. Kinsey, Wardell B. Pomeroy, Clyde E. Martin, and Paul H. Gebhard, *Sexual Behavior in the Human Female*, Philadelphia: W. B. Saunders Company, 1953, pp. 348–9; Leslie A. Westoff and Charles F. Westoff, *From Now to Zero: Fertility, Contraception and Abortion in America*, Boston: Little, Brown and Co., 1971, pp. 23–24.

while men, who would prefer more, underestimate the actual frequency.[5] From the beginning of marriage, the differential interest of husband and wife in sex is a problem for many couples.

One might hypothesize that there would be a direct relationship between mutual high sex desire on the part of both husband and wife and good marital adjustment. Research shows, however, that the situation is not that simple. Wallin and Clark found that maritally satisfied husbands perceived their wives to be similar to themselves in preferred frequency of coitus more often than did maritally dissatisfied husbands. The relationship did not hold equally well for wives, however.[6] Further light was thrown on this situation by Clifford Adams in a study of 150 women who had been married for an average of about eight years. He found that the wives' sexual adjustment was substantially related to their marital happiness but that the relationship between the wives' sexual responsiveness and their marital happiness was very low.[7] Thus, the relationship between frequency of desire for coitus, sexual adjustment, and marital adjustment appears to be more complicated among women than among men.

It appears likely that perceived marital adjustment among men is linked closely to the frequency and satisfactoriness of sexual intercourse. Since most women desire intercourse less frequently than their husbands—and since most men value sex highly—responsiveness on the part of the wife directly facilitates the husband's adjustment. Among women, however, sexual adjustment may depend on how well things are going in other areas of the marriage more than vice versa. Men incline to evaluate marriage in terms of sex, while women tend to evaluate sex in terms of marriage.

Although most young married men desire intercourse more frequently than their wives do, there are some cases where the reverse is true. Moreover, with the general trend toward equality between the sexes, it appears reasonable to expect that the number of women who are highly responsive is increasing. Wallin and Clark studied 604 married couples to determine the relative ac-

---

[5] In general, research shows that husband and wife agree more closely in their estimates of sexual aspects of their relationship than of other nonsexual aspects. See, Bruce Thomason, "Extent of Spousal Agreement on Certain Non-Sexual and Sexual Aspects of Marital Adjustment," *Marriage and Family Living* 17 (Nov. 1955), pp. 322–4.

[6] Paul Wallin and Alexander Clark, "Marital Satisfaction and Husbands' and Wives' Perception of Similarity in their Preferred Frequency of Coitus," *Journal of Abnormal and Social Psychology* 57 (Nov. 1958), pp. 370–73. See also George Levinger, "Systematic Distortion in Spouses' Reports of Preferred and Actual Sexual Behavior," *Sociometry* 29 (Sept. 1966), pp. 291–9.

[7] Clifford R. Adams, *An Informal Preliminary Report on Some Factors Relating to Sexual Responsiveness of Certain College Wives*, Mimeo., 1953.

ceptability of marriages in which the husband's sex drive was stronger, the drives of the partners were equal, and in which the wives' sex drives were stronger. They found that a cultural norm is operative in which equality of sex drive in husband and wife or a stronger drive in the husband are acceptable, but a stronger drive on the part of the wife is not.[8] Apparently, husbands want their wives to be responsive, but not more responsive than they are.

Perhaps the most objective measure of the satisfaction of women in marital intercourse is to be found in the regularity with which they achieve orgasm. Table 2 presents data showing the proportions of marital coitus leading to orgasm during the first, fifth, tenth, fifteenth, and twentieth years of marriage. The table shows that, during the first year of marriage, one-quarter of the women failed to achieve orgasm at all and approximately half of the women achieved it less than 60 per cent of the time. Approximately four women out of every ten almost always achieved orgasm. In subsequent years of marriage, the proportion never experiencing coital orgasm declines but, even during the 20th year, some 11 per cent of women are still found in this category. At the other extreme, the proportion of women almost always having orgasm rises with length of time married. At the maximum, however, fewer than half of all women are found in this category.[9]

Kinsey and his associates found certain general correlates of the frequency with which married couples have coitus and of the frequency of the wife's experiencing orgasm. Interestingly, the data indicate that the frequency of marital coitus has declined over the last several decades. In the age group 16–20, for example, the median frequency dropped from 3.2 per week among women born before 1900 to 2.6 per week among the group born from 1900 to 1909.[10] Similar trends were found among other age groups. The rates stabilized among women born after 1909 and further declines are not evident. These figures probably should be interpreted with some caution because of the difficulty of comparing recall data from women born before 1900 with

[8] Paul Wallin and Alexander Clark, "Cultural Norms and Husbands' and Wives' Reports of their Marital Partners' Preferred Frequency of Coitus Relative to Their Own," *Sociometry* 21 (Sept. 1958), pp. 247–54.

[9] A study of marital adjustment among blacks yielded findings similar to these findings for white women. King found that 131 out of 418 Negro wives reported that they always had orgasm in marital intercourse; 160 said that they usually experienced orgasm, 107 said they sometimes did, and 20 reported that they never experienced orgasm. See Charles E. King, "The Sex Factor in Marital Adjustment," *Marriage and Family Living* 16 (Aug. 1954), pp. 237–40. A study of Puerto Rican women indicated that over one-third of them got real enjoyment from sex relationships. See J. Mayone Stycos, *Family and Fertility in Puerto Rico: A Study of the Lower Income Group*, New York: Columbia University Press, 1955.

[10] Op. cit. pp. 358–9, 397.

TABLE 2. *Percentage of Marital Coitus Leading to Female Orgasm, by Length of Marriage.*

PER CENT OF COITUS WITH ORGASM	YEAR OF MARRIAGE				
	1st	5th	10th	15th	20th
None	25	17	14	12	11
1–29	11	13	14	16	13
30–59	13	15	13	11	12
60–89	12	15	17	16	17
90–100	39	40	42	45	47
Number of Cases	2244	1448	858	505	261

Source: Alfred C. Kinsey, Wardell B. Pomeroy, Clyde E. Martin, and Paul H. Gebhard, *Sexual Behavior in the Human Female*, Philadelphia: W. B. Saunders Company, 1953, p. 408.

recall data from women born several decades later. Assuming that the reported decline is real, the most likely explanation is that men of the older generation were more likely to have intercourse on a schedule determined by their own needs and with less regard for their wives' needs or interests. The more recent generations of men appear to restrict their activity somewhat in terms of their wives' interests.

The only other variable which appears significantly related to the frequency of marital intercourse is that of religious devoutness. Interestingly, in this case, the association is with the husband's religiosity and not with the wife's. Since the husband is usually the more aggressive partner in sexual activity, perhaps this should not be surprising. The data comparing religiously active Protestants with religiously inactive Protestants show that, at each age level, the inactive men report higher frequencies of marital intercourse. Between the ages of 21 and 25, inactive Protestants report a median frequency of 2.5 per week while the active group reports a frequency of only 2.2 per week.[11] What effect differences in frequency of marital intercourse among different religious groups have on marital or sexual adjustment has not been adequately studied. In general, the data do not show that the proportion of marital coitus producing female orgasm is lower among the more devout.

As might be expected from the data presented in Table 2, Kinsey and his associates found that the proportion of marital coitus that produces female orgasm increases steadily with age, at least up to age 50. Adequate data on the responsiveness of older women are not available. This *proportionate in-*

---

[11] Alfred C. Kinsey, Wardell B. Pomeroy, and Clyde E. Martin, *Sexual Behavior in the Human Male*, Philadelphia: W. B. Saunders Company, 1948, p. 482.

crease in orgasm experience must be seen, of course, in the context of a steadily decreasing frequency of sexual intercourse with age and an absolute decline in the frequency of marital orgasm.

The data also show that orgasm in marital coitus is related to the decade of the woman's birth, her father's occupational class, and her educational level. The likelihood of achieving orgasm at all, the likelihood of achieving orgasm within any five-year period, and the proportion of marital intercourse producing orgasm all are higher among women born in more recent decades, among those whose fathers followed upper-white-collar or professional occupations, and among those with more formal education. The widely held stereotype that regards lower-class women as being sexually more responsive appears simply to be wrong.

A recent retabulation of the Kinsey data on 1026 women living in intact marriages showed a correlation between the regularity with which the wives achieved orgasm and their marital happiness. Approximately 60 per cent of the wives who reported achieving orgasm from 90 to 100 per cent of the time also reported their marriages to be very happy. At the other extreme, only 4 per cent of the wives who never reach orgasm reported very happy marriages, and 19 per cent of the no-orgasm group said that their marriages were very unhappy. Gebhard concludes that the strong correlation between female orgasm and marital happiness probably is causal in both directions; the more responsive women are happier and regular orgasm brings happiness.[12]

In summary, research evidence shows some variation in the frequency of marital coitus and in the proportion of coitus producing orgasm in the wife. Increasing length of time married and upper economic and educational status appear to be associated with more female responsiveness. The evidence is also clear, however, that most husbands early in marriage desire intercourse more frequently than their wives do and that a significant proportion of wives are not as responsive as either they or their husbands think that they should be.

LACK OF RESPONSIVENESS IN WOMEN

That lack of sexual responsiveness in women is associated with problems in marriage is a widespread idea that has found support in research findings. Rainwater, summarizing findings from studies of four different lower-class groups in the United States, England, Puerto Rico, and Mexico, states that women use a variety of techniques to cut down on the frequency of marital intercourse. They feign sleep, menstruation, and illness; they throw up to their

[12] Paul H. Gebhard, "Factors in Marital Orgasm," *Journal of Social Issues* 22 (April 1966), pp. 88–95.

husbands the possibility of pregnancy; and they seek to prolong the period of abstinence before and after the birth of children. Some of them also provoke arguments with the husband that give them an excuse for not being affectionate.[13] Middle-class women may be more subtle in their attempts to regulate the frequency of sexual intercourse, but the testimony of many middle-class husbands indicates that some of the same techniques are employed.

When the wife's lack of responsiveness is either extreme or consistent, the term, frigidity, often is applied. Vincent points out that although some extreme cases of frigidity may be due to personality disturbances or physiological impairments, many cases can be explained in interactional terms. In marriages across social class lines, for example, a wife who is not aloof to sex relationships as such may be repulsed by her husband's sexual values and attitudes. If she has married a lower-status man she may find him crude and vulgar. If she has married into a higher class, on the other hand, she may come, in time, to suppress her own sexuality if it is out of harmony with the considerate and gentle attentions of her husband.[14]

Vincent refers to the lack of sexual responsiveness in situations such as this as symptomatic frigidity. The difficulty is not sexual alone but is symptomatic of much wider and more basic differences in life. He goes on to give other illustrations of symptomatic frigidity.

In some cases, couples may come to define the wife as being frigid simply because her interest in sex does not come up to some arbitrary level they have been led to believe is normal and desirable. A husband and wife, for example, who have been relatively satisfied with their sex life may suddenly define themselves as having a problem upon discovering that most couples their age have intercourse more frequently. Vincent refers to this kind of problem as being caused by the "tyranny of the majority norm." [15] If the couple had not become aware of the idealized standard they might never have thought of themselves as having a problem.

Closely related is the general problem of overemphasis upon technique in love-making and the glorification of mutual orgasm as the criterion for defining a good sex relationship. Many of the so-called marriage manuals, in seeking to educate people to some of the basic facts of anatomy and physiology, have encouraged a mechanical approach to the sexual arousal of the

[13] Lee Rainwater, "Marital Sexuality in Four Cultures of Poverty," *Journal of Marriage and the Family* 26 (Nov. 1964), pp. 457–66.

[14] Clark E. Vincent, "Social and Interpersonal Sources of Symptomatic Frigidity," *Marriage and Family Living* 18 (Nov. 1956), pp. 355–60.

[15] Ibid. p. 356.

partner that tends to rob the relationship of love, spontaneity, and fun.[16] Some wives complain bitterly of being able to tell when their husbands are turning from page 37 to page 38! Rather than being more fully aroused by such techniques, some wives increasingly reject sex altogether.

Sexual responsiveness in women appears to be much more situationally determined than among men. Women who are harassed with child care duties, women who feel unloved by their husbands, women who are worried about finances or whatever, women who doubt their own personal worth— all are likely to be at least temporarily unresponsive. If such conditions persist, the condition may become almost irreversible. Men, who would not respond to the same pressures in the same way, often cannot understand their wives' reactions and apply the label "frigid" to them in both anger and dismay.

Finally, misunderstanding by wives of the nature of their husbands' sex needs sometimes leads them to stereotype those needs and to withdraw from meeting them. There is a widespread impression that men use sex only for physical satisfaction and not for the expression of love. This impression is likely to be particularly vivid in a wife whose husband wants to make up a quarrel by going to bed with her. Her own desire having been completely eliminated by the upset of the quarrel, she cannot imagine that her husband's proposal for sex is his means of showing her that he loves her and reassuring himself of her love in return. Instead, she feels "used" and withdraws from sex even more.

This by no means exhausts the range of interpersonal factors that works to maintain the difference in sex desires between husband and wife early in marriage. But the fact is that a difference commonly exists at the beginning of marriage. The nature of the sex pattern that is established between the couple often represents a compromise between the greater sexual interest of the husband and the lesser sexual interest of the wife. The wife is likely to regard her husband as somewhat oversexed and the husband often finds his wife to be disappointing.

SUBSTITUTE OUTLETS

As already shown in Table 1, the frequency of marital intercourse tends to be highest at younger ages and to decline steadily with the passage of time. For husbands this has manifold significance. To some degree the decreasing frequency of marital intercourse reflects physiological processes of aging and

---

[16] See Dennis Brissett and Lionel S. Lewis, "Guidelines for Marital Sex: An Analysis of Fifteen Popular Marriage Manuals," *The Family Coordinator* 19 (Jan. 1970), pp. 41–8; and Nelson N. Foote, "Sex As Play," *Social Problems* 1 (April 1954), pp. 159–63.

decreased frequency of sexual activity of any sort. Kinsey and his co-workers found that male sexual activity reaches its peak in adolescence and then drops steadily with increasing age.

Some psychological causation operates here too. A kind of psychological fatigue develops as a function of the wife's lack of responsiveness and the husband's frustration over being discouraged by her. In addition, there is loss of interest in endlessly repeating the same sexual experience. The opportunities for trying new techniques, new positions, and new situations must eventually come to an end.

The decrease in frequency of marital intercourse often represents more than physiological and psychological fatigue, however. Many males whose sexual urges are quite strong find substitute outlets. The commonest of these substitute outlets is masturbation. At lower educational levels some 30 to 40 per cent of married men engage in masturbation at some time, while among those who have attended college almost 70 per cent do so. These college-educated married men may masturbate as often as once or twice per week.[17]

Almost as widespread as masturbation is extramarital sexual intercourse. Kinsey estimates the proportion of men who ultimately become involved at about 50 per cent. Again differences are found by educational level. The highest incidences for those with less formal education appear at the younger age levels and decrease steadily with age. Among college-educated men, on the other hand, not more than 15 to 20 per cent are involved at younger age levels. The proportion who are involved increases steadily with age until approximately 27 per cent are having extramarital intercourse by age 50. Among these same college-educated men the frequencies of extramarital intercourse are not more than once every two or three weeks between 16 and 30 years of age, but climb to almost once a week at age 50.[18]

Obviously marital intercourse accounts for only part of the sexual activity of married men. Among college-educated men, marital coitus supplies about 85 per cent of the total outlet during the early years of marriage but, by age 55, it is accounting for only 62 per cent of the total outlet. Apparently, college-educated men as they grow older are likely to conclude that the restraints on their early sexual involvements were not justified and frequently deal with their wives' lack of adequate responsiveness by finding other partners.[19]

The situations of wives in relation to the declining frequency of marital intercourse with age are quite different from those of their husbands. Their initial lack of responsiveness, much of which is due to repressive early training,

[17] *Sexual Behavior in the Human Male*, op. cit. pp. 273–7.
[18] Ibid. p. 587.
[19] Ibid. pp. 567–8.

tends to give way to increasing sexual interest as they become more experienced. Kinsey estimates that women may reach a peak of sexual responsiveness at about 30 years of age and that this higher level of sexual interest is then maintained essentially without diminution until the fifties or even the sixties. At some point in this process, the desires of the wife for marital intercourse may come to surpass in frequency those of the husband. Wives, too, develop alternate sources of sexual satisfaction.

The proportion of women who are active in masturbation at given age levels varies widely by educational level, being much higher at the higher educational levels. The active incidence of masturbation to orgasm by married women between the ages of 21 and 25 is close to 30 per cent for women with college and postgraduate educations. By age 31–35, it has climbed to 34 per cent among college-level women and to 40 per cent among those with some graduate education. The percentages continue to climb at least through the age period 36–40 with a high of 48 per cent of graduate-school-educated women masturbating in the age period from 41 to 45 years.[20] One can only conclude that many of these women are now being forced to seek sexual satisfaction which they cannot get from their husbands.

Emotional boredom pushes most unfaithful American spouses into adultery, according to a new study in the Kinsey vein. . . .

A condensation of Morton Hunt's book, The Affair . . . said that half of the men interviewed for the survey and two-thirds of the women gave the same reason. Emotional boredom, they said, led to a loss of self-esteem. An affair restored some of that esteem by proving that they were still attractive to the opposite sex.

Noting that Hunt estimated that 60 per cent of married men and 35 to 40 per cent of married women have affairs. . . . Dr. Paul Gebhard of the Institute for Sex Research . . . said, "This is a change— but not a revolution."

—St. Petersburg Times, August 27, 1969.

As with men, some women become involved in extramarital intercourse. Relatively few are involved during their teens and early twenties, and the majority who do become involved early in adulthood are women from the lower educational levels. The proportion of women who have engaged in extramarital coitus rises from 7 per cent in the teens to 16 per cent by age

---

[20] *Sexual Behavior in the Human Female*, op. cit. p. 181.

30, 23 per cent by age 35, and to a maximum of 26 per cent by age 40. The proportion who are having such relationships during any one age period is, of course, somewhat lower. Between 16 and 20 years of age, only 6 per cent are actively involved; the percentage climbs to 9 per cent between 21 and 25 years, to 14 per cent between 26 and 30, and to 17 per cent between 31 and 35. It then remains relatively constant to about age 45.

There are differences in the proportion of women involved, by educational level (see Table 3). Not until age 25 have college-educated women become

TABLE 3. *Percentage of Women with Experience in Extramarital Intercourse, by Educational Level and Age.*

AGE	TOTAL SAMPLE	EDUCATIONAL LEVEL		
		9–12	13–16	17+
18	8	6	6	
19	7	8	4	
20	6	7	6	6
25	9	10	10	7
30	16	16	16	17
35	23	21	26	25
40	26	24	31	27
45	26	22	29	27

Source: Alfred C. Kinsey, Wardell B. Pomeroy, Clyde E. Martin, and Paul H. Gebhard, *Sexual Behavior in the Human Female*, Philadelphia: W. B. Saunders Company, 1953, p. 440.

involved in as large numbers as women of less formal education. By age 35, more college-educated women have become involved and the gap continues to widen through age 45. The percentage of college-level women who have had extramarital coitus reaches a high of 31 per cent at age 40.[21] Thus, we see that both men and women at the higher educational levels are more likely to become involved in extramarital sex relationships after several years of marriage. It appears ironic that, among the couples who should be most able to communicate adequately with one another, noncommunication in the sexual area should be so pervasive.

In spite of widespread interest in the topic, relatively little research has been directed toward assessing the impact of extramarital affairs upon marriage relationships. Kinsey reports that the extramarital activities of the women in his sample not infrequently led to emotional involvements that interfered with their relationships with their husbands. Difficulty was least

[21] Ibid. pp. 439–40.

likely when the husbands did not know of the relationships, and crises often developed when the spouses learned of the affairs.

One interesting study which bears directly upon this matter was done by Neubeck and Schletzer among former students at the University of Minnesota. These researchers interviewed each partner in 40 upper-middle-class marriages where the spouses were approximately 30 years old at interview and most of whom had three children. The respondents were queried about both actual extramarital sexual involvements and about fantasied involvements. Two general conclusions were reached. First, the persons who had become sexually involved were not so controlled by their consciences and were thus able to find extramarital sex relationships acceptable. Second, the group who became involved in fantasy only were more controlled by their consciences and used fantasy as a substitute.[22]

In many ways, the situation with regard to sexual adjustment in marriage may be likened to that involving total marital adjustment. Most couples report their sexual adjustment to be good. In the Burgess and Wallin study, for example, 73 per cent of the husbands and 61 per cent of the wives reported receiving complete relief from sexual desire through marital coitus.[23] Yet along with these reassuring reports must be considered the steadily decreasing frequency of intercourse as marriages continue, some degree of orgasm incapacity in women, and the resort of both men and women to other sources of sexual satisfaction. It appears that the level of communication between many husbands and wives about sexual matters leaves something to be desired and that, if anything, the communication becomes poorer as the marriage continues.

FAMILY PLANNING AND CHILD-BEARING

Nearly one out of every two couples produces a child during the first year of marriage, and at least 90 per cent of all couples now produce at least one child before they reach the end of their reproductive years. Curiously, the proportion of couples who remain permanently childless appears to have been dropping during the very period when improvement in contraceptive methods logically would have made the choice to remain childless easier and, hence, more likely. As recently as 1950, 17 per cent of native-born, white wives aged 45–49 had not produced a child. Among native-born, white wives reach-

[22] Gerhard Neubeck and Vera M. Schletzer, "A Study of Extra-Marital Relationships," *Marriage and Family Living* 24 (Aug. 1962), pp. 279–81.

[23] Ernest W. Burgess and Paul Wallin, *Engagement and Marriage*, Philadelphia: J. B. Lippincott Company, 1953, p. 669.

ing 45–49 years in 1965, however, more than 90 per cent had produced at least one child.[24]

These figures do not seem to be completely consistent with the transition from a large rural family system to a small urban one. Let us take a brief look at what has been happening.

RECENT TRENDS IN FAMILY SIZE

Adequate data on family size in the United States are available for about the last 100 years. These data show that from 1860 to 1930 birth rates and the size of families steadily declined. In 1871, the crude birth rate (the number of births per 1000 population) was 37; by 1900 it had declined to 29; and by 1930 it was down to about 19. During that same time period the number of persons per household in the United States declined from 5.1 to 4.1.

Birth rates stayed at rather low levels until the end of World War II, when a rush of marriages deferred during both the depression of the 1930's and the war began to produce rapidly increasing numbers of births. The crude birth rate climbed to 25 in 1946. A better indication than the crude birth rate of what has been happening here is revealed, however, by changing preferences in family size.

During the 1940's, the American Institute of Public Opinion asked a national sample of women how many children they considered to be ideal. Again in 1955 and 1960, carefully drawn national samples of married women were asked the same thing. In all three time periods, about 90 per cent of the women stated that they wanted either two, three, or four children. The proportions wanting two children steadily declined, however, while the proportions wanting four children steadily increased. In 1960, the proportion wanting four children was higher than the proportion wanting any other number.[25]

NUMBER OF CHILDREN AND MARITAL ADJUSTMENT

A whole series of studies have attempted to ferret out the relationship between marital adjustment and the number of children that parents have. Most

[24] Ronald Freedman, Pascal K. Whelpton, and Arthur A. Campbell, *Family Planning, Sterility and Population Growth*, New York: McGraw-Hill Book Company, 1959, pp. 46–7.

[25] Ibid; and Pascal K. Whelpton, Arthur A. Campbell, and John E. Patterson, *Fertility and Family Planning in the United States*, Princeton, New Jersey: Princeton University Press, 1966.

of these studies have failed to find any consistent relationships.[26] Two pre-World War II studies found that couples with either one or two children were happier than couples who had more children, reflecting perhaps the congruence between child-bearing patterns and the prevailing child-bearing values during this period.[27]

Just after World War II, two additional studies yielded findings that tended to corroborate the inverse relationship between family size and marital adjustment. Reed reported data collected in 1941 from 860 relatively fecund Indianapolis couples. Dividing the couples into good adjustment and poor adjustment groups, Reed found an inverse relationship between marital adjustment and number of children. Twice as many couples who had no children at all reported happy marriages as did couples who had four or more living children. Moreover, the proportion of couples reporting happy marriages declined steadily with each additional child. More one-child families reported happiness than two-child families did, and so on. The largest single break occurred between three-child and four-child families, indicating that this may be a critical point for the adjustment of the parental couple.[28]

The second study was a study of 346 married college-student couples residing in married-student housing in 1950. In this case, the inverse relationship between marital adjustment and number of children appeared to be related to the fact that nearly two-thirds of the couples had unplanned children and that many of the husbands (38 per cent) believed that their children interfered with their college work.[29]

A study of 731 urban and 178 farm wives in the Detroit area in 1955 showed that the mothers of three children were better satisfied with their marriages than were mothers who had either more or fewer children.

[26] Jessie Bernard, "Factors in the Distribution of Success in Marriage," *American Journal of Sociology* 40 (July 1934), p. 51; Katherine B. Davis, *Factors in the Sex Life of Twenty-two Hundred Women*, New York: Harper and Brothers, 1929; Gilbert V. Hamilton, *A Research in Marriage*, New York: Boni, 1929: Harvey J. Locke, *Predicting Adjustment in Marriage: A Comparison of a Divorced and a Happily Married Group*, New York: Henry Holt and Company, 1951; and Lewis M. Terman, *Psychological Factors in Marital Happiness*, New York: McGraw-Hill Book Company, 1938.

[27] Ernest W. Burgess and Leonard S. Cottrell, Jr., *Predicting Success or Failure in Marriage*, New York: Prentice-Hall, 1939. R. O. Lang, *The Rating of Happiness in Marriage*, Unpublished M.A. Thesis, University of Chicago, 1932.

[28] Robert B. Reed, "Social and Psychological Factors Affecting Fertility: The Interrelationship of Marital Adjustment, Fertility Control, and Size of Family," *The Milbank Memorial Fund Quarterly* 25 (Oct. 1947), pp. 383–425.

[29] Harold T. Christensen and Robert E. Philbrick, "Family Size as a Factor in the Marital Adjustments of College Couples," *American Sociological Review* 17 (June 1952), pp. 306–12.

The mothers of more than three or four children often reported that they wished they had not had so many.[30] Again it appears significant that there is an association between marital adjustment and correspondence between preferred number of children and actual child-bearing experience.

Finally, a secondary analysis of data from 600 high school students and 1984 mothers in the state of Washington showed families of three or four children to rank lower on several measures than did families of one and two children.[31]

In summary, it appears that studies of the influence of children on marital adjustment need to take into account the relationship between child-bearing preferences and child-bearing experience. This was illustrated by the early Burgess and Cottrell study which showed that childless couples who wanted children had the highest proportion falling in the good-adjustment category. Intermediate proportions had good adjustment where there was relative correspondence between preferences and experience; and the lowest proportions of well-adjusted marriages were found among those couples who had more children than they wanted.

FAMILY PLANNING

There have been several studies dealing with family planning in the United States and with the relationship between success in family planning and other aspects of the marital relationship. We will report data from several of those studies here.

The most recent and comprehensive study was the National Fertility Study conducted in 1965 and involving interviews with a national probability sample of 5600 married women.[32] One of the facts confirmed by this study was that

[30] Robert O. Blood, Jr. and Donald M. Wolfe, *Husbands and Wives: The Dynamics of Married Living*, The Free Press of Glencoe, Illinois, 1960, pp. 262–3.

[31] F. Ivan Nye, John Carlson, and Gerald Garrett, "Family Size, Interaction, Affect, and Stress," *Journal of Marriage and the Family* 32 (May 1970), pp. 216–26. See also, Gerry E. Hendershot, "Familial Satisfaction, Birth Order, and Fertility Values," *Journal of Marriage and the Family* 31 (Feb. 1969), pp. 27–33; Eleanore B. Luckey and Joyce K. Bain, "Children: A Factor in Marital Satisfaction," *Journal of Marriage and the Family* 32 (Feb. 1970), pp. 43–4; and Susan M. Stolka and Larry D. Barnett, "Education and Religion as Factors in Women's Attitudes Motivating Childbearing," *Journal of Marriage and the Family* 31 (Nov. 1969), pp. 740–50.

[32] Westoff and Westoff, op. cit. A probability sample is a carefully drawn sample in which the probability that any given unit of the population will be included in the sample is known. This knowledge makes it possible to estimate the error that derives from sampling. The results of surveys based upon probability samples, assuming that the quality of other aspects of the survey is high, may be used with special confidence.

about one-third of American couples are limited in their ability to have children; they are subfecund. Most of the 11 per cent of all couples who are definitely sterile have had operations that make conception impossible. Some of these operations are done with contraceptive intent and some are done for other medical reasons. The large number of such operations, however, was and still is a surprise.

There is a tendency for sterilization operations to be associated with lower socioeconomic and educational status and with advancing age of the wife. By age 35-39, one out of every six wives has had such an operation. That there is some association of such operations with contraceptive intent is indicated by the fact that another national study reported that 37 per cent of the couples who had used contraceptives before the last pregnancy reported that the last pregnancy was an accident.[33]

Since this study was published there has been increased attention given to the growing use of vasectomy (surgical sterilization of the male) as a means of contraception. Two separate studies done in California, one primarily of working-class subjects and one primarily of upper-middle-class subjects, found that most of the men involved were under 30 years of age and had about three children on the average. Very few men in either sample had more than four children. In both samples, the overwhelming majority thought that the operation had been beneficial. Most would recommend the operation to others, and the conclusion was that they generally had acted out of rational considerations and were relatively free of unconscious neurotic concerns about the consequences of the operation.[34] In the light of these findings it appears that

[33] Freedman, Whelpton, and Campbell, pp. 28–9. A study of 48 women in North Carolina who had been sterilized indicated that almost all of them had welcomed the operation because it gave them a safe, permanent method of contraception. Moreover, there were virtually no adverse reactions on the part of these women after the operation. See Moya Woodside, "Psychological and Sexual Aspects of Sterilization in Women," *Marriage and Family Living* 9 (Spring 1949), pp. 72–3.

[34] Judson T. Landis and Thomas Poffenberger, "The Marital and Sexual Adjustment of 330 Couples Who Chose Vasectomy as a Form of Birth Control," *Journal of Marriage and the Family* 27 (Feb. 1965), pp. 57–8; Thomas Poffenberger and Shirley B. Poffenberger, "Vasectomy as a Preferred Method of Birth Control: A Preliminary Investigation," *Marriage and Family Living* 25 (Aug. 1963), pp. 326–30; Thomas Poffenberger, "Two Thousand Voluntary Vasectomies Performed in California: Background Factors and Comments," *Marriage and Family Living* 25 (Nov. 1963), pp. 469–74; David A. Rodgers, Frederick J. Ziegler, and Patricia Rohr, "Sociopsychological Characteristics of Patients Obtaining Vasectomies from Urologists," *Marriage and Family Living* 25 (Aug. 1963), pp. 331–5. Some contrary evidence indicating that men may tend to exaggerate the beneficial effects of vasectomy and to underestimate its undesirable consequences was found in David A. Rodgers, Frederick J. Ziegler, John Altrocchi, and Nissim Levy, "A Longitudinal Study of the Psycho-Social Effects of Vasectomy," *Journal of Marriage and the Family* 27 (Feb. 1965),

sterilization is being used increasingly for contraceptive purposes at many different social levels. The increasing use of vasectomy reflects the fact that it is a much simpler and less expensive surgical procedure than is sterilization of the female (salpingectomy). The threat to masculinity which was believed to be inherent in such procedures a decade or two ago, by and large, does not seem to be showing up.

Not only did the Growth of American Families study show that up to one-third of all married couples may be subfecund, it also showed that childlessness and subfecundity are closely associated. The authors report that few couples today are voluntarily childless. Of 51 childless couples in the sample who had been married 15 years or longer, 96 per cent were classified as subfecund, with 67 per cent being either definitely or probably sterile. This contrasts strongly with the situation discovered in a major fertility study before World War II which found that 40 per cent of the couples who were childless wanted it that way and used contraception regularly.[35]

To understand other findings of this study, it is necessary to know and keep in mind the five basic categories into which the couples were classified. Those categories, with brief explanations, are shown in Figure 2. Roughly two out of three couples were classified as fecund, there being no reason to suspect impaired fertility. The 12 per cent classified as semifecund will have some difficulty having children, the 7 per cent who are probably sterile are unlikely to have children in the future, and the 10 per cent who are definitely sterile will have no more children. The 5 per cent who are classified as of indeterminate fecundity contain unknown proportions of fecund and subfecund couples.

The vast majority of couples in this study either had used, were using, or planned to use contraception. Many of them had not used contraception from the beginning of marriage, however. About half of all users did not begin until after the first pregnancy and some 18 per cent did not begin until after at least the second pregnancy. By the latter part of the child-bearing period, virtually all couples were either contraceptive users or were classified as subfecund.

It appears that many couples begin marriage without having given serious consideration to the use of contraception. Some 70 per cent of the sample couples who had at least one pregnancy before using contraception reported that they wanted the pregnancies they had under these circumstances. Most

---

pp. 59–64. The reactions of physicians to the contraceptive use of vasectomy is reported in Judson T. Landis, "Attitudes of Individual California Physicians and Policies of State Medical Societies on Vasectomy for Birth Control," *Journal of Marriage and the Family* 28 (Aug. 1966), pp. 277–83.

[35] Freedman, Whelpton, and Campbell, p. 46.

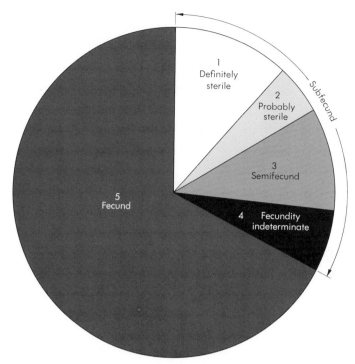

FIGURE 1. *Per cent distribution by fecundity, for all couples.*

1. *Definitely Sterile.* Couples reporting physical or medical conditions making pregnancy impossible.
2. *Probably Sterile.* Couples for whom a birth seems to be improbable on the basis of specific medical evidence.
3. *Semifecund.* Couples who had not conceived at a "normal" rate although the wives did not know of any physiological limitation to reproduction.
4. *Fecundity Indeterminate.* Couples who cannot be classified as to fecundity on the basis of available information. The wives report that they use a douche soon after intercourse, but for cleanliness only. They do not acknowledge practicing contraception.
5. *Fecund.* Couples for whom there is no evidence of impaired fecundity. All couples not included in one of the four subfecund categories.

Source: Ronald Freedman, Pascal K. Whelpton, and Arthur A. Campbell, *Family Planning, Sterility and Population Growth*, New York: McGraw-Hill Book Company, 1959, pp. 21–6.

of the others were "surprised" that the first pregnancy appeared so early.[36] Some of the couples did not experience a pregnancy even though contraception was not practised and it was thus that subfecundity became evident.

As marriages progress, the use or nonuse of contraception is related to fecundity status. The likelihood that contraception will be used increases with

[36] Ibid. p. 63.

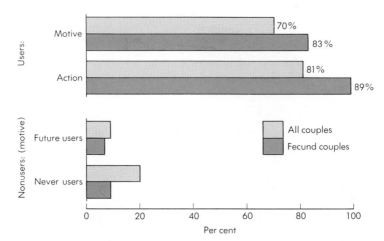

FIGURE 2. *Percentage who have used, will use, and will not use contraception, for all couples and fecund couples.*

Source: Ronald Freedman, Pascal K. Whelpton, and Arthur A. Campbell, *Family Planning, Sterility and Population Growth,* New York: McGraw-Hill Book Company, 1959, p. 62.

each succeeding pregnancy. The data on this point are summarized in Figure 3. The data are presented separately for fecund couples and for all couples. The contraceptive users are also separated into "motive" users and "action" users. Motive users are those who acknowledge that they practise contraception, while action users are those who say that they douche for purposes of cleanliness only. When all of the couples are considered together, 70 per cent have practised contraception on a motive basis and 81 per cent have done so on an action basis. When only the fecund couples are considered, the figures are even higher; 83 per cent were motive users and 89 per cent were action users. When intentions for future use are added, the percentages of fecund couples who are users become 90 per cent on a motive basis and 94 per cent on an action basis.

The nearly universal use of contraception by fecund couples does not ensure that they will have completely planned families. Freedman and his associates divide their sample into three groups: those with completely planned fertility, those with partially planned fertility, and those with excess fertility (see Figure 4).

The couples with partially planned fertility were of several different sorts. Most of them had had one or more pregnancies but had not planned all of their pregnancies by stopping the use of contraception. Some of these couples had never used contraception, some had used it occasionally, and some had

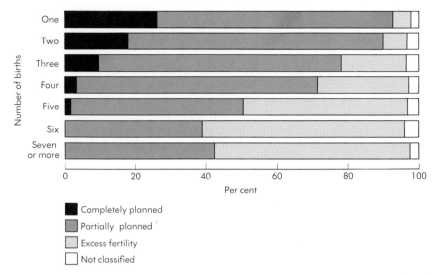

FIGURE 3. *Per cent distribution by fertility planning status, for all couples, by number of births.*

Source: Ronald Freedman, Pascal K. Whelpton, and Arthur A. Campbell, *Family Planning, Sterility and Population Growth*, New York: McGraw-Hill Book Company, 1959, p. 82.

used it regularly but had experienced unexpected pregnancies. Some pregnancies had developed long before they were desired, but none of the children thus born was defined as unwanted. Two-thirds of the couples were classified in the partially planned fertility category.

Excess fertility was defined by the last pregnancy being unwanted by the husband, or wife, or both. Some of these couples had used contraception and some had not. If they had tried to use contraception, ultimately they had failed. Thirteen per cent of all couples fell into this category. As can be seen in Figure 4, excess fertility is associated with large families. While a few couples with only one or two children had not wanted that many, the excess fertility percentage doubled in three-child families, and a majority of the couples with five, six, or seven children had not wanted so many.

As might be expected, these general findings for all 2713 couples do not apply equally well to all subgroups within the United States population. Specifically, important differences were found by religion, by economic and educational status, and by the working status of the wife.

Freedman and his associates hypothesized that Roman Catholics would make less effective use of family planning than other Americans; that Jews, because of their generally high educational and occupational status and their concentration in urban areas, would make especially effective use of contraception; and that Protestants would fall in between. This prediction was borne out.

The majority of Catholic couples either had used family planning or expected to do so in the future. Seventy per cent of fecund Catholic wives were past users and an additional 10 per cent were classified as future users. Some 47 per cent of the Catholic users had confined themselves to the rhythm method, the use of which is approved by the church. About 30 per cent of all Catholic couples had used methods unacceptable to the church. The proportion of Catholic couples using other than church-approved methods tended to increase with age and with the unsuccessful use of the rhythm method. Among fecund Catholics who had been married for at least 10 years, 50 per cent had used a method other than rhythm. Freedman comments: "It is almost certain, however, that some of the couples who used a method which the church condemns as sinful did so in order to have no more children than they could care for properly—a motive which is endorsed by the church." [37]

That Catholic religious affiliation is a powerful determinant of family-planning practices is shown in several ways. First, those Catholics who attend church regularly are less likely to be users than are those who do not attend regularly. This difference holds for all income and educational groups. The old assumption that Catholic-Protestant differences will be eliminated as their economic statuses are equated appears not to be true. Instead, Catholics tend to use increased income to adhere more closely to the teachings of the church. Finally, expected family size is larger among Catholics and fewer Catholic couples achieve completely planned fertility. The average expected number of children among the Catholic wives was 3.4 while, for Protestants, it was only 2.9. [38] Only half as many Catholic couples as Protestant couples had achieved completely planned families.

Significant relationships were found between income and education and family planning. In general, low income and low education depressed the proportion of couples who were contraceptive users. Where the husband's income was under $3000 and the wife had only a grade-school education the percentage of users was 40 per cent or less. By contrast, 85 to 90 per cent of the couples with incomes of over $6000 and college educations were users. In the joint effect of income and education on family planning, the influence of the wife's education was found to be especially important. The authors conclude that

[37] Ibid. p. 183.

[38] Ibid. p. 284. See also Ronald Freedman, Pascal K. Whelpton, and John W. Smit, "Socio-Economic Factors in Religious Differentials in Fertility," *American Sociological Review* 26 (Aug. 1961), pp. 608–14.

higher education is associated with the wife's facing her problems more rationally and aspiring to a style of life that requires the planning of her family.

Finally, the Growth of American Families study found that both fecundity and family planning are associated with the wife's holding a job outside the home. Fecundity impairments were much more common among working wives; only 58 per cent of working wives versus 69 per cent of nonworking wives were classified as fecund. Of wives who had worked five years or more after marriage, only 43 per cent were fecund. Among the large number of young married women who work, apparently those who are subfecund are more likely to keep on working. In addition, some proportion of sterile or subfecund wives probably goes to work because they do not have enough children to keep them occupied at home.[39]

Not all working wives are subfecund, however. Among fecund couples, those where the wife is working are much more likely to plan their families effectively. Forty-two per cent of the fecund contraceptive users had completely planned fertility among those couples where the wife worked. Only 25 per cent of fecund nonworking wives completely planned their families. Apparently the motivation for the wife to work is strong enough among some couples that they attain real efficiency in family limitation.

In summary, the Growth of American Families study shows that virtually all fecund American couples use contraception. Only a minority, however, use it from the beginning of marriage and successfully plan all of their children. Slightly over one-tenth of the population is harassed with excess fertility, one-tenth of the population is sterile, and up to another 25 per cent are subfecund. The incidence of sterility in the population probably is growing due to the increasing use of sterilization operations for contraceptive purposes by couples who have already had all of the children they want. The successful use of contraception is directly correlated with economic and educational status, with Roman Catholics constituting something of an exception. Working wives tend either to be subfecund or to be effective family planners.[40]

In the context of these generally reliable data for the total United States population, let us now examine some of the findings of a less quantitative study that throw considerable light on the relationship between family planning and

---

[39] Ibid., pp. 51–3. For an excellent discussion of this point and an analysis of factors encouraging larger middle-class families, see Lois W. Hoffman and Frederick Wyatt, "Social Change and Motivations for Having Larger Families: Some Theoretical Considerations," *Merrill-Palmer Quarterly* 6 (July 1960), pp. 235–44.

[40] For accounts of the impact of the pill upon contraceptive practice, see Warren O. Nelson, "The Physiology of Reproduction and its Relation to the Regulation of Fertility," *Marriage and Family Living* 25 (Feb. 1963), pp. 74–80; and Westoff and Westoff, op. cit.

the general and specifically sexual roles that men and women play in marriage. Rainwater interviewed, in depth, 409 men and women from 257 different marriages. The respondents were mostly from Chicago, Cincinnati, and Oklahoma City and were selected to provide approximately equal numbers of upper-middle, lower-middle, upper-lower, and lower-lower class persons. Quotas of Catholics were included within each of the class groups.[41]

First of all, marital roles were found to vary by social class. Upper-middle-class couples tended to have joint conjugal role relationships in which there are many shared activities between husband and wife.[42] Although there may be a division of labor between them, each spouse is actively interested in the duties of the other. Most of their leisure time is spent together. The lower-middle-class couples were about equally divided between those who had joint role relationships and an intermediate type in which there is some sharing of tasks and activities and also some segregation of roles. The trend toward role segregation continues as we move downward in social class until the majority of lower-lower-class couples followed segregated conjugal roles. Such segregated roles involve the husband and wife coordinating their daily activities, but with each largely going his own way. There is no special value seen in sharing.

The joint or segregated marital roles were reflected in general means of solving marital problems, in the pattern of sex relationships, and in family-planning practices. Joint role relationships generally involved the solving of problems through discussion, compromise, and mutual accommodation. These techniques, which were associated with a generally high level of marital satisfaction, stood in marked contrast to the lack of effective communication in segregated role relationships. Segregated roles often were accompanied by a good bit of dissatisfaction with the marriage.

The level of sexual gratification was found to vary by social class and by the type of role organization, particularly in the lower class. Lower-class women were more likely to report dissatisfaction with the sex relationship than were middle-class women, and lower-class women whose marriages were characterized by role segregation were the most dissatisfied of all. Such women tended to define sex as being primarily for the satisfaction of men and often considered their husbands to be inconsiderate of the wife's feelings.

[41] Lee Rainwater, *Family Design: Marital Sexuality, Family Size, and Contraception,* Chicago: Aldine Publishing Company, 1965. For an overview of differences in family planning patterns between the lower and middle classes, see Frederick S. Jaffe, "Family Planning and Poverty," *Journal of Marriage and the Family* 26 (Nov. 1964), pp. 467–70.

[42] The idea of marital roles ranging from "joint" to "segregated" was developed in Elizabeth Bott, *Family and Social Network,* London: Tavistock Publications, 1957, pp. 53–5.

Although it dealt with lower-class couples only, an earlier report of this same general study described patterns of sex relationships and of family planning which may have relevance for much of middle-class society also. There is abundant impressionistic evidence that many of the same dynamics—in more muted form, perhaps—operate in middle-class marriages.

Of the 96 women interviewed in this part of the study, about one-half were Protestant, one-third were Catholic, 5 per cent were Jewish, and a few had no religious affiliation. Rainwater classified them into four types according to their patterns of family planning: the early planners, the "do nothing" group, the sporadic users, and the late "desperate" planners.

The early planners often do not begin the use of contraception until after one or two pregnancies, but they do act before they have achieved their ideal family size and they are reasonably effective in their contraceptive efforts. Although specific figures are not given, this apparently is a rather small group. The "do nothing" group probably is self-explanatory. It represents the opposite end of the continuum from the early planners and includes couples who have had several children and still make no use of contraception. Like the early planners, it is a small group. Many are Roman Catholics who place value upon having large families.

The largest single group were the sporadic or careless contraceptive users. Most of them had used several different types of contraceptives but had not been able to use any of them effectively. They want to limit the number of their children but they are not able to translate that motivation into any consistent program of action. Communication between the husband and wife is poor and the wives often feel victimized by their husbands. They also tend to blame their failures entirely upon the contraceptives used rather than upon themselves.

The last category of late "desperate" planners often had been sporadic users earlier in their marriages. Having had all of the children they want, or more than they want, they have now become effective contraception users out of sheer desperation. Significantly, the device or technique that they now use effectively often is one of the ones that they failed with earlier.[43]

These categories "make sense" in terms of the statistical patterns reported from the larger, more representative Growth of American Families study. Not only do they make sense alone, however, but Rainwater has also effectively linked these patterns to a group of psychosexual factors in the style of life of these couples. Specifically, he further classifies the couples into three groups:

[43] Lee Rainwater and Karol K. Weinstein, *And the Poor Get Children: Sex, Contraception, and Family Planning in the Working Class,* Chicago: Quadrangle Books, 1960, pp. 29–42.

(1) those in which both husband and wife derive considerable gratification from sex relations; (2) those in which the wife's pleasure is subject to interference from other concerns; (3) and those in which the wife receives little gratification and intercourse is performed for the husband's satisfaction.

The first pattern, Rainwater describes as being one of mutuality. Both husband and wife enjoy sex and it is an important element in their relationship. Over two-thirds of this group—which constituted just under half of the total sample—had intercourse three or more times per week. There was an openness in their discussions of family planning, they cooperated in using contraception, and their family planning generally was effective. The women involved had little difficulty using feminine methods of contraception and assumed much responsibility in relation to it.

The second group constituted something less than one-third of the total number of couples and were labeled as "repressive compromisers." Three-fourths of this group reported having intercourse fewer than three times per week and with variable results. When things are going well in the marriage in general and in the woman's daily life, she may be a willing, responsive participant in sex. But when there are problems with the children, money, or conflict with the husband, she is unable to be interested or responsive. Such women tend not to have very positive images of their husbands but concentrate, instead, upon their negative virtues—"He doesn't drink"; "He doesn't gamble"; "He's good to the kids." Fewer of these couples were effective users of contraception, tending in that respect to be like members of the third category.[44]

The most negative conceptions of sex and of their husbands were held by the women whom Rainwater called "active rejectors." Constituting nearly one-third of the sample, 18 out of 19 wives reported having intercourse fewer than three times per week. They react to sex with disgust, fear, or anxiety, and regard it merely as an unpleasant duty. Many of these wives complain of their husbands' drinking, bad tempers, sloppiness and low moral standards, and lack of consideration for their wives. A most interesting question here, of course, is to what degree these husbands really are different from the husbands of the women in the other two categories. Whatever the causation, communication in these marriages is very poor and few are effective in family planning. Most of the women are repulsed by the idea of handling their genitals for the use of contraception and insist that the responsibility is the husband's.

[44] For a somewhat different, but supportive, conceptualization of this situation, see Nicholas Babchuk and Angelo La Cognata, "Crises and the Effective Utilization of Contraception," *Marriage and Family Living* 22 (Aug. 1960), pp. 254–8. See also, Charles H. Hawkins, "What's Good in a Contraceptive Method?" *The Family Coordinator* 19 (Jan. 1970), pp. 49–56.

What these findings indicate, of course, is that the effectiveness of contraception and family planning do not depend simply upon the technical efficiency of the methods used. Instead, both sexual interaction and family planning vary with the kind and amount of communication between the husband and wife.[45] This communication is a function of the larger roles the spouses play in relation to one another. In general, communication, sexual satisfaction, and success in family planning all are better at middle-class levels than at lower-class levels. More needs to be known about variations in these phenomena within given class levels.

PREGNANCY AND CHILD-BEARING

Apparently, at least 70 per cent of all pregnancies are welcomed by the prospective parents.[46] It seems likely that, under these circumstances, the pregnancy experience would be a generally rewarding one. Conversely, it seems logical that unplanned and unwanted pregnancies would be accompanied by problems of adjustment. If this is true, however, apparently it is later pregnancies, rather than the first one, that create problems. Poffenberger and Landis studied this situation in detail and several other studies have contributed to our understanding of it.

The first pregnancies of 212 students' wives at Michigan State University were classified into those where the wives had not wanted the conceptions, those where they had not tried to achieve or avoid the conceptions, and those where the conceptions were sought. During the first trimester of pregnancy, there were more feelings of unhappiness and more emotional upset among those who had not wanted to conceive. But by the second trimester these differences had virtually disappeared, indicating that most couples quickly make their peace with the fact of the first pregnancy whether it was planned or not. The amount of nausea experienced by the wives during pregnancy was not related to whether the child was planned, and there were no relationships between planning status and the ease or difficulty of delivery.[47] Brodsky, studying student wives at the University of Florida, found that the

---

[45] For theoretical development of this thesis and empirical support from a different lower-class culture, see Reuben Hill, J. Mayone Stycos, and Kurt W. Back, *The Family and Population Control: A Puerto Rican Experiment in Social Change*, Chapel Hill: University of North Carolina Press, 1959.

[46] Ronald Freedman, Pascal K. Whelpton, and Arthur A. Campbell, *Family Planning, Sterility and Population Growth*, op. cit. p. 63.

[47] Shirley Poffenberger, Thomas Poffenberger, and Judson T. Landis, "Intent Toward Conception and the Pregnancy Experience," *American Sociological Review* 17 (Oct. 1952), pp. 616–20.

self-acceptance of pregnant women did not differ significantly from that of wives who were not pregnant.[48]

The Michigan study did show that pregnancy often has some effect upon couples' sex adjustments. Fifty-eight per cent of the 212 couples indicated that their sex adjustment had not been affected, but about 24 per cent believed their adjustment to have been adversely effected, while some 18 per cent stated that their adjustment had improved. In general, those who had had good sex adjustment before the pregnancy continued to have good adjustment. Where previously poor adjustment improved, the improvement might have occurred without the pregnancy or it might have been linked to the pregnancy. Some husbands and wives described themselves as becoming more considerate and sympathetic toward one another during the pregnancy. Where poorer adjustment accompanied the pregnancy it was frequently explained in terms of the added responsibilities that pregnancy and child-bearing entailed; the wife sometimes became too busy and too tired to be as interested in sex. There also was a general tendency for the frequency of sex desire of both husband and wife to decrease during the pregnancy and to remain lower after the birth of the child than it had been before the pregnancy. Fear of another pregnancy hindered sex adjustment after the birth, and sex adjustment was better in those cases where the wife had confidence in the contraceptive subsequently used.[49]

Both studies of family planning and general knowledge would lead us to expect that the effects of subsequent pregnancies and particularly unwanted pregnancies would be different. That this is true is verified by data collected by Kinsey and his associates. They found that some pregnancies at each birth order are terminated by induced abortion. Only about 10 per cent of second pregnancies were so terminated, 16 per cent of third pregnancies, 19 per cent of fifth pregnancies, and 34 per cent of sixth pregnancies ended in induced abortion.[50]

The abortion situation in the United States has been changing rapidly as 17 states have liberalized their abortion laws. The number of therapeutic

[48] Stanley L. Brodsky, "Self-Acceptance in Pregnant Women," *Marriage and Family Living* 25 (Nov. 1963), pp. 483–4. See also William R. Rosengren, "Social Sources of Pregnancy as Illness or Normality," *Social Forces* 39 (March 1961), pp. 260–67; and William R. Rosengren, Social Instability and Attitudes Toward Pregnancy as a Social Role," *Social Problems* 9 (Spring 1962), pp. 371–8.

[49] Judson T. Landis, Thomas Poffenberger, and Shirley Poffenberger, "The Effects of First Pregnancy upon the Sexual Adjustment of 212 Couples," *American Sociological Review* 15 (Dec. 1950), pp. 766–72.

[50] Paul H. Gebhard, Wardell B. Pomerov, Clyde E. Martin, and Cornelia V. Christenson, *Pregnancy, Birth and Abortion*, New York: Harper and Brothers, 1958, p. 136.

(legal) abortions has risen dramatically—over 180,000 in New York State in one year—and, although reliable figures are not available, it is believed that the number of illegal (criminal) abortions has dropped correspondingly.

The trend toward legalization of abortion appears, also, to have further diminished the emotional consequences for the women involved. This is particularly significant in view of the fact that, even at the time of the Kinsey studies, 82 per cent of the married women who had been aborted reported no unfavorable consequences.[51]

Obviously, reactions to pregnancy vary with the number of pregnancies and whether the pregnancy is desired or not. Most early pregnancies appear to be wanted and to produce only minor effects on the marital relationship. Later pregnancies, after the couple have had all the children they want, are more likely to have negative repercussions and to end in illegal abortion.

If there is justification for conceiving of pregnancy as possibly crisis-producing in marriage, there also is justification for reasoning that childbirth may sometimes produce a marital crisis. Le Masters, reasoning that the adding of a new member of the family could be expected to upset the existing adjustment between husband and wife, studied 46 middle-class couples who were having their first child. He found that 38 of the 46 couples (83 per cent) reported an "extensive" or "severe" crisis in adjusting to the birth of the child. Since 35 of these 38 children were "desired" or "planned," the crisis could not be attributed to the fact of an unwanted pregnancy. Neither could the crises be attributed to poor marital adjustment or to psychiatric problems. Instead, Le Masters concluded that these parents had romanticized parenthood and were essentially unprepared for the reality of having a baby in the home. The mothers often complained of feeling tired, of being confined to their homes, and of having to give up social activities and employment outside the home. The fathers also complained of financial pressures, of worry about another pregnancy, and of lessened sexual interest on the part of their wives.[52] These findings led Le Masters to hypothesize that parenthood, rather than marriage, is the focal point for the romantic complex in American culture.

Two other studies have been published which attempted to confirm or refute Le Masters's findings. Dyer studied 32 middle-class couples in Houston, Texas, and reached conclusions very similar to Le Masters's. Fifty-three per cent of his couples experienced extensive or severe crisis after the birth of their first child. These crises which involved the reorganization of pre-existing role

---

[51] *Ibid.*, pp. 203–11.

[52] Ersel E. Le Masters, "Parenthood as Crisis," *Marriage and Family Living* 19 (Nov. 1957), pp. 352–5.

relationships often lasted for several months. Both Le Masters and Dyer found that the large majority of couples eventually made satisfactory recovery from the crises.[53]

Hobbs's study differed somewhat from the two earlier studies and suggested additional complications in the study of parenthood as crisis. His sample was not limited to middle-class couples and was contacted much sooner after the birth of the child. Whereas Dyer's and Le Masters's couples were contacted from two to five years after the birth of the child, Hobbs's couples had babies averaging only about ten weeks of age. At this early period, only 13 per cent reported experiencing even moderate crisis and 87 per cent were classified as falling into the slight-crisis category.[54] Hobbs quotes Feldman as saying that the low proportion of couples experiencing crisis at this early period may be due to what he calls a "baby honeymoon." Feldman believes that couples experience early elation over parenthood, but that after four to six weeks a period of crisis begins to set in.[55] All investigators appear to agree that whatever trauma is involved in early parenthood is successfully resolved by most couples within a few years.

PATTERNS OF CHILD-REARING

The sociological study of child-rearing covers a vast area—too vast for full treatment here.[56] In the concluding section of this chapter, we shall summarize research from just one of the many areas of sociological interest—that having to do with the values that middle-class parents attempt to instill in their children, with a brief look at differences between middle-class and lower-class patterns.

Sociological research into patterns of child-rearing has developed essentially since World War II. One of the first studies, and one that set a pattern for

---

[53]Everett D. Dyer, "Parenthood as Crisis: A Re-Study," *Marriage and Family Living* 25 (May 1963), pp. 196–201.

[54] Daniel F. Hobbs, Jr., "Parenthood as Crisis: A Third Study," *Journal of Marriage and the Family* 27 (Aug. 1965), pp. 367–72. For confirmation and extension of these findings, see Daniel F. Hobbs, Jr., "Transition to Parenthood: A Replication and an Extension," *Journal of Marriage and the Family* 30 (Aug. 1968), pp. 413–17; and Arthur P. Jacoby, "Transition to Parenthood: A Reassessment," *Journal of Marriage and the Family* 31 (Nov. 1969), pp. 720–27.

[55] Feldman also found that the advent of the first child begins a critical period in the marital relationship. See Harold Feldman, *Development of the Husband-Wife Relationship: A Research Report*, Cornell University, Mimeograph, no date.

[56] For an excellent summary and synthesis of much of this literature, see Edward Z. Dager, "Socialization and Personality Development in the Child," in Harold T. Christensen, ed., *Handbook of Marriage and the Family*, Chicago: Rand McNally, 1964, pp. 740–81.

future research, was done in Chicago of the child-rearing practices of 48 middle-class and 52 lower-class mothers. This study found that middle-class parents were more rigid in infant-care practices than were lower-class parents; they were more likely to schedule feed, to wean early, and to toilet-train early. Differences were more pronounced by social class than by race, with middle-class white and Negro practices being more similar than were the practices of either middle-class group to either lower-class group. The researchers concluded that middle-class parents were generally stricter than lower-class parents and that ". . . middle-class children are subjected earlier and more consistently to the influences which make a child an orderly, conscientious, responsible and tame person." Middle-class children were seen as suffering more frustration of their impulses than were lower-class children.[57]

At about the same time, Duvall studied 433 Chicago women who were members of mothers' groups. She found that middle-class mothers defined a "good" child as one who is happy and contented, loves and confides in his parents, shares and cooperates with others, and is eager to learn. Working-class mothers placed less emphasis upon these traits and emphasized, instead, that the child should be neat and clean, that he should respect and obey adults, and that he be honest, polite, and fair.[58]

Over the next decade or so, a whole series of studies were done, some of which yielded findings consistent with those of the two earlier studies and some of which showed flatly contradictory findings.[59] One major study of 375 Boston-area mothers found that middle-class mothers were not more rigid but were more lenient than lower-class mothers. The middle-class mothers were more permissive in the areas of toilet training, dependency, sex training, and the expression of aggression. Middle-class mothers also appeared to be

---

[57] Allison Davis and Robert J. Havighurst, "Social Class and Color Differences in Child-Rearing," *American Sociological Review* 11 (Dec. 1946), pp. 698–710.

[58] Evelyn M. Duvall, "Conceptions of Parenthood," *American Journal of Sociology* 52 (Nov. 1946), pp. 190–92. See also Rachel A. Elder, "Traditional and Developmental Conceptions of Fatherhood," *Marriage and Family Living* 11 (Summer 1949), pp. 98–100, 106; and Ruth Connor, Helen F. Greene, and James Walters, "Agreement of Family Member Conceptions of 'Good' Parent and Child Roles," *Social Forces* 36 (May 1958), pp. 353–8.

[59] Ethelyn H. Klatskin, "Shifts in Child Care Practices in Three Social Classes Under an Infant Care Program of Flexible Methodology," *American Journal of Orthopsychiatry* 22 (Jan. 1952), pp. 52–61; Martha S. White, "Social Class, Child-Rearing Practices, and Child Behavior," *American Sociological Review*, 22 (Dec. 1957), pp. 704–12; Richard A. Littman, Robert A. Moore, and John Pierce-Jones, "Social Class Differences in Childrearing: A Third Community for Comparison with Chicago and Newton," *American Sociological Review* 22 (Dec. 1957), pp. 694–704; and Walter E. Boek, Marvin B. Sussman, and Alfred Yankhauer, "Social Class and Child Care Practices," *Marriage and Family Living* 20 (Nov. 1958), pp. 326–33.

less punitive, less restrictive in the activity permitted in the home, and more permissive of free-ranging activity outside the home.[60]

The conflict over whether middle-class parents are more permissive or more strict than lower-class parents was resolved by Bronfenbrenner, who reanalyzed much of the data from earlier studies. He made the social class groupings more consistent from study to study and estimated the approximate dates at which each pattern of findings had been secured. In so doing, he found that there had been a gradual shift in child-care practices. Before World War II it did indeed appear that middle-class mothers were more rigid. By the end of World War II, however, the situation had been reversed and middle-class mothers were more permissive than lower-class mothers.[61]

The shift in the relationship between middle-class and lower-class child-rearing practices appears to have occurred within the context of a general shift toward more permissiveness at all social levels. It will be recalled from earlier chapters that Western society has a long history of children being under the complete domination of their parents, particularly of their fathers. Even in the immediate premodern era, parents were supposed to be strict disciplinarians whose duty it was to break the will of the child, to make him submissive, and to train him in the denial of his innate evil impulses. Early in the present century in the United States there began to appear a massive child-guidance literature which, by the 1930's, was advocating more permissive child-rearing. Parents were urged to assume friendly, loving roles and to allow their children to develop "naturally" and at their own pace. Bronfenbrenner's analysis showed a close correspondence between the general trend toward permissiveness in child-rearing and the practices recommended in the child care literature.[62]

Differences between the middle and lower classes in the characteristics believed to be desirable in children appear to have persisted through the period of the general trend toward permissiveness. In a recent series of studies, Kohn found that middle-class mothers valued happiness, considerateness, and

---

[60] Robert R. Sears, Eleanor E. Maccoby, and Harry Levin, *Patterns of Child-Rearing*, Evanston, Illinois: Row, Peterson and Company, 1957.

[61] Urie Bronfenbrenner, "Socialization and Social Class Through Time and Space," in Eleanor E. Maccoby, Theodore M. Newcomb, and Eugene L. Hartley, eds., *Readings in Social Psychology*, New York: Henry Holt, 1958, pp. 400–424. See also Donald G. McKinley, *Social Class and Family Life*, New York: The Free Press of Glencoe, 1964; and William H. Sewell, "Social Class and Childhood Personality," *Sociometry* 24 (Dec. 1961), pp. 340–46, 358–61.

[62] Ibid. See also Gerald R. Leslie and Kathryn P. Johnsen, "Changed Perceptions of the Maternal Role," *American Sociological Review* 28 (Dec. 1963), pp. 919–28; and Martha Wolfenstein, "The Emergence of Fun Morality," *Journal of Social Issues* 7 (1951), pp. 15–25.

self-control in their children, while lower-class mothers were more likely to value neatness, cleanliness, and obedience.[63] This evidence would seem to show that changes in child-care practices are not caused by changes in mothers' expectations for their children.

Perhaps the most provocative thesis yet developed to explain recent changes in United States child-rearing patterns is presented by Miller and Swanson in their book, *The Changing American Parent*.[64] They assume an increasingly dominant middle-class way of life and that the way in which the family is integrated into the economic structure will be a major influence on the family's child-rearing philosophy. Particularly, the values and way of life of the parents are seen as being molded by their experiences in that part of the economic structure within which the father works. The characteristics or traits that are rewarded in this setting are emphasized in child-rearing. The parents treat their children the same way they treat themselves and others, in line with their values and expectations.

To operationalize this thesis, Miller and Swanson defined two different types of middle-class "integrational settings:" an *individuated-entreprenurial*, and a *welfare-bureaucratic* setting. The concept of the individuated entrepreneur appears to be based, at least in part, on a rural-urban dichotomy in which it is proposed that urbanites meet one another in highly segmented roles, relate to one another in a superficial competitive way, lack close and continuing contacts, and become isolated and lonely. When these experiences are linked with a type of occupation that involves risk-taking, is subject to the fluctuations of the market place, and is dependent upon personal judgment and manipulative skill to stay in business, the concept of the individuated entrepreneur emerges. This type of orientation the authors attribute to the older middle classes who put a premium on self-control, rational behavior, denial of present gratifications for future gains, and an active manipulative approach to the environment.[65]

For research purposes, families were classified as entrepreneurial if they met any of the following five criteria: (1) if the husband was self-employed; (2)

[63] Melvin L. Kohn, "Social Class and Parental Values," *American Journal of Sociology* 64 (Jan. 1959), pp. 337–52; and Melvin L. Kohn, "Social Class and Parent-Child Relationships: An Interpretation," *American Journal of Sociology* 68 (Jan. 1963), pp. 471–80. For needed cautions in the conduct of research in this area, see Kathryn P. Johnsen and Gerald R. Leslie, "Methodological Notes on Research in Childrearing and Social Class," *Merrill-Palmer Quarterly* 11 (Oct. 1965), pp. 345–58.

[64] Daniel R. Miller and Guy E. Swanson, *The Changing American Parent*, New York: John Wiley and Sons, 1958.

[65] For this summary and critique of *The Changing American Parent*, the author is indebted to Kathryn P. Johnsen, "Trends in Child-Rearing Advice Compared with Actual Parental Practices," paper prepared for research seminar on the family.

if he received at least half of his income from profits, fees, or commissions; (3) if he worked in an organization having only two levels of supervision; (4) if either the husband or wife was born on a farm; or (5) if either was born outside the United States.

The concept of welfare bureaucracy was based on an emerging pattern in large-scale organizations which the authors believe is modifying the older individually oriented society. Bureaucracy, in this context, implies a high degree of specialization and supervision governed by a coded set of rules, and "welfare" implies that the organization offers security to its members. The authors see the values of persons, so integrated, as stemming from the special demands made upon the personnel of such organizations. These demands include the steady, faithful performance of duty, without rewards for the exercise of imagination or initiative, these traits being desirable only if they are under the control of the organization. Excessive drive and competition are discouraged. Employees must not be too aggressive or too ambitious. In the organization, people are supposed to find each other's presence so mutually rewarding and so lacking in threat that they feel wholly comfortable and seek to preserve their happy, productive state. To fit into this secure world, children should be warm, friendly, and supportive of others. As adults they will have less need for strict consciences or internal controls, since as members of large organizations they will be supervised and guided carefully.

Miller and Swanson see the whole of American society moving gradually toward the bureaucratic integrational setting, in which a more relaxed approach to parenthood is spreading; where methods of discipline will be physical or external (rather than internal) because internal controls are neither necessary nor wanted in the bureaucratic system. Thus the family becomes the means of supplying the economic system with the kind of personalities it needs to operate.

To test this thesis, the authors classified as bureaucratic those families where: (1) both husband and wife were urban-born; (2) the husband worked for someone else in an organization with three or more supervisory levels; and (3) their income was primarily in the form of wages or salary. Four hundred seventy-nine white, middle-class Detroit mothers constituted the basic sample, with comparisons between the two middle-class groups being based upon 99 mothers in the entrepreneurial category and 86 in the bureaucratic category.

Several kinds of predictions were made. First it was predicted that the entrepreneurial mothers would emphasize development of internal controls in their children through earlier bowel training, scheduled feeding, not immediately tending to a crying baby, and through the use of symbolic rather than physical punishment. It was also predicted that bureaucratic mothers would be more permissive of thumb-sucking and sexual exploration, would place less emphasis on the achievement of independence, and would not emphasize differences between male and female occupations.

The authors concluded that their findings generally bore out their predictions and their over-all thesis. They found that the entrepreneurial mothers were more likely to begin bowel training by the time the baby was ten months old, were more likely to feed the baby on a schedule, were more likely to delay giving attention to a crying baby, and were more likely to use symbolic forms of punishment. The entrepreneurial mothers also were more likely to use harsh means to stop thumb-sucking, to feel it necessary to do something when the child touched his sex organs, to believe it good to leave the child with a competent person because the mother benefits, to agree that the child should be on his own as soon as possible, and to feel that only boys should perform activities traditionally associated with their sex among adolescents. The authors stated, ". . . we consider it correct and conservative to conclude that our prediction is upheld. Entrepreneurial middle-class mothers are more likely than those in a bureaucratic integration to use practices which emphasize self-control in training children." [66]

The Miller and Swanson research is open to a number of criticisms. The classification of families as entrepreneurial was based too heavily upon rural or foreign birth with the result that a portion of the results may be due to rural-urban differences. [67] The assumption that competition and ambition are no longer valued as such is unproven. The comparisons between the two groups of middle-class mothers often were based upon small numbers, the mothers had children of different ages, the integration setting used was the current one rather than the one applying when the child was an infant, the items used to test the thesis may not have been the best ones, and so on.

At this stage it does not appear warranted to say that the Miller and Swanson thesis has been adequately tested. Neither, of course, has it been disproven. It has been shown that there has been a pervasive trend toward more permissive child-rearing at both middle-class and lower-class levels. The Miller and Swanson thesis is provocative and is generally in accord with the functionalist view of the nature of the middle-class American family.

SUMMARY

This chapter deals with the general areas of sex adjustment, family planning, pregnancy, child-bearing, early child-rearing, and some of the interrelations among them.

[66] Op. cit., p. 98. A recent study challenges this conclusion. See Jack L. Franklin and Joseph E. Scott, "Parental Values: An Inquiry Into Occupational Setting," *Journal of Marriage and the Family* 32 (Aug. 1970), pp. 406–9.

[67] Urie Bronfenbrenner, op. cit.

At marriage, husbands typically desire sexual intercourse more frequently than their wives do and the adjustment reached generally represents something of a compromise. Husbands appear prone to evaluate their marriages in terms of the sex adjustment, while wives are more likely to evaluate the sex adjustment in terms of how things are going in other areas of marital interaction.

One kind of sexual problem in marriage is illustrated by some degree of orgasm incapacity in a substantial proportion of women. The proportion of women regularly experiencing orgasm increases with age even though the frequency of sexual intercourse is declining. Orgasm performance also is related to decade of birth and to economic and educational level. The relative lack of sexual responsiveness in wives may be due to a variety of interactional factors in the marriage and tends both to cause and to accompany breakdown in marital communication.

Both men and women show some tendency to find substitute outlets for marital intercourse. Among men, continued masturbation and the development of extramarital intercourse are common. At lower educational levels, extramarital intercourse is most common during the early years of marriage, while at higher educational levels the proportion who are so involved continues to increase up to age 50. The involvement of women in both masturbation and extramarital coitus follows the development of sexual responsiveness. Particularly at higher educational levels, the peak participation comes during the thirties and forties.

Most young couples move quickly into child-bearing. Although the long-term trend in child-bearing has been downward, there has been an upsurge since World War II, with most couples now wanting two, three, or four children.

There have been a number of studies of the relationship between number of children and marital success which have shown generally that there tends to be an inverse relationship. In part, this apparent relationship is due to the especially deleterious effect of excess child-bearing. Children, up to the preferred number, may contribute to marital happiness, while children beyond the preferred number cause strife and problems.

The vast majority of couples make some effort at family planning. Recent national studies have yielded the following findings. First, up to 10 per cent of all couples are sterile and up to one-third are of impaired fecundity. Second, childlessness and subfecundity are closely related; relatively few couples abstain voluntarily from child-bearing. Third, about half of all contraceptive users do not begin until they have experienced at least one pregnancy. Fourth, by the end of the child-bearing period virtually all couples are either contraceptive users or are subfecund. Fifth, in spite of contraception, only about one couple out of five is successful in planning both the number and spacing of all children. Sixth, Roman Catholics are somewhat less effective contraceptive users than non-Catholics, and higher-status Catholics are most likely to follow the teachings of the church. Seventh, success in family planning is positively associated with economic and educational status. And, finally, both subfecundity and successful family planning were found to be associated with the wife holding a job outside the home.

Another study of middle- and lower-class couples throws light on some of the relationships between marital roles, sex adjustment, and family planning. Joint marital roles involving adequate communication between husband and wife tend to be associated with good sex adjustment and with effective family planning. Segregated marital roles are more often associated with lack of sexual responsiveness in the wife, depreciation of the husband, and ineffective family planning.

The impact of pregnancy and child-bearing upon the marital relationship also has been studied. Most first pregnancies either are desired beforehand or quickly accepted. Few differences appear in the adjustment to pregnancy between couples who had planned the pregnancy and those who had not. Variable effects of pregnancy upon sex adjustment are reported; slightly over half of all couples report no effect while some report improvement and some report deterioration. There does appear to be a tendency for the frequency of sexual intercourse to decrease during the latter part of pregnancy and to remain lower after the birth of the child.

Subsequent pregnancies are less often welcomed than the first one, and the proportion of couples resorting to abortion increases with succeeding pregnancies. The vast majority of these abortions are illegal but, among married women at least, appear more often to be welcomed than to produce undesirable consequences.

Studies show that the birth of the first child often produces a crisis in the home. The new arrival forces the restructuring of marital roles and some time often is required to do this. Most couples do achieve such readjustment after awhile.

Sociological research into patterns of child-rearing indicates that there has been a general trend toward more permissiveness over the last 30 to 40 years. During that period, also, the relative positions of the middle and lower classes have been reversed; whereas, formerly, middle-class parents appeared stricter than lower-class parents, the reverse has been true since World War II.

One recent study has postulated a basic shift in middle-class conditions of life that encourages permissive child-rearing. It is argued that the old middle class emphasized ambition, competitiveness, risk-taking, and the development of internal controls in the individual. By contrast, the new middle class, which is oriented toward participation in large-scale organizations, emphasizes the ability to get along comfortably with other people in the organization. Child-rearing patterns, it is argued, are changing accordingly.

SUGGESTED READINGS

Bartell, Gilbert D., *Group Sex: A Scientist's Eyewitness Report on the American Way of Swinging*, New York: Peter H. Wyden, Inc., 1971. A social anthropological report based upon direct interaction with more than 280 swingers in the central part of the United States.

Benson, Leonard, *Fatherhood: A Sociological Perspective*, New York: Random House, 1968. A well-documented analysis of parental interaction with one another and with their children. Unique analysis of the father's role in the family.

Dager, Edward Z., "Socialization and Personality Development in the Child," in Harold T. Christensen, ed., *Handbook of Marriage and the Family*, Chicago: Rand McNally and Co., 1964, pp. 740–81. One of the best summaries and interpretations of the available data on child-rearing.

Kohn, Melvin L., *Class and Conformity*, Homewood, Illinois: The Dorsey Press, Inc., 1969. A monograph focusing upon the relation between social class and child-rearing practices. Based upon the findings of three separate research projects.

Le Masters, Ersel E., *Parents in Modern America: A Sociological Analysis*, Homewood, Illinois: The Dorsey Press, 1970. The first systematic, comprehensive sociological analysis of parenthood in the United States. Contains chapters on minority group parents and parents without partners.

Neubeck, Gerhard, ed., *Extramarital Relations*, Englewood Cliffs, New Jersey: Prentice-Hall, Inc., 1969. A varied collection of essays on a formerly taboo topic. Contains a section on causes and effects of extramarital relations.

Ritchie, Oscar W., and Koller, Marvin R., *Sociology of Childhood*, New York: Appleton-Century-Crofts, 1964. A recent textbook that deals with socialization in the context of family experience.

FILMS

A Planned Parenthood Story (Mayo-Video, 113 West 57th St., New York), 18 minutes. Produced for the Planned Parenthood Federation of America. Deals with a young couple who lost two babies in rapid succession because the wife had not regained her strength after the birth of their third living child. They learn of the service of "Planned Parenthood" and are able to space the arrival of their next baby. During the clinic scenes, the action shows how other services of "Planned Parenthood" are carried on.

Children (*Time-Life* Films, 43 West 16th Street, New York, 10011), 45 minutes. Compares the ways in which different societies bring up children and teach them to behave properly. Asks whether it is vital for mothers to spend all their waking hours with their children.

Children's Emotions (McGraw-Hill Book Company, Text-Film Division, 330 West 42nd St., New York 10036), 22 minutes. Major emotions of childhood —fear, anger, jealousy, curiosity, joy. What parents can do to lessen fears, promote child's happiness and natural development.

Unfolding (American Documentary Films, 336 West 84th Street, New York 10024; or 379 Bay Street, San Francisco 94133), 18 minutes. An esthetic expression of human sexuality from a woman's point of view.

Whose Life? (CCM Films, Inc., 866 Third Avenue, New York 10022), 30 minutes. An original drama about abortion and the problems that arise when a wife and mother decides that she doesn't want any more children.

QUESTIONS AND PROJECTS

1. What is the relationship between age and marital sexual intercourse? What interpretation would you place upon the discrepancies between husbands and wives in reported frequencies of intercourse?

2. How widespread is lack of sexual responsiveness among American women? What are some of the social origins of this lack of responsiveness?

3. What is, perhaps, the commonest sex-adjustment problem confronted by young married couples? Does the nature of this problem tend to change with time? If so, how?

4. What associations do there appear to be between sexual frustration in marriage and participation in extramarital intercourse? Are these purely biological frustrations? Use data by social class to show that they are not.

5. What does research show about the relationship between number of children and marital adjustment? What factor, other than simply the number of children a couple have, needs to be taken into account in explaining the effect of children upon marital adjustment?

6. What proportion of American couples appears to be sterile? To be subfecund? What has research shown about the effects of the use of vasectomy as a means of birth control?

7. What technical problems must be faced when estimating exactly what proportion of American couples use contraception? How do motive users differ from action users? Summarize the available data on the extent of contraceptive use; by religion; by social class.

8. How does success in family planning appear to be related to the general process of communication between husband and wife? How does sexual adjustment fit into the picture?

9. What does research show about the adjustment of couples to the first pregnancy? How do statistics on abortion indicate a different pattern of reaction to subsequent pregnancies?

10. What evidence is there for assuming that the birth of the first child is likely to produce a crisis in the marital relationship? What sort of time sequence appears to be involved? Are most such crises successfully resolved?

11. What trends have been occurring in American child-rearing patterns over the past three or four decades? What social-class differences existed in the past? At present?

12. Describe the thesis developed by Miller and Swanson to explain recent changes in child-rearing patterns. Has this thesis been adequately proven or disproven? Relate this thesis to the concept, developed earlier in this book, of the middle-class family model.

17	*Marriage in the Middle Years*

. . . A review of the research literature and reports on husband-wife relationships has turned up the interesting and salient fact that conversation, "just plain talk" between husbands and wives almost never happens. A general social apartheid between the sexes has also shown up. . . .

There have been, in effect, only two alternatives the sexes have had: either they hopped into bed or they turned their backs on one another. The only times there has been good talk between the sexes socially were when a determined effort was made to achieve it, as in the Renaissance or in the 18th-century salons. The sexes have loved one another but not . . . liked one another. Companionship requires people to like one another.

Marital companionship cannot, therefore, be taken for granted. It is not something that just naturally happens, the "natural" outcome of marriage. For many if not most marriages, the "natural" course of events leads away from companionship; after the intense relationship based on love and sex has tapered off, it is not companionship that takes its place but a parallelism in which each goes his or her own way with a minimum of communication. Study after study has shown this of higher as well as lower socio-economic levels. People become habituated to one another, but this is a far cry from companionship. The objective of companionship between husbands and wives in addition to sexual compatibility is surely brand new, a luxury item. That husbands and wives like as well as love one another, enjoy one another's company—this is a very exalted conception of marriage. . . .[1]

THIS quotation, from a distinguished family sociologist, makes several explicit and implicit judgments about the nature of marriage in general and American marriage in particular. First is the implied judgment that both men and women often find their marital relationships

[1] Jessie Bernard, "Developmental Tasks of the NCFR—1963–1988," *Journal of Marriage and the Family* 26 (Feb. 1964), pp. 33–4.

wanting. Communication in many marriages, she indicates, is woefully inadequate, the apparent intimacy of the sex relationship disguising the fact that there is little significant communication of other sorts in the relationship. Second is the judgment, supported by research, that there tends to be a decrease in communication between husbands and wives the longer they are married. And, third, she describes marital relationships as being characterized by parallelism and habit rather than companionship. The author is talking, of course, of marriages that have passed the honeymoon and early adjustment stages. She is talking about marriage in the middle years.

In an earlier chapter, we learned that while most people describe themselves as being happily married, marital adjustment is a complex thing. Some conflict appears to be inevitable in marriage just as it is in other areas of life. Some couples succeed quickly in reducing conflict to a bare minimum, some drive it underground, and other relationships appear to depend—if not to thrive—on it. Existing concepts of marital adjustment tend to be couched in terms of middle-class norms, defining as good marriages those in which there is relative absence of overt conflict and at least outward conformity to conventional standards of behavior. But such marriages have variable outcomes. Some produce husbands, wives, and children who are vibrant, creative, and truly alive, while others appear to involve their members in neurotic intrigue or simply stifle potentials for growth and development.

Implicit in the earlier discussion was the implication that marital adjustment is a process and not simply a state. Reference back to Chapter 9 and the discussion of the family life cycle shows that married couples spend an average of only two years together before their first child is born, some half-dozen years in child-bearing, about 20 years in child-rearing, and another 20 years before the husband reaches retirement. Whereas in that discussion the phrase, families in the middle years, was used to refer only to the period following the marriages of the children and before the husband's retirement, a somewhat different usage is employed here. In this chapter the phrase, the middle years, will be used to cover the whole range of marital adjustment from the early child-rearing years up to the husband's retirement. The emphasis will be not so much upon any specific period in marital life as upon the changes which take place in marriages over this very large part of the life cycle.

Marriage as a Developmental Process

A potentially useful approach to the analysis of marital adjustment has been originated by Nelson Foote, who conceives of mate selection in terms of matching husband and wife in phases of development rather than in terms of particular traits brought by the partners to the marriage.[2] He assumes that the matching of personalities is a continual process and that personalities continue to change throughout adult life. Correlatively, he questions whether it is possible to determine, at the time of marriage, whether a given match will prove to be a good one or a bad one. Changes that occur in the partners during the marriage itself may be just as important.

Foote cites several kinds of evidence to support his view. Studies of the stresses faced by couples undergoing enforced separation are a case in point. The prolonged separation of couples by military service has been shown to strain the relationship between them and to require very complex readjustments at the time of reunion.[3] Other kinds of separation, such as those required by migration, employment, or confinement in institutions, have similar effects. In less drastic circumstances, the significant involvement of both husband and wife in different groups in the community during the day may provide them with accumulations of experience that they cannot satisfactorily share with one another in the few evening hours they have together.

The implication that there are forces encouraging couples to grow apart finds support in popular interpretations of causes for divorce. One frequently hears it said that one of the spouses—almost always the husband—outgrew the other. The husband's occupation frequently forces him into a variety of new experiences and into extensive contact with members of the opposite sex who, in time, may come to share more significant aspects of his daily life than does his wife. This appears to be one of the major challenges facing wives in the middle-class family model, and one of which women are becoming more and more aware.[4]

Foote points out that, although we emphasize the fact that more marital separations appear to occur during the first year of marriage than during any other, other averages suggest that marriages ending in divorce deteriorate over a considerable period of time.[5] The median length of marriages ending in divorce, he suggests, may be about three years, while the mean length may be as long as ten years. Some divorces occur even after 20 or 30 years of marriage. Such figures indicate that simple mismatching is not adequate to

[2] Nelson N. Foote, "Matching of Husband and Wife in Phases of Development," *Transactions of the Third World Congress of Sociology, International Sociological Association* 4 (1956), pp. 24–34, as reprinted in Marvin B. Sussman, ed., *Sourcebook in Marriage and the Family*, Boston: Houghton Mifflin Company, 1963, pp. 15–21.

[3] Reuben Hill, et al., *Families Under Stress: Adjustment to the Crises of War Separation and Reunion*, New York: Harper and Brothers, 1949.

[4] William H. Whyte, Jr., *The Organization Man*, Garden City, New York: Doubleday and Company, 1956, p. 401.

[5] Thomas P. Monahan, "Is Childlessness Related to Family Stability?" *American Sociological Review* 20 (Aug. 1955), pp. 446–56.

account for all divorces. Foote states that "a better hypothesis would be that those who were sufficiently matched to marry became sufficiently unmatched to unmarry." [6]

A useful analogy may also be made between marriage and friendship. Friendship, presumably, is one component in marriage and any given marriage may be expected to improve or worsen as friendship between the partners prospers or withers. Significantly, there are, for most people, few lifelong friendships outside of marriage. Instead, friendships develop, change, and decline over the life cycle. As Foote points out, little is known about the development and decline of friendships and no more is known about the development and maintenance of friendship in marriage. It appears plausible that friendship, both in and out of marriage, depends upon shared common interests; and since interests change over time, the continuance of friendships rests partly upon the continual development of new common interests. The more marriage in our society comes to center on companionship and friendship, the more crucial it becomes that spouses be capable of sharing new common interests. This ability probably is little related to conventional social homogamy between husband and wife but may be related instead to some sequence of developmental stages in the individual.

The whole notion of a sequence of developmental stages in marriage has been conceptualized by Farber, who describes the family as a set of mutually contingent careers. That people—particularly men—pass through a progression of statuses in connection with their occupations is well recognized. It is also widely recognized that changes in a man's occupational career impinge directly upon his relationships with his family. Farber extends the notion of career, as an orderly progression of statuses, to all members of the family and he sees careers as being not only occupational but also familial, recreational, and so on. Significant changes, then, in any aspect of any career of any family member impinge upon the careers of other family members. In this sense, the family is seen not only as a set of careers but as a set of intercontingent careers. [7]

The concept of marriage as a set of mutually contingent careers does not require that the husband and wife both pursue careers outside of the home, nor does it assume any other kind of invariant relationship between them. It regards personal happiness as an unsatisfactory criterion of marital success both because it is unstable over time and because happiness is affected by too many variables apart from the quality of the marital relationship. It hypothesizes that the judgments that spouses make of their marriages may depend as

[6] Nelson N. Foote, op. cit. p. 17.

[7] Bernard Farber, *Family: Organization and Interaction*, San Francisco: Chandler Publishing Company, 1964, pp. 334-5.

much upon prospects for the future as upon the present condition of the relationship. If there is a single variable that predicts the future development of a marriage, Foote believes that it may be communication—the degree to which husband and wife are truly able to communicate with one another when they are together.

Foote acknowledges that his conception of the nature of modern marriage is a demanding one. It is not necessarily a discouraging one, however. He points out that the segment of the United States population which makes the most stable marriages—the professional class—is also the one in which the concept of marriage as a set of mutually contingent careers emerges most clearly. He implies that the number and proportion of stable, rewarding marriages may increase as the trend toward professionalization of the larger society continues.

THE TREND OF MARITAL ADJUSTMENT

Only within the past 15 years has empirical research begun to assess the changes in marital adjustment patterns that occur after the early years of marriage. Within this period, however, a number of studies have appeared, based upon a variety of populations, that trace the trend in adjustment over 5, 10, to 20 or more years of marriage. Some of the specific findings of the major studies follow. Without exception, they show that the high levels of commitment characteristic of early marriage are not commonly maintained. The data indicate that marriage as a set of mutually contingent careers may be more of an ideal than of an accomplished fact. However marital adjustment is conceived, the long-term trend apparently is downward.

LONGITUDINAL STUDIES OF MARITAL ADJUSTMENT

One of the few truly longitudinal studies of marital adjustment is Burgess and Wallin's study of 1000 engaged couples whom they attempted to follow through early marital adjustment and into middle life. As has been reported earlier, only 666 of the engaged couples actually married and were available for study after four to six years of marriage. Further sample losses occurred up to 1954, when some 400 couples were restudied after they had been married up to 20 years. [8]

---

[8] Ernest W. Burgess, and Paul Wallin, *Engagement and Marriage*, Philadelphia: J. B. Lippincott Co., 1963. It is not possible fully to assess the biasing effects of this sample loss. It can be reported, however, that there were no significant differences in marital adjustment scores in the early 1940's between the 400 couples who were studied for the third time and the other 266 couples.

A portion of the results of the comparison of 400 couples after about 5 years of marriage and again after nearly 20 years of marriage is shown in Table 1. The statistical procedures involved in the computation of the gains or losses in marital adjustment need not concern us here; suffice it to say that positive figures indicate gains in marital adjustment while negative figures indicate drops in adjustment. Only the figures followed by asterisks are large enough to be regarded as statistically significant.

First, it should be noted that an overwhelming proportion of the figures both for husbands and for wives are negative. Moreover, 13 of the negative

TABLE 1. *Gains in Marital Adjustment from Early to Middle Years of Marriage on Eighteen Indices, 400 Couples.*

	GAIN FROM EARLY TO MIDDLE YEARS	
	Husbands	Wives
A. Marital Satisfaction		
Marital adjustment	−4.63 *	−5.42 *
Love	−2.01 *	−2.87 *
Permanence	−2.12 *	−2.64 *
Consensus	−2.26 *	−2.37 *
Marriage complaints (absence of) ...	−1.59	−2.09 *
Own happiness	−1.13	−1.42
Sexual adjustment	−1.14	−0.93
B. Marital Type		
Sharing of interests and activities	−3.84 *	−4.56 *
Frequency of sexual intercourse	−2.31 *	−2.13 *
Traditionalism	−1.86	−1.76
Attitudes to having children	−0.04	−0.72
Dominance	0.79	−0.26
C. Personal Characteristics		
Idealization of mate's personality	−0.60	−0.67
Personal growth gains due to marriage	−0.16	−0.36
Non-neuroticism or autonomy	−0.24	−0.12
Rating of own personality traits	−1.07	−0.34
Rating of mate's personality traits ...	0.34	−1.31
Number of felt personality needs	1.45	1.25

* Statistically significant changes at the 0.05 level of confidence or better; the standardized gains are numerically equivalent to z-scores between actual mean change and hypothesized no mean change.

$$\text{Gain} = \frac{\Sigma D}{\sqrt{\dfrac{\Sigma D^2 - (\Sigma D)^2}{N-1}}}, \text{ where D=time period two score−time period one score}$$

Source: Peter C. Pineo, "Disenchantment in the Later Years of Marriage," *Marriage and Family Living* 23 (Feb. 1961), p. 4.

figures are statistically significant while none of the positive figures is large enough to achieve significance. The data suggest a large and pervasive drop in marital adjustment.

The greatest losses are to be found within the category of indices labeled marital satisfaction. All signs are negative and 9 out of 14 are statistically significant. Pineo, who did the analysis, believes that this is a phenomenon of such magnitude that the phrase, loss of satisfaction, "is insufficient to express the fact that this is a process which appears to be generally an inescapable consequence of the passage of time in a marriage." [9] He conceptualizes the process of decreasing marital satisfaction as being one of "disenchantment."

This disenchantment appears to be inevitable and need not have its roots in idealization of the partner or the relationship prior to marriage. That it is a general process rather than a series of independent changes is indicated by two things. First, there is a definite association between the losses experienced by the husbands and those experienced by the wives. Second, changes on any one score tend to be associated with changes on the other scores.

Pineo uses the general idea of marriage as a developmental process to develop a theory that disenchantment sets in after the early years of marriage, stating explicitly that personality changes in the partner and changes in the context in which the marriage will operate cannot be determined before the wedding. What ordinarily happens is that people marry on the basis of a "good fit" between them at the time. When they are already well matched, the changes that inevitably occur after marriage are far more likely to worsen that fit than to improve it. As Pineo puts it, "The deviant characteristics which provided the grounds upon which the marriage was contracted begin to be lost, as later changes tend toward the population mean and the couples become more and more like ones who married at random rather than by choice." [10]

"You study one another for three weeks, you love each other three months, you fight for three years, you tolerate the situation for 30."

—André de Missan

---

[9] Peter C. Pineo, "Disenchantment in the Later Years of Marriage," *Marriage and Family Living* 23 (Feb. 1961), p. 6. For a comprehensive final report on the results of the third wave of interviews, see Jan Dizard, *Social Change in the Family*, University of Chicago, Community and Family Study Center, 1968.

[10] Pineo, "Disenchantment," op. cit. p. 7.

One possibility, of course, is that the drop in general marital adjustment might be a function of a drop in personal adjustment over the same time period—a function of the general process of aging. The data, however, contradict this hypothesis. Some changes in personal adjustment were detected over the study period, but personal adjustment was as likely to improve as to worsen and there was no general association between a drop in personal adjustment and a drop in marital adjustment.[11]

It should be pointed out that the general drop in marital adjustment indicated by the figures in Table 1 should not be interpreted to mean that *all* couples suffered a drop in adjustment. Some couples actually improved their adjustment, many appeared not to have changed significantly, and some, of course, declined in adjustment. Unfortunately, the authors who report these data do not give us detailed figures on this point. Dentler and Pineo do indicate that 75 per cent of the husbands maintained their early levels of adjustment, with only 25 per cent changing significantly. Among those who changed, two-thirds changed from high to low adjustment.

In addition to the general drop in marital satisfaction, some other interesting conclusions may be drawn from the data in Table 1. For one thing, the greatest drop outside that in general marital adjustment occurs in the sharing of interests and activities. Since these couples had already been married a few years at the time of the first measurement, this drop cannot be attributed to the fact of marriage alone. It seems more likely that it is associated with child-rearing and the many duties which child-rearing imposes upon the parents.

A significant decrease occurs also in the frequency of sexual intercourse, with the results of this decrease being different for husbands than for wives. Among wives the decrease may occur without an accompanying drop in general satisfaction. About a fourth of all husbands, however, also experience a drop in sexual adjustment and in marital adjustment.[12]

Two other items, those on "traditionalism" and on "dominance," indicate paradoxical shifts in the nature of marital interaction. There is a general decrease in the traditionalism of both husbands and wives with the passage of time. Yet, husbands also tend to become more dominant and wives tend to become more submissive. Couples appear to give lip-service to the ideal of equalitarian relationships between men and women but, as they grow older, relationships between them actually become more authoritarian. Both Pineo

[11] Ibid. p. 8; and Robert A. Dentler and Peter Pineo, "Sexual Adjustment, Marital Adjustment and Personal Growth of Husbands: A Panel Analysis," *Marriage and Family Living* 22 (Feb. 1960), pp. 45–8.
[12] Ibid. pp. 46–7.

and Goode have analyzed this situation in terms of the power which tends to accrue to middle-class husbands as a function of their high incomes and occupational prestige.[13] A real irony exists in the fact that lower-class couples who are more likely to endorse verbal norms of dominance and submission are actually more equalitarian because of the relatively greater economic power of the wife, while equalitarian-oriented middle-class couples actually have relationships based more on dominance and submission.

Finally, it should be noted that there were significant differences in several areas between those couples who experienced a general drop in marital adjustment and those who did not. Those who had dropped in adjustment were far more likely to regret their marriages and to state that they would not marry the same person again. They were also more likely to report decreases in the frequency of kissing and confiding and to indicate less reciprocity in the settlement of disagreements. The couples who did not suffer disenchantment showed no significant drops in these areas. Ninety-nine per cent would marry the same person again and also reported no decrease in frequency of kissing. Ninety-nine per cent continued to confide in their spouses, and 96 per cent settled their disagreements by give and take.[14]

The couples originally studied by Burgess and Wallin were married, of course, in the late 1930's and early 1940's. It could be that the general drop in marital adjustment found among them was characteristic of that particular generation. Changes in circumstances might not produce the same pattern in succeeding generations of marriages. To check that possibility, let us examine another study—done on a much smaller scale—that was completed in 1965.

Marriage is like hot mustard—many a man praises it with tears in his eyes.

Luckey studied, in 1957, two groups of 40 married couples each, who were classified as being satisfactorily or unsatisfactorily married on the basis of marital-adjustment scale scores.[15] The couples, selected from among former University of Minnesota students, had been married for a mean average of

13 Peter C. Pineo, op. cit. p. 8; and William J. Goode, *World Revolution and Family Patterns*, New York: The Free Press of Glencoe, 1963, pp. 20-22.

14 Peter C. Pineo, op. cit. p. 5.

15 Eleanore B. Luckey, "Perceptional Congruence of Self and Family Concepts as Related to Marital Interaction," *Sociometry* 24 (Sept., 1961), pp. 234–50.

7.7 years. In 1963 the husbands and wives were studied again through marital-adjustment scales and questionnaires. Responses were received from 36 wives in the Satisfied group, 34 wives in the Unsatisfied group, and 31 husbands from each of the two groups.[16]

Changes in marital adjustment between the seventh and thirteenth years of marriage were measured by changes in marital-adjustment scale scores. When the two groups were analyzed together, both husbands and wives were found to make lower scores in 1963 than they did in 1957. Thus the results of this study are consistent with those of the earlier, larger study just reported.

Luckey's findings are presented separately for the originally Satisfied and Unsatisfied groups in Table 2. There it can be seen that the scores of the

TABLE 2. *Number of Couples Showing Increases and Decreases in Marital Satisfaction Between the Seventh and Thirteenth Years of Marriage.*

	INCREASE	DECREASE	TOTAL
Satisfied couples (7th year)	5	18	23
Unsatisfied couples (7th year)	13	9	22
Total	18	27	45 *

* Includes only those couples where completed questionnaires were received from both husband and wife.

Source: Bethel L. Paris and Eleanor B. Luckey, "A Longitudinal Study in Marital Satisfaction," *Sociology and Social Research* 50 (Jan. 1966), pp. 212–23.

Satisfied couples were more likely to decline than to increase over the six-year period, while for the originally Unsatisfied couples the reverse was true; the scores of poorly adjusted couples tended to increase. There are at least two possible explanations for this difference. First, the Satisfied couples, by virtue of having higher aspiration levels for their marriages, may be less likely to discover that their actual experience lives up to their expectations. Second, the scores of the Satisfied group are so high in the first place that they really have only one direction to go. By the same token, the low scores of the Unsatisfied group may have to increase if the prospect of divorce is to be avoided. This interpretation is strengthened by the fact that three of the original Unsatisfied couples actually had been divorced during the six-year period.

OTHER COMPARATIVE STUDIES OF MARITAL ADJUSTMENT

A number of other recent studies that have involved studying couples married for different lengths of time—rather than following the same couples

[16] Bethel L. Paris and Eleanore B. Luckey, "A Longitudinal Study in Marital Satisfaction," *Sociology and Social Research* 50 (Jan. 1966), pp. 212–23.

through time—have yielded data that inferentially support the findings of the two longitudinal studies already reported. These inferential studies include data from lower socio-economic groups as well as from middle-class couples.

The study by Blood and Wolfe, referred to in earlier chapters, of 731 city families and 178 farm families in the Detroit area provides a variety of relevant data. These data were derived from interviewing systematic samples of wives who ranged from 21 years to more than 60 years of age and who had been married from less than one to more than 40 years. Comparisons with United States Census data indicate that the samples generally were representative of the Detroit-area population and covered virtually the whole range of socio-economic and occupational statuses.[17]

The authors describe time as a corrosive influence, wearing away at the strength of marriages. Of those women who had been married for two years or less, 52 per cent described themselves as being very satisfied with their marriages and none said that they were notably dissatisfied. Among those who had been married 20 years or longer, however, only 6 per cent remained fully satisfied with their marriages and 21 per cent were conspicuously dissatisfied. Much of the dissatisfaction, according to the authors, reflects decreases in the number of things that spouses do for and with each other. Many husbands and wives permit their marriages to go to seed. Middle-aged people find satisfaction in children, in jobs, in their friends, and elsewhere, but they seldom find as much satisfaction in one another.

The decline in wives' satisfaction with their marriages is shown graphically in Figure 1. The wife's marital satisfaction is computed by weighting her reported satisfaction with her standard of living, companionship, understanding, love and affection, the congruity between her expected and desired number of children, and by the relative importance that she attaches to each of these five aspects of marriage. As the graph shows, wives' reported satisfaction declines steadily with increasing length of time married. Satisfaction is at a maximum during the first two years of marriage and decreases through at least the next 30 years.

A woman marries in the hope of having a lifelong lover and discovers too late, that she merely has a boarder who is most difficult to please.

—Myrtle Reed.

---

[17] Robert O. Blood, Jr. and Donald M. Wolfe, *Husbands and Wives: The Dynamics of Married Living*, The Free Press of Glencoe, Illinois, 1960, pp. 5–7, 263–73.

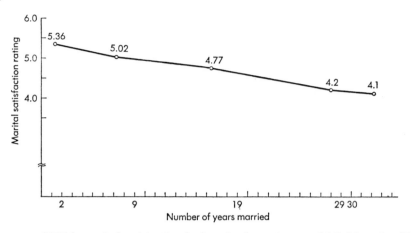

FIGURE 1. *Wife's marital satisfaction by length of marriage, 556 Michigan families.*

Source: Robert O. Blood, Jr. and Donald M. Wolfe, *Husbands and Wives: The Dynamics of Married Living,* The Free Press of Glencoe, Illinois: 1960, p. 264.

More of the Detroit-area wives chose companionship in doing things together with the husband as the most valuable aspect of marriage than chose love, understanding, standard of living, or the opportunity to have children. Companionship apparently is the most important thing to them in marriage. Companionship too, however, tends to decline at least through the middle years of marriage. The mean satisfaction scores of wives with their companionship with their husbands declined from 4.26 during the honeymoon period to 3.99 during the preschool stage of the family life cycle, to 3.91 during the pre-adolescent stage, to 3.76 during the period when they had adolescent children, and to 3.50 when there were adult but still unmarried children in the home.[18] As Blood and Wolfe put it, companionship is primarily characteristic of young couples and of older couples who are newly-weds. Couples's appreciation of each other reaches a peak during the honeymoon and declines as the partners come to take each other for granted, to deplete the stock of new experiences that they can share together, and as they come to find companionship vicariously in their children or even in watching television.

That wives tend, with time, to turn away from their husbands is illustrated by their responses to questions concerning how they handle small emotional crises in their lives. Blood and Wolfe asked both the city and farm wives, "After you've had a bad day, what do you do to get it out of your system?" The results are shown in Table 3. Most often the wives coped with their problems by sitting down and relaxing, by going to bed early, by reading and watch-

[18] Ibid. pp. 150–56.

TABLE 3. *How City and Farm Wives in the Detroit Area Tend To Cope with "A Bad Day."*

WIFE'S REACTION	CITY WIVES	FARM WIVES
Get away from house	14%	14%
Housework	9	10
Solitary distraction at home	10	11
Passive relaxation at home	23	38
Oral indulgence	2	3
Turn to religion	3	4
Positive interaction with husband	5	3
Positive interaction with others	7	6
Negative interaction with husband	3	0
Negative interaction with others	18	9
Other or N.A.	6	2
Total	100	100
Number of families	731	178

Source: Robert O. Blood, Jr. and Donald M. Wolfe, *Husbands and Wives: The Dynamics of Married Living*, The Free Press of Glencoe, Illinois, 1960, p. 185.

ing television, or by going for a walk. Only 8 per cent of the city wives and 3 per cent of the farm wives specifically mentioned their husbands in response to this question. And of the 8 per cent of city wives, almost half tended to attack their husbands rather than turn to them for comfort. Some small consolation may be gained from the fact that the wives who took out their frustrations on someone else were also more likely to choose persons other than the husband for that purpose. The picture is softened somewhat, too, by the fact that one-fifth of the wives reported that they almost always tell their husbands of their problems and an additional one-fourth or more usually do so.[19]

The right to nag is one of the consolations of marriage.

—Will Durant.

A recent study of 58 marriages in which the husbands followed blue-collar occupations, had gone only through high school, and were under 40 years of age bears out some of Blood and Wolfe's findings. Komarovsky's study of blue-collar marriage involved intensive case studies in which the wives were interviewed for at least four hours and the husbands for at least two hours. She

[19] Ibid. p. 190.

found, first of all, that about one-third of the husbands and wives in her sample could hardly be called friends since they did not share their hurts, worries, and dreams with one another. When the wives were asked, "What helps you when you feel bad, unhappy or worried about something, or generally low?," they mentioned a total of 278 different aids but mentioned the husband only 22 per cent of the time. Forty-four per cent of the group did not mention their mates at all. High-school graduates were more likely to share their feelings with their spouses than were those with less formal education, and communication between mates tended to decline with the number of years married.[20]

Komarovsky also found that two-thirds of the wives had at least one person other than the husband in whom they confided. In 35 per cent of the cases these other confidants, who were most often female kinsmen, shared some aspect of the wives' lives more fully than did the husbands.

An additional study of the general trend of marital adjustment through the middle years has been reported by Harold Feldman, who secured questionnaires from two samples of 120 couples each. He describes these couples as being well educated and middle or upper class. Most of the couples were in their first marriages and most of the wives were not working outside the home. His findings on the trend of marital adjustment may be summarized as follows. Marital discussions are most frequent early in marriage and decline with the passage of time. Couples, as they move into the middle years, may not need to communicate verbally with each other because they understand one another without the necessity for talk, or they may find each other less interesting, or they may simply have less to talk about.[21]

The most recent report of the general trend of marital adjustment comes from Luckey, who studied 80 couples who had been married from two to 21 years. She found that marital adjustment scores were negatively correlated with the number of years married, and that the longer couples were married the less favorable personality qualities each partner saw in his mate. As she phrased it, ". . . subjects in happy marriages tended to see their spouses less admirably, while those in unhappy marriages tended to see their spouses as being more undesirable," with the passage of time.[22]

[20] Mirra Komarovsky, *Blue-Collar Marriage*, New York: Random House, 1964, pp. 140–86.

[21] Harold Feldman, *Development of the Husband-Wife Relationship: A Research Report*, Cornell University, no date, p. 119. See also, Wesley R. Burr, "Satisfaction with Various Aspects of Marriage Over the Life Cycle: A Random Middle Class Sample," *Journal of Marriage and the Family* 32 (Feb. 1970), pp. 29–37; and Boyd C. Rollins and Harold Feldman, "Marital Satisfaction Over the Family Life Cycle," *Journal of Marriage and the Family* 32 (Feb. 1970), pp. 20–28.

[22] Eleanore B. Luckey, "Number of Years Married as Related to Personality Perception and Marital Satisfaction," *Journal of Marriage and the Family* 28 (Feb. 1966), pp. 44–8.

> *There's one consolation about matrimony. When you look around you can always see somebody who did worse.*
>
> —Warren H. Goldsmith.

The weight of all this evidence is impressive. Several sophisticated studies have yielded a remarkably consistent pattern showing a tendency for marital adjustment, measured in a variety of ways, to decline steadily from almost the beginning of marriage at least up to the point where children are grown and leave the home. The conclusion seems inescapable that romance is closely linked to novelty in the majority of relationships. On the other hand, it should not be overlooked that, in almost all of the studies cited, a sizable proportion of marriages continued to be characterized by closeness, affection, and effective communication. Some proportion of marriages even seems to improve in communication and empathy as the years go by. A major task for future research is to determine what factors account for some marriages' being able to withstand the corrosive effects of time.

Marriage, of course, does not typically end with the middle years, and there are data available on the trend of adjustment during the postparental years which help put the findings reported here into broader perspective. These data on the latter stages of the family life cycle will be presented in a later chapter. Of relevance to the analysis of marriage during the middle years, however, remain at least two more topics: the allocation of power and the division of labor within the family; and the effects of working wives and mothers upon family relationships.

THE ENACTMENT OF MARITAL ROLES

Just as marital adjustment does not end with the middle years, so marital roles do not begin in the middle years. The roots of both marital adjustment and marital roles are formed in childhood, develop in early marriage, and change through the middle years right on into old age. There are at least two kinds of justification, however, for analyzing marital roles in connection with the middle years of marriage. First is the fact that the years of child-rearing and the postparental years before retirement so greatly outnumber those in all other stages of the family life cycle combined. Second is the fact that middle-class people, at least, seem to become acutely conscious of the roles they play during this period. Adolescents anticipate marital roles and young marrieds play them, but middle-aged people wrestle with problems of role definition in an especially self-conscious way.

If we think back to the theories of family structure developed earlier in this book, it becomes apparent that conflicting interpretations might be placed upon whatever roles husbands and wives play in marriage and that those roles should be expected to vary with the stage of the family life cycle. Implicit in the defunctionalization theory is the belief that husband-wife roles are becoming more equalitarian and that the companionship that should develop in these circumstances is a mainstay of modern marriage. Functionalist theory places somewhat more emphasis upon the value of a relatively clear division of labor between husband and wife and tends to link family stability with subordination of other family interests to the requirements of the husband's occupational role. Theories to be maximally useful, of course, should be supported by empirical data. Let us see what research shows.

MARITAL ROLE EXPECTATIONS

Several studies have been done in an attempt to see what kinds of marital role expectations young men and women carry into marriage. Two studies of high-school students by Dunn and Moser using a Marriage Role Expectation Inventory showed a general trend toward equalitarian relationships. However, there were differences by sex of the respondent and by the area of marital interaction under consideration. The endorsement of equalitarian norms was least noted in the two areas that were most clear-cut in the older male-dominated family system—those specifying that the husband should be the breadwinner and the wife should be the homemaker. More girls than boys believed that the wife should play the traditional housewife role and most of the girls did not anticipate employment outside the home.[23]

Two other studies of appropriate husband-wife roles as seen by college students yielded findings generally consistent with the studies of high-school students. Lovejoy's study of Washington State University students showed that sex roles in the family today are not so clearly defined as they once were and showed that both men and women believe that decision-making should be more of a joint matter than it was in their own families of orientation.

[23] Marie S. Dunn, "Marriage Role Expectations of Adolescents," *Marriage and Family Living* 22 (May 1960), pp. 99–104; and Alvin J. Moser, "Marriage Role Expectations of High School Students," *Marriage and Family Living* 23 (Feb. 1961), pp. 42–3. See also Lamar T. Empey, "Role Expectations of Young Women Regarding Marriage and a Career," *Marriage and Family Living* 20 (May 1958), pp. 152–5; John Kosa, Leo D. Rachiele, and Cyril O. Schommer, "Marriage, Career, and Religiousness Among Catholic College Girls," *Marriage and Family Living* 24 (Nov. 1962), pp. 376–80.

Women were shown to have moved farther in this direction than men, suggesting the possibility of conflict in marriage.[24] Dyer and Urban's study of a group of Mormon students, who might be expected to be more traditionally oriented than most students, found that there was less agreement on marital roles between single men and women students than between married students. They also found generally equalitarian attitudes, with the areas of finances and the performance of household tasks still to be more traditional.[25]

The question may properly be asked, of course, what relationship there is, if any, between the marital-role conceptions of adolescents and unmarried college students and the roles which men and women actually play both early in marriage and later on. Some inferential data are available on this question in studies by Kirkpatrick and Hobart and by Motz. Kirkpatrick and Hobart sought to see what changes occurred in relationships as couples moved from favorite date to marriage. In the area of marital roles, they found that there was less disagreement among married couples than between engaged couples, less disagreement between engaged couples than between steady-dating couples, and so on. They tended to interpret these facts as indicating that people choose to marry persons holding similar role expectations rather than in terms of changes in role expectations occurring during courtship.[26]

Motz queried married college-student couples and found that husbands and wives tend to define marital roles in much the same way. Husbands are expected to be concerned about meeting their wives' personality needs and to carry their share of household, parental, and social responsibilities. In contrast with the companionate role deemed appropriate for husbands, wives are expected to be subordinate to their husbands and to concentrate on the care of husband, children, and home.[27]

---

[24] Debi D. Lovejoy, "College Student Conceptions of the Roles of the Husband and Wife in Family Decision-Making," *Family Life Coordinator* 9 (Mar.-June 1961), pp. 43-6.

[25] William G. Dyer and Dick Urban, "The Institutionalization of Equalitarian Family Norms," *Marriage and Family Living* 20 (Feb. 1958), pp. 53-8. See also Genevieve M. Wise and Don C. Carter, "A Definition of the Role of Homemaker by Two Generations of Women," *Journal of Marriage and the Family* 27 (Nov. 1965), pp. 531-2.

[26] Clifford Kirkpatrick and Charles Hobart, "Disagreement, Disagreement Estimate, and Non-Empathetic Imputations for Intimacy Groups Varying from Favorite Date to Married," *American Sociological Review* 19 (Feb. 1954), pp. 10-19.

[27] Annabelle B. Motz, "Conceptions of Marital Roles by Status Groups," *Marriage and Family Living* 12 (Fall 1950), pp. 136, 162. See also Alver H. Jacobson, "Conflict of Attitudes Toward the Roles of the Husband and Wife in Marriage," *American Sociological Review* 17 (April 1952), pp. 146-50; Carl J. Couch, "The Use of the Concept 'Role' and Its Derivatives in a Study of Marriage," *Marriage and Family Living* 20 (Nov. 1958), pp. 353-7; Theodore Johannis, Jr., "Roles of Family Members," in Iowa State University Center for Agricultural and Economic Development, *Family Mobility in Our Dynamic Society*, Ames, Iowa: Iowa State University Press, 1965, pp. 69-79; William F. Kenkel and

A TYPOLOGY OF MARITAL ROLES FOR WOMEN

As we turn from the marital role expectations held by the young, and the expectations held by the newly married, to the continuing ways in which husbands and wives relate to one another, the situation becomes infinitely more complicated. One way to look at the situation is to conceptualize role patterns that are provided by the society for wives. Kirkpatrick specifies three general roles for married women, each role carrying certain privileges and certain obligations.[28]

The wife-mother role is the traditional role of the married woman in Western society, the kind of role that one associates, perhaps, with one's mother and one's grandmother. Child-rearing is important in it and maternal qualities are to be found in the relationship with the husband as well as in the relationship with children. The wife's interests are expected to center in the home, she is supposed to yield her own interests in favor of her husband's, and especially to defer to the requirements of his job. In return, the wife is entitled to gentle affection and respect from husband and children, she has limited authority within the home, and she has security. She may not be abused or divorced without grave cause. In the event of divorce, she should be entitled to alimony.

The companion role, Kirkpatrick describes as being essentially a leisure-class phenomenon. It emphasizes continuation of the romantic relationship with the husband and the sharing of pleasure between the pair. The wife is both entitled and required to be well dressed, well groomed, and sexually attractive. She spends her free time in leisure and educational activity but has, as a primary responsibility, the cultivation of social contacts advantageous to her husband. She receives a maximum of chivalrous attention but her security depends upon her maintaining her attractiveness and upon the social, personal, and sexual gratifications she provides to her husband.

The third culturally prescribed role is that of the partner. Here the emphasis is upon the sharing of economic support of the family by the husband and wife. This newest of the three roles assumes that the wife works outside the home for pay. In consequence, she has financial independence and is entitled to acceptance by her husband as an equal, to have equal authority in the home, and to be exempt from one-sided domestic service to the husband. A

Dean K. Hoffman, "Real and Conceived Roles in Family Decision Making," *Marriage and Family Living* 18 (Nov. 1956), pp. 311–16; and Eugene A. Wilkening and Denton E. Morrison, "A Comparison of Husband and Wife Responses Concerning Who Makes Farm and Home Decisions," *Marriage and Family Living* 25 (Aug. 1963), pp. 349–51.

[28] Clifford Kirkpatrick, *The Family: As Process and Institution*, New York: The Ronald Press Company, 1963, pp. 168–9.

single standard of social and sexual behavior prevails. Wives, in this case, give up any claims to chivalrous attention from the husband and children. They do not depend upon their husbands for financial support and, in the event of divorce, they are not entitled to alimony or support.

It probably is obvious that these three conceptualizations are ideal types; they are polar conceptions that are useful as reference points against which to measure the roles which living women actually play in marriage. They are not meant to be actual descriptions of behavior.

One approach to the use of these ideal types is to regard them as providing alternatives among which women—with the aid and influence of their husbands—choose as they enter marriage. And undoubtedly some freedom of choice exists. It is also possible that there are other choice points, as at the time when the last child enters school, when the husband receives a major promotion, when the last child marries, and so on. Undoubtedly some husbands and wives exercise a good bit of conscious choice in marital roles as the years go by. Given the inevitability also of some cultural determination of behavior, including choices, it appears likely that there may be certain common, if not typical, patterns that couples tend to fall into. There may even be common sequences that occur at different stages in life.

EARLY MARRIAGE ROLES

It is the author's impression that a very large proportion of young couples begin married life with the wife playing a very mixed role—a combination, perhaps, of the wife-partner-companion roles. The companion aspects of the role were described in the chapter on marital adjustment and center around the sex and affectional relationship between the couple. Although precise statistics are not available, it is also known that a large percentage of young married women work for pay. In spite of the difficulty of having to adjust quickly in so many areas, many of these young relationships have a good deal going for them. Both the husband and wife are preoccupied with their sexual and romantic relationship and receive great satisfaction from it. In addition, they are often relatively well off financially. Even though the husband's income may be lower than it will be later on, the two incomes afford a good standard of living, providing the opportunity to acquire possessions, to indulge in leisure pursuits, and even to save.

The partner aspects of the role may be less threatening to the husband than they would be at other times in the marriage because they are defined as temporary and because they permit the husband apparently to live up to his equalitarian ideals. Frequently there is some agreement that the wife will work until a specified goal is attained: until debts are paid off, a new car is purchased, a down payment on a home secured, and so on. The wife's income, or a large portion of it, may be saved while the husband's income is used for living expenses, and neither spouse conceives of the wife as a breadwinner.

There are, however, certain factors making for instability and strain in this situation. The companionship aspects of the role are threatened from two sources. First of these is the wife's tendency to become less interested in the sex relationship. Data in the last chapter have already shown that, after an initial adjustment period, most wives desire sex less frequently than their husbands do. As their wives tend to withdraw somewhat from this aspect of the relationship, husbands fairly typically react with anger, hurt, and withdrawal also.

Husbands, too, contribute to the deterioration of the companionship part of the role. The norms of the larger society, and of the masculine subculture in particular, encourage men to invest themselves wholeheartedly in their occupational roles—even at the expense of their marital roles. Young wives, who formed expectations for marital roles on the basis of courtship behavior, understandably are bewildered and hurt by their husbands' apparent loss of interest in them. This may reinforce their loss of interest in being approached sexually by their husbands.

In some instances, there probably is some threat, too, from the wife's performance of the partner role. Young women, trained in independence, may assert themselves against their husbands' control of all of the family income. Even if the wife is very careful to avoid this, any feelings of personal inadequacy that the husband has may be aggravated by the paycheck which she brings home each week.

Fundamental alteration of the wife-companion-partner role probably is accomplished in the majority of cases by the fact of the wife's bearing a child. Nearly half of all couples produce a child during the first year, and almost nine out of ten ultimately bear a child. Wives ordinarily quit their jobs during pregnancy and, toward the latter stage at least, the sex relationship is interfered with further. We also saw in the last chapter that the frequency of sexual intercourse tends to remain lower after the birth of the child.

THE TRADITIONAL WIFE-MOTHER ROLE

The demands of parenthood and of the husband's occupation tend to take precedence over romance and most wives fall into a rather traditional wife-mother role. How conscious most husbands are of dissatisfaction over this turn of events is impossible to say. Some minor resentment may be common but satisfactions on the job and in parenthood provide substitutes. Similarly, and more drastically, wives are likely to bestow the tender emotions, to which their husbands are not completely receptive, upon the child or children.

With the passage of time many couples tend to take on parental roles, not only with their children but also with one another. Husbands bestow a gentler affection and respect upon their wives and wives defer to and take security in their husbands, almost as they once did in their fathers. This subtle shift in roles is well illustrated by the practice of husbands coming to call their wives by terms such as "mother," "mom," and "momma," and wives referring to their husbands as "father," "dad," or "poppa." It is natural enough, of course, for parents to aid their children in assuming the proper roles toward the parents by using these forms of address, but the point is that there is often more to it than this. Without being aware of it, the spouses actually assume childlike nurturant and succorant roles toward one another.

Many people apparently find considerable and lasting satisfaction in these quasi-parental marital roles. There probably is a certain comfort in no longer having to be virile and aggressive or attractive and seductive. Moreover, the couple now enact roles part of which they knew, from a different vantage point, in their own childhood. Whatever nostalgia attached to those aspects of childhood now attaches to the marriage relationship.

It seems plausible that many couples live out most of their lives in this situation. Judging from the data reported in the first section of this chapter, there probably is a gradual trend toward emotional withdrawal that accompanies aging. There should be, according to this logic, a tendency for relationships between the pair to become increasingly hierarchically structured also. The husband as "father" should become more dominant and the wife as "mother" should control her children but defer to her husband.

A whole series of studies has provided data that bear upon this point and which show the situation to vary with the occupational status of the husband and with age. White-collar workers consistently have more power over their wives than do blue-collar workers, and the husband's power increases directly with his income (see Figure 2). That income and the power that is associated with affluence is a crucial variable is suggested by the fact that husbands in native-born American families have more power than husbands in foreign-born families. In spite of the patriarchal traditions of many European nations, husbands in immigrant families often are of relatively low economic status and have less power than husbands in native-born families who give lip service

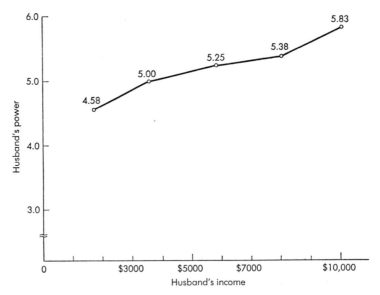

FIGURE 2. *Husband's mean power by income, Detroit area couples.*

Source: Robert O. Blood, Jr. and Donald M. Wolfe, *Husbands and Wives: The Dynamics of Married Living,* The Free Press of Glencoe, Illinois, 1960, p. 31.

to equalitarian standards.   As might be expected, Negro husbands have less power than white husbands.[29]

Figure 3 presents data on the husband's power by stage of the family life cycle and by whether or not the couple has children. The most striking fact

[29] Nicholas Babchuk and Alan P. Bates, "The Primary Relations of Middle-Class Couples: A Study in Male Dominance," *American Sociological Review* 28 (June 1963), pp. 377–84; Robert O. Blood, Jr., and Donald M. Wolfe, "Negro-White Differences in Blue-Collar Marriages in a Northern Metropolis," *Social Forces* 48 (Sept. 1969), pp. 59–64; Richard Centers, Bertram H. Raven, and Aroldo Rodrigues, "Conjugal Power Structure: A Re-examination," *American Sociological Review* 36 (April 1971), pp. 264–78; David M. Heer, "The Measurement and Bases of Family Power: An Overview," *Marriage and Family Living* 25 (May 1963), pp. 133–9; Clinton E. Phillips, "Measuring Power of Spouse," *Sociology and Social Research* 52 (Oct. 1967), pp. 35–49.

Another series of studies has provided data on comparisons between the United States and other countries. See Michel Andrée, "Comparative Data Concerning the Interaction in French and American Families," *Journal of Marriage and the Family* 29 (May 1966), pp. 337–44; Eugen Lupri, "Contemporary Authority Patterns in the West German Family: A Study in Cross-National Validation," *Journal of Marriage and the Family* 31 (Feb. 1969), pp. 134–44; Hyman Rodman, "Marital Power in France, Greece, Yugoslavia, and the United States: A Cross-National Discussion," *Journal of Marriage and the Family* 29 (May 1967), pp. 320–24; and Constantina Safilios-Rothschild, "The Study of Family Power Structure: A Review 1960–1969," *Journal of Marriage and the Family* 32 (Nov. 1970), pp. 539–52.

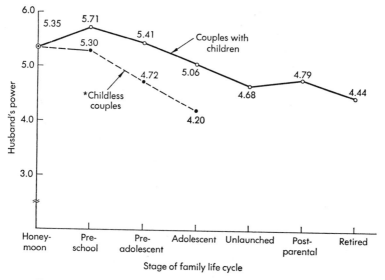

FIGURE 3. *Husband's power by stage in family life cycle, Detroit area couples.*

* Data for childless couples were tabulated separately by equivalent length of marriage through 22 years of marriage. After 22 years, data on the childless couples are merged with those on the childbearing couples for the remaining stages of the family life cycle.

Source: Robert O. Blood, Jr. and Donald M. Wolfe, *Husbands and Wives: The Dynamics of Married Living*, The Free Press of Glencoe, Illinois, 1960, p. 42.

is that wives in childless families have relatively more power, during the first 22 years of marriage at least, than do wives with children. Undoubtedly this is linked to the fact that childless wives are more likely to continue working and have relatively greater economic power than do wives with children. Blood and Wolfe state that "the continued participation of the wife in the occupational world accelerates her own maturity toward decision-making resourcefulness. So the childless wife's need for one-sided dependence is less and her skill in independent decision-making greater." [30]

Among couples with children, the process of becoming a mother appears

[30] Blood and Wolfe, *Husbands and Wives*, op. cit., p. 42. See also Robert O. Blood, Jr., and Robert L. Hamblin, "The Effect of the Wife's Employment on the Family Power Structure," *Social Forces* 36 (May 1958), pp. 347–52; David M. Heer, "Dominance and the Working Wife," in F. Ivan Nye and Lois W. Hoffman, eds., *The Employed Mother in America*, Chicago: Rand McNally and Company, 1963, pp. 251–62. A provocative and rigorous study by Hoffman suggests that the wife's employment may lead to more dominance by the husband in marriages where both spouses are ideologically committed to male dominance. See Lois W. Hoffman, "Effects of the Employment of Mothers on Parental Power Relations and the Division of Household Tasks," *Marriage and Family Living* 22 (Feb. 1960), pp. 27–35.

to increase the wife's dependence upon her husband. As the children grow older, the wife's dependence upon her husband gradually lessens. The slight increase in the husband's power after the children are grown and before retirement is difficult to interpret but may be related to insecurity on the part of the wife in response to the husband's rapid aging and the specter of his imminent death. It will be recalled from our earlier discussion of the family life cycle that the longevity of wives is greater than that of husbands. The subsequent drop in the husband's power with retirement undoubtedly is linked with his loss of earning capacity.

Although many couples may live out their lives comfortably in quasi-parental roles, one of the great changes in American family life in the twentieth century may center on the inadequacy of this life pattern for growing numbers of couples. Two generations ago many people literally were "old" by the age of 40 and were quite content with their "mama" and "papa" roles. Now, however, apparent youth and vitality often are sustained through the fifties and even beyond. Marriages must last through a much longer period in which husbands and wives may seek the emotional gratifications associated with youth and young adulthood.

One prevalent sign of dissatisfaction with these traditional roles probably is to be found in the development of extramarital affairs by middle-class persons roughly between the ages of 30 and 50. The development of affairs by persons at these ages cannot be explained in terms of absolute sexual deprivation, for all of the evidence points to less biological sex need and less sex capacity after the early twenties. What may happen is that the incipient marital dissatisfaction experienced by husbands and wives as they move into parenthood becomes focused either in growing personal unhappiness, the availability of a partner for an affair, or in some combination of the two. Even persons to whom illicit relationships are anathema may succumb to their yearnings to recapture the intensity of premarriage and early married relationships. Current societal definitions of extramarital affairs in terms of immorality tend to obscure the meanings that such relationships have for marriages and in the lives of the persons involved.

We do not know, of course, what proportion of couples live out their lives in quasi-parental roles or what proportion of marriages end in separation or divorce as a function of frustration encountered in connection with those roles. It does appear that the growing employment of married women after their children have reached school age and after they have left home is bringing about some shifts in marital roles for the couples involved. A growing number of women are moving into what might be called a wife-mother-partner role.

WORKING WIVES AND MOTHERS

The percentage of married women living with their husbands and working outside the home has been increasing irregularly for the last 30 years. In 1940, the percentage was only 15 per cent. By the end of World War II, the figure was approximately 20 per cent, and, by 1960, it had climbed to 31 per cent. Since 1960, the percentage has fluctuated upward, reaching a high of 41 per cent in 1970.

The distribution of working married women by age is shown in Table 4.

TABLE 4. *Per Cent of Married Women in the Labor Force, by Age, 1970.*

AGE	PER CENT
16 to 19 years	36.0
20 to 24 years	47.4
25 to 34 years	39.3
35 to 44 years	47.2
45 to 64 years	44.1
65 years and over	7.9

Source: Adapted from U. S. Bureau of the Census, *Statistical Abstract of the United States: 1971*, Washington, D. C., p. 213.

Although the association of age with length of time married is far from perfect, the table clearly shows that the percentage of married women who work drops off in the early child-rearing years and then climbs to its highest level as the children grow older and leave the home. Over 40 per cent of married women between the ages of 35 and 65 years of age work outside the home.[31] Reference back to Figure 3 will also show that the power which the husband exercises over the wife tends to decline during these years.

Effects of the Wife's Employment upon Marital Adjustment. Several studies have sought to determine directly the effects of the wife's employment on marital adjustment. Blood, reanalyzing data from the Detroit Area Study, concluded that employment of the wife decreases her housekeeping duties and increases the husband's sharing in those duties. In a sizable number of

[31] A national survey based upon a careful probability sample confirmed these statistics. In the survey, working mothers, as compared to nonworking mothers, were more likely to be between 35 and 49 years of age, not to have children of preschool age, and to have higher family incomes. See Sheila Feld, "Feelings of Adjustment," in F. Ivan Nye and Lois W. Hoffman, eds., op. cit. pp. 331-51.

families, this produces conflict over marital roles. Working wives from low-income families tended to report more marital satisfaction than did nonworking wives. Where the husband's income was $5000 or more, however, the reverse was true; the working wives reported less marital satisfaction.[32] Blood was not able to take into account the husband's reaction to his wife's employment.

Nye collected data from 1993 mothers in the state of Washington and found that there was much more conflict in marriages where mothers were employed. Not only did the mothers report more conflict with their husbands, but adolescent children of the mothers verified their mothers' reports. Some of Nye's data are summarized in Table 5. Whether the criterion of conflict was the frequency of quarreling, having separated one or more times, or having considered the possibility of divorce, the working mothers showed up the poorest in every case.

In a suburb of Washington, D. C., a six-year-old child was surprised to find that his playmate's mother was at home one noon, preparing lunch. The six-year-old piped up: "What's the matter with your mother? Can't she work?"

Of all the social verities that have recently been called into question, none has crumbled quite so rapidly as the belief that a woman's place is in the home—full time. Today a record of 43% of all U. S. women—32 million strong—are in the nation's labor force. . . . They now constitute 37.5% of the work force and more are streaming into the job market every day. . . .

The most dramatic change has occurred among married women. Only 30% of them were in the nation's work force a decade ago; today, more than 40% of them are. The new trend is partly due to male willingness; one recent survey showed that half the men questioned would not object if their wives took a job. . . .

An increasing number of them have abandoned the notion that children need a full-time mother. Just under 50% of all U. S. women who have school-age children also hold down jobs; so do 30% of women who have children under six years of age.

. . . the rise of working women is caused at least as much by their desire for respect as for cold cash. If the trend to working mothers seems uncaring and unwise, defenders of it point out that a second paycheck often allows fathers to spend more time with their children.

---

[32] Robert O. Blood, "The Husband-Wife Relationship," in F. Ivan Nye and Lois W. Hoffman, eds., op. cit. pp. 282–305. See also Robert N. Whitehurst and Edward Z. Dager, "The Lower-Class Working Mother: Some Findings from a Small Sample Comparison Study," paper presented to National Council on Family Relations, Toronto, October 1965.

Not only is Dad freed of some pressure to work overtime and struggle for promotion, but he also feels an obligation to get home and help mother with the chores.

—Reprinted by permission from *Time*, The Weekly Newsmagazine; copyright Time, Inc., 1971.

Nye's findings contradict Blood's findings concerning variations in marital adjustment by socio-economic status. Nye found that any adverse effect of maternal employment on marital adjustment is less among higher socio-economic groups than among lower socio-economic groups. The difference almost disappeared among the higher income and educational groups. Nye also found that dissatisfaction with the wife's employment by either the husband or the wife was associated with poor marital adjustment. He cautions that a husband's dissatisfaction may be either a cause of poor marital adjust-

TABLE 5. *Employment Status of Mother and Various Criteria of Marital Adjustment.*

CRITERIA OF MARITAL ADJUSTMENT [1]	NOT EMPLOYED (N=400)		EMPLOYED (N=199)	
	Number	Per Cent	Number	Per Cent
Conflict				
Argued	183	45.8	103	51.6
Quarreled *	30	7.6	26	13.4
Permanence				
Lived apart *	46	11.6	33	16.7
Considered divorce *	178	46.6	133	60.1
Happiness				
"Was unhappy"	80	20.7	52	26.8
Satisfaction				
"Was dissatisfied"	110	28.9	56	28.3

[1] Categories are as follows.
  Arguing: sometimes or oftener in at least four areas
  Quarreling: fairly often or more frequently
  Lived apart: one or more times following a quarrel
  Considered divorce: all responses except never
  Happiness: partly unhappy, unhappy, and very unhappy
  Satisfaction: partly or less satisfied.
* Indicates statistical significance.
Source: F. Ivan Nye, "Marital Interaction," in F. Ivan Nye and Lois W. Hoffman, eds., *The Employed Mother in America*, Chicago: Rand McNally and Company, 1963, p. 268.

ment or a result of the poorer marital adjustment produced by the wife's working. [33]

Feld, analyzing data from 438 wives who were part of a national sample, generally confirmed Nye's findings. She discovered that, with educational level and family income controlled, working mothers show more marital unhappiness than do their housewife counterparts. She, too, points out that it is impossible to determine the direction of cause and effect from these data. The tendency to unhappiness may result in the wife's seeking employment, or the fact of her employment may lead to problems in the marital relationship. [34]

Effects of Working Mothers Upon Children. The connection between maternal employment and problems of marital adjustment undoubtedly has contributed to widespread public awareness of working mothers as a social problem. Perhaps as important in the public mind, however, is a series of alleged connections between maternal employment and undesirable effects upon the children. It has been variously claimed that the children of working mothers are more likely to become delinquent, that they are more anxious, more prone to antisocial behavior, more likely to make a poor adjustment in school, and so on. Fortunately, a growing body of research permits us to put many such generalizations to the test of empirical evidence.

The research on the effects of maternal employment upon children has been ably summarized by Hoffman, who points out that research does not support the assumption of general meaningful differences between the children of working and nonworking mothers. Scattered pieces of research have reported significant differences, but these probably are due to chance because they are so few among the many tests made and because they have not been verified in repeat studies. [35] Hoffman cautions against interpreting this lack of general associations to mean that maternal employment has no effects at all,

[33] F. Ivan Nye, "Marital Interaction," in F. Ivan Nye and Lois W. Hoffman, eds., op. cit. pp. 263–81.

[34] Op. cit. See also Leland J. Axelson, "The Marital Adjustment and Marital Role Definitions of Husbands of Working and Nonworking Wives," *Marriage and Family Living* 25 (May 1963), pp. 189–95; Artie Gianopulos and Howard E. Mitchell, "Marital Disagreement in Working Wife Marriages as a Function of Husband's Attitude Toward Wife's Employment," *Marriage and Family Living* 19 (Nov. 1957), pp. 373–8; David A. Gover, "Socio-Economic Differential in the Relationship Between Marital Adjustment and Wife's Employment Status," *Marriage and Family Living* 25 (Nov. 1963), pp. 452–8; Harvey J. Locke and Muriel Mackeprang, "Marital Adjustment and the Employed Wife," *American Journal of Sociology* 54 (May 1949), pp. 536–8; and Robert C. Williamson, "Socio-Economic Factors and Marital Adjustment in an Urban Setting," *American Sociological Review* 19 (April 1954), pp. 213–16.

[35] Lois W. Hoffman, "Effects on Children: Summary and Discussion," in F. Ivan Nye and Lois W. Hoffman, eds., op. cit. pp. 190–212.

however. She argues, instead, that only research that imposes careful controls will reveal what relationships actually exist.

The concept of maternal employment, Hoffman states, is too broad a variable to be used without the imposition of controls. She summarizes studies that have imposed controls by social class, by full-time versus part-time employment, by age of child, by sex of child, and by the mother's attitude toward her employment.

Three studies provide some evidence that there is a relationship between maternal employment and juvenile delinquency among middle-class youth but not among lower-class youth. Using a delinquency scale, Nye found that the children of working mothers were more likely to be delinquent than were the children of nonworking mothers. Nye's sample was predominately middle-class, however, and when the findings were controlled by class they were found to hold only for the middle-class respondents.[36] Glueck and Glueck, using contact with the police as the criterion of delinquency and studying only lower-class youth, found no relationship between full-time employment of the mother and delinquency.[37] In a third study, Gold compared the children of blue-collar and white-collar families and found a relationship between maternal employment and delinquency only within the white-collar group.[38]

These statistical correlations do not answer, of course, the question of why maternal employment is related to delinquency in the middle class and not in the lower class. Perhaps the nature and conditions of maternal employment are different in the two classes. Perhaps the effects upon family structure are different. It remains for future research to tell.

Research generally supports the position that part-time employment has a favorable effect upon the adjustment of adolescent children. Three separate studies have found such an association.[39] It appears likely that the factors leading the mothers of adolescents into part-time employment are quite dif-

[36] F. Ivan Nye, "The Adjustment of Adolescent Children," in F. Ivan Nye and Lois W. Hoffman, op. cit. pp. 133–41.

[37] Sheldon Glueck and Eleanor Glueck, "Working Mothers and Delinquency," *Mental Hygiene* 41 (July 1957), pp. 327–52.

[38] M. Gold, *A Social-Psychology of Delinquent Boys*, Ann Arbor, Michigan: Institute for Social Research, 1961.

[39] Elizabeth Douvan, "Employment and the Adolescent," in F. Ivan Nye and Lois W. Hoffman, op. cit. pp. 142–64; F. Ivan Nye, "Adolescent-Parent Adjustment: Age, Sex, Sibling Number, Broken Homes, and Employed Mothers as Variables," *Marriage and Family Living* 14 (Nov. 1952), pp. 327–32; F. Ivan Nye, "The Adjustment of Adolescent Children," op. cit. See also Evan T. Peterson, "The Impact of Maternal Employment on the Mother-Daughter Relationship," *Marriage and Family Living* 23 (Nov. 1961), pp. 355–61; and Prodipto Roy, "Maternal Employment and Adolescent Roles: Rural-Urban Differentials," *Marriage and Family Living* 23 (Nov. 1961), pp. 340–49.

ferent from those leading the mothers of younger children into full-time employment. Whereas the latter group are likely to be of lower socio-economic status and under considerable pressure to work to help support their families, the former group are much more likely to work as a matter of choice. Women who work by choice, who still have time for the accomplishment of their household duties, and who are not under financial pressure may be more likely both to derive satisfaction from their work and to compensate for working by presenting a positive role model to their children. The part-time employment presents less of a threat to the husband and father than full-time employment would and, yet, the status of the mother is raised. Such mothers, since they have outside interests, may be more likely also to grant to adolescents the increasing freedom which they need.

Long-established belief has it that it is especially detrimental for mothers to work while their children are very young. There is also some evidence that the lot of working mothers of young children is harder; they are more likely to be under financial pressure and their children require a good deal of physical care and supervision. By and large, however, research to date has failed to support the idea of adverse effects of maternal employment upon young children.[40] Few significant differences have been found. Maternal employment during the child's preschool years appears to have no observable effects at later ages, and the mother's work history appears to make little difference; no effects have been found to be related to whether the mother works continuously or only intermittently. Whether the expectations that people hold concerning the effects of maternal employment upon young children simply are wrong or whether research simply has not uncovered such effects cannot be said for sure.

Logically, the effects of maternal employment might be different for boys than for girls and evidence generally indicates that this is so. A series of studies has shown that girls' concepts of themselves and their concepts of appropriate female roles differ when their mothers work. The daughters of working mothers have been shown to make fewer differentiations between the household tasks deemed appropriate for men and women to perform, to see women as less restricted to their homes, and to be more favorable to the employment of women. Such girls are also more likely to wish to work themselves when

[40] Lee G. Burchinal, "Personality Characteristics of Children," in F. Ivan Nye and Lois W. Hoffman, op. cit. pp. 106–21; and from the same source: F. Ivan Nye, Joseph B. Perry, Jr., and Richard H. Ogles, "Anxiety and Anti-Social Behavior in Preschool Children," pp. 82–94; Kathryn S. Powell, "Personalities of Children and Child-Rearing Attitudes of Mothers," pp. 125–32; and Alberta E. Siegel, Lois M. Stolz, Ethel A. Hitchcock, and Jean Adamson, "Dependence and Independence in Children," pp. 67–81.

they are older and have children.[41] Hoffman concludes that working mothers provide role models which their daughters are likely to admire and to emulate.

The effects of maternal employment upon the personality development of sons are less clear. Although there is some pattern in the findings obtained, the results generally have not achieved statistical significance. For this reason, the following should be considered more to represent hypotheses than to constitute definite findings. One study, by Douvan, indicates that lower-class boys of working mothers are least likely to name their fathers as the persons they most admire.[42] Since lower-class men are least able to support their families without their wives' assistance, the sons' low estimates of their fathers may stem from the perceived general inadequacy of the fathers rather than from any direct effects of the mothers' employment. Both the mothers' employment and the sons' negative evaluations of their fathers may reflect general lower-class conditions of life.

A second study yielded statistically nonsignificant but consistent findings to the effect that the young sons of working mothers were more dependent and obedient, were less self-reliant and less sociable, and were more likely to seek succorance from adults.[43] Hoffman also found that the sons of working mothers are more dependent upon their teachers,[44] and data from a study by Rouman suggest that the sons of working mothers are more likely to be sent for counseling for withdrawal problems than for any other kind of problem.   Until further research modifies it, a tenable hypothesis appears to be that maternal employment is associated with adequate self-concepts and less traditional femininity among girls and with dependency, lack of aggression, and low achievement among boys.

Finally, the mother's attitude toward her employment appears to be an important variable. Two studies show that when the mother is satisfied with her employment, the relationship between her and her children is likely to be warm and satisfying. There is even some suggestion that mothers in this category may overindulge their children because they feel a little guilty about working. Among mothers who are dissatisfied with their employment, rela-

[41] Elizabeth M. Almquist and Shirley S. Angrist, "Role Model Influences on College Women's Career Aspirations," *Merrill-Palmer Quarterly* 17 (July 1971), pp. 263–79.

[42] Elizabeth Douvan, op. cit. See also, Karl King, Jennie McIntyre, and Leland J. Axelson, "Adolescents' Views of Maternal Employment as a Threat to the Marital Relationship," *Journal of Marriage and the Family* 30 (Nov. 1968), pp. 633–7.

[43] Alberta E. Siegel, Lois M. Stolz, Ethel A. Hitchcock, and Jean Adamson, op. cit.

[44] Lois W. Hoffman, "Mother's Enjoyment of Work and Effects on the Child," in F. Ivan Nye and Lois W. Hoffman, op. cit. pp. 95–105.

[45] J. Rouman, "School Children's Problems as Related to Parental Factors," *Journal of Educational Research* 50 (Oct. 1956), pp. 105–12.

tionships with their children are less rewarding and the children are more likely to be burdened with too many household tasks.[46]

The New Feminists: Revolt Against Sexism

. . . Most middle-aged or older women take a skeptical if not down-right hostile view of the new movement, if they have heard of it at all. But younger women, part of a rebellious generation, are fertile grounds for the seeds of discontent. They are also having fewer babies, looking ahead to living longer, and thinking more about careers. A study of 10,000 Vassar alumnae showed that most graduates of the mid-'50s wanted marriage, with or without a career, while in the mid-60s most were insisting on a career, with or without marriage. . . .

—Reprinted by permission from *Time*, The Weekly Newsmagazine. Copyright © Time, Inc. 1969.

In summary, it may be repeated that research generally contradicts the idea of there being generally significant differences between the children of work-ing and nonworking mothers. Maternal employment operates in interaction with too many other variables to be studied alone. Scattered pieces of research that have utilized adequate controls indicate that there may be some relation-ships with juvenile delinquency at middle-class levels, that part-time maternal employment has a favorable effect upon the adjustment of adolescent chil-dren, and that the effects upon younger children may vary by sex. Any general conclusion to the effect that maternal employment is undesirable appears unwarranted.

Further Implications of the Partner Role. There seems to be little doubt but that the relationships between husbands and wives are different where the wives steadily work outside the home than where they stay in the traditional wife-mother role. Research shows us that working wives have more nearly equalitarian relationships with their husbands and that the division of labor, particularly in relation to household tasks, is not so sharp. In some instances, at least, the wife's working is associated with feelings of well-being on her part

---

[46] Elizabeth Douvan, op. cit., and Lois W. Hoffman, "Mother's Enjoyment of Work and Effects on the Child," op. cit. See also, Doris K. Katelman, and Larry D. Barnett, "Work Orientations of Urban, Middle-Class, Married Women," *Journal of Marriage and the Family* 30 (Feb. 1968), pp. 80–88; and Constantina Safilios-Rothschild, "The Influence of the Wife's Degree of Work Commitment Upon Some Aspects of Family Organization and Dynamics," *Journal of Marriage and the Family* 32 (Nov. 1970), pp. 681–91.

and with approval from husband and children. The historical trend in the United States certainly seems to be in this direction.

The full effects of this wifely role upon husband, children, and marital adjustment still are not known. The wife's working is only one of many factors influencing these relationships. The effect probably varies, too, with the nature of the wife's work and the degree of her identification with it.

The situation of middle-class wives who work at least partly in the search for personal fulfillment is quite different from that of lower-class wives who work out of dire necessity and whose jobs are more likely to be tedious and exhausting.

Within the past few years in the United States, there has been a resurgence of effort to provide women with equal occupational opportunities with men and to promote a redefinition of marital roles that would assign equal responsibility to husbands and wives for performance of household duties and child care.[47] The fact that the more shrill elements of the women's liberation movement have adopted the rhetoric of revolution and have sometimes appeared to be anti-men and anti-family should not be permitted to obscure the importance of the movement.

A women's equal rights amendment to the constitution is nearer to adoption than it has been for many decades, and serious efforts are being made by federal agencies to make redress for past de facto discrimination against women. Employers who receive federal funds are being required to show "affirmative action" in recruiting women into higher paying jobs of responsibility, in raising their salaries accordingly, and in granting them equal opportunities for promotion and advancement.

At this writing, it is too early to tell how widespread support for the women's liberation movement really is. Its core certainly exists among rather well-educated middle-class women who already are involved in professional work and who are especially sensitive to the subtle and not-so-subtle discrimination they encounter. Their efforts to align themselves politically with lower-class women and black women appear not to be very successful so far. Then there is the vast majority of American women who may share some of the ambivalence and disappointment of the women's lib group but who show little inclination to join the movement.

It seems likely that the continuing pressure in America toward a more

[47] Dean Knudsen, "The Declining Status of Women: Popular Myths and the Failure of Functionalist Thought," *Social Forces* 48 (Dec. 1969), pp. 183–93; Alice Rossi, "Women In Science: Why So Few?," in Bernard C. Rosen, Harry J. Crockett, and Clyde Z. Nunn, eds., *Achievement in American Society* (Cambridge: Schenkman, 1969), pp. 470–86; and Charles I. Schottland, "Government Economic Programs and Family Life, *Journal of Marriage and the Family* 29 (Feb. 1967), pp. 71–123.

democratic society will result in more women playing the partner role in the future. It appears likely, too, that there are special problems associated with that role.

Evidence presented in the last chapter suggested that these are likely to be marriages that produce fewer than the average number of children. Whatever the nature of the cause-and-effect relationship involved, such couples are less likely to have the bond of a continuing interest in children to buttress whatever else is between them.

There is impressionistic evidence also to suggest that many men and women tire of a continuing full-partner relationship. Women, as they grow older, may become nostalgic over the full joys of parenthood which they feel to have been denied them and they may come increasingly to doubt their femininity. Moreover, the same husbands who rationally admire their wives' accomplishments may long for the lost romance of youth and for the apparently warm and comfortable marriage relationships that they think they see enjoyed by men who have less talented wives. The phenomenon of the successful career woman cast aside by her husband for a less able but more dependent woman is far from unknown. Unfortunately, no data are available to indicate what proportions of full-partner marriages turn out in these various ways.

THE RE-EMERGENCE OF THE COMPANION ROLE?

The foregoing discussion almost makes it appear that the romantic, erotic, and companionship aspects of man-woman roles disappear with marriage, never to be recovered. And, as the data have shown, there is some truth to this. The frequency with which couples have sexual intercourse declines steadily with increasing age, wives report steadily declining satisfaction with the companionship they have with their husbands, and the impact of parenthood usually is such as to de-emphasize romantic companionship in favor of the more placid relationships of mother and father.

At the same time, certain trends in American society appear to be facilitating a new emphasis upon companionship aspects of the marital role.

Startling changes have been occurring in health, longevity, and the structure of the family life cycle. As recently as 40 years ago, many husbands and wives were physically old and tired before their children were grown. Now, by contrast, the parents of married children often appear nearly as young, energetic, and forward-looking as their offspring. Married people in their forties, fifties, and even sixties desire love, companionship, and sexual satisfaction.[48]

[48] Helena Z. Lopata, "The Life Cycle of the Social Role of the Housewife," *Sociology and Social Research* 51 (Oct. 1966), pp. 5–22.

Increasingly, couples appear to be searching for ways to prevent the disappearance of romance from their lives, or to recapture it once they sense that it has been lost. The ubiquitousness of baby-sitters and the emphasis upon parental recreation apart from the activities shared with children attest to what is happening here. As the children grow older, there is more time and more energy for spouses to invest in one another. Based again upon impressionistic evidence rather than upon hard data, we might hypothesize an emerging marital role for women that emphasizes companionship with the husband as the primary focus even through the child-bearing and child-rearing years. Most of these marriages produce children and in many cases the wives also work. Consequently what emerges is not simply a companionship role but a multifaceted one which might be designated a COMPANION-mother-partner role.[49]

Many apparent advantages accrue to women who can play such a role. First, they are likely to take full advantage of the increases in longevity and health to remain alert to and interested in the full world around them. In a literal sense, they remain young, attractive, and interesting people. At the same time, they escape the disadvantage inherent in playing a simple companionship role, that disadvantage being that ultimately youth and charm must fade. Men who have—and who value—only romantic companionship with their wives must eventually find that their wives compare unfavorably with younger women. The case of such wives being replaced in their husbands' affections, if not in actual matrimony, is well known. But wives whose relationships with their husbands are buttressed by common identification with the lives of their children are likely to be much more secure. Wives who combine romantic companionship with parenthood—and perhaps with employment—may have the best of all possible worlds.

It must be acknowledged, however, that there are problems here, too. First of all, such a multifaceted role may be too demanding for many women. Few

---

[49] For some provocative articles bearing directly or indirectly upon this theme, see Laurence L. Falk, "Occupational Satisfaction of Female College Graduates," *Journal of Marriage and the Family* 28 (May 1966), pp. 177–85; Nelson N. Foote, "New Roles for Men and Women," *Marriage and Family Living* 23 (Nov. 1961), pp. 325–9; Kenneth Kammeyer, "The Feminine Role: An Analysis of Attitude Consistency," *Journal of Marriage and the Family* 26 (Aug. 1964), pp. 295–305; Norman Kiell and Bernice Friedman, "Culture Lag and Housewifemanship: The Role of the Married Female College Graduate," *Journal of Educational Sociology* 31 (Oct. 1957), pp. 87–95; George C. Myers, "Labor Force Participation of Suburban Mothers," *Journal of Marriage and the Family* 26 (Aug. 1964), pp. 306–11; Mildred W. Weil, "An Analysis of the Factors Influencing Married Women's Actual or Planned Work Participation," *American Sociological Review* 26 (Feb. 1961), pp. 91–6; and Robert S. Weiss and Nancy M. Samelson, "Social Roles of American Women: Their Contribution to a Sense of Usefulness and Importance," *Marriage and Family Living* 20 (Nov. 1958), pp. 358–66.

would dispute that any one of the three aspects of this role is demanding enough to occupy most women. Perhaps it is too much to ask of women that they be all things to their husbands. Secondly, there is a possibility that the maternal aspect of this combination role may suffer. Popular belief has it that the traditional wife-mother role, even if it involved suffering for the husband, was good for the children. If wives increasingly insist upon dividing their attentions between husband and children, there is at least the theoretical possibility that the children may suffer. Unfortunately, there are no data that bear directly upon this question. The most relevant data—those relating to working mothers—have been summarized earlier.

THE CHALLENGE OF THE FUTURE

The phrase "marriage in the middle years" has new meaning today. The steady deterioration of marital relationships which research has shown to be characteristic up to now is out of harmony with the facts of twentieth-century existence. Most people do not enter old age before their child-rearing duties are ended. Instead, they may have some 20 years of fairly vigorous adulthood ahead of them. What this means, as far as marital roles are concerned, is that the settling down into marriage that may have been appropriate a generation or two ago is appropriate no longer.

Marriage today requires flexibility in roles and change over the family life cycle. There is no assurance that the pattern of adjustment achieved during the pre-child-bearing years will work equally well a few years later. Neither is there assurance that the kind of adjustment arrived at during the child-bearing years will sustain couples through child-rearing and beyond. Marital roles increasingly are becoming multidimensional, with the emphasis on the various dimensions shifting with the passage of time.[50]

Both men and women appear to be more demanding today in what they expect of marriage. They will not be denied the romance of youth, the satisfactions of parenthood, the challenge of work achievement, or the contentment of secure marital relationships. Marriage, too, is more demanding. It is expecting much for two people to remain in love and to be friends for as long as 40 or 50 years. In no other area do we expect so much of human relationships.

SUMMARY

This chapter focuses upon marital adjustment and changes in marital adjustment as couples move from the child-bearing through the child-rearing

[50] Shirley S. Angrist, "Role Constellation as a Variable in Women's Leisure Activities," *Social Forces* 45 (March 1967), p. 423.

years, and even beyond. Marital adjustment is seen as a process rather than as a state, and the events of 5, 10, and 20 years after the marriage ceremony are seen as changing it significantly. It is useful to conceptualize marriage as a set of mutually contingent careers in which couples may grow closer together or move farther apart.

Both longitudinal and cross-sectional studies of marital adjustment show that there is a tendency for couples to grow farther apart with the passage of time. There is a gradual drop in marital adjustment scores, in marital satisfaction, in the frequency of sexual intercourse, and in the adequacy of marital communication. Nor are these changes simply a function of aging, for there is no comparable drop in personal adjustment scores. What happens to many marriages may be conceptualized as a process of disenchantment in which the "goodness of fit" that prevailed between the couple at the time of marriage gradually is lost. Not all marriages suffer this fate, however. A smaller percentage of marriages appears to improve in communication and empathy as time goes by.

Middle-class couples probably are most self-conscious about the roles which men and women should play in marriage, but, to some degree, this is a problem which must be faced by all couples at all stages of the family life cycle. Research shows that marital roles are anticipated by adolescents and by young, unmarried adults, and that both sexes tend to endorse rather equalitarian norms.

Perhaps most young couples begin married life with the wife playing a mixed wife-partner-companion role to her husband. Romantic elements loom large in the relationship, and many young wives work outside the home. The husband's increasing preoccupation with his job and the wife's lesser sexual interest tend gradually to de-emphasize the companionship aspects of the relationship, but the factor which most often precipitates major change probably is pregnancy.

With the birth of the first child, many wives fall into the traditional wife-mother role and husbands also assume increasingly parental attitudes not only to their children but also to their spouses. Many couples live out most of the rest of their lives in this situation, some with obvious satisfaction and others with increasing unrest. Many extramarital affairs probably are to be interpreted as attempts to recapture some of the companionship aspects of preparental marital roles.

Research indicates that the middle years of marriage are likely to be accompanied by increasing dominance on the part of the husband and greater dependence on the part of the wife. These trends are most obvious where the husbands are occupationally most successful, in families where there are children, and vary somewhat erratically over the life cycle.

The proportion of wives who work outside the home has been increasing irregularly over the past 25 years. The percentage of working wives drops off somewhat during the early child-bearing years and then reaches a high point when the wives are between 35 and 65 years of age. Research shows that the gainful employment of wives is associated with the sharing of household tasks and conflict over marital roles.

Contrary to widespread belief, there appear to be few, if any, gross relationships between maternal employment and the adjustment of children. Carefully controlled studies have suggested that there may be a relationship between maternal employment and juvenile delinquency among middle-class children but not among lower-class children. There is some evidence, also, that part-time maternal employment is positively correlated with the adjustment of adolescent children.

Maternal employment appears to influence the self-concepts of both sons and daughters, but in different ways. The daughters of working mothers appear likely to develop adequate self-concepts, to make minimal distinctions between the household tasks deemed appropriate for men and women, and to anticipate employment themselves when they are older. The evidence concerning sons is less convincing but suggests that sons of working mothers have less admiration for their fathers, are more obedient, and less independent and self-reliant.

A most important variable appears to be the mother's attitude toward her employment. When she is satisfied, the relationship between her and her children is likely to be warm and rewarding. When she is dissatisfied, the relationship with her children suffers.

Even when wives work, most of them subordinate their occupational roles to their wifely roles and continue in some deference to their husbands. How many wives play a fully competitive role in the occupational system is unknown. Some do. And some such marriages appear to work out well for all concerned. Wives who elect to play a full economic-partner role in marriage often are denied the satisfactions of parenthood and run the risk of their husbands becoming interested in less talented but more domestic women.

Recent trends in American society have included greater emphasis upon maintaining the companionship aspects of marital roles. Greater longevity and longer apparent youthfulness encourage this trend. Wives who manage to combine parenthood with continuing companionship with their husbands appear to have a special advantage. This multifaceted role is a demanding one, however, and not all wives may be capable of managing it. What should be true of American marriage in the future is that it will require much more flexibility and much more virtuosity in marital roles than it did in the past.

SUGGESTED READINGS

Blood, Robert O., Jr., and Wolfe, Donald M., *Husbands and Wives: The Dynamics of Married Living*, The Free Press of Glencoe, Illinois, 1960. A report of research on the marriages of city and farm families in Wayne County, Michigan.

Epstein, Slyvia F., *Woman's Place: Options and Limits in Professional Careers*, Berkeley and Los Angeles: University of California Press, 1970. One of the best analyses of women's occupational roles in American society. Reasoned arguments supported by hard data.

Komarovsky, Mirra, *Blue-Collar Marriage*, New York: Random House, Inc., 1964. Comprehensive study of marital adjustment among 58 working-class couples.

Nye, F. Ivan, and Hoffman, Lois W., eds., *The Employed Mother in America*, Chicago: Rand McNally and Company, 1963. A comprehensive symposium summarizing recent research on working wives, the effects upon their children, upon their marriages, and upon the women themselves.

Reeves, Nancy, *Womankind: Beyond the Stereotypes*, Chicago: Aldine, 1971. Presents traditional images of women and shows their inadequacy in modern society. Textual analysis accompanied by a set of parallel readings.

Scanzoni, John H., *Opportunity and the Family*, New York: The Free Press, 1970. A research monograph that analyzes the relation between marital roles and integration of the family into the economic-opportunity structure.

Veroff, Joseph, and Feld, Sheila, *Marriage and Work in America: A Study of Motives and Roles*, New York: Van Nostrand Reinhold Company, 1970. Presents the results of research by two psychologists into the interrelationships between work roles and family roles. For the serious student.

FILMS

A Family Affair (International Film Bureau, 332 S. Michigan Ave., Chicago 01274), 30 minutes. The story of a middle-aged couple whose relationships are strained to the breaking point. Shows how the breaking up of a marriage can be averted with the help of a marriage counselor.

Children of Change (Affiliated Film Board, Inc., 164 E. 38th St., New York 10016), 31 minutes. Discusses the problem of working mothers and their children during the day, and the activities of these children in day-care centers. Reviews values of an effective day-care program for children.

Radcliffe Blues (American Documentary Films, 336 West 84th Street, New York 10024; or 379 Bay Street, San Francisco 94133), 23 minutes. A woman speaks on women's rights, alienation, and radicalization.

The New Prime of Life (Indiana University, Bloomington, Ind.), 12 minutes. Shows a white collar worker during two stages of his life: as a young ambitious junior executive, and 25 years later as an office manager. Illustrates how the man's values and outlook on life change with maturity. The man develops new interests and learns to adjust to the disappointments in life.

QUESTIONS AND PROJECTS

1. What is meant by the phrase, "marriage as a developmental process"? What are the implications for mate selection? How may marriage be conceived of as a set of mutually contingent careers?

2. What does research show about the trend of marital adjustment through the middle years? How does the term, disenchantment, describe what happens to most marriages? Are these changes a direct function of aging? How do you know? Do all couples decline in marital adjustment?

3. Are marital roles anticipated in adolescence and young adulthood? What expectations do people typically carry into marriage?

4. Define the "wife-mother," "partner," and "companion" roles as ideal types. How may they be used in the study of actual marital roles?

5. Describe the typical roles played in marriage by young couples. What forces operate to bring about change in these roles?

6. What roles do couples typically play during the child-bearing and early child-rearing years? What do we know about the satisfactions attendant upon playing such roles? Do these roles appear to provide lasting satisfaction for some couples?

7. Describe the power relationhips that typically obtain between husband and wife during the middle years. What influence does economic status have? What influence does child-bearing have?

8. What appear to be the major effects upon marital adjustment of the wife's working outside the home? What inferences, if any, can be made about cause and effect?

9. What does research show, in general, about the effects of maternal employment upon the adjustment of children? What findings have been yielded by studies imposing careful controls? Are all of the effects of maternal employment known?

10. Are there successful marriages where the wife plays a full economic-partner role? Are there any special hazards in such marriages? If so, what are they?

11. What factors in American society may be contributing to greater emphasis upon the companionship aspects of marital roles? What advantages inhere in combining a companionship role with parental roles? Are there any problems in such a combination role? If so, what are they?

12. Take a poll of the class. Determine what marital-role expectations the students hold. Are there differences by sex? Are there differences by the work experience of the students' mothers? Are your findings in accord with the data presented in this chapter?

18 | *Divorce and Desertion*

Pretending marriage is for life was fine when people died young and vigorous men could bury three wives and put nice gravestones over all of them. You also found the woman who, if she were vigorous, would bury three husbands. . . . But . . . today . . . people stay alive so long. I think the longer people live and the more diverse their experience, the less likely it is that two people will stay married a lifetime. You see, if people get married at 20, they then have a reasonable expectation of being married for 50 years. The contemplation of 50 years together makes people less willing to tolerate an unsatisfactory marriage.[1]

VIRTUALLY everyone has read statements to the effect that the United States has the highest divorce rate in the world. In that bald form the statement happens to be false but that doesn't stop it from being repeated and reprinted endlessly. Perhaps this is because the statement is more often intended to convey a feeling than to communicate a fact. The feeling, of course, is that divorce rates in the United States are so high as to threaten the existence of the family itself. Where divorce rates are concerned, most people seem to think unknowingly in terms of defunctionalization theory: if only we could go back to the family system of old, divorce rates would be lowered and the stability of the family would be enhanced. There is, however, the competing view espoused by functional theorists that high divorce rates are inevitable in modern society and that such high divorce rates are quite consistent with a basically stable family system. Our purpose in this chapter is not to address ourselves to this debate directly but to examine the available data to see what meaning may be attached to divorce and desertion in modern American society.

[1] Margaret Mead, "We Must Learn to See What's Really New," *Life Magazine* (Aug. 1968), p. 34. © Time, Inc. 1968.

INTERCULTURAL PERSPECTIVE ON DIVORCE

When people try to evaluate American divorce rates, they usually compare them with the divorce rates of other large nations, and certainly such comparisons are useful. It should not be forgotten, however, that most of the world's societies are small, preliterate ones and that they have something to teach us, too, about the range of family practices that is consistent with the over-all stability of the system.

As with other family practices, the most useful comparative data on divorce in preliterate societies have been assembled by George Murdock. He points out that all societies have institutionalized provisions for ending marriages as well as for establishing them in the first place, and that divorce rates in about 60 per cent of all preliterate societies are higher than those found in the contemporary United States.[2]

Nor is there any particular relationship between divorce rates in preliterate societies and other symptoms of social disorganization. High divorce rates can be, and are, associated with stable family systems where there are clear norms specifying what happens to husband, wife, and children after the divorce. In brief, it is generally provided that the husband and wife should be reabsorbed by their respective kin groups. The children continue to live with the lineage of which they are a part and do not suffer unduly from the separation of their parents.

Statements that the United States has the world's highest divorce rate generally have, as their referent, large nations. And it is true that the United States today has the highest divorce rate of any large nation. It has not always been this way (see Table 1). Japan, for example, had a higher divorce rate than did the United States up to 1920. High Japanese divorce rates were associated with a patriarchal, patrilineal, extended family system similar in many respects to that of traditional China. Divorce reflected the fact that the young bride was not satisfactory to her in-laws. The family system itself was quite stable and not until that system began to break down did divorce rates begin to fall. Japan's divorce rate today remains relatively high, but—opposite to the experience of the United States—the process of urbanization and a shift toward a conjugal family system have been associated with a falling divorce rate.

Historically, divorce rates have been high also in Moslem countries, where men were permitted to divorce their wives simply by saying three times, "I

---

[2] George P. Murdock, "Family Stability in Non-European Cultures," *Annals of the American Academy of Political and Social Science* 272 (Nov. 1950), p. 197.

TABLE 1. *Divorces per 1000 Marriages in Selected Countries,*
1900–1969.

COUNTRY	YEAR							
	1900	1910	1920	1930	1940	1950	1960	1969
U. S.	75.3	87.4	133.3	173.9	165.3	231.7	258	307.5
Germany	17.6	29.9	40.7	72.4	125.7	145.8	106.8	151.8*
England & Wales			8.0	11.1	16.5	86.1	68.	110.3**
Australia	13.6	12.4	20.4	41.2	41.6	97.3	87.9	100.9**
France	26.1	46.3	49.4	68.6	80.3	106.9	94.3	107.6*
Sweden	12.9	18.4	30.5	50.6	65.1	147.7	178.6	209.5**
Iran						194	211	173.7	101.3**
Egypt				269	273	273	228.7	222.6**
Japan	184	131	100	98	76	100	80.1	90.9
Algeria	352	288	396	286	292	161***	n.a.	n.a.

* figure is for 1967
** figure is for 1968
*** figure is for 1955

Source: Figures for 1900 through 1950 are from William J. Goode, "Family Disorganization," in Robert K. Merton and Robert Nisbet, eds., *Contemporary Social Problems,* New York: Harcourt, Brace, Jovanovich, Inc., 1971, p. 482. Figures for 1960 forward are calculated from *United Nations Demographic Yearbooks,* 16th Issue, 1965, and 21st Issue, 1970.

divorce thee." In 1900 the divorce rate in Algeria (the only Moslem country for which reliable data are available) was roughly four times as high as in the United States.[3] As in Japan, modernization in Algeria has been accompanied by falling divorce rates and, during the 1940's, Algeria's rate fell below that of the United States. Fragmentary data indicate that divorce rates in the less modern Moslem nations remain very high today.

In summary, divorce rates vary drastically from one society to another, and, in the same society, they may vary drastically over time. There is no necessary relationship between divorce rates and either family or societal stability; high divorce rates may reflect family breakdown or they may reflect societally prescribed ways of eliminating disruptive influences. In world perspective, the United States falls in the large group of societies having relatively high divorce rates. Striking increases in United States divorce rates have accompanied urbanization, industrialization, and the shift to a conjugal family system.

[3] William J. Goode, *World Revolution and Family Patterns,* New York: The Free Press of Glencoe, 1963, pp. 155–62.

The Divorce Rate in the United States

THE HISTORICAL TREND

The emergence of divorce in the American colonies was described in Chapter 7. It will be remembered that the attitude toward divorce was more liberal in New England than in the southern colonies, but that even in New England divorce often required legislative enactment, and the number of divorces granted was small.

Actual statistics on the frequency of divorce in the United States began to become available only about a century ago. These statistics, a few of which are presented in Table 2, show an inexorable rise both in the number of divorces and in the rate of divorces per 1000 marriages. In 1860, there were fewer than 8000 divorces in all of the United States. By 1900 there were 55,000 and, in 1970, there were over 715,000 divorces.

Part of the increase in the number of divorces, of course, is to be accounted for simply by the growth of the population. It would be quite possible, in a growing nation, for the number of divorces to climb without there being any increase in the probability that any given marriage would end in divorce. The right-hand column of Table 2, however, shows that the number of divorces per 1000 marriages in the United States also has been climbing. In 1920, there were only 8.0 divorces per 1000 marriages. By 1969, the rate was 13.4.

TABLE 2. *United States Divorce and Annulment Rates, 1920–1970*

YEAR	NUMBER OF DIVORCES	DIVORCE AND ANNULMENT RATE PER 1000 EXISTING MARRIAGES
1920	171,000	8.0
1930	196,000	7.5
1940	264,000	8.8
1946	610,000	17.8
1950	385,000	10.3
1960	393,000	9.2
1965	479,000	10.6
1970	715,000	N.A. [1969 —13.4]

Source: U. S. Bureau of the Census, *Statistical Abstract of the United States: 1971* (Washington, D. C.), p. 60; and *Historical Statistics of the United States, Colonial Times To 1957*, Series B-9, p. 22.

THE INFLUENCE OF WAR AND THE ECONOMY

While the long-term trend in the divorce rate has been markedly upward, the increases have not been uniform from year to year or from decade to decade. The years 1930 and 1933 had lower divorce rates than prevailed during the 1920's, and the years 1945 and 1946 had higher divorce rates than existed either before or since that time. These fluctuations only suggest the influences of wars and recessions that more complete statistics would show in detail.

Wars tend to be followed by sharp increases in divorce rates and then by a return to the level of the prewar trend. As early as the Civil War this phenomenon was evident. There were 7380 U.S. divorces in 1860. In 1862, the number was down to 6230. In 1865, the number was 10,090 and the peak of 11,530 divorces was reached in 1866. The number of divorces then dropped off and did not reach the 1866 level again until 1871.

A somewhat similar pattern was observed after World War I. From 116,254 divorces in 1918, the number jumped to 141,527 in 1919 and to 171,000 in 1920. The number in 1921 was back down to 156,580 and dropped still further in 1922. The experience of World War I also demonstrated that this is not strictly an American phenomenon. England, France, and Germany all had relatively greater increases in divorce in 1919 and 1920 than did the United States. All three of these European countries also experienced decreases in the number of divorces during the early 1920's.

World War II saw fluctuations in the number of U.S. divorces from month to month but gradually increasing numbers until 1946, when a total of 610,000 divorces was recorded. Today, twenty years later, that figure has finally been surpassed. The divorce rate in 1946 was 17.8 per 1000 marriages. By 1950, the divorce rate dropped back almost to immediate pre-World War II levels, where it hovered until 1963. Since 1963, it has been on the rise again.

Explanations for these relationships between war and divorce rates are not difficult to find. A major factor probably is the large number of wartime marriages that are contracted after only very short acquaintance. Such marriages probably would produce a large number of divorces even without the direct effects of war. The war itself, however, separates many couples for long periods of time. In some instances, couples, who formerly were close, simply grow apart. In other cases, wartime separation merely establishes separate existences for couples whose marriages had been held together only by habit and inertia. In addition, many lonely spouses are thrown together with persons of the opposite sex under conditions that encourage extramarital involvement. Relatively few of these persons institute divorce actions while the war is actually in progress but many of them do so when the war is ended and re-adjustment must be achieved. Finally, the strains of postwar reunion them-selves often are great. Some formerly stable marriages break under this addi-tional strain.[4]

In addition to war, economic depressions also have marked effects upon divorce rates. The relative influences of a major depression and a major war are shown in Figure 1, which covers the great depression of the 1930's and

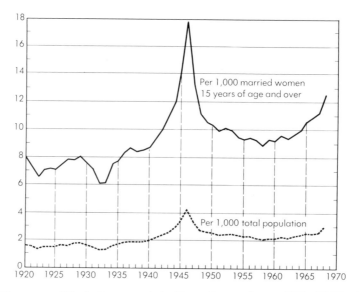

FIGURE 1. *The Influences of the Great Depression and World War II upon United States Divorce Rates*

World War II. It will be seen that the depression depressed divorce rates markedly, although not so much as World War II inflated them. Before the stock market crash in 1929 there were 201,468 divorces, or a rate of 7.9 divorces per 1000 marriages. At the depth of the depression in 1933 there were 40,000 fewer divorces and the divorce rate had dropped to 6.1. From 1933 until the start of World War II, again both the number of divorces and the divorce rate climbed steadily.[5]

Explanations for the effect of depressions upon divorce rates are, again, not hard to find. The process of securing a divorce is costly and many people

[4] Reuben Hill, *Families Under Stress*, New York: Harper and Brothers, 1949.

[5] Paul H. Jacobson, *American Marriage and Divorce*, New York: Rinehart and Com-pany, 1959, pp. 89–91.

simply cannot afford it during a depression. Beyond that, divorce requires the establishment of separate households, a division of property, and the establishment of specific terms for the support of any children who may be involved. These requirements tax most persons' financial resources even during periods of prosperity and often become prohibitive in bad times. Great financial hardship may tend to draw together some couples who might otherwise become alienated but, if it does, apparently the effect is short-lived. For, although divorce rates drop during the depression itself, they rise rapidly as the depression comes to an end.

PRESENT STATUS AND FUTURE PROSPECTS

Popular concern with the interpretation of divorce rates often manifests itself in estimates of the probability that any given marriage will end in divorce. Just as the rate of divorces per 1000 marriages has been increasing, so have estimates of the probability of divorce for individual couples. In 1940, before World War II, one divorce occurred for each six marriages contracted.

There was one divorce for every 3.8 marriages in 1946, and in 1970 there was one divorce for every 3 marriages.[6] This would seem to indicate that the probability of any given marriage ending in divorce is about one in three or four, and this estimate is widely quoted.

Actually, to state that the probability of any given marriage ending in divorce is one in three or four is misleading. This was clearly demonstrated by Monahan, who analyzed divorce rates in Iowa by whether the divorce was granted to persons who had been married only once or to persons who had experienced an earlier divorce. The data showed that divorce rates among those who had remarried following divorce are higher than among the first married and that the probability of divorce among persons in their first marriages is substantially below the national average. For Iowa, 1953–55, Monahan found that primary marriages had a lifetime divorce ratio of only 16.6 per 100 marriages whereas the ratio for all marriages was 21.9.[7] A Census Bureau study conducted in 1967 again found that the probability of divorce in first marriages is about one in six.

We have already seen that the long-term trend in American divorce rates

[6] Actually, it is unrealistic to compare divorces granted in any one year to marriages contracted during that year, because most of the persons being divorced were married during earlier years. A more adequate procedure relates divorces to the average number of marriages occurring during the preceding ten years. See Ray E. Baber, *Marriage and the Family*, New York: McGraw-Hill Book Company, 1953, pp. 448–50.

[7] Thomas P. Monahan, "The Changing Nature and Instability of Re-Marriages," *Eugenics Quarterly* 5 (Aug. 1958), pp. 73–85.

is upward, and, although predictions are hazardous, the prospect is that the upward trend will continue for some time to come. The number of divorces will continue to climb if only because the population is growing. In all probability the divorce rate will rise also.

After the post-World War II peak, divorce rates dropped and remained fairly stable for the period from 1955 through 1962. Then they began to climb again. From 413,000 divorces in 1962, there were 479,000 in 1965 and 523,000 in 1967. Since 1967, the increase has accelerated until there were 715,000 divorces in 1970. The number of divorces in 1970 was an all-time peak and the divorce rate was the second highest on record, approaching that set in 1946.

THE DISTRIBUTION OF DIVORCE

The preceding section, by pointing out differences in the divorce rates of first-married and remarried persons, indicated that the probability of divorce is not spread evenly throughout the United States population. The significance of this particular difference will be pursued in the next chapter on "Remarriages." Here, we will analyze the influences of region, race, economic status, length of time married, and parental status upon divorce rates.

VARIATIONS BY RURAL-URBAN STATUS AND BY REGION

In the decennial census of population, information is secured on the current marital status of persons enumerated. These data show that divorced persons are overrepresented in urban areas and underrepresented in rural areas. In part, these data probably reflect a higher probability of divorce under conditions of uban living; the lesser likelihood of divorce under rural, particularly farm, conditions of living has been pointed out earlier in this book. In part also, however, these statistics undoubtedly reflect a tendency of rural persons to migrate to urban areas before, during, or after a divorce. There is little place for divorced persons, particularly women, in a farm economy, whereas life in cities caters more nearly to married and unmarried persons alike.

Divorce rates also vary by region of the country, tending to increase from east to west. In 1960, the divorce rate was lowest in the northeast, followed by the north central region, then by the south and, finally, by the west. The rate was almost four times as high in the west as in the northeast.

Several factors help to account for these regional variations, but a full explanation does not exist. One factor undoubtedly is a difference in attitudes and values; something of a frontier tradition including rootlessness lingers on in the west. The age distribution of the population varies, with more younger, divorce-prone, persons being found in the west. Some western states also grant relatively more migratory divorces to eastern residents who come west for precisely that purpose. Finally, the ethnic and religious composition of the population has something to do with it; Roman Catholics particularly are overrepresented in northern and eastern sections of the country.[8]

In a recent, brilliantly conceived study, Fenelon offers another structural explanation of these variations. He suggests that divorce rates may be a function of the social costs that are involved. States having a large number of migrants in their populations may be characterized by a lower degree of social integration and there may be fewer effective sanctions against divorce. Analysis of state and regional variations in divorce rates strongly supports his hypothesis.[9]

VARIATIONS BY RACE

Strange as it may seem, the data available on divorce rates by race are so inadequate as to render hazardous any unqualified generalizations about the relative rates of whites and Negroes. The data come from two sources: from the decennial censuses, and from very incomplete reports made to the National Vital Statistics Division by those states included in the Divorce Registration Area.

The decennial census data refer only to persons who report themselves as separated or divorced at the time of enumeration. Not only are these figures subject to error, but they do not include persons who have been divorced and who have remarried. For what they are worth, the figures for 1960 show that 2.4 per cent of all nonwhite males were then divorced while the corresponding percentage for white males was 2.1. The differences between white and nonwhite females were greater, with 3.6 per cent of the nonwhite and only 2.7 percent of the white females reporting divorced status.

Even more striking were the differences in the figures for separations. The percentage of nonwhite separated males was more than five times (5.6 per cent to 1.0 per cent) that of white males. The separation rate of nonwhite

[8] See Paul C. Glick, "Marriage Instability: Variations by Size of Place and Religion," *The Milbank Memorial Fund Quarterly* 41 (Jan. 1963), pp. 43–55; and Kenneth L. Cannon and Ruby Gingles, "Social Factors Related to Divorce Rates for Urban Counties in Nebraska," *Rural Sociology* 21 (March 1956), pp. 34–40.

[9] Bill Fenelon, "State Variations in United States Divorce Rates," *Journal of Marriage and the Family* 33 (May 1971), pp. 321–7. See also Henry Pang and Sue M. Hanson, "Highest Divorce Rates in Western United States," *Sociology and Social Research* 52 (Jan. 1968), pp. 228–36.

females was over six times (8.3 per cent to 1.3 per cent) that of white females.[10] Thus the decennial census data indicate that divorce rates may be somewhat higher, and separation rates may be much higher, among nonwhites than among whites.

Data from the Divorce Registration Area are improving but still are woefully inadequate. The DRA is made up of 26 states in which local courts forward data on all divorces to their state health departments which, in turn, send systematic samples of these records to the National Vital Statistics Division. Unfortunately for our purposes, many of these records omit information pertaining to race.

Very fragmentary data for the period from 1939 through 1950 suggest that divorce rates may have been higher among whites than among blacks until 1942, when the relationship appears to have been reversed and Negro rates came to average 20 per cent higher than those of whites.

Why these relationships should have changed over time requires explanation, and a plausible explanation is available. It appears likely that Negro divorce rates recently have come to reflect, more accurately than they did before, the actual rate of marital disruption. The factors described in Chapter 10 that encouraged the use of desertion among blacks as a solution to family problems probably held down the divorce rate.

There is evidence, too, that Negro divorce rates are more sensitive to economic conditions than are white divorce rates. Blacks hold fewer middle-class jobs where employment is relatively secure and are much more likely to be laid off or fired during periods of economic recession. Jacobson, using divorce rates for the state of Virginia, demonstrated that nonwhite divorce rates were higher than white divorce rates during the prosperous period between 1918 and 1928. During the depression decade from 1929 through 1940, by contrast, nonwhite divorce rates were lower than those among whites. The same reversal occurred in the state of Mississippi.

Jacobson concludes that the upsurge in Negro divorce rates after World War II also has been associated with economic prosperity. Higher incomes have permitted blacks to hire lawyers and to file formal divorce proceedings. Divorce helps black men to protect their incomes from separated wives, and opens to black women possibilities of alimony and child support.[11]

A sample survey of 22,000 households by the Bureau of the Census, in 1957, confirmed the fact that greater percentages of blacks than whites now experi-

---

[10] "Trends in Divorce and Family Disruption," *Health, Education, and Welfare Indicators*, August 1963, pp. 11–12.

[11] Op. cit. p. 102–3.

ence divorce. Some 19.8 per cent of nonwhite males and 19.9 per cent of nonwhite females reported that they had experienced a divorce. The corresponding percentages among whites were only 14.1 and 16.7.[12]

VARIATIONS BY SOCIO-ECONOMIC STATUS

At least four major studies have demonstrated that there is generally an inverse correlation between socio-economic status and divorce rates. Regardless of the criterion of socio-economic status used, there appear to be more divorces at the bottom of the socio-economic structure and the rate steadily declines as we move upward.

Hillman, using 1950 census data on divorced status at the time of enumeration and broad occupational categories, found that men who were private household workers and service workers had the highest proportion of divorces; laborers had rates that were nearly as high. The proportion of divorces dropped through the middle-class, white-collar occupations and was lowest of all among professionals, managers, and proprietors. The occupation of farming was in a class by itself. As might be imagined, the divorce rate among farm owners and farm managers was less than half that among proprietors, managers, and officials.[13]

In a study of 425 Detroit-area women who had been divorced from 2 to 26 months, Goode calculated an index of proneness to divorce by the husbands' occupational status. The index was figured by dividing the percentage of divorced husbands in each occupational category by the percentage of all Detroit men in that category.[14] The results, shown in Table 3 are consistent with Hillman's findings. Divorce rates are lowest at the top of the occupational structure, with professionals and proprietors contributing barely more than half their proportionate share. Not until we drop down to semiskilled and operatives do we find any group exceeding its proportionate share. Finally, the unskilled have almost twice as many divorces as their share in the population as a whole.

[12] National Office of Vital Statistics, *Special Reports* 45 (1957), p. 298. For a penetrating analysis of the interrelationships among family stability and race, see Charles V. Mercer, "Interrelations Among Family Stability, Family Composition, Residence, and Race," *Journal of Marriage and the Family* 29 (Aug. 1967), pp. 456–60.

[13] Farm laborers, interestingly, had high divorce rates like other laborers rather than low divorce rates like farm owners. See, Karen G. Hillman, "Marital Instability and Its Relation to Education, Income, and Occupation: An Analysis Based on Census Data," in Robert F. Winch, Robert McGinnis, and Herbert R. Barringer, eds., *Selected Studies in Marriage and the Family*, New York: Holt, Rinehart, and Winston, 1962, pp. 603–8.

[14] William J. Goode, *After Divorce*, The Free Press of Glencoe, Illinois, 1956, pp. 46–7.

TABLE 3. *Index of Proneness to Divorce by Occupation,*
Based on 425 Detroit Area Divorces.

OCCUPATIONAL CATEGORY	INDEX
Professional and proprietary	67.7
Clerical, sales, service	83.2
Skilled, foremen	74.1
Semiskilled, operatives	126.1
Unskilled	179.7

Source: Reprinted with permission of The Free Press of Glencoe from William J. Goode, *After Divorce,* copyright © 1956 by The Free Press, A Corporation.

Goode's Detroit findings were generally confirmed by Kephart in an independent study of 1434 Philadelphia divorce cases. Working from the divorce records themselves, Kephart found that the upper occupational levels were clearly underrepresented in divorce actions, the middle-level occupations were represented roughly in accord with their proportions of the population, and lower-level occupations were greatly overrepresented.[15]

Finally, Monahan has analyzed 4449 divorce cases for the state of Iowa and found evidence to support the generalizations deriving from the three studies already cited. He found professional persons, officials, managers, and owners to contribute less than their share of divorces. The clerical and sales group contributed almost exactly their expected share, and laboring groups contributed up to four times their share. Farmers had the lowest divorce rates of all.[16]

The four studies reported so far have all used occupation as the index of socio-economic status. Goode and Hillman, however, also used both education and income as indexes and found the same inverse relationship between these measures and divorce rates as exists between occupation and divorce rates. When education is used as an index, however, some striking anomalies appear. Hillman found that the relationships discovered hold for white males only, and Goode found that when education is used as the index the relationships are reversed for blacks and whites. Among blacks, the higher the educational level up to college graduation, the higher the divorce rate. Blacks who

[15] William M. Kephart, "Occupational Level and Marital Disruption," *American Sociological Review* 20 (Aug. 1955), pp. 456–65. For a sophisticated analysis based upon 1960 census data, see Phillips Cutright, "Income and Family Events: Marital Stability," *Journal of Marriage and the Family* 33 (May 1971), pp. 291–306.

[16] Monahan found Iowa farm laborers to have very low divorce rates, also. The conflict in findings here between Monahan's and Hillman's studies has not yet been reconciled. See Thomas P. Monahan, "Divorce by Occupational Level," *Marriage and Family Living* 17 (Nov. 1955), pp. 322–4.

actually finish college again have low divorce rates, approximating those of blacks who have very little formal education. It may be that blacks with more formal education are more likely to use attorneys and courts in the solution of their marital problems and are less likely to resort to desertion. The low divorce rates among black college graduates may reflect the next stage in this process: the eventual tendency for middle-class norms to have more salience than those associated with race.

The general relationships between socio-economic status and divorce rates probably reflect basic differences in the conditions of life at upper-, middle-, and lower-class levels. Although there is a widespread stereotype of carefree living at lower-class levels, the opposite situation seems actually to exist. Lower-class people appear to be more beset by problems of all sorts. Divorce is only one of them.

VARIATIONS BY LENGTH OF TIME MARRIED

One of the hazards in tracing changes in divorce rates is that there may be apparent increases in the yearly rates without there being any long-term changes in the proportion of the population actually becoming divorced. This may happen if the average duration of marriages to divorce shortens. In this case, the earlier divorces would cause the yearly rates to show temporary increases. Unfortunately, the available data on length of marriage to divorce are too fragmentary to show conclusively what has been happening here.

A second problem is that the duration of marriage to the date of divorce is not so useful a measure as is the duration of marriage to the time of separation. The period of separation before a divorce decree is granted may vary from only a few weeks to many years.[17]

Getting married is a good deal like going into a restaurant with friends. You order what you want, and then when you see what the other fellow has got you wish you had taken that.

—Clarence Darrow.

Several major studies have dealt with the problem of the duration of marriage to divorce and have produced—in spite of the use of different populations and different time periods—generally consistent results. The earliest of

[17] Thomas P. Monahan, "When Married Couples Part: Statistical Trends and Relationships in Divorce," *American Sociological Review* 27 (Oct. 1962), pp. 625-33.

these, by Jacobson, was based upon data collected from almost 700 county and state offices and from the National Office of Vital Statistics for divorces and annulments granted from 1940 to 1948. This study showed that the increases in divorce rates between 1941 and 1946 were greatest among couples who had been married five years or less. The divorce rate for this early-marriage group literally doubled. Increases occurred among marriages of longer duration, also, but the relative increase was smaller for each succeeding five years of marriage. After 20 years of marriage, however, the divorce rate in 1946 was still 40 per cent higher than it had been in 1941.

Jacobson's study also showed that more divorces occurred during the third year of marriage than during any other. After the third year, the divorce rate dropped steadily through the seventh year. After the seventh year, the decline continued but less rapidly. Some divorces were granted, however, after 50 years of marriage.[18]

Mention has already been made of Kephart's study of 1434 Philadelphia divorces between 1937 and 1950. In that study, the author sought to summarize fragmentary data from early government reports and also to determine the duration of marriage to the point of separation as well as to divorce. He hypothesized that the patterns to separation and to divorce would be different and that these patterns would vary by first marriages and remarriages and by race.

The Census Bureau released striking statistical evidence today that mother knows best: people who marry young are twice as likely to be divorced as are somewhat older couples.

. . . the Bureau found that within 20 years of marriage, 28 per cent of men who married before the age of 22 had been divorced. This compared with only 13 per cent among men who married when they were older.

The figures were nearly identical for women. Among those who married before their 20th birthday, 27 per cent had been divorced, compared with 14 per cent of those who married after. . . .

The study showed that about 15 per cent of the men and about 17 per cent of the women had been divorced. Among blacks, the figures were 28 per cent for men and 31 per cent for women.

—Jack Rosenthal, "Young Love Fades Fast, Divorce Statistics Suggest," The New York Times, Oct. 11, 1971. © 1971 by the New York Times Company. Reprinted by permission.

---

[18] Paul H. Jacobson, "Differentials in Divorce by Duration of Marriage and Size of Family," American Sociological Review 15 (April 1950), pp. 235-44.

Kephart presented figures on the duration of marriage to divorce for 1932, the last year in which national figures were available, and which again showed the third year of marriage to produce more divorces than any other. The rate tended to decline thereafter. Kephart pointed out that the difference in the median time period from separation to divorce was 4.6 years. More separations occurred during the first year of marriage than any other, and most divorces took place during the second and fourth years of marriage. Forty per cent of all the couples had separated within the first three years of marriage, and both separation and divorce rates declined with the passage of time.[19]

The Philadelphia study produced two other general findings worthy of note. First is the fact that the average duration of marriage to divorce is longer in first marriages than in remarriages. Where either partner had been married before, the median time to separation was 3.4 years and to divorce was 7.1 years. The comparable medians for first marriages were 5.4 years and 10.4 years.

Kephart also found that the interval from separation to divorce is significantly longer among Negroes than among whites. The median times to separation were almost equal—4.9 years for Negroes and 5.1 years for whites. The median time to divorce, however, was 5.4 years longer for Negroes, the figures being 9.5 years and 14.9 years. This is consistent, of course, with the acknowledged greater reliance of Negroes upon separation as a means of marital disruption.

All divorces in the state of Wisconsin in 1957 were analyzed by Monahan, who also traced changes in length of time to separation and divorce from the middle 1800's. He, too, found the maximum number of separations to occur during the first year of marriage and the maximum number of divorces to occur within the first three years. Using the arithmetic mean, rather than the median, as the average, he found that the interval to separation may have increased slightly over the years from 7.7 years in 1887–1906 to 8.4 years in 1957. By contrast, the interval from separation to divorce appears to have shortened slightly, from 2.7 years in 1887–1906 to 1.3 years in 1957.[20]

The most recent data available come from the Survey of Economic Opportunity conducted in 1967 by the Bureau of the Census, and involving the

[19] Kephart makes the important point that the apparent decline in divorce rates in succeeding years of marriage is, in part, a function of the increasing death rate. Even if divorces were equally prevalent at all years of marriage, the number would decline during each successive year because of the increase in the number of deaths. See William M. Kephart, "The Duration of Marriage," *American Sociological Review* 19 (June 1954), pp. 287–95.

[20] Thomas P. Monahan, "When Married Couples Part: Statistical Trends and Relationships in Divorce," op. cit.

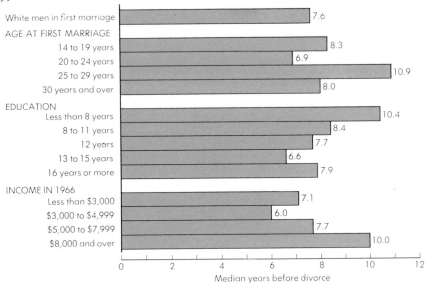

FIGURE 2. *Median Duration of First Marriage for Divorced*
White Men by Selected Characteristics, 1960–1966.

Source: U. S. Bureau of the Census, forthcoming report from the 1967 Survey of Economic Opportunity.

study of 28,000 households. These data, the first for the entire United States, show the median interval from first marriage to divorce to be 7.7 years for men and 7.9 years for women. Half the divorces occur between 3 years and 15 years of marriage. Figure 2 shows the median interval for white men between first marriage and divorce by age at marriage, education, and income.[21]

VARIATIONS BY PARENTAL STATUS

Crude statistics collected early in this century made it appear that the possibility of divorce was many times as great among childless couples as among couples with children. Cahen, for example, concluded that some 71 per cent of childless marriages ended in divorce while only 8 per cent of marriages with children did so.[22] For some time, no one seriously questioned these extreme figures and the conclusion was widely accepted that childlessness and divorce are causally associated.

Gradually, however, flaws in the statistics became apparent. The basic unit

[21] Paul C. Glick and Arthur J. Norton, "Frequency, Duration and Probability of Marriage and Divorce," *Journal of Marriage and the Family* 33 (May 1971), pp. 307–17.

[22] Alfred Cahen, *Statistical Analysis of American Divorce*, New York: Columbia University Press, 1932, p. 113.

of "children" had been variously defined to refer to the number of children ever born to a marriage, to the number of children living in the family, to the number of minor children, to the number of children affected by the decree, and so on. Moreover, it was discovered that the apparent childlessness of divorcing couples might be largely a function of the duration of marriage to divorce. Both childlessness and divorce are most common early in marriage; hence the relationship between them might be spurious.[23]

We do not know what the relationship between childlessness and divorce was several decades ago. Perhaps child-bearing was more of a deterrent to divorce then than it is now. We do know that the more refined the statistics become, the less of a relationship appears. And we do know that the proportion of divorces granted to couples with minor children in the home has been increasing fairly rapidly.

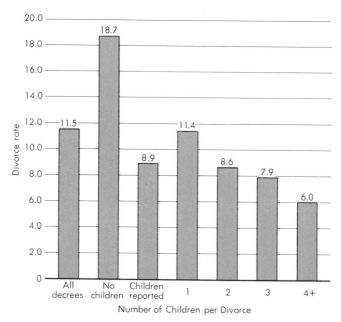

FIGURE 3. Divorce Rate by Number of Children Reported—per 1000 Couples With a Given Number of Children, The United States, 1960.

Source: National Center for Health Statistics, Children of Divorced Couples: United States, Selected Years (Washington, D. C.), Series 21, Number 18, February, 1970, p. 3.

[23] Thomas P. Monahan, "Is Childlessness Related to Family Stability?" American Sociological Review 20 (Aug. 1955), pp. 446–56.

Both the number of children affected by divorce and the proportion of divorces involving children have been increasing. In 1948, for example, there were an estimated 322,000 children involved in parental divorces. By 1955, the number had climbed to 347,000 and, by 1965, it was 630,000. It should be remembered that these increases were occurring during a period when the number of divorces was relatively stable. This means that both the proportion of couples with children and the number of children per divorce have been rising.

From 1955 to 1965, it is estimated that the proportion of divorces involving children increased from 48 per cent to 59.8 per cent. The number of children per divorce ranged from one to eight or more (see Figure 3), and the percentages varied by region of the country. Sixty-nine per cent of divorcing couples in the Northeast reported children, compared to only 54 per cent in the South.

Thus, it seems quite clear that children are no longer—if they ever were—an effective deterrent to divorce. What the effects of divorce on children are will be dealt with in a later section of this chapter.

DESERTION

Before proceeding with analysis of the actual divorce process in the United States and with the effects of divorce upon spouses and children, we shall digress to include a second major form of marital disruption—that of desertion. By its very nature, desertion is difficult to study. Deserting spouses do not register with the courts or any other official body. To the contrary, they seek to lose themselves in anonymity.

There is not even any clear definition of what desertion is. The Bureau of the Census uses the term, marital separations, and defines these as including "couples with legal separations, those living apart with intentions of obtaining a divorce, and other persons permanently or temporarily estranged from their spouse because of marital discord." Kephart estimates that the number of such separated couples runs into the millions, while Monahan estimates that at least three in every hundred married couples are truly separated and another large group of couples live together in a state of extreme marital discord.

Basically, there are three sources of statistics on recorded cases of desertion in the United States: applications to social agencies for aid to dependent children; applications to courts for the support of wife and children by the husband; and divorce cases where desertion is presented as the legal ground for divorce. Statistics on aid to dependent children show that as many as one and one-half million children may be receiving aid because their fathers are separated from their families. Desertion is the second most frequently used legal ground for divorce in the United States, with an estimated 112,000 such cases having been heard in 1946 and 66,000 in 1965.

Kephart and Monahan have done the most adequate research to date on the social characteristics associated with desertion, both men working with data from the Philadelphia Municipal Court. In general, their findings include the following. First, the occupational distribution in desertion cases is strikingly similar to that in cases of divorce. Rates are highest in the unskilled and semiskilled occupations and tend to decrease as we move up the occupational ladder. Second, desertion rates appear to be higher among Catholics than among non-Catholics. This may be due to a combination of factors. For one thing, Catholics are disproportionately represented in the occupational groups having the highest desertion and divorce rates. For another, the religious proscription of divorce for Catholics may force more Catholics into desertion as the only available alternative. Third, blacks are overrepresented and whites are underrepresented in desertion cases. This, of course, has roots in history and reflects the differential distribution of blacks and whites in the occupational structure. Finally, there are much more likely to be minor children present in the home in desertion cases than in divorce cases.[24]

We have already indicated that the term "desertion" is used to refer to several different kinds of phenomena. At least two of them merit further discussion here.

One kind of desertion appears to be largely a lower-class phenomenon and to be associated with excess child-bearing. This is the kind of desertion that is sometimes referred to as "the poor man's divorce."[25] The deserting party usually is the husband and often the desertion occurs during or just after a pregnancy. The husband, unable to cope with his problems, simply leaves and does not return. This leaves his wife and children destitute and forces them to turn to the courts or to social agencies to gain support.

. . . A poor youth . . . is likely to marry younger, diminishing his chance of completing education or job training. Children come sooner, adding to financial and marital strain. A family quickly finds itself in the situation Mirra Komarovsky describes in "Blue-Collar Marriage":

[24] William M. Kephart, "Occupational Level and Marital Disruption," op. cit., and Thomas P. Monahan, "Is Childlessness Related to Family Stability?" op. cit.

[25] Kephart and Monahan have pointed out that this phrase is a misnomer. Desertion does not legally end a marriage and neither partner is free to remarry unless a divorce is subsequently obtained. See William M. Kephart and Thomas P. Monahan, "Desertion and Divorce in Philadelphia," *American Sociological Review* 17 (Dec. 1952), pp. 719–27.

"A 33 year-old man, a bottler in a beer company, struggles to support his wife and three children on $3,000-a year pay. He does not like his job, but he also feels that he cannot risk giving up a secure job." Though comparatively young, the family is trapped.

The man's alternative is to become what Researcher Hylan Lewis has called a "marriage dropout." It becomes clear that the father can never earn enough, and things are not so sweet at home anyway. At the third or fourth pregnancy, he deserts. Or his wife, conscious of his failure and her own misery, precipitates a divorce. (Lewis has pointed out that although middle-class women may not be happy in their marriages, they can at least settle for being kept comfortably. A poor woman does not have this to settle for.) When each member of the couple remarries, they take trouble along—children already requiring support and, sometimes, the idea that escape is an ultimate solution for any further trouble. . . .

—Alvin L. Schorr, "Program for the Social Orphans," *New York Times Magazine*, March 31, 1966, p. 101. © 1966 by The New York Times Company. Reprinted by permission.

Historically, American society has been ill-prepared to cope with this kind of desertion. Either social agencies assumed the support of the family—and supporting them at a very inadequate level—or the courts sought to locate the husband and to return him to his family under criminal indictment. To bring the husband and father back in this fashion often made things worse rather than better. If reconciliation were not already impossible, the bitterness created by this situation often made it so. The husband might literally be put in jail until he made some token gesture toward supporting his family. In the meantime, he could not earn, his family was not better off, and the state was saddled with the expense of keeping him in jail. Soon after he was released from jail, he was likely to disappear again.[26]

The situation began to improve somewhat in 1949 when the Family Location Service in New York got together with other groups to sponsor a uniform dependents' support law which has now been adopted in every state and territory.[27] These new laws permit the wife to go into a family court, instead of a criminal court, from which papers are sent to a corresponding court in the

[26] For a recent analysis of the ineffectiveness of sanctions, see Kenneth W. Eckhardt, "Deviance, Visibility, and Legal Action," *Social Problems* 15 (Spring 1968), pp. 470–77.

[27] Thomas P. Monahan, "Family Fugitives," *Marriage and Family Living* 20 (May 1958), pp. 146–51.

state where the deserting husband has been located. The second court then determines how much the husband can and should pay for his family's support, collects the money, and forwards it to the wife through the court in her own state. The husband and wife may also be urged toward reconciliation by referring them to counseling agencies in their own communities.[28]

If anything, this lower-class pattern of desertion may be becoming less common as living standards increase. A second widespread form of desertion probably has become more common over the past few decades. This "desertion" is to some degree fictitious and involves the use of desertion as legal grounds for divorce. In states where desertion is a legal ground for divorce, some couples agree ahead of time to live apart in order to obtain the legal grounds. In Philadelphia, Kephart reported finding cases of "desertion" where the husband was simply living in a different apartment or in a different building on the same street from his wife. In some one-third of Philadelphia desertion and nonsupport cases, the spouses were still living in the same household. A most striking finding was that, over the past 30 years, the number of new desertion and nonsupport cases in the courts was almost twice the number of divorces granted during that period.[29] It appears likely that many of the nonsupport cases stemmed from the first kind of desertion described above and that many of the desertion cases involved the use of "desertion" as preliminary to divorce.

THE DIVORCE PROCESS IN THE UNITED STATES

So far in this chapter we have examined divorce in cross-cultural perspective, surveyed the trend in divorce in the United States, analyzed the distribution of divorce among different segments of the population, and taken a brief look at desertion. We have yet to survey the impact of divorce upon spouses and upon children. To do that, however, requires some knowledge of how the divorce process actually works. For there is reason to believe that aspects of the divorce process may produce as much strife within families as does the fact of divorce itself.

New York's state divorce rate, for years the lowest in the nation, has more than tripled in the first two years of a liberalized matrimonial law.

[28] For an overview of counseling agencies and programs, see Gerald R. Leslie, "The Field of Marriage Counseling," in Harold T. Christensen, ed., *Handbook of Marriage and The Family,"* Chicago: Rand McNally and Company, 1964, pp. 912–43.
[29] William M. Kephart and Thomas P. Monahan, op. cit. p. 719.

> From an average of fewer than 4,000 divorces granted because of adultery, the only permitted ground under the old law, state courts are now processing more than 18,000 divorces on this and five additional grounds. . . .
>
> —*The New York Times*, Jan. 4, 1970.

Divorce law in the United States is state law and there are as many sets of divorce law as there are jurisdictions—some 51, including all the states plus the District of Columbia. Divorce law, and all of domestic-relations law for that matter, is state law because the United States Constitution does not grant the power to enact such law to the federal government. All powers not specifically granted to the federal government by the Constitution are reserved to the several states.

LEGAL GROUNDS FOR DIVORCE

All states in the United States now sanction divorce. Until 1966, the state of New York granted divorce for adultery only, but New York's grounds have been broadened to five: adultery, cruelty, abandonment, imprisonment, and living apart for two years after a formal separation decree. At the other extreme, Kentucky grants divorce on any one of twenty different legal grounds, and over the whole United States as many as forty different legal grounds are in use.[30]

In spite of the variety of legal grounds available in most states, the overwhelming proportion of divorces are granted either on grounds of cruelty or for desertion. About 52 per cent of all U. S. divorces are granted on grounds of cruelty in some form or other. The laws of some states specifically require that there must be extreme physical cruelty, while other laws specify only that there must be mental distress. In practice, the courts tend to interpret the term, cruelty, very loosely, and cruelty is widely used because it is a relatively unobjectionable ground for divorce.

About 23 per cent of U. S. divorces are granted on grounds of desertion, which, we saw in the last section, is often fictitious. Many couples live apart, but with knowledge of one another's whereabouts, in order to have grounds

[30] Frances Kuchler, *The Law of Marriage and Divorce*, Dobbs Ferry, New York: Oceana Publications, 1963.

for divorce. Again, desertion is widely used because it is relatively unobjectionable.

The third most widely used legal ground for divorce, non-support, is used in about 4 per cent of all divorces. Adultery is used in only about 1 per cent of all cases.[31] Since adultery is ground for divorce in all states, and since New York previously granted divorce for adultery only, this is somewhat surprising. Many more marriages than this are adulterous, of course. And it appears likely that adultery has occurred and is known in many cases where divorces are granted for cruelty or desertion. The use of adultery as grounds for divorce obviously carries a stigma that most couples try to avoid.

One more point which needs to be made here is that there is little apparent relationship between the number of legal grounds for divorce and the number of divorces granted in a state.[32] The number of divorces granted in a state appears far more to be a function of the way in which the divorce laws are administered than of the laws themselves. This leads directly into consideration of the adversary system underlying the administration of United States law.

THE ADVERSARY SYSTEM

In order for a divorce to be legally granted in most states, one spouse must bring charges against the other in court, which charges, if proven, constitute legal grounds for divorce in that state. Moreover, the spouse who brings the charges, the plaintiff in the suit, must not himself or herself be guilty of any offense that is grounds for divorce. Thus, the law requires that there be a guilty party and an innocent party, a situation which seldom if ever obtains in marriage.

In truth, of course, people do not generally seek divorce because one of them has committed adultery or been cruel to the other; they seek divorce because they have concluded that they can no longer live together. By this time, it is very likely that both spouses have treated one another in ways that constitute legal grounds for divorce and that both partners, if reluctantly, are agreed that a divorce should be sought and granted. Yet, if it should be called to the

---

[31] Paul C. Glick and Hugh Carter, *Marriage and Divorce: A Social and Economic Study*, Cambridge, Mass.: Harvard University Press, 1970, pp. 367–8.

[32] Alexander Broel-Plateris, "Associations Between Marriage Disruption, Permissiveness of Divorce Laws, and Selected Social Variables," in Ernest W. Burgess and Donald J. Bogue, eds., *Contributions to Urban Sociology*, Chicago: University of Chicago Press, 1964, pp. 512–26.

attention of the judge that both partners have agreed to the divorce, this constitutes collusion and he is legally bound to deny the divorce.

In practice, the legal requirements are winked at. More often than not, the husband and wife agree to seek a divorce, their attorneys get together to work out the terms of the divorce, the attorneys present a recommended settlement to the judge, and he accepts it with or without minor modification. Something around 85 per cent of U. S. divorces are uncontested; the defendant spouse simply does not appear in court and is assumed to be guilty by default.

The significance of the adversary system for our purposes—beyond the fact that it involves judge, attorneys, and the couple in a tacit conspiracy to ignore the law—is that in spite of the efforts of all concerned to keep trauma to a minimum and to make the divorce as therapeutic as possible, the whole process tends to generate strife and bitterness. The husband and wife ordinarily have agreed that a divorce is necessary but there are likely to be feelings of hurt, rejection, shame, and anger in them before they even approach attorneys. The attorneys, in turn, are bound by legal ethics to obtain the best possible settlements for their clients. In addition to deciding which partner is to be charged with what legal offense and how this is to be proved in court, bargaining must take place to determine who gets the house, the furniture, the automobile, and so on. Custody and support arrangements have to be worked out for any children involved and it must be decided whether the wife is entitled to alimony. Before the negotiations are completed, what may have started out as an attempt by both partners to reach an equitable solution often has degenerated into bitter conflict.

Virtually all authorities in the field are agreed that much of the vindictiveness which has traditionally been associated with divorce in the United States is traceable to the hostilities that are engendered by the divorce process itself. A few states have begun to do something about it. Three states—Alaska, New Mexico, and Oklahoma—grant divorces on grounds of incompatibility which does not automatically imply moral fault on the part of either spouse.

Since 1969, three additional states have gone even further. Texas revised its whole divorce code and has added "insupportability" as grounds for divorce. This means divorce without fault and based upon mutual agreement of incompatibility. California has scrapped the term, divorce, in favor of "dissolution of marriage" which is granted on grounds of "irreconcilable differences" which have caused the irremediable breakdown of the marriage. The law also provides for the substantially equal division of property and bases alimony upon the length of the marriage and the earning ability of both spouses. In 1971, Florida also passed a "no-fault" divorce law.

MIGRATORY DIVORCE

People have long sought to get around the strict divorce requirements of their own states by traveling to other states or countries with more lenient laws. Reno, Nevada, has long been famed as a divorce center, as has Juarez, Mexico. Reno's popularity has dropped with the passage of the new California law, and Mexico has recently gone out of the divorce business. Haiti and the Dominican Republic have leaped into the breech, however, and the migratory divorce pattern goes on.

The problem (or the solution, if one happens to be seeking a migratory divorce) stems from the fact that divorce laws vary from one state to another and from the fact that the United States Supreme Court has held that the full faith and credit clause in the Constitution applies in the field of domestic relations as well as in relation to business contracts. This clause, which was designed to prevent people from escaping contractual obligations by moving from one state to another, holds that any legal status that accrues to a person by virtue of his residence in one state shall be legally binding in any and all states to which he may subsequently move. As applied in this case, it means that a person who is legally divorced in Nevada or Idaho or elsewhere must have his divorced status recognized by New York or any other state to which he subsequently moves.

Haiti and the Dominican Republic . . . are competing for the "quickie" divorce business abandoned by Mexico. The Caribbean countries changed their laws this year . . . to allow foreign visitors to obtain quick divorces following the closing of the Ciudad Juarez divorce factory, which had been processing as many as 30,000 couples a year. . . .

With similar laws and equivalent fees, lawyers and politicians in the two countries are striving for faster and smoother service and better publicity to give them the edge in bidding for divorce business from the East Coast of the United States. . . .

The new divorce legislation is almost identical to the old Mexican law, to insure recognition by the same states in the United States that recognized Mexican decrees.

In both cases, husband and wife must consent to the divorce, usually on grounds of mutual incompatibility, and one spouse must attend the court hearing. The other party is represented by a local lawyer. Any

*separation agreement must be drawn up in the United States before
the local proceedings begin. . . .*

> —Alan Riding, "Hispaniola Offers 'Quickie' Divorces," *The New
> York Times*, Sept. 5, 1971. © 1971 by the New York Times Com-
> pany. Reprinted by permission.

Confusion arises when it appears that people take up residence in states with
short residence requirements for divorce for the specific purpose of securing
a divorce under that state's more lenient laws. The traffic between New York,
with its stringent divorce laws, and Nevada, with its six weeks' residence requirement, has been widely publicized. Because there are many borderline
cases and because no statistics are kept on this matter, it is not known exactly
how much migratory divorce occurs. Jacobson estimates migratory divorces at
somewhere between 3 and 5 per cent of the total number of divorces.[33] In
addition to Nevada and Idaho, disproportionately large numbers of divorces
are granted in Florida, Alabama, Paris, and the Virgin Islands.

Most migratory divorces are binding simply because the parties are agreed
to the divorce and no one challenges them. Occasionally, however, one of the
spouses does bring suit in a court in his home state to have the migratory
divorce secured by his partner declared invalid. A few such cases have eventually reached the United States Supreme Court, and that court has held that
courts in one state have the right to review court decisions in other states to
determine whether the courts in those states had jurisdiction under their own
laws. The attempt obviously is to get away from the practice of establishing
phony legal residence for purposes of divorce. The question has not yet been
completely resolved. Most migratory divorces are binding simply because they
go unchallenged. When suit is brought, most cases are resolved in state courts,
and there is no unanimity of practice among these; certain types of migratory
divorces may be accepted as binding in some states but not in others. Finally,
the Supreme Court has not been consistent in its rulings. As a consequence,
there are literally hundreds of thousands of people in the United States who
have had migratory divorces whose marital statuses are potentially in legal
jeopardy.

THE CONSEQUENCES OF DIVORCE

Most societies tend to define divorce as being undesirable, and the United
States is no exception. On the one hand, there is the tendency to associate

[33] Paul H. Jacobson, *American Marriage and Divorce*, op. cit. p. 109.

divorce with threat to the stability of the family and of the larger society. And, on the other hand, divorce is assumed to have grave consequences for the men, women, and children caught up in it. The first part of this concern was dealt with in the beginning of this chapter and requires no further treatment here. The second part—the presumed effects upon adults and children—has been rather extensively researched in recent decades. We will first present the major findings of this research on the consequences for the marital partners, and then we will examine the alleged effects of divorce upon their children.

CONSEQUENCES FOR THE MARITAL PARTNERS

Perhaps the most sensitive analyst of the effects of divorce upon marital partners was Willard Waller, who brought to an early classic study the same combination of brilliant insight and lack of methodological rigor that we have witnessed in his studies of dating and marital adjustment. Waller focused upon the emotional aspects of adjustment to divorce and described a series of typical stages that many people go through.

First, he said, comes shock associated with the realization that one is actually being divorced. Although there may be full intellectual understanding of the situation, separation and divorce frustrate deeply rooted habits in a fashion that is quite painful. What happens here may be likened to the experience of an amputee who finds that the amputated limb that isn't there still hurts. Dozens of times during the day, activities that formerly were routine must be faced consciously and with nostalgia for the comfort and well-being that attended their performance in better days.

This disruption of habits is accompanied by some ambivalence toward both the partner and oneself. Self-preservation may demand that increased bitterness be felt toward the spouse and that he or she be blamed for the failure of the marriage. At the same time, the former partner may appear in some ways to be more desirable than before; even formerly disliked traits in the partner may come to be admired. An analogous ambivalence may be found in attitudes towards oneself. On the one hand, one's every action may be justified and held to demonstrate one's superiority to the former spouse. On the other hand, there may be nagging feelings of failure and a compulsive focusing of attention on what one might have done differently to avoid the breakup.

There is, of course, disruption of established sexual patterns on both physical and emotional levels. Some persons appear to react by suppressing or repressing all sexual desire. This may or may not be associated with bitterness which is generalized to all members of the opposite sex. Many persons after the initial shock of divorce, however, appear to go through a period of relatively promiscuous experimentation with sex that has overtones both of revenge upon the former spouse and some degradation of self. Casual sexual affairs may represent some combination of these along with attempts to reassure oneself of one's desirability and of one's sexual adequacy.

Finally, there is the need to adjust to the loss of other relationships in addition to that with the former spouse, to make new friends, and to establish a new pattern of life. Alienation from the spouse is accompanied by alienation from many of one's friends, some of whom have taken sides in the divorce and all of whom serve as reminders of the relationship that is now dead. Without a spouse, one also becomes "a fifth wheel" at most of the social gatherings one formerly enjoyed. Gradually one has to develop new friendships with people who do not know of the former relationship and whose circumstances of life are consistent with one's own.

TWO POINTS OF VIEW

"Alimony is an anachronism and has been one for years," says a suburban Connecticut lawyer who has helped unmarry many Fairfield County couples. "Understand, I'm not talking about child support. I mean strictly alimony—the salary paid to a woman for the sole reason that she was once married. Alimony originated centuries ago when a woman had little chance to earn her own livelihood. In fact, women of so-called 'good' families simply couldn't work for a living. Most didn't know how to, and social custom forbade it anyway. So it was only fair to make a man support his ex-wife. Today an able bodied woman can get a job as easily as a man can. Why should she get a free ride through life?" . . .

"Sure, I could get a job," says an attractive Manhattan divorcee in her mid-40's. "But what kind of job? Listen, I married right after college. I agreed to be my husband's cook and housekeeper and raise his children. I voluntarily gave up any chance of training for a career, and in return my husband agreed to share his salary with me as it grew. This is the deal a man and woman make when they marry. Now that my husband doesn't want me around anymore, I'm over 40 and not trained to be anything but maybe a $75-a-week Gal Friday. My husband's salary is nearly 10 times that much. Is it fair to let him wriggle out of the deal and drop me back to a working girl's income?" . . .

—Max Gunther, "The Fraternity of Crippled Men,"
New York Times Magazine, September 19, 1965, p. 34.
© 1965 by The New York Times Company. Reprinted by permission.

The period of adjustment to divorce, according to Waller, is accompanied by much frustration and unhappiness. Gradually, however, the pains ease away and new habits are developed to replace the old. Gradually, new friends are acquired and one's needs for love and affection are directed toward new partners. Some persons become permanently blocked at some stage in this process, but most eventually form new relationships that replace the old.[34]

In sharp contrast, methodologically, to Waller's analysis of readjustment to divorce is a recent study, by Goode, of 425 Detroit-area mothers who had been divorced from 2 to 26 months at the time of interview. Goode sought to test hypotheses to the effect that: (1) divorce is traumatic; (2) most divorcées are neurotic; (3) divorce often is secured for trivial reasons; (4) adequate readjustment following divorce is rare; (5) there are undesirable effects of the divorce upon children.[35]

To try to understand some of the basic causes of divorce, Goode asked these 425 women why they got the divorce. The general themes covered in their responses are shown in Table 4. The themes, of course, are broad. "Drinking" covers all stated objections of the wives to their husbands' drinking and not just that "he drank too much." Similarly, "relatives" covers all complaints concerning one or the other's families, and "complex" refers to some combination of the other listed themes. These complaints probably should not be

TABLE 4. *The Main Causes of Their Divorces as Viewed by 425 Detroit Mothers.*

COMPLAINT THEME	PER CENT OF RESPONSES	PER CENT OF RESPONDENTS
Nonsupport	13	33
Authority	12	32
Complex	12	31
Drinking	12	30
Personality	11	29
Home life	9	25
Values	8	21
Consumption	8	20
Triangle	6	16
Miscellaneous	4	12
Desertion	3	8
Relatives	2	4
Number of complaints	1110	

Source: Reprinted with permission of The Free Press of Glencoe from William J. Goode, *After Divorce*, copyright © 1956 by The Free Press, A Corporation.

[34] Willard Waller, *The Old Love and the New: Divorce and Readjustment*, Carbondale, Illinois: Southern Illinois University Press, 1967 (Originally published in 1930).

[35] William J. Goode, *After Divorce*, op. cit., pp. 15–17.

taken too literally, both because they represent the wives' perceptions of the causes rather than objectively determined causes and because a somewhat similar list of complaints might be given by women who were not divorced from their husbands. What is clear from Table 4 is that the perceived causes of divorce generally are not trivial ones. Most of these women saw their divorces as having stemmed from quite serious marital problems.

Goode also found that divorce is preceded by a long period of conflict and that the securing of a decree is the final result of a decision process that lasts for an average of about two years. One-third of the respondents reported waiting more than two years from the time they first seriously considered divorce before actually filing suit.

A paradoxical situation emerged in connection with attempts to discover which of the two partners first wanted the divorce and which of them first suggested divorce. More often than not, the husband was the first to desire divorce but the wife was first to suggest it. Goode explains it this way. Men, by virtue of their relative dominance in the family, their greater freedom of action, and their lesser commitment to the family, are more likely to come consciously to desire a divorce. This desire and the behaviors that lead to it tend to produce some guilt feelings, however. As a consequence, the husband does not ordinarily press for divorce but unwittingly assumes a pattern of behavior that eventually forces his wife to ask for and even insist upon divorce. He becomes disinterested and obnoxious. Sixty-two per cent of the wives first suggested divorce, in 13 per cent of the cases it was a mutual decision, and in one-fourth of the cases the husband first suggested divorce.[36]

This study also yielded data bearing upon the trauma which Waller earlier had found to be associated with divorce. The respondents were divided into high- and low-trauma groups on the basis of answers to questions concerning the impact of the divorce upon sleeping, health, loneliness, work efficiency, memory difficulties, smoking, and drinking. Thirty-seven per cent of the respondents showed little appreciable increase in symptoms and were classified as low-trauma cases. In about two-thirds of the cases, however, there was definite evidence of an increase in personal difficulty. Interestingly, the time of greatest difficulty was not at the time of or following the issuance of the divorce decree. The period of greatest trauma was the time of final separation. The divorce decree may announce the end of the marriage to the world at large, but the greatest personal crisis and the effective end to the marriage for the spouses, their kin, and their friends, comes at the time of final separation.

Apparently, most of these women experienced little or no discrimination

36 Ibid. pp. 133–45.

against themselves as divorced persons. On the average only 30 per cent reported experiencing any discrimination at all, and the percentage declined steadily with the age of the woman involved.[37] By contrast, 54 per cent of the women who had been divorced for 26 months had already remarried and 50 per cent of the remainder had steady dates. Over half of all the divorcées claimed to have kept their old circle of friends after the divorce, and most of the others had found new friends whom they believed to be equal to or better in quality than their old friends.

Surprisingly, even the financial adjustment of these women failed to bear out the belief that divorce works continuing hardship. In most of the cases, there was little property to be divided and the wife got most of it. Where there was a house and furniture, the wife most often got them. The husbands were generally ordered to pay child support, but since their incomes often were low the payments tended to be low also. About half of all the husbands made their support payments "always" or "usually," but 40 per cent of them made them "rarely" or "never." As contact between the former spouses dwindled, the support payments tended to become less regular.

On the average, the divorced women had almost as much income, from all sources, as their husbands had earned during their marriages. Moreover, the women's incomes increased with the length of the time since the divorce, most of which increase was associated with remarriage. There was, of course, a large difference in income between those women who had remarried and those who had not. When the women's perceptions of their economic situations were considered, however, the differences were smaller. The remarried women tended to judge themselves as being better off than during their first marriages and better off than their objective financial situations would indicate. Among those who had not remarried, the tendency was to view their financial situations as worse than objective conditions would indicate, but, even here, the financial attractiveness of the marriage continues to fade. More of these women come to believe that the period while they were separated from their husbands was better than either the time of the marriage or now.

Thus, Goode's careful recent analysis of adjustment to divorce supports Waller's analysis at some points and contradicts it at others. He did find that the majority of couples reach the decision to divorce only reluctantly over a long period of time; that for most of them there is considerable trauma involved; that a minority experience some discrimination and may be, for a time, almost without friends; and that there is some economic deprivation.

---

[37] *Ibid.*, pp. 184–8. For a good summary of the literature on one-parent families, see Jane K. Burgess, "The Single-Parent Family: A Social and Sociological Problem," *The Family Coordinator* 19 (April 1970), pp. 137–44.

On the other hand, Goode found that most of the divorcées kept their former friends or made other equally desirable friendships, that most of them quickly moved back into dating activities and remarriage, and that their estimates of their financial situations tended to change accordingly.

If divorce is a mixed blessing, it must be acknowledged that there may also be problems involved in remaining married. Mathews and Mihanovich, for example, studied 984 Catholic respondents and found that couples who made low scores on the Burgess and Wallin marriage-adjustment schedule have both more problems and more serious problems than those who made higher scores. Neither did they find any tendency for the number of problems to decrease with length of time married.[38] Landis found that, the unhappily married, those who married young, those who are indifferent to religion, and those with more formal education are more likely to resort to divorce.[39]

Finally, Le Masters studied 36 couples whose marriages had been characterized by chronic conflict for at least ten years. He found that evidence of personal disorganization could be found in one or both spouses in 75 per cent of the cases. Symptoms of such personal disorganization included alcoholism, psychosomatic illness, neurotic or psychotic behavior, occupational problems, and extramarital affairs. He found no evidence that these couples were able to improve their marriages over time and found that the husbands were more likely to suffer personality damage from their marriages than were the wives.[40]

Landis has pointed out that another possible effect of divorce is to increase the likelihood of divorce in succeeding generations of the same families. He found that if neither set of grandparents is divorced, only 15 per cent of their children become divorced. If one set of grandparents is divorced, 24 per cent of the next generation is divorced. And, if both sets of grandparents are divorced, the probability of divorce in the next generation rises to 38 per cent.[41] At first glance, these figures seem to suggest that divorce within families is highly contagious. However, Peterson has correctly pointed out that these statistics should be regarded with caution until controls for social class

[38] Vincent D. Mathews and Clement S. Mihanovich, "New Orientations on Marital Maladjustment," *Marriage and Family Living* 25 (Aug. 1963), pp. 300–304.

[39] Judson T. Landis, "Social Correlates of Divorce or Nondivorce Among the Unhappy Married," *Marriage and Family Living* 25 (May 1963), pp. 178–9.

[40] Ersel E. Le Masters, "Holy Deadlock: A Study of Unsuccessful Marriages," *Midwest Sociologist* 21 (July 1959), pp. 86–91. See also William H. Clements, "Marital Interaction and Marital Stability: A Point of View and a Descriptive Comparison of Stable and Unstable Marriages," *Journal of Marriage and the Family* 29 (Nov. 1967), pp. 697–702.

[41] Judson T. Landis, "The Pattern of Divorce in Three Generations," *Social Forces* 34 (March 1956), pp. 213–16.

are imposed. It may be that the marital failures of succeeding generations are more social class-linked than divorce-linked.[42]

CONSEQUENCES FOR CHILDREN

Over the years, there has been even more public concern for the presumed effects of divorce upon the children involved than there has been for the welfare of their parents. And the presumed effects upon the children have almost always been bad. Adults, knowing something of the trauma of divorce for themselves and their peers, have generally assumed that children must suffer far more, that they must suffer a loss of emotional and financial security that could not help but make a deep impression upon their lives. Over the years too, of course, the number and proportion of children caught up in parental divorces has been increasing. The proportion of divorces involving minor children today hovers around 60 per cent. In 1935, there were only 68 children involved in every 100 divorces. By 1948, there were 74, and by 1957 there were 100. Today, over 700,000 children see their parents divorced each year.

Judson Landis has inquired into the actual trauma experienced by children at the time of parental divorce and has confirmed the fact that such trauma is widespread. He studied 295 university students of previously divorced parents, finding, initially, that 112 of them were too young at the time of divorce to remember any trauma associated with it. Surprisingly, 19 per cent of the remaining respondents had considered their families to be closely united before they learned of the impending parental divorce and 24 per cent reported that there had been no open conflict in the family. In only 22 per cent of the cases was there constant open conflict between the parents.

The reactions of the children to the divorce depended greatly upon their previous evaluations of the parental marriages and their own security in their families. Over half of the children from openly unhappy homes reacted by thinking that divorce was the best thing for all concerned. Over half of those who had believed their homes to be happy, on the other hand, reported that they were unhappy and upset. Two out of five of this latter group simply couldn't believe what was happening to them. After the divorce, the same split evaluation occurred between the children who had thought their homes to be happy and those who knew them to be unhappy: those from apparently

[42] James A. Peterson, "Catastrophes in Partnership: Separation, Divorce, and Widowhood," in Seymour M. Farber, Piero Mustacchi, and Roger H. L. Wilson, eds., *Man and Civilization: The Family's Search for Survival*, New York: McGraw-Hill Book Company, 1965, p. 76.

happy homes reported either no change in feelings of security and happiness or a change to feeling less secure and less happy; respondents from unhappy homes reported shifts in the direction of greater happiness and greater security.

Almost half of these youngsters (44 per cent) reported that they felt themselves "used" by one or both of their parents after the divorce. The parents played on their children's sympathy, tried to get information from them about the other parent, told untrue things about the other parent, and sought to involve the children in continuing quarrels.

Over the long haul, one effect of the divorce was to increase the feelings of closeness of the children to their mothers and to increase the emotional distance between them and their fathers. Undoubtedly this is associated with the mother's having custody. One cost of divorce for fathers apparently is loss of closeness with their children regardless of the nature of the situation that precipitates the divorce.

Finally, Landis found that about one-fifth of the children experienced feelings of shame that their parents were divorced and one out of six felt inferior to other children. Some 15 per cent talked to others as though their parents were not divorced or avoided the subject. One out of ten lied about the whereabouts of the other parent.[43]

Apparently there is foundation for the belief that children suffer trauma from divorce just as adults do. So, also, is there reason to think that the amount of trauma is related to the previously perceived quality of the family relationships: where the child has perceived the home to be a happy one, the trauma is great; where the home has been very unhappy, trauma may be less conspicuous than a sense of relief that the conflict is over.

Goode's study of divorced Detroit mothers provides further data on this matter. He classified the mothers according to the amount of trauma which they experienced in connection with the divorce and then related the problems they had with their children to it. As might be expected, the greater the trauma, the higher the proportion of mothers who admitted that, at some time, their children had been hard to handle. Eighty-one per cent of the mothers admitted to worrying before the divorce about the effects upon the children. However, 55 per cent reported no increase in problems afterwards with their children. Eighteen per cent said that the children were harder to handle during the separation or immediately following the divorce, 13 per cent said they had been at their worst during the marriage itself, and only 14 per cent thought that they were harder to handle at the time of interview.[44]

[43] Judson T. Landis, "The Trauma of Children When Parents Divorce," Marriage and Family Living 22 (Feb. 1960), pp. 7-13.

[44] Op. cit. pp. 317-21.

Goode also sought to determine whether the mothers thought their children to be better off or worse off following the divorce. The weight of evidence, he concluded, indicated that the vast majority of the mothers believed them to be better off. Three-fourths of all the mothers who had remarried stated that their children were better off at the time of interview, and another 15 per cent said that their life was about the same. Only 8 per cent thought that the children were worse off in the second marriage than in the first one. Among the women who had not remarried, 57 per cent put their children in the care of relatives while they worked. Of all the mothers who used outside help, 65 per cent thought that their children received "excellent" care, 24 per cent said that it was "good," 8 per cent said it was "average," and only 4 per cent acknowledged that it was "poor."

One series of studies has tended to show that broken homes contribute more than their share to the problem of juvenile delinquency. The Gluecks, for example, used matched samples of delinquent and nondelinquent youngsters and found that about 9 per cent of the delinquents but only 6 per cent of the nondelinquents had divorced parents. What was more surprising, however, was that homes where one parent had been widowed or where the parents were separated contributed even more significantly to the ranks of the delinquent.[45]

Although several studies have essentially confirmed the findings of the Gluecks, sociologists have been reluctant to draw firm conclusions about the relationship between divorce and delinquency for at least two reasons. First is the fact that both delinquency and divorce are heavily concentrated in lower socio-economic strata; the apparent relationship between them may be largely spurious, with both stemming from other conditions of lower-class living. Second, there is a strong suggestion that family disorganization, rather than divorce, may be the crucial variable. The findings of the Gluecks regarding the effects of widowhood and separation suggest this. A study by Browning of delinquent and nondelinquent boys in Los Angeles led him to the same conclusion. He states that his findings "support the hypothesis that delinquents are as likely to come from disorganized but structurally unbroken homes as they are from broken homes." [46]

[45] Sheldon Glueck and Eleanor Glueck, *Unraveling Juvenile Delinquency*, New York: The Commonwealth Fund, 1951. See also Thomas P. Monahan, "The Trend in Broken Homes Among Delinquent Children," *Marriage and Family Living* 19 (Nov. 1957), pp. 362–5; and F. Ivan Nye, "Adolescent-Parent Adjustment: Age, Sex, Sibling Number, Broken Homes, and Employed Mothers as Variables," *Marriage and Family Living* 14 (Nov. 1952), pp. 327–32.

[46] Charles J. Browning, "Differential Impact of Family Disorganization Upon Male Adolescents," *Social Problems* 8 (Summer 1960), p. 43.

These results point to the fact that the negative impact of divorce upon children may be no greater than would be the effect of parents continuing to live together in an unhappy marriage. On the contrary, at least four studies have shown that unhappy, unbroken homes may have more deleterious effects upon children than do broken homes.[47]

The most recent of these studies may be used to represent the findings and the point of view. Burchinal studied seventh- and eleventh-grade children and their parents in Cedar Rapids, Iowa, around 1960, securing data from 98 per cent of the students and 91 per cent of the parents. The families were separated into unbroken, broken, and reconstituted types and controls were imposed for socio-economic status. Virtually no significant differences were found for either boys or girls in either personality characteristics or social relationships. Burchinal sums up the meaning of his findings and the current state of our knowledge in this area as follows:

. . . Inimical effects associated with divorce or separation . . . were almost uniformly absent in the populations studied. Acceptance of this conclusion requires the revision of widely held beliefs about the detrimental effects of divorce upon children. Many persons will quarrel with the results of this study —and similar results from other studies as well—by pointing to their obvious limitations. It is true that data were limited to the type collected by questionnaires or obtained from school records. It is also true that some children will suffer extreme trauma because of divorce or separation and consequent withdrawal of one parent, and, for some, their development will be affected deleteriously. However, even in these cases it is difficult to assess whether the difficulty occurs because of divorce or whether it reflects the conflict preceding the divorce and separation. Nevertheless, for the adolescents in the seventh and eleventh grades in one metropolitan area, there is no question that in terms of variables measured, family dissolution . . . was not the overwhelming influential factor that many have thought it to be. . . .[48]

Summary

All societies provide for divorce. Divorce rates vary widely from one society to another, and there is no apparent relationship between divorce rates and

[47] Lee G. Burchinal, "Characteristics of Adolescents from Unbroken, Broken, and Reconstituted Families," *Journal of Marriage and the Family* 26 (Feb. 1964), pp. 44–51; Judson T. Landis, "A Comparison of Children from Divorced and Nondivorced Unhappy Marriages," *Family Life Coordinator* 11 (July 1962), pp. 61–5; Paul H. Landis, *The Broken Home in Teenage Adjustment*, Pullman, Washington: Agricultural Experiment Station Bulletin No. 542, June, 1953; and F. Ivan Nye, "Child Adjustment in Broken and in Unhappy Unbroken Homes," *Marriage and Family Living* 19 (Nov. 1957), pp. 356–61.
[48] Op. cit.

other symptoms of societal breakdown. More than half of all preliterate societies have higher divorce rates than does the United States, and until recently several large nations had higher divorce rates also. Our divorce rate has been climbing steadily, however, and now is the highest of any modern nation.

The long-term trend both in the number of divorces and the divorce rate in the United States has been upward. The rate of climb has been unevenly affected by wars and depressions. Wars tend to be followed by sharp increases in divorce rates and then by a return to the level of the prewar trend. Depressions depress divorce rates temporarily and then are followed by a rapid rise.

There are, currently, about 715,000 divorces in the United States each year, or about 13.4 per 1000 existing marriages. The probability that first marriages currently being contracted will end in divorce is about one in six; the probability is somewhat higher in the case of remarriages. The number of divorces is certain to continue to rise. If the rate continues to rise also, it will not be long before the level attained just after World War II is reached again.

Divorced persons are overrepresented in urban areas and underrepresented in rural areas. Probably this reflects both the greater likelihood of divorce under urban living conditions and a tendency for divorced persons to migrate to cities. Divorce rates tend to increase from east to west across the country, reflecting differences in attitudes and values, and in the age, ethnic, and religious composition of the population.

The relative divorce rates among whites and Negroes appear to have been changing. As blacks have come to rely less upon separation, their divorce rates have been rising rapidly and now exceed those of whites. A greater proportion of blacks are found in the lower socio-economic strata, and there is a general inverse correlation between socio-economic status and divorce rates. Whether occupation, education, or income is used as the criterion of economic status, the relationship holds.

Several studies have shown that more separations occur during the first year of marriage than during any other. The time lag from the time of separation to divorce results in the peak number of divorces occurring from the second to the fourth year of marriage. The mean interval to divorce is longer, of course, and is around seven to eight years. The length of marriage to divorce is longer in first marriages than in remarriages and is longer among blacks than among whites.

Refined statistics indicate less of a relationship between childlessness and divorce than formerly was believed to exist. There may be from one and one-half to two times the probability that a childless marriage will end in divorce over a marriage with children. Both the number and proportion of divorces involving children have been increasing. In 1970, there were about 715,000 children involved in the divorces granted. The proportion of divorces in which minor children were involved was about 60 per cent. Having children no longer appears to be a very effective deterrent to divorce.

Desertion both constitutes an additional form of marital disruption and often serves as a prelude to divorce. Adequate statistics on desertion do not exist, but the figures that are available suggest that: the occupational distribution of desertion cases is similar to that of divorce cases, Catholics have higher rates than non-Catholics, and Negroes have higher rates than whites. One frequent form of desertion is found among lower-class groups and is associated with excess childbearing. An increasing percentage of "desertions" may be fictitious as couples choose to use desertion as legal grounds for divorce.

Divorce law in the United States is state law. Legal grounds in the various states range up to 40 in number, with 75 per cent of all divorces being granted on grounds of cruelty or desertion. These are widely used because they have little stigma associated with them, and their use tells us little about the actual causes of divorce. Most divorce law is administered through the adversary system, which again conceals the true causes of divorce and which works to create more bitterness between the already embattled spouses.

Migratory divorces apparently number from 3 to 5 per cent of all divorces. Although such divorces frequently involve the open flouting of state laws, most of them are valid because they go unchallenged. Some court decisions, however, have held that obviously migratory divorces are invalid, and the whole situation is in need of clarification.

The effects of divorce upon the marital partners include some trauma at the time of and after the divorce. There is a painful severing of former habit patterns, ambivalence toward both the partner and oneself, feelings of failure, interference with established sexual patterns, and the need to form new relationships outside the marriage. Empirical studies have confirmed the trauma, finding it to be greater at the time of final separation than at the time of the divorce decree.

Divorce seldom appears to be secured on frivolous grounds, and a long period of time generally elapses from the first serious consideration of divorce to the actual issuing of a decree. The evidence suggests that husbands more often than not desire the divorce first but that they generally maneuver their wives into being the ones to ask for the divorce. Studies of divorced women show that most do not feel themselves discriminated against as divorcées, most keep their former friends, most make an adequate financial adjustment, and most remarry.

Studies of unhappy couples who do not seek divorce indicate that the many serious problems they have do not lessen with the passage of time and that the partners suffer some personality damage in such marriages. Statistics showing that divorce perpetuates itself in succeeding generations of the same families should be used with caution because of the possible contaminating influence of social-class background.

Divorce often produces trauma in the children of divorcing parents as well as in the adults directly involved. The effects are particularly pronounced where the children have believed their parents' marriages to be happy. Following the divorce, children tend to become closer emotionally to their mothers, who usually have custody, and to become more distant emotionally from their fathers. Where the parental home was obviously unhappy, the children often experience relief when the divorce is final.

Most mothers worry about the effects of divorce upon their children, but most experience no increase in problems with the children after the divorce. Mothers who remarry generally believe their children to be better off in the second marriage, and those who have not remarried generally are satisfied with their child-care arrangements.

Several studies have shown that broken homes and juvenile delinquency are associated. However, the correlation appears to be with all forms of broken homes, including those that are emotionally broken but structurally intact, and not just with divorce-broken homes. More research needs to be conducted. In the meantime, predictions of dire effects of divorce upon children appear not to be warranted.

SUGGESTED READINGS

Bradway, John S., ed., "Progress in Family Law," special issue of *The Annals of the American Academy of Political and Social Science*, (May 1969). Contains articles on divorce, desertion, annulment, alimony, and the family court. An excellent reference source.

Carter, Hugh, and Glick, Paul C., *Marriage and Divorce: A Social and Economic Study*, Cambridge, Mass.: Harvard University Press, 1970. A monograph of the American Public Health Association containing the most recent data on patterns and variations in divorce in the United States.

Ferriss, Abbott L., *Indicators of Change in the American Family*, New York: Russell Sage Foundation, 1970. One product of the growing effort to develop social indicators of the state of American society. Contains sections on divorce, marital status, and dependency as indicators of the state of the American family.

Goode, William J., *Women in Divorce*, New York: The Free Press, 1965. A reissue of the classic study published in 1956 under the title, *After Divorce*. Still the most definitive study of adjustment to divorce in the United States.

Hill, Reuben, and Hansen, Donald A., "Families Under Stress," in Harold T. Christensen, ed., *Handbook of Marriage and the Family*, Chicago: Rand McNally and Company, 1964, pp. 782–819. Summary of theory and research in the broad area of family crises. Includes desertion and divorce as two forms thereof.

O'Neill, William L., *Divorce in the Progressive Era*, New Haven: Yale University Press, 1967. A fascinating historical study of changing attitudes toward divorce.

Peterson, James A., "Catastrophes in Partnership: Separation, Divorce, and Widowhood," in Seymour M. Farber, Piero Mustacchi, and Roger H. L. Wilson, eds., *Man and Civilization: The Family's Search for Survival*, New York: McGraw-Hill Book Company, 1965, pp. 73–80. A brief but penetrating analysis of the meaning of desertion and divorce in the United States.

FILMS

Being in Love (NET Film Service, Indiana University, Bloomington, Ind.). Film opens with two brothers meeting in a restaurant. One brother plans to divorce his wife to marry a woman he has met in business. Psychotherapist discusses the possibilities of success for such a second marriage and questions whether the man is mature in his attitudes.

In Time of Trouble (McGraw-Hill Book Company, Text-Film Division, 330 West 42nd St., New York 10036), 14 minutes. The story of a couple whose happy marriage is jeopardized by a lack of understanding of each other's needs. The advisability of seeking outside help is stressed.

Marriage Under Stress: The Causes of Divorce (Time-Life Films, 43 West 16th Street, New York 10011), 40 minutes. Shows the pressures that force couples apart. Discusses what happens when a marriage finally is over, including the chances of and problems in remarriage.

This Charming Couple (McGraw-Hill Book Company, Text-Film Division, 330 West 42nd St., New York 10036), 19 minutes. Focuses on a frequent cause of broken marriages—false ideas of romantic love. Follows the courtship of two young people who refuse to evaluate each other's good qualities and shortcomings in a realistic, adult fashion. Because they are in love with "love" and not with each other, their marriage is doomed to fail.

QUESTIONS AND PROJECTS

1. What is the relationship between the divorce rate in a society and the stability of the society?
2. How does the divorce rate in the United States compare to the divorce rates of preliterate societies? Of modern societies?
3. Describe the long-term trend in American divorce rates. Describe the influence of wars and depressions. What is the level of the current divorce rate? What are the prospects for the future?

4. Analyze variations in United States divorce rates by rural-urban residence, region, race, socio-economic status, length of time married, and parental status. Try to account for the variations you have just described by reference to sociological theory, history, or just plain common sense.

5. What basic patterns does desertion take in the United States? How is desertion distributed in the population? What does understanding of it contribute to our knowledge of family disruption?

6. What is meant by the adversary system in relation to divorce? How does this system complicate divorce for the persons involved? What is the relationship between causes of divorce and legal grounds for divorce?

7. Define the term, migratory divorce. How is migratory divorce related to the full faith and credit clause of the Constitution? What is the approximate incidence of migratory divorce? What is its legal status?

8. Analyze the impact of divorce upon the emotions, habits, and self-concepts of the marital partners.

9. What does research show about the way in which people decide to secure a divorce? What does it show about their adjustment following divorce? What is the situation of unhappily married couples who avoid divorce?

10. What factor is significantly related to the amount of trauma which children experience over their parents' divorces? What does research show about behavior problems in children following divorce? About economic problems? About child-care arrangements?

11. What appear to be the relative effects of happy homes, unhappy unbroken homes, and broken homes upon children?

12. Arrange a visit to a local court where divorce cases are being heard. If possible, have the judge talk with the group about how he views the divorce cases moving through his court. Is he in sympathy with present legal procedures? What changes would he favor?

19 | *Remarriages*

Case 2: High Stability. Subject is 19 years old; the mother, a beautician, is 41. He was three or four at the time of the divorce and 6 at the time of remarriage. The new father, now 39, is a tool maker; he was unmarried at the time of marriage to the subject's mother. There are three children of the new marriage, two girls, now 6 and 8, and a boy 12. The relationships among the children are warm and cordial. The own father remarried some 5 years ago, and subject has had no contact with him since that time.

The subject was too young to have any reaction to his parents' divorce. His first reaction to the second marriage of the mother was one of indifference; he already knew the new father. His present attitude is "glad." He liked the new father from the beginning and now considers him "like a real father." He reports that the new father, in turn, has always been like a regular father to him. Comment: "I think of my father as a big brother; I work with him in his business."

Case 3: Low Stability. Subject was 3 at the time of the divorce; he was 13 when his mother, who is now 49, married a widowed man, some 16 years her senior, with three children, a son, now 36, and two daughters, also in their thirties. The new father had been born in England. The mother is a teacher, the new father in business. The own father is unemployed; he has not remarried. All the adults are Protestant.

Subject was too young to have had an attitude toward the divorce; he was, and remains, indifferent toward the second marriage. At first he liked the new father, but at the present his attitude is only "fair." He likes his father's children, but reports close relationships with only one, a sister. He has no contact with the other sister, and reports that she is indifferent toward him. Relationships with the brother are "not so good underneath . . . there is an undercurrent of disfavor" on the part of the brother toward subject. Subject reports that the attitude of his new father was indifferent at first and at present time remains indifferent with "occasional disputes."

. . . Stepfather slightly old-fashioned, domineering. Occasional disputes over use of car and spending money. Stepfather wants subject to take over his business but he doesn't want to. Mother takes subject's part in disputes; is irritated at husband, but gets over it. There is a workable relationship. The subject was a little reserved at first; later thawed out and talked as if something had been on his mind. It had; the last weekend he'd wrecked the car.

Case 7: New Mother Salvages Family. . . . Although the husband still loved his [first] wife, the crisis was not so great as might have been expected, since he had seen the situation building up over the years and had more or less expected this end. His adjustment was aided, too, by his fairly soon developing a new interest in the form of an attachment for a family friend. The son was old enough to have seen it coming, too, and therefore he found it relatively easy to adjust to. The daughter suffered the severest crisis. She was bewildered and confused. Her mother, who was living in the same city, met her occasionally and bought her things or took her to dinner and the movies. The daughter could not decide where her allegiance belonged. Several times she went to live with her mother, but after a few weeks she would return to her father. . . .

The father married the family friend about a year after the divorce. The children had known her for a number of years and were fond of her. She seemed to be the factor that pulled all the loose ends together. In the three or four years since their marriage, the children have come to love her more than their own mother. The daughter commented, "For the first time in my life I know that when I get home from school there will be a mother and a hot dinner waiting for me, instead of a note and a can of beans." [1]

THESE three excerpts are taken from one of the very few comprehensive studies of remarriages that have yet been done. Each views a remarriage through the eyes of children of one of the partners. If they indicate that there are many complications in such marriages, they cannot begin to convey the variations that actually exist. Some remarried couples are 20 years of age, some are 40, and some are 60. Some remarriages follow divorce and some follow widowhood. In some cases there are no children. Sometimes one partner brings children from the prior marriage and sometimes both do so. In addition, there may be children on one or both sides who live with the former spouse or elsewhere. The children may range from infancy to middle-aged adulthood and, eventually, there may be "your children," "my children," and "our children." Remarriages vary along other dimensions too. This chapter will analyze some of them.

The fact that there has been so little study of remarriages tells us something about the nature of American society. The oversight cannot be attributed to

[1] Jessie Bernard, *Remarriage: A Study of Marriage*, New York: Dryden Press, 1956, pp. 323–8.

the lack of significance of such marriages, for they are numerous and conspicuous, and they have both more and different problems than first marriages.
That they have been virtually ignored for so long apparently reflects the
tenacity with which the United States holds onto the ideal of the permanent
monogamous family—"until death do us part." Even when death does the
parting, there is a widespread stereotype of an aging widow who lives out her
life keeping the memory of her husband alive for herself, her children, and her
grandchildren. No one questions that many such cases exist. But when one
considers the incidence and nature of remarriage objectively, the total situation looks quite different.

The Incidence and Nature of Remarriage

TYPES OF REMARRIAGES

We have already indicated that the term, remarriage, covers a number of
different kinds of marriages. The various combinations that can be achieved
through the use of previous marital status, presence or absence and age of
children, age, and so on, are too complicated for full presentation here. Some
idea of the range may be gleaned, however, from Table 1, which presents
types of remarriage in terms of previous marital status alone. Either the bride
or the groom, of course, may be single, previously divorced, or previously
widowed, making eight possible combinations in all. If it is recognized that
either or both spouses may have been both divorced and widowed prior to
the present remarriage, the number of possible combinations is considerably
larger. With so many combinations deriving from the use of previous marital
status alone, it is easy to see that dozens of variations would emerge if we
were to add such elemental variables as children, age, economic status, and
religion.

Table 1 also shows the distribution of remarriages among the eight types
for two separate populations, a Seattle group studied by Bowerman and a
group of 2009 cases studied by Bernard. More methodological detail on
the Bernard study, which was a very comprehensive one, will be presented later in the chapter. For now, some idea of the incidence of various types of remarriage may be seen in the percentages in Table 1. It
will be noted that the highest percentages consistently involve at least one
partner who has been divorced previously. The largest number of cases in the
samples combined is found in the "single man-divorced woman" category.
Almost equally numerous are those marriages involving two previously divorced persons. "Divorced man-single woman" marriages come next, with no

TABLE 1. *The Distribution of Remarriages by Previous Marital Status in Two Populations.*

PREVIOUS MARITAL STATUS	1947 CASES IN UTOPOLIS*		13,088 CASES IN SEATTLE	
Divorced man-single woman	20.7%	(403)	18.2%	(2,397)
Divorced man-widowed woman	4.5	(87)	5.4	(721)
Divorced man-divorced woman	16.4	(319)	23.3	(3,057)
Single man-divorced woman	21.5	(419)	29.8	(3,917)
Single man-widowed woman	9.0	(176)	8.0	(1,046)
Widowed man-single woman	12.9	(251)	3.4	(459)
Widowed man-widowed woman	9.3	(182)	6.8	(797)
Widowed man-divorced woman	5.6	(110)	5.2	(694)

* Utopolis is a hypothetical community constructed around 2009 remarriages which are assumed to be the total remarried population of the community. Previous marital status was unknown in 62 of the 2009 cases studied.

Source: Jessie Bernard, *Remarriage: A Study of Marriage*, New York: Dryden Press, 1956, p. 9; and Charles E. Bowerman, "Assortative Mating by Previous Marital Status, Seattle, 1939–1946," *American Sociological Review* 18 (April 1953), p. 171.

other type approaching in frequency these top three. At the other extreme, the lowest percentages are found consistently to involve persons who have been previously widowed. No claim is made that these two populations accurately represent the total United States population but, as succeeding sections will show, there are good reasons why remarriages occur most often following divorce and least often following widowhood.

THE TREND IN REMARRIAGES

Before 1900 the incidence of remarriage in the United States was relatively low. About nine-tenths of all marriages were first marriages, and most of the remarriages that did occur involved widowed persons. As the divorce rate began to climb to high levels, the remarriage rate began to rise and the pattern changed. More of the growing percentage of remarriage occurred among previously divorced persons.

Most of the change took place after World War I. In 1917, for example, 87.4 per cent of all grooms were entering marriage for the first time, 8 per cent had been widowed, and 4.5 per cent had been divorced. By 1960, only 77 per cent of brides and grooms were entering marriage for the first time, about 6 per cent were marrying after having been widowed, and between 16 and 17 per cent were remarrying following divorce.[2]

[2] Hugh Carter and Paul C. Glick, *Marriage and Divorce: A Social and Economic Study*, Cambridge, Mass.: Harvard University Press, 1970, pp. 82–3. For Canadian data, see Benjamin Schlesinger, and Alex Macrae, "Remarriages in Canada: Statistical Trends," *Journal of Marriage and the Family* 32 (May 1970), pp. 300–303.

The increasing incidence of remarriage following divorce is easy enough to understand, but, at first glance, the declining proportion of remarriage among the widowed may appear surprising. It does not, however, reflect a lesser tendency on the part of the widowed to remarry but a combination of the greater number of divorced people in the total population and the changing age composition of the widowed population. Increased longevity during this century, particularly among males, tends to postpone widowhood to the older ages when remarriage is less likely.

THE INCIDENCE OF REMARRIAGE

There are two different ways of stating remarriage rates, just as, in Chapter 14, we pointed out that there are two different ways of calculating mixed marriage rates. We may figure a remarriage rate for couples or a remarriage rate for persons.

Using data supplied by Glick, Bernard has stated the remarriage rate for couples as follows. Out of every 100 married couples in the United States, almost one-fifth involve remarriage for one or both partners. In 7 couples out of 100, both partners have been married before. In an additional 11 couples, one of the two spouses has been married before. In all, 18 marriages out of 100 involve at least one remarried person.[3]

The incidence of remarriage among individuals is figured by taking the total number of remarried people in the 100 marriages referred to above—14 people in the 7 marriages where both partners are remarried and 11 people who are remarried to formerly single persons—and calculating the percentage that the 25 remarried people are of the total 200 people in the 100 marriages. This gives, of course, a remarriage rate of 12.5 per cent for individuals.

It should be kept in mind that remarriage rates figured on the basis of all existing marriages, as we have figured them, understates the frequency of remarriage at the present time and the likelihood of remarriage in the future. It is estimated that between 20 and 25 per cent of all persons marrying recently have been entering marriage for the second or subsequent time.

RACE AND REMARRIAGE

At least two factors should lead us to expect higher remarriage rates among blacks than among whites. First is the higher divorce rate among blacks;

---

[3] Jessie Bernard, op. cit. p. 45; and Paul C. Glick, "First Marriages and Remarriages," *American Sociological Review* 14 (Dec. 1949), pp. 726–34.

and second is the higher Negro death rate. Both these factors should increase the proportion of blacks who become eligible for remarriage.

The expectation is borne out. According to the 1967 Survey of Economic Opportunity conducted by the U. S. Bureau of the Census, approximately 30 per cent of the blacks sampled had been married twice, compared with only 17 per cent of the whites. Four per cent of the blacks, but only 2 per cent of the whites had been married three or more times.[4] For as long as there are significant differences between the marital dissolution rate and death rate of blacks and whites, these differences will continue.

AGE AT REMARRIAGE

Carter and Glick have presented statistics on age at marriage and remarriage for the states in the Marriage Registration Area for 1963. The median age at first marriage for men was 23.0 and for women was 20.5. At remarriage, however, the median ages were 36.4 for men remarrying after a divorce and 57.9 for widowers. Women averaged 34.7 years at remarriage following divorce, and widows averaged 53.2 years at remarriage.[5] Obviously, the remarrying population is considerably older than those who are marrying for the first time.

That remarriage generally involves older persons was confirmed by Bernard's study of 2009 remarriages that formed the total remarried population of a hypothetical community termed Utopolis. She found that the average age of divorced men at the time of remarriage was 36.8 years and the average for women was 33.7 years (see Table 2).[6]

Similar findings appear when the remarriages of widowed persons are considered, with the ages at remarriage being slightly older than in the case of divorced persons. Bernard's study showed widowed men to be an average of 45.4 years old and widowed women to be an average of 41.0 years old at the time of remarriage.

An important fact to keep in mind then is that most remarriages involve men and women in their middle years. Although there are men and women remarrying at 20 and 25 years of age, most remarriages occur among people who are not starry-eyed adolescents. Typically they are in their thirties and

[4] Paul C. Glick and Arthur J. Norton, "Frequency, Duration, and Probability of Marriage and Divorce," *Journal of Marriage and the Family* 33 (May 1971), p. 309.
[5] Carter and Glick, op. cit. p. 84.
[6] Jessie Bernard, op. cit. p. 11.

TABLE 2. *Summary of Data on Divorced Women and Men in 2009 Cases of Remarriage.*

	DIVORCED WOMEN (N=849)	WIDOWED WOMEN (N=445)	DIVORCED MEN (N=809)	WIDOWED MEN (N=543)
Average age at time of study	34.7 (825)	42.6 (415)	44.2 (752)	53.3 (514)
Average age at first marriage	21.4 (560)	21.9 (351)	24.0 (560)	24.3 (351)
Average age at termination of first marriage	27.6 (739)	34.5 (351)	32.9 (662)	40.9 (449)
Average duration of first marriage	5.8 (696)	11.5 (321)	7.0 (612)	16.5 (393)
Average interval between marriages	4.6 (761)	6.2 (440)	2.5 (649)	3.4 (443)
Per cent who remarried within one year	8.4 (761)	1.6 (440)	12.8 (649)	3.4 (443)
Average age at second marriage	33.7 (796)	41.0 (399)	36.8 (733)	45.4 (496)
Average number of children by first marriage	1.25 (849)	1.74 (442)	1.39 (809)	1.97 (547)
Per cent with no children by first marriage	c. 40.0	c. 25.0	c. 40.0	c. 20.0

* The number of individuals whose responses are tabulated is 2645; the 1249 previously unmarried persons whose partners are remarried persons are not included. In 62 marriages, data on the previous marital status of one or both spouses were unavailable.

Source: Jessie Bernard, *Remarriage: A Study of Marriage*, New York: Dryden Press, 1956, pp. 11–12.

forties. We should at least entertain the hypothesis that the factors that lead them into remarriage are quite different from those motivating first marriages.

THE JOINT EFFECTS OF AGE AND PREVIOUS MARITAL STATUS

The joint influences of age and previous marital status upon remarriage are shown graphically in Figure 1. The remarriages of persons up to 35 years of age overwhelmingly occur following divorce. After age 35, the proportion of remarriages involving widowed persons begins to climb rapidly, until beyond age 55 the number of such remarriages is far greater than the number following divorce. Of the total number of persons remarrying in 1959, about three-fourths had been divorced and one-fourth had been widowed. A slightly higher percentage of the men had been divorced and a slightly higher percentage of the women had been widowed.

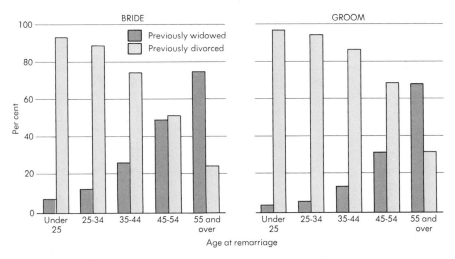

FIGURE 1. *Remarriages by previous marital status of bride and groom, by age: 28 states, 1959.*

Source: "Trends in Divorce and Family Disruption," *Health, Education, and Welfare Indicators*, August 1963, p. 14.

PROBABILITIES OF MARRIAGE AND REMARRIAGE

What may come as a surprise to many people is that, at any age, persons who have been married before have higher probabilities of remarrying than single persons have of getting married for the first time! Empirical verification of this fact is provided in Table 3. This table, which gives marriage rates during given age periods by previous marital status and separately for men and women, shows that during the age period 20–24 the likelihood that a divorced woman will remarry is more than twice as great as the chance that a single woman will marry. At older ages the differences tend gradually to increase in favor of the previously divorced women. Sufficiently large numbers of cases to compare widows become available during the age period, 25–29. At that age, and for each succeeding age, we see that widows are more likely to remarry than single women are likely to marry originally, but are less likely to remarry than divorcées are. The ages at which adequate numbers of cases for divorced and widowed men become available are slightly older than among women but precisely the same pattern is found. Divorced men have a greater probability of remarrying than do widowed men, and, age by age, single men have the lowest probabilities of all of marrying.

We cannot be certain of the reason for the greater probability of remarriage

TABLE 3. *Marriage Rates* by Previous Marital Status,*
Age at Marriage, and Sex, 1950–1953.

AGE AT MARRIAGE	MALE			FEMALE		
	Single	Divorced	Widowed	Single	Divorced	Widowed
14–17	6			47		
18–19	65			192		
20–24	190			220	515	
25–29	177	518		139	359	223
30–34	101	368		78	171	117
35–44	36	322	97	43	126	50
45–54	20	110	85	7	62	19
55–64	10	74	37	2	41	6
65 and over	4	24	8	1	13	2

* Rates per 1000 population. Rate not shown where base is less than 200,000.
Source: Hugh Carter, Paul C. Glick, and Sarah Lewit, "Some Demographic Characteristics of Recently Married Persons: Comparisons of Registration Data and Sample Survey Data," *American Sociological Review* 20 (April 1955), p. 170.

than of first marriage at each age'level, but the following explanation appears plausible. One of the developmental tasks facing people in adolescence and early adulthood consists of the necessity for establishing meaningful relationships with members of the opposite sex that will, in the course of time, lead to the emotional and physical intimacy that precede marriage. Divorced persons, even though their first marriages fail, have at least demonstrated their ability to form relationships of some intimacy. Widowed persons, of course, have done this without the imputation of failure in the first marriage, the reason for their remarriage rate being lower than that of divorced persons being mainly the advanced ages at which widowhood most often occurs. Single persons, while they may be defined by many people as being morally superior to and better adjusted than divorced persons, may not have achieved a heterosexual orientation adequate enough to eventuate in marriage. Moreover, with each increase in age beyond the early twenties, the chances that such a heterosexual orientation ever will be achieved diminishes rapidly.

Table 3 also shows that divorced men have greater probabilities of re-

---

Findings from a new Census Bureau study of 28,000 U. S. households, and covering the whole adult lifetime of those surveyed, has yielded the following findings.
– about 15 per cent of the men and 17 per cent of the women had been divorced. Among Blacks, the figures were 28 per cent for men and 31 per cent for women.

- about three-fourths of all divorced men and three-fifths of all divorced women eventually remarry.
- men are more likely to remarry than women during any given year. The odds for men are 17 in 100, for women 13 in 100.
- the chances of remarriage are particularly low among the poorest men and among those who have been divorced for more than five years.

---

marrying, at every age level, than divorced women do. More than one divorced man out of every three in his early thirties remarried while less than one woman out of five did so. Between the ages of 45 and 54, one divorced man out of 10 remarried but only one woman out of 20 did so. Bernard has calculated the total remarriage rates of divorced men and women of varying ages and comes up with the following probabilities. "Of 100 grooms in the 45–49 age bracket, 10 will remarry: of 100 brides in this age group, only 3–4 in 100 will remarry. The remarriage rate for men past 55 is five times that for women the same age." [7]

The explanations for this disparity probably are several. During the middle years, men who are heads of families need wives to help care for their homes and children. Where the situation is reversed and the woman has the children, however, the opposite situation prevails; men are reluctant to assume the burden of the woman's children. Moreover, middle-aged women have to compete with the greater physical attractiveness of younger women. As we move into the older ages, the differential longevity of men and women begins to increase in effect. There develops a gross shortage of men eligible for remarriage.

There is some indication that the traditional difference in remarriage rates for men and women is lessening. Statistics for both Massachusetts and Iowa suggest that this may be happening. [8] If so, it may reflect at least two things. First, the trend toward smaller families may be lessening the deterrent effect of children upon the remarriage of women. Second, the trend toward equality between the sexes may be increasing the acceptability of those women as marital partners.

INTERVAL TO REMARRIAGE

The interval between the ending of the first marriage and remarriage depends upon how the first marriage is terminated. The intervals for both

[7] Ibid. p. 55.
[8] Thomas P. Monahan, "One Hundred Years of Marriages in Massachusetts," *American Journal of Sociology* 56 (May 1951), pp. 538–9.

divorced and widowed persons tend to be relatively short but are considerably shorter in the case of divorce.

Jacobson reports that one-third of the women who remarry following divorce do so within one year. Almost half remarry within two years and approximately two-thirds remarry within five years. He estimates slightly longer intervals for men but that three-fifths of the men who remarry after divorce do so within five years.[9] Slightly shorter intervals are implied in Glick's findings, from survey data and from data collected by the National Office of Vital Statistics, that three-fourths of all divorced persons remarry within five years.[10]

Bernard's analysis of 849 divorced women and 809 divorced men in the hypothetical city of Utopolis showed that the average intervals between first and second marriages were 4.6 years and 2.5 years, respectively (see Table 2). She also quotes, with approval, Landis's statement that "the large proportion of divorced persons who remarry so quickly makes one suspect that students of the family . . . have discounted too heavily the notion of the man on the street that most divorces take place so that one or both parties may be free to marry a person already selected." [11]

The interval from widowhood to remarriage varies both by sex and by age. Widowers remarry sooner than widows, and the disparity increases with increasing age. In Bernard's 2009 remarriages, the average interval was 3.4 years for 543 widowers and 6.2 years for 445 widows (see Table 2).

COURTSHIP AND WEDDING BEHAVIOR IN REMARRIAGES

In New Haven, Connecticut, Hollingshead studied 900 couples, 715 of whom were being married for the first time and 185 of whom had at least one partner marrying for the second or a subsequent time. The courtship pattern, he found, was determined, more than anything else, by whether the woman had been married before. Women who had been married before had courtships, before engagement, of about one year's duration. Where the woman had not been married before, the pre-engagement courtship lasted an average of almost a year and a half, irrespective of whether the man had been married before. Similarly, women who were remarrying were less likely to have a formal engagement period, were less likely to receive an

[9] Paul H. Jacobson, *American Marriage and Divorce*, New York: Rinehart and Company, 1959, pp. 69–70.

[10] Op. cit.

[11] Paul H. Landis, "Sequential Marriage," *Journal of Home Economics* 42 (Oct. 1950), p. 626; as quoted in Jessie Bernard, op. cit. p. 66.

engagement ring, and, if engaged, were likely to be engaged for a shorter time before the marriage (see Table 4).

TABLE 4. *Selected Behavioral Traits Associated with the Courtship and Wedding by Marriage Type.*

BEHAVIORAL TRAIT	MARRIAGE TYPE			
	First marriage for both	Woman married before	Man married before	Both married before
Number of months dating before engagement	17.7	13.4	17.3	12.2
Number of months engaged	10.3	6.9	9.0	4.9
Percentage engaged	89.4	69.4	74.1	53.8
Percentage with engagement ring	83.9	59.7	63.8	43.1
Percentage with formal wedding	69.7	4.8	29.3	6.2
Percentage with church wedding	81.3	22.6	44.8	24.6
Number of wedding guests	172	34	77	30
Percentage of cases where bride's family paid for wedding	45.7	14.8	23.1	3.1

Source: August B. Hollingshead, "Marital Status and Wedding Behavior," *Marriage and Family Living* 14 (Nov. 1952), pp. 310–11.

Wedding behavior also tended to vary much more according to whether the bride was remarrying than according to whether the groom was remarrying. Only about 5 per cent of the remarrying brides had formal weddings and only 20–25 per cent had church weddings. Four-fifths of the first weddings were church weddings, and 45 per cent of those where a previously married man was marrying a single woman were church weddings. In addition, there were fewer wedding guests and the wife's family was much less likely to pay for the wedding if she were remarrying (see Table 4).[12]

THE SUCCESS OF REMARRIAGES

After having studied the chapter on marital adjustment, the student should be prepared to understand that it is equally difficult to estimate the degree of success achieved in remarriages. What criteria are we to use? Divorce rates? Duration of marriage to divorce? Marital-happiness estimates? Marital-adjustment scores? Achievement in other areas of life? There is no general agreement on what good remarriages are any more than there is agreement on

[12] August B. Hollingshead, "Marital Status and Wedding Behavior," *Marriage and Family Living* 14 (Nov. 1952), p. 310.

what good first marriages are. In general, the data on success in remarriage are even scantier than those available for first marriages, but some comparisons may be made.

DIVORCE FROM REMARRIAGE

The most definitive study of divorce rates among remarriages has been made by Monahan, using data for the entire state of Iowa during the period 1953–55. During those three years there were 70,901 marriages and 15,502 divorces in the state, the ratio of divorces per 100 marriages being 21.9.[13] Monahan's data are summarized in Figure 2.

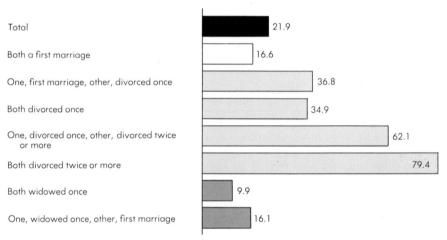

FIGURE 2. *Ratio of divorces per 100 marriages by previous marital background, Iowa, 1953–55.*

Source: Thomas P. Monahan, "The Changing Nature and Instability of Remarriages," *Eugenics Quarterly* 5 (June 1958).

As reported in the last chapter, Monahan found the ratio of divorces per 100 marriages to be only 16.6 where both husband and wife were in their first marriages. Figure 2 also shows the ratios to be low where one or both partners had been previously widowed. When divorce is used as the criterion, remarriage following widowhood is quite successful. At least two sets of inferences might reasonably be drawn from these data. First, there is probably some basis for assuming that widowed persons often are reasonably well adjusted

[13] Thomas P. Monahan, "The Changing Nature and Instability of Remarriages," *Eugenics Quarterly* 5 (June 1958), pp. 73–85. See also Thomas P. Monahan, "How Stable Are Remarriages?," *American Journal of Sociology* 57 (Nov. 1952), pp. 280–88.

persons and their prior experience with marriage was not too bad. While there are malcontents and bitterly unhappy people among the widowed, undoubtedly they are fewer in number than in the general population. Such persons logically should be expected to approach remarriage with values, attitudes, and skills that would predispose them to achieve satisfaction in their new relationships. Second, the lower divorce rate among the remarriages of widowed persons must also reflect the older ages of such persons. Even those remarried couples who are unhappy with one another are not in as good a position to undergo divorce as younger persons would be.

The findings on divorce rates among previously divorced persons, in Figure 2, are startling. The divorce rate where either partner or both partners have been divorced once is over twice as high as in first marriages. Where either one or both have been divorced more than once, the rate doubles again. Where both partners had been divorced at least twice previously, fully 79 per cent of the remarriages ended in divorce.

Those figures seem to suggest that marital adjustment involves a rigorous selection process and that failure to make the necessary adjustments in the first marriage lessens considerably the probability that they will be made in a second marriage. Failure a second time greatly lessens the probability of permanence in a third marriage, and so on. This lends support to the position of those people who maintain that divorce often reflects personality problems in the persons involved and that there is a hard core of essentially neurotic people who go through a series of marriages and divorces.

Monahan does point out that the probability of divorce in remarriage may appear somewhat exaggerated by the fact that the duration of marriage to divorce is shorter in remarriages. The duration of marriage to divorce is shorter in second marriages than in first marriages, is shorter in third marriages than in second marriages, and so on.[14] This could not, however, account for any considerable portion of the differences found.

Landis supports Monahan's conclusions about the higher divorce rates among remarriages. He reported that second marriages are about 50 per cent more risky than first marriages and that women are somewhat poorer risks for remarriage than men are.[15] Other fragmentary studies all support the fact that remarriages have higher divorce rates.

The explanation for higher divorce rates in remarriages may be sociological as well as psychological. The status of divorced persons in American society is, at best, uncomfortable. They feel out of place in most social groups and

[14] Thomas P. Monahan, "The Duration of Marriage to Divorce: Second Marriages and Migratory Types," *Marriage and Family Living* 21 (May 1959), pp. 134-8.

[15] Paul H. Landis, op. cit. p. 627.

remain aware of the threat which their divorced status presents to others. Family members, friends, and even their children are likely to pressure divorced persons toward remarriage. As a consequence, many divorced persons begin dating again before they are emotionally ready for it and remarry after very short intervals. Our knowledge of courtship and mate selection makes it appear that such marriages might be more divorce-prone even without the complicating effects of an earlier divorce.[16]

It might also prove instructive, in the future, to have data broken down by socio-economic status. We do not yet know whether the remarriages of middle-class persons are as unstable as those of the population generally. There is at least the possibility that second and third divorces are more heavily concentrated at the bottom of the socio-economic structure than first divorces are. Such an hypothesis would be consistent with the data on adjustment in second marriages to be reported in the next section.

ADJUSTMENT IN REMARRIAGES

At least three major studies have provided data on the quality of remarriages. The higher divorce rates among remarriages should not blind us to the fact that the vast majority of remarriages—as with the vast majority of first marriages—do not end in divorce.

Harvey Locke, in his study of predicting marital adjustment by comparing happily married with divorced persons, secured data on 21 happily married persons who had remarried following widowhood and upon 146 divorced persons who had remarried. He tested the hypothesis that both bereaved and divorced persons are less well adjusted in their second marriages than once-married persons are in their first marriages.[17]

Locke reasoned that widowed persons in remarriages would tend to idealize their former mates and would find that their present mates suffered by comparison. The data, however, did not support this reasoning. The mean marital-adjustment score of the widowed-remarried persons was 169.7, while it was only 166.8 among those in their first marriages. Thus, Locke was forced to conclude that remarriages after widowhood are as happy as first marriages. He explained this finding as follows. Widowed and then remarried persons probably are highly adaptable or they would not have entered their second mar-

---

[16] Remarriages also are more likely to be interreligious marriages. See Erich Rosenthal, "Divorce and Religious Intermarriage: The Effect of Previous Marital Status Upon Subsequent Marital Behavior," *Journal of Marriage and the Family* 32 (Aug. 1970), pp. 435–40.

[17] Harvey J. Locke, *Predicting Adjustment in Marriage: A Comparison of a Divorced and a Happily Married Group*, New York: Henry Holt and Company, 1951, pp. 298–309.

riages; if they are more adaptable, then they should adjust to the requirements of their second marriages in spite of idealization of the deceased spouse.

Turning to analysis of the marital adjustments of the 146 persons remarried following divorce, Locke found that approximately 45 per cent rated their second marriages to be "very happy" and another 32 per cent said they were "happy." A summary of his findings, along with comparable data from the Burgess and Cottrell and Terman studies of first marriages, is shown in Table 5. The 76.7 per cent of the remarriages that were reported to be either very

TABLE 5. *Marital Happiness Ratings in First Marriages and Remarriages.*

HAPPINESS RATINGS	526 ILLINOIS FIRST MARRIAGES	792 CALIFORNIA FIRST MARRIAGES		146 REMARRIAGES
		Husbands	Wives	
Very happy or happy	63.1%	82.5%	85.2%	76.7%
Average	14.4	12.9	9.2	12.3
Unhappy or very unhappy	21.5	4.6	5.6	11.0
Totals	99.0	100.0	100.0	100.0

Source: Ernest W. Burgess and Leonard S. Cottrell, Jr., *Predicting Success or Failure in Marriage,* New York: Prentice-Hall, 1939, p. 32; Lewis M. Terman, *Psychological Factors in Marital Happiness.* New York: McGraw-Hill Book Company, 1938, p. 78; and Harvey J. Locke, *Predicting Adjustment in Marriage: A Comparison of a Divorced and a Happily Married Group,* New York: Henry Holt and Company, 1951, p. 302.

happy or happy is actually higher than Burgess and Cottrell found among Illinois couples and nearly as high as Terman reported for California couples. The pattern is similar when the average and unhappy categories are considered. On the basis of this evidence, Locke concluded that the divorced persons in his study were fairly good risks for subsequent marriages.

Locke and Klausner also have reported data from a smaller study comparing 47 divorced and remarried persons with 64 once-married persons in the Los Angeles area. Using the Burgess and Cottrell marriage-adjustment scale, they found that almost equal proportions of the remarried and once-married groups fell into "good" and "fair" marital-adjustment categories.[18] Interestingly, in this study, remarried men made lower adjustment scores than remarried women did, directly contradicting Landis's assertion that women are poorer risks for remarriage than men are. Both of these sex comparisons were

[18] Harvey J. Locke and William J. Klausner, "Marital Adjustment of Divorced Persons in Subsequent Marriages," *Sociology and Social Research* 33 (Nov. 1948), pp. 97–101.

based upon fragmentary data, and the only thing that can be said at this point is that research has yet to demonstrate whether men or women make better adjustment in remarriages.

The extensive study by Goode of the readjustments following divorce of 425 Detroit-area mothers also yielded some data on the quality of remarriages, particularly in relation to the perceived quality of these same women's first marriages. Goode correctly points out that his data on adjustment in remarriage are not definitive because none of these women had been remarried for longer than two years. He also emphasized that the most relevant comparison for previously divorced persons is not between the quality of their remarriages and the quality of all first marriages but between their own first and second marriages.

A full 87 per cent of the women in Goode's sample, who had remarried, claimed that their second marriages were "much better" than their first ones, and an additional 8 per cent said that their second marriages were "a little better." [19] The relatively high value placed upon their remarriages by these women also was shown when they replied to the question, "Would you try to tell me how you think your life would be today, in general, if you hadn't got a divorce?" Eighty-two per cent said, without qualification, that things would have been "worse" or "the same" as during the first marriage.

Finally, Bernard has analyzed the quality of remarriages thoroughly in connection with her study of the entire remarried population of the hypothetical community of Utopolis. First of all, she points out that there may not be any indication, in the higher divorce rate among remarriages, that remarriages are of poorer quality than first marriages. Divorce is a learned behavior pattern and persons who have overcome the societal taboo and been through the experience once may be more likely to use divorce again if their remarriages do not measure up to exceptionally high standards. According to this point of view, remarried persons may demand more from their new marriages and may more quickly dissolve them if their high expectations are not fulfilled. Thus, those remarriages that survive may be relatively more satisfying than most first marriages. [20]

Many analyses of divorce and remarriage have emphasized the stability of basic personality characteristics and the apparent contribution of personality problems to divorce. When we talk about "the divorce-prone" this is what we have in mind. On the other hand, even if basic personality does not change—and this assumption is being more and more frequently questioned—the way in which personality is expressed in behavior certainly does change over time.

[19] William J. Goode, *After Divorce*. Glencoe, Illinois: The Free Press, 1956, pp. 331–42.
[20] Op. cit. pp. 270–72.

Bernard analyzed three sets of factors which may conduce to greater success in remarriages.

First, an unhappy first marriage, although it may be a very painful experience, may contribute directly to the success of the second marriage. Both men and women learn, through their divorces, something about what produced the failure of their marriages. At the simplest level, there are skills such as those involved in housekeeping and in earning a living. By the time of her second marriage the wife is likely to be proficient at everything from cooking to managing a budget. Similarly, her husband is likely to have achieved a stable pattern of occupational adjustment to which both he and the new wife are accommodated. More significantly, remarried persons are likely to have increased their competence in interpersonal relationships, to have acquired more of such elusive qualities as maturity, wisdom, and tolerance. Although remarried persons may not compare favorably with the general population in these characteristics, they often are better prepared to make a success of their second marriages than they were to be successful in their first ones.

Second, it appears likely that failure in a first marriage often produces changes in the motivational structure of personality. Here we encounter a paradox. We have already stated that one divorce experience makes a second one easier and more acceptable and that this helps to account for the higher divorce rate in remarriages. At the same time, failure in a first marriage appears to make many people determined and even desperate to succeed in the second one. We saw, in Chapter 16, how many couples with a history of failure in contraceptive practice become efficient family planners when they decide that they have had all of the children that they can stand. Similarly, men and women who remain basically committed to marriage and family life in spite of divorce may acquire a near all-conquering will to succeed in the second one. The motivation may be mixed: the will to achieve the benefits of a stable family life and the will to remove the stigma of failure; but it may also be quite effective.

Third, and finally, the changes that are associated with aging may work to the benefit of partners in remarriages. We saw, in Chapter 14, that there is evidence that marriages among very young couples encounter special problems and that those who are somewhat older when they marry are less likely to divorce and tend to make higher scores on marital-adjustment scales. Most persons are beyond 30 years of age at the time of remarriage and are likely to have worked through—as much as they ever will—the rebelliousness and irresponsibility of youth. If people approaching middle-age are unlikely ever to achieve the passionate commitment to one another of youth, they are more likely to accept one another as they are and not to view each flaw in one another as a catastrophe. The comfort and security that probably are more characteristic of middle-aged marriage may produce deep and lasting satisfaction.

Being young is a fault which improves daily.

—Swedish proverb.

Bernard also sought to acquire insight into the nature of success in remarriage by comparing marriages that were judged to be "extremely successful" with marriages reported to be either "below average" or "extremely unsuccessful." In general, she found conventionality, higher social class, lack of hostility toward the first spouse, favorable attitudes of children to the remarriage, favorable attitudes of parents to the remarriage, and favorable community attitudes to the remarriage all to be associated with success. Let us look briefly at each of these groups of factors.

Both men and women who had entered their first marriages before age 20 were less likely to be reported as successful in their second marriages. Bernard reasoned that the early first marriages might be conceived of as an index of impulsiveness or unconventionality that would work against success in remarriage also. In like fashion, it was reasoned that persons who remarried immediately following divorce were behaving unconventionally while those who waited at least a year before remarrying were behaving much less impulsively. No interval before remarriage proved to be unfavorably associated with success in remarriage. Those persons who reported that their first marriages were successful (generally widows and widowers) were also more likely to be reported as successful in their remarriages.

The measures of social class used included both education and type of occupation. Some college education on the part of either the husband or wife was associated with success in remarriage, while less formal education and working at clerical, skilled, semiskilled, and service jobs were unfavorably associated.

Hostility toward one's own first spouse or toward the first spouse of the present mate proved to be unfavorably related to success. The presence of such negative attitudes could reflect, of course, either continuing emotional involvement with the former partner or some interference by the former spouse in the new marriage. In either case, the effects would be unfavorable. Friendliness toward the former spouses was not associated statistically with success in remarriage.

Custody arrangements for children of the first marriages were not associated with the quality of the remarriage except where there was alternating custody between the two parents. The adjustment of men also was affected unfavorably where their former wives had exclusive custody. As might be expected, the new marriages fared better where children of the former marriage were favorably inclined toward the new marriage and toward the new partner.

The importance of group support in influencing the success of remarriages also was indicated by findings with regard to parental attitudes and community attitudes. Approval of the new marriage, both by one's own parents and by the new spouse's parents, was associated with success; disapproval by either or both sets of parents was unfavorable. The same thing was true with regard to community attitudes. In this case, however, there was a closer association between community approval of the woman's remarriage and marital success than between community approval of the man's remarriage and marital success.[21]

THE EFFECTS OF REMARRIAGE UPON CHILDREN

Among Bernard's 2009 cases of remarriage, about 60 per cent of both men and women who remarried following divorce had children by their first marriages; among those who remarried following widowhood, from 75 to 80 per cent had children by their first marriages. The average number of children in all cases was between one and two (see Table 2). In this section, we shall summarize what sociologists have learned about the adjustment of these children in the context of the new marriage.

American attitudes toward remarriage undoubtedly are complicated by the existence of a widespread negative stereotype of stepparents. The "wicked stepmother," particularly, is prominent in the fairy tales that parents read to their children, and, for many people, the word, stepmother, calls forth an image of a cold, harsh figure who shows favoritism to her own children over those of her husband and in relation to whom the usual emotions are fear and hatred. The folk characterization of the stepfather is less clear, reflecting, perhaps, the existence of greater numbers of stepmothers than stepfathers. When he does appear, the figure presented by the stepfather often is that of an aloof, unconcerned, intolerant person who puts up with his wife's children only because he must do so. With long-standing stereotypes such as these and the relatively recent emergence of remarriage as a large-scale phenomenon, it is not surprising that the literature on relationships between stepparents and stepchildren is scanty.[22]

[21] Ibid. pp. 284–94, 355–60.
[22] See William C. Smith, *The Stepchild*, Chicago: University of Chicago Press, 1953.

One of the earliest studies to present hard data on the adjustment of children in remarriages was Nye's study of 780 boys and girls in high school in the state of Washington. He compared the adjustment of children in broken, unhappy unbroken, and reconstituted families and found little evidence to support the idea of special problems between stepparents and stepchildren. Instead, he found few apparent differences in child adjustment to broken homes, to homes in which there was only one parent, and homes that had been reconstituted through remarriage. In all three cases, the adjustment of children was better than in unhappy, unbroken homes. Twenty-nine per cent of the remarriages studied were found to fall into the happiest parent interaction tercile, and the conclusion was reached that "there are differences between the two categories of families with the differences favoring the 'reconstructed' family including a stepparent, or the 'partial' family composed of one parent and child or children." [23]

A second study, by Bowerman and Irish, gathered data from 2145 stepchildren who were junior- or senior-high-school students in Washington, Ohio, and North Carolina. Using the felt affection of the children for parents and stepparents and feelings of discrimination and rejection as criteria, they found evidence to support the view that reconstituted families provide a less favorable environment for children than do intact families. The adjustment of these children toward their stepparents was poorer than toward the real parent of the same sex. Adjustment to stepfathers usually was better than adjustment to stepmothers. Moreover, stepparents more often were believed to discriminate among the children, and stepchildren were more likely to feel rejected both by the natural parent and by the stepparent.[24]

Although Nye's study and this one are not directly comparable, there is no doubt that, if their findings do not conflict directly, at least they present quite different segments of reality. The hypothesis is suggested that children experience generally the best adjustment in intact homes, that there are more adjustment problems in reconstructed homes, and still more adjustment problems in unhappy but structurally intact homes.

That this may be the case also is suggested by Burchinal's research, using seventh- and eleventh-grade students and their parents in Cedar Rapids, Iowa. He classified the families into five types: unbroken families; broken families headed by the mother; and three types of reconstituted families—those consisting of fathers and stepmothers, those consisting of stepfathers and mothers,

[23] F. Ivan Nye, "Child Adjustment in Broken and in Unhappy Unbroken Homes," *Marriage and Family Living* 19 (Nov. 1957), pp. 356–61.

[24] Charles E. Bowerman and Donald P. Irish, "Some Relationships of Stepchildren to Their Parents," *Marriage and Family Living* 24 (May 1962), pp. 113–21.

and those in which both parents had divorced and remarried. Selected measures of personality adjustment and selected measures of social relationships were then compared among students in the five family types.[25]

In general the findings were of no striking differences in the adjustment of children in the five family types. There were no differences on any of the personality measures, in participation in school or community activities, in school-grade point averages, in the number of schoolmates the respondent thought liked him or her, in attitudes toward school, or, among girls, how many of their schoolmates they liked. A few significant differences appeared. Students from unbroken homes were absent the least number of days from school and those from broken homes were absent the greatest number of days. It was also found that boys living with their fathers and stepmothers reported liking fewer of their schoolmates than was true among any of the other family types.

William Goode points out that even when we establish the fact of a relationship between divorce and/or remarriage and certain personality or social characteristics of children we still have not determined that divorce and remarriage have any effects upon children. The problems, whatever they may be, may be caused by the same set of factors that predisposed the parents to divorce in the first place. The establishment of cause-and-effect relationships simply has not been done as yet.

Goode's own analysis of remarriage among divorced mothers in the Detroit area indicated that most of the remarried mothers were satisfied with their children and with the children's adjustment. He concludes that remarriage tends to regularize the position of the children following whatever trauma was associated with the divorce and that, in most ways, reconstituted families are similar to unbroken families. Tensions between children and the new parent are believed to decrease with time.[26]

Bernard reports on a study carried out by graduate students at Pennsylvania State University in which Bernreuter Personality Inventory scores were obtained for 59 young men and women who lived in families where there had been a remarriage. Since norms on this test are available for college students, the scores of the children of remarriages could be measured against those norms. On none of the three scores contained within the inventory—stability, self-sufficiency, or dominance—did the children of remarriages differ significantly from the general college population. When tests were made separately for students whose parents' remarriages followed divorce and bereavement,

[25] Lee G. Burchinal, "Characteristics of Adolescents from Unbroken, Broken, and Reconstituted Families," *Journal of Marriage and the Family* 26 (Feb. 1964), pp. 44–51.

[26] Op. cit. pp. 307, 339–341.

again no significant differences were found. The data did not support the view that divorce leaves children more disturbed than does bereavement.[27]

Concluding that most remarriages are not harmful to children, Bernard explains this situation in terms of three different factors: (1) the attitudes of the children to the remarriage; (2) the new parent as a salvaging force; and (3) the inherent resiliency of human nature.

The Utopolis data showed that most children, whether the first marriage was broken by divorce or death, tend to be in favor of the remarriage of the parent with whom they are living. Even adult children seem generally to support their parents' remarriages. The only partial exceptions were found where custody of the children alternated between the parents and where the remarriage of a father appeared to threaten the children's interest in his property.

The stereotype of the unfeeling stepparent was contradicted in the Utopolis data by both men and women who provided the wisdom, love, and understanding to help their stepchildren compensate for whatever trauma had been associated with divorce. Interestingly, these effects were found more often in remarriages following divorce than in those following widowhood. The stepparent replacing a deceased parent was much more likely to be resented than the stepparent replacing a divorced parent.

Finally, Bernard emphasizes the inherent toughness of the human organism. She points out that most persons, whether their parents' marriages have been broken or not, undergo some traumatic childhood experiences. Most persons cope effectively with these factors and may even emerge stronger for them. Perhaps only when there is a compounding of unfortunate experiences is personality damage likely to result. It stands to reason that the effects of divorce or death of a parent and remarriage should be different in the lives of middle-class children whose lives otherwise are safe and secure, than in lower socio-economic groups whose problems are compounded by minority-group status and social and personal pathologies of other sorts. Perhaps the greatest increases in our understanding of the effects of remarriage upon children will come when we are able successfully to control for the variable of economic status.[28]

THE DYNAMICS OF REMARRIAGE

Up to now we have analyzed the incidence and nature of remarriage, the degree of success encountered in it, and its effect upon children. Our approach has been analytic and statistical. When we are dealing with phenomena that

[27] Op. cit. pp. 306–11.
[28] Ibid. pp. 318–23.

we know well—phenomena to which we have been intimately exposed over long periods of time—most of us are capable of applying broad generalizations to the actual experiences of living men and women. When we come to re-marriage, however, we have reached a point in family experience with which only a minority of college students have had direct, sustained contact. Re-marriage, to most 20-year-olds who are convinced that their own marriages will be successful and life-long, may be about as academic as the family system of a preliterate society on another continent. To put some descriptive meat upon the statistical bones, let us look briefly at some of the dynamics of remarriage.

THE DYNAMICS OF COURTSHIP

We saw earlier in the chapter that courtship among persons who are re-marrying—particularly among women who are remarrying—tends to be con-siderably shorter than among the young and inexperienced. Where a triangle situation has existed before divorce, this may help to explain the short court-ship, but there are several reasons for thinking that this is not the major ex-planation. First is the shorter courtships among remarrying women than among remarrying men. Stripped of its sentimental overtones, courtship may be described as convincing the woman involved to enter a sanctioned sex re-lationship. Where the woman is sexually rather inexperienced, this apparently involves a great deal of circumlocution; coquettishness is the order of the day. In remarriage, however, both the man and the woman know the woman to be sexually experienced. The man feels a freedom to approach his partner that would have been unthinkable before a first marriage. For the woman, the cultural taboos upon sexual experience have long since been overcome. She has long ago adopted a fully heterosexual pattern of life and has little reason to fear the consequences of a sex relationship now.

Not that courtship before remarriage becomes a sexual orgy. Far from it. The tonicity of the relationship and the erotic content of the relationship are likely to be lower than among previously unmarried persons. The couple are older and their sex needs—particularly those of the man—may be somewhat less frequent and less imperious than among younger people. The couple also have had enough marital experience to be somewhat better able to place sex in proper proportion to other aspects of marriage. Thus we have a paradox. Courtship before remarriage tends quickly to become sexually explicit and the percentage of couples who have sexual intercourse is extremely high.[29] Yet

[29] Adequate data on this point are not available. Terman reported the figure for women to be beyond 80 per cent as long as 30 years ago. See Lewis M. Terman, *Psychological Factors in Marital Happiness*, New York: McGraw-Hill Book Company, 1938, p. 418.

the fact of having had sexual intercourse is not likely to lead to guilt or to alter seriously the probability of marriage. Sex, once intercourse is begun, is likely to occupy less of the time and attention of the couple than among younger persons.

Nor should sex be singled out as *the* area in which couples courting before remarriage are more intimate. In fact, they may tend to anticipate most of the conditions of married life. While a young swain ordinarily takes most of his meals before seeing his girl or ritually takes her out for a hamburger or an elaborate meal, older couples are likely to take a good portion of their evening meals, at least, together. Among other things, the man is looking for a cook. The woman, who is used to cooking for a man, may find satisfaction in doing so and may use her culinary competence as a major inducement to the man to marry her. She is likely also to assume some wifely responsibility for his clothing and his living quarters; doing laundry, mending, and even cleaning for him. In turn, the man often assumes some financial responsibility in relation to the woman. He may buy part or all of the groceries, he may buy clothing for her in a way that would be considered to be in very bad taste if done by a younger man. He may even make a regular financial contribution to the maintenance of her household.

Where there are children present, they are likely to figure prominently in the courtship. If marriage is to occur, both the man and the woman must woo one another's children. Marriage may occur over the opposition of children, but it is somewhat unlikely and, in the eyes of both partners, certainly undesirable. Consequently both partners during courtship are likely to move into quasi-parental roles in relation to any young children the other may have. These roles include concerted efforts at the development of affection, but they also include everything from changing diapers, to bathing, to spanking, and to having the children accompany their parents on "dates."

With quasi-marital and quasi-parental roles developing so easily in courtship and with the demands that those roles reflect indicating the need for marriage, it should not be surprising that courtship before remarriage is often relatively short. There are many variations from this pattern, of course. When the couples are younger and there are no children involved, their courtships may be virtually indistinguishable from those of persons marrying for the first time. At the other extreme, where there are grown children, particularly of the man, who fear the loss of property interests if he remarries, the courtship may be greatly complicated by outside resistance. Among the divorced and widowed, also, are to be found a certain number of people who want companionship but are loathe to remarry. Among some of them, the courtship may reach some plateau where one or both are relatively comfortable and may remain there over a long period of time.

Remarriages, once decided upon, are likely to come about more quickly and to be accomplished with less fanfare than first marriages. Weddings are less likely to be church weddings, invited guests usually are fewer, and the ceremony is more likely to be performed by a civil official. There is less aura of people being initiated into a new realm of experience, and, although it may not be consciously recognized, the role of the principals looms much larger in the remarriage ceremony. In first marriages, the emphasis is more on the ritual—upon the ceremony itself—and the young man and woman are somewhat dwarfed by the pomp and mysticism associated with it. In second marriages, by contrast, the ceremony often is viewed simply as giving sanction to a relationship that already exists or would exist, in different form perhaps, whether or not official provision were made for it.

THE DYNAMICS OF MARITAL ADJUSTMENT

Adjustment in remarriages is both like and unlike adjustment in first marriages. There is the need to establish new habits and roles and to affirm the primacy of the emotional ties between the new husband and wife. Adjustments must be worked out in each of the conventional areas—sex, in-laws, money, friends, religion, and so on. But there are differences too.

At least one of the partners is not a beginner—there is a storehouse, as it were, of knowledge and experience upon which to draw. The spouses are likely to be older and to have worked through most of the authority problems that are so prominent in young adulthood. In some ways, at least, the man is likely to be more sure of his manhood and the woman to be more sure of herself as a woman.

But there are scars, too, resulting from the death or divorce that made the remarriage possible. And, usually, there are more people involved; in addition to the primary families of the new husband and wife, there may be up to two former spouses, and there may be up to two sets of children. If nothing else, most remarriages are more crowded than most first marriages.

The initial marital adjustments probably are made more quickly in remarriages than in first marriages. As already described, quasi-marital and quasi-parental roles are more likely to have been established before the marriage ceremony takes place. In some ways, too, the spouses are less likely to be threatened by the moods of their partners. Middle-aged people often know, as younger people seldom can, that the partner's being too tired to go out, or for sex, or being just plain grouchy does not automatically reflect upon oneself. On the other hand, what emotional crises do develop early in remarriages—and all of the conventional ones do to some degree—have more potential for disrupting the marriage. Paradoxically, remarried couples both adjust quicker and divorce quicker than do first-married couples.

Sex Adjustment. The sex adjustment in remarriages probably binds the pair together more comfortably than in first marriages. With the greater likelihood of intimate sexual knowledge of one another before marriage, remarriages may be more selective in the first place; it is difficult to imagine middle-aged people entering a marriage when they have reason to think that the sex relationship will not be satisfactory.[30]

Most of the sexual disabilities suffered by young wives in first marriages probably are not experienced by older women in remarriages. Wives in remarriage are more likely to be comfortable with their own bodies and with those of men. They are not likely to be squeamish or easily offended; they are likely to sympathize with the sexual needs of their husbands when they are greater than the wives' own; and there is far less likely to be a significant difference in sexual need. The man's needs typically have been declining with age [31] while the woman's capacity for sexual expression has been increasing.

No figures are available on the frequency of marital intercourse by age and remarried status, but we might hazard the hypothesis that, age for age, the frequency of intercourse is higher in remarriages than in first marriages. There are at least two reasons for this. First is the fact that, at a given age level, the remarriages will be of shorter duration. Novelty certainly gives stimulus to sexual participation, and in remarriages there has been less time for the novelty to wear off. Second, sexual participation in remarriage is less likely to suffer the debilitating effects of gross differences in sexual need and of being used as a focus for conflicts originating in other areas of the marriage.

Social Life. In some other areas of adjustment, remarriages are much more likely to suffer some disadvantage. The social life of remarried couples, for example, often has to undergo considerable reorganization. The specific pat-

---

[30] Benjamin Schlesinger, "Remarriage as Family Reorganization for Divorced Persons—A Canadian Study," *Journal of Comparative Family Studies* 1 (Autumn 1970), pp. 101–18.

[31] The fact that the sexual needs of men tend to decline with age should not be over-emphasized. Several studies have shown that many males remain sexually active and competent well into old age. A survey by *Sexology* magazine, for example, reported that 70 per cent of the married men over 65 years of age engaged in sexual intercourse regularly and led satisfying sexual lives. See Gustave Newman and Claude R. Nichols, "Sexual Activities and Attitudes in Older Persons," *Journal of the American Medical Association* 173 (May 1960), pp. 33–5; William H. Masters and Virginia E. Johnson, *Human Sexual Response*, Boston: Little, Brown, 1966, pp. 248–9; and Mark Tarail, "Sex Over 65," *Sexology* (Feb. 1962), pp. 440–45.

terns may vary according to whether one or both partners are being remarried and whether the new marriage follows death or divorce, but certain general observations may be offered.

In many instances, the new couple will encounter resistance from among old friends. Friends of a first-married man or woman entering marriage with someone who has been married before may think the match inappropriate and convey their distaste for the relationship to the couple. Or the widowed person who has remarried may find that acquaintances interpret it as betrayal of the memory of the deceased spouse. Those who remarry following divorce are even more likely to encounter social disapproval. Even the so-called "innocent party" who did not want the divorce and who, until now, has been the object of sympathy may suddenly find himself or herself the object of some disapproval. In the case of the more aggressive partner in the divorce, or where there has been a triangle, there is almost certain to be censure from outsiders.

Most remarried couples attempt to cope, for a time, with the cool attitudes of their social groups and some eventually win a greater degree of approval for the new marriage. It goes without saying, however, that strains are produced in the marriage. It is not pleasant to find oneself in disapproval by people whose opinions have mattered in the past. Whether the couple attempt to ignore such disapproval or whether they acknowledge it openly, their relationship becomes a source of pain to them.

It seems likely that most couples solve the problem to some degree by giving up some old friendships and making new ones among people who were not acquainted with the former marriage(s) and who accept the new relationship simply for what it is. It is not as simple to do this, however, as it sounds. For the months or even years that the change takes, remarried couples suffer some disability that most first-married couples do not. A significant number of couples find it necessary either to change jobs or to move away, or both, in order to escape the offended feelings of former associates.

Adjustment to Former Partners. That remarriages are more crowded than first marriages has been mentioned. In a real sense, the first marriage partners of the new spouses are parties to the remarriage also. Although they are not physically present, they intrude on the new marriage in subtle and not-so-subtle ways.

Where one of the parties in the new marriage has been widowed, the spouse may find himself or herself competing with the memory of the former partner. Countless analyses of bereavement have pointed out that there is a tendency —particularly where the former marriage was happy, but even when it was not too satisfactory—for the surviving spouse gradually to build up an idealized image of the deceased partner. The unpleasantnesses of earlier days tend to be forgotten while the good things are remembered, and the deceased spouse takes on an image larger than life. In remarriage, the new spouse, however desirable he or she may be, may be compared with this idealized image and found wanting.

In extreme forms of this problem there may be numerous daily reminders of the former relationship. The new spouse may actually have moved into the house or apartment formerly shared with the deceased partner. Out of habit, he or she may occasionally be called by the former partner's name. Or there may be photographs of the former partner unthinkingly displayed in prominent places, or mementoes of the former life that are treasured to the distress of the new spouse. The competition with memories is particularly difficult, because the norms of our society hold that one should not feel animosity toward a deceased person. The new spouse must woo his partner away from memories without appearing to be trying to do so.

When the remarriage has followed divorce, one must cope with the physical being of the former spouse rather than with memories. If the former spouse was the reluctant partner in the divorce, he or she may still carry a torch and may literally be a rival in the new relationship. There are instances of former spouses waging, for months and years, battles to regain their partners. While the probability of the divorced spouse's actually being successful is small, considerable threat is likely to be felt by the new spouse.

Intrusion by the former spouse is likely, whether or not there remains any emotional attraction, when there are children involved. If the new marriage has custody of the children, then the former spouse usually must be permitted some entrée for visits with them. If the former spouse has custody, then he or she must be placated in order that continuing contacts with the children not be jeopardized. The necessity for such continuing contacts affords an aggrieved former spouse the opportunity to make demands that annoy the new partners and create strain.

Becoming a New Family. The foregoing sections probably have made it clear that adjustments in remarriages tend to be most complicated when there are children present from one or both of the preceding marriages. For Utopolis, Bernard found that about 21.5 per cent of the men and 23.4 per cent of the women had children by a previous marriage, and in 5.6 per cent of the cases both the new husband and wife had children. Following divorce, the typical situation was for a mother and her children to secure a new husband and father. Following widowhood, on the other hand, it was typically a father and his children who secured a new wife and mother.[32]

[32] Op. cit. pp. 211–12.

Marital adjustment may be viewed as a process whereby the separate value systems, attitudes, and habit patterns of the spouses yield to a new and joint way of life. That many people do not give up old patterns easily is illustrated by the greater prevalence of conflict early in most marriages. In remarriages with children, the situation is more complicated because there are more people involved. Beyond that, the presence of other people who may be drawn into witting or unwitting alliances may strengthen one's resistance to change and prolong the time required for it to occur.

A wedding ceremony, by itself, does little to weld two families into one. Instead, what happens is that the two families take up common residence but attempt unknowingly to continue their old ways of life. This is almost bound to bring them into conflict. It happens in different ways.

First, when there are children present, they share with their natural parent a host of experiences and memories that are not shared by the other partner and his or her children, if such are present. In the normal course of conversation, and without any intent of so doing, one of the partners tends to be relegated to the role of outsider. He or she has not shared the common experiences, be they joyous, sentimental, or sad. The partner who is left out, unless he or she be exceptionally patient and wise, may react defensively. He may try to compete for the center of attention in the group, he may retaliate by attacking the group or one of its members, or he may withdraw emotionally and set the family on an alienation course.

Far more directly, there is a strong tendency for alliances to develop within the family. By their very nature, family ties are particularistic, and the pattern of special consideration that has grown up between a parent and children over the years is not easily or automatically extended to the new spouse and his or her children. Each partner justifiably feels that the other shows favoritism to his own natural children. Again it takes wisdom for the couple to realize what is happening and to prevent it from developing into a destructively rivalrous situation.

The potential for conflicts in reconstituted families is both greater and less than in first marriages. The tolerance that comes with age and experience must be balanced against the involvement of children in whatever conflict exists; the parents may be moved to greater wisdom by having jointly to deal with the demands made by their children, and, at the same time, the children may carry the fray with a vigor that only the young possess.

Just as earlier shared family experiences tend to work against the solidarity of the new family, so does time and new experience work for it. For months, or even years, customary remembrances tend to go back to a time when this family did not exist. But eventually the pattern of shared experience comes to outweigh the separate experiences and the group remembers the things that "we" did together or which happened to "us." Those "other things" happened a long time ago and no longer seem real or important.

Similarly, a new set of affectional relationships develops. A stepparent may come to be as cherished as the natural parent, and the relationship may draw special strength from the fact that it was worked out without the accident of birth. The stepparent, too, may cease to distinguish between my children, your children, and our children. The terms, Mom, and Dad, and son, and daughter may come to apply as naturally to sociological children as to biological ones. With or without benefit of legal adoptive procedures, a common family culture comes into existence.

At what point reconstituted families become more like than unlike original families it is impossible to say. It would be absurd to state that differences do not continue to exist. The relative strengths and problems of reconstituted and original families is a topic that is just beginning to be explored.

Summary

Remarriages are by no means a homogeneous phenomenon. Only one, or both, of the partners may be remarrying. The remarriage may follow bereavement or divorce or both. There may or may not be children from one or both of the earlier marriages.

Until about the end of World War I, remarriage in the United States was uncommon and most of it took place following widowhood. As divorce rates rose, however, so did rates of remarriage following divorce. Just after World War II, the remarriage rate for marriages was almost 20 per cent and that for individuals was about 12.5 per cent. Remarriage rates are continuing to climb, and it is estimated that between 20 and 25 per cent of all persons marrying recently have been marrying for the second or a subsequent time.

Remarriage rates are higher among blacks than among whites. This reflects both the higher death rate and the higher divorce rate among blacks. As black families come to approximate the middle-class model, their remarriage rates are expected to decline somewhat.

Men who are remarrying tend to be about 13 years older than men who are marrying for the first time; women who are remarrying are about 10 years older. The difference between the ages of bride and groom also is about twice as great in remarriages as in first marriages. Up to about 35 years of age, most remarriages follow divorce; after age 35, the number of remarriages following bereavement climbs rapidly.

Most divorced persons remarry. In fact, age for age, divorced persons have higher probabilitiies of remarrying than single persons do of getting married for the first time. Again, age for age, widowed persons are more likely to wed than single persons are. Divorced persons have the highest probabilities of marrying, widows and widowers come next, and single persons have the poorest chances of all. Divorced and widowed men also have greater probabilities of remarriage than divorcees and widows do.

Intervals to remarriage tend to be relatively short and to be shorter following divorce than following bereavement. Up to three-fourths of all divorced persons remarry within five years. Remarriages generally follow shorter courtships than first marriages do, more of the ceremonies are civil ceremonies, and there is less pomp and formality than in first weddings. The fact of remarriage for the woman is more important in determining the type of courtship and wedding than is the fact of remarriage of the man.

Studies show that remarriages following divorce have higher divorce rates than first marriages do and remarriages following bereavement have lower divorce rates than first marriages do. The probability of divorce from remarriage increases directly with the previous divorce experience of either partner. Two or more divorces on either side suggests the existence of personality problems that militate against success in any future marriage.

Studies of adjustment among remarried couples yield a different pattern of findings. Happiness ratings and marital-adjustment scores generally do not show remarriages to be less satisfactory than first marriages. The vast majority of remarried persons state that their second marriages are better than their first ones were. It appears that, even if basic personality structure is not amenable to change, the way in which personality is expressed in behavior may change in second marriages. Three factors working to make second marriages successful are the learning which occurred during the first marriage, changes in motivation which follow an unsuccessful first marriage, and changes that are associated with increasing age and social maturity.

Research into the effects of remarriage upon children indicates that adjustment is better than in broken homes or emotionally broken homes but perhaps not so good as in happy, intact homes. Most remarried mothers report themselves to be satisfied with their children's adjustment, and personality testing of such children generally fails to show important differences between them and children from intact homes.

The dynamics of courtship and adjustment in remarriage differ from those same phenomena in first marriages. Prior marital experience on the part of the woman changes courtship more than does that same experience on the part of the man. Before remarriage, couples are more likely to be intimate sexually but may devote less exclusive attention to sex than first-marrying couples do. Also, before remarriage, couples may come to play quasi-marital roles in many different areas of life and may assume quasi-parental roles as well.

Adjustment in remarriages is similar in many ways to adjustment to first marriages. There are the same general areas in which adjustment must be made, and the new couple must establish a common way of life. Adjustment differs from that in first marriages, too. Neither of the pair may be beginners and there may be more in-laws and children to be dealt with. Emotional crises may develop more quickly and may either be resolved more quickly or rapidly lead to divorce.

The reorganization of the couple's social life may be troubling initially. Some rejection by former friends often is encountered and some frustration experienced. Part of the solution usually involves making new friends who have no ties with the former marriage(s). Sometimes, too, the problem is alleviated by moving to a new location and/or taking a new job.

Then there are former marital partners who intrude on the new relationship. Deceased former spouses intrude symbolically and divorced partners often intrude directly. Particularly where there are children from a former marriage, contacts must be maintained with the divorced spouse.

Adjustment in remarriages probably is most complicated when there are children present from a former marriage. The parent and his or her children inevitably share with one another more than they do with the new spouse. This can lead to rivalry or to emotional withdrawal. In more extreme cases, alliances may develop within the new family which threaten its solidarity as a group. With time, however, these divisive forces tend to yield to the accumulating shared experience in the new family and to the developing affectional relationships within it. Remarriages remain different from first marriages, but the nature of the continuing differences has not yet been analyzed adequately.

SUGGESTED READINGS

Bernard, Jessie, *Remarriage: A Study of Marriage*, New York: Dryden Press, 1956. The most exhaustive study of remarriages that has yet been made. Deals both with the statistics and the dynamics of remarriage.

Engelson, James, and Engleson, Janet, *Parents Without Partners*, New York: E. P. Dutton, 1961. A guide for divorced, widowed, or separated parents written by a remarried couple who had been members of the organization, Parents Without Partners, Inc.

Fanshel, David, *Foster Parenthood: A Role Analysis*, Minneapolis: University of Minnesota Press, 1966. Report of a study of child care by foster parents. Analyzes these people by the way they perceive their roles, the satisfactions they derive from them, and the problems involved.

Goode, William J., *After Divorce*, Glencoe, Illinois: The Free Press, 1956. Chapters 18–22 deal with problems of dating, courtship, and remarriage.

Monahan, Thomas P., "The Changing Nature and Instability of Remarriages," *Eugenics Quarterly* 5 (June 1958), pp. 73–85. The most definitive work to date on divorce rates comparing first marriages and remarriages.

Simon, Anne W., *Stepchild in the Family: A View of Children in Remarriage*, New York: The Odyssey Press, 1964. The author, who has been a step-grand-child, a stepchild, and a stepmother, analyzes the problems encountered in remarriages that involve children.

QUESTIONS AND PROJECTS

1. The term, remarriage, refers to a number of different marriage types. Specify as many types of remarriage as you can.
2. What is the approximate incidence of remarriage in the United States today? Specify the relationship between the variables of age and previous marital status to patterns of remarriage.
3. What intervals ordinarily occur between death of a spouse, or divorce, and remarriage? What are the probabilities that divorced and widowed persons will remarry as compared to the probability that single people will marry?
4. What differences exist in length of courtship and type of wedding between first-marrying and remarrying couples? Which has more influence—the previous marital status of the bride, or of the groom?
5. How does the divorce rate in remarriage compare with that in first marriage? What careful qualification needs to be made here? What effect do successive divorces have upon the likelihood of divorce in a subsequent marriage?
6. Are findings of studies of adjustment in remarriage consistent with divorce statistics? How? How do you explain this?
7. What bases are there for thinking that any given person's adjustment in a remarriage may be different from his adjustment in his first marriage? What bases are there for thinking that it may not be different?
8. What does research show about the personality adjustment of children in remarriages compared with those living in intact families?
9. How are the dynamics of courtship before remarriage likely to differ from those which precede first marriages? Evaluate the statement that "remarrying couples are more likely to be preoccupied with sex."
10. Why is reorganization of the couple's social life often necessary after remarriage? How is this likely to come about?
11. How do former partners intrude upon the new marriage? What differences exist between remarriages following bereavement and those following divorce? What difference does the presence of children make?
12. What is the meaning of the phrase, becoming a new family, as applied to remarriages? What complications are likely to be encountered here? What factors operate in favor of the new marriage?

20 | *The Postparental Phase*

. . . of the 42 million married couples in the United States, little more than half have children at home; of these childless couples, more than two-thirds are in the post-parental category; that is, as many as 15 million couples. And of these, most would consider themselves middle-aged, not aged. . . .

From the standpoint of the individual, the newness of the problem of enjoying his life with his mate for that 20-year period before retirement will in part be mitigated and in part be aggravated by the fact that nearly his whole generation will be going through the experience simultaneously. The kinds of places that such couples like to go are likely to be crowded, as with the tourists who deplore the other tourists. On the other hand, to be free to go to parties, to travel, to have the opportunity to try new ventures without care of children to interfere, and while energy is still abundant, is a blessing that is somehow enhanced by sharing the discoveries with others similarly situated.

The nature of the experience will differ in some ways according to whether one is a man or a woman. For the man, if his work has gone well, he will be at the peak of his career. Those 20 years may thus be a harvest of the fruits of previous study, trials and investment of effort. A peculiar new challenge, however, has arisen to confront many men in their middle years, the grim threat of being superseded by the younger generation midway in their careers, sometimes many years before their retirement. The obsolescence of knowledge and skills is accelerating at such a pace that periodic retraining is becoming the price that will be exacted of all who do not wish to be superseded, even cast aside by the labor market.

. . . The problem of what happens to masculine ego and marital role when a man is conquered by his juniors is one that students of the family have barely begun to explore. What happens to sexual potency when the masculine ego is damaged? Or does not external stress make conjugal life the central value—a sanctuary from the rat race—for many in our time? What role can a wife play in coaching her husband through the tribulations of learning a new vocation in middle-age . . . ?

Grandparenthood, especially for the grandmother—once in-law relations get straightened out—is still at moments almost an ecstatic experience. Esthetically it may be superior to parenthood, offering more of the joys with fewer of the problems, more perspective with less involvement. . . . Of course, if the generations are separated by geographical distance . . . the amount of time per week or year the grandmother can spend with her grandchildren is limited and sporadic. But she can be a grandmother for 20 to 30 years and thus recapitulate vicariously every phase of her grandchildren's development. She cannot, however, without sad consequences, directly take the place of their actual mother. And so the woman who becomes a grandmother at 45, as millions nowadays do, really does need to substitute some equally worthwhile and satisfying activity. . . .[1]

IT is no accident that the article from which the quotation above was taken is titled, "New Roles for Men and Women," for the patterns which it discusses virtually did not exist a very few decades ago. Increases in longevity and prolongation of the family life cycle have drastically altered the way of life and adjustment problems of people from their mid-forties to their seventies and eighties.

If the student will refer back to the discussion of the family life cycle in Chapter 9, he will see that both husbands and wives average less than 50 years of age at the time of the marriage of their youngest child. There are, then, in the neighborhood of 15 years before the husband's retirement and as long as 30 years before the marriage is broken by the death of one of the spouses. The postparental phase of married life is on the average as long as all the earlier stages put together.

This chapter deals with the phase of married life which begins with the marriage of the youngest child and lasts until the marriage is broken by death. It is a long stage and is roughly divisible into two parts: the part which lasts until the husband's retirement from work, and the postretirement phase.

CONTINUING MARITAL ADJUSTMENT

Not too much has been written about the relations between husbands and wives after the marriages of their children, and even less has been substantiated by empirical research. It is widely recognized that the postparental phase gives to couples the opportunity to rediscover one another and to do all of the things that they could not do earlier in life because of responsibilities to the children. At the same time, it is feared that the parallel adjustments which they have made during the child-rearing years tend to perpetuate themselves after the children have gone. Husbands frequently are portrayed as becoming even more engrossed in their work and less available to their wives. Wives, in turn, are described as lonely and frustrated in their attempts to find new

[1] Nelson N. Foote, "New Roles for Men and Women," *Marriage and Family Living* 23 (Nov. 1961), pp. 326–7.

meaning in life. Women's clubs and civic duties are seen as providing less than satisfactory outlets.

Unfortunately, we have no reliable information on the proportions of couples who follow these different paths of adjustment. There are some empirical data, however, on the continuing trend of marital adjustment after the middle years. The most comprehensive data come from Blood and Wolfe's Detroit-area study, referred to in earlier chapters, and from a study of 312 Minneapolis-area families by Reuben Hill. Hill's study covered three generations of nuclear families in the same family lines and thus affords a unique opportunity to compare intergenerational patterns. The grandparent generation in the study were between 60 and 80 years of age, the parents were between 40 and 60, and the married children were from 20 to 30 years old.[2]

LOVE AND COMPANIONSHIP

It will be recalled, from Chapter 17, that both longitudinal and cross-sectional studies have shown a general drop in marital adjustment and satisfaction, beginning early in marriage and continuing through the middle years. The data from the Detroit-area study, presented in Figure 1, show that the process does not end during the middle years but continues through the postparental years and right on into retirement. Figure 1 presents, separately,

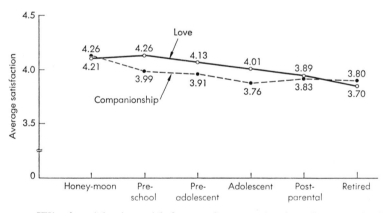

FIGURE 1. *Wives' satisfaction with love and companionship, by stage in family life cycle.*

Source: Data used with permission of The Free Press of Glencoe from Robert O. Blood, Jr. and Donald M. Wolfe, *Husbands and Wives: The Dynamics of Married Living,* copyright © 1960 by The Free Press, A Corporation.

[2] Reuben Hill, *et. al., Family Development in Three Generations,* Cambridge, Mass.: Schenkman Publishing Company, Inc., 1970.

wives' satisfaction with love and with companionship in their marriages. In both cases, the scores are distinctly lower than during the early child-bearing and child-rearing years.[3] Satisfaction with love in the relationship continues to decline steadily from the high point reached during the preschool years, while satisfaction with companionship shows a very modest increase after the children are gone. Thus there is some empirical basis for the idea that married couples tend to turn back toward one another when their children leave home. The most striking thing, however, is that the increase in companionship scores is so small. It is still lower during the postparental years than during the first 15 years, or so, of marriage.

POWER RELATIONSHIPS

Other changes in the relationship accompany the gradual drop in satisfaction with love and companionship. The Detroit data on changes in the power relationship of husband and wife were presented in Figure 3 of Chapter 17 and showed that the husband's power tends to rise during the postparental but preretirement years and then to fall after he retires. The authors interpret these findings as probably indicating that the gradual drop in the husband's power during the child-rearing years reflects his increasing preoccupation with his job rather than his family. After the departure of the children, his power may tend to increase again because of his wife's realization that he is likely to precede her in death. Still virile and fulfilling his role as breadwinner, his power is enhanced by the wife's realization that she may lose him. Retirement changes drastically the husband's status as income-provider and removes much of the prestige which attached to his occupational role. The husband's power during retirement is less than at any other time in the family life cycle.

Hill's Minneapolis study provides some interesting data on the distribution of power in relationships of young marrieds, their parents, and their grandparents (Table 1). In this case, the respondents were asked to specify who makes final decisions in several different areas of marital decision-making, and, at the same time, the interviewers independently rated who did most of the

[3] The magnitude of this decline should not be overemphasized. Havighurst, for example, has shown that the age period from 40 to 70 constitutes a kind of plateau period during which social adjustment remains relatively constant. See Robert J. Havighurst, "The Social Competence of Middle Aged People," *Genetic Psychology Monographs* 56 (Nov. 1957), pp. 297–373.
Other studies have shown that the postparental but preretirement period is a more crucial one in the adjustment of wives than in the adjustment of husbands. See Irwin Deutscher, "The Quality of Postparental Life: Definitions of the Situation," *Journal of Marriage and the Family* 26 (Feb. 1964), pp. 52–9.

TABLE 1. *Family Authority Patterns, by Generation, Minnesota Families*

AUTHORITY PATTERN	SELF-REPORTED			OBSERVER REPORTED		
	GRAND-PARENT	PARENT	MARRIED CHILD	GRAND-PARENT	PARENT	MARRIED CHILD
Husband-Centered	22	12	15	34	24	41
Equalitarian	69	82	80	28	47	42
Wife-Centered	9	6	5	38	29	18
Total	100	100	100	100	100	100
No. of Families	94	100	107	74	90	96

Source: Adapted from Reuben Hill, *et. al., Family Development in Three Generations,* Cambridge, Mass.: Schenkman Publishing Co., Inc., 1970, p. 48.

talking, who exercised most influence, and who seemed to have the last word in the joint interview situation. The self-reports of the couples differed considerably from the interviewer evaluations.

According to the three generations of couples themselves, the vast majority at each generational level had equalitarian relationships. The respondents also indicate an increase in husband-centered and in wife-centered relationships in the parental and grandparental generations. Although the inference is that the power relationships within couples change as they move through the family life cycle, it should be remembered that these are cross-sectional data; they come from three separate generations, not from the same couples followed through time.

The interviewers provide far lower estimates of the proportion of equalitarian relationships at each generational level. They also report substantial increases in the proportions of wife-centered relationships at the parental and grandparental levels. Since Hill's data on the grandparental generation are not presented by retirement status, his findings cannot be compared directly with Blood's. Both studies, however, show shifts away from equalitarian norms among older couples and the increasing power of the wife in later years.

ROLE SPECIALIZATION

In one other area of marital role-taking the Michigan and Minnesota studies provide roughly comparable data. Blood and Wolfe developed a measure of role specialization to determine the degree to which husband and wife share the various tasks involved in maintaining a home and the degree to which each performs the tasks which he deems most consistent with his sex

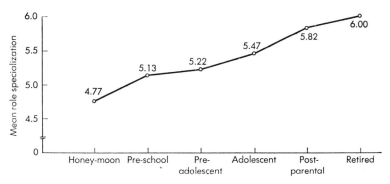

FIGURE 2. *Role specialization by stage in family life cycle.*

Source: Data used with permission of The Free Press of Glencoe from Robert O. Blood, Jr. and Donald M. Wolfe, *Husbands and Wives: The Dynamics of Married Living,* copyright © 1960 by The Free Press, A Corporation.

role. The results of this analysis, by stages of the family life cycle, are shown in Figure 2.

The figure shows that there is more sharing of tasks during the honeymoon period than at any time thereafter. A large number of wives are working for pay, outside the home, during this period. As wives move out of gainful employment and into child-bearing and child-rearing, they begin to specialize more in the traditional wifely tasks. Husbands, freed from many domestic tasks, also concentrate more on the traditional masculine tasks. This trend continues throughout child-rearing and into the postparental years. During the postparental years the trend continues, and the differentiation of marital roles reaches its peak during the postretirement years.[4]

Hill, in Minneapolis, sought not only to determine the degree to which men stick to the traditional manly tasks of earning a living, working in the yard, doing repair jobs, and so on; he developed measures of both role specialization and role conventionality. Role conventionality refers to men doing only traditional men's work and women doing only traditional women's work. Role specialization refers to the degree to which there is some shifting about in the performance of various tasks or the degree to which role differentiation is rigidly adhered to.

In Table 2, it can be seen that role specialization in the Minnesota sample tends to increase over the generations. High specialization increases markedly from the married child to the parental to the grandparental generation. Cor-

---

[4] This increase in role differentiation often is accompanied by feelings of loneliness on the part of wives. See Leland J. Axelson, "Personal Adjustment in the Post-parental Period," *Marriage and Family Living* 22 (Feb. 1960), pp. 66–8.

TABLE 2. *Role Specialization and Role Conventionality*
by Generation, Minnesota Families

ROLE SPECIALIZATION	GRANDPARENT PER CENT	PARENT PER CENT	MARRIED CHILD PER CENT
High specialization, husband or wife always do certain household tasks	78	65	57
Medium specialization, spouses usually but not always do the same specified tasks	14	29	37
Low specialization, great shifting about, in who does tasks	8	6	6
Total	100	100	100
Number of families	99	100	107
Role Conventionality			
Both conventional in doing sex-typed tasks, and combination where wife conventional, husband crossing line	42	21	17
Husband conventional and wife crossing line, and combinations where both cross line	33	62	70
Combinations of conventionality, line crossing and systematic role reversals	26	17	13
Total	100	100	100
Number of Families	98	100	107

Source: Adapted from Reuben Hill, *et al.*, *Family Development in Three Generations*, Cambridge, Mass.: Schenkman Publishing Company, Inc., 1970, p. 49.

respondingly, medium role specialization is more than halved over the generations.

When we look at role conventionality, the situation is more complicated. The number of conventional couples does increase steadily from 17 per cent in the married-child generation to 42 per cent in the grandparental generation. However, unconventionality increases, too, in the older generations. The most unconventional pattern increases from 13 per cent in the married-child generation to 26 per cent in the grandparental generation. There is no completely satisfactory explanation for this latter finding. The fact that increased unconventionality is found in the parental generation also suggests that some couples may become increasingly flexible with the passage of time. In the grandparental generation, disabilities that come with infirmity or illness may produce role reversals in couples who, until then, have played conventional roles.

In summary, the available evidence indicates that the disenchantment experienced by couples after the early years of marriage tends to continue right on into old age. While marital-adjustment scores, as such, are not available for couples during the postparental years, wives report steadily decreasing satisfaction in the love relationships with their husbands. This drop in love satisfaction may be compensated for, to some degree, by slight increases in satisfaction with the companionship aspects of the relationship after the children are gone.[5] Even if they do so with considerably diminished ardor, many couples do appear to turn back toward one another during their declining years.

Shifts in the power relationship between husband and wife, and changes in the roles which the spouses play, also are found in the postparental years. The husband's power appears to increase after the children leave, at least up to the time of his retirement from the occupational world. When he ceases to work, his power declines again and more relationships become wife-centered. Paradoxical shifts appear in the roles played by the couple. On the one hand, the role specialization begun in earlier years becomes sharper, with each spouse tending to perform, alone, the tasks which are culturally prescribed for his sex. On the other hand, there also appear more cases where there are almost complete role reversals. Some older couples appear to be less bound by expectations regarding the sex division of labor, and some of them obviously restructure their relationships in accord with developing physical limitations.

MARITAL DYNAMICS

The ways in which spouses relate to one another during the postparental years may be as varied as those that characterize early marriage and the middle years. Certainly there is a great deal of continuity as couples move from one stage in life to another. There are differences, too, however, as the special problems of aging emerge.

There is ample reason to think that the transition to postparental status either may be smooth and uneventful or it may be traumatic. Moreover, the transition may be unequally made by the two partners; one partner may take things in stride and the other be thrown into an emotional tailspin.

At one extreme, some couples literally do "stay together for the benefit of the children." The marriage, or entrance into college, of the last child may signal, for the parents, the end of a long period of distasteful obligation.

[5] Marvin B. Sussman, "Activity Patterns of Post-Parental Couples and Their Relationship to Family Continuity," *Marriage and Family Living* 17 (Nov. 1955), pp. 338–41.

Divorce may soon follow; and widespread experience attests to the fact that it may come as a great shock to virtually unsuspecting children. Or, surprisingly, couples who have longed for the day when they might be free of marital bonds find themselves immobilized when the opportunity finally appears. In spite of their professed wishes to be free, they may be sufficiently dependent upon one another that some other rationalization must be found for continuing the marriage. Essentially neurotic relationships may be clung to for the blend of pain and satisfaction that they bring.

At the other extreme is found an increasing proportion of couples who anticipate the day when they will be relieved of responsibility for children and thus enabled to enjoy the full fruits of whatever financial and other success life has brought. A diminishing proportion of couples define parenthood as the *prime* goal in life. Not that parenthood has been devalued, for few couples are content to do without it. But, increasingly, parenthood is viewed as occupying only one portion of the vigorous adult years—the ages from 20 to 45 or so.

And mixed with its joys are the seemingly unending frustrations of being tied down. Coping with the need for baby-sitters, a continuous round of infectious illnesses, school schedules that discourage travel, the competing schedule demands of budding adolescents, financial demands for everything from braces to summer camps, to college expenses and weddings—some couples can hardly wait for the day when they may be free to indulge their own desires without hindrance.

Just a measure of privacy and quiet after hectic years of crowded family living may have overwhelming appeal—the opportunity to carry on an uninterrupted conversation, to be able to watch one's own favorite TV shows, and to have the daily schedule determined by one's own, instead of the children's, needs. Luxuries, from new clothes, to automobiles, to extended vacations, may be afforded. For couples in this situation, the postparental years may represent years of fulfillment rather than years of decline.

The postparental years are not without problems, of course. The data on continuing marital adjustment presented early in this chapter indicate a tendency for many spouses to live somewhat parallel rather than truly intertwined lives. On the average, marital satisfaction is lower than in earlier years.

The Preretirement Years. As was discussed in Chapter 11 in the section on in-law relationships, the immediate postparental years often appear more unsettling for wives than for husbands. The marriage of children does not occasion any drastic change in the daily routines of most husbands. The husbands continue to spend a large share of their waking hours at work. Moreover, assuming even modest occupational success, these are rewarding years for men. Their incomes, their prestige, and their power are at maximum. Even if the pain of "losing one's children" is severe, men have a means of nearly full escape into their work.

Their wives' situation, of course, is much different. Women who formerly found that there were not enough hours in the day to accomplish their work suddenly are burdened heavily with time. Only so much time can be devoted to the diminished demands of housekeeping. When the wife seeks to fill her time with added attention to her husband, often she finds him both physically and emotionally unavailable; his escape into work makes her feel more alone than ever.

There are alternatives available to mothers whose children have flown the nest. Some women seek fulfillment, and escape, in paid employment. And for some of them, this is quite successful. On the other hand, middle-aged women who wish to work face handicaps. They *are* middle-aged and have lost the fresh appeal of younger women. Moreover, they are likely to be essentially untrained, or their earlier training is likely to have been lost and become out of date. As a consequence, the work available to them often is unskilled and rather poorly paid.

When the husbands' incomes are high enough that their wives are not tempted to seek paid employment, one or another combination of community service and an expanded social life often fill the available hours. Many community agencies—the United Funds, the Red Cross, hospital auxiliaries, and many more—almost depend upon such voluntary service for their very existence. Then there are the women's organizations in the churches, fund drives for worthy causes, and special community projects to absorb time and energy. And in the lulls in between there are always shopping, lunch, and the ubiquitous bridge game.

Some women appear to thrive on this kind of existence. Virtually everyone knows such women who are healthy, hearty, and content. Equally true, however, is the fact that community service and social life sometimes take on a compulsive quality that appears to mask basic dissatisfaction and frustration. It is no accident that such women are a favorite subject of cartoonists.

Basic to women's problems at this stage of life appears to be the enforced recognition of age. It was pointed out earlier that women are regarded as most desirable somewhere around the age of 20 and that age brings decreasing attractiveness. When a woman's children marry, it not only deprives her of established routines and sources of emotional satisfaction but also signals the end of the productive period of her life. Much has been written but, still, little is known about how women respond to aging during the middle years.

Some women—witness the clichéd joke about women who remain at 29 years of age for a decade or more—appear to experience distress over aging quite early in adult life. It stands to reason that the transition to being over 40 years old is more difficult, and that seeing one's children begin their reproductive lives is more threatening yet. For women in the postparental years, the physical symptoms of the menopause reinforce the feelings of becoming old and useless.

Thus, the postparental years often are years of emotional crisis for women. Some wives busy themselves with activities, some make inordinate demands upon the time and affection of their husbands, and some refuse to let go of their children. The meddlesome mother-in-law may frequently be a lonely, frightened woman who unknowingly seeks to recapture youth by living through her children and grandchildren. The puzzled spouse and children alternate between opposition to and pity over her behavior.

The Years Following Retirement. Most men face compulsory retirement from work at somewhere around 65 years of age. There are exceptions of course—professional people, farmers, and the self-employed, to mention a few. But, increasingly in the modern world, men work in large organizations with regular retirement policies.

The adjustments that married couples make to retirement may not be as variable as the adjustments that may be made in earlier years, for, if nothing else, physical limitations are becoming increasingly prominent. Then, too, the accumulating habit cage makes it less likely that there will be extreme deviation from earlier adjustment patterns.

Certainly couples vary, however, in their preparation for retirement. Some couples plan enthusiastically for retirement, just as some couples anticipate the marriage of their children so that they may have more time together and the opportunity to carry out long-delayed plans. Particularly when their income is adequate, retired couples may seek the good life. In genuine affluence, world travel is possible. On a more modest level, there still may be the winter cottage in Florida or California and the summer place at a northern lake or in the mountains. Retirement may make it possible to make frequent and regular visits to children and grandchildren who now live in distant localities. It is also possible to leave again when the pleasures of the visit wane.

Other couples, of number undetermined, who have not the energy or the income to live so well are relatively content to stay on in their old homes and not have to cope with the demands of either other family members or the world of work. They may visit their children occasionally or be visited by them. Disengagement from much of the world around them is the hallmark of such couples, who socially are becoming aged whether or not they are older chronologically than the more active couples discussed above.[6]

[6] Elaine Cumming and William E. Henry, *Growing Old: The Process of Disengagement,* New York: Basic Books, 1961.

For still other couples, the prospect of retirement is filled with threat. Either the husband or wife or both may fear that the shaky equilibrium of their marriage will be upset by the adjustments that must be made when the husband is no longer out of the home for most of the day. And, although a steadily expanding proportion of retired couples has adequate income through social security, corporation retirement programs, and savings, retirement to some, means severe economic deprivation. Problems of adjustment between husband and wife may be complicated by the threat of becoming dependent either upon children or upon public agencies.

If the preretirement years are more often troublesome for the wife, those following retirement may be equally difficult for the husband. Men in our society appear to have their roles defined, more than anything else, by their status as breadwinners. Up until retirement, most men achieve whatever measure of self-respect they possess from their jobs. Their relationships with their wives are influenced significantly by their success at work, and work often becomes an escape from full involvement in the family situation.

Upon retirement, all of this is likely to be changed drastically. In at least two ways the retired man is faced with the necessity of making radical adjustments: adjustments in self-concept, and adjustment in the daily routines of living.

The threat to the husband's self-concept is of major importance by itself, and may also be the major determinant of how he adapts his daily routines following retirement. For many years the man has had an ingrained concept of himself as, for example, an executive, a salesman, or a clerk. Regardless of the relative prestige attaching to his occupation, the occupational identification has brought him self-respect at some level. He has had the strength and security that come from being the breadwinner.

Upon retirement, however, he is no longer executive, salesman, or clerk. In the eyes of his co-workers, his wife, and himself, suddenly he is old and no longer of great use. The frontal assault on his self-concept is most likely to come from outsiders. Former friends on the job now exclude him and no longer show him respect. To them, and to others who did not know him on the job, he is now "old-timer," perhaps, to be patronized a bit but not to be taken too seriously.

Of great importance is the attitude taken by his wife. If her conception of him remains that which she had before, then the husband may be able to hold on to his self-concept in spite of lack of support for it from other people. If, however, she is threatened personally by his retirement or if she takes advantage of the opportunity to be hostile toward him, the husband must either capitulate or insulate himself against all outside opinions.

It appears likely that many men struggle through a period of severe ambivalence trying to find a new self-concept that is consistent with their retired status. The easiest time of it, perhaps, may be had by those men of high status or expertise who continue to do some consulting work even after formal retirement. Their situation is not greatly different from that of some farmers, independent businessmen, and professionals who do not face absolute retirement at any particular age. Such people may be able to hold onto their occupational self-concepts into very old age.

A second alternative is to adopt a full-time leisure role. For those who can manage it, extravagant and expensive leisure such as that involving foreign travel still affords the retired man high status. It is his occupational success that makes such leisure possible, and he may generally conceive of himself as a retired lawyer or banker rather than simply as a retired person. Full-time leisure may be had on a much more modest basis, of course, but it is much less likely to bring lasting satisfaction. The man who devotes himself full-time to woodworking or gardening is likely to define himself and to be defined by others as just filling time—he is doing busy-work rather than truly being busy.

There's no point in being young unconsciously, and the young are necessarily young unconsciously. The only fun in being young is knowing you are young and glorying in it accordingly; and no one ever did that. In fact, you can't begin to do it until you're old.

—E. V. Lucas.

A third alternative is to identify with old age itself. Some retired persons cease trying to hold onto earlier associations with other people and confine themselves almost exclusively to relationships with other retired people. The men (and women) whose days come to center on the activities of the Golden Age Clubs and the Senior Citizens' Clubs provide the best example. While there may be macabre overtones in this pattern of adjustment, simple observation of these groups in action indicates that the organizations become a consuming interest for at least some of their members.[7]

Adjustments in daily routine are implied in these adjustments of self-concepts, but there is more to it than that. Before retirement the husband typically leaves the house for eight or more hours each working day. Week-

---

[7] Some research has shown identification with old age to be associated with maladjustment. See Bernard S. Phillips, "A Role Theory Approach to Adjustment in Old Age," *American Sociological Review* 22 (April 1957), pp. 212–17.

ends may be anticipated for the time to be spent together, but many couples are ready to return to their regular routines by Monday morning. By now, the wife has adapted to the absence of children in the home and has developed a new schedule to fill her days. The husband's routines center on his work, and many husbands have difficulty coping with too much time away from work.

Retirement abruptly ends the core of the husband's routines and throws him into the home on a 24-hour-a-day basis. The only schedule he has for this kind of living is his usual relaxed weekend schedule that he can only tolerate for a few days at a time. Soon he becomes restive for things to do, demanding time and attention from his wife, perhaps seeking to aid her in the performance of her household tasks, or expecting her to defer to the demands of whatever projects around the home that he embarks upon. As he seeks to adjust both self-concept and routine to the fact of retirement, the stress seldom improves his disposition, and many wives find themselves living with men who are most difficult to please.

Although the husband may be affected most profoundly by retirement, it often ushers in a crisis for the wife too. As indicated above, she may find herself trying to cope with a husband who makes impossible demands upon her time and her patience. He keeps the home in turmoil, he disrupts her schedule and makes it impossible for her to get things done, and he constantly is under foot. Even his efforts to assist her with household tasks do more to disrupt her schedule than anything else.[8]

When the wife responds to these annoyances with annoyance, as she is wont to do, the husband's self-concept is threatened further and some acute conflict reminiscent of the first months of marriage often emerges. Either or both partners may complain to their grown children, or to friends, and the family may even appear on the verge of disruption. Seldom does disruption occur, however. Years of resolving crises have provided the stamina to handle this one, too, and at retirement age there really are few alternatives. Gradually, shifts in self-concept and routine occur, and most couples settle into their new patterns with a growing sense of relief. As old age—with prospects for infirmity and death—draws closer, many couples become dependent upon one another as they have never been before.

THE KIN NETWORK

Earlier chapters, particularly Chapter 11, have shown that married couples in the United States actually maintain a complex network of relationships

[8] John A. Ballweg, "Resolution of Conjugal Role Adjustment After Retirement," *Journal of Marriage and the Family* 29 (May 1967), pp. 277–81.

with other kin. Within this network, relationships between parents and their married children are particularly prominent. Research shows a comprehensive pattern of mutual aid in which a variety of goods and services are exchanged and in which the direction of flow is slightly more often from parents to children.[9] In Chapter 11 it was shown that mutual aid continues to 60 years of age or older, but the implications of there being three adult generations of the same family were not systematically examined.

With postparental status often being achieved by couples between 45 and 50 years of age, it follows that many families today have two living post-parental generations. The younger of these two generations is likely to be in full vigor and at the height of whatever financial success they will achieve; the older generation usually has passed the age of retirement. In Table 3, Hill presents data from the Minneapolis study that specify the amount of help given and received by all three generations in five different areas—economic, emotional, household management, child care, and illness.

It is apparent, in Table 3, that the parental generation stands at the center of the mutual aid network. In four of the five areas, the parents are more involved in giving aid than are either the grandparental or married-child generations. Moreover, even in the management of illness, the parental generation gives as much help as it receives. The married-child generation comes next, giving more help than it receives in three of the areas—emotional gratification, household management, and help in time of illness. As was also pointed out in Chapter 11, the married-child generation receives a great deal of financial help and help with the care of children. The grandparents are mainly on the receiving end of the situation. The area of child care is not relevant for them, of course, and in all other areas they receive substantially more assistance than they give.

Hill summarized these data by inferring the ways in which each of the three generations perceives its position and function in the family network. For the married-child generation, he says, there is both considerable giving and receiving; for them the situation is one of high reciprocity and interdependence. The parental generation is more affluent and supportive and occupies a kind of patron status in relation to the other generations. The grandparents are meager givers and high receivers. Theirs is almost a dependency status.

---

[9] A recent report actually shows retired parents giving more help to married children than they receive from them. See Gordon F. Streib, "Intergenerational Relations: Perspectives of the Two Generations on the Older Parent," *Journal of Marriage and the Family* 27 (Nov. 1965), pp. 469–76.

TABLE 3. *Help Given and Received in Various Areas by Generation, Minnesota Sample.*

| | ECONOMIC | | EMOTIONAL GRATIFICATION | | HOUSEHOLD MANAGEMENT | | CHILD CARE | | ILLNESS | |
	Gave	Received	Gave	Received	Gave	Received	Gave	Received	Gave	Received
Grandparents	26%	34%	23%	42%	21%	52%	16%	0%	32%	61%
Parents	41	17	47	37	47	23	50	23	21	21
Married children	34	49	31	21	33	25	34	78	47	18
Totals	100% *	100%	100%	100%	100%	100%	100%	100%	100%	100%

* Some percentages do not add to 100 because of rounding.

Source: Adapted from Reuben Hill, *et al*, *Family Development in Three Generations*, Cambridge, Mass.: Schenkman Publishing Company, Inc., 1970, p. 67.

THREE-GENERATION FAMILIES

The kin network in American society appears to exist in spite of—or in consequence of—a widespread trend toward the nuclear family as the basic residential unit. The traditional extended family has virtually disappeared from the American scene, and three-generation families—with grandparents, parents, and children living together—typically are regarded as undesirable deviations from the norm. Perhaps because of this, relatively little study has been devoted to either the frequency with which grandparents live with their children or what the adjustment patterns are in those cases where doubling up does occur.

No nation-wide statistics are available to indicate how many parents live with their children. United States census figures do give some estimate, however, of the sharing of households with relatives generally. These statistics show that from 1910 up to 1947 there was an increase in related families "doubling-up" in the same dwelling. In 1947, almost 10 per cent of all families were sharing their households with other families.[10] Since 1947, the sharing of households declined again, and, by 1955, had dropped below the 1910 level. In 1955, some 3.5 per cent of all married couples did not have households of their own; by 1970, the figure was 1.4 per cent.[11]

Several factors appear to account for the doubling-up which increased up to 1947. One factor, undoubtedly, was the large concentration of ethnic groups in the population who had strong extended family traditions.[12] The concentration of rural and rural-oriented persons in the population also was still relatively large.[13] Most important in the increases up to 1947, which ran counter to the emerging norms on maintenance of separate residence, undoubtedly were the frequent financial necessity to double-up during the depression of the 1930's, the shortages of construction materials during and shortly after World War II, the number of "war wives" who lived with one set of parents while their husbands were gone, and the postwar boom in marriages without a corresponding increase in available housing.

These statistics refer to the doubling-up of all family groups and not just with the extent to which grandparents double up with their children and

[10] Thomas P. Monahan, "The Number of Children in American Families and the Sharing of Households," *Marriage and Family Living* 18 (Aug. 1956), pp. 201–3.

[11] U. S. Bureau of the Census, *Statistical Abstract of the United States: 1970*, Washington, D. C., 1971, p. 36.

[12] John Kosa, Leo D. Rachiele, and Cyril O. Schommer, "Sharing the Home With Relatives," *Marriage and Family Living* 22 (May 1960), pp. 129–31.

[13] William M. Smith, Jr., "Family Plans for Later Years," *Marriage and Family Living* 16 (Feb. 1954), pp. 36–40.

grandchildren. The U. S. Census reported that there were 1,994,000 three-generation families in 1960, with only 1,245,000 of these involving a parent living with offspring and grandchildren.[14] The number of families who experience three-generation living *at some time* during the life cycle is considerably larger, and the proportion of aged persons who live with their children is substantial.

Carol Stone collected data from 5102 junior- and senior-high-school students in Washington, finding that only 318, or 6 per cent, of those students lived in households with one or more of their grandparents. She found that in more than half of these cases, the grandmother alone lived with the family; in one-fifth of the cases the grandfather lived with the family; and in only about 30 per cent of the cases were both grandparents present. Thus, in only about 2 per cent of the total sample were there three-generation families.[15]

Koller, studying three-generation family patterns in Ohio, found their numbers to be so small that he finally resorted to studying them wherever he could find them, rather than drawing them systematically from a sample of families in a given community. In attempting to sample one community, for example, he found that only 16 of 62 families could be classified as being concerned with three-generation living in any way. Moreover, those 16 cases were divided into three groups: those who were concerned with three-generation living in the past only; those who were living in three-generation families at the time; and those who expected to establish a three-generation household in the future. He also found that three-generation families ordinarily do not last long. Most of them lasted from one to five years before the parent or parents died.[16]

As a proportion of all families, three-generation families are not numerous. When viewed from the standpoint of the aging grandparents, however, they are much more common. Shanas estimates that a third of the old people, who have children, live with one child or another.[17] A U. S. Census sam-

---

[14] Hugh Carter and Paul C. Glick, *Marriage and Divorce: A Social and Economic Study,* Cambridge, Mass.: Harvard University Press, 1970, p. 159. See also Karen Kay Petersen, "Demographic Conditions and Extended Family Households: Egyptian Data," *Social Forces* 46 (June 1968), pp. 531-7.

[15] Carol L. Stone, "Three-Generation Influence on Teen-Agers' Conceptions of Family Culture Patterns and Parent-Child Relationships," *Marriage and Family Living* 24 (Aug. 1962), pp. 287-8.

[16] Marvin R. Koller, "Studies of Three-Generation Households," *Marriage and Family Living* 16 (Aug. 1954), pp. 205-6.

[17] Ethel Shanas, "Living Arrangements of Older People in the United States," *The Gerontologist* 1 (March 1961), pp. 27-9.

ple survey showed that one-fourth of married couples over 65 lived with their children, one-third of separated, divorced, and widowed men did so, and nearly one-half of separated, divorced, and widowed women did so.[18] Undoubtedly, the exact proportions vary from one locality to another and, more significantly, with the age and marital status of the grandparents. The loss of a mate and increasing age make living with kin more likely. Thus, we may conclude that upwards of one-fourth of persons over 65 who have children live with their children. Most of these cases involve grandparents of advanced age, and, because of that advanced age, three-generation living typically lasts only a few years.

There is no question but what the weight of opinion in the United States is against three-generation living. Speaking from a theoretical framework, Parsons states: "It is impossible to say that with us it is 'natural' for any other group than husband and wife and their dependent children to maintain a common household. . . . It is, of course, common for other relatives to share a household with the conjugal family but this scarcely ever occurs without some important elements of strain. For independence is certainly the preferred pattern for an elderly couple, particularly from the point of view of the children." [19]

Among the general population, apparently from half to over 90 per cent say that it is better for children to live separately.[20] Even among aged women living alone, more than half take this position. William Smith, using data from households in two Pennsylvania cities, reports that only 14 per cent thought that it was a good idea for older persons to live with relatives, 50 per cent said that it would work sometimes, and 35 per cent stated flatly that it was "no good." [21]

One of the few studies reporting on reactions to actual three-generation living is Koller's study of 30 families in Ohio and Virginia. He reports that his respondents recognized such living as hazardous, requiring the combined virtues of diplomat, statesman, and saint. Oldsters, he says, who have had authority in the past find it difficult to give up power to their own children.

[18] Ernest W. Burgess, "The Older Generation and the Family," in Wilma Donahue and Clark Tibbitts, eds., The New Frontiers of Aging, Ann Arbor: University of Michigan Press, 1957, pp. 161–2.

[19] Talcott Parsons, "Age and Sex in the Social Structure of the United States," American Sociological Review 7 (October 1942), p. 616.

[20] Alvin L. Schorr, "Current Practice of Filial Responsibility," in Robert F. Winch, Robert McGinnis, and Herbert R. Barringer, Selected Studies in Marriage and the Family, New York: Holt, Rinehart, and Winston, 1962, p. 424.

[21] William M. Smith, Jr., "Family Plans for Later Years," Marriage and Family Living 16 (Feb. 1954), pp. 36–40.

Their married children in turn resent this intrusion upon their authority over their own lives and their own children. Three-generation families were most likely to be created when the wife's mother moved into the home, and conflict between the two women over management of the home was common.

Sharp issue with the American bias against three-generation living, and with both the theoretical arguments and data in support of that bias, has been taken by Schorr. He points out that methodologically more adequate studies in England tend to challenge this view,[22] and that American data show only that three-generation living may cause problems, not that it necessarily does so.[23]

Schorr turns to the writing of Ernest Burgess, rather than to that of Parsons, for his interpretation of three-generation living. He quotes Burgess: "Where both parents and children elect to live together, the arrangement may work out more or less satisfactorily. Where the wife is working, the mother-in-law often takes on the major charge of the household responsibilities. She may be happy to function as a babysitter. . . . Although there may be some disagreements, these tend to be minor, and both generations report the relationship as satisfying."[24] Summing up the argument, Schorr concludes that "there can be no question that there are potential strains when parents and adult children live together. But potential strains are inherent in any living situation—in work, in rearing children, in marrying. If technical and popular literature confined themselves to the strains intrinsic to each of these activities, would we conclude that we should give them up?"[25]

And so the argument goes. Structurally, the American family system has little place in it for aged parents. Apparently the socialization process, in this instance, works well, for the vast majority of both older and middle-aged persons favor the grandparents' maintaining their independence and living alone. Economic trends in the society are consistent with this pattern. The development of social security, company retirement plans, medicare, and the like have gone far to remove the burden of poverty which formerly accompanied old age. As more aging couples can maintain their independence financially, more of them prefer independent living too.

On the other hand, there comes a time when many people are forced to

[22] Elizabeth Bott, *Family and Social Network*, London: Tavistock Publications, 1957, p. 218.

[23] Alvin L. Schorr, op. cit. p. 425.

[24] Ernest W. Burgess, "Family Living in the Later Decades," *The Annals of the American Academy of Political and Social Science* 279 (Jan. 1952), pp. 111–12.

[25] Op. cit. pp. 425–6. See also Alvin L. Schorr, "Filial Responsibility and the Aging," in Hyman Rodman, ed., *Marriage, Family, and Society: A Reader*, New York: Random House. 1965, pp. 186–97.

cope with biological decline and death. Couples in their fifties and sixties, and sometimes in their seventies, may still be hale and hearty; but each passing year threatens both emotional and financial security. Between the ages of 55 and 64, one woman out of every five is a widow. Between 65 and 74, two-fifths are widows; and past 75, 70 per cent are widows.[26] Old people living alone are far less likely to value their independence, and feelings of filial responsibility loom larger within their children. Even without death, illness or financial necessity frequently produces three-generation living. This produces strain. But, as Schorr points out, strain is inherent in living itself. This particular strain has its counterpart at every other stage in the family life cycle.

PARENT-CHILD DYNAMICS

An implicit theme running through our discussion of marital adjustment in the preretirement and retirement years, and through the analysis of the continuing kin network, has been that these phenomena are progressive in character. It is one thing to talk of postparental couples who are in their forties and fifties, another thing with couples who have reached retirement age, and still another with couples who are truly aged. Perhaps nowhere is this more evident than in the changing relationships between parents and their adult children.

We have already shown that the parental generation—in the context of grandparents, parents, and married children—stands at the center of the mutual-aid network. They give aid in a variety of areas and on a substantial scale. They conceive of themselves as being powerful, independent, and interested in promoting their adult children's welfare.

This orientation still prevailing among parents who have reached approximately 69 years of age was shown clearly in Streib's study of 1500 families. He reports data from 1287 men who were married and still living with their wives. Seven hundred and forty-nine of the men were retired and 538 were still working.[27] Attitudes toward occupational achievement, upward social mobility, mutual aid, and continuing close interpersonal relationships were studied.

Most of the parents explicitly acknowledged that it was important for their children to do well occupationally. They approved of their children going to college and moving to remote sections of the country when their
required it. They recognized that such moves threaten the maintenance

Bulletin, Metropolitan Life Insurance Company, 47 (May 1966), pp. 3–4.
eib, "Family Patterns in Retirement," *Journal of Social Issues* 14 (No.

TABLE 4. *Differential Success of Parents and Children as Related to Family Relationships and Solidarity.**

	NUMBER OF CHILDREN WHO HAVE BEEN MORE SUCCESSFUL IN EARNING A LIVING AND GETTING AHEAD IN LIFE		
	All (263)	Most or Some (184)	None (157)
See children:			
Often	78%	74%	75%
Sometimes	17	17	20
Hardly ever	3	5	3
Since leaving home, children in close contact:			
All	94%	77%	84%
Some	4	20	13
None	2	3	3
Children with families, kept in close contact:			
All	93%	77%	85%
Some	6	19	12
None	1	4	3
Form close family group with children:			
Very close	79%	67%	73%
Somewhat close	18	27	23
Not close	3	1	4
Children offered financial help:			
All	70%	33%	37%
Some	18	44	26
None	10	23	32
Willingness of children to make sacrifices:			
Very willing	72%	58%	64%
Somewhat willing	23	37	32
Not willing	2	3	2
Children have less respect than they should for parents:			
Agree	5%	8%	10%
Disagree	94	91	90
Undecided	1	2	—

* Table presents data for retired persons living with spouse who have children. The findings are identical for persons who are still employed.

Percentages may not equal 100 due to rounding errors or small percentage of no-answer category.

Source: Gordon F. Streib, "Family Patterns in Retirement," *Journal of Social Issues* 14 (No. 2, 1958), p. 51.

of family ties, and they believed that their children should not ignore their responsibilities to the parents. However, they were prepared to cope with problems of this sort rather than to stand in the way of their children's advancement. Parents who had retired were a little less likely than those who were still working to emphasize achievement norms, but the vast majority of both the retired and working groups did so.

That the parents' assessment of their situation was realistic was indicated by the actual family experience of those whose children had achieved a higher level of occupational success than the parents had. Upward mobility appeared not to have adversely affected relationships between parents and children (see Table 4). The more successful children were more likely to keep in close touch with their parents, were more likely to offer financial aid, and were more willing to make sacrifices for their parents.

Finally, when the parents were asked what they considered the children's major responsibility to the parents to be, the vast majority emphasized the maintenance of affectional and social ties over the offering of financial help. Here, however, we begin to see more clearly the effects of retirement status and lowered income. Retired parents were somewhat more likely than parents who were still working to say that financial ties are as important as affectional ties. Moreover, the percentages who emphasized financial help, while still small, were greatest at the lowest income levels. In this, perhaps, we begin to see changes in parent-married child relationships as the parents move into old age.

Paul and Lois Glasser, working with data from a sample of persons about 70 years of age who had approached a family service agency for help, concluded that the problems faced by these elderly persons could be conceptualized as those of role reversal. Parents, they state, who must turn to their children for material aid are dependent upon their children much as the children were dependent upon them earlier in life. The children tend to become like parents to their own parents and the parents become like children of their own children. For many persons of both generations, this leads to role conflict and personal problems.[28]

The Glassers were working with a clinical population and specifically warned that their findings might not apply to a general population. Data from just such a general population have been provided by Albrecht, who took a representative sample of parents over 65 years of age in a midwestern community of 7000 persons. She found that 85 per cent of these aging parents maintained roles associated with independence or responsibility and that 15 per cent showed dependence, distance, or neglect.[29] She further classified the parents into independent, responsible, dependent, and distant or lone groups.

[28] Paul H. Glasser and Lois N. Glasser, "Role Reversal and Conflict Between Aged Parents and Their Children," *Marriage and Family Living* 24 (Feb. 1962), pp. 46-51.

[29] Ruth Albrecht, "Relationships of Older Parents With Their Children," *Marriage and Family Living* 16 (Feb. 1954), pp. 32-5. See also Ruth Albrecht, "Relationships of Older

The independent parents were those who had allowed their children to become independent adults. They maintained close affectional and social relationships with them, but neither dominated them nor were dominated by them. Most of these parents maintained separate households but occasionally lived next door. Some of them had remarried in their later years and concentrated on their new marital relationships rather than upon their children. As a group, the independent persons were able to incorporate in-laws into the family without feeling threatened, they maintained interests that gave them something in common with the younger generation, they gave and accepted favors easily, and they showed pride in their children by bragging about them to nonfamily members.

By contrast, the responsible parents still maintained some degree of responsibility for the second generation. In some large families, there still were adult children in the home after the parents had passed age 65. Various other circumstances—the late adoption of a young child, remarriage and the acquisition of young stepchildren, prolonged education in preparation for a profession, and the return of sons from the armed forces—combined to prolong the years of parental responsibility in some families. Many of these families were ethnic families in which traces of the old, large family system still survived. In others, there were hints of personality needs in the parents which caused them to hold on long after most other parents had let go.

The dependent parents were the ones who had suffered role reversals. Constituting only 6 per cent of the parents, they were, of course, older. Some of them maintained separate residences and some lived with their children. Many had been widowed. The basis for their classification as dependent was that they required social attention, economic aid, or physical care from their children. They represented the ultimate stage in the family life cycle.

Finally, there were the lone or distant parents, the widowed men and women who seldom see their children. There were actually more parents in this category—9 per cent—than in the preceding one. Most of these people are in homes for the aged. Some feel that they have been deserted by their children, and some, interestingly, resisted their children's efforts to care for them, apparently preferring life in the old people's home to life with their children. This would be a most interesting group upon which to do further research. It appears that many of them had never had close relationships with their families or that these had been broken a long time ago. Since some of the

People with Their Own Parents," *Marriage and Family Living* 15 (Nov. 1953), pp. 296-8; and Ruth Albrecht, "The Parental Responsibilities of Grandparents," *Marriage and Family Living* 16 (Aug. 1954), pp. 201-4.

children in this case were stepchildren, we might entertain the hypothesis that here is a little recognized cost of remarriage.

GRANDPARENTHOOD

So far, little has been said about the relationships between middle-aged and older couples and their young grandchildren, or the significance of grand-parenthood for marital and personal roles. The fact that relationships between grandparents and grandchildren ordinarily are mediated through parents should not blind us, however, to the importance of these relationships in their own right.

The preparation for and reaction to grandparenthood often differ between men and women. They differ, too, according to whether grandparenthood is achieved relatively early in life or later on.

There is evidence that some women, particularly when grandchildren come relatively early, are markedly ambivalent about them. When women marry, on the average, before age 21 and begin bearing their children soon after, some of them are due to become grandmothers by age 40 and many more of them do so by age 45. Where the marriage of the daughter has been accompanied by threats to the mother's conception of herself as a young, attractive woman, the threat posed by grandparenthood may be even greater. Most people know grandmothers who refuse to be called by that term and who insist that their grandchildren refer to them by pet terms of some sort. The status of the grandchild, as grandchild, may be virtually ignored by the grandmother, who concentrates, instead, on maintaining an image of herself as too young to have such a status.

Probably, more often, middle-aged women find, in the arrival of grandchildren, the opportunity to resume the maternal role directly and to gain more entrée to the lives of their children and their spouses. Even before the baby is born, the grandmother-to-be reassumes a role of authority as she counsels her daughter or daughter-in-law on the management of the pregnancy. In addition, she is permitted to buy clothing and other items for the new arrival, or to make some of them if she is so inclined.

Grandmothers frequently care for the new mother, her baby, and her family during the immediate postnatal period, making the grandmother the person who first diapers, bathes, and otherwise cares for the baby outside the brief intervals while the mother does so. After she returns to her own home, she is permitted and, indeed, is expected to continue a grandmotherly concern for the mother's well-being and the grandchild's care. Thus grandmotherhood often is a major part of the middle-aged woman's solution to the loss of her children through marriage. As grandmother, she acquires a new sense of importance and usefulness. Moreover, she experiences again most of the joys of parenthood without having to cope with its exacting demands. Entering her children's homes as visitor and/or baby-sitter, she can indulge herself and her grandchildren; when her energy or her patience wane, she has simply to leave and go to her own quiet home.

The adjustments made by grandmothers in their middle years do not change appreciably as they grow older. Unlike their husbands, they do not have to cope with the threat of retirement. They continue essentially the same roles right on into old age. Their care of grandchildren usually is welcomed, and they can slow the pace down gradually as their own physical and emotional needs dictate.

The status of grandfather, in middle age, appears to have much less impact. Some men appear to resist the role of grandparent just as some women do, but for them it is likely to be less of a problem. Aging, during the middle years, does not present as much threat to men; indeed aging during this period often is associated with occupational and financial success. Moreover, the man's overwhelming identification with his job up until the time of retirement forestalls the role of grandfather being of major importance to him. Grandchildren may be a source of pride and may constitute pleasant momentary diversions, but they do not stand quite at the center of the universe.

Retirement again brings great changes. Without jobs to claim most of their energy, many grandfathers identify much more completely with their young grandchildren. They begin to want to visit with them, to take them for walks, to buy them things, and otherwise to participate in their care.

I love the acquaintance of young people; because, in the first place, I don't like to think of myself growing old. In the next place, young acquaintances must last longest, if they do last; and then, sir, young men have more virtue than old men; they have more generous sentiments in every respect.

—Samuel Johnson.

Cavan properly points out that the role of older grandfather in American culture is essentially maternal in nature. Unless the child's father is dead or absent, the grandfather is not permitted to be an authority figure to his grandchild or to be the source of his financial support. Instead, the grandfather baby-sits, plays with the child, and generally aids the mother in caring for him. Such a role is not likely to appeal to a younger man, and even the retired grandfather may have difficulty accepting it. On the other hand, the status of grandfather is an envied one and grandfathers are permitted to display a tenderness and sentiment toward grandchildren that are not permitted to men in virtually any other circumstance. Both grandfathers and grandchildren often derive great satisfaction from this relationship which is uncomplicated by any emphasis upon discipline.[30]

WIDOWHOOD

With but few exceptions, the family life cycle ends in widowhood. Although young people seldom can imagine it, one partner in each pair is destined to live out the last part of his life alone—at least without his marital partner. Moreover, as shown in Chapter 9, the period of widowhood lasts, on the average, from 8 to 16 years.

For some 25 years now, the number of widows in the United States has been increasing by more than 100,000 per year, and the total number of widows is now more than nine and one-half million.[31] The disparity between the number of widows and widowers has been widening. Fifty years ago the ratio was about two to one; today widows outnumber widowers by about four to one. Widowers are much more likely to change their status through remarriage, making the problem of widowhood in the United States an overwhelmingly feminine phenomenon.

That widowhood presents serious problems probably is obvious, but there are empirical data, also, which verify this fact. Bellin and Hardt, for example, studying 1803 people over 65 in upstate New York, found that rates of mental disorder were significantly higher among the widowed than among the still-married. These higher rates of mental illness were related not only to widowhood but also to advanced age, physical ill health, and other variables.[32] A

---

[30] "Self and Role Adjustment in Old Age," op. cit. pp. 393–4. For a provocative discussion of emerging roles in grandparenthood, see Bernice L. Neugarten and Karol K. Weinstein, "The Changing American Grandparent," *Journal of Marriage and the Family* 26 (May 1964), pp. 199–204.

[31] "Widows and Widowhood," *Statistical Bulletin*, Metropolitan Life Insurance Company, 47 (May 1966), pp. 3–4.

[32] Seymour S. Bellin and Robert H. Hardt, "Marital Status and Mental Disorders Among the Aged," *American Sociological Review* 23 (April 1958), pp. 155–62. See also, Helena Znaniecki Lopata, "Loneliness: Forms and Components," *Social Problems* 17 (Fall 1969), pp. 248–62.

report by Ilgenfritz based upon experience in a community guidance center also emphasizes that widows suffer from fears of being alone and from loss of self-esteem as women in addition to the many practical problems related to living alone.[33]

Problems associated with widowhood are partly a function of increasing age, but not completely so. This was demonstrated by Zena Blau in a study of almost 1000 people over 60 years of age in two areas of New York State. She found, first, that extensive association with friends is an important mechanism of adjustment to old age and widowhood. People over 70 who were still married were less likely to report high friendship participation than were younger married people. This decline did not occur among widowed men or women, however. In fact, older widowed persons often had more significant friendship associations than did younger ones.[34] How can this seeming paradox be explained?

We long for youth chiefly because we like being alive, and youth, rather than any later age, is the extreme opposite of death.

—Robert Lynd.

The key to the situation was found in the status of widowed persons relative to the status of most other persons in their age group. Since friends tend to be of about the same age, people who are widowed before most of their age-mates find themselves with a different pattern of experience and with different interests than their fellows. Without the bonds of common experiences and interests, friendships suffer. With more advanced age, widowhood becomes common and it is the still-married people who now are relatively deviant and isolated. Thus it appears that whatever maladjustment is associated with widowhood is not a function of widowhood and advancing age alone but is also a function of the individual's position in a total social group. The individual's strategic position in relation to other people of his or her age can make adjustment either much harder or considerably easier.

Widowhood for women is, in some ways, comparable to retirement from work among men. The death of the husband severely jolts the wife's image of

[33] Marjorie P. Ilgenfritz, "Mothers on Their Own: Widows and Divorcees," *Marriage and Family Living* 23 (Feb. 1961), pp. 38–41.

[34] Zena S. Blau, "Structural Constraints on Friendships in Old Age," *American Sociological Review* 26 (June 1961), pp. 429–31.

herself as a wife and as a person. She is denied the opportunity to maintain her competence as companion to her husband and housekeeper for others. If she continues to live alone and remains active, she is likely to receive admiration from other people. If she is not able to do this, her children are likely to offer her a home. This probably is the most common origin of the three-generation family situation.[35]

As already pointed out, three-generation families present problems for the younger generation of adults in them. They also present problems for the aging widow. The younger adults have established themselves in the positions of authority in the family, and often they admit an aging widow in a subordinate and virtually functionless capacity. Patronized by their children and by other people, and denied the opportunity to be useful, many aging widows deteriorate rapidly both in health and in outlook on life. Most three-generation families do not last very long.

Some families are wise enough to recognize that aging parents need to retain their self-respect by being admitted to the household, if at all, as full and responsible partners. Under these circumstances it appears likely that many of the problems widely associated with old age in the United States may be avoided or at least ameliorated.

There is no escape. The life cycle of the family, as with the individual, must end in death. By this time, the family life cycle of the next generation usually is well along.

SUMMARY

Increasing numbers of couples have completed the child-rearing and child-launching stages of the family life cycle by the time they are 45 or 50 years of age. Most such couples remain vigorous, healthy, and alert. Although they may seem ancient to their children, they do, in fact, often have a third of their lives ahead of them.

Empirical data show that the gradual drop in marital adjustment begun in earlier years continues into the postparental stage. The satisfaction that wives report with the love of their husbands declines steadily into old age. Companionship-satisfaction scores show a modest increase after the children are gone,

[35] For useful analyses of the roles of the widowed, see Felix M. Berardo, "Widowhood Status in the United States: Perspective on a Neglected Aspect of the Family Life-Cycle," *The Family Coordinator* 17 (July 1968), pp. 191–203; Felix M. Berardo, "Survivorship and Social Isolation: The Case of the Aged Widower," *The Family Coordinator* 19 (Jan. 1970), pp. 11–25; Bernard J. Cosneck, "Family Patterns of Older Widowed Jewish People," *The Family Coordinator* 19 (Oct. 1970), pp. 368–73; and Benjamin Schlesinger, "The Widowed as a One-Parent Family Unit," *Social Science* 46 (Jan. 1971), pp. 26–32.

suggesting that husbands and wives do tend to turn back toward one another slightly.

Changes in power relationships occur, too, with husbands tending to gain in power up to retirement but losing power thereafter. Interviewer reports, even more than self-estimates, emphasize the tendency for wives to increase in power as couples move into old age. The roles played by the spouses tend to become more specialized with increasing age, men coming to play the traditional masculine role and women coming to play the traditional feminine role. However, role unconventionality increases, too, with age. Many couples adapt flexibly to the limitations imposed by illness and infirmity.

Some couples make the transition to post-parental status uneventfully, while for others it is traumatic. Some generally unsatisfactory marriages break under the strain; others continue in neurotic interdependence. Increasing numbers of couples anticipate pleasantly their release from parental burdens and embark upon a life of relative leisure and companionship.

Adjustment, at this stage, often appears harder upon women than upon men. Women whose children have flown the nest may find themselves with too much time on their hands, with too few opportunities to use their energies constructively, and confronted with a conception of themselves as old.

A comparable crisis period for men follows retirement. Husbands suddenly are deprived of their chief source of status, define themselves, and are defined by others, as being old and useless. They face the necessity both of revising their self-concepts drastically and of developing new daily routines. Some fortunate men are able to develop a leisure role, and some come to identify with old age itself. Temporary conflict often develops between husband and wife until new definitions and new routines are worked out.

The kin network at this stage may involve three adult generations—grandparents, parents, and married children. The parental generation stands at the center of the network, giving aid to the other two generations.

As grandparents become dependent, many three-generation families appear. As a proportion of all families, three-generation families are not common; but the proportion of persons over 65 who live with their children is substantial. There is a widespread bias against three-generation living in American society, and data show that there often is conflict in such families. On the other hand, there is not evidence of more serious strains here than exist within other family units at other stages of the family life cycle.

Most grandparents prefer to remain independent and specifically emphasize the importance of their adult children being upwardly mobile. Both their expectations and actual experience data show that such upwardly mobile families are likely to be successful in maintaining close family ties and patterns of mutual aid. The older the grandparents become, the more likely they are to emphasize the importance of mutual aid.

Relationships between grandparents and parents are quite variable. Some grandparents are comfortable with their children's independence and some seek to prolong dependence upon themselves. Some grandparents become dependent in turn, and there may be a complete reversal of roles between the generations. In up to 10 per cent of the cases, there may be estrangement and virtual loss of contact between the generations.

Relationships between grandparents and young grandchildren also are variable. Some relatively young grandparents tend to reject their grandparent status. More often, women use grandmotherhood to regain some aspects of the maternal role. The role of grandfather becomes more prominent following retirement, when the grandfather, too, often assumes some responsibility for child care. These relationships may be very satisfying to all three generations.

The family life cycle usually ends in widowhood. Associated with extreme old age, widowhood often is problem-ridden. Evidence indicates, however, that problems are a function of the total social situation and not of aging alone. The widowed persons are, most frequently, women who suffer then a drastic change of status comparable to that produced by retirement for men. Some widows carry on quite independently and some quickly become dependent. According to the wisdom of the people involved, the final years in the life cycle may either be tragic or continually rewarding.

SUGGESTED READINGS

Duvall, Evelyn M., *Family Development*, Philadelphia, J. B. Lippincott Company, 1971. Uses the developmental task concept to analyze family change over the life cycle. Has chapters on middle age and aging.

Hill, Reuben, Foote, Nelson, Aldous Joan, Carlson, Robert, and Macdonald, Robert, *Family Development in Three Generations: A Longitudinal Study of Changing Family Patterns of Planning and Achievement*, Cambridge, Mass.: Schenkman Publishing Co., Inc., 1970. Comprehensive report of a research project involving the repeated interviews of three generations of the same 300 families. Seeks to develop a theory of family development.

Riley, Matilda W., Foner, Anne, and Associates, *Aging and Society: An Inventory of Research Findings*, New York: Russell Sage Foundation, 1968. Brings together the total social science knowledge of aging. Chapters 7 and 23 deal specifically with the family.

Rosow, Irving, *Social Integration of the Aged*, New York: The Free Press, 1967. Brilliant sociological analysis, based upon extensive research, of how old people maintain integration in the social system. Emphasizes the importance of ties with family members and with friends of the same age.

Shanas, Ethel, and Streib, Gordon F., eds., *Social Structure and the Family: Generational Relations*, Englewood Cliffs, New Jersey: Prentice-Hall, 1965. An interdisciplinary symposium which focuses upon the three-generation family. Emphasizes the role relationships of older family members.

Tunstall, Jeremy, *Old and Alone: A Sociological Study of Older People*, London: Routledge and Kegan Paul, Ltd., 1966. Analyzes the minority of older people who are alone and lonely in three Western countries. Emphasizes the disruptive effects of death of the spouse.

FILMS

A Place to Live (Dynamic Films, 405 Park Ave., New York 10022), 24 minutes. A documentary study of the aged and their social needs. The problem of one man, forced to live with children and grandchildren, is set forth. A suggested solution is shown—a home designed especially for elderly people—a place where activities provide a sense of usefulness and responsibility.

Adventure in Maturity (The University of Oklahoma, Norman, Okla.), 22 minutes. A woman has resigned herself to a rocking-chair existence where she can dream about the "good old days." She is stimulated by a woman friend, older than she, to learn about the opportunities for older women in her community. She discovers women whose mature years are filled with service for others and satisfactions for themselves.

Aging (NET Film Service, Indiana University, Bloomington, Ind.). Two elderly Jewish gentlemen, playing cards, reveal their attitudes toward life. Psychotherapist asserts that the greatest evil dealt to the elderly in modern times is the idea that an old person is functionless. Having an old person as a useful participant in a domestic situation is mutually beneficial to child, parent, and grandparent.

Death (*Time-Life Films*, 43 West 16th Street, New York, 10011), 45 minutes. Shows how different societies cope with death. Contrasts the open disposition of corpses in India with the secretive disposal of bodies in England. Includes practices in New Guinea, Hong Kong, and among the Botswana.

Old Age (*Time-Life Films*, 43 West 16th Street, New York, 10011), 45 minutes. Looks at the ways in which people in various countries cope with old age. Emphasizes the role of the family in providing protection against loneliness and destitution.

Three Grandmothers (National Film Board of Canada, Mackenzie Building, Toronto), 29 minutes. From Nigeria, Brazil, and Saskatchewan, three portraits comparing the role of the grandmother in the family and the community.

QUESTIONS AND PROJECTS

1. What research evidence is there to indicate the trend of marital adjustment during the postparental years? What is the trend with regard to wives' satisfaction with their husbands' love? With companionship?

2. Specify the changes that occur in the power relationships between husband and wife. What happens with regard to role specialization? How do you account for the changes in role conventionality?

3. Which partner usually experiences greater adjustment problems in the immediate postparental period? Why? What is the nature of these problems?

4. Which partner ordinarily experiences greater adjustment problems following retirement? Why?

5. In what two main areas must retired husbands make adjustments? What are some of the life styles adopted by retired men?

6. How are the wife's attitudes important in influencing the husband's adjustment to retirement? What problems are likely to be posed for her by the husband's retirement?

7. Describe the mutual-aid patterns typically existing among grandparents, parents, and married children.

8. Roughly what proportion of American families are three-generation families? What proportion of people over 65 live in such families? Typically, what is their composition? How long do they last? What adjustment problems do they face? Do they have more or fewer problems than other families?

9. How do parents over 65 typically view their relationships with their adult children? What values do they emphasize? How realistic are their expectations?

10. How may grandparenthood be dysfunctional in the lives of women? How may it be functional? Which pattern is more common?

11. Describe the typical grandfather role for middle-aged men. For retired men. What is meant by the statement that "the grandfather role is a maternal role"?

12. What evidence is there that widowhood brings special problems? How do friendships play a part in the adjustment to widowhood? What conditions influence the balance between tragedy and satisfaction at the end of the life cycle?

Name Index

683

Subject Index

DATE DUE